DOCTRINAL INSIGHTS TO THE

BOOK OF MORMON

DOCTRINAL INSIGHTS TO THE
BOOK OF MORMON

VOLUME TWO
JACOB THROUGH ALMA

Compiled by
K. DOUGLAS BASSETT, PhD

CFI
Springville, Utah

This is not an official publication of The Church of Jesus Christ of Latter-day Saints. The opinions and views expressed herein belong solely to the author and do not necessarily represent the opinions or views of Cedar Fort, Inc. Permission for the use of sources, graphics, and photos is also solely the responsibility of the author.

ISBN 13: 978–1–59955-055-8

Published by CFI, an imprint of Cedar Fort, Inc., 2373 W. 700 S., Springville, UT, 84663
Distributed by Cedar Fort, Inc., www.cedarfort.com

LIBRARY OF CONGRESS CATALOGING-IN-PUBLICATION DATA

Doctrinal insights to the Book of Mormon / compiled by Doug Bassett.
   p. cm.
  Includes index.
  ISBN-13: 978-1-59955-055-8
  1. Book of Mormon—Commentaries. 2. Church of Jesus Christ of Latter-day Saints—Doctrines. I. Bassett, Doug.
  BX8627.D63 2007
  289.3'22—dc22
                    2007013260

Cover design by Nicole Williams
Cover design © 2007 by Lyle Mortimer
Typeset by Annaliese B. Cox

Printed in the United States of America

10 9 8 7 6 5 4 3 2 1

Printed on acid-free paper

PREFACE

Because of a health condition I have dealt with for many years, I find that sleep does not come easily. I have discovered that by studying the Book of Mormon and the talks by the Brethren, I feel the peace I need to be able to obtain the necessary rest.

This three-volume commentary is the result of that study. My wife, Arlene, and I worked out a tag-team relationship regarding our Book of Mormon study. As I study night after night, alone in my library at home, I underline those statements by the Brethren and scholars that help to define the various verses within the Book of Mormon. When I finally am able to sleep, there is a stack of books sitting next to the computer with pages turned over, waiting for my wife to read the next day. After reading the quotes, she follows my directions found in the margins of the text and types them into the computer. What you will read is the sum total of my research over the course of many years and Arlene's patient typing each day.

This book is "old school" in the sense that it involves just reading books and talks with no Internet searches or computer-assisted programs. It is not a stubborn rebellion against technology, but rather it is simply the way I study.

My unending thanks go out to my sweet wife for her love of the scriptures and her desire to type these quotes.

May our labor of love with the Book of Mormon be a blessing to your life.

JACOB

Jacob 1:6 • WE ALSO HAD MANY REVELATIONS

We cannot force spiritual things. . . . Our life's purpose to obtain experience and to develop faith would be frustrated if our Heavenly Father directed us in every act, even in every important act. . . .

Even in decisions we think very important, we sometimes receive no answers to our prayers. This does not mean that our prayers have not been heard. It only means that we have prayed about a decision which, for one reason or another, we should make without guidance by revelation. . . .

Thus, a person who seeks guidance on which of two different ways he should pursue to get even with a person who has wronged him is not likely to receive revelation. Neither is a person who seeks guidance on a choice he will never have to make because some future event will intervene. . . .

On one occasion, my wife and I prayed earnestly for guidance on a decision that seemed very important. No answer came. We were left to proceed on our own best judgment. We could not imagine why the Lord had not aided us with a confirming or restraining impression. But it was not long before we learned that we did not have to make a decision on that question because something else happened that made a decision unnecessary. The Lord would not guide us in a selection that made no difference.

No answer is likely to come to a person who seeks guidance in choosing between two alternatives that are equally acceptable to the Lord. . . . Similarly, the Spirit of the Lord is not likely to give us revelations on matters that are trivial. I once heard a young woman in a testimony meeting praise the spirituality of her husband, indicating that he submitted every question to the Lord. She told how he accompanied her shopping and would not even choose between different brands of canned vegetables without making his selection a matter of prayer.

That strikes me as improper. I believe the Lord expects us to use the intelligence and experience He has given us to make these kinds of choices. When a member asked the Prophet Joseph Smith for advice on [a] particular matter, the Prophet stated:

"It is a great thing to inquire at the hands of God, or to come into His presence; and we feel fearful to approach Him on subjects that are of little or no consequence" (*Teachings of the Prophet Joseph Smith*, 22). . . .

When a choice will make a real difference in our lives—obvious or not—and when we are living in tune with the Spirit and seeking God's guidance, we can be sure we will receive the guidance we need to attain our goal.

(Dallin H. Oaks, *With Full Purpose of Heart* [Salt Lake City: Deseret Book, 2002], 162–163)

Jacob 1:7 • ENTER INTO HIS REST
(Refer in this text to Alma 37:34; Moroni 7:3.)

Jacob 1:13–14 • NEPHITES, LAMANITES
(Refer in this text to Helaman 11:24.)

The Book of Mormon is careful to specify that the terms Lamanite and Nephite are used in a loose and general sense to designate not racial but political (Moroni 1:9), military (Alma 43:4), religious (4 Nephi 38), and cultural (Alma 53:10, 15; 3:10–11) divisions and groupings of people. The Lamanite and Nephite division was tribal rather than racial, each of the main groups representing an amalgamation of tribes that retained their identity (Alma 43:13; 4 Nephi 36).

(Hugh Nibley, *Since Cumorah* [Salt Lake City: Deseret Book, 1976], 246)

Plainly it [Book of Mormon] is meant for us, as it reminds us many times; it is the story of what happened to the Nephites—and we are the Nephites.

(Hugh Nibley, *Since Cumorah* [Salt Lake City: Deseret Book, 1976], 390–391)

———

The Lamanites in the Book of Mormon represent a designation given to a group simply because they are the people who "seek to destroy the people of Nephi." Throughout the Book of Mormon, the term "Lamanite" is used in widely different contexts suggesting variously political, military, religious, and cultural distinction from the Nephites. Thus the label Lamanite must not necessarily suggest a racial difference, as many have suggested. . . .

The fact to be aware of in understanding the meaning of Nephite or Lamanite in the Book of Mormon is that eventually neither term connoted race, color, creed, political persuasion, or national origin.

(Kirk Holland Vestal and Arthur Wallace, *The Firm Foundation of Mormonism* [Los Angeles, CA: LL Company, 1981], 101–102)

Jacob 1:18 • PRIESTHOOD AMONG THE NEPHITES
(Refer in this text to 2 Nephi 5:26.)

The Melchizedek Priesthood was the only priesthood held by the Nephites for the first 634 years of their . . . existence. There were, of course, none of the tribe of Levi among them, and the Levites were the only ones anciently who held the lesser priesthood.

(Bruce R. McConkie, *The Promised Messiah* [Salt Lake City: Deseret Book, 1978], 412)

Jacob 1:19; 2:2 • MAGNIFY OUR OFFICE UNTO THE LORD

The Prophet Joseph Smith was once asked, "Brother Joseph, you frequently urge that we magnify our callings. What does this mean?" He is said to have replied, "To magnify a calling is to hold it up in dignity and importance, that the light of heaven may shine through one's performance to the gaze of other men. An elder magnifies his calling when he learns what his duties as an elder are and then performs them."

(Thomas S. Monson, *Ensign*, May 2006 [Salt Lake City: The Church of Jesus Christ of Latter-day Saints, 2006], 56)

Jacob 1:19; 2:2; 3:10 • THEIR SINS UPON OUR HEADS IF WE DON'T TEACH
(Refer in this text to 2 Nephi 4:5–6.)

President John Taylor said on one occasion, speaking to the brethren of the priesthood: "If you do not magnify your callings, God will hold you responsible

for those you might have saved, had you done your duty." This is a challenging statement. If I by reason of sins of commission or omission lose what I might have had in the hereafter, I myself must suffer and, doubtless, my loved ones with me. But if I fail in my assignment as a bishop, a stake president, a mission president, or one of the General Authorities of the Church—if any of us fail to teach, lead, direct, and help to save those under our direction and within our jurisdiction, then the Lord will hold us responsible if they are lost as the result of our failure."

(Hugh B. Brown, in Conference Report, Oct. 1962 [Salt Lake City: The Church of Jesus Christ of Latter-day Saints, 1962], 84)

———

Surely we would be condemned if one of our associates in life should stand in the presence of the Great Judge and say of us that we could have taught him the gospel, if we had made an effort. . . . Let none of us, my brethren and sisters, be justly accused in that way.

(*The Teachings of George Albert Smith*, ed. by Robert and Susan McIntosh [Salt Lake City: Bookcraft, 1996], 31)

———

And I say to you Seventies and you Elders, Awaken up! God has placed the priesthood upon you, and he expects you to magnify it. . . . We want some manhood, and some priesthood and power of God to be manifested in Israel. . . . And I pray God, the Eternal Father, to waken up these Elders, that the spirit of their mission may rest upon them, and that they may comprehend their true position before God. . . .

If you do not magnify your callings, God will hold you responsible for those whom you might have saved had you done your duty.

(John Taylor, *Journal of Discourses* [London: Latter-day Saints' Book Depot, 1880], 20:23)

———

What a responsibility it is to hold this heavenly, this eternal, this everlasting Priesthood! And we shall have to give an account of it. Apostles, Seventies, High Priests, Elders, and all men who bear any portion of this Priesthood that has been given unto us, will be held responsible for it. . . .

We will be condemned if we do not fulfil it. We shall find it out when we get to the other side of the veil. . . . I think our hearts are set too much upon the things of this world. We do not appreciate, as men bearing the Holy Priesthood . . . the mighty responsibility we are under to God and high heaven. . . .

If we . . . use that priesthood for any other purpose under heaven but to build up the Kingdom of God . . .

our power will fall. . . . A good many men have undertaken . . . to build themselves up. . . . You may say amen to their power and authority. . . . You cannot use the priesthood for any other purpose under heaven but to build up the kingdom and do the will of God; and when you attempt to do otherwise your power will be taken from you. . . .

Let . . . man use that priesthood for any other purpose than the building up of the kingdom of God, . . . and the heavens withdraw themselves, the power of the priesthood departs.

(*Teachings of Presidents of the Church—Wilford Woodruff* [Salt Lake City: The Church of Jesus Christ of Latter-day Saints, 2004], 39–41)

Jacob 2 • THE SENSITIVITY OF JACOB

Jacob's sensitivity is never more tenderly expressed than in his denunciation of sexual immorality. While he warns of the dire consequences of fornication and adultery (see Jacob 2:27–33; 3:12), he is mostly concerned with the sufferings of the victims. He declares that the Lord has "seen the sorrow, and heard the mourning . . . [and] the cries of the fair daughters." He chastises those who have caused such sorrow, saying: "Ye have broken the hearts of your tender wives . . . ' and the sobbings of their hearts ascend up to God. . . . Many hearts died, pierced with deep wounds" (Jacob 2:31–35).

Expressions such as these reveal Jacob as one attuned to sorrow and suffering. . . . Characteristic of Jacob is his discomfort with confrontational speech. Revealing his sensitivity to suffering, he consistently apologizes for the necessary harshness of his words. Jacob often emphasizes that he would rather comfort and console than chastise and rebuke. . . . Jacob 2:2–11 records ten amazingly compassionate verses of apology before beginning a strong call for repentance. . . .

In many ways, Jacob's tender heart is much like the Savior's. Shusaku Endo, the Japanese novelist and biblical scholar, said of Jesus: "The interest of Jesus extended to the ones who wept for the harsh realities of life: the sick and the lame crawling out of the huts. . . . His heart ached at the sight. Love and sympathy flowed from him like blood from a deep wound. We in our own hearts know how we are attracted to glamorous and beautiful people and how we easily close our eyes to those who are filthy and ugly. It was different with Jesus" (Shusako Endo, *A Life of Jesus*, trans. Richard A. Schuchert (New York: Paulist Press, 1973), 62).

Apparently, it was also different with Jacob. Perhaps this is why, when the name of Christ was revealed to the Nephites, Jacob was the first to receive that knowledge (see 2 Ne. 10:3).

(Chris Conkling, *Ensign*, Feb. 1992 [Salt Lake City: The Church of Jesus Christ of Latter-day Saints, 1992], 9–10)

Jacob . . . told the men of his day that it grieved him to speak so boldly in front of their sensitive wives and children. But notwithstanding the difficulty of the task, he said he had to speak to the men about this subject because God had commanded him (see Jacob 2:7–11). I do so for the same reason.

In the second chapter of the book that bears his name, Jacob condemns men for their "whoredoms" (vv. 23, 28). He told them they had "broken the hearts of [their] tender wives, and lost the confidence of [their] children, because of [their] bad examples before them" (v. 35).

What were these grossly wicked "whoredoms"? No doubt some men were already guilty of evil acts. But the main focus of Jacob's great sermon was not with evil acts completed, but with evil acts contemplated.

Jacob began his sermon by telling the men that "as yet [they had] been obedient unto the word of the Lord" (Jacob 2:4). However, he then told them he knew their thoughts, that they were "beginning to labor in sin, which sin appeareth very abominable . . . unto God" (v. 5). "I must testify unto you concerning the wickedness of your hearts" (v. 6), he added. Jacob was speaking as Jesus spoke when He said, "Whosoever looketh on a woman to lust after her hath committed adultery with her already in his heart" (Matthew 5:28; see also 3 Nephi 12:28; D&C 59:6; 63:16).

(Dallin H. Oaks, *Ensign*, May 2005 [Salt Lake City: The Church of Jesus Christ of Latter-day Saints, 2005], 87–88)

Jacob 2:5 • I CAN TELL YOU CONCERNING YOUR THOUGHTS

(Refer in this text to Alma 12:3–7.)

Jacob 2:7, 9 • TENDER FEELINGS

I had just received a phone call telling me of a friend's death in an accident. I was sitting in the living room with tears streaking down my cheeks. Our young son, Cory, saw the tears as he passed in the hallway. I learned that he had anxiously assumed the tears were because he had disappointed me in some way. He didn't know about the phone call. Brethren, we underestimate how genuinely and frequently our children want to please us.

(Neal A. Maxwell, *Ensign*, May 2004 [Salt Lake City: The Church of Jesus Christ of Latter-day Saints, 2004], 45)

Jacob 2:8; 3:2; 6:7 • THE PLEASING WORD OF GOD

In the world today we are victims of many who use

their tongues as sharp swords. . . . We as members of the Church need to be reminded that the words "Nay, speak no ill" are more than a phrase in a musical context but a recommended way of life (see *Hymns*, no. 233). . . .

How far adrift we have allowed ourselves to go from the simple teaching "If you can't say something good about someone or something, don't say anything." . . .

We need to get back to the basic principle of recognizing the good and the praiseworthy within the family. Home evening needs to be reemphasized and used as a tool or foundation for wholesome communication and teaching, but never as an opportunity to bash other family members, neighbors, teachers, or Church leaders. Family loyalty will emerge when we reinforce the good and the positive and bridle our negative thoughts as we seek after those things that are of good report. . . .

Whatever happened to giving each other the benefit of the doubt? Whatever happened to hoping that another person would succeed or achieve? Whatever happened to rooting for each other? . . .

Imagine what could happen in today's world . . . if each of us would vow to cherish, watch over, and comfort one another.

(Marvin J. Ashton, in Conference Report, Apr. 1992 [Salt Lake City: The Church of Jesus Christ of Latter-day Saints, 1992], 23–25)

You're better than you think you are, really. Do you know that? Yes, you are. You're great. . . . Believe in yourselves. Believe in your capacity to do some good in this world. . . . I know of your problems as young people. I know you worry. I know you're concerned. You worry what kind of a job you're going to get. You worry what your major should be in school. You worry whether you're going to make it. You're worried about who you're going to marry, where you're going to live, all of those things. You worry about money and nearly everything else, don't you? These are days of worry and concern for you. But they are days of such tremendous opportunity. . . .

Don't go around tearing people down. The Lord doesn't want that. He doesn't want us to spend our time destroying others. He expects us to build and sustain and cultivate and nurture and strengthen our associates. Wonderful things happen when you go forth with that kind of attitude. . . .

Believe in the innate goodness of people.

(*Discourses of President Gordon B. Hinckley*, 1995–99 [Salt Lake City: The Church of Jesus Christ of Latter-day Saints, 2004], 1:381–383, 385, 387)

Jacob 2:8, 9, 35 • WOUND

Jacob uses some words in ways no other Book of Mormon writer uses them. For example, of thirty-one times *wound* or a variant is used, twenty-four refer to physical wounds. Only the seven used by Jacob refer to a "wounded soul."

(Chris Conkling, *Ensign*, Feb. 1992 [Salt Lake City: The Church of Jesus Christ of Latter-day Saints, 1992], 7)

Jacob 2:13–17 • PRIDE, RICHES
(Refer in this text to 2 Nephi 9:28–30; Alma 1:6; 3 Nephi 6:10–16.)

There will come a time, however, in the history of the Saints when they will be tried with peace, prosperity, popularity and riches.

(Daniel H. Wells, *Journal of Discourses* [London: Latter-day Saints' Book Depot, 1878], 19:367)

Pride is essentially competitive in nature. . . . In the words of C. S. Lewis: "Pride gets no pleasure out of having something only out of having more of it than the next man. . . . It is the comparison that makes you proud: the pleasure of being above the rest. Once the element of competition has gone, pride has gone" (*Mere Christianity* [New York: Macmillan, 1952], 109–10). . . .

Pride is ugly, It says, "If you succeed, I am a failure." . . .

Pride is the great stumbling block to Zion. I repeat: Pride is the great stumbling block to Zion.

(Ezra Taft Benson, in Conference Report, Apr. 1989 [Salt Lake City: The Church of Jesus Christ of Latter-day Saints, 1989], 4–7)

Continuing with the words of Paul, "For the love of money is the root of all evil" (1 Tim. 6:10). It is the love of money and the love of those things which money can buy which destroys us. We all need money to supply our needs. But it is the love of it which hurts us, which warps our values, which leads us away from spiritual things and fosters selfishness and greed.

(Gordon B. Hinckley, *Ensign*, May 1997 [Salt Lake City: The Church of Jesus Christ of Latter-day Saints, 1997], 49)

Today we are basking in the lap of luxury, in the like of which we have never seen in the history of the world. It would seem that probably this is the most severe test of any we have ever had in the history of the Church.

(Harold B. Lee, Address to Church Employees, 13 Dec. 1973)

The worst fear I have about this people is that they will get rich in this country, forget God and His people, wax fat, and kick themselves out of the Church and go to hell. This people will stand mobbing, robbing, poverty, and all manner of persecution, and be true. But my greater fear . . . is that they cannot stand wealth.

(Brigham Young, *Life of a Pioneer*, James S. Brown [Salt Lake City: George Q. Cannon and Sons, 1990], 122–123)

I have been in homes of rich people. I have never seen any tears of joy shed because of anything they could purchase with their money, but I have been in groups of missionaries and groups of Saints, when for hours at a time there was not a dry eye there; just because the spirit of God was there.

(LeGrand Richards, in Conference Report, Apr. 1952 [Salt Lake City: The Church of Jesus Christ of Latter-day Saints, 1952], 113–114)

I remember reading the results some time ago of a national survey which attempted to summarize the responses as to what brings happiness. . . . Most people felt money was a significant part of happiness. The author's research, however, indicated that money alone seldom, if ever, resulted in true happiness. . . . It's important to have sufficient money for our needs, but beyond that, money has little to do with true happiness.

(W. Eugene Hansen, *Ensign*, Nov. 1993 [Salt Lake City: The Church of Jesus Christ of Latter-day Saints, 1993], 81)

Money never goes as far as you want it to, . . . you just cannot get enough of what you do not need, and . . . it is not possible to buy happiness at a store or through a catalog. . . . Everything that you take with you into the next life is everything that money cannot buy. . . .

I love the story our prophet, President Gordon B. Hinckley, relates about a conversation he had with his wife, Marjorie, on the eve of their wedding. He was anxious about the economic realities of their marriage. He had totaled his assets and realized that he had less than $150 and, even more alarming, that he made only $185 a month. Marjorie put his fears to rest. She replied that "she had hoped for a husband and now she found out she was getting $150 too." "This will work out wonderfully," she told him. "If you've got $150, we're set." And, as you well know, they were.

(Mary Ellen Smoot, *"Everything Money Cannot Buy,"* Satellite Broadcast, 3 Feb. 2002, Brigham Young University [Salt Lake City: The Church of Jesus Christ of Latter-day Saints, 2002], 1–2)

Some years ago, Elder ElRay L. Christiansen told about one of his distant Scandinavian relatives who joined the Church. He was quite well-to-do and sold his lands and stock in Denmark to come to Utah with his family. For a while he did well as far as the Church and its activities were concerned, and he prospered financially. However, he became so caught up in his possessions that he forgot about his purpose in coming to America. The bishop visited him and implored him to become active as he used to be. The years passed, and some of his brethren visited him and said, "Now, Lars, the Lord was good to you when you were in Denmark. He has been good to you since you have come here. . . . We think now, since you are growing a little older, that it would be well for you to spend some of your time in the interests of the Church. After all, you can't take these things with you when you go."

Jolted by this remark, the man replied, "Vell, den, I vill not go." But he did! And so will all of us!

(James E. Faust, in Conference Report, Oct. 2002 [Salt Lake City: The Church of Jesus Christ of Latter-day Saints, 2002], 19–20)

It seems to be the hardest thing in the world for people to grow in wealth and keep the spirit of the gospel (RSM, 24:628).

(Heber J. Grant, *Gospel Standards*, comp. by G. Homer Durham [Salt Lake City: An Improvement Era Publication, 1942], 31)

Money in and of itself is not an evil, but as Paul taught Timothy, it is the love of money that is the root of all evil (1 Tim. 6:10). There are some of the wealthy who deal with their prosperity very well, using their resources to bless others and build the kingdom. For many, however, wealth presents major difficulties. . . .

The more our hearts and minds are turned to assisting others less fortunate than we, the more we will avoid the spiritually cankering effects that result from greed, selfishness, and overindulgence. Our resources are a stewardship, not our possessions. I am confident that we will literally be called upon to make an accounting before God concerning how we have used them to bless lives and build the kingdom. . . .

How much should we give? I appreciate the thought of C. S. Lewis on this subject. He said: "I am afraid the only safe rule is to give more than we can spare. . . . If our charities do not at all pinch or hamper us, . . . they are too small. There ought to be things we should like to do and cannot do because our charitable expenditure excludes them" (*Mere Christianity* [New York: Macmillan, 1952], 67).

(Joe J. Christensen, *Ensign*, May 1999 [Salt Lake City: The Church of Jesus Christ of Latter-day Saints, 1999], 9, 11)

The great trouble is that there are many people who, as they grow and increase in the things of this world, set their hearts upon them and lose the Spirit of the Lord. Therefore, that which is counted by the world as success is failure; because if a man starts out for a prize and . . . after laboring nearly a lifetime for that prize, certainly his life has been a failure. . . . The appetite for money grows upon a man, increases and strengthens unless he is careful, just as much as the appetite for whiskey. It gets possession of him, and he loves the money instead of loving it only for the good that he can do with it.

(Heber J. Grant, *Teachings of Presidents of the Church* [Salt Lake City: The Church of Jesus Christ of Latter-day Saints, 2002], 125)

I can stand at a window in my house and see horses gently grazing in our pasture. As I look beyond our property, I can see our neighbors working in their yard. Extending my perspective farther, I behold the clean, blue water of the reservoir just north of our small town. But if I apply a special type of silver paint to the glass, my view of the world around me changes considerably. Because of this special paint, my window becomes a mirror. As I try to look out my window, I no longer see the world as it is; I see only myself. This is the challenge for all of us who find excess silver in our lives. Instead of viewing the world as it is, this silver may change our perspective to the point that we may not be able to see beyond our own self-indulgent desires. If our hearts are turned inward, it doesn't take much silver to blind us to the world outside our own house. But if our souls are in tune with the needs of others, if we truly care about our fellowman, then we can use whatever silver the Lord blesses us with to bless the lives of God's children in and outside our own homes.

(Jack R. Christianson and K. Douglas Bassett, *Life Lessons from the Book of Mormon* [Salt Lake City: Deseret Book, 2003], 124–125)

Jacob 2:18–19 • THE LORDS PROGRAM FOR WEALTH

Gold does not corrupt man; it is in the motive of acquiring that gold that corruption lies.

(David O. McKay, *Treasures of Life*, 174–175).

Perhaps because he grew up with Laman and Lemuel, the sin Jacob condemns most vigorously is pride—especially pride caused by excessive riches and learning. Indeed, Jacob's condemnations of this sin are

among the most powerful in all scripture. Unlike many today who frown on too much learning but never fear growing rich, Jacob teaches the opposite: "To be learned is good if they hearken unto the counsels of God. But wo unto the rich" (2 Ne. 9:29–30). Ironically, we are permitted to seek riches only if we intend to give them away (see Jacob 2:17–19).

(Chris Conkling, *Ensign*, Feb. 1992 [Salt Lake City: The Church of Jesus Christ of Latter-day Saints, 1992], 8)

Jacob 2:23–28 • PLURAL MARRIAGE

1. *Why did the Lord command people to practice plural marriage?* (Jacob 2:30; Deut. 25:5; Gen. 16:1–3 & D&C 132:34–35).

2. *Who decided when a person was to practice plural marriage?* (D&C 132:7).

I hold the keys of this power in the last days; for there is never but one on earth at a time on whom the power and its keys are conferred; and I have constantly said no man shall have but one wife at a time, unless the Lord directs otherwise.

(*Teachings of the Prophet Joseph Smith*, comp. by Joseph Fielding Smith [Salt Lake City: Deseret Book, 1976], 324)

---

3. *Did the Saints practice plural marriage because there were more women than men?*

The most common of these conjectures is that the Church, through plural marriage, sought to provide husbands for its surplus of female members. The implied assumption in this theory, that there have been more female than male members in the Church, is not supported by existing evidence. On the contrary, there seems always to have been more males than females in the Church.

(John A. Widtsoe, *Evidences & Reconciliations* [Salt Lake City: Bookcraft, 1987], 307–309)

---

4. *Is plural marriage essential for exaltation?* (D&C 49:16).

Plural marriage is not essential to salvation or exaltation. Nephi and his people were denied the power to have more than one wife and yet then could gain every blessing in eternity that the Lord ever offered to any people. In our day, the Lord summarized by revelation the whole doctrine of exaltation and predicated it upon the marriage of one man to one woman (D&C 132:1–28). . . . All who pretend or assume to engage in plural marriage in this day, when the one holding the keys has withdrawn the power by which they are performed, are guilty of gross wickedness.

(Bruce R. McConkie, *Mormon Doctrine* [Salt Lake City: Bookcraft, 1966], 578–579)

———————

The first principle of the gospel is faith in the Lord Jesus Christ. Faith means trust—trust in God's will, trust in His way of doing things, and trust in His timetable. . . .

People who do not accept continuing revelation sometimes get into trouble by doing things too soon or too late or too long. The practice of plural marriage is an example.

(Dallin H. Oaks, *With Full Purpose of Heart* [Salt Lake City: Deseret Book, 2002], 207–208)

Jacob 2:24, 27; 3:5 • CONCUBINES

In modern times a concubine is a woman who cohabits with a man without being his wife. But from the beginning of creation, all down through the history of God's dealings with his people, including those with the house of Israel, concubines were legal wives married to their husbands in the new and everlasting covenant of marriage (D&C 132:1, 37–39, 65). Anciently they were considered to be secondary wives, that is, wives who did not have the same standing in the caste system then prevailing as did those wives who were not called concubines. There were no concubines connected with the practice of plural marriage in this dispensation, because the caste system which caused some wives to be so designated did not exist.

(Bruce R. McConkie, *Mormon Doctrine* [Salt Lake City: Bookcraft, 1966], 154)

———————

By definition, a concubine would be either a woman kept for lewd purposes or a lawful wife of a lower social standing than her husband's other wife or wives (see also Mosiah 11:2). Hagar, plural wife of Abraham, would be an example of the latter, inasmuch as Abraham did only that which he was commanded (D&C 132:37). The offense to which Jacob made reference was the Nephites' consorting either with paramours or with wives improperly taken.

(Robert Millet and Joseph McConkie, *Doctrinal Commentary on the Book of Mormon* [Salt Lake City: Bookcraft, 1988], 2:20)

HOW DID THE BRETHREN FEEL TOWARD PLURAL MARRIAGE?

[Joseph Smith] . . . knew the commandment of the Almighty to him was to go forward—to set the example, and establish Celestial plural marriage. He knew that he had not only his own prejudices and prepossessions to combat and overcome, but those of the whole

Christian world stared him in the face; but God, who is above all, had given the commandment, and he must be obeyed, yet the Prophet hesitated and deferred from time to time, until an angel of God stood by him with a drawn sword, and told him that, unless he moved forward and established plural marriage, his Priesthood would be taken from him and he should be destroyed.

(Eliza R. Snow, *Biography and Family Record of Lorenzo Snow* [Reprint of 1884 edition, *Deseret News*, 1975], 69–70)

———————

If any man had asked me what was my choice when Joseph Smith revealed the doctrine, . . . I would have said, "let me have but one wife." . . . It was the first time in my life that I desired the grave, and I could hardly get over it for a long time.

(Brigham Young; as quoted in *Comprehensive History of the Church*, ed. by B. H. Roberts [Orem, Utah: Sonos Publishing, 1991], 2:201–203)

———————

I had always entertained the strict ideas of virtue, and I felt as a married man that this was to me, outside of this principle, an appalling thing to do. The idea of going and asking a young lady to be married to me when I had already a wife! I had always entertained the strictest regard of chastity. . . . With the feelings I had entertained, nothing but a knowledge of God, and the revelations of God, and the truth of them, could have induced me to embrace such a principle as this.

(John Taylor, *The Life of John Taylor* [Salt Lake City: Deseret Book, 2002], 100)

Jacob 2:35; 3:10 • NEGATIVE EXAMPLE OF FATHERS
(Refer in this text to Mosiah 25:12; Alma 39:11; 2 Nephi 4:5–6.)

Consider this sobering forecast: "About 40 percent of U.S. children will go to sleep in homes in which their fathers do not live" (David Blankenhorn). Some estimate this will rise to 60 percent. This same commentator has written, "Fatherlessness is the engine driving our most urgent social problems, from crime to adolescent pregnancy to domestic violence" (ibid.). Such outcomes, brothers and sisters, unfortunately, constitute America's grossest national product, produced in the slums of the spirit created by spreading secularism!

(Neal A. Maxwell, *Ensign*, May 1995 [Salt Lake City: The Church of Jesus Christ of Latter-day Saints, 1995], 67)

———————

A word to adults and parents. Elder Bruce R. McConkie's father counseled that when we violate any commandment, however small, our youth may choose to violate a commandment later on in life perhaps 10 times or 100 times worse and justify it on the basis of the small commandment we broke (Conversation with Brit McConkie).

(Vaughn J. Featherstone, *Ensign*, Nov. 1999 [Salt Lake City: The Church of Jesus Christ of Latter-day Saints, 1999], 14)

———————

Sometimes bad examples, or "the uncertain sound of the trumpet," which children receive in the home comes in the form of criticism of Church authorities, or in speaking kind words and thoughts outside the home but within it speaking words which are harsh and brusque. The sound is unclear if children observe the payment of tithing when and if it is convenient, or if they hear justifications for not paying it in moments when faith weakens. It is a distorted sound when they see that observance of the Sabbath depends on which sport event is scheduled for the day, or if the weather is ideal for an outing.

Those who act in this manner can be compared to the person whom President Hugh B. Brown described when he said, "He who knows the precepts and neglects to obey them is like one that lights a candle in the darkness and then closes his eyes" (*Relief Society Magazine*, Oct. 1969, 725).

(Angel Abrea, in Conference Report, Apr. 1984 [Salt Lake City: The Church of Jesus Christ of Latter-day Saints, 1984], 97–98)

Jacob 3:1 • PRAY UNTO HIM WITH EXCEEDING FAITH

In a theological school held in Kirtland during the winter of 1834–35, Heber C. Kimball related a story of simple faith that touched a responsive cord in the Prophet's heart and revealed the quality of faith which he possessed. Kimball's little daughter had broken a saucer and for the act was promised a whipping, to be administered by her mother when she returned from a visit on which she was just starting. While her mother was away, the girl went out under an apple tree and prayed that her mother's heart might be softened so that the promised punishment might not be administered. Mrs. Kimball was very careful to fulfill her promises to her children, but upon returning she had no disposition to chastise her child. Later the child told her mother that she had prayed to God that she might not receive the whipping. "Joseph wept like a child on hearing this simple narrative and its application," Kimball reported.

In the Prophet's reaction may be found a key to his nature. He, too, knew the power of childlike faith. Hence the narration of that simple incident deeply touched him. At another time he sat down to eat a scanty

meal of corn bread, and prayed, "Lord, we thank Thee for this johnny cake, and ask Thee to send us something better. Amen." Before the bread had been eaten, a man came to the door and asked if Joseph were home, and upon being informed that he was, said, "I have brought you some flour and a ham." After thanking the man and blessing him for the gift, the Prophet turned to his wife and said, "I knew the Lord would answer my prayer."

(Hyrum L. Andrus, *Joseph Smith, the Man and the Seer* [Salt Lake City: Deseret Book, 1970], 58–59)

Jacob 3:2 • FEAST UPON HIS LOVE

The Prophet Joseph taught us what it means to feast on the scriptures. He said that the Book of Mormon would get a man "nearer to God by abiding by its precepts, than by any other book" (*History of the Church*, 4:461) You will grow closer to the Lord and love Him more. That is the promise in Jacob 3:2. . . .

You and those you love will receive the word of God by obeying it. That will allow them to feel His love. That is one of the great blessings of the gift of the Holy Ghost. When we feel that love, we can know that our course in life is approved of God. That is the feast of the delicious fruit described in the Book of Mormon (see 1 Nephi 11:21–23; 15:36).

(Henry B. Eyring, in Conference Report, Oct. 2003 [Salt Lake City: The Church of Jesus Christ of Latter-day Saints, 2003], 96)

Jacob 3:7 • HUSBANDS LOVE WIVES, WIVES LOVE HUSBANDS
(Refer in this text to 1 Nephi 5:2, 7; Enos 1:1–3.)

The way we treat our wives could well have the greatest impact on the character of our sons. If a father is guilty of inflicting verbal or physical abuse in any degree on his companion, his sons will resent him for it, perhaps even despise him for it. But interestingly enough, when they are grown and marry, they are likely to follow the same pattern of abuse with their wives. There is an urgent need in our society for fathers who respect their wives and treat them with sweet, tender love.

Recently I heard of a father who foolishly called his beautiful, intelligent wife "stupid" and "dumb" in a most degrading manner for some small mistake she innocently made. The children listened, embarrassed and frightened for their mother. She was belittled in front of those that she loved most. Although an apology and forgiveness were expressed, there still remained the hurt and shame of a senseless moment.

The Spirit of the Lord cannot be expected to bless our lives if we persist in being angry, callous, and cruel to our mates. We cannot expect our sons to develop respect and gentleness toward their mothers if we do not provide them a proper example. President David O. McKay said, "The most important thing a father can do for his children is to love their mother" (quoted from Theodore Hesburgh, *Reader's Digest,* Jan. 1963, 25; in *Richard Evans' Quote Book* [1971], 11).

(F. Melvin Hammond, in Conference Report, Oct. 2002 [Salt Lake City: The Church of Jesus Christ of Latter-day Saints, 2002], 107)

Jacob 3:7 • LOVE THEIR CHILDREN

Too often, out of our own frustration and weakness, we raise our hands to strike our children, usually in an attempt to protect our own selfish pride. Every child needs to be disciplined. Not only do they need it; they expect it; they want it. Discipline gives direction and teaches self-control, but in all discipline there should be a sense of righteous judgment and pure love.

When I was a little boy, my widowed mother gave me the most severe discipline possible. She said, with tears in her eyes, "My son, I am so disappointed in you." The pain in my heart was more than I could bear. A thousand lashes could not have cut me so deeply. I knew that such a rebuke could only have been made to me out of her pure love, for if there was one thing that I was certain of, it was that my mother loved me. I resolved never again to be subject to the disappointment and the broken heart of an angel mother. I believe that I have succeeded in that resolve.

(F. Melvin Hammond, in Conference Report, Oct. 2002 [Salt Lake City: The Church of Jesus Christ of Latter-day Saints, 2002], 108)

Jacob 4:6–7 • OUR WEAKNESS AND THE POWER OF THE LORD

(Refer in this text to Ether 12:26–27.)

Jacob 4:6 • SPIRIT OF PROPHECY

Each of us is privileged to receive prophetic revelation illuminating future events in our lives, such as a Church calling we are to receive. To cite another example, after our fifth child was born, my wife and I did not have any more children. After more than ten years, we concluded that our family would not be any larger, which grieved us. Then one day, while my wife was in the temple, the Spirit whispered to her that she would have another child. That prophetic revelation was fulfilled a year and a half later with the birth of our sixth child, for whom we had waited thirteen years.

(Dallin H. Oaks, *With Full Purpose of Heart* [Salt Lake City: Deseret Book, 2002], 151)

It is the privilege of every man and woman in this kingdom to enjoy the spirit of prophecy, which is the Spirit of God; and to the faithful it reveals such things as are necessary for their comfort and consolation, and to guide them in their daily duties.

(Wilford Woodruff, *Deseret News*, 30 July 1862, 33; as quoted in Julie B. Beck, *Ensign*, May 2006 [Salt Lake City: The Church of Jesus Christ of Latter-day Saints, 2006], 13)

Jacob 4:10 • TAKE COUNSEL FROM HIS HAND

Many in various illnesses have measured their recovery in such small degrees and over so many days— like the hand-over-hand climb out of a steep gravel pit. But Jesus' empathy is not merely a matter of detached intellectual familiarity. He helps us, hand over hand, because He understands personally that through which we pass. No wonder we should acknowledge His hand.

(Neal A. Maxwell, *One More Strain of Praise* [Salt Lake City: Bookcraft, 1999], 38)

Jacob 4:12 • WHY NOT SPEAK OF THE ATONEMENT OF CHRIST?

"Why not speak of the atonement of Christ?" (Jacob 4:12). Brothers and sisters, given man's true self-interest, why should we really speak much of anything else?

(Neal A. Maxwell, *Ensign*, Nov. 1986 [Salt Lake City: The Church of Jesus Christ of Latter-day Saints, 1986], 52–54, 59)

Jacob 4:13 • THE SPIRIT SPEAKETH TRUTH AND LIETH NOT

When President Elaine Jack was called in 1990, and Chieko Okazaki and I became her counselors, we humbly sought to be instruments . . . for our sisters throughout the world. We were well aware that their circumstances vary greatly. . . . We centered on Jacob chapter 4, verse 13. . . . We knew that women struggling to clarify their identities could best do that not by comparing themselves to other women but by understanding their important place as full and equal partners with men in receiving, in righteousness, the saving ordinances established by Christ. We saw that men and women are baptized, are offered the gift of the Holy Ghost, partake of the sacrament, and make sacred covenants in the temples of the Church in exactly the same ways. We would not try to describe an ideal Mormon woman. We would seek instead to teach that Christ is our model and that as we are filled with his love, we are his disciples.

(Aileen H. Clyde, *Ensign*, Nov. 1993 [Salt Lake City: The Church of Jesus Christ of Latter-day Saints, 1993], 92)

Jacob 4:13 • THINGS AS THEY REALLY ARE . . . AS THEY REALLY WILL BE

The temple is the matchless setting for receiving priesthood blessings. . . . Priesthood authority assures that the covenants we make in the temple are everlasting. . . . When we attend the temple, we are blessed with knowledge of "things as they really are and of things as they really will be" (Jacob 4:13).

(Elaine L. Jack, *Ensign*, Nov. 1996 [Salt Lake City: The Church of Jesus Christ of Latter-day Saints, 1996], 77–78)

In a time when many perceive truth as relative, a declaration of absolute truth is not very popular, nor does it seem politically correct. . . . Testimonies of things how "they really are" (Jacob 4:13) are bold, true, and vital because they have eternal consequences for mankind. . . . A testimony of the restored gospel of Jesus Christ will always include these clear and simple truths:

•   God lives. He is our loving Father in Heaven, and we are His children.
•   Jesus Christ is the Son of the living God and the Savior of the world.
•   Joseph Smith is the prophet of God through whom the gospel of Jesus Christ was restored in the latter days.
•   The Book of Mormon is the word of God.
•   President Gordon B. Hinckley, his counselors, and the members of the Quorum of the Twelve Apostles are the prophets, seers, and revelators in our day.

(Dieter F. Uchtdorf, *Ensign*, Nov. 2006 [Salt Lake City: The Church of Jesus Christ of Latter-day Saints, 2006], 38)

Jacob 4:14 • LOOKING BEYOND THE MARK

They were apparently afflicted with a pseudosophistication and a snobbishness that gave them a false sense of superiority over those who came among them with the Lord's words of plainness. . . . They must have reveled in speculative and theoretical matters that obscured for them the fundamental spiritual truths. . . . There are other ways in which many of us often look beyond the mark. Sometimes we focus too much of our attention and energy upon our temporal wants, not only to entertain ourselves and gratify our physical appetites, but also to gain recognition, position, and power. We can become so consumed by the pursuit of these things that we sacrifice the sweetness and enduring peace of mind that are found in spiritual well-being, in well-nurtured family relationships, and in the love and respect of friends and associates.

(Dean L. Larsen, in Conference Report, Oct. 1987

[Salt Lake City: The Church of Jesus Christ of Latter-day Saints, 1987], 12–13)

We are "looking beyond the mark" (Jacob 4:14), therefore, when, figuratively speaking, we are more interested in the physical dimensions of the cross than what was achieved thereon by Jesus. Or, when we neglect Alma's words of faith because we are too fascinated by the light-shielding hat reportedly used by Joseph Smith during some of the translating of the Book of Mormon.

(Neal A. Maxwell, *First Nephi, The Doctrinal Foundation* [Provo, Utah: BYU Religious Studies Center, 1988], 5)

So many times young people are enticed to go to the very edge or even beyond it. With only a precarious toehold, it is easy to be seriously injured or even die. Life is too precious to throw away in the name of excitement, or, as Jacob said in the Book of Mormon, "looking beyond the mark." You young people may think that you are indestructible and that you are going to live forever. In a few years you will learn that this is not so. . . . Of even more danger is to put your souls at risk by dabbling in drugs or other mind-abusing substances to "get a buzz." Some of you may think that you will discover your strengths and abilities by living on the edge. . . . Your strengths and identity will come from honoring your priesthood, developing your talents, and serving the Lord.

(James E. Faust, *Ensign*, Nov. 1995 [Salt Lake City: The Church of Jesus Christ of Latter-day Saints, 1995], 45–46)

[An example of how we can look beyond the mark.] We should remember that our family relationships—even more than our church callings—are the setting in which the most important part of that development can occur. . . .

I hope th[is] . . . will cause our local leaders to reduce their concentration on statistical measures of actions and focus more on what our brothers and sisters *are* and what they are striving to *become*.

(Dallin H. Oaks, *With Full Purpose of Heart* [Salt Lake City: Deseret Book, 2002], 41)

Some persons write General Authorities asking when we will be returning to Missouri or how we should plan to build up the New Jerusalem. Others want to know details about the Celestial Kingdom, such as the position of a person who lives a good life but never ever marries.

I don't know the answers to any of these questions. What I do know is that persons worrying about such things are probably neglecting to seek a firmer understanding and a better practice of the basic principles of the gospel that have been given to them with words of plainness by the scriptures and by the servants of the Lord.

If we neglect the words of plainness and look beyond the mark, we are starting down a path that often leads to a loss of commitment and sometimes to a loss of faith. There is enough difficulty in following the words of plainness, without reaching out for things we have not been given and probably cannot understand.

On our refrigerator at home Sister Oaks has posted these wise words of Sister Elisa Wirthlin: "Don't complicate the simplicities of the gospel with questions that are not in harmony with simple truths."

(Dallin H. Oaks, "Be Wise," BYU–Idaho Devotional, Nov. 7, 2006, 2 of 10)

Jacob 4:14 • DESPISED WORDS OF PLAINNESS

Ancient Israelites despised words of plainness and sought for things they could not understand (Jacob 4:14). Thus, Isaiah spoke without simplicity and plainness.

(Victor L. Ludlow, *Unlocking The Old Testament* [Salt Lake City: Deseret Book, 1981], 151)

Jacob 4:15–18 • A STONE, THE SURE FOUNDATION
(Isaiah 28:16.)

The prophecy that the stone would be rejected by the Jews is also found in Psalms 118:22 and is quoted by the Savior in the New Testament (see Matt. 21:42). In the Book of Mormon, Jacob quoted the allegory of Zenos to show how the rejected stone would become the head of the corner (see Jacob 4:15–18).

(Monte S. Nyman, *Great Are the Words of Isaiah* [Salt Lake City: Bookcraft, 1980], 104)

———————

In each new temple we have had a cornerstone ceremony in harmony with a tradition that goes back to ancient times. Before the general use of concrete, the foundation walls of the building were laid with large stones. A trench would be dug, and stones would be placed as footings. Starting at a point of beginning, the foundation wall would be run in one direction to a cornerstone; then the corner would be turned and the wall run to the next corner, where another stone was placed, from which the wall would be run to the next corner, and from there to the point of beginning. In many instances, including the construction of early temples in the Church, cornerstones were used at each junction point of the walls and put in place with ceremony. The final stone was spoken of as the chief cornerstone, and its placement became the reason for much celebration. With this cornerstone in position, the foundation was ready for the superstructure. Hence the analogy that Paul used in describing the true Church. . . . (Ephesians 2:19–21).

We have basic cornerstones on which this great latter-day Church has been established by the Lord and built, "fitly framed together." . . .

I mention first the chief cornerstone, whom we recognize and honor as the Lord Jesus Christ. The second is the vision given the Prophet Joseph Smith when the Father and the Son appeared to him. The third is the Book of Mormon, which speaks as a voice from the dust with the words of ancient prophets declaring the divinity and reality of the Savior of mankind. The fourth is the priesthood with all of its powers and authority, whereby men act in the name of God in administering the affairs of His kingdom. . . .

Each of these cornerstones is related to the others, each connected by a foundation of apostles and prophets, all tied to the chief cornerstone, Jesus Christ. On this has been established His Church, "fitly framed together" for the blessing of all who will partake of its offering (see Ephesians 2:20–21).

(Gordon B. Hinckley, *Ensign*, Feb. 2004 [Salt Lake City: The Church of Jesus Christ of Latter-day Saints, 2004], 3–4, 7)

Jacob 4:18 • ANXIETY
(Refer in this text to Mosiah 4:27; 3 Nephi 11:3–5.)

In today's overloaded society, some of the healing agents that our parents enjoyed seem not to be at work in our lives. Fewer and fewer are able to relieve stress by working with their hands and by tilling the soil. The increasing demands, the diversity of voices, the entreating sales pitches, the piercing noises, the entanglement of many personal relationships can rob our soul of the peace they need to function and survive. Our hurry to meet the relentless demands of the clock tears away at our inner peace. The pressures to compete and survive are great. Our appetite for personal possessions seems enormous. The increasing forces that destroy the individual and family bring great sadness and heartbreak.

(James E. Faust, *Ensign*, May 1992 [Salt Lake City: The Church of Jesus Christ of Latter-day Saints, 1992], 6)

———————

Only as we seek to be purged of selfishness and of concern for recognition and wealth can we find some sweet relief from the anxieties, hurts, pains, miseries, and concerns of this world.

(James E. Faust, *Ensign*, May 1995 [Salt Lake City: The Church of Jesus Christ of Latter-day Saints, 1995], 63)

In this school environment, you are not immune from pressures which relate to schoolwork—tensions and problems—and the long list of attendant emotionally-oriented difficulties and disorders—insecurity, worry, stress, confusion, dependency, suspicion, withdrawal, fear . . . If you happen to hit a good sorry mood once in a while, relax and enjoy it—it is a good sign that you are normal. It is all right to worry about things now and again, I suppose, but when you get worried about being worried, that is when you are getting off the track.

(Boyd K. Packer, BYU Devotional, 4 Oct. 1966, 3, 6)

It is not work that kills men; it is worry. Work is healthy; you can hardly put more upon a man than he can bear. Worry is rust upon the blade. . . . Fear secretes acids; but love and trust are sweet juices.

(Henry Ward Beecher; as quoted in Hugh B. Brown, *You and Your Marriage* [Salt Lake City: Bookcraft Inc., 1960], 175)

We are indoctrinated that somehow we should always be instantly emotionally comfortable. When that is not so, some become anxious—and all too frequently seek relief from counseling, from analysis, and even from medication.

It was meant to be that life would be a challenge. To suffer some anxiety, some depression, some disappointment, even some failure is normal.

Teach our members that if they have a good, miserable day once in a while, or several in a row, to stand steady and face them. Things will straighten out.

(Boyd K. Packer, in Conference Report, Apr. 1978 [Salt Lake City: The Church of Jesus Christ of Latter-day Saints, 1978], 139–140)

We know that some anxiety and depression is caused by physical disorders, but much (perhaps most) of it is not pain of the body but of the spirit. Spiritual pain resulting from guilt can be replaced with peace of mind.

(Boyd K. Packer, *Ensign*, May 2001 [Salt Lake City: The Church of Jesus Christ of Latter-day Saints, 2001], 23)

Because we have not immersed and washed our-

selves in those living waters which flow from the Book of Mormon, we have not enjoyed faith like the ancients, that faith which strengthens resolve and provides courage and peace in a time of unrest. So much of the stress and fear and apprehension and exhaustion that now exist in society is so very unnecessary; ours could be the right to that lifting and liberating Spirit which produces hope and peace and rest.

(Robert Millet, Know the Book of Mormon Seminar, Brigham Young University, 2 June 1990, 3)

I have come to know that in this age of anxiety, and sometimes selfishness, there are not many of us willing to forego comforts or hard-earned security in order to concern ourselves with the welfare of others outside of our immediate circle of acquaintance. But some are—and some do.

(F. Burton Howard, in Conference Report, Apr. 1981 [Salt Lake City: The Church of Jesus Christ of Latter-day Saints, 1981], 95)

When we're too anxious we won't be able to gather new information, think clearly about the problem, explore our options, give calm and clear feedback to others, and find creative solutions that consider the needs of all. And fear can run amok, flooding our system with adrenaline and hijacking our neo-cortex—the thinking part of the brain.

Usually, anxiety is a mean trickster. It signals you to pay attention, but it also turns your brain to oatmeal, narrows and rigidifies your focus, and obscures the real issues from view. Anxiety tricks you out of the "now" as you obsessively replay and regret the past and worry about the future. It tricks you into losing sight of your competence and your capacity for love, creativity, and joy. . . . Anxiety interferes with self-regard and self-respect. . . . It can dig a big negative groove in your brain and make it impossible for you to hang on to a positive thought for more than five seconds. It can affect your body in ways that can feel crippling. . . .

When you're anxious, doom-and-gloom fantasies tend to permeate your day, and reach a fever pitch when you're lying in bed. Your anxious mind . . . will hook on to some dire, worst-case scenario . . . these thoughts grip you in a way that accomplishes nothing except to make you feel miserable and powerless.

(Harriet Lerner, PhD, *Fear and Other Uninvited Guests* [New York: Harpers Collins, 2004], 54–58)

Here was a prophet, in the temple, preaching the doctrines of the kingdom, and he was concerned about losing the Spirit over something as simple as anxiety. Even the worthy prophet Jacob could not be sensitive to the promptings of the Spirit when anxiety was a part of his life.

I had grown up assuming that the companionship of the Spirit was the reward for the absence of sin; that not participating in drugs, alcohol, sexual sin, and so forth would allow the Spirit to permeate our lives. Jacob seemed to be suggesting that it takes more than reacting to the negative—we must also be proactive toward the Spirit, even in our attitude. Thus, the prophetic reminder to maintain a disposition that rises above something as simple as anxiety.

(K. Douglas Bassett, *The Barber's Song* [Springville, Utah: Cedar Fort, 2005], 126)

Jacob 5 • JACOB'S ATTEMPT TO ANSWER THE QUESTION HE POSES IN 4:17

I have a key by which I understand the scriptures. I enquire, what was the question which drew out the answer.

(*Teachings of the Prophet Joseph Smith*, comp. by Joseph Fielding Smith [Salt Lake City: Deseret Book, 1976], 276)

Jacob 5 • THE ALLEGORY OF ZENOS

Olive trees do have to be pruned and cultivated diligently; the top branches are indeed the first to wither, and the new shoots do come right out of the trunk; the olive is indeed the most plastic of trees, surpassing even the willow in its power to survive the most drastic whacking and burning; a good olive tree is greatly cherished, and no end of pains are taken to preserve it even through many centuries, for really superior fruit is very rare and difficult to obtain and perpetuate; the ancient way of strengthening the old tree (especially in Greece) was to graft in the shoots of the oleaster or wild olive; also, shoots from valuable old trees were transplanted to keep the stock alive after the parent tree should perish; to a surprising degree the olive prefers poor and rocky ground, whereas rich soil produces inferior fruit; too much grafting produces a nondescript and cluttered yield of fruit; the top branches if allowed to grow as in Spain and France, while producing a good shade tree, will indeed sap the strength of the tree and give a poor crop; fertilizing with dung is very important, in spite of the preference for rocky ground, and has peen practised since ancient times; the thing to be most guarded against is bitterness in the fruit. All these points . . . are duly, though quite casually, noted in Zenos's Parable of the Olive Tree.

(Hugh Nibley, *Since Cumorah* [Salt Lake City: Deseret Book, 1976], 269–270)

But we have something in the Book of Mormon that, if we did not have any other truth expressed in it, would be sufficient evidence of the divinity of this book. I have reference to the fifth chapter of Jacob. . . . I think that as many as ninety-nine out of every hundred who read the Book of Mormon, read this parable through without grasping the fulness and meaning of it. And I think this is one of the greatest passages in the Book of Mormon. . . . No matter how many times you have read the Book of Mormon, . . . take a few minutes at some convenient time and sit down and just read carefully every word in the fifth chapter of the Book of Jacob. . . . No greater parable was ever recorded. . . . I tell you, my brothers and sisters, Joseph Smith did not write it. That was written by the inspiration of the Almighty. . . . When you read that chapter through if you cannot say in your soul, "this is absolutely a revelation from God," then there is something wrong with you.

(Joseph Fielding Smith, *Answers to Gospel Questions* [Salt Lake City: Deseret Book, 1972], 4:203–207)

Israel is a tame olive tree. It is an olive tree that begins to decay. The branches that are dying are cut off. But the gardener takes certain of those branches off that tree that seem to be decaying and plants them in all parts of the Lord's vineyard. And the Lord says, "I will take these branches and plant them in the distant parts of my vineyard. Have my servants attend to them. The old tree seems to be dying and we shall see if we can't take these severed branches and raise fruit." Not only that, but they took some of the branches and grafted them in to all the wild olive trees. Who were the wild olive trees? The Gentiles. And so the Lord sent his servants to all parts of this vineyard, which is the world, and planted these branches of the tree. As they grew, they bore fruit. In the course of time, some of these branches began to wither and decay. And the Lord nurtured them. He had his servants dig around them, cultivate them, care for them the best they knew how, and yet some of them practically died. Others bore fruit. Then comes the time of the harvest. The Lord says, "I will cultivate my field for the last time. These branches that I have taken to various parts of the world are dying. I'll gather the fruit and do the best I can with them." . . . the House of Israel, . . . in its native land . . . began to die. So the Lord took branches like the Nephites, like the lost tribes, and like others that the Lord led off that we do not know anything about, to other parts of the earth. He planted them all over his vineyard, which is the world. No doubt he sent some of these branches into Japan, into Korea, into China. No question about it, because he sent them to all parts of the world. . . . What's the use of going out among the Chinese, the Japanese, the Koreans, and the people of the Far East to preach the gospel to them? The answer: because they are branches of the tree, they are of the house of Israel. The Lord took the branches of the tree, grafted them into the wild olives, the Gentiles, and is bringing the Gentiles into the gospel of Jesus Christ.... Are we going to preach the gospel in Korea, in Japan, in China? Yes, we are. Why? Because the blood of Israel is there.... [The Lord] scattered [Israel] over the whole face of the earth. So now the Gentiles are sanctified by the blood of Abraham.

(Joseph Fielding Smith, *Answers to Gospel Questions* [Salt Lake City: Deseret Book, 1972], 4:203–207)

JACOB	SYMBOLS	EXPLANATION
5:3	Vineyard	(Jacob 6:3)
5:3	Tame Olive Tree	(Jacob 5:3)
5:4	Master of the Vineyard	(D&C 104:86)
5:6	Main Top	(Footnote 6a)
5:7	Wild Olive Tree	(Roman 11:13, 17, 19)
5:7	Servant	(Amos 3:7; D&C 1:38)

JACOB	EVENTS	EXPLANATION
5:3	Decay of tame olive tree	(Footnote 3d)
5:8	Take away many of these young and tender branches	(Footnote 8a)
5:9	Graft in the branches of wild olive tree	(1 Ne. 10:14; 15:13; 2 Ne 30:2)
5:14	Hid branches of tame olive tree in nethermost parts of the vineyard.	(Hosea 8:8; 1 Ne. 10:12; 15:12; 22:3–4)
5:17	Fruit born following the grafting of the wild olive branches	(Gal. 3:7–9, 29)
5:24–25	Planted natural branches in a good spot of ground	(Footnote 25a; Alma 26:36)
5:25	Part of the tree hath brought forth tame fruit	(Jacob 5:45; Hel.15:3)
5:25	Part of the tree hath brought forth wild fruit	(Jacob 5:45; Hel. 15:4)
5:29	A long time passed ... the Lord ... said unto his servant	(D&C: 103:21)
5:32	The wild branches have produced fruit, "there is none of it which is good."	(JS—H. 1:19)
5:43	This last that "I did plant in a good spot of ground."	(Jacob 5:25)
5:44	"Cut down that which cumbered this spot of ground."	(Footnote 44a)
5:45	"They have overcome the good branch"	(Morm. 8:2)
5:48	How could the branches have overcome the roots?	(Footnote 48a)
5:52	Graft branches back into tame olive-tree	(1 Ne. 10:14)
5:61–62; 6:2	"Call servants that we might labor"	(D&C 24:19; 88:84; Larsen, in Conference Report, Apr. 1983, 33)
5:72, 74–75	What makes missionaries successful?	(Jacob 6:3)
5:77	"Evil fruit shall again come into my vineyard"	(Joseph Fielding Smith, *Answers to Gospel Questions*, 4:206; "That means there will be some apostasy.")

The parable of Zenos, recorded by Jacob in chapter five of his book, is one of the greatest parables ever recorded. This parable in and of itself stamps the Book of Mormon with convincing truth. No mortal man, without the inspiration of the Lord, could have written such a parable. It is a pity that too many of those who read the Book of Mormon pass over and slight the truths which it conveys in relation to the history, scattering, and final gathering of Israel....

In brief, it records the history of Israel down through the ages, the scattering of the tribes to all parts of the earth; their mingling with, or being grafted in, the wild olive trees, or in other words the mixing of the blood of Israel among the Gentiles by which the great blessings and promises of the Lord to Abraham are fulfilled (see Gen. 22:16–18)....

This remarkable parable portrays how, as branches of the olive tree (Israelites) were carried to all parts of the earth (the Lord's vineyard) and grafted into the wild olive trees (the Gentile nations). Thus they are fulfilling the promise that the Lord had made.

Today Latter-day Saints are going to all parts of the world as servants in the vineyard to gather this fruit and lay it in store for the time of the coming of the Master.

This parable is one of the most enlightening and interesting in the Book of Mormon. How can any person read it without feeling the inspiration of this ancient prophet?

(Joseph Fielding Smith, *Answers to Gospel Questions*, comp. and ed. by Joseph Fielding Smith Jr. [Salt Lake City: Deseret Book, 1972], 4:141–142)

Jacob 5:7, 11, 13, 32, 46, 47, 51, 66 • IT GRIEVETH ME

An almost haunting declaration of this divine devotion is laced through these seventy-seven verses in the eight-fold repetition of the line "it grieveth me that I should lose this tree." This long parable does outline Israel's history, but soon enough the attentive reader senses a much more personal story coming from the printed page—the grief and the godly pain of a father anguishing over the needless destruction of His family.

(Jeffrey R. Holland, *Heroes from the Book of Mormon* [Salt Lake City: Bookcraft, 1995], 37)

Jacob 5:32 • BROUGHT FORTH FRUIT, NONE OF IT GOOD

This morning we went to Delft [in the Netherlands] to see that historic and beautiful and attractive city, the place of the many, many canals. It was very interesting to go to Delft and visit those two old churches there that go way back through the centuries. One's called the Old Church, one's called the New Church. They both looked old.

It was interesting to reflect there. . . . [The Lord said] to the boy prophet, "Having a form of godliness, but they deny the power thereof" (Joseph Smith—History 1:19). That's exactly what I was thinking about as we were in those old churches—a form of godliness but no life in their worship. I know why the Lord restored this gospel in this great dispensation.

(*Discourses of President Gordon B. Hinckley*, 1995–99 [Salt Lake City: The Church of Jesus Christ of Latter-day Saints, 2004], 1:427)

Jacob 5:33–35 • THE TREE PROFITETH ME NOTHING

The master is concerned that the roots are now supporting branches that bring forth evil fruit; or in other words, the Lord is disappointed that the people grafted into the covenant have turned away to doing evil works.

(John L. Fowles, *The Book of Mormon—Tenth Annual Symposium* [Provo, Utah: The Church of Jesus Christ of Latter-day Saints, 1986], 34)

Jacob 5:41, 47, 49 • WHAT COULD I HAVE DONE MORE?

There is much more here than simply the unrav-eling of convoluted Israelite history. Of greater significance in this allegory is the benevolent view of God that it provides. He is portrayed here as one who repeatedly, painstakingly, endlessly tries to save the work of His hands and in moments of greatest disappointment holds His head in His hands and weeps, "What could I have done more for my vineyard?" (Jacob 5:41, 47, 49). This allegory is a declaration of divine love, of God's unceasing effort as a father laboring on behalf of His children.

(Jeffrey R. Holland, *Heroes from the Book of Mormon* [Salt Lake City: Bookcraft, 1995], 37)

———————

That vivid moment in the Book of Mormon allegory of the olive tree, when after digging and dunging, watering and weeding, trimming, pruning, transplanting, and grafting, the great Lord of the vineyard throws down his spade and his pruning shears and weeps, crying out to any who would listen, "What could I have done more for my vineyard?"

What an indelible image of God's engagement in our lives! What anguish in a parent when His children do not choose Him nor "the gospel of God" He sent! How easy to love someone who so singularly loves us!

(Jeffrey R. Holland, in Conference Report, Oct. 2003 [Salt Lake City: The Church of Jesus Christ of Latter-day Saints, 2003], 74)

Jacob 5:49–51 • DESIRES OF THE RIGHTEOUS

The servant pleads with him to spare it a little longer, and the master consents. Not wanting to lose the trees, he extends the time for more labor. This shows that the righteous can influence the Lord. He blesses men according to the desires of their hearts. . . . On one occasion Jesus was going to leave, but he perceived that the people desired him to stay a little longer with them. His bowels were filled with compassion towards them, and he healed their sick, lame, and blind (see 3 Nephi 17:5–8). Righteous servants can influence the Lord through desires and faith, just as the servant does in the allegory.

(John L. Fowles, *The Book of Mormon—Tenth Annual Symposium* [Provo, Utah: The Church of Jesus Christ of Latter-day Saints, 1986], 34)

Jacob 5:61–62; 6:2 • CALL SERVANTS THAT WE MIGHT LABOR

It is properly referred to as the "fullness of times" (D&C 112:30). It is the period during which the Lord and his servants will make the final great effort to take the message of truth to all the peoples of the earth and to reclaim the descendants of ancient Israel who have lost their true identity.

The prophet Zenos, whom Jacob quotes in the Book of Mormon, compares this effort to the work of the laborers who prune and nurture a vineyard and gather its fruit for the last time. . . .

You have come to the earth when the foundation has been laid for this great work. The gospel has been restored for the last time. The Church has been established in almost every part of the world. The stage is set for the final dramatic scenes to be enacted. You will be the principal players. You are among the last laborers in the vineyard. This is the yoke that is set upon your necks. This is the service for which you are chosen.

(Dean L. Larsen, in Conference Report, Apr. 1983 [Salt Lake City: The Church of Jesus Christ of Latter-day Saints, 1983], 47)

Jacob 5:75 • YE SHALL HAVE JOY WITH ME BECAUSE OF THE FRUIT OF MY VINEYARD

I learned as a 12-year-old boy the Boy Scout Oath: "On my honor I will do my best to do my duty to God and my country and to obey the Scout Law; to help other people at all times; to keep myself physically strong, mentally awake, and morally straight" (*Boy Scout Handbook*, 10th ed. [1990], 5). Now, that great opening statement, "On my honor, I will do my best"—that is all you have to worry about in missionary service. Do your very best, and the Lord will take care of the fruit of your service.

You have to know that every time you bring a convert into this Church you bless a life—not one life, if he or she remains faithful, but many lives, for that which you do becomes the fruit of generations yet to come. All of us here are the fruit of missionary work.

(*Discourses of President Gordon B. Hinckley*, 1995–99 [Salt Lake City: The Church of Jesus Christ of Latter-day Saints, 2004], 1:404–405)

Jacob 5:77 • EVIL FRUIT SHALL AGAIN COME INTO MY VINEYARD

There are a few teachers within the Church who while courting apostasy still want to remain members in the Church, for being members makes them more effective in misleading the Saints. But their day of judgment is coming. . . .

The Lord has stated that his Church will never again be taken from the earth because of apostasy. But he has also stated that some members of his Church will fall away.

(Ezra Taft Benson, in Conference Report, Oct. 1964 [Salt Lake City: The Church of Jesus Christ of Latter-day Saints, 1964], 58)

We have been assured that in this last dispensation of the fulness of times, there will be no universal apostasy. When the Lord appears again in his glory, he will find a people who will have remained faithful and who will be ready to receive him and join with him in the completion of his work.

But the fact that there will not be a complete apostasy in this last dispensation does not mean all who have received the gospel and become members of the Church will remain faithful.

(Dean L. Larsen; as quoted in *The Book of Mormon: Alma, The Testimony of the Word*, ed. by Monte S. Nyman and Charles D. Tate [Provo, Utah: Religious Studies Center, BYU, 1992], 5)

Jacob 6 • JACOB'S COMMENTARY CONCERNING THE ALLEGORY OF ZENOS

Jacob 6:5 • ARM OF THE LORD
(Refer in this text to 2 Nephi 19:13–17.)

The "arm of the Lord" is a commonly used metaphor for the power of God in the Bible in the context of creation (see Jeremiah 32:17), in the redemption of Israel from Egypt (see Exodus 15:16; Deuteronomy 4:34), and in his deliverance of Israel in the last days (see Isaiah 40:10; 52:10). In the Book of Mormon, the image of the "arm of the Lord" occurs in the context of the restoration of the gospel and the coming forth of the Book of Mormon (see 1 Nephi 22;10–11; Enos 1:13), and the "arm of mercy" is associated with the power of the Atonement on behalf of the repentant (see Jacob 6:5; Mosiah 29:20; Alma 19:36).

(David Rolph Seely, *The Book of Mormon: The Foundation of Our Faith* [Salt Lake City: Deseret Book, 1999], 206)

Jacob 6:10 • FIRE AND BRIMSTONE
(Refer in this text to 2 Nephi 9:16.)

Jacob 6:11 • THE STRAIT GATE
(Refer in this text to 2 Nephi 31:17–18; 1 Nephi 8:20.)

Jacob 6:12 • BE WISE

I carry in my daily date book a few brief memo sheets. . . . One sheet almost worn out now has nothing more on it than Jacob 6, verse 12: "O be wise; what can I say more?" Be wise enough to accept appropriate discipline and guidelines. Be wise enough to say the right words at the right time to the right person. . . . Ever bear in mind that Jesus was the wisest of the wise, even brilliant, in his relationships with people. . . . President Spencer W. Kimball, on one occasion a few years ago, asked me to accompany him to the Utah State Prison. . . . I learned much from a prophet who was wise. . . . We were greeted by the warden and taken to his office. . . . Two inmates were invited to come in and meet with us. They were in their prison garb and looked hard. I felt very uneasy when the steel door closed behind them and we were left with the two of them. . . . President Kimball shook their hands before we all sat down. This was followed by a brief period of intense silence. The prisoners were looking at the floor. President Kimball was looking at them, and I was looking at him. After this awkward period of silence was over, President Kimball started off with what seemed to me to an unusual approach. The thought crossed my mind that he could say: "What are you in here for? Why did you do it? When do you get out? You ought to be ashamed of yourselves," or "What is your previous record?" . . . He looked at the one, and said to my surprise: "Tell me about your mother." The prisoner responded and told President Kimball and others of us assembled about his mother. . . . President Kimball finally looked at the other prisoner and said: "What does your father do for a living?" He too responded with comments, and the Prophet gave complete attention and listened intently. . . . They looked at him, responded, and looked in his face while he gently listened. . . . Word had spread that President Spencer W. Kimball was at the prison visiting, and some of the media were outside the doors waiting for pictures and conversation with President Kimball. [He] . . . invited some of the press into the room with a cameraman. One reporter said, "President Kimball, we'd like to have a picture of you talking to these two inmates." President Kimball granted the interview by standing up promptly and getting between the two prisoners as the picture was taken. I recall as though it were yesterday what he said after the picture was taken. He shook one hand and then the other and said, "Thank you, boys, for letting me have my picture taken with you." One of these hardened prisoners was in for murder and the other one for grand larceny. To say they were touched and responsive is an understatement. I will never forget the impact of this visit upon me and my future. A wise, gentle prophet conducted his interview without embarrassment, without ridicule, and without condemnation . . . interviewing, counseling, instructing, and touching lives with wisdom.

(Marvin J. Ashton, BYU University Conference, 24–25 Aug. 1992)

Jacob 7 • SHEREM: AN ANTI-CHRIST

(Refer to Korihor lesson in this text, Alma 30.)

Jacob 7:19 • THE UNPARDONABLE SIN

(Refer to "Deny the Holy Ghost" in this text, Alma 39:5–6.)

Jacob 7:26 • MOURNING OUT OUR DAYS

(Refer in this text to 3 Nephi 23:11.)

That scripture has always fascinated me. It's as if Jacob lets down his hair and, in one paragraph, gives us a candid, frank look at how he feels about his life, which is drawing to a close. He could have painted a rosy picture of things, but he tells us his life was one tribulation after another and that he and his people are "mourning out [their] days." Life was no picnic for the descendents of Lehi who settled in the Promised Land.

I believe it is those types of candid comments in our journals that will be of most interest to our ancestors. They will enjoy reading about events and other things in our lives, but the glimpses into our deepest thoughts and innermost feelings will capture their attention because they will get to know who we really are.

(Val Hale, "Publish or Perish," LDSSA Devotional Address, Orem LDS Institute, 20 Jan. 2006)

Jacob 7:27 • ADIEU

The Prophet Joseph Smith's use of the word "adieu" has created considerable interest among Book of Mormon students. The use of the French word should create no problems since it is widely used in English.

(Sidney B. Sperry, *Book of Mormon Compendium* [Salt Lake City: Bookcraft, 1968], 267)

————————

Some anti-LDS critics of the Book of Mormon have raised the question as to how Jacob could possibly have used such a word as adieu when this word clearly comes from the French language, which was not developed until hundreds of years after the time of Jacob. Such critics evidently overlook the fact that the Book of Mormon is translation literature, and Joseph Smith felt free in his translation to use any words familiar to himself and his readers that would best convey the meaning of the original author. It is interesting to note that there is a Hebrew word *Lehitra'ot*, which has essentially the same meaning in Hebrew as the word adieu has in French. Both of these words are much more than a simple farewell; they include the idea of a blessing. Would it be unreasonable to remind these critics that none of the words contained in the English translation of the book of Jacob were used by Jacob himself? These words all come from the English language, which did not come into existence until long after Jacob's time!

(Daniel H. Ludlow, *A Companion to Your Study of the Book of Mormon* [Salt Lake City: Deseret Book, 1976], 163)

ENOS

Enos 1:1–3 • PARENTAL RESPONSIBILITY

(Refer in this text to 2 Nephi 4:5–6; Mosiah 25:12; Alma 56:47–48, Helaman 5:5.)

Sometimes as I go throughout the Church, I think I am seeing a man who is using his church work as a kind of escape from family responsibility. And sometimes when we've talked about whether or not he's giving attention to his family, his children and his wife, he says something like this: "Well I'm so busy taking care of the Lord's work that I really don't have time." And I say to him, "My dear brother, the greatest of the Lord's work that you and I will ever do is the work that we do within the walls of our own home." Now don't you get any misconception about where the Lord's work starts. That's the most important of all the Lord's work. And you wives may have to remind your husbands of that occasionally. That here in the home—family home night—you must see to it that all the principles are involved so that father takes his place and doesn't neglect the children.

(Harold B. Lee, Address to Seminary and Institute Personnel, BYU, 8 July 1966)

———————

No other success can compensate for failure in the home.

(David O. McKay, *Improvement Era*, June 1964 [Salt Lake City: The Church of Jesus Christ of Latter-day Saints, 1964], 445)

———————

We emphasize that the greatest work you will do will be within the walls of your home. . . . It is not uncommon for responsible parents to lose one of their children, for a time, to influences over which they have no control. They agonize over rebellious sons or daughters. They are puzzled over why they are so helpless when they have tried so hard to do what they should. It is my conviction that those wicked influences one day will be overruled. "The Prophet Joseph Smith declared—and he never taught a more comforting doctrine—that the eternal sealings of faithful parents and the divine promises made to them for valiant service in the Cause of Truth, would save not only themselves, but likewise their posterity. Though some of the sheep may wander, the eye of the Shepherd is upon them, and sooner or later they will feel the tentacles of Divine Providence reaching out after them and drawing them back to the fold. Either in this life or the life to come, they will return. They will have to pay their debt to justice; they will suffer for their sins; and may tread a thorny path; but if it leads them at last, like the penitent Prodigal, to a loving and forgiving father's heart and home, the painful experience will not have been in vain. Pray for your careless and disobedient children; hold on to them with your faith. Hope on, trust on, till you see the salvation of God" (Orson F. Whitney, in Conference Report, Apr. 1929, 110) . . . When parents keep the covenants they have made at the altar of the temple, their children will be forever bound to them. President Brigham Young said [*Discourses of Brigham Young*, 208]: "Let the father and mother, who are members of this Church and Kingdom, take a righteous course, and strive with all their might never to do a wrong, but to do good all their lives; if they have one child or one hundred children go, they are bound up to their parents by an everlasting tie, and no power of earth or hell can separate them from their parents in eternity; they will return again to the fountain from whence they sprang."

(Boyd K. Packer, *Ensign*, May 1992 [Salt Lake City: The Church of Jesus Christ of Latter-day Saints, 1992], 68)

———————

An ancient grandmother lived with her daughter and grandson. As she grew frail and feeble, instead of being a help around the house, she became a constant trial. She broke plates and cups, lost knives, spilled water. One day, exasperated because the old woman had broken another precious plate, the daughter sent the grandson to buy his grandmother a wooden plate. The boy hesitated because he knew a wooden plate would humiliate his grandmother. But his mother insisted, so off he went. He returned bringing not one, but two wooden plates. "I only asked you to buy one," his mother said. "Didn't you hear me?" "Yes," said the boy. "But I bought the second one so there would be one for you when you get old."

(Thomas S. Monson, *Ensign*, May 1993 [Salt Lake City: The Church of Jesus Christ of Latter-day Saints, 1993], 62)

———————

God has placed within us a will, and we should be satisfied to have it controlled by the will of the Almighty. . . . It has been the custom of parents to break the will until it is weakened, and the noble, God-like powers of the child are reduced to a comparative state of imbecility and cowardice. Let that heaven-born property of human agents be properly tempered and wisely directed, instead of pursuing the opposite course, and it will conquer in the cause of right. Break not the spirit of any person, . . . until God shall reign within us to will and do his good pleasure.

(*Discourses of Brigham Young*, comp. by John A. Widtsoe [Salt Lake City: Deseret Book, 1954], 264)

———————

Sometimes some parents mistakenly feel that they can relax a little as to conduct and conformity . . . thinking that a little laxness or indulgence won't matter—or they may fail to teach or to attend Church, or may voice critical views. Some parents sometimes seem to feel that they can ease up a little on the fundamentals without affecting their family or their family's future. But if a parent goes a little off course, the children are likely to exceed the parent's example.

(Richard L. Evans, in Conference Report, Oct. 1964 [Salt Lake City: The Church of Jesus Christ of Latter-day Saints, 1964], 135–136)

———————

One new father wrote: "Often as I watch my son watch me, I am taken back to moments with my own dad, remembering how vividly I wanted to be just like him. I remember having a plastic razor and my own can of foaming cream, and each morning I would shave when he shaved. I remember following his footsteps back and forth across the grass as he mowed the lawn in summer.

"Now I want my son to follow my lead, and yet it terrifies me to know he probably will." . . .

At a vulnerable moment in young Nephi's life, his prophetic future was determined when he said, "I did believe all the words which had been spoken by my father" (1 Ne. 2:16). At the turning point of the prophet Enos's life, he said it was "the words which I had often heard my father speak" (Enos 1:3), which prompted one of the great revelations recorded in the Book of Mormon. And sorrowing Alma the Younger, when confronted by the excruciating memory of his sins, "remembered also to have heard [his] father prophesy . . . concerning the coming of . . . Jesus Christ, a Son of God, to atone for the sins of the world" (Alma 36:17). That brief memory, that personal testimony offered by his father at a time when the father may have felt nothing was sinking in, not only saved the spiritual life of this, his son, but changed forever the history of the Book of Mormon people.

(Jeffrey R. Holland, *Ensign*, May 1999 [Salt Lake City: The Church of Jesus Christ of Latter-day Saints, 1999], 15–16)

———————

Spencer W. Kimball said in an area conference: "Most people are largely the result of their home environment, good or bad. As Lehi said, on the brink of the grave, to his children, 'I know that if ye are brought up in the way ye should go, ye will not depart from it' (2 Nephi 4:5). Our conclusions must therefore be taking life at its best and life at its worst; the difference seems to be the catalyst of love and family solidarity."

(British Area in Conference Report, Aug. 1971, 82; as cited in Jack R. Christianson and K. Douglas Bassett, *Life Lessons from the Book of Mormon* [Salt Lake City: Deseret Book, 2003], 77)

———————

Not long after we were married, we built our first home.

. . . The first of many trees that I planted was a thornless honey locust. . . . It was so supple that I could bend it with ease in any direction. I paid little attention to it as the years passed.

Then one winter day, . . . I chanced to look out the window at it. I noticed that it was leaning to the west, misshapen and out of balance. . . . I went out and braced myself against it as if to push it upright. But the trunk was now nearly a foot in diameter. . . . It seemed to say, "You can't straighten me. It's too late. I've grown this way because of your neglect, and I will not bend."

Finally in desperation I took my saw and cut off the great heavy branch on the west side. The saw left an ugly scar, more than eight inches across. . . . I had cut off the major part of the tree, leaving only one branch growing skyward.

More than half a century has passed since I planted

that tree. . . . The other day I looked at the tree. It is large. Its shape is better. . . . But how serious was the trauma of its youth and how brutal the treatment I used to straighten it.

When it was first planted, a piece of string would have held it in place against the forces of the wind. . . .

I have seen a similar thing, many times, in children whose lives I have observed. The parents who brought them into the world seem almost to have abdicated their responsibility. The results have been tragic. A few simple anchors would have given them the strength to withstand the forces that have shaped their lives. Now it appears it is too late.

(*Teachings of Gordon B. Hinckley* [Salt Lake City: Deseret Book, 1997], 419–20)

We need to make our homes a place of refuge from the storm, which is increasing in intensity all about us. Even if the smallest openings are left unattended, negative influences can penetrate the very walls of our homes. Let me cite an example.

Several years ago I was having dinner with my daughter and her family. The scene is all too common in most homes with small children. My daughter was trying to encourage her young, three-year-old son to eat a balanced meal. He had eaten all the food on his plate that he liked. A small serving of green beans remained, which he was not fond of. In desperation, the mother picked up a fork and tried to encourage him to eat his beans. He tolerated it just about as long as he could. Then he exclaimed, "Look, Mom, don't foul up a good friendship!"

Those were the exact words he heard on a television commercial a few days earlier. Oh, what impact advertising, television programs, the Internet, and the other media are having on our family units!

(L. Tom Perry, in Conference Report, Apr. 2003 [Salt Lake City: The Church of Jesus Christ of Latter-day Saints, 2003], 42)

I speak carefully and lovingly to any of the adults of the Church, parents or otherwise, who may be given to cynicism or skepticism, who in matters of whole-souled devotion always seem to hang back a little. . . . I say, please be aware that the full price to be paid for such a stance does not always come due in your lifetime. No, sadly, some elements of this can be a kind of profligate national debt, with payments coming out of your children's and grandchildren's pockets in far more expensive ways than you ever intended it to be. . . .

Parents simply cannot flirt with skepticism or cynicism, then be surprised when their children expand that flirtation into full-blown romance. . . .

Not long ago Sister Holland and I met a fine young man who came in contact with us after he had been roaming around through the occult and sorting through a variety of Eastern religions, all in an attempt to find religious faith. His father, he admitted, believed in nothing whatsoever. But his grandfather, he said, was actually a member of The Church of Jesus Christ of Latter-day Saints. "But he didn't do much with it," the young man said. "He was always pretty cynical about the Church." From a grandfather who is cynical to a son who is agnostic to a grandson who is now looking desperately for what God had already once given his family!

(Jeffrey R. Holland, in Conference Report, Apr. 2003 [Salt Lake City: The Church of Jesus Christ of Latter-day Saints, 2003], 90–91)

President McKay . . . had a powerful influence as a loving father. When one of his sons, David Lawrence, was a young boy, he accompanied his father in a horse-drawn carriage. "We forded a swollen river in a thunderstorm," David Lawrence later recalled, "and got caught between that river and a mountain torrent. I thought the end of the world had come, and started to cry. Father held me on his lap in his arms all night until we were rescued in the morning. It's hard to disobey a man who loves you and puts his arms around you." . . .

"Our parents' expectations provided the path for us to follow, and our love for them provided an irresistible motivation for us to walk that path. We learned to love them because they first dearly loved each other and us."

(*Teachings of Presidents of the Church—David O. McKay* [Salt Lake City: The Church of Jesus Christ of Latter-day Saints, 2003], 153)

We receive a testimony of the Gospel by obeying the laws and ordinances thereof; and our children will receive that knowledge exactly the same way; and if we do not teach them, . . . they will never receive this knowledge. I have heard people say that their children were born heirs to all the promises of the new and everlasting covenant, and that they would grow up in spite of themselves, with a knowledge of the Gospel. I want to say to you that this is not a true doctrine. . . . We find that it is laid down to the Latter-day Saints, . . . as a law, that they should teach their children.

(*Teachings of President of the Church—Heber J. Grant* [Salt Lake City: The Church of Jesus Christ of Latter-day Saints, 2002], 201)

The most potent influence over the mind of a child to persuade it to learn, to progress, or to accomplish anything, is the influence of love. More can be accomplished for good by unfeigned love, in bringing up a child, than by any other influence that can be brought to bear upon it. A child that cannot be conquered by the lash, or subdued by violence, may be controlled in an instant by unfeigned affection and sympathy. I know that is true. . . . Govern the children, not by passion, by bitter words or scolding, but by affection and by winning their confidence.

If you can only convince your children that you love them, that your soul goes out to them for their good, that you are their truest friend, they, in turn, will place confidence in you and will love you and seek to do your bidding and to carry out your wishes with your love. But if you are selfish, unkindly to them, and if they are not confident that they have your entire affection, they will be selfish, and will not care whether they please you or carry out your wishes or not, and the result will be that they will grow wayward, thoughtless and careless. . . .

If children are defiant and difficult to control, be patient with them until you can conquer by love, and you will have gained their souls, and you can then mould their characters as you please.

(*Teachings of Presidents of the Church—Joseph F. Smith* [Salt Lake City: The Church of Jesus Christ of Latter-day Saints, 1998], 299)

———

Twas a sheep not a lamb that strayed away
In the parable Jesus told,
A grown-up sheep that strayed away
From the ninety and nine in the fold.
And why for the sheep should we seek
And earnestly hope and pray?
Because there is danger when sheep go wrong;
They lead the lambs astray.
Lambs will follow the sheep, you know,
Wherever the sheep may stray.
When sheep go wrong, it won't take long
'Til the lambs are as wrong as they.
And so with the sheep we earnestly plead
For the sake of the lambs today,
For when sheep are lost, what a terrible cost
The lambs will have to pay!

("The Echo," C. C. Miller, quoted in Ben B. Banks, *Ensign*, Nov. 1999 [Salt Lake City: The Church of Jesus Christ of Latter-day Saints, 1999], 10)

———

If the home inflicts harshness, abuse, uncontrolled anger, dishonesty, immorality, and disloyalty, the fruits will be certain and discernible and, in all likelihood,

repeated in the generation that follows. If, on the other hand, there is forbearance, forgiveness, respect, consideration, kindness, mercy, and compassion, the fruits again will be discernible and they will be rewarding.

(Gordon B. Hinckley, *Standing for Something* [New York: Times Books, 2000], 158)

———

The things you say, the tone of your voice, the anger or calm of your words—these things are noticed by your children and by others. They see and learn both the kind and the unkind things we say or do. Nothing exposes our true selves more than how we treat one another in the home. . . .

Even when we think we are doing no harm by our critical remarks, consequences often follow. I am reminded of a boy who handed a donation envelope to his bishop and told him it was for him. The bishop, using this as a teaching moment, explained to the boy that he should mark on the donation slip whether it was for tithing, fast offerings, or for something else. The boy insisted the money was for the bishop himself. When the bishop asked why, the boy replied, "Because my father says you're one of the poorest bishops we've ever had."

(Joseph B. Wirthlin, *Ensign*, May 2005 [Salt Lake City: The Church of Jesus Christ of Latter-day Saints, 2005], 27)

———

Have expectations for your children. We had a curfew and told our sons that the Holy Ghost goes to bed at midnight. When they didn't come home, a few times the Holy Ghost told me to go out and find them. That surprised a few of their dates! We laugh about that now—but I must admit, laughter comes easier as they have grown older.

Be there for your children. Sit on the bed and enjoy the late-night talks—try to stay awake! Pray for the Lord to inspire you. Forgive often. Choose your battles. Testify frequently of Jesus Christ and His goodness and of the Restoration. And most of all, let them know of your trust in the Lord.

(Bonnie D. Parkin, *Ensign*, Nov. 2005 [Salt Lake City: The Church of Jesus Christ of Latter-day Saints, 2005], 109)

Enos 1:4 • PRAYER, HUNGER, REAL INTENT

I have been driven many times to my knees by the overwhelming conviction that I had nowhere else to go.

(Abraham Lincoln; as quoted in Ezra Taft Benson, *A Nation Asleep* [Salt Lake City: Bookcraft, 1963], 42)

To those of us who would pay pennies toward our unfathomable debt, we remember Enos, who, like many of us, had great need. Like many sons of good families, he strayed. How heinous were his sins I do not know, but they must have been grievous. . . . Here is no casual prayer; here no trite, worn phrases; here no momentary appeal. All the day long, with seconds turning into minutes, and minutes into hours, and hours into an "all day long." But when the sun had set, relief had still not come, for repentance is not a single act nor forgiveness an unearned gift. So precious to him was communication with, and approval of, his Redeemer that his determined soul pressed on without ceasing. . . . Could the Redeemer resist such determined imploring? How many of you have thus persisted? How many of you, with or without serious transgressions, have ever prayed all day and into the night? Have you ever wept and prayed for many hours? How many of you have prayed for five hours? for one? for thirty minutes? for ten?

(Spencer W. Kimball, *BYU Speeches of the Year*, 11 Oct. 1961 [Provo, Utah: BYU Press, 1997], 8–9)

In answer to my first prayer, no answer came. The faith was there, I felt, to the extent that I could exert it. The need was there, I felt certainly no doubt about that, but was the worthiness? I could always think of something, as I prayed night after night without an answer, . . . and so I continued to pray, feeling that when I could make myself worthy of an answer, I would get it. It was after I had been praying nightly for five years that the whole family . . . attended a Sunday School entertainment. My class rendered its number, followed by another that sang, and I remember some of the words of that song: "Keep on asking, God will answer by and by." To me that was a revelation. I kept on praying. Some four years later, in the latter part of the month of August, 1887, in my nineteenth year, after I had been praying nightly for nine long years with all the earnestness of my soul for this special blessing, I was alone in the bedroom, and I said, half aloud, "O Father, wilt thou not hear me?" I was beginning to get discouraged. Then, brethren, something happened. The most glorious experience that I have received came. In answer to my question I heard as distinctly as anything I ever heard in my life the short, simple word: "Yes." Simultaneously my whole being, from the crown of my head to the soles of my feet, was filled with the most joyous feeling of elation, of peace and certainty that I could imagine a human being could experience. I sprang from my knees, and jumped as high as I could, and shouted: "O Father, I thank thee." At last an answer had come. I knew it.

(Joseph F. Merrill, in Conference Report, Apr. 1944 [Salt Lake City: The Church of Jesus Christ of Latter-day Saints, 1944], 151–152)

I have a longtime friend. . . . Occasionally, to find relief from the stress of his responsibilities, he would partake of substances forbidden by the Word of Wisdom. As the stress in his life increased, so did his consumption of alcohol. Indeed, he was becoming a prisoner to alcohol. One afternoon he felt the enticing of the Spirit prompting him to overcome this addiction. . . . He . . . drove to a very secluded spot far removed from the city. There he knelt in humble prayer and pled with the Lord with all the energy of his heart for added strength to overcome this addiction, which robbed his spirituality and threatened to destroy his very soul. He remained on his knees for a very long time, and eventually a sweet, purifying spirit began to distill upon his soul, cleansing him from any desire to drink and fortifying him with a firm resolve to keep the commandments. A spiritually sensitive bishop noticed a change in my friend and extended a call for him to work with the young Aaronic Priesthood brethren of the ward. He was a natural, enthusiastic leader of youth, and about a year later he was called to be the new bishop, dearly loved by all . . .

(Spencer H. Condie, *Ensign*, Nov. 1993 [Salt Lake City: The Church of Jesus Christ of Latter-day Saints, 1993], 16)

Enos 1:1–5 • THE CYCLE OF GROWTH

The very first verse contains the key to starting anyone's spiritual growth, namely, a feeling of gratitude. Enos recognized the great blessing of having good parents who taught him correct principles, and he acknowledged this as a blessing from God.

It is interesting that this feeling of gratitude is also the first recorded expression of Nephi, and thus the actual beginning of the Book of Mormon. To my mind, this sets a very important precedent or pattern for us; that is, spiritual growth begins with gratitude. If we do not recognize that we have been blessed, or if we do not feel gratitude for our blessings, we simply cannot grow spiritually.

One of the most consistent themes in the Savior's life was His constant expression of gratitude to His Father. How often we read in the scriptures the phrase, "Father, I thank thee!" . . .

Thus having achieved a grateful heart, he was prepared to take the next step, which I have chosen to term humility. . . .

Verses 2–4 express this step very well. As Enos pondered on the blessing of having good parents who taught him correct principles, the importance of those principles "sunk deep" into his heart. The deeper they sank, the more he knew that his life must be in harmony with God in order for him to experience "the joy of the saints." Because of the humility that followed his gratitude he was able to see clearly that his life was not fully in tune with the Spirit of God and that he must do something about it.

Humility is largely a recognition of our own inadequacies as well as a recognition that we need outside help to achieve the joy that is the end of our existence, namely, eternal life. As Enos sensed this truth his soul "hungered" to achieve that goal.

I have a feeling that this was not the first time he had wondered, or prayed about these things, but his account explains that this was the time he resolved to seriously do something about it. . . . Like Enos, we will only achieve our goal when we are determined enough to do whatever is necessary to reach it. . . .

Because of his gratitude and his humility and his determination, he knew what he must do, so he "kneeled down before [his] Maker," and "cried unto him in mighty prayer and supplication" for the welfare of his soul (see verse 4). He was beginning the third step of the cycle of spiritual growth, that is, putting forth great effort to bring his life into tune with God's will. . . .

After he had paid the necessary price in effort and sincerity, he received his heart's desire, as recorded in verse 5: "And there came a voice unto me saying: Enos, thy sins are forgiven thee, and thou shalt be blessed."

(John H. Groberg, *Heroes from the Book of Mormon* [Salt Lake City: Bookcraft, 1995], 48–50, 54)

———

We cannot find Enos-like faith without our own wrestle before God in prayer. I testify that the reward is worth the effort. Remember the pattern: (1) hear the word of God, spoken and written by His servants; (2) let that word sink deep into your heart (Enos 1:3); (3) hunger in your soul for righteousness (Enos 1:4); (4) obediently follow gospel laws, ordinances, and covenants; and (5) raise your voice in mighty prayer and supplication, asking in faith to know that Jesus Christ is our Savior (Enos 1:4). I promise that if you do these things sincerely and unceasingly, the words Christ spoke to His disciples will be fulfilled in your life: "Ask, and it shall be given you; seek, and ye shall find; knock, and it shall be opened unto you" (Matt. 7:7).

(Robert D. Hales, in Conference Report, Oct. 2004 [Salt Lake City: The Church of Jesus Christ of Latter-day Saints, 2004], 74)

Enos 1:2, 9, 13 • THE PROGRESSIVE DIMENSIONS OF PRAYER

Very often the Twelve and the First Presidency pray together. When President Kimball takes his turn to be voice, he generally includes this phrase in his prayers:

"Bless our enemies. Help us to understand them, and them to understand us." He doesn't ask for vengeance or retaliation, just for understanding so differences can be resolved. Perhaps, family differences and neighborhood problems could be resolved if we would follow our prophet's example and pray for patience and forgiveness.

(Marvin J. Ashton, in Conference Report, Apr. 1985 [Salt Lake City: The Church of Jesus Christ of Latter-day Saints, 1985], 59)

———

Here is another important pattern which is followed by the prophets and which we must follow also:
1. First praying for the welfare of our own souls and doing what is necessary to achieve that.
2. Then praying for the welfare of our family and friends and doing what is necessary to help them.
3. Then praying for the welfare of all others, including those who some may term our enemies, and doing all we can to help them.

If we cannot honestly follow this pattern we still have a distance to go to be as God would have us be and feel and love as He would have us feel and love.

(John H. Groberg, *Heroes from the Book of Mormon* [Salt Lake City: Bookcraft, 1995], 56)

Enos 1:4 • ALL THE DAY . . . AND NIGHT

I once read that scripture to a woman who laughed and said, "Imagine anybody praying all night and all day." I replied, "My dear sister, I hope you never have to come to a time where you have a problem so great that you have to so humble yourself. I have; I have prayed all day and all night and all the next day and all the next night, not always on my knees but praying constantly for a blessing that I needed most."

(Harold B. Lee, *Improvement Era*, Oct. 1966 [Salt Lake City: The Church of Jesus Christ of Latter-day Saints, 1966], 898)

Enos 1:5, 10 • THE VOICE OF THE LORD CAME INTO MY MIND

We do not have the words (even the scriptures do not have the words) which perfectly describe the Spirit. The scriptures generally use the word voice, which does not exactly fit. These delicate, refined spiritual communications are not seen with our eyes, nor heard with our ears. And even though it is described as a voice, it is a voice that one feels, more than one hears.

(Boyd K. Packer. *Ensign*, Jan. 1983 [Salt Lake City: The Church of Jesus Christ of Latter-day Saints, 1983], 52)

———

Thus the Lord, by revelation, brings into our mind

as though a voice were speaking. May I bear humble testimony, if I may be pardoned, to that fact? I was once in a situation where I needed help. The Lord knew I needed help and I was on an important mission. I was awakened in the hours of the morning as though someone had wakened me to straighten me out on something that I had planned to do in a contrary course, and there was clearly mapped out before me as I lay there that morning, just as surely as though someone had sat on the edge of my bed and told me what to do. Yes, the voice of the Lord comes into our minds and we are directed thereby.

(Harold B. Lee, *BYU Speeches of the Year*, 15 Oct. 1952 [Provo, Utah: BYU Press, 1997])

———————

Each first Thursday of the month is a day for fasting and the bearing of testimony by the General Authorities of the Church. . . . We hold our monthly testimony meeting in an upper room of the Salt Lake Temple. . . . The Thursday of which I speak was June 1, 1978. . . .

The question of extending the blessings of the priesthood to blacks had been on the minds of many of the Brethren over a period of years. . . . It had become a matter of particular concern to President Spencer W. Kimball. . . .

On this occasion he raised the question before his Brethren—his Counselors and the Apostles. . . . We joined in prayer in the most sacred of circumstances. President Kimball himself was voice in that prayer. . . . For me, it felt as if a conduit opened between the heavenly throne and the kneeling, pleading prophet of God who was joined by his Brethren. The Spirit of God was there. And by the power of the Holy Ghost there came to that prophet an assurance that the thing for which he prayed was right, that the time had come, and that now the wondrous blessings of the priesthood should be extended to worthy men everywhere regardless of lineage.

Every man in that circle, by the power of the Holy Ghost, knew the same thing. . . .

No voice audible to our physical ears was heard. But the voice of the Spirit whispered with certainty into our minds and our very souls.

It was for us, at least for me personally, as I imagine it was with Enos, . . . [in] (Enos 1:10).

(Gordon B. Hinckley, *Ensign*, Oct. 1988 [Salt Lake City: The Church of Jesus Christ of Latter-day Saints, 1988], 69–70)

———————

When a very young child in the home of my youth, I was fearful at night. I traced it back to a vivid dream when two Indians—some Indians used to come up there—came into the yard. I ran to the house for pro-

tection, and one of them shot an arrow and hit me in the back. Only a dream, but I felt that blow, and I was very much frightened, for in the dream they entered, one a tall one, and a smaller one, and sneered and frightened Mother.

I never got over it. Added to that were the fears of Mother, for when Father was away with the herd or on some mission, Mother would never retire without looking under the bed; so burglars were real to me, or wicked men who would come in and attempt to injure Mother and the young children. . . .

One night I could not sleep. . . . I fancied I heard noises around the house. Mother was away in another room. . . . I became terribly fearful, and I decided that I would do as my parents had taught me to do—pray. I thought I could not pray without getting out of bed and kneeling, and that was a terrible test. But I finally did bring myself to get out of bed and kneel and pray to God to protect Mother and the family. And a voice as clearly to me as mine is to you said, "Don't be afraid. Nothing will hurt you." Where it came from, what it was, I am not saying. You may judge. To me it was a direct answer, and there came an assurance that I should never be hurt in bed at night.

(David O. McKay, *Cherished Experiences from the Writings of President David O. McKay*, comp. by Clare Middlemiss [Salt Lake City: Deseret Book, 1955], 17–18)

———————

The Spirit of God speaks to our spirits. The Lord does not communicate to us very often through our natural senses, but when He speaks He speaks to the immortal part; the spirit of man receives the communications the Lord sends to His children, and we must therefore be in harmony to receive them.

(*Teachings of Presidents of the Church—Joseph F. Smith* [Salt Lake City: The Church of Jesus Christ of Latter-day Saints, 1998], 202–203)

———————

Once . . . I prayed through the night to know what I was to choose to do in the morning. . . . I knew what choice looked most comfortable to me. I knew what outcome I wanted. But I could not see the future. I could not see which choice would lead to which outcome. So the risk of being wrong seemed too great to me.

I prayed, but for hours there seemed to be no answer. Just before dawn, a feeling came over me. More than at any time since I had been a child, I felt like one. My heart and my mind seemed to grow very quiet. There was a peace in that inner stillness.

Somewhat to my surprise, I found myself praying, "Heavenly Father, it doesn't matter what I want. I don't care anymore what I want. I only want that Thy will be done. That is all that I want. Please tell me what to do."

In that moment I felt as quiet inside as I had ever felt. And the message came, and I was sure who it was from. It was clear what I was to do. . . .

Only when my heart has been still and quiet, in submission like a little child, has the Spirit been clearly audible to my heart and mind.

(Henry B. Eyring, *Ensign*, May 2006 [Salt Lake City: The Church of Jesus Christ of Latter-day Saints, 2006], 16)

Enos 1:7 • HOW IS IT DONE?

Enos . . . asked that eternal question, "Lord, how is it done?" (Verse 7).

The Lord explained that it was done because of his faith in Christ. That is the way all eternal blessings come to any of us. While the scripture doesn't specifically state it, I feel that Enos must have humbly asked, at least in his heart, "And what else should I do?"

President Howard W. Hunter gave additional support to this feeling when he said, "Any time we experience the blessings of the Atonement in our lives, we cannot help but have a concern for the welfare of others" (Seminar for New Mission Presidents, June 1994).

Enos's humility was rewarded with an understanding that his own family and his own people needed the same blessings he had just received, that is, a forgiveness of sins and the accompanying feeling of love from our Father in Heaven.

(John H. Groberg, *Heroes from the Book of Mormon* [Salt Lake City: Bookcraft, 1995], 56)

Enos 1:10 • I WILL VISIT ACCORDING TO THEIR KEEPING THE COMMANDMENTS

"I will visit thy brethren according to their diligence in keeping my commandments. . . ." There you have, in simple language, a great principle: It isn't the Lord who withholds himself from us. It is we who withhold ourselves from him because of our failure to keep his commandments.

(Harold B. Lee, in Conference Report, Oct. 1966 [Salt Lake City: The Church of Jesus Christ of Latter-day Saints, 1966], 117)

───────

When you received your confirmation, you were commanded to receive the Holy Ghost. He was not obligated to seek you out. . . . If our lives are responsive and clean, if we are reaching and cultivating, the Holy Ghost will come, and we may retain him and have the peace his presence thus affords.

(Spencer W. Kimball, *BYU Speeches of the Year*, Oct. 1961 [Provo, Utah: BYU Press, 1997], 7)

Enos 1:13–18 • THE IMPORTANCE OF SCRIPTURE

(Refer in this text to 1 Nephi 4:12–13; Omni 1:17.)

Enos 1:14 • DESTROY OUR RECORDS

We might think that destroying the Nephites would have been enough. Why would they be concerned about destroying the Nephite records too? Perhaps it was because the Lamanites remembered Nephi's and Lehi's prophecies that those records would be a powerful tool in converting Lamanites to the Nephite beliefs. If so, they would want to eliminate even that possibility by wiping out the books.

(Noel B. Reynolds, *Rediscovering The Book of Mormon*, ed. by John L. Sorenson and Melvin J. Thorne [Salt Lake City: Deseret Book, 1991], 223)

Enos 1:20 • OUR LABORS WERE VAIN

His labors may have seemed vain to him and the other Nephite missionaries, but any honest effort put forth in proclaiming the truth is never in vain. First of all, this diligent effort obviously brought great blessings to Enos and his fellow workers; and second, through his faith and the faith of many others the record of the Book of Mormon was preserved and is now having a marvelous influence for good not only among the Lamanites but also among all people of the earth.

(John H. Groberg, *Heroes from the Book of Mormon* [Salt Lake City: Bookcraft, 1995], 56)

Enos 1:27 • IN CHRIST I WILL FIND REST

Peace in this world always comes after the receiver has done the works of righteousness. . . . This is the way peace comes in this world. It can be obtained no other way. The promised peace . . . emanates from Christ. He is the source of it. His spirit is the essence of it.

(Marion G. Romney, in Conference Report, Apr. 1967 [Salt Lake City: The Church of Jesus Christ of Latter-day Saints, 1967], 80–82)

JAROM

Jarom 1:5 • SABBATH DAY
(Refer in this text to Mosiah 13:16, 18–19.)

We have become a nation of pleasure seeking Sabbath breakers.

(Ezra Taft Benson, *A Nation Asleep* [Salt Lake City: Bookcraft, 1963], 44)

––––––––––

There isn't anybody in this Church who has to buy furniture on Sunday. . . . There isn't anybody in this Church who has to buy a new automobile on Sunday. . . . There isn't anybody in this Church who, with a little care and planning, has to buy groceries on Sunday. . . . I don't think we need to patronize the ordinary business merchants on the Sabbath day. Why do they stay open? To get customers. Who are those customers? Well, they are not all nonmembers of this Church.

(Gordon B. Hinckley, Heber City/Springville, Utah, Regional Conference, Priesthood Leadership Meeting, 13 May 1995)

––––––––––

The Sabbath of the Lord is becoming the play day of the people. It is a day of golf and football on television, of buying and selling in our stores and markets. Are we moving to mainstream America as some observers believe? In this I fear we are. What a telling thing it is to see the parking lots of the markets filled on Sunday in communities that are predominantly LDS. Our strength for the future, our resolution to grow the Church across the world, will be weakened if we violate the will of the Lord in this important matter.

(Gordon B. Hinckley, *Ensign*, Nov. 1997 [Salt Lake City: The Church of Jesus Christ of Latter-day Saints, 1997], 69)

––––––––––

What fits the purpose of the Sabbath? Here are a few suggestions: Activities that contribute to greater spirituality; essential Church meetings in the house of prayer; acquisition of spiritual knowledge—reading the scriptures, Church history and biographies, and the inspired words of the Brethren; resting physically, getting acquainted with the family, relating scriptural stories to children, bearing testimonies, building family unity; visiting the sick and aged shut-ins; singing the songs of Zion and listening to inspired music; paying devotions to the Most High—personal and family prayer; fasting, administrations, father's blessings; preparing food with singleness of heart—simple meals prepared largely on Saturday. . . . I don't believe that it is possible to keep our spirituality on a high plane by spending our Sabbaths on the beach, on the golf course, . . . or in our own homes . . . looking at television.

(*Teachings of Ezra Taft Benson* [Salt Lake City: Bookcraft, 1988], 439)

––––––––––

The Lord said: "Remember the Sabbath day, to keep it holy" (Ex. 20:8) and made Sabbath day observance a sign between Him and the people to indicate their obedience (see Ex. 31:13–17). That commandment and sign have never been rescinded. In our day, standards for keeping the Sabbath day holy are lowered a little at a time by some individuals until practically anything seems to become acceptable. The sign between the Lord and His covenant people is trampled underfoot as Church members skip Sunday meetings to seek recreation at lakes and beaches, in the mountains, at sports arenas, and at theaters. Parking lots at supermarkets and discount stores often are full on Sundays. Many store owners feel compelled to open their doors on Sundays because of the demand for the merchandise and services. The people who misuse the Sabbath lose the blessings of spiritual food and growth promised to those who keep this commandment.

(Joseph B. Wirthlin, *Ensign*, Mar. 1993 [Salt Lake City: The Church of Jesus Christ of Latter-day Saints, 1993], 71)

In Hebrews the term Sabbath means "rest." . . . The Sabbath day is given throughout the generations of man for a perpetual covenant. It is a sign between the Lord and his children forever. . . . It is a day not for lavish banqueting but a day of simple meals and spiritual feasting; . . . a day when maid and mistress might be relieved from the preparation. . . . A day when employer and employee, master and servant may be free from plowing, digging, toiling. It is a day when the office may be locked and business postponed, and troubles forgotten. . . . A day to study the scriptures, . . . a day to nap and rest and relax, a day to visit the sick, a day to preach the gospel, a day to proselyte, a day to visit quietly with the family and get acquainted with our children, a day for proper courting, a day to do good. . . . The Savior . . . recognized also that the ox might get into the mire or the ass fall into the pit; but neither in the letter nor in the spirit did he ever approve the use of the Sabbath for ordinary and regular work or for amusements and play.

(*Teachings of Spencer W. Kimball*, ed. by Edward L. Kimball [Salt Lake City: Bookcraft, 1982], 215–216)

Members of The Church of Jesus Christ of Latter-day Saints recognize Sunday as the Sabbath in commemoration of the fact that Christ came forth from the grave on Sunday, and the Apostles commenced meeting thereafter on the first day of the week (see John 20:1–6; Luke 24:1; Mark 16:1; Matt. 28:1; Acts 20:7). . . . Let's not shop on Sunday. One way we avoid this is by planning ahead. Fill up the gas tank on Saturday. Acquire the needed groceries for the weekend on Saturday. Don't you be the means of causing someone to work on Sunday because you patronize their establishment. . . . The justification for and reason often cited by the owners and operators of such businesses is to be competitive, to conform to corporate policy, and so on. I well remember an interview President Spencer W. Kimball once had with a faithful Church member. It went like this: "What is your occupation?" And [the man] said, "I operate a service station." And I asked, "Do you operate on the Sabbath?" His answer was, "No, I do not." "Well, how can you get along? Most service station operators seem to think they must open on the Sabbath." "I get along well," he said. "The Lord is good to me." "Do you not have stiff competition?" I asked. "Yes, indeed," he replied. "Across the street is a man who keeps open all day Sunday." "And you never open?" I asked. "No, sir,"

he said, "and I am grateful, and the Lord is kind, and I have sufficient for my needs" (*Teachings of Spencer W. Kimball*, 227). What are the promises and blessings of the Lord to those who honor the Sabbath day . . . ? The fulness of the earth is yours, the land will be blessed with rain and will yield its increase, there will be peace in the land, and God will magnify His faithful people, have respect for them, and establish His covenant with them (see D&C 59:16–19; Lev. 26:2–6, 9).

(Earl C. Tingey, *Ensign*, May 1996 [Salt Lake City: The Church of Jesus Christ of Latter-day Saints, 1996], 10–12)

We have requested priesthood leaders to minimize administrative meetings on the Sabbath so that families may engage in worship and family time. Our hope is that you will use this time to attend your meetings, render Christian service, visit family members, hold family home evenings, and study the scriptures.

(Ezra Taft Benson, in Conference Report, Apr. 1984 [Salt Lake City: The Church of Jesus Christ of Latter-day Saints, 1984], 7)

The consolidated meeting schedule was implemented largely in order to provide several more Sabbath hours for families. Therefore take time to be together as families to converse with one another, to study the scriptures, to visit friends, relatives, and the sick and lonely. This is also an excellent time to work on your journals and genealogy.

(*Teachings of Spencer W. Kimball*, ed. by Edward L. Kimball [Salt Lake City: Bookcraft, 1982], 221)

Years ago a father asked Elder ElRay L. Christiansen (1897–1975), Assistant to the Twelve Apostles, what name Elder Christiansen could suggest for the man's newly acquired boat. Elder Christiansen suggested, "Why not call it The Sabbath Breaker?" I'm confident the would-be sailor pondered whether his pride and joy would be a Sabbath breaker or a Sabbath keeper. Whatever his decision, it no doubt left a lasting impression upon his children.

(Thomas S. Monson, *Ensign*, Apr. 2006 [Salt Lake City: The Church of Jesus Christ of Latter-day Saints, 2006], 4)

Jarom 1:9–12 • NEPHI'S FREEDOM THESIS
(Omni 1:6; Mosiah 1:7; 2:22; Refer in this text to 1 Nephi 2:20.)

OMNI

To this point, the Book of Mormon covers a period of 239 years in 139 pages. Omni covers possibly 231 years in 3 pages. What happened? (Omni 1:30; Jarom 1:2, 14).

Omni 1:1–3 • I AM A WICKED MAN

All he did was lay his life on the line so that others would be free to make decisions he didn't make.

(Marion D. Hanks, personal notes from general conference.)

Omni 1:13, 27, 28 • NEPHITE DIRECTIONS
(Refer in this text to 1 Nephi 3:9.)

The concept of going "up" when you go north and of going "down" when you go south is of relatively recent origin, and thus was not used by the Nephites. When the Nephites stated they went from Nephi down to Zarahemla, they were referring to elevation and not to direction. Zarahemla was definitely lower in elevation than Nephi because the river Sidon had its head in the land of Nephi but flowed down through the center of the land of Zarahemla (Alma 16:6–7; 22:27–29).

(Daniel H. Ludlow, *Companion to Your Study of the Book of Mormon* [Salt Lake City: Deseret Book, 1976], 169)

Omni 1:17 • THEY BROUGHT NO RECORDS WITH THEM
(Refer in this text to 1 Nephi 4:12–13.)

The Mulekites, who migrated to the American continent shortly after Lehi and his family left Jerusalem, failed to bring with them any sacred scriptures or records. Omni recorded the condition of a nation without scriptures: [Omni 1:17]. Even more serious than their continuous contentions and wars and the corruption of their language was the tragedy that they did not know the Savior. The pattern is the same for individuals as it is for nations. Without searching the scriptures, they cease to know the Savior.

(L. Lionel Kendrick, *Ensign*, May 1993 [Salt Lake City: The Church of Jesus Christ of Latter-day Saints, 1993], 14)

Words of Mormon

What are the Words of Mormon doing here when Omni was written about 130 BC and Words of Mormon was written about AD 385, and the book which follows Words of Mormon, (Mosiah) begins approximately at 130 BC?

The Words of Mormon were apparently written near the end of Mormon's life for the purpose of connecting two major records [large & small plates of Nephi.] . . . So that a gap would not occur in the history of the Nephites, Mormon included the major events of the lifetime of King Benjamin in The Words of Mormon, thus connecting the account on the small plates of Nephi with Mormon's abridgment of the book of Mosiah.

(Daniel H. Ludlow, *Companion to Your Study of the Book of Mormon* [Salt Lake City: Deseret Book, 1976], 170)

Words of Mormon 1:3 • I SEARCHED AMONG THE RECORDS

When Joseph got the plates, the angel instructed him to carry them back to the hill Cumorah, which he did. Oliver says that when Joseph and Oliver went there, the hill opened, and they walked into a cave, in which there was a large and spacious room. . . . They laid the plates on a table; it was a large table that stood in the room. Under this table there was a pile of plates as much as two feet high, and there were altogether in this room more plates than probably many wagon loads; they were piled up in the corners and along the walls. . . .

I tell you this as coming not only from Oliver Cowdery, but others who were familiar with it, and who understood it just as well as we understand coming to this meeting.

(Brigham Young, *Journal of Discourses* [London: Latter-day Saints' Book Depot, 1878], 19:38)

Words of Mormon 1:5–7 • FOR A WISE PURPOSE . . . I DO NOT KNOW

(Refer in this text to Mosiah 1:6–7.)

At the beginning of the Book of Mormon history, Nephi had been commanded to make two separate sets of plates. After starting what would be known as the large plates of Nephi, he was later commanded to make a set of more religious records, known as the small plates of Nephi (1 Ne. 9:2, 4 and 1:17). After Nephi's death, the large plates remained with the kings down to the time of Mormon, while the small plates went to Jacob and his posterity until the time of Amaleki, who gave them to King Benjamin. Thus the two sets of plates were back into the possession of one person. After Mormon had completed his abridgment of five hundred years of Nephite history, he may have been somewhat surprised to find the small plates of Nephi, which largely duplicated his efforts. Instead of keeping only one of the sets of records, Mormon was prompted to include the small plates with his abridgment, without really knowing why (see verse 7). He apparently did not know what would happen to his records after they would come into the hands of Joseph Smith. After Joseph Smith received the plates of Mormon, he had completed the translation of 116 pages of manuscript, which comprised Mormon's abridgment from the time of Lehi down to King Benjamin. After the loss of these pages by Martin Harris, the Lord commanded the Prophet to translate further in the plates of Mormon without retranslating the first portion. However, since the small plates contained a more spiritual account of the same time period, the teachings of greatest value were not lost for the readers of the Book of Mormon. In order for this more spiritual record to be available, Nephi first had to start the small plates, and Mormon had to include them with his abridgment. We can be thankful today that Mormon had the courage to follow his spiritual promptings so that these valuable teachings are now part of our contemporary scripture.

(Victor L. Ludlow; as quoted in *Studies in Scripture*, ed. by Kent P. Jackson [Salt Lake City: Deseret Book, 1987], 7:203)

———————

At least six times in the Book of Mormon the phrase "for a wise purpose" is used in reference to the making, writing, and preserving of the small plates of Nephi (see 1 Nephi 9:5; Words of Mormon 1:7; Alma 37:2, 12, 14, 18). We know one such wise purpose—the most obvious one—was to compensate for the loss of the earlier mentioned 116 pages of manuscript. But it strikes me that there is a 'wiser purpose' than that. . . . The key to such a suggestion is in verse 45 of Section 10. . . . He says, "Behold, there are many things engraven upon the [small] plates of Nephi which do throw greater views upon my gospel." So clearly . . . it was not tit for tat, this for that—you give me 116 pages of manuscript and I'll give you 142 pages of printed text. Not so. We got back more than we lost. And it was known from the beginning that it would be so. We do not know exactly what we missed in the 116 pages, but we do know that what we received on the small plates was the personal declarations of three great witnesses [Nephi, Jacob, and Isaiah], . . . testifying that Jesus is the Christ. . . . I think you could make a pretty obvious case that the sole purpose of the small plates was to give a platform for these three witnesses. After all, their writing constitutes a full 135 pages of what is only a 145-page record.

(Jeffrey R. Holland, CES Symposium, BYU, 9 Aug. 1994)

———————

When Mormon found among the records delivered into his keeping the "Smaller Plates of Nephi," he was so well pleased with their contents that he placed the whole of them with the abridgment he had made from the larger Nephite records. . . . By the addition of the Smaller Plates of Nephi to Mormon's abridgment of the Larger Plates, it will be observed that there was a double line of history for a period of about 400 years. Therefore, when, through carelessness and breaking his agreement with the Prophet, Martin Harris lost the translation of the first part of Mormon's abridgment, and those into whose hands the manuscript had fallen designed to change it and destroy the claims of the Prophet to inspiration in translating it—under divine direction he translated the Smaller Plates of Nephi, and let that translation take the place of the one which had been stolen, and thus the plan of the conspirators against the work was thwarted.

(B. H. Roberts, *New Witness for God* [Salt Lake City: Deseret Book, 1950], 2:384)

MOSIAH

The lack of a preface for the book of Mosiah in the present Book of Mormon is probably because the text takes up the Mosiah account some time after its original beginning. The original manuscript of the Book of Mormon, written in Oliver Cowdery's hand, has no title for the Book of Mosiah. It was inked in later, prior to sending it to the printer for typesetting. The first part of Mormon's abridgment of Mosiah's record . . . was evidently on the 116 pages lost by Martin Harris.

(John A. Tvedtnes, *Rediscovering the Book of Mormon*, ed. by John L. Sorenson and Melvin J. Thorne [Salt Lake City: 1991], 33)

Mosiah 1:1–2 • THIRD PERSON AUTHORSHIP

Note that the main story in the book of Mosiah is told in the third person rather than in the first person as was the custom in the earlier books of the Book of Mormon. The reason for this is that someone else is now telling the story and that 'someone else' is Mormon. With the beginning of the book of Mosiah we start our study of Mormon's abridgment of various books that had been written on the large plates of Nephi (3 Nephi 5:8–12). The book of Mosiah and the five books that follow—Alma, Helaman, 3 Nephi, 4 Nephi, and Mormon—were all abridged or condensed by Mormon from the large plates of Nephi, and these abridged versions were written by Mormon on the plates that bear his name, the plates of Mormon. These are the same plates that were given to Joseph Smith by the angel Moroni on September 22, 1827.

(Daniel H. Ludlow, *Companion to Your Study of the Book of Mormon* [Salt Lake City: Deseret Book, 1976], 173)

Mosiah 1:4 • BRASS PLATES, EGYPTIANS
(Refer in this text to 1 Nephi 3:19.)

The statement that "Lehi . . . having been taught in the language of the Egyptians therefore he could read" the engravings on the brass plates of Laban quite clearly indicates these plates were written in the Egyptian language. Thus they were almost certainly not started until after the flood and the tower of Babel, as there was no Egyptian language before those events. The brass plates were probably not started until after the Israelites went down into Egypt in the days of Joseph, although the writers on these plates may have had access to records that had been written earlier.

(Daniel H. Ludlow, *A Companion to Your Study of the Book of Mormon* [Salt Lake City: Deseret Book, 1976], 173)

Perhaps the phrase "language of the Egyptians" in [this] verse means the same thing that Nephi meant when he spoke of the language of his father (and thus the language of the Book of Mormon) as consisting of "the learning of the Jews and the language of the Egyptians" (1 Nephi 1:2). That is to say, the Nephite record reflected the Hebrew culture and background of the Jews, but was written in Egyptian characters. In the present context, then, the brass plates may have been records of Hebrew prophets and their prophecies, all recorded in an Egyptian script.

(Robert L. Millet, "The Brass Plates: An Inspired and Expanded Version of the Old Testament," in *The Old Testament and the Latter-day Saints*, 421–22; as quoted in Joseph Fielding McConkie and Robert L. Millet, *Doctrinal Commentary on the Book of Mormon* [Salt Lake City: Bookcraft, 1988], 2:130)

Mosiah 1:6–7 • PLATES OF NEPHI
(Refer in this text to Words of Mormon 1:5–7.)

It appears the large plates of Nephi were kept and expanded by the kings, but the small plates of Nephi were kept by the prophets, and were not expanded. . . .

The first important change that took place at the time of King Benjamin was that the small plates of Nephi became full, and this separate spiritual record was given to King Benjamin for safe keeping (Omni 1:25). . . . A second important change during the time of King Benjamin was that the large plates of Nephi were now used to record both secular and spiritual events. There was no longer a separate spiritual record being kept; therefore preachings, visions, and prophecies, etc., were included in the large plates.

(Rex C. Reeve, Jr., *First Nephi, The Doctrinal Foundation*, BYU Religious Studies Center, 106)

Mosiah 1:11–12; 5:8–12 • A NAME GIVEN

As his followers, we cannot do a mean or shoddy or ungracious thing without tarnishing his image. Nor can we do a good and gracious and generous act without burnishing more brightly the symbol of him whose name we have taken upon ourselves.

(Gordon B. Hinckley, *Be Thou an Example* [Salt Lake City: Deseret Book, 1981], 90)

"These are they who are not valiant in the testimony of Jesus; wherefore, they obtain not the crown over the kingdom of our God" (D&C 76:79). These enter into the terrestrial glory.

Who are they? All who refuse to receive the fulness of the truth, or abide by the principles and ordinances of the everlasting gospel. They may have received a testimony; they may be able to testify that they know that Jesus is the Christ; but in their lives they have refused to accept ordinances which are essential to entrance into the celestial kingdom. They have refused to live the gospel, when they knew it to be true; or have been blinded by tradition; or for other cause have not been willing to walk in the light.

In this class we could properly place those who refuse to take upon them the name of Christ, (D&C 181–28; 20:37; Mosiah 5:7–14; Alma 5:38–39) even though they belong to the Church. . . .

They may live clean lives; they may be honest, industrious, good citizens, and all that; but they are not willing to assume any portion of the labor which devolves upon members of the Church, in carrying on the great work of redemption of mankind.

(Joseph Fielding Smith, *Doctrines of Salvation*, comp. by Bruce R. McConkie [Salt Lake City: Bookcraft, 1955], 11:28–29)

One of the greatest messages that I ever received was from President Harold B. Lee. I was a young man visiting Salt Lake City, and he asked me to come by his office. He knew something I didn't know—that some-

one would be asking me to represent their organization. He put both of his hands on my shoulders, looked me directly in the eye, and said, "Be careful who you give your name to."

I believe that the Lord Jesus Christ is very careful whom He gives His name to. When we go into the waters of baptism, we take upon us His name and promise that we will always be obedient. Every time we take the sacrament, we remind ourselves that we will always remember Him, that we will take His name upon us, and that we will always keep His commandments.

(Robert D. Hales, in Conference Report, Oct. 1985 [Salt Lake City: The Church of Jesus Christ of Latter-day Saints, 1985], 27)

Mosiah 2

In order to understand the full impact of King Benjamin's address, we must examine the setting that drew it forth. Mormon, writing some four centuries later, informed us about King Benjamin and the circumstances that led to his last great sermon (see W of M 1:12–18; Mosiah 1:1–2:8). Benjamin did not inherit a comfortable situation when be became the king of the Nephite peoples. It was a time of war, with armies of the Lamanites coming down against the Nephites. King Benjamin led his people in battle, wielding the sword of Laban with his own hand. Thousands were killed, and eventually the Lamanites were driven out of the land (see W of M 1:13–14). . . .

During the kingship before Benjamin's reign, the Nephites had incorporated the Mulekite people, whose language was different and whose knowledge of Jehovah and the Mosaic law had been corrupted. Teaching them a new language and a new religion and having that settle in would have been difficult and time-consuming (see Omni 1:14–19). Mormon said that besides the wars with the Lamanites, there were "contentions among his [Benjamin's] own people." Mormon also explained that there were "false Christs," "false prophets," and "false preachers and teachers" among the people. "Many dissensions" also arose, and the people were described as stiffnecked (W of M 1:12, 15–17). . . .

With the assistance of holy prophets, whom he sustained, and through his own personal righteousness, King Benjamin brought a complete turnaround among his people. . . (W of M 1:18).

(*Selected Writings of Gerald N. Lund* [Salt Lake City: Deseret Book, 1999], 220–221)

Mosiah 2–6 • YEAR RITE

There is a detailed description of a coronation in the Book of Mormon that is paralleled only in ancient nonbiblical sources, notably Nathan ha-Babli's description of the coronation of the Prince of the Captivity. The Book of Mormon version in Mosiah 2–6 (c. 125 BC) is a classic account of the well-documented ancient "Year Rite": (a) The people gather at the temple, (b) bringing firstfruits and offerings (Mosiah 2:3–4); (c) they camp by families, all tent doors facing the temple; (d) a special tower is erected, (e) from which the king addresses the people, (f) unfolding unto them "the mysteries" (the real ruler is God, etc.); (g) all accept the covenant in a great acclamation; (h) it is the universal birthday, all are reborn; (i) they receive a new name, are duly sealed, and registered in a national census; (j) there is stirring choral music (cf. Mosiah 2:28; 5:2–5); (k) they feast by families (cf. Mosiah 2:5) and return to their homes.

(*Collected Works of Hugh Nibley*, ed. by S. Ricks, J. Welch, et al. [Salt Lake City, 1985], 6:295–310; as quoted in *Encyclopedia of Mormonism*, ed. by Daniel H. Ludlow [New York: Macmillan Publishing, 1992], 1:189)

Mosiah 2:9 • TO TRIFLE WITH THE WORDS

Last week I was talking with a member of the Quorum of the Twelve about comments we had received on our April conference talks. My friend said someone told him, "I surely enjoyed your talk." We agreed that this is not the kind of comment we like to receive. As my friend said, "I didn't give that talk to be enjoyed. What does he think I am, some kind of entertainer?" Another member of our Quorum joined the conversation by saying, "That reminds me of the story of a good minister. When a parishioner said, 'I surely enjoyed your sermon today,' the minister replied, 'In that case, you didn't understand it.' " . . .

A message given by a General Authority at a general conference . . . is not given to be enjoyed. It is given to inspire, to edify, to challenge, or to correct. It is given to be heard under the influence of the Spirit of the Lord, with the intended result that the listener learns from the talk and from the Spirit what he or she should do about it.

King Benjamin understood that principle and explained it. His great sermon that is recorded in the first few chapters of the Book of Mosiah begins with these words:

My brethren, all ye that have assembled yourselves together, you that can hear my words which I shall speak unto you this day; . . . I have not commanded you to come up hither to trifle with the words which I shall speak, but that you should hearken unto me, and open your ears that ye may hear, and your hearts that ye may understand . . . (Mosiah 2:9).

As this prophet-king taught, when we come to hear a servant of the Lord, we are not "to trifle with the words" that he speaks. It is our duty to open our ears to hear and our hearts to understand. And what we should seek to understand is what we should do about the message. I feel sure that is what King Benjamin meant, because he said later in his great message, "And now, if you believe all these things see that ye do them" (Mosiah 4:10).

(Dallin H. Oaks, *The Dedication of a Lifetime*, CES Broadcast, Oakland, California, 1 May 2005)

Mosiah 2:14 • TAXATION

Burdensome, unjust taxation is a form of theft. King Benjamin realized that a government has no more right to steal from its citizens than the citizens have to steal from one another.

(Rodney Turner; as quoted in *Studies in Scripture*, ed. by Kent P. Jackson [Salt Lake City: Deseret Book, 1987], 7:211)

Mosiah 2:16–17 • SERVICE
(Refer in this text to Alma 17:18.)

Continue to seek opportunities for service. Don't be overly concerned with status. Do you recall the counsel of the Savior regarding those who seek the "chief seats" or the "uppermost rooms"? "He that is greatest among you shall be your servant" (Matt. 23:6, 11). It is important to be appreciated. But our focus should be on righteousness, not recognition; on service, not status. The faithful visiting teacher, who quietly goes about her work month after month, is just as important to the work of the Lord as those who occupy what some see as more prominent positions in the Church. Visibility does not equate to value.

(Howard W. Hunter, *Ensign*, Nov. 1992 [Salt Lake City: The Church of Jesus Christ of Latter-day Saints, 1992], 96–97)

When we understand why we serve we will not worry about where we serve.

(Howard W. Hunter, BYU Devotional, 2 Sept. 1990)

People serve one another for different reasons. . . . [1] Some serve for hope of earthly reward. Such a man or woman may serve in a Church position or in private acts of mercy in an effort to achieve prominence or cultivate contacts that will increase income or aid in acquiring wealth. Others may serve in order to obtain worldly honors, prominence, or power. . . . The scriptural word for gospel service "for the sake of riches and honor" is priestcraft (Alma 1:16). . . . [2] Another reason for service . . . is that which is motivated by a desire to obtain good companionship. We surely have good associations in our Church service, but is that an acceptable motive for service? . . . Persons who serve only to obtain good companionship are more selective in choosing their friends than the Master was in choosing his servants. [3] Some serve out of fear of punishment. The scriptures abound with descriptions of the miserable state of those who fail to follow the commandments of God. . . . [4] Other persons serve out of a sense of duty or out of loyalty to family, friends, or traditions. I would call such persons 'good soldiers.' They instinctively do what they are asked, without question. . . . Such persons . . . do much good. We have all benefited from their good works. . . . Service of this character is worthy of praise and will surely qualify for blessings, especially if it is done willingly and joyfully. . . . [5] One such higher reason for service is the hope of an eternal reward. This hope . . . is one of our most powerful motivations. . . .

The above five motives for service have a common deficiency. In varying degrees each focuses on the actor's personal advantage, either on earth or in the judgment to follow. Each is self-centered. There is something deficient about any service that is conscious of self. A few months after my calling to the Council of the Twelve, I expressed my feelings of inadequacy to one of the senior members of my quorum. He responded with this mild reproof and challenging insight: "I suppose your feelings are understandable. But you should work for a condition where you will not be preoccupied with yourself and your own feelings and can give your entire concern to others, to the work of the Lord in all the world." Those who seek to follow [the Savior's] . . . example must lose themselves in their service to others. . . . [6] If our service is to be most efficacious, it must be unconcerned with self and heedless of personal advantage. It must be accomplished for the love of God and the love of his children. . . . Here we learn that it is not enough to serve God with all of our might and strength. He who looks into our hearts and knows our minds demands more than this. In order to stand blameless before God at the last day, we must also serve him with all our heart and mind.

(Dallin H. Oaks, *Pure in Heart* [Salt Lake City: Bookcraft, 1988], 38–49)

———————

On November 5, 1985, after nearly 12 years serving as President of the Church, Spencer W. Kimball passed away. At the time of his passing, President Kimball's counselor President Gordon B. Hinckley declared: "It has been my great privilege and opportunity to work at President Kimball's side in the harness of the work of the Lord. On one occasion I tried to slow him down a little, and he said, 'Gordon, my life is like my shoes—to be worn out in service.' He so lived, He so died. He

has gone to the company of Him whose servant he was, even the Lord Jesus Christ, of whom he bore witness and testimony."

(*Teachings of Presidents of the Church—Spencer W. Kimball* [Salt Lake City: The Church of Jesus Christ of Latter-day Saints, 2006], xxxvi)

———————

Service to others deepens and sweetens this life while we are preparing to live in a better world. It is by serving that we learn how to serve. When we are engaged in the service of our fellowmen, not only do our deeds assist them, but we put our own problems in a fresher perspective. When we concern ourselves more with others, there is less time to be concerned with ourselves! In the midst of the miracle of serving, there is the promise of Jesus that by losing ourselves, we find ourselves!

(Spencer W. Kimball, *Ensign*, July 1978 [Salt Lake City: The Church of Jesus Christ of Latter-day Saints, 1978], 3–7)

———————

Sometimes, because of the pressures of the world around us, our service projects become self service projects rather than selfless service projects. . . . Of all influences that cause men to choose wrong, selfishness is undoubtedly the strongest. Where it is the Spirit is not.

(William R. Bradford, in Conference Report, Oct. 1987 [Salt Lake City: The Church of Jesus Christ of Latter-day Saints, 1987], 80–83)

———————

I speak of that service which is given without expectation of monetary reward. Most of the troubles of the world come because of human greed. What a therapeutic and wonderful thing it is for a man or woman to set aside all consideration of personal gain and reach out with strength and energy and purpose to help the unfortunate, to improve the community, to clean up the environment and beautify our surroundings.

(Gordon B. Hinckley, *Ensign*, Aug. 1992 [Salt Lake City: The Church of Jesus Christ of Latter-day Saints, 1992], 5)

———————

Service . . . is the golden key which unlocks the doors to celestial halls. . . . Wise undershepherds, in helping others to partake of the bread of life and the living water, seek neither acclaim nor accolade. The honors of men are of no consequence to them.

(Alexander B. Morrison, *Ensign*, May 1992 [Salt Lake City: The Church of Jesus Christ of Latter-day Saints, 1992], 14)

———————

Many great people I know work for much less money than they are worth because service is a greater value to them than money. Whatever career or profession you pursue, consider the value of service.

(Janette C. Hales, BYU Devotional, 16 Mar. 1993)

———————

Love is a potent healer. Realizing that, Satan would separate you from the power of the love of God, kindred, and friends. . . . He would lead you to feel that the walls are pressing in around you and there is no escape or relief. He wants you to believe you lack the capacity to help yourself and that no one else is really interested. . . . His strategy is to have you think you are not appreciated, loved, or wanted so that you in despair will turn to self-criticism, and in the extreme to even despising yourself and feeling evil when you are not. . . . If you have such thoughts, break through those helpless feelings by reaching out in love to another in need. That may sound cruel and unfeeling when you long so much for healing, but it is based upon truth. Paul taught, "Bear ye one another's burdens, and so fulfil the law of Christ" (Gal. 6:2). Love comes by learning how to give it to another in a spirit of trust. If you feel deprived of love, that is difficult. Yet sustained concern and support of others will engender their interest and love. You will feel needed. You become an instrument through which the Lord can bless another.

(Richard G. Scott, *Ensign*, May 1994 [Salt Lake City: The Church of Jesus Christ of Latter-day Saints, 1994], 8–9)

———————

Position in the Church does not exalt anyone, but faithfulness does. On the other hand, aspiring to a visible position—striving to become a master rather than a servant—can destroy the spirit of the worker and the work. Occasionally confusion exists regarding servants and masters. The Bible reports that a group of men "had disputed among themselves, who should be the greatest" among them. Jesus said, "If any man desire to be first, the same shall be last of all, and servant of all" (Mark 9:34–35). . . . The word servant comes from the Greek noun diakonos, which means "one who executes the commands of another, especially of a master," Diakonos is the Greek word from which the English word deacon is derived.

(Russell M. Nelson, *Ensign*, May 1996 [Salt Lake City: The Church of Jesus Christ of Latter-day Saints, 1996], 15–16)

———————

I believe we will never lose anything in life by giving service, by making sacrifices, and doing the right thing.

The true key to happiness in life is to labor for the happiness of others. I pity the selfish man who has never experienced the joy which comes to those who receive the thanks and gratitude of the people whom they may have aided in the struggle of life. . . .

I am converted to the thought that the way to peace and happiness in life is by giving service. Service is the true key, I believe, to happiness. . . . When we perform any acts of kindness, they bring a feeling of satisfaction and pleasure into our hearts, while ordinary amusements pass away.

It is a God-given law that in proportion to the service we give, in proportion to what we do in this Church and out of it—what we are willing to sacrifice for the Church and for those to whom we owe our loyalty outside of Church activity—we shall grow in the grace of God and in the love of God, and we shall grow in accomplishing the purposes of our being placed here on the earth.

(*Teachings of President of the Church—Heber J. Grant* [Salt Lake City: The Church of Jesus Christ of Latter-day Saints, 2002], 143–144)

———————

A less serious worldly tradition that conflicts with gospel culture is the idea of upward or downward movement in positions. In the world, we refer to the up or down of promotions or reductions. But there is no up or down in Church positions. We just move around. A bishop released by proper authority and called to teach in Primary does not move down. He moves forward as he accepts his release with gratitude and fulfills the duties of a new calling—even one far less visible.

I saw a memorable example of this a few months ago in the Philippines. I visited a ward in the Pasig stake, near Manila. There I met Augusto Lim, whom I had known in earlier years as a stake president, a mission president, a General Authority, and president of the Manila temple. Now I saw him serving humbly and gratefully in his ward bishopric, second counselor to a man much younger and much less experienced. From temple president to second counselor in a ward bishopric is a beautiful example of the gospel culture in action.

(Dallin H. Oaks, in Conference Report, Oct. 2003 [Salt Lake City: The Church of Jesus Christ of Latter-day Saints, 2003], 40–41)

———————

The bandage for a sufferer of leprosy arrived at LDS Humanitarian Center in an ordinary plastic bag. It looked like the many hundreds of others: made by hand from white, cotton thread, three inches wide by four feet long.

Like other similar bandages, this one was sturdy, designed so it would not stick to sores like flat bandages can, and could be sterilized for reuse. These bandages, while relatively easy to make, can take more than 40 hours to complete.

But there was something special about this bandage. At the top, the stitches were tight and orderly. About half way down, the stitches became increasingly uneven and loose. After another few inches, the stitches once again became even.

Attached to the bandage was a small note written by hand that said:

"Just a note about this bandage. I know it's not the most perfect bandage you've ever seen, but it was made by my younger sister (age 46) who died of breast cancer in February. She worked on this right up till the end. . . . She was determined to finish it, but died before it was finished. I finished it for her. Even though it looks a little funny, no bandage was ever done with more love, effort, or perseverance."

The letter was not signed. There was no indication of who this woman was or where she was from.

All that can be surmised is that during her time of greatest affliction, this woman performed a simple act of kindness, something that would bring relief to a stranger. One stitch at a time—hour after hour—in her final and most troubling hours, her thoughts and hands were devoted to easing the pain of another.

In the great events of world history, the making of a bandage for a leprosy patient may not merit a mention. But perhaps beyond the veil, angels rejoice in a simple act of charity that serves as a symbol of all that is best within us.

(Nell K. Newell, Welfare Services, *Church News*, 8 Jan. 2005, 16)

———

A few years ago I had been assigned with other General Authorities to attend a series of area conferences in New Zealand and Australia. Initially, the leader of our group was to have been President Spencer W. Kimball. However, because of the need for some emergency surgery, he could not travel with us, so President N. Eldon Tanner led the group in his place.

Each day during the trip President Tanner telephoned President Kimball in his hospital room to get a report on his condition and to give a brief report of the conferences in which we were participating. After the daily call to Salt Lake City, President Tanner would always give us a report on the President's condition. We were anxious and appreciated these brief messages.

Once, after we had been out for five or six days, President Tanner made his usual call to the hospital in Salt Lake City. However, this day he had no report for us. When we asked if he had talked to the President, he told us he had tried, but President Kimball wasn't in his room. "Where was he?" we asked. "They weren't sure; they couldn't find him," President Tanner said. "They thought he might have gone down to the next floor of the hospital to visit the sick."

To paraphrase a statement made by Wendell Phillips, it may be accurately said, "How prudently most men sink into nameless graves, while now and then a few *forget themselves* into immortality."

(William Jennings Bryan, *The Prince of Peace* [Independence: Zion's Printing and Publishing, 1925]; as quoted in H. Burke Peterson, in Conference Report, Apr. 1985 [Salt Lake City: The Church of Jesus Christ of Latter-day Saints, 1985], 81–82)

———

It is not enough for any of us to get a job and feverishly work to produce income that leads only to personal comfort. We may gain some recompense in all of this, but we will not gain the ultimate satisfaction. When we serve others, we best serve our God.

Generally speaking, the most miserable people I know are those who are obsessed with themselves. By and large, if we complain about life, it is because we are thinking only of ourselves. For many years, there was a sign on the wall of a shoe shop I patronized that read: "I complained because I had no shoes until I saw a man who had no feet." The most effective medicine for the sickness of self-pity is to lose ourselves in the service of others. . . .

The best cure for weariness is the challenge of helping someone who is even more tired. One of the great ironies of life is this: He or she who serves almost always benefits more than he or she who is served.

(Gordon B. Hinckley, *Standing for Something* [New York: Times Books, 2000], 56)

———

You elders perhaps have one of your number sick, and his crop needs harvesting. Get together and harvest it. One of you members has a son on a mission, and his funds are getting low. Just ask if you can be of help to him. Your thoughtfulness he will never forget. Such acts as these are what the Savior had in mind when he said, "Inasmuch as ye do it unto the least of these my brethren, ye do it unto me" (see Matt. 25:40). There is no other way that you can serve Christ. You can kneel down and pray to him, that is good. You can plead with him to give you his guidance through the Holy Spirit—yes, we do that and must do it. We have to do it. But it is these practical, daily visits in life, it is the controlling of our tongue, in not speaking evil of a brother, but speaking well of him, that the Savior marks as true service.

(*Teachings of Presidents of the Church—David O. McKay* [Salt Lake City: The Church of Jesus Christ of Latter-day Saints, 2003], 120)

Mosiah 2:20–25 • YE ARE INDEBTED TO HIM

We are told that we are unprofitable servants, and so we are, if we think of trying to pay our Savior back for what he has done for us, for that we never can do; and we cannot by any number of acts, or a full life of faithful service, place our Savior in our debt.

(Joseph Fielding Smith, *Doctrines of Salvation*, comp. by Bruce R. McConkie [Salt Lake City: Bookcraft, 1954], 1:15)

It is not for me to rise up and say that I can give to the Lord, for in reality I have nothing to give. . . .

We are not our own, we are bought with a price, we are the Lord's; our time, our talents, our gold and silver, our wheat and fine flour, our wine and our oil, our cattle, and all there is on this earth that we have in our possession is the Lord's. . . .

I would not give the ashes of a rye straw for the man who feels that he is making sacrifice for God. We are doing this for our own happiness, welfare and exaltation, and for nobody else's. This is the fact, and what we do, we do for the salvation of the inhabitants of the earth, not for the salvation of the heavens, the angels, or the Gods. . . .

We own nothing but the talents God has given to us to improve upon, to show him what we will do with them.

(*Discourses of Brigham Young*, comp. by John A. Widtsoe [Salt Lake City: Deseret Book, 1954], 176–177)

I believe that one of the greatest sins of which the inhabitants of the earth are guilty today is the sin of ingratitude. . . . We see a man raised up with extraordinary gifts, or with great intelligence, and he is instrumental in developing some great principle. He and the world ascribe his great genius and wisdom to himself. He attributes his success to his own energies, labor and mental capacity. He does not acknowledge the hand of God in anything connected with his success, but ignores him altogether and takes the honor to himself; this will apply to almost all the world. In all the great modern discoveries in science, in the arts, in mechanics, and in all material advancement of the age, the world says, "We have done it." The individual says, "I have done it," and he gives no honor or credit to God. Now, I read in the revelations through Joseph Smith, the prophet, that because of this, God is not pleased with the inhabitants of the earth but is angry with them because they will not acknowledge his hand in all things (D&C 59:21).

(Joseph F. Smith, *Gospel Doctrine* [Salt Lake City: Deseret Book, 1975], 270)

Mosiah 2:21 • LENDING YOU BREATH

Master spoke of the "second mile" and told us to go there (see Matt. 5:41). Why? Because he wants to bless us. So he put all the blessings in the second mile, but we must go where they are before we get them.

The first mile, we owe: that's what we are getting paid for. Recently I mentioned that to an elder who was hardly meeting the minimums, He responded, "Paid? I'm not getting paid."

I said, "Oh? You can breathe can't you?"

"Yes."

"You think you have that coming to you or something? King Benjamin says the Lord is preserving you from day to day by granting you breath—even supporting you from moment to moment" (see Mosiah 2:21). Do we ever thank the Lord for the fact we can breathe? No, not usually, until we get to where we can't breathe. Then we call upon him in a panic.

(Hartman Rector, Jr., *Ensign*, May 1979 [Salt Lake City: The Church of Jesus Christ of Latter-day Saints, 1979], 30)

Mosiah 2:25–26, 4:2, 5, 11 • LESS THAN THE DUST
(Refer in this text to Jacob 2:21; Alma 26:12; Helaman 12:7.)

[Regarding man] science tells us that without the spirit about all that is left is a quantity of water, fat enough to make about seven bars of soap, sulphur enough to rid one dog of fleas, iron enough for a large nail, magnesium for one dose, lime enough to whitewash a chicken coop, phosphorous sufficient to tip some 2200 matches, potassium enough to explode a toy cannon, sugar to fill a shaker, and little more. But with a spirit directing mental processes and physical maneuvers man is "little lower than the angels" and is "crowned . . . with glory and honour" (Psalm 8:5). And yet man in his vanity and impudence has taken unto himself the glory of all his accomplishments, set himself up as God and, as has been said, has even "created God in his (man's) own image." It is as if the Boulder Dam should say: "I am powerful. I hold back great quantities of water. Parched land becomes fertile and productive because of me. There were no builders. I am the great cause and responsible to no power."

(*Teachings of Spencer W. Kimball*, ed. by Edward L. Kimball [Salt Lake City: Bookcraft, 1982], 27)

The animal, vegetable, and mineral kingdoms abide the law of their Creator; the whole earth and all things pertaining to it, except man, abide the law of their creation. . . . We tame the animals and make them do our drudgery and administer to our wants in many ways, yet man alone is not tamed—he is not subject to his Great Creator. Our ignorant animals are faithful to us, and will do our bidding as long as they have any strength; yet man, who is the offspring of the Gods, will not become subject to the most reasonable and self-exalting principles. How often have we witnessed a faithful animal conveying his master home so drunk that he could not see his way or sit up; yet his faithful animal will plod through mud, shun stumps, trees, and bad places, and land him safely at home.

(Brigham Young, *Journal of Discourses* [London: Latter-day Saints' Book Depot, 1862], 9:246–247)

These are the words of the late Malcolm Muggeridge, British author, journalist and television commentator.

"I may, I suppose, regard myself, or pass for being, a relatively successful man. People occasionally stare at me in the streets—that's fame. I can fairly easily earn enough to qualify for admission to the higher slopes of the Internal Revenue—that's success. Furnished with money and a little fame even the elderly, if they care to, may partake of trendy diversions—that's pleasure. It might happen once in a while that something I said or wrote was sufficiently heeded for me to persuade myself that it represented a serious impact on our time—that's fulfillment. Yet I say to you—and I beg you to believe me—multiply these tiny triumphs by a million, add them all together, and they are nothing—less than nothing . . . measured against one draught of that living water Christ offers to the spiritually thirsty."

(Malcolm Muggeridge; as quoted in *With Full Purpose of Heart, Messages by Dallin H. Oaks* [Salt Lake City: Deseret Book, 2002], 74–75)

Mosiah 2:27 • A CLEAR CONSCIENCE BEFORE GOD
(Refer in this text to 2 Nephi 9:14; Mosiah 4:3.)

With all my heart I urge you wonderful young people not to take a secret shame with you to your marriage. You may never be able to forget it. You will want to go through life with the strength that comes from a clear conscience, which will permit you one day to stand before your Maker and say, "My soul is pure." Self-denial is not restrictive. It is liberating. It is the pathway to freedom. It is strength.

(James E. Faust, in Conference Report, Apr. 2000 [Salt Lake City: The Church of Jesus Christ of Latter-day Saints, 2000], 56)

Mosiah 2:32 • AVOID CONTENTION
(Refer in this text to 3 Nephi 11:28–30.)

Mosiah 2:36 • WITHDRAW YOURSELVES FROM THE SPIRIT OF THE LORD
An important aspect of baptism by the Spirit may

frequently be overlooked in our spiritual development.

"We should . . . endeavor to discern when we withdraw [ourselves] from the Spirit of the Lord, that it may have no place in [us] to guide [us] in wisdom's paths that [we] may be blessed, prospered, and preserved" (Mosiah 2:36). Precisely because the promised blessing is that we may always have His Spirit to be with us, we should attend to and learn from the choices and influences that separate us from the Holy Spirit.

The standard is clear. If something we think, see, hear, or do distances us from the Holy Ghost, then we should stop thinking, seeing, hearing, or doing that thing. If that which is intended to entertain, for example, alienates us from the Holy Spirit, then certainly that type of entertainment is not for us. . . .

I recognize we are fallen men and women living in a mortal world and that we might not have the presence of the Holy Ghost with us every second of every minute of every hour of every day. However, the Holy Ghost can tarry with us much, if not most, of the time—and certainly the Spirit can be with us more than it is not with us.

(David A. Bednar, *Ensign*, May 2006 [Salt Lake City: The Church of Jesus Christ of Latter-day Saints, 2006], 30)

Mosiah 3:7 • CHRIST'S SUFFERING
The Father withdrew His spirit from His Son, at the time he was to be crucified. . . . at the very moment, at the hour when the crisis came for him to offer up his life, the Father withdrew Himself, withdrew His Spirit, and cast a veil over him. That is what made him sweat blood [in Gethsemane]. If he had had the power of God upon him he would not have sweat blood. . . .

(Brigham Young, *Journal of Discourses* [London: Latter-day Saints' Book Depot, 1856], 3:206)

We know that an angel came from the courts of glory to strengthen him in his [Christ's] ordeal, and we suppose it was mighty Michael [Adam] who foremost fell that mortal man might be. As near as we can judge, these infinite agonies—this suffering beyond compare—continued for some three or four hours.

(Bruce R. McConkie, in Conference Report, Apr. 1985 [Salt Lake City: The Church of Jesus Christ of Latter-day Saints, 1985], 10)

All of the anguish, all of the sorrow, and all of the suffering of Gethsemane recurred during the final three hours on the cross, the hours when darkness covered the land.

(Bruce R. McConkie, *The Mortal Messiah* [Salt

Lake City: Deseret Book, 1981], 4:footnotes, 232)

This sacrifice . . . took place in Gethsemane when he sweat great gouts of blood from every pore . . . And it also took place as he hung on the cruel cross of Calvary. During the last three hours of that agonizing ordeal, while darkness overspread the land, all the pains and suffering of Gethsemane returned.

(Bruce R. McConkie, *A New Witness for the Articles of Faith* [Salt Lake City: Deseret Book, 1985], 109)

Many thought that if there is suffering [from Christ] there surely must be guilt. Indeed, there was plenty of guilt here—a whole world of it—but it fell upon the only utterly sinless and totally innocent man who had ever lived. . . .

He who most deserved peace and was the Prince of Peace had peace taken from him. He who deserved no rebuke, let alone physical abuse, went under the lash that his taking of such stripes might spare us such pain if only we would repent. The total cost of such combined spiritual and physical suffering is incalculable. Yet the iniquities, including the sorrows and sadness, of every mortal being who ever has lived or will live in this world were laid across one lonely set of shoulders. In the most magnificent display of strength ever known in the world of human endeavor, they were carried until full payment had been made.

(Jeffrey R. Holland, *Christ and the New Covenant* [Salt Lake City: Deseret Book, 1997], 91–92)

Mosiah 3:11 • THOSE WHO DIE WITHOUT THE GOSPEL

(Refer in this text to Moroni 8:8–22.)

Mosiah 3:15–27 • GOD'S JUSTICE

JUSTICE requires that God must be a God of order and that he must be just and impartial. MERCY agrees with justice; however, mercy introduces the possibility of vicarious payment of the laws that have been transgressed (or broken). The Law of mercy paraphrased: Whenever a law is broken a payment (or atonement) must be made; however, the person does not need to make payment if he will repent and if he can find someone who is both able and willing to make payment. Note that the Law of MERCY insists the demands of JUSTICE be met fully.

(Daniel H. Ludlow, *Companion to Your Study of the Book of Mormon* [Salt Lake City: Deseret Book, 1976], 176–177)

Mosiah 3:16–18 • LITTLE CHILDREN

(Refer in this text to Moroni 8:8–22.)

Mosiah 3:19 • THE NATURAL MAN

The natural man is the earthy man who has allowed rude animal passions to overshadow his spiritual inclinations.

(Spencer W. Kimball, in Conference Report, Oct. 1974 [Salt Lake City: The Church of Jesus Christ of Latter-day Saints, 1974], 160–161)

At the one end of the spectrum, the natural man may be a person bent on lasciviousness; he may be one who loves Satan more than God and thereby is carnal, sensual, and devilish. . . . At the other end of the spectrum, the natural man may well be a "nice man," a moral and upright person bent upon benevolence. Such a person, acclimated to the present fallen world, still does not enjoy the enlivening powers of the Holy Ghost and does not enjoy the sanctifying power of Christ's covenants and ordinances. Even though the light of Christ is making an impact on him, he has not followed it into the Lord's full gospel truths. . . . And what of members of the Church of Jesus Christ of Latter-day Saints? Are any of us "natural" beings? We can answer that question, perhaps, by examining some broad characteristics of the natural man: **1.** *The natural man is unable or unwilling to perceive spiritual realities* (1 Cor. 2:14; Alma 26:21; *Journal of Discourses* 1:2). **2.** *The natural man is proud.* President Benson explained: "We pit our will against God's. When we direct our pride toward God, it is in the spirit of my will and not thine be done. . . . The proud wish God would agree with them" (*Ensign*, May 1989, 4). **3.** *The natural man is overly competitive and externally driven.* "Such people are tempted daily to elevate [themselves] above others and diminish them." There is no pleasure in "having something," only in "having more of it than the next man" (*Ensign*, Benson, May 1989, 4). **4.** *The natural man yields himself to the harsh and the crude.*

(Robert Millet, *Ensign*, June 1992 [Salt Lake City: The Church of Jesus Christ of Latter-day Saints, 1992], 8–9)

The virtue . . . of heroic proportions, consists in being able to overcome disgust, for the love of Jesus. . . . The ability to go beyond what is merely natural.

This is what happened to Saint Francis of Assisi. Once, when he ran into a leper who was completely disfigured, he instinctively backed up. Right away he overcame the disgust he felt and kissed the face that was completely disfigured. What was the outcome of this? Francis felt himself filled with tremendous joy. He felt totally in control of himself.

And the leper went on his way praising God.

(Jose Luis Gonzalez-Balado, *Mother Teresa—In My Own Words* [New York: Gramercy Books, 1996], 4)

———————

There is an old story . . . which told of the experience of a great artist who was engaged to paint a mural for the cathedral in a Sicilian town. The subject was the life of Christ. For many years the artist labored diligently, and finally the painting was finished except for the two most important figures, the Christ child and Judas Iscariot. He searched far and wide for models for those two figures.

One day while walking in an old part of the city he came upon some children playing in the street. Among them was a twelve-year-old boy whose face stirred the painter's heart. It was the face of an angel—a very dirty one, perhaps, but the face he needed.

The artist took the child home with him, and day after day the boy sat patiently until the face of the Christ Child was finished.

But the painter failed to find a model for Judas. For years, haunted by the fear that his masterpiece would remain unfinished, he continued his search.

One afternoon, in a tavern, the painter saw a gaunt and tattered figure stagger across the threshold and fall to the floor, begging for a glass of wine. The painter lifted him up and looked into a face that startled him. It seemed to bear the marks of every sin of mankind.

"Come with me," the painter said, "I will give you wine, food, and clothing."

Here at last was his model for Judas. For many days and parts of many nights the painter worked feverishly to complete his masterpiece.

As the work went on, a change came over the model. A strange tension replaced the stuporous languor, and his bloodshot eyes were fixed with horror on the painted likeness of himself. One day, perceiving his subject's agitation, the painter paused in his work, saying, "My son, I'd like to help you. What troubles you so?"

The model sobbed and buried his face in his hands. After a long moment he lifted pleading eyes to the old painter's face.

"Do you not then remember me? Years ago I was your model for the Christ Child!"

After relating the story, President McKay said, "Well, the story may be fact or fiction, but the lesson it teaches is true to life. The dissipated man made a wrong choice in his youth, and in seeking gratification in indulgence sank ever lower and lower until he wallowed in the gutter."

(*Teachings of Presidents of the Church—David O. McKay* [Salt Lake City: The Church of Jesus Christ of Latter-day Saints, 2003], 11–12)

———————

The word natural, when applied to man, is used differently in the scriptures than it is by the world. Usually natural, or by nature, indicates an inherent part of our makeup, something we are born with. The scriptures, however, clearly teach that natural man means fallen or sinful man.

(*Book of Mormon—Student Manual, Religion 121 and 122* [Salt Lake City: The Church of Jesus Christ of Latter-day Saints, 1989], 55)

———————

As with any selfish, or "natural," man—sacrifice is never convenient.

The natural man has a tendency to think only of himself—not only to place himself first, but rarely, if ever, to place anyone else second, including God. For the natural man, sacrifice does not come naturally. He has an insatiable appetite for more. His so-called needs seem to always outpace his income so that having "enough" is forever out of reach.

(Lynn G. Robbins, *Ensign*, May 2005 [Salt Lake City: The Church of Jesus Christ of Latter-day Saints, 2005], 34)

Mosiah 3:19 • BECOMETH A SAINT

The word saint is tied to the Hebrew root Kadosh, which means to separate, to be apart from, and to become sacred and holy (Hebrew, and English Lexicon, Brown, Driver, Briggs, 872). In all dispensations of time the Lord's people have been called Saints, thus emphasizing that they are a people who have separated themselves from that which is worldly and are seeking through obedience to the laws and ordinances of the gospel to become a holy people.

(R. Millet and J. F. McConkie, *Doctrinal Commentary on the Book of Mormon* [Salt Lake City: Bookcraft, 1987], 2:153)

Mosiah 3:19 • BECOMETH AS A CHILD

Nobody grows old by merely living a number of years. People grow old by deserting their ideals, their faith. There is always the love of wonder, a childlike appetite for what is next, and the joy of your life. You are as young as your faith, as old as your doubt; as young as your self-confidence, as old as your fear or despair. In the center of our heart is a recording chamber, and so long as it receives messages of beauty, hope, cheer, courage, and faith, so long are we young.

(David B. Haight, *Ensign*, Nov. 1983 [Salt Lake City: The Church of Jesus Christ of Latter-day Saints, 1983], 25)

———————

A father shared an experience he had with his eight-year-old daughter. He said:

"While I was contemplating remarks for my sacrament meeting talk on 'Becoming like Little Children,'" I asked my daughter why we needed to become like little children. She responded, "Because we are all little children compared to Jesus, and because little children have a good imagination."

Surprised by the last part of her answer, he asked why we need a good imagination. She replied, "So we can imagine Jesus in the Garden of Gethsemane and on the cross, and when we take the sacrament we can think about Him."

(Coleen K. Menlove, in Conference Report, Oct. 2002 [Salt Lake City: The Church of Jesus Christ of Latter-day Saints, 2002], 13)

Recently our daughter and son-in-law were preparing to enjoy an evening together. They were rushing around trying to get ready and give the babysitter some last-minute instructions. They didn't really notice the sad countenance of one of the children and the tears in the eyes of another until they were at the door, ready to leave. They realized that their children were apprehensive about their mommy and daddy being away from them. So their parents gathered their four precious children around them. Their daddy asked them to put their hands out in front of them. All eight tiny hands were extended. Mom and Dad then kissed each hand and told them that when they missed them or they were frightened or needed to feel their love, they could put their little hands up to their cheeks and they would be able to feel Mommy's and Daddy's presence anytime. They were so happy, and when our daughter and son-in-law left, they saw four little children standing at the window with smiles on their faces and hands on their cheeks.

They trusted their parents. They knew they were loved.

Just as little children trust, each of us must have that same childlike, unreserved trust. We must all remember that we are sons and daughters of God and that He loves us very much. If we truly understand who we are, we will have an unfailing source of hope and comfort.

(W. Craig Zwick, in Conference Report, Oct. 2003 [Salt Lake City: The Church of Jesus Christ of Latter-day Saints, 2003], 37–38)

Those of us who arrive at the years of accountability are here to develop and to be tried and tested, to see if we can so live as to regain the state of innocence and purity which we enjoyed as children, and thereby be qualified to go where God and Christ are.

(Bruce R. McConkie, *Ensign*, Apr. 1977 [Salt Lake City: The Church of Jesus Christ of Latter-day Saints, 1977], 4)

When our oldest son was about three, he would kneel with his mother and me in our evening prayer. I was serving as the bishop of the ward at the time, and a lovely lady in the ward, Margaret Lister, lay perilously ill with cancer. Each night we would pray for Sister Lister. One evening our tiny son offered the prayer and confused the words of the prayer with a story from a nursery book. He began: "Heavenly Father, please bless Sister Lister, Henny Penny, Chicken Licken, Turkey Lurkey, and all the little folks." We held back the smiles that evening. Later we were humbled as Margaret Lister sustained a complete recovery. We do not demean the prayer of a child. After all, our children have more recently been with our Heavenly Father than have we.

(Thomas S. Monson, in Conference Report, Apr. 1984 [Salt Lake City: The Church of Jesus Christ of Latter-day Saints, 1984], 20–21)

From the standpoint of faith, sincerity, and abiding trust, the prayer of an innocent child will surely receive most ready response from a loving Father.

(*Teachings of Presidents of the Church—David O. McKay* [Salt Lake City: The Church of Jesus Christ of Latter-day Saints, 2003], 75)

Most of us want to be strong. We may well see being like a child as being weak. Most parents have wanted their children at times to be less childish. . . .

But King Benjamin, who understood as well as any mortal what it meant to be a man of strength and courage, makes it clear that to be like a child is not to be childish. It is to be like the Savior, who prayed to His Father for strength to be able to do His will and then did it. Our natures must be changed to become as a child to gain the strength we must have to be safe in the times of moral peril.

(Henry B. Eyring, *Ensign*, May 2006 [Salt Lake City: The Church of Jesus Christ of Latter-day Saints, 2006], 15)

Mosiah 3:19 • SUBMIT TO HIS FATHER

The entry for January 28, 1972, concerns my two-year-old son and reads in part:

"Matthew supplied me a lesson. He cried, I thought without reason, in bed tonight. He asked several times if I'd blow his nose for him or hold the tissue while he blew his nose. After three or four trips, I stalked into his room and asked, 'Do you want me to spank you?' He nodded yes. I asked again, this time illustrating with my raised hand. He said, 'Yes.' Suddenly, my heart melted as I realized he trusted me so much that if I thought a spanking would help his problem, that's what he wanted. I rocked him for a while and then realized to my further softening that he had a stuffed nose from a cold that was just beginning. That had been his discomfort. I got some tissues for him, gave them to him in bed, and told him to blow as much as he would like. He said, 'Thanks.' I went away a chastened man."

Here was a two-year-old giving anew an example of King Benjamin's discourse (Mosiah 3:19). . . .

Clearly, Matthew and other children start out as King Benjamin says they must finish: submissive. But we make the mistake, too often, of putting our efforts and concerns as parents into keeping them submissive to us and to our leadership. We forget that King Benjamin phrased the problem for us differently: how do we transfer that natural submissiveness of our children to the Lord Jesus Christ? . . .

An older Matthew is going to look quizzically at me someday when I say, "Even though all your friends are dressing that way, it's better that you don't." Oh, what a test of faith that will be for him! Will he choose to change clothes then, as he chose the spanking?

(Henry B. Eyring, *Because He First Loved Us* [Salt Lake City: Deseret Book, 2002], 161–163)

Mosiah 3:19 • INFLICT

Use of the word inflict suggests customized challenges and tutoring that require an added and special submissiveness.

(Neal A. Maxwell, *One More Strain of Praise* [Salt Lake City: Bookcraft, 1999], 13)

Mosiah 4:1–2 • FALLEN TO THE EARTH

(Refer in this text to 1 Nephi 21:23.)

Mosiah 4:2–3 • A REMISSION OF THEIR SINS

(Refer in this text to Mosiah 5:2, 7.)

This process of obtaining a remission of one's sins is further outlined in . . . the aftermath of King Benjamin's mighty discourse about Jesus Christ, his divine Sonship and atoning sacrifice. Following this message, we are told how the saints in King Benjamin's time receive a remission of their sins: FIRST: "They . . . viewed themselves in their own carnal [worldly] state. . . ." NEXT: "They all cried aloud with one voice, saying: O have mercy, and apply the atoning blood of Christ that we may receive forgiveness of sins, and our hearts may be purified. . . ." FINALLY: "After they had spoken these words the Spirit of the Lord came upon them, and they were filled with joy, having received a remission of their sins, and having peace of conscience, because of the exceeding faith which they had in Jesus Christ. . . ."

This is the manner by which the saints in all ages have come to be converted.

(Ezra Taft Benson, *Charge to Religious Educators* [Salt Lake City: The Church of Jesus Christ of Latter-day Saints, 1982], 48–54)

Often the most difficult part of repentance is to forgive yourself. Discouragement is part of that test. Do not give up. That brilliant morning will come. Then "the peace of God, which passeth . . . understanding" comes into your life once again. Then you, like Him, will remember your sins no more. How will you know? You will know!

(Boyd K. Packer, *Ensign*, Nov. 1995 [Salt Lake City: The Church of Jesus Christ of Latter-day Saints, 1995], 20)

Mosiah 4:3 • PEACE OF CONSCIENCE

(Refer in this text to 2 Nephi 9:14; Mosiah 2:27.)

A beautiful little blind girl was sitting on the lap of her father in a crowded compartment in a train. A friend seated nearby said to the father, "Let me give you a little rest," and he reached over and took the little girl on his lap.

A few moments later the father said to her, "Do you know who is holding you?"

"No," she replied, "but you do." . . .

Our trust and our relationship with our Heavenly Father should be one similar to that of the little blind girl and her earthly father. When sorrow, tragedy, and heartbreaks occur in our lives, wouldn't it be comforting if when the whisperings of God say, "Do you know why this has happened to you?" we could have the peace of mind to answer "No, but you do." . . .

Just as the little girl could sit peacefully on the stranger's lap because her father knew him, so we can find peace if we know our Father and learn to live by his principles.

(Marvin J. Ashton, in Conference Report, Oct. 1985 [Salt Lake City: The Church of Jesus Christ of Latter-day Saints, 1985], 86–87, 90)

Mosiah 4:10 • SEE THAT YE DO THEM

Sometimes we get so busy discussing the doctrines that *talking* about them almost becomes a substitute for *applying* them. . . .

Nephi's "I will *go and do*" leads to action and brings results (1 Nephi 3:7; emphasis added). Its counterpart, "I will *stay here and moodily contemplate* my navel," stirs no souls, indicative of those who are willing to serve the Lord but only in an advisory capacity.

(Neal A. Maxwell, *Whom The Lord Loveth* [Salt Lake City: Deseret Book, 2003], 27–28)

The Apostle James wrote, "Be ye doers of the word, and not hearers only, deceiving your own selves" (James 1:22). King Benjamin taught, "And now, if you believe all these things see that ye do them" (Mosiah 4:10). And in modern revelation the Lord declares, "If you will that I give unto you a place in the celestial world, you must prepare yourselves by doing the things which I have commanded you and required of you" (D&C 78:7).

(Dallin H. Oaks, in Conference Report, Oct. 2004 [Salt Lake City: The Church of Jesus Christ of Latter-day Saints, 2004], 49)

Mosiah 4:14–16 • TEACH YOUR CHILDREN
(Refer in this text to 2 Nephi 4:5–6; Enos 1:1–3; Mosiah 25:12; Alma 56:47–48.)

The Church has established two special times for families to be together. The first is centered around the proper observance of the Sabbath day. This is the time we are to attend our regular meetings together, study the life and teachings of the Savior and of the prophets. "Other appropriate Sunday activities include (1) writing personal and family journals, (2) holding family councils, (3) establishing and maintaining family organizations for the immediate and extended family, (4) personal interviews between parents and children, (5) writing to relatives and missionaries, (6) genealogy, (7) visiting relatives and those who are ill or lonely, (8) missionary work, (9) reading stories to children, and (10) singing Church hymns" ("Suggestions for Individual and Family Sabbath-Day Activities," *Ensign*, Mar. 1980, 76).

The second time is Monday night. We are to teach our children in a well-organized, regular family home evening. No other activities should involve our family members on Monday night.

(L. Tom Perry, in Conference Report, Apr. 2003 [Salt Lake City: The Church of Jesus Christ of Latter-day Saints, 2003], 44)

Do not let your children's clothing lie underfoot when you undress them at night, but teach your boys and girls, when they come into the house, to find a place for their hats, cloaks, and bonnets, that, when they want them, they can put their hands upon them in a moment. When they take off their boots and shoes, let them be deposited where they can be found. . . .

I believe in indulging children, in a reasonable way. If the little girls want dolls, shall they have them? Yes. . . . Let the girls learn to cut and sew the clothing for their dolls, and in a few years they will know how to make a dress for themselves and others. Let the little boys have tools, and let them make their sleds, little wagons, &c.; and when they grow up, they are acquainted with the use of tools and can build a carriage, a house, or anything else.

(Brigham Young, *Journal of Discourses* [London: Latter-day Saints' Book Depot, 1862], 9:173)

What we desire is to have Church programs serve Church members, not the reverse. . . . There is a difference between being "anxiously engaged" and busy work. . . . Wards and stakes exist primarily to help members live the gospel in the home. Then we can understand that people are more important than programs, and that Church programs should always support and never detract from gospel-centered family activities. . . .

Auxiliary leaders and teachers of youth should ask . . . How can we schedule meetings, practices, and activities to avoid disrupting home relationships and responsibilities, and to allow time for family activities?

Our commitment to home-centered gospel living should become the clear message of every priesthood and auxiliary program, reducing, where necessary, some of the optional activities that may detract from proper focus on the family and the home. . . .

As local Church leaders cautiously conserve the time that families can spend together, we say to both parents and children, "Come back home." Parents should spend less time in clubs, bowling alleys, banquets, and social gatherings, and more time with their children. Young men and women must balance their involvement in school and other social activities with supportive participation in family activities and appropriate time in the home.

All should work together to make home a place where we love to be.

(Spencer W. Kimball, *Ensign*, May 1978 [Salt Lake City: The Church of Jesus Christ of Latter-day Saints, 1978], 101)

One woman . . . wrote:
"Right after my divorce, I determined that I was going to give my children the *best* of everything. . . . I would provide well for them. . . . I would substitute in every way for their father. I would take them on picnics, build them a tree house, and play baseball with them. I would not allow them to suffer because of our divorce.

"I baked, sewed, ran, played, wrestled. I cleaned, I ironed. I was busy being both mother and father for them.

"One evening I put the three of them in the bathtub together while I finished a chore. Then I came back, soaped the youngest, rinsed him, lifted him from the tub, and stood him on a bath mat while I wrapped a towel around him. Then I carried him off to the bedroom to put his pajamas on and tuck him into bed. I repeated the process with his brother and then his sister.

"As I bent down to kiss them goodnight, my older son said, 'Sing us a song, please.'

" 'Which one?' I asked.

" ' "Rudolph"!' said the youngest immediately.

" 'No, "Johnny Appleseed," ' said his brother.

"Then their sister said, 'Sing, "Stay Awake."'

" 'I can see if I stay to sing one song, I'll be singing for an hour, and I don't have an hour to spare. So goodnight.' I turned off the lights.

" 'Please sing just one song, Mommy. You can choose the song.'

" 'What about our prayers?'

"Firmly, I replied, 'I said goodnight and I mean goodnight.'

"As I walked bock to the bathroom to tidy up, I thought of how grateful they would be someday when they were old enough to understand how much I had done for them!

"As I entered the room I stopped short. There on the bath mat were three perfect sets of damp footprints. For one brief moment I thought I saw standing in the footprints the spirits of those precious children I had just tucked into bed. In that instant I saw the foolishness of my ways. I had been so busy providing for the physical needs of their mortal bodies that I was neglecting their spirits. I knew then that I had a sacred obligation to nourish both. If I were to clothe them in the latest fashions and give them all that money could buy and fail to tend to their spiritual needs, I could not justifiably account for my awesome responsibility as their mother.

"Humbled, I went back to their bedroom. We knelt together in prayer. We all four climbed up on the boys' big bed and sang song after song until I was the only one awake to sing."

(Barbara B. Smith, in Conference Report, Apr. 1982 [Salt Lake City: The Church of Jesus Christ of Latter-day Saints, 1982], 115–116)

A few years ago I had been assigned to tour a mission in another land. Before our first meeting with the missionaries, I asked the mission president if there were any particular problems I needed to attend to. He told me of one missionary who had made his mind up to go home early—he was very unhappy. "Could I help him?" I asked. The president wasn't sure.

As I was shaking hands with the missionaries before the meeting, it wasn't hard to tell which one wanted to leave. I told the president if he didn't mind I'd like to speak to the young man after the meeting. As I watched him during the meeting, about all I could think of was the big piece of gum he had in his mouth. After the meeting this tall young missionary came up to the stand.

"Could we visit?" I asked.

His response was an inference that he couldn't care less.

We went to the side of the chapel. We sat together as I gave him my very best speech on why missionaries should not go home early. He kept looking out the window, paying absolutely no attention to me.

Off and on we were in meetings together for two days. One time he even sat on the front row and read the newspaper as I talked. I was baffled and unnerved by him. By now it appeared to me that he should go home—and soon! I'd been praying for a way to reach him for two days, but to no avail.

The last night after our meeting I was visiting with some folks in the front of the chapel. Out of the corner of my eye I saw the elder. At that very moment I had a feeling about him enter my heart that I had not yet experienced. I excused myself, went over to him, took his hand, looked him in the eye, and said, "Elder, I'm glad I've become acquainted with you. I want you to know that I love you."

Nothing more was said as we separated. As I started out the chapel door for our car, there he stood again. I took his hand again, put my arm around him, looked up in his eyes and said, "What I said to you before, I really mean. I love you; please keep in touch with me."

Spirit communicates to spirit. It was then that his eyes filled with tears and this boy said simply, "Bishop Peterson, in all my life I can never remember being told 'I love you.' "

Now I knew why he was confused, disturbed, insecure, and wanted to leave the mission field.

In speaking of a son or daughter, some will say, "He ought to know I love him. Haven't I done everything for him? I buy him clothes, give him a warm home, an education, and so on." Make no false assumptions: unless the person feels that the need has been filled, the parent's responsibility has not been accomplished.

We must make an even clearer effort to communicate real love to a questioning child. The giving of love from a parent to a son or daughter must not be dependent on his or her performance. Ofttimes those we think deserve our love the least need it the most.

Remember this scriptural admonition to parents. . . . (Mosiah 4:14–15).

May I suggest that parents' teachings will be listened to more intently and be more closely heeded if they are preceded by and woven together with that golden fiber of love. If our words are to be remembered they must be accompanied and followed by considerate, thoughtful actions that cannot be forgotten.

Many are waiting for the other to take the first step, to make the first overture. If you are a parent or a child, a husband or wife who has been waiting for the other to give some expression first, please listen to this.

One of the most effective secrets for happiness is contained in the fourth chapter of 1 John, verse 19. It is only eight words long—listen carefully: "We love him, because he first loved us." This will cause a change to happen because it is right. Do you get the message? "He first loved us." Your children will love you; your brothers and sisters will love you; your eternal companion will love you—because you first loved them. Now I don't mean it will all happen in a day, a week, or a year. But it will happen.

(H. Burke Peterson, *Ensign*, May 1977 [Salt Lake City: The Church of Jesus Christ of Latter-day Saints, 1977], 68–69)

From our lessons learned in Primary we remember the poem entitled "Which Loved Best?"

"I love you, Mother," said little [John];
Then, forgetting his work, his cap went on,
And he was off to the garden swing,
And left her the water and wood to bring.
"I love you, Mother," said rosy Nell—
"I love you better than tongue can tell";
Then she teased and pouted full half the day,
Till her mother rejoiced when she went to play.
"I love you, Mother," said little Fan;
"Today I'll help you all I can;
How glad I am that school doesn't keep!"
So she rocked the babe till it fell asleep.
Then, stepping softly, she fetched the broom,
And swept the floor and tidied the room;
Busy and happy all day was she,
Helpful and happy as child could be.
"I love you, Mother," again they said,
Three little children going to bed;
How do you think that Mother guessed
Which of them really loved her best?

(Joy Allison, *The World's Best Loved Poems* [New York: Harper and Row, 1955], 243–44)

Years pass. Childhood vanishes. Truth remains. The transition from Primary's poems to today's truths is not difficult. True love continues to be an outward expression of an inward conviction.

(Thomas S. Monson, in Conference Report, Oct. 1985 [Salt Lake City: The Church of Jesus Christ of Latter-day Saints, 1985], 43–44)

Mosiah 4:16–23 • ADVICE TO THE AFFLUENT
(Refer in this text to Jacob 2:13–17.)

It is better to feed ten impostors than to run the risk of turning away one honest petition.

(Joseph Smith; as quoted in the *Collected Works of Hugh Nibley*, [Salt Lake City: Deseret Book, 1989], 9:226)

Suppose that in this community there are ten beggars who beg from door to door for something to eat, and that nine of them are imposters who beg to escape work. . . . [What is your choice?] To give food to the ten, . . . or to repulse the ten because you do not know which is the worthy one? You will all say, administer charitable gifts to the ten, rather than turn away the only truly worthy . . . person among them. If you do this, it will make no difference in your blessings, whether you administer to worthy or unworthy persons, inasmuch as you give alms with a single eye to assist the truly needy.

(*Discourses of Brigham Young*, comp. by John A. Widtsoe [Salt Lake City: Deseret Book, 1954], 274)

What difference is it to us what our lot may be, whether we abound in wealth, or whether we have to struggle with grim poverty. . . It will soon be with the rich as if they were not rich, and with the poor as if they had not to struggle—all will find a level in the grave.

(John Taylor, *The Gospel Kingdom*, ed. by G. Homer Durham [Salt Lake City: Bookcraft, 1987], 20)

One evening at dusk as I left the Church Administration Building, a man approached me and, with alcohol on his breath, asked if I was a General Authority. When I said yes, he immediately fell to his knees and requested a blessing.

I hesitated as several thoughts went through my mind. First, I thought of the words in Matthew 6:5, which says, "And when thou prayest, thou shalt not be as the hypocrites are: for they love to pray . . . in the corners of the streets, that they may be seen of men."

I also thought of how I could avoid the situation, and Luke 10:31–32 came to mind: "And by chance there came down a certain priest that way: and when he saw him, he passed by on the other side. And likewise a Levite, when he was at the place, came and looked on him, and passed by on the other side."

I thought, "Should I pass by 'on the other side'? It wouldn't be appropriate to give him a blessing on the street with all these people nearby. Also, as soon as I give him the blessing, he will probably ask for a contribution." At that moment, I remembered the words of Mosiah 4:16–19. . . .

Then I gave him a blessing. When I finished, he stood up, hugged me, pushed himself away leaving his hands on both my shoulders, and looking me in the eye said, "Thank you, brother. I really needed that." Then he turned and walked away. . . .

The point I really want to make concerns what I wish I could now say to the man. . . . At the time, I had doubted his sincerity. I had worried about appearances. I had thought about walking on the other side. I assumed he would ask for a handout. But his faith in asking for a blessing and his expression of gratitude . . . touched me in ways that have brought about needed changes in my thinking and behavior.

Let us remember the phrase from the wall in Kingston, Jamaica: "Blessed are those who can give without remembering and those who can receive without forgetting." . . . I pray that in my own case that may also be the result, that I received a man's thanks without forgetting the lesson he taught me.

(Stephen A. West, *Ensign*, Feb. 2004 [Salt Lake City: The Church of Jesus Christ of Latter-day Saints, 2004], 63–64)

———

Many years ago, my parents lived in a very modest home in the northern end of the state of Utah. One morning, my mother answered a knock at the door and was confronted there by a large, frightening-looking man, who asked her for money.

She said, "We have no money." . . .

He pressed his demands, . . . finally saying, "I am hungry; I would like to get something to eat."

"Well," she said, "if that is the case then I can help you." So she hurried to the kitchen and fixed him a lunch. And I am sure it was the most modest of provisions. She could tell as she gave him the lunch at the door that he was not pleased, but with little resistance he took the lunch and left.

She watched him as he went down the lane through the gate and started up the road. He looked back, but he did not see her standing inside the door, and as he passed the property line, he took the lunch and threw it over the fence into the brush. . . .

She was angered; she was angered at the ingratitude. . . . She was angered that he was so ungrateful.

The incident was forgotten until a week or two later; she answered another knock at the door. There stood a tall, raw-boned teenage boy, who asked about the same question in essentially the same words: "We need help; we are hungry. Could you give us some money; could you give us some food?"

But somehow the image of the first man appeared in her mind and she said, "No," excusing herself: "I am

sorry. I am busy; I cannot help you today. I just cannot help you." What she meant was, "I won't. I won't. I won't be taken in again."

Well, the young man turned without protest and walked out the gate, and she stood looking after him. It wasn't until he passed through the gate that she noticed the wagon, the father and mother and the other youngsters, and as the boy swung his long legs into the wagon he looked back rather poignantly; the father shook the reins and the wagon went on down the road. She hesitated just long enough so that she could not call them back.

From that experience she drew a moral by which she has lived and which she has imparted to her children, and though that was, I suppose, nearly fifty years ago, there has always been just a tiny hint of pain as she recalled the incident with this moral: "Never fail to give that which you have to someone who is in need."

I stress . . . your obligation to give that which you possess to any who may be in need. . . . I urge you to resolve with me that never so long as we live would anyone be hungry, spiritually or physically, that we could aid and assist.

(Boyd K. Packer, *Memorable Stories and Parables by Boyd K. Packer* [Salt Lake City: Bookcraft, 1997], 45–47)

———

In every big city we have those who are beaten down and left by the roadside—those who are homeless, destitute, hungry, and sick. Some say that by giving them money we only support their habit of drug or alcohol addiction, thus enabling them to continue a lifestyle they have chosen. It is so easy to judge these individuals and, like Job's friends, speculate about all the mistakes they have made in their lives that brought this great misery upon them (see Job 22; Mosiah 4:17). . . .

Remember that the Savior was homeless, had only the clothes on His back, and was often hungry. What would He do? There is no question what He would do. He would show mercy and minister unto them.

There are many ways to help the homeless, including the contribution of time, goods, and money to humanitarian groups, soup kitchens, or agencies that deal with these problems. Nevertheless, it seems to me that we must also show mercy unto them.

(William W. Parmley, in Conference Report, Oct. 2003 [Salt Lake City: The Church of Jesus Christ of Latter-day Saints, 2003], 98)

———

Do not ever belittle anyone, including yourself, nor count them, or you, a failure, if your livelihood has been modest. Do not ever look down on those who labor in occupations of lower income. There is great dignity and worth in any honest occupation. Do not use the word menial for any labor that improves the world or the people who live in it.

There is no shame in any honorable work. . . .

There will be many who struggle through life with small ownership and low income who discover, because they have been decent, the meaning of the scripture, "He that is greatest among you," let him be "the least and the servant of all" (Matt. 23:11; D&C 50:26).

(Boyd K. Packer, in Conference Report, Apr. 1982 [Salt Lake City: The Church of Jesus Christ of Latter-day Saints, 1982], 121)

I sincerely believe if we do everything in our power to be obedient to the will of God, we and our families will never lack. If we are obedient as true followers of Christ and share what we have with those less fortunate than we, the Lord will keep his promise to watch over us and care for us.

(Theodore M. Burton, in Conference Report, Apr. 1974 [Salt Lake City: The Church of Jesus Christ of Latter-day Saints, 1974], 91–92)

We should love them . . . [the poor] and serve them, with utter respect. . . .

We treat the poor like they are a garbage bag in which we throw everything we have no use for[.] Food we do not like or that is going bad—we throw it there.

Perishable goods past their expiration date, and which might harm us, go in the garbage bag: in other words, go to the poor. An article of clothing that is not in style anymore, that we do not want to wear again, goes to the poor.

This does not show any respect for the dignity of the poor . . . but to consider them less than our equals. . . .

Today it is very fashionable to talk about the poor. Unfortunately, it is not fashionable to talk with them.

(Jose Luis Gonzalez-Balado, *Mother Teresa—In My Own Words* [New York: Gramercy Books, 1996], 15, 23)

A few years ago, my wife and I served as a resource to a little inner-city branch of the Church. . . .

During a discussion the members were having in Sunday School concerning when you should give to those who ask you for aid. One of the members . . . raised his hand and told us of the following experience. As he had been walking home in the neighborhood, he had been approached by a man who put a pistol to his chest and demanded all his money. Our member took the money from his pockets and handed it over to the man and then said, "If you need the money that badly, I have more." He opened his briefcase and took out additional money,

which he gave to the robber, saying, "Understand, you are not taking this from me; I am giving it to you in the name of the Lord because you need it." He said the robber looked at him in amazement, put the pistol in his belt, and said, "Where do you live? I'm going to walk you home because you're too good a man to be on these streets, and you are not safe here."

As they started to walk to the member's apartment, suddenly they were surrounded by police cars because a woman had seen the holdup from her apartment window and had called the police. The police arrested the robber and took him away. Having been the victim, this member was asked to be a witness later at the trial of the robber. At the trial, he testified that although the robber had demanded his money, he had told him that he gave the money to him in the name of the Lord and that if the robber needed it that badly, he wanted him to have it.

(Stephen A. West, *Ensign*, May 1999 [Salt Lake City: The Church of Jesus Christ of Latter-day Saints, 1999], 28–29)

When we fast, brethren and sisters, we feel hunger. And for a short time, we literally put ourselves in the position of the hungry and the needy. As we do so, we have greater understanding of the deprivations they might feel. When we give to the bishop an offering to relieve the suffering of others, we not only do something sublime for others, but we do something wonderful for ourselves.

(Joseph B. Wirthlin, *Ensign*, May 2001 [Salt Lake City: The Church of Jesus Christ of Latter-day Saints, 2001], 74)

The Lord commands that we not covet our own property (see D&C 19:26). In many places we are blessed to have Deseret Industries. We can teach our children to go through their closets regularly and share their clothing while it is still in style, allowing others to dress fashionably too.

(Carol B. Thomas, *Ensign*, May 2001 [Salt Lake City: The Church of Jesus Christ of Latter-day Saints, 2001], 64)

Mosiah 4:24–25 • ADVICE TO THE POOR

[Those] who have been denied blessings . . . in this life—who say in their heart, "If I could have done, I would have done, or I would give if I had, but I cannot for I have not"—the Lord will bless you as though you had done, and the world to come will compensate for those who desire in their hearts the righteous blessings that they were not able to have because of no fault of their own.

(Harold B. Lee, *Ye Are the Light of the World* [Salt Lake City: Deseret Book, 1974], 298)

Mosiah 4:24 • IF I HAD I WOULD GIVE

Some months ago my wife drove down to Provo for her customary weekly visit with her mother, who had been ill for some time. On this particular day her mother had been having an unusually difficult time, and didn't have the strength to hold up her head, or even open her eyes. Though she was physically restricted, she was very alert mentally, and as my wife was caring for her many needs of the day she visited with her about family and friends. My wife held her mother's head up with one hand while she fed her with the other, and during the meal their conversation turned to one of our daughters and her husband who have five children under the age of seven. My wife commented to her mother that three of our daughter's children had chicken pox at the same time. The fact that this little mother was unusually busy was obvious. My mother-in-law stopped eating, thought for a moment, and then in a weak, almost inaudible voice said, "I feel so sorry for Robin. I wish I could go to her home and help her." A few moments later, as my wife pondered this wish, she observed, "You know, Mother, I think in your case wanting to is enough. Surely you will receive a blessing for service and selflessness as though you went to her home and helped." . . .

It is my feeling that, after all is said and done, it will be the intent of the heart by which we shall be judged.

(H. Burke Peterson, in Conference Report, Apr. 1985 [Salt Lake City: The Church of Jesus Christ of Latter-day Saints, 1985], 84)

Mosiah 4:25; 13:24 • GREED, COVET

A friend recently confided that he had lost heavily in a get-rich-quick scheme because he couldn't turn off his greed valve. Wanting more and more—living beyond one's income—makes many of us susceptible to the dishonest promoter. The plan that offers exorbitant rewards or gives you and only you a once-in-a-lifetime deal is to be avoided.

Use of important, well-recognized names or undue reference to special community or religious affiliations are often used to gain confidence and open the door to sales deceptions.

Avoid those who want immediate decisions or cash right now. All worthwhile investment opportunities can bear deliberation and scrutiny.

(Marvin J. Ashton, in Conference Report, Apr. 1982 [Salt Lake City: The Church of Jesus Christ of Latter-day Saints, 1982], 12)

Brothers and sisters, beware of covetousness. It is one of the great afflictions of these latter days. It creates greed and resentment. Often it leads to bondage, heartbreak, and crushing, grinding debt.

The number of marriages that have been shattered over money issues is staggering. The amount of heartbreak is great. The stress that comes from worry over money has burdened families, caused sickness, depression, and even premature death. . . .

Debt is a form of bondage. It is a financial termite. When we make purchases on credit, they give us only an illusion of prosperity. We think we own things, but the reality is, our things own us.

Some debt—such as for a modest home, expenses for education perhaps for a needed first car—may be necessary. But never should we enter into financial bondage through consumer debt without carefully weighing the costs. . . .

Spend less than you earn. . . . All too often a family's spending is governed more by their *yearning* than by their *earning.* They somehow believe that their life will be better if they surround themselves with an abundance of things. All too often all they are left with is avoidable anxiety and distress. . . .

Those who use credit cards to overspend unwisely should consider eliminating them. It is much better that a plastic credit card should perish than a family dwindle and perish in debt. . . .

Often people make purchases today based upon optimistic predictions of what they hope will happen tomorrow. . . . Our Heavenly Father expects that we do more with our riches than build larger barns to hold them. Will you consider what more you can do to build the kingdom of God? Will you consider what more you can do to bless the lives of others and bring light and hope into their lives?

(Joseph B. Wirthlin, *Ensign*, May 2004 [Salt Lake City: The Church of Jesus Christ of Latter-day Saints, 2004], 40–43)

[J. Reuben Clark Jr. said,] "Interest never sleeps nor sickens nor dies; it never goes to the hospital; it works on Sundays and holidays; it never takes a vacation. . . . Once in debt, interest is your companion every minute of the day and night; you cannot shun it or slip away from it; you cannot dismiss it; it yields neither to entreaties, demands, or orders; and whenever you get in its way or cross its course or fail to meet its demands, it crushes you."

(As quoted in Joseph B. Wirthlin, *Ensign*, May 2004 [Salt Lake City: The Church of Jesus Christ of Latter-day Saints, 2004], 41)

Mosiah 4:27 • ORDER, SPIRITUAL PACE, BALANCE
(Refer in this text to Jacob 4:18; 3 Nephi 11:3–5.)

If you had asked me, "Can a person accept too many callings in a branch or a ward and get too overloaded in terms of the time left for family, work, community, and so forth," the answer would be yes, in the sense that you ask. But if we ask ourselves, "Am I doing quite enough to help further the Lord's work," then our answer must be no. Most of us can do a better job of managing our time and our talents than we do, but it is important to do as the Lord suggested—to run no faster than we are able. When we run faster than we are able, we get both inefficient and tired. . . . I have on my office wall a wise and useful reminder by Anne Morrow Lindberg concerning one of the realities of life. She wrote, "My life cannot implement in action the demands of all the people to whom my heart responds." That's good counsel for us all, not as an excuse to forgo duty, but as a sage point about pace and the need for quality in relationships.

(Neal A. Maxwell, *Deposition of a Disciple* [Salt Lake City: 1976], 57–58)

A few weeks ago, President McKay related to the Twelve an interesting experience. . . . He said it is a great thing to be responsive to the whisperings of the spirit, and we know that when these whisperings come it is a gift and our privilege to have them. They come when we are relaxed and not under pressure of appointments. (I want you to mark that.) The President then took occasion to relate an experience in the life of Bishop Wells, former member of the Presiding Bishopric. A son of Bishop Wells was killed in Emigration Canyon on a railroad track. . . . His boy was run over by a freight train. Sister Wells was inconsolable. She mourned during the three days prior to the funeral, received no comfort at the funeral, and was in a rather serious state of mind. One day soon after the funeral services while she was lying on her bed relaxed, still mourning, she says that her son appeared to her and said, "Mother, do not mourn, do not cry. I am alright." He told her that she did not understand how the accident happened and explained that he had given the signal to the engineer to move on, and then made the usual effort to catch the railing on the freight train, but as he attempted to do so his foot caught on a root and he failed to catch the hand rail, and his body fell under the train. It was clearly an accident. Now listen. He said that as soon as he realized that he was in another environment he tried to see his father, but couldn't reach him. His father was so busy with the duties in his office he could not respond to his call. Therefore, he had come to his mother. He said to her, "You tell father that all is well with me, and I want you not to mourn anymore."

(Harold B. Lee, an address given to the Seminary & Institute Faculty, BYU, 5 July 1956)

Our lives can become cluttered by many things. Some are obvious, such as material things, the stuff we collect. . . . How well I know that we can surround ourselves with the material things to the extent that we have no time for the spiritual. Look around and you will see all the gadgets and toys and the nice and the fun things that cause us to squander and pay, and to wander and play. Other things that clutter our lives and use up our time are not as obvious as the material. They are more subtle and just seem to evolve, taking control of us. . . . Nothing suits the devil better than to become a silent partner with us. . . . He also knows that while in mortality we are subject to time. If by his subtle means he can become our silent partner, he can then influence us to make wrong choices that use up our time unwisely and prevent us from doing that which we should. We give our lives to that which we give our time.

(William R. Bradford, in Conference Report, Apr. 1992 [Salt Lake City: The Church of Jesus Christ of Latter-day Saints, 1992], 38)

[Young People] can have all these blessings if they are in control of themselves and if each one takes the experiences in proper order: first some social get acquainted contacts to develop social skills, then a mission, then courting, then temple marriage and a family, and then schooling and degrees and business. Now the sequence of these things is very serious. If one gets them tipped around topsy-turvy, if some get married first, many of the other dreams fall flat. But if they will take them one at a time in proper order and sequence, they may have all of them. They don't need to choose among them; they merely time them.

(Spencer W. Kimball, *Charge to Religious Educators* [Salt Lake City: The Church of Jesus Christ of Latter-day Saints, 1982], 43–47)

Are there so many fascinating, exciting things to do or so many challenges pressing down upon you that it is hard to keep focused on that which is essential? When things of the world crowd in, all too often the wrong things take highest priority. . . . Satan has a powerful tool to use against good people. It is distraction. He would have good people fill life with "good things" so there is no room for the essential ones.

Find retreat of peace and quiet where periodically you can ponder and let the Lord establish the direction of your life. Each of us needs to periodically check our bearings and confirm that we are on course. Sometimes soon you may benefit from taking this personal inventory:

What are my highest priorities to be accomplished while on earth?

How do I use my discretionary time? Is some of it

consistently applied to my highest priorities?
Is there anything I know I should not be doing? If so,
I will repent and stop it now.

In a quiet moment write down your responses. Analyze them. Make any necessary adjustments.

Put first things first.

(Richard G. Scott, *Ensign*, May 2001 [Salt Lake City: The Church of Jesus Christ of Latter-day Saints, 2001], 7, 9)

———

I am convinced that if Satan can't influence us to sin outright, the next best thing he can do is fill our lives with so much clutter that he becomes our silent partner, so silent that too often we are unaware of his influence in speeding up the pace of our lives and camouflaging our priorities.

(Jack R. Christianson and K. Douglas Bassett, *Life Lessons from the Book of Mormon* [Salt Lake City: Deseret Book, 2003], 221)

———

There is power in steadiness and repetition. And if we can be led by inspiration to choose the right small things to change, consistent obedience will bring great improvement.

(Henry B. Eyring, *The Lord Will Multiply the Harvest* [An Evening with Elder Henry B. Eyring, 6 Feb. 1998], 3)

———

This is a noisy and busy world that we live in. Remember that being busy is not necessarily being spiritual. . . .

Do we allow influences into our homes that drive the Spirit from our homes? The type of entertainment that we permit into our homes will certainly have an impact on the power of the Holy Ghost. Much of the entertainment of the world is offensive to the Holy Ghost. Surely we should not watch movies or television shows that are filled with violence, vulgar language, and immorality.

(Joseph B. Wirthlin, in Conference Report, Apr. 2003 [Salt Lake City: The Church of Jesus Christ of Latter-day Saints, 2003], 27–28)

———

When I was around thirteen and my brother ten, Father had promised to take us to the circus. But at lunchtime there was a phone call; some urgent business required his attention downtown. We braced ourselves for disappointment. Then we heard him say [into the phone], "No, I won't be down. It'll have to wait."

When he came back to the table, Mother smiled. "The circus keeps coming back, you know," [she said].

"I know," said Father. "But childhood doesn't."

(Arthur Gordon, *A Touch of Wonder* [1974], 77–78; as quoted in Thomas S. Monson, in Conference Report, Apr. 2003 [Salt Lake City: The Church of Jesus Christ of Latter-day Saints, 2003], 20–21)

———

A computer can be a useful and indispensable tool. But if we allow it to devour our time with vain, unproductive, and sometimes destructive pursuits, it becomes an entangling net.

Many of us enjoy watching athletic contests, but if we can recite the statistics of our favorite players and at the same time forget birthdays or anniversaries, neglect our families, or ignore the opportunity to render acts of Christlike service, then athletics may also be an entangling net. . . .

When our work consumes us to the point where the spiritual dimensions of life are neglected, work can also be an entangling net.

Some have been ensnared in the net of excessive debt. The net of interest holds them fast, requiring them to sell their time and energies to meet the demands of creditors. They surrender their freedom, becoming slaves to their own extravagance. . . .

Our lives are so easily filled with appointments, meetings, and tasks. . . . Sometimes we feel that the busier we are, the more important we are—as though our busyness defines our worth. . . . We can spend a lifetime whirling about at a feverish pace, checking off list after list of things that in the end really don't matter. . . .

We can easily get our lives out of balance.

(Joseph B. Wirthlin, in Conference Report, Apr. 2002 [Salt Lake City: The Church of Jesus Christ of Latter-day Saints, 2002], 15–16)

———

We need at times to strive to focus on the basic purposes of our work so that mere busyness does not create the illusion that we are effective when we are not.

Merely attending meetings may be busyness, but to get something accomplished is the purpose of our call. . . .

Avoid the tendency to crowd too many meetings in on the Sabbath day. . . . It would be a mistake simply to rush in to fill up the time with more meetings.

(*The Teachings of Spencer W. Kimball*, ed. by Edward L. Kimball [Salt Lake City: Bookcraft, 1982], 492–493)

———

William M. Allred . . . stated that some straitlaced people had problems with the Prophet Joseph playing ball with the boys. Said Allred, referring to the Prophet [Joseph Smith]:

"He then related a story of a certain prophet who

was sitting under the shade of a tree amusing himself in some way, when a hunter came along with his bow and arrow, and reproved him. The prophet asked him if he kept his bow strung up all the time. The hunter answered that he did not. The prophet asked why, and he said it would lose its elasticity if he did. The prophet said it was just so with his mind, he did not want it strung up all the time" (*Juvenile Instructor*, 1 Aug. 1892, 472).

(James E. Faust, in Conference Report, Apr. 1984 [Salt Lake City: The Church of Jesus Christ of Latter-day Saints, 1984], 94)

———

President McKay, I remember, said to us once, in speaking to the Council of the Twelve . . . "Brethren, we need to meditate more." Those were his words. We need to take time to meditate. It's so hard. We have been cruising the highways in this part of the world. . . . And I've had one impression—the whole world's going mad. Traffic! Everywhere you go! . . . But we don't meditate. We don't take time to think. . . . We passed a sign on one of these roads that said Walden's Pond, with an arrow. And I thought, "Poor old Henry Thoreau would go crazy if he saw what was happening on the highways around his pond." The speed at which we live. Slow down, at least for an hour or two. . . .

President McKay used to tell a story of General Gordon on a campaign in Africa. Every morning there was a white handkerchief dropped at his tent door, in the front, on the ground. And the whole army under his direction knew that when that flag was on the ground in front of his tent, General Gordon was in communing with the Lord, and nobody, regardless of the emergency, dared disturb him during that time.

(*Discourses of President Gordon B. Hinckley*, 1995–99 [Salt Lake City: The Church of Jesus Christ of Latter-day Saints, 2004], 1:333–334)

———

I have known persons who began their academic studies with great momentum, but as time went by did not continue to invest the time they needed in their studies because they supposed . . . if they simply did their church work the Lord would bless them to achieve their academic objectives. . . .

I remember a graduate student who used his church service as a means of escape from the rigors of his studies. He went beyond what we call church-service time and became almost a full-time church-service worker, consistently volunteering for every extra assignment and giving help that was greatly appreciated in the various organizations and activities of the Church, but finally failing in his studies and blaming his failure on the excessive burden of his church work. His strength became his downfall.

Similarly, I remember the concerns President Harold B. Lee expressed to me when I was president of Brigham Young University. Shortly before the Provo Utah Temple was dedicated, he told me of his concern that the accessibility of the temple would cause some students to attend the temple so often that they would neglect their studies. He urged me to work with Brigham Young University stake presidents to make sure that the students understood that even something as sacred and important as temple service needed to be done in wisdom and order so that the students would not neglect the studies that should be the major focus of their time during their student years.

(Dallin H. Oaks, *With Full Purpose of Heart* [Salt Lake City: Deseret Book, 2002], 173–174)

———

We don't have to be fast; we simply have to be steady and move in the right direction. We have to do the best we can, one step after another.

In my younger days, I loved to run. Although it may be hard for you to believe it, I did. And I did win a few races. I'm not so fast anymore. In fact, I'm not sure how well I would do in a race if the only contestants were the member of the Quorum of the Twelve.

My ability to run is not so swift now. While I am looking forward to that future time when, with a resurrected body, I can once again sprint over a field and feel the wind blowing through my hair, I do not dwell on the fact that I cannot do it now.

That would be unwise. Instead, I take steps that I can take. Even with the limitations of age, I can still take one step at a time. To do what I can is all my Heavenly Father now requires of me. And it is all He requires of you, regardless of your disabilities, limitations, or insecurities.

John Wooden was perhaps the greatest college basketball coach in the history of the game. He had four full undefeated seasons. His teams won 10 national championships. At one point, he had a streak of 88 consecutive wins.

One of the first things Coach Wooden drilled into his players was something his father had taught him when he was a boy growing up on a farm. "Don't worry much about trying to be better than someone else," his father said. "Learn from others, yes. But don't just try to be better than they are. You have no control over that. Instead try, and try very hard, to be the best that you can be. That, you have control over."

Let me cite a hypothetical example of a dear sister in any ward, the one who has perfect children who never cause a disturbance in church. She is the one working on her 20th generation in her family history, keeps an immaculate home, has memorized the book of Mark, and makes wool sweaters for the orphaned children in Romania. No disrespect, of course, intended for any of these worthy goals. Now, when you get tempted to throw your hands in the air and give up because of this dear sister, please remember you're not competing with her any more than I'm competing with the members of the Quorum of the Twelve in winning a 50-yard dash.

The only thing you need to worry about is striving to be the best you can be. And how do you do that? You keep your eye on the goals that matter most in life, and you move towards them step by step.

(Joseph B. Wirthlin, *Ensign*, Nov. 2001 [Salt Lake City: The Church of Jesus Christ of Latter-day Saints, 2001], 26)

———————

We must not confuse means and ends. The vehicle is not the destination. If we lose sight of our eternal goals, we might think the most important thing is how fast we are moving and that any road will get us to our destination. The Apostle Paul described this attitude as "hav[ing] a zeal of God, but not according to knowledge" (Romans 10:2). Zeal is a method, not a goal. Zeal—even a zeal toward God—needs to be "according to knowledge" of God's commandments and His plan for His children.

(Dallin H. Oaks, *With Full Purpose of Heart* [Salt Lake City: Deseret Book, 2002], 180)

———————

While we may be able to answer honestly all of the temple recommend questions and be worthy to enter the temple, it is also true that the pace of our lives can keep us from the daily companionship of that Spirit we so desire. In Mosiah 4:27, King Benjamin encouraged each of us to run life's race with diligence. His words remind us that life's race is not a sprint but a long-distance race. Unlike a sprint, a long-distance race must be run at a pace that allows us to finish strong, or as the scriptures say, "endure [to] the end" (1 Nephi 13:37).

The Lord referred to this concept following the loss of the 116-page manuscript, when he counseled the Prophet Joseph Smith: "Do not run faster or labor more than you have strength" (D&C 10:4). "But," one might say, "what about the words of Spencer W. Kimball about lengthening our stride?" I would suggest that, even in a long distance race, the runner must lengthen his stride; he just doesn't do it so early in the race that he has no second wind—becoming exhausted so that he cannot endure to the end.

Words from the book of Hebrews echo this same theme: "Let us run with *patience* the race that is set before us" (Hebrews 21:1; emphasis added). Patience is not required in a sprint.

(K. Douglas Bassett, *The Barber's Song* [Springville, Utah: Cedar Fort, 2005], 127–128)

Mosiah 4:30; 5:13 • WATCH YOUR THOUGHTS, WORDS, DEEDS

(Refer in this text to Alma 12:14; 3 Nephi 12:27–29; Moroni 7:4–11.)

We cannot indulge in swearing. We cannot be guilty of profanity; we cannot indulge in impure thoughts, words, and acts and have the Spirit of the Lord with us.

(Gordon B. Hinckley, *Ensign*, May 1997 [Salt Lake City: The Church of Jesus Christ of Latter-day Saints, 1997], 49)

———————

If men's secret acts shall be revealed it is likely that their secret thoughts will also be revealed. . . . The one who harbors evil thoughts sometimes feels safe in the conviction that these thoughts are unknown to others. . . . Accordingly, men's deeds and thoughts must be recorded in heaven, and recording angels will not fail to make complete recordings of our thoughts and actions. We pay our tithing and the bishop records it in his book and gives us a receipt. But even if the entry fails to get in the ward record, we shall have full credit for the tithes we paid. There will be no omissions in the heavenly records, and they will all be available at the day of judgment.

(Spencer W. Kimball, *The Miracle of Forgiveness* [Salt Lake City: Bookcraft, 1969], 108)

———————

Control your thoughts. No one steps into immorality in an instant. The first seeds of immorality are always sown in the mind. When we allow our thoughts to linger on lewd or immoral things, the first step on the road to immorality has been taken. I especially warn you against the evils of pornography. Again and again we hear from those caught in deep sin that often the first step on their road to transgression began with pornographic materials.

(Ezra Taft Benson, *BYU Speeches of the Year*, 1987–88 [Provo, Utah: BYU Press, 1997], 51–52)

———————

A priesthood holder is temperate. This means he is restrained in his emotions and verbal expressions. He does things in moderation and is not given to overindulgence. In a word, he has self-control. He is the master of his emotions, not the other way around. A priesthood holder who would curse his wife, abuse her with words or actions, or do the same to one of his own children is guilty of grievous sin. "Can ye be angry, and not sin?" asked the Apostle Paul (JST Ephesians 4:26). If a man does not control his temper, it is a sad admission that he is not in control of his thoughts. . . . A priesthood holder is to be patient. Patience is another form of self-control. . . . Patience is composure under stress. . . . A priesthood holder who is patient will be tolerant of the mistakes and failings of his loved ones. Because he loves them, he will not find fault nor criticize nor blame. . . . A priesthood holder is kind. Kindness pardons others' weaknesses and faults. Kindness is extended to all—to the aged and the young, to animals, to those low of station as well as the high. These are the true attributes of the divine nature.

(Ezra Taft Benson, *Ensign*, Nov. 1986 [Salt Lake City: The Church of Jesus Christ of Latter-day Saints, 1986], 47)

———————

If we entertain temptations, soon they begin entertaining us.

(Neal A. Maxwell, in Conference Report, Apr. 1987 [Salt Lake City: The Church of Jesus Christ of Latter-day Saints, 1987], 88)

———————

Talking about or looking at immodest pictures of a woman's body can stimulate powerful emotions. It will tempt you to watch improper videocassettes or movies. . . . Work at keeping your thoughts clean by thinking of something good. The mind can think of only one thing at a time. Use that fact to crowd out ugly thoughts. Above all, don't feed thoughts by reading or watching things that are wrong. If you don't control your thoughts, Satan will keep tempting you until you eventually act them out.

(Richard G. Scott, *Ensign*, Nov. 1994 [Salt Lake City: The Church of Jesus Christ of Latter-day Saints, 1994], 37)

———————

[Prov. 23:7] Unclean thoughts lead to unclean acts. I remember going to President McKay years ago to plead the cause of a missionary who had become involved in serious sin. I said to President McKay, "He did it on an impulse." The President said to me: "His mind was dwelling on these things before he transgressed. The thought was father to the deed. There would not have been that impulse if he had previously controlled his thoughts."

(Gordon B. Hinckley, *Ensign,* May 1996 [Salt Lake City: The Church of Jesus Christ of Latter-day Saints, 1996], 48)

———————

I had read somewhere of a young couple who settled in the wilderness. While the man cleared the land, his wife tended things about the homestead. Occasionally, the cow would get into the garden, and the husband would complain. One day, as he left to get supplies, he said in a sarcastic way, "Do you think you'll be able to keep the cow in while I am gone?" . . . That night a terrible storm arose. Frightened by thunder, the cow escaped into the woods. Several days later the husband returned to an empty cabin and an apologetic note: "A storm came up, and the cow got out. I am so sorry, but I think I can find her." He searched; neither had survived. The author concluded the incident with these words:

> Boys flying kites haul in their white-winged birds;
> You can call back your kites, but you can't call back
>   your words.
> 'Careful with fire' is good advice, we know;
> 'Careful with words' is ten times doubly so.
> Thoughts unexpressed will often fall back dead.
> But God Himself can't kill them, once they are said.

(Boyd K. Packer, in Conference Report, Oct. 1987 [Salt Lake City: The Church of Jesus Christ of Latter-day Saints, 1987], 18)

———————

The fundamental reason why the Lord has instructed us to conduct worthiness interviews in His Church is to teach us to keep the commitments we make. In short, we are to be trained during this season of mortal probation to master ourselves (see Alma 34:33–37) to live with integrity and be true to our covenants. Worthiness interviews are conducted in a spirit of loving concern for each son and daughter of a loving God. These interviews represent the rehearsal stage for final judgment. Such interviews are a blessing, a choice opportunity to account to the Lord through His authorized servants for the sacred stewardship we all have to "watch [ourselves], and [our] thoughts, and [our] words, and [our] deeds."

(Joseph B. Wirthlin, *Ensign*, May 1997 [Salt Lake City: The Church of Jesus Christ of Latter-day Saints, 1997], 16)

———————

We understand that we will live a postmortal life of infinite duration and that we determine the kind of life it will be by our thoughts and actions in mortality. Mortality is very brief but immeasurably important. . . . We can compare our lives with the flight of a spaceship. When its motor is started up, its trajectory is monitored precisely. Any deviation from its decreed course is corrected immediately. Even a fraction of a degree off course would carry it many miles from its destination if not corrected. The longer the correction is delayed, the greater will be the required adjustment. Can you imagine how far off course we can become without course corrections? . . . Our course on earth is . . . determined by the decisions we make each day. We cannot separate our thoughts and actions now from their effects on the future.

(Joseph B. Wirthlin, *Ensign*, May 1998 [Salt Lake City: The Church of Jesus Christ of Latter-day Saints, 1998], 14–16)

———————

You tell me what you think about when you do not have to think, and I'll tell you what you are.

(David O. McKay, "My Young Friends . . .," comp. by Llewelyn R. McKay [Salt Lake City: Bookcraft, 1973], 29)

———————

A number of years ago I went with a brother to tow in a wrecked car. . . . The car was demolished; the driver, though unhurt, had been taken to the hospital for treatment of shock and for examination.

The next morning he came asking for his car, anxious to be on his way. When he was shown the wreckage, his pent-up emotions and disappointment, sharpened perhaps by his misfortune, exploded in a long stream of profanity. So obscene and biting were his words that they exposed years of practice with profanity. . . .

One of my brothers crawled from beneath the car, where he had been working with a large wrench. He too was upset, and with threatening gestures of the wrench . . . he ordered the man off the premises. "We don't have to listen to that kind of language here," he said. And the customer left, cursing more obscenely than before.

Much later in the day he reappeared, subdued, penitent, and avoiding everyone else; he found my brother.

"I have been in the hotel room all day," he said, "lying on the bed tormented. I can't tell you how utterly ashamed I am for what happened this morning. My conduct was inexcusable. I have been trying to think of some justification, and I can think of only one thing. In all my life, never, not once, have I been told that my language was not acceptable. I have always talked that way. You were the first one who ever told me that my language was out of order."

Isn't it interesting that a man could grow to maturity, the victim of such a vile habit, and never meet a protest? How tolerant we have become, and how quickly we are moving. A generation ago writers of newspapers, editors of magazines, and particularly the producers of motion pictures, carefully censored profane and obscene words.

(Boyd K. Packer, in Conference Report, Sept.–Oct. 1967 [Salt Lake City: The Church of Jesus Christ of Latter-day Saints, 1967], 126–127)

———————

To enable us to keep our minds centered on righteousness, we should consciously elect to ponder the truths of salvation in our hearts . . . call on ourselves to preach a sermon. I have preached many sermons walking along congested city streets, or tramping desert trails, or in lonely places, thus centering my mind on the Lord's affairs and the things of righteousness; and I might say they have been better sermons than I have ever preached to congregations.

If we are going to work out our salvation, we must rejoice in the Lord. We must ponder his truths in our hearts.

(Bruce R. McConkie, in Conference Report, Oct. 1973 [Salt Lake City: The Church of Jesus Christ of Latter-day Saints, 1973], 56)

———————

When you learn to control your thoughts, you will be safe.

One man I know does this: Whenever an unworthy thought tries to enter his mind, he brushes his thumb against his wedding ring. That breaks the circuit and for him becomes an almost automatic way to close out unwanted thoughts and ideas.

(Boyd K. Packer, *Ensign*, Nov. 1999 [Salt Lake City: The Church of Jesus Christ of Latter-day Saints, 1999], 24)

———————

All evils to which so many become addicted begin in the mind and in the way one thinks. Experience teaches that when the will and imagination are in conflict, the imagination usually wins. What we imagine may defeat our reason and make us slaves to what we taste, see, hear, smell, and feel in the mind's eye. The body is indeed the servant of the mind.

In his widely acclaimed essay *As a Man Thinketh*, James Allen reinforced what Jesus so beautifully proclaimed. Mr. Allen wrote:

"Man is made or unmade by himself; in the armoury of thought he forges the weapons by which he destroys himself; he also fashions the tools with which he builds for himself heavenly mansions of joy and strength and peace. By the right choice and true application of thought, man ascends to the Divine Perfection; by the abuse and wrong application of thought, he descends below the level of the beast. Between these two extremes are all the grades of character, and man is their maker and master. . . .

"All that a man achieves and all that he fails to achieve is the direct result of his own thoughts" (New York: Thomas Y. Crowell, n.d., 8–9, 34).

(Joseph B. Wirthlin, in Conference Report, Apr. 1982 [Salt Lake City: The Church of Jesus Christ of Latter-day Saints, 1982], 34)

———————

What a man continually thinks about determines his actions in times of opportunity and stress. A man's reaction to his appetites and impulses when they are aroused gives the measure of that man's character. . . .

Man is responsible not only for every deed, but also for every idle word and thought. Said the Savior:

Every idle word that men shall speak they shall give account thereof in the day of judgment (Matthew 12:36).

(*Teachings of Presidents of the Church—David O. McKay* [Salt Lake City: The Church of Jesus Christ of Latter-day Saints, 2003], 87)

———————

It really matters what you listen to, what you look at, what you think, say, and do. Select music that will strengthen your spirit. Control your speech; keep it free from profanity and vulgarity. Follow the teachings of this proverb: "My mouth shall speak truth; and wickedness is an abomination to my lips.

"All the words of my mouth are in righteousness; there is nothing . . . perverse in them" (Proverbs 8:7–8).

(Russell M. Nelson, in Conference Report, Oct. 1985 [Salt Lake City: The Church of Jesus Christ of Latter-day Saints, 1985], 41)

———————

Recently I was in a department store trying on shoes. Four young men were looking at what they labeled missionary shoes. It was evident at least two of the young men had received mission calls and were there to find shoes suitable for missionary service. I was surprised by a barrage of crude terms with a few profanities which seemed to routinely roll off their tongues. When they noticed there was someone else nearby, I heard one say, "Hey, guys, we better clean up our language," as he motioned with his head in my direction. . . .

Profanity and priesthood are not compatible. Neither is profanity compatible with missionary service. Profane and crude terms, if part of our conversation, need to be eliminated from our vocabularies. Conversation is one of the windows to our souls.

(H. David Burton, in Conference Report, Apr. 2000 [Salt Lake City: The Church of Jesus Christ of Latter-day Saints, 2000), 49)

———————

The great over-all struggle in the world today is, as it has always been, for the souls of men. Every soul is personally engaged in the struggle, and he makes the fight with what is in his mind. In the final analysis the battleground for each individual is within himself. Inevitably he gravitates toward the subjects of his thoughts. Ages ago the wise man succinctly put this great truth thus: "As he thinketh in his heart, so is he" (Proverbs 23:7). . . .

If we would avoid adopting the evils of the world, we must pursue a course that will daily feed our minds with, and call them back to, the things of the spirit. I know of no better way to do this than by reading the Book of Mormon. . . . (Psalm 119:97–105).

I am persuaded that it is irrational to hope to escape the lusts of the world without substituting for them as the subjects of our thoughts the things of the spirit. . . .

I counsel you to make reading in the Book of Mormon a few minutes each day a lifelong practice. . . . I am persuaded by my own experience and that of my loved ones, as well as by the statement of the Prophet Joseph Smith, that one can get and keep closer to the Lord by reading the Book of Mormon than by reading any other book.

(Marion G. Romney, *Learning for the Eternities*, comp. by George J. Romney [Salt Lake City: Deseret Book, 1977], 82–85)

———————

I want to tell you of one way you can control your thoughts. . . .

The mind is like a stage. Except when we are asleep, the curtain is always up. Always there is some act being performed on that stage. . . .

Have you noticed that, without any real intent on your part and almost in the midst of any performance, a shady little thought may creep in from the wings and endeavor to attract your attention? These delinquent little thoughts, these unsavory characters, will try to upstage everybody. If you permit them to go on, all other thoughts, of any virtue, will leave the stage. You will be left, because you consented to it, to the influence of unworthy thoughts. . . .

What do you do at a time like this, when the stage of your mind is commandeered by these imps of unclean thinking? . . .

Let me suggest that you choose from among the sacred music of the Church one favorite hymn. . . .

Now, go over it in your mind very thoughtfully a few times. Memorize the words and the music. Even though you have had no musical training, even though you do not play an instrument, and even though your voice may leave something to be desired, you can think through a hymn. . . . I have stressed how important it is to know that you can only think of one thing at a time. Use this hymn as your emergency channel. Use this as the place for your thoughts to go. Anytime you find that these shady actors have slipped in from the sideline of your thinking onto the stage of your mind, think through this hymn. "Put the record on," as it were, and then you will begin to know something about controlling your thoughts. . . . It will change the whole mood on the stage of your mind. Because it is clean and uplifting and reverent, the baser thoughts will leave.

While virtue, by choice, will not endure the presence of filth, that which is debased and unclean cannot endure the light.

Virtue will not associate with filth, while evil cannot tolerate the presence of good. . . .

At first this simple little procedure may seem to you so trivial as to be unimportant and ineffective. With a little experimenting, you will learn that it is not easy, but it is powerfully effective.

(*Memorable Stories and Parables by Boyd K. Packer* [Salt Lake City: Bookcraft, 1997], 79–81)

Mosiah 5:2, 7 • A MIGHTY CHANGE OF HEART
(Refer in this text to Mosiah 27:24–26.)

Being born again, comes by the Spirit of God through ordinances.

(*Teachings of the Prophet Joseph Smith*, comp. by Joseph Fielding Smith [Salt Lake City: Deseret Book, 1976], 162)

_____

Mere compliance with the formality of the ordinance of baptism does not mean that a person has been born again. No one can be born again without baptism, but the immersion of water and the laying on of hands to confer the Holy Ghost do not of themselves guarantee that a person has been or will be born again. The new birth takes place only for those who actually enjoy the Gift or companionship of the Holy Ghost, only for those who are fully converted, who have given themselves without restraint to the Lord.

(Bruce R. McConkie, *Mormon Doctrine* [Salt Lake City: The Church of Jesus Christ of Latter-day Saints, 1966], 100–101)

_____

In addition to the physical ordinance of baptism and the laying on of hands, one must be spiritually born again to gain exaltation and eternal life.

(Ezra Taft Benson, *Ensign*, July 1989 [Salt Lake City: The Church of Jesus Christ of Latter-day Saints, 1989], 2–3)

_____

(For most of us) this process is usually slow. The unusually quick ones make their way into scripture.

(Bruce R. McConkie, *BYU Speeches of the Year*, 1976 [Provo, Utah: BYU Press, 1997])

_____

Let us recognize that to be spiritually born of God and receive the baptism of fire and of the Holy Ghost is, as the scriptures attest, a glorious and wonderful event that prepares us to pursue eternal life. But it does not immediately translate us into perfect beings ready for celestial glory. It does not mean that we will never make a mistake or sin again. Hence, we see the great need to apply the principle of repentance continuously as we strive daily to serve God and keep his commandments.

(David W. Hellem, *Ensign*, June 1992 [Salt Lake City: The Church of Jesus Christ of Latter-day Saints, 1992], 12)

_____

That change comes today to every son and daughter of God who repents of his or her sins, who humble themselves before the Lord, and who seek forgiveness and remission of sin by baptism. . . . Yet many of us who have received that witness, that new birth, that change of heart, while we may have erred in judgment or have made many mistakes, and often perhaps come short of the true standard in our lives, we have repented of the evil, and we have sought from time to time forgiveness at the hand of the Lord; so that until this day the same desire and purpose which pervaded our souls when we were baptized and received a remission of our sins, still holds possession of our hearts, and is still the ruling sentiment and passion of our souls. Though at times we may be stirred to anger, and our wrath move us to say and do things which are not pleasing in the sight of God, yet instantly on regaining our sober senses and recovering from our lapse into the power of darkness, we feel humble, repentant, and to ask forgiveness for the wrong that we have done to ourselves, and per-chance to others.

(Joseph F. Smith, *Gospel Doctrine* [Salt Lake City: Deseret Book, 1975], 96–97)

_____

Conversion basically represents the transformation from the "natural man" to becoming the "man of Christ" (Mosiah 3:19; Helaman 3:29; see also 2 Corinthians 5:17). It is a labor which takes more than an afternoon.

The outcomes of this ongoing process include having "no more disposition to do evil, but to do good continually" (Mosiah 5:2).

(Neal A. Maxwell, in Conference Report, Apr. 2003 [Salt Lake City: The Church of Jesus Christ of Latter-day Saints, 2003], 73)

_____

Conversion does not normally come all at once, even though the scriptures give us dramatic accounts. It comes in stages, until a person becomes at heart a new person. Being "born again" is the scriptural term. It is a change of both how we think and how we feel. . . .

You will notice their words are very similar to the commitments you make in the baptismal covenant (see D&C 20:37).

The blessings and promises of conversion are received by covenant through baptism and confirmation and all the ordinances of the temple and the priesthood. Then by continued repentance and obedience and faithful keeping of the covenants made, the fruits of conversion grow and develop in one's life. . . .

It is through this total conversion experience that we truly come to personally know and feel the character and greatness of God. It is the means whereby we become not only servants of the Lord but His friends as well. To the Saints of the early restoration period, the Lord defined His relationship with them: "And again I say unto you, my friends, for from henceforth I shall call you friends" (D&C 84:77). . . .

Knowing God and becoming His friend comes with the conversion process. Enos found it. King Benjamin's subjects found it. Alma found it. It is available to all who will repent and obey the commandments. This conversion is an intimate and intensely personal experience. It is about relationships. It involves awakening the Spirit of Christ, which is in all men and women (see D&C 84;45–46; 88:11).

(Dale E. Miller, in Conference Report, Oct. 2004 [Salt Lake City: The Church of Jesus Christ of Latter-day Saints, 2004], 12–14)

Mosiah 5:7 • HIS SONS

You may enjoy music, athletics, or be mechanically inclined, and someday you may work in a trade or a profession or in the arts. As important as such activities and occupations can be, they do not define who we are. First and foremost, we are spiritual beings. We are sons of God.

(David A. Bednar, *Ensign*, Nov. 2005 [Salt Lake City: The Church of Jesus Christ of Latter-day Saints, 2005], 47)

Mosiah 5:8 • NO OTHER NAME . . . WHEREBY SALVATION COMETH

. . . Jesus is uniquely our "advocate with the Father," that He pleads for us, and that He makes intercession for us (see 1 John 2:1; 2 Nephi 2:9; Mosiah 5:8; D&C 32:3; 45:3; 62:1; 110:4). . . .

Jesus' personal role is unique in yet another way: "For the Father judgeth no man, but hath committed all judgment unto the Son" (John 5:22). "Jesus, our Redeemer," has earned this special standing, entitling Him not only to plead for us but also to judge us, which His unique suffering made possible by virtue of His agonies during the Atonement (see Mosiah 15:8; D&C 45:3–5). Thus, by His suffering and by divine investiture, in one sense Jesus is both advocate and judge!

Only an omniscient, all-loving God could have both roles of advocate (pleading for the petitioner) and judge (deciding the ultimate fate of the petitioner).

(Neal A. Maxwell, *One More Strain of Praise* [Salt Lake City: Bookcraft, 1999], 33)

Mosiah 5:13 • THE MASTER WHOM HE HAS NOT SERVED
(Refer in this text to Mosiah 2:16–17.)

The minute a man stops supplicating God for his spirit and directions just so soon he starts out to become a stranger to him and his works. When men stop praying for God's spirit, they place confidence in their own unaided reason, and they gradually lose the spirit of God, just the same as near and dear friends, by never writing to or visiting with each other, will become strangers.

(*Teachings of Presidents of the Church—Heber J. Grant* [Salt Lake City: The Church of Jesus Christ of Latter-day Saints, 2002], 174)

If we do not know the doctrines, do not honestly count our blessings, and do not serve and think about the Lord, then we become estranged from Him (Mosiah 5:11–13). It is our decision—entirely.

There is yet another pervasive cause of such distancing: "Despair cometh because of iniquity" (Moroni 10:22). . . . If His love is unfelt by us, it is because we have taken our phone off the hook, having in one way or another let ourselves become "past feeling" (Ephesians 4:19; 1 Nephi 17:45; Moroni 9:20).

If *unfelt* by us, it is not because God's love is *unoffered*.

(Neal A. Maxwell, *Whom The Lord Loveth* [Salt Lake City: Deseret Book, 2003], 43–44)

An inspired prophet saw service as the way we come to want what the Lord wants. He wrote, "For how knoweth a man the master whom he has not served, and who is a stranger unto him, and is far from the thoughts and intents of his heart?" (Mosiah 5:13). . . .

You may be assured that He knows you and your capacity to grow. He has prepared you. Calls will stretch you, often at the start and always over their course, but He will give you the Holy Ghost to be your companion. The Holy Ghost will tell you what to do when your own abilities and efforts are not enough (see John 14:26). . . . The call is an invitation to become like Him (see 3 Nephi 27:27).

You might well ask, "How will seeing my call that way make me more confident of success?" The answer is that seeing it in that lofty way will make it more likely that you will go for help to the only source that is never-failing.

(Henry B. Eyring, in Conference Report, Apr. 2000 [Salt Lake City: The Church of Jesus Christ of Latter-day Saints, 2000], 81–82)

Mosiah 5:23 • YE ARE IN THE HANDS OF GOD

While most of our suffering is self-inflicted, some is caused by or permitted by God. This sobering reality calls for deep submissiveness, especially when God does not remove the cup from us. In such circumstances, when reminded about the premortal shouting for joy as this life's plan was unfolded (see Job 38:7), we can perhaps be pardoned if, in some moments, we wonder what all the shouting was about.

For the faithful, what finally emerges is . . . the reassuring realization that we are in the Lord's hands! But, brothers and sisters, we were never really anywhere else! . . .

Perhaps the realization of being in God's hands comes fully only as we ponder the significance of the prints in the hands of our submissive Savior (see 3 Nephi 11:14–15).

(Neal A. Maxwell, in Conference Report, Apr. 1985 [Salt Lake City: The Church of Jesus Christ of Latter-day Saints, 1985], 91–92)

Mosiah 7:27 • CHRIST . . . THE FATHER OF ALL THINGS

Some of you may wonder why the Son is occasionally referred to as "the Father." The designation used for any man can vary. Every man here is a son but may also be called "father," "brother," "uncle," or "grandfather," depending on conversational circumstance. . . . Because Jesus was our Creator, He is known in scripture as "the Father of all things" (Mosiah 7:27; see also 15:3; 16:15; Helaman 14:12; Ether 3:14). But please remember, as the First Presidency taught, "Jesus Christ is not the Father of the spirits who have taken or yet shall take bodies upon this earth, for He is one of them. He is The Son, as they are sons or daughters of Elohim" (James R. Clark, comp. *Messages of the First Presidency of the Church of Jesus Christ of Latter-day Saints* [Salt Lake City: Bookcraft, 1965–75], 5:34).

(Russell M. Nelson, *A Book of Mormon Treasury—Gospel Insights from General Authorities and Religious Educators* [Salt Lake City: Deseret Book, 2003], 25, 31)

Mosiah 8:14–17 • A SEER

A seer is a prophet selected and appointed to possess and use these holy interpreters [the Urim and Thummim]. . . . The President of the Church holds the office of seership (D&C 107:92; 124:94, 125). Indeed, the apostolic office itself is one of seership, and the members of the Council of the Twelve, together with the Presidency and Patriarch to the Church, are chosen and sustained as prophets, seers, and revelators to the Church. If there are seers among a people, that people is the Lord's. Where there are no seers, apostasy prevails (Isa. 29:10; 2 Ne. 27:5).

(Bruce R. McConkie, *Mormon Doctrine* [Salt Lake City: Bookcraft, 1966], 700–701)

———————

One can trust a seer because a seer may see the heavens open. He may see the great vision of God working in all his majesty. He may see the fulness of truth as it is revealed to him by God who makes no mistakes. . . . The seer can bear personal testimony, not based on books, not based on scholarship, not based on tradition, but based on the evidence of things that God himself can reveal to him in an actual experience with Deity. He may receive a revelation from God by actually seeing and hearing and being instructed in the real truth.

A seer then is one who may see God, who may talk with God, who may receive personal instruction from God. Our prophet is a seer and a revelator. . . . I was taught this doctrine by Elder Marion G. Romney, who told me that the Lord will never let his prophet, the seer, lead his people astray. . . .

How grateful, my brothers and sisters, we should be that God in the fulness of his grace has given us a living prophet to guide us to Him; even more that God has given us a seer, for this seer and prophet reveals personal testimony to young and old alike that Jesus is in very deed the risen Savior, the Living God. . . .

Of this I bear sacred testimony, for under conditions too sacred to mention here God has given me witness three times in the temples that David O. McKay is truly and indeed a prophet of God, a seer, and I bear you this testimony.

(Theodore M. Burton, in Conference Report, Sept./Oct. 1961 [Salt Lake City: The Church of Jesus Christ of Latter-day Saints, 1961], 121–122)

Mosiah 8:17 • THINGS WHICH ARE NOT KNOWN SHALL BE MADE KNOWN

Why does the prophet say to young people, "Don't date until you're sixteen"? What does he "see" that we may not? I heard of a mother who said, "If my daughter is not going steady by the time she's fourteen—how will she ever get a date for the school dances?" I could just weep, because I know a bishop is very likely to see that girl down the road, as she comes to him to confess serious transgressions. If she's going steady at fourteen, there will usually be problems later. Why? Because youth are not yet mature enough to understand the powers of sexual attraction and how easily young couples can get into moral trouble. But the prophet understands. The prophet can see things that other people cannot see, and he has counseled the youth not to date until the age of sixteen. . . . A prophet and seer can foresee how to help our youth avoid moral tragedy.

(*Selected Writings of Gerald N. Lund* [Salt Lake City: Deseret Book, 1999], 106)

Mosiah 9:3 • OVERZEALOUS
(Refer in this text to Mosiah 4:27.)

The overzealous tend to judge others by their own standard. True excellence in gospel living—compliance with the established laws and ordinances in a quiet and patient manner—results in humility, in greater reliance upon God, and in broadening love and acceptance of one's fellow man. What I am doing in the name of goodness ought to bring me closer to those I love and serve, ought to turn my heart toward people, rather than causing me to turn my nose up in judgmental scorn and rejection. The greatest man to walk the earth, the only fully perfect human being, looked with tenderness and compassion upon those whose ways and actions were less than perfect.

(Robert Millet, CES Symposium, Aug. 1993)

In the context of Zeniff's experience, we may define overzealous as making decisions too quickly without approval of those in authority and without full consideration of the consequences of our actions. An overzealous person is quick to do his own will and slow to consider the Lord's will. . . .

The Book of Mormon gives no hint that Zeniff sought out the will of the Lord in prayer or even a visit with his spiritual leaders concerning this risky decision to move. It is not hard for anyone who has a sense of the relationship between the Nephites and Lamanites at that point in history to see the potential downside in his decision to move to the land of the Lamanites without seeking appropriate confirmation. But without consideration of the consequences of such a move, Zeniff and his colony moved forward.

(Jack R. Christianson and K. Douglas Bassett, *Life Lessons from the Book of Mormon* [Salt Lake City: Deseret Book, 2003], 223–224)

Virgil I. Grissom, lieutenant colonel of the United States Air Force. He spoke on travel in space. In 1965 he became the world's first astronaut to maneuver his spacecraft while orbiting.

"You can't just step on the gas out there," Gus Grissom said. "In fact, one craft gains on another by slowing down." He explained that a decrease in speed brings the craft closer to the earth. The orbit is thus shortened, and the craft gains by "riding closer to the rail."

Gus Grissom talked of space travel. He could have described how to get ahead on earth, too. Many a man moves out front by slowing down and putting better personal control on his course in life, even as Grissom skillfully maneuvered in orbiting.

(Wendell J. Ashton, *To Thine Own Self . . .* [Salt Lake City: Bookcraft, 1972], 50)

Everybody today seems to be in a hurry. No one has any time to give to others: children to their parents, parents to their children, spouses to each other.

World peace begins to break down in the homes.

(Jose Luis Gonzalez-Balado, *Mother Teresa—In My Own Words* [New York: Gramercy Books, 1996], 50)

[Brigham Young] This is the counsel I have for the Latter-day Saints to day. Stop, do not be in a hurry. . . . You are in too much of a hurry; you do not go to meeting enough, you do not pray enough, you do not read the Scriptures enough, you do not meditate enough, *you are all the time on the wing, and in such a hurry that you do not know what to do first.* . . . Let me reduce this to a simple saying—one of the most simple and homely that can be used—"Keep your dish right side up," so that when the shower of porridge does come you can catch your dish full.

(*Deseret News*, 5 June 1872, 248; as quoted in Keith B. McMullin, in Conference Report, Oct. 2002 [Salt Lake City: The Church of Jesus Christ of Latter-day Saints, 2002], 103; italics added)

I have come to realize that in order to save my own life, I had to save yours as well. I know now that it is not so much the haste of one's journey but rather what he does along the way which determines whether he will arrive at his destination.

(F. Burton Howard, in Conference Report, Apr. 1981 [Salt Lake City: The Church of Jesus Christ of Latter-day Saints, 1981], 97)

Our lives have become intensely fast-paced, filled with busyness and a frantic flitting about that was uncharacteristic of earlier ages. Everything from increased mobility to a plethora of time-saving devices has enticed us to pack our lives with so many activities and pursuits that too many of us have lost sight of something that it is of critical importance to families—time together.

(Gordon B. Hinckley, *Standing For Something* [New York: Times Books, 2000], 152)

The world is so noisy. There are voices everywhere trying to influence us. We all need time to think. We need to drown out the clamor and noise and simply be quiet. We need time to ponder and meditate, and to contemplate the deeper things of life. We need time to read and to immerse ourselves in the thoughts of great minds.

Our lives are so busy. We run from one thing to another. We wear ourselves out with our studies and our social lives and our pursuit of money. . . . We are entitled to spend some time with ourselves. We need to spend time out in nature where we can think and breathe deeply and feel the earth and listen to the sounds of the ocean or the woods or the mountains. . . .

I ask you to think about all of the time you spend in front of your computer, maybe surfing the Internet, or plugged in to video games, or watching some of the inane programs and sports contests on television. I am not anti-sports. I enjoy a good football or basketball game. But I have seen so many men and women become addicted to sports or the Internet or video games. . . . I believe their lives would be richer and more rewarding if at least occasionally they would get up from watching a game that will be forgotten tomorrow, get up from surfing one more web site, and spend a little time reading and thinking and simply Being Still.

They would be blessed if they would occasionally ride out into the darkness at night, look at the stars, and ponder their place in the world. . . .

The scriptures admonish: "Be still, and know that I am God" (Psalm 46:10).

(Gordon B. Hinckley, *Way To Be!* [New York: Simon & Schuster, 2002], 103–106)

———————

Are there parts of our lives that we could rest for a season in an effort to renew our souls so we can be more productive, especially in the ways that matter most to the Lord? . . .

[Think of] the last time you remodeled any part of your house, and see how many additional electrical outlets you added to each room. Then think about where you have added extension cords with four to six more outlets to provide power for new electrical devices. Despite all [the] . . . new laborsaving devices, I would guess your life is more, not less, complicated. . . .

For many television is robbing them of valuable family time. . . .

Unfortunately, with the blessings of the new information age also come challenges, as evil influences have a new medium of transmission and new ways of infiltrating our minds. Worldly influences enter our homes in new shapes and forms to challenge our resolve to use our time wisely and for the Lord's purposes.

Perhaps we could . . . call "time-out." . . . Determine . . . that we will discontinue those activities that are of little value and worth that might even jeopardize our eternal welfare.

(L. Tom Perry, *Ensign*, Nov. 1999 [Salt Lake City: The Church of Jesus Christ of Latter-day Saints, 1999], 75–76)

Mosiah 11:2 • WALK AFTER THE DESIRES OF HIS OWN HEART, SELFISHNESS

The distance between constant self-pleasing and self-worship is shorter than we think. Stubborn selfishness is actually rebellion against God, because, warned Samuel, "stubbornness is as . . . idolatry" (1 Samuel 15:23). Selfishness is much more than an ordinary problem because it activates all the cardinal sins! . . . The selfish individual has a passion for the vertical pronoun *I*. Significantly, the vertical pronoun *I* has no knees to bend, while the first letter in the pronoun *we* does.

(Neal A. Maxwell, in Conference Report, Oct. 1990 [Salt Lake City: The Church of Jesus Christ of Latter-day Saints, 1990], 15–16; emphasis added)

———————

Many years ago I was in a professional association with two older, more experienced men. . . . One day, one associate sought our help on a complex matter. As soon as the issue had been explained, the first thing the other associate said was, "What's in it for me?" When his old friend responded so selfishly, I saw the look of pain and disappointment on the face of the one who had invited our help. The relationship between the two was never quite the same after that. Our self-serving friend did not prosper, as his selfishness soon eclipsed his considerable gifts, talents, and qualities. . . .

During my professional career I helped the heirs of a noble couple settle their estate. The estate was not large, but it was the fruit of many years of hard work and sacrifice. Their children were all decent, God-fearing people who had been taught to live the saving principles of the Savior. But when it came to dividing up the property, a dispute developed about who should get what. Even though there was nothing of great value to fight about, feelings of selfishness and greed caused a rift among some of the family members that never healed and continued into the next generation. . . . I learned from this that selfishness and greed bring bitterness and contention. . . .

We torture our souls when we focus on getting rather than giving. . . . I learned that selfishness has more to do with how we feel about our possessions than how much we have.

(James E. Faust, in Conference Report, Oct. 2002 [Salt Lake City: The Church of Jesus Christ of Latter-day Saints, 2002], 18–19)

Selfishness is much more than an ordinary problem because it activates all the cardinal sins! It is the detonator in the breaking of the Ten Commandments.

By focusing on oneself, it is naturally easier to bear false witness if it serves one's purpose. It is easier to ignore one's parents instead of honoring them. It is easier to steal, because what one wants prevails. It is easier to covet, since the selfish conclude that nothing should be denied them.

It is easier to commit sexual sins, because to please oneself is the name of that deadly game in which others are often cruelly used. The Sabbath day is easily neglected, since one day soon becomes just like another. If selfish, it is easier to lie, because the truth is conveniently subordinated.

The selfish individual thus seeks to please not God, but himself. He will even break a covenant in order to fix an appetite.

Selfishness has little time to regard the sufferings of others seriously, hence the love of many waxes cold.

(Neal A. Maxwell, in Conference Report, Oct. 1990 [Salt Lake City: The Church of Jesus Christ of Latter-day Saints, 1990], 15)

A selfless person is one who is more concerned about the happiness and well-being of another than about his or her own convenience or comfort, one who is willing to serve another when it is neither sought for nor appreciated, or one who is willing to serve even those whom he or she dislikes. A selfless person displays a willingness to sacrifice, a willingness to purge from his or her mind and heart personal wants, and needs, and feelings. Instead of reaching for and requiring praise and recognition for himself, or gratification of his or her own wants, the selfless person will meet these very human needs for others. . . .

There is another word that sounds almost like the one we have been using. However, it is an ugly word. It describes a characteristic of satanic proportions. . . . The word is *selfish*. . . . A selfish person is often one who refers to "I," "me," and "mine" rather than to "we," "ours," "yours," or "theirs." This person is anxious to be in the limelight, to be on center stage in life's little dramas. He or she may be a poor listener, or a conversation monopolizer. Selfishness is the great unknown sin. No selfish person ever thought himself to be selfish. . . .

At a dinner or in a group, notice yourself. Do you take up a large share of the conversation time? . . . Sincere and sensitive acts in behalf of *others* are the mark of the selfless.

(H. Burke Peterson, in Conference Report, Apr. 1985 [Salt Lake City: The Church of Jesus Christ of Latter-day Saints, 1985], 82–83)

Some grow bitter or anxious when it seems that not enough attention is being paid to them, when their lives would be so enriched if only they paid more attention to the needs of others.

The answer lies in helping to solve the problems of those around us rather than worrying about our own, living to lift burdens even when we ourselves feel weighed down, putting our shoulder to the wheel instead of complaining that the wagons of life seem to be passing us by.

Stretching our souls in service helps us to rise above our cares, concerns, and challenges. As we focus our energies on lifting the burdens of others, something miraculous happens. Our own burdens diminish. We become happier. There is more substance to our lives.

(David S. Baxter, *Ensign*, Nov. 2006 [Salt Lake City: The Church of Jesus Christ of Latter-day Saints, 2006], 14)

Mosiah 11:19 • BOASTING IN THEIR OWN STRENGTH

When threatened, we become anti-enemy instead of pro-kingdom of God. . . . We forget that if we are righteous the Lord will either not suffer our enemies to come upon us (and this is the special promise to the inhabitants of the land of the Americas) or he will fight our battles for us.

(Spencer W. Kimball, *Ensign*, June 1976 [Salt Lake City: The Church of Jesus Christ of Latter-day Saints, 1976], 6)

Men of the world are in the world only because they adopt the philosophy of the world which is the philosophy of self sufficiency. It is not a humble philosophy—it is highly egotistical. It makes men themselves for the solution of all question. . . . It requires courage to come out of the world and adopt the philosophy of faith. Sometimes it subjects one to ridicule and the contempt of friends which are harder for most men to endure than physical pain; but because a thing is hard to do or hard to believe is no assurance that it is not right.

(Stephen L Richards, in Conference Report, Apr. 1935 [Salt Lake City: The Church of Jesus Christ of Latter-day Saints, 1935], 30)

Mosiah 12:20–24; 15:11–18 • HOW BEAUTIFUL UPON THE MOUNTAINS
(Isaiah 52:7–10; Refer in this text to Mosiah 27:35–37; 3 Nephi 20:40.)

One cannot help but wonder as to the motivation behind the question. Did the high priest actually desire understanding of the verses? [21–24] Or, rather, was he essentially saying: "I thought that the prophet Isaiah had said that blessed are those who declare *good* tidings and bring *peaceful* salutations. Why is your message so negative, so pessimistic, and why are you so prone to such gloomy prophecy?"

Abinadi nevertheless treated the questioner with enough respect as to suggest a direct answer; the answer would, however, not be given at the moment (see Mosiah 15:11–18).

(Robert L. Millet, *A Symposium on the Book of Mormon* [Salt Lake City: The Church of Jesus Christ of Latter-day Saints, 1986], 98)

———————

I had great joy yesterday in hearing of the call of Elder Helio da Rocha Camargo, our companion and fellow member of the Church. Brother Camargo and his wife were stalwart, faithful people before they joined the Church. They had been brought up in the nurture and admonition of the Lord. Brother Camargo was a graduate of the military academy of Brazil. Later, still a young man, he became a Methodist minister. . . . One evening two young men called at his home. He said that the first thing he noticed was the huge feet of one of the young men. He looked upward from the feet until he found the face of the tallest North American he had ever met. He was not at first impressed with the beauty of either the feet or the face. However, he invited the young men in, and in the process of their presentation they left him a copy of the Book of Mormon.

On a subsequent visit they inquired if he had read the book. He explained that he had read considerable, making notes of the things with which he did not agree. The elder then suggested that it was not in keeping with a book of scripture to read it to see what was wrong with it, but that it should be read as Moroni says, "with a sincere heart" and "real intent," having "faith in Christ" and desiring to know the truth of the book (see Moro. 10:4).

Brother Camargo said he found it necessary to read the book again. In the process the Spirit witnessed to him that it was the true word of God, and he joined the Church with his family. He sometimes refers to the scripture in Isaiah 52:7 which says, "How beautiful upon the mountains are the feet [those huge missionary feet] of him that bringeth good tidings, that publisheth peace; . . . that sayeth unto Zion, Thy God reigneth!" The truth he has found has brought similar beauty to the feet of three of his sons as they have served as missionaries.

(William Grant Bangerter, *Ensign,* May 1985 [Salt Lake City: The Church of Jesus Christ of Latter-day Saints, 1985], 64–65)

———————

Not long ago, President Gordon B. Hinckley, in a commencement address at BYU–Hawaii, admonished graduates to "stop seeking out the storms and enjoy more fully the sunlight" (*Church News*, 3 July 1983, 10). He pointed out that we can be negative and look for the ugly in life and the faults and failings of those around us, or we can develop positive attitudes and see the beautiful in life and the good, the strong, the decent, and the virtuous in people, which brings joy and happiness. It is a matter of attitude. . . .

The Lord has told us that we can be beautiful, even like a temple. In 1 Corinthians he said, "Know ye not that ye are the temple of God, and that the Spirit of God dwelleth in you?" (1 Cor. 3:16) . . .

As we live righteous and unselfish lives, the Spirit of the Lord enters our souls and then radiates from us. We become beautiful, even as a holy temple is beautiful.

(Keith W. Wilcox, *Ensign,* May 1985 [Salt Lake City: The Church of Jesus Christ of Latter-day Saints, 1985], 27)

———————

The imagery embodied in the poetry of Isaiah 52:7–10 is that of watchmen on a city wall who witness the approach and arrival of a messenger who travels on foot. Walled cities were commonplace in ancient Israel and throughout the ancient Near East, and watchmen, or lookouts, were regularly posted above city gates. The job security and probably the life of a watchman depended on his ability to remain alert to anyone or anything approaching his city, especially things appearing suspicious in nature. . . .

What is fascinating about Isaiah's use of imagery here is that not only does he mention a messenger or herald, but he also focuses on the messenger's feet with the notation that they are "beautiful." Feet are not generally considered among the more attractive body parts; they are functional, yes, but not beautiful. What did Isaiah intend by this description?

Interestingly, the word rendered "beautiful" in verse 7 is the Hebrew term *na'wu* (from the rarely attested verbal root *N'H*), the word from which Joseph Smith coined the city name "Nauvoo." This particular form is used only here and in Song of Solomon 1:10, where it is rendered "comely" in the KJV.

Since walking on dirt roads with sandal-shod feet was the major form of transportation for most people in ancient Israel, feet were not only quite visible but required daily washing and attention. The cleansing and care of a guest's feet was long considered a basic act of hospitality. However, despite the importance of foot care in ancient Israel, when Isaiah described the messenger's feet on the mountains as "beautiful," he was probably not suggesting that the arriving herald had remarkably clean and well-manicured feet!

It is not the condition of the feet but their observable activity, their *progress,* that is being emphasized by the description "beautiful." . . . The focus of the passage is on the delivery of the message as well as on the arrival of the messenger.

(Dana M. Pike, *Isaiah in the Book of Mormon,* ed. by Donald W. Parry and John W. Welch [Provo, Utah: Foundation for Ancient Research and Mormon Studies, 1998], 254, 258)

———————

Abinadi recited and interpreted Isaiah 53 because his accusers, the priests of Noah, had challenged him to explain the meaning of Isaiah 52:7–10. What was the thrust of their challenge? It appears that the priests intended, by their direct examination of Abinadi, to catch him in conflict with that scripture and thereby convict him of false prophecy—a capital offense under the law of Moses (see Deut. 18:20). In essence, they were apparently asking Abinadi why he bore tidings of doom and destruction when Isaiah had declared that the beautiful and true prophet brings good tidings and publishes peace: "How beautiful upon the mountains are the feet of him that bringeth *good* tidings" (Mosiah 12:20–22, emphasis added). Isaiah gave cause for great joy: "They shall see eye to eye when the Lord shall bring again Zion; break forth into joy" (Mosiah 12:22–24), and yet Abinadi had brought nothing but bad tidings of destruction.

Abinadi's rebuttal was an extensive and brilliant explanation of the true essence of redemption and how it brings good tidings to those who accept Christ (see Mosiah 12:29–37 and chapters 13–16).

(John W. Welch, *Isaiah in the Book of Mormon,* ed. by Donald W. Parry and John W. Welch [Provo, Utah: Foundation for Ancient Research and Mormon Studies, 1998], 294)

———————

The cause to which I speak is of missionary work as couples. . . . There has never been a greater need than now for an army of mature couples to go out into every far corner of this earth and retain the fruit of the harvest. . . .

I think we will not be tested in the way the pioneers were tested. They were called to leave all worldly possessions, homes, even family and loved ones to cross the prairies to dry and desolate, forbidding lands. They buried their babies, children, and companions on the Great Plains in shallow, unmarked graves. Physically, they suffered beyond belief, nor can tongue tell the sad, pitiful story. . . .

There is a need—*not* to leave homes forever, but for a time—then return and reap the rich harvest of the faithful labor. Your children and grandchildren will be blessed. . . . "How beautiful upon the mountains are the feet of him that bringeth good tidings; that publisheth peace" (Mosiah 12:21).

(Vaughn J. Featherstone, *Ensign,* May 1992 [Salt Lake City: The Church of Jesus Christ of Latter-day Saints, 1992], 42)

———————

Anciently, a watchman was responsible to keep the surrounding country under surveillance from a spot on the watchtower, to identify any hostile force that invaded the land, and to warn citizens of the invasion. Only when he recognized the danger and warned them of their peril could citizens take measures to protect their lives. . . . (Ezek. 33:2–6).

As conquering enemies destroy physical life, sin destroys spiritual life. But those who are sick enough to die, when warned of their danger, might save their lives through repentance. And thus one might see why the Lord would call Ezekiel to be a watchman—to warn citizens of their soul-destroying dangers. If they heeded his warning and repented, they would live. If not, they would die spiritually—but he would not be responsible for their deaths; he would have fulfilled his calling and delivered his own soul.

(Keith H. Meservy, *Ensign,* Apr. 1992 [Salt Lake City: The Church of Jesus Christ of Latter-day Saints, 1992], 60)

Mosiah 12:35 • NO OTHER GOD BEFORE ME

Selfishness is self-worship. In its various gradations, it is a violation of the first commandment: "Thou shalt have no other gods before me" (Exodus 20:3). Such selfishness can smother our chances of keeping the second commandment. The problem is further exacerbated when we act to "please ourselves" or even seek to set ourselves up "for a light" (Romans 15:1; 2 Nephi 26:29).

(Neal A. Maxwell, *Whom The Lord Loveth* [Salt Lake City: Deseret Book, 2003], 70)

Mosiah 13:3 • I WON'T DIE BEFORE MY TIME

Stories such as these do not mean that the servants of God are delivered from all hardship or that they are always saved from death. Some believers lose their lives in persecutions, and some suffer great hardships as a result of their faith. But the protection promised to the faithful servants of God is a reality. . . .

(Dallin H. Oaks, *Ensign,* Nov. 1992 [Salt Lake City: The Church of Jesus Christ of Latter-day Saints, 1992], 39)

———————

[A blessing given from Joseph Smith Sr. to his son Joseph, as recorded by the Prophet's mother.] "You shall even live to finish your work." At this Joseph cried out, weeping, "Oh! my father, shall I?" "Yes," said his father, "you shall live to lay out the plan of all the work which God has given you to do. This is my dying blessing upon your head in the name of Jesus. . . ."

(*History of Joseph Smith by His Mother, Lucy Mack Smith* [Salt Lake City: Bookcraft, 1958], 309–310)

Many people die before their time because they are careless, abuse their bodies, take unnecessary chances, or expose themselves to hazards, accidents and sickness (Eccl. 7:17).

(Spencer W. Kimball, *Faith Precedes the Miracle* [Salt Lake City: Deseret Book, 1973], 103)

[June 24, 1834, Zion's Camp] This night the cholera burst forth among us, . . . even those on guard fell to the earth with their guns in their hands, so sudden and powerful was the attack of this terrible disease. . . . The disease seized upon me like the talons of a hawk, and I said to the brethren: "If my work were done, you would have to put me in the ground without a coffin."

(Joseph Smith, *History of the Church of Jesus Christ of Latter-day Saints* [Salt Lake City: Deseret Book, 1976], 2:114)

The Father's plan comprehends and is inlaid with His personal plans for each of us, including our individual . . . trial. . . . Only a few people seem to have known something of their longevity and personal timetables. . . .

We trust in the timing of the Lord, and, meanwhile, know that the days and years of righteous individuals will not be numbered less.

(Neal A. Maxwell, *One More Strain of Praise* [Salt Lake City: Bookcraft, 1999], 10–11)

It has been said that the death of a righteous man is never untimely because our Father sets the time. I believe that with all my soul.

(Spencer W. Kimball, *Ensign*, Dec. 1985 [Salt Lake City: The Church of Jesus Christ of Latter-day Saints, 1985], 33)

May I say for the consolation of those who mourn, and for the comfort and guidance of all of us, that no righteous man is ever taken before his time. In the case of the faithful saints, they are simply transferred to other fields of labor. The Lord's work goes on in this life, in the world of spirits, and in the kingdoms of glory where men go after their resurrection.

(Joseph Fielding Smith [in his remarks at the funeral services for Elder Richard L. Evans])

Mosiah 13:4 • APOSTATE ATTITUDE, ANGER AGAINST THE TRUTH
(Refer in this text to Alma 21:3.)

When a corrupt man is chastised he gets angry and will not endure it.

(*Teachings of the Prophet Joseph Smith*, comp. by Joseph Fielding Smith [Salt Lake City: Deseret Book, 1976], 195)

Mosiah 13:11–26 • THE TEN COMMANDMENTS

Some have mistakenly supposed that the Ten Commandments were a part of the law of Moses. In fact, they are a part of the higher law or the fulness of the gospel. This is illustrated by their reiteration to us as part of the restoration of all things (see D&C 59:5–12). The Ten Commandments were a part of the fulness of the gospel as first given to Moses on Sinai. Though the higher priesthood and its ordinances were taken from Israel because of her transgressions, when Moses returned to Sinai to receive what we know as the law of Moses the Ten Commandments were retained as a part of Israel's covenant with God.

(R. Millet and J. F. McConkie, *Doctrinal Commentary on the Book of Mormon* [Salt Lake City: Bookcraft, 1988], 2:216)

Mosiah 13:15 • THE NAME OF GOD IN VAIN

Those who routinely take the name of God in vain and resort to filthy, crude language only advertise the poverty of their vocabularies. . . .

I will never forget coming home from school one day as a first-grader. I threw my books on the table and took the name of the Lord in vain, expressing my relief that school was out for the day. Mother heard me and was horrified. Without uttering a word, she took me by the hand and led me to the bathroom, pulled out a clean washcloth and a bar of soap, told me to open my mouth, and preceded to wash my mouth with that terrible soap. I blubbered and protested. She stayed at it for what seemed a long time, and then said, "Don't let me ever hear such words from your lips again."

The taste was terrible. The reprimand was worse. I have never forgotten it. How can one profane the name of God and then kneel before Him in prayer? Profanity separates us from Him who has supreme power to help us. Profanity wounds the spirit and demeans the soul.

(Gordon B. Hinckley, *Standing for Something* [New York: Times Books, 2000], 51–52)

Be clean in thought. Do not use filthy language. There is so much filthy language that is used by high school students, isn't there? Everywhere you run into it, isn't that so? Filthy, dirty language. Do not use it. You are members of The Church of Jesus Christ of Latter-day Saints. You cannot afford to use filthy language. The Lord expects something more of you than that. Stand above it. When you use filthy language, it says that you do not have vocabulary enough to express yourself without reaching down into the gutter for words. . . . Whatever you do, do not use His name in vain. He said, when Jehovah's finger wrote upon the tablets of stone: "Thou shalt not take the name of the Lord thy God in vain; for the Lord will not hold him guiltless that taketh his name in vain" (Exodus 20:7). Do not take the name of the Lord in vain. Never, never, never.

I have told this story before, which I heard from President Kimball. When he was very sick he was coming out of an operation, and they placed him on a gurney to take him to the intensive care room. The young man who was wheeling the gurney hit the corner of the elevator and let out an oath, using the Lord's name in vain. President Kimball, who was barely conscious, said, "Please, please, you are talking of my friend." The young man said, "I'm sorry." Do not take the name of the Lord in vain.

You boys hold the priesthood. You girls have obligations likewise as members of this Church. Be clean in thought and in word and in deed.

(*Discourses of President Gordon B. Hinckley*, 1995–99 [Salt Lake City: The Church of Jesus Christ of Latter-day Saints, 2004], 1:396–397)

———————

You boys and girls, you be careful. . . . No profanity in your lives. Where you go to school, there are so many who use foul and sleazy language. You can't afford to do that; you are members of this great Church. None of that filthy language. Never take the name of the Lord in vain, for God will hold him responsible who taketh His name in vain. Be better than those around you.

I talked with a policeman last night in Quebec. He said when he first joined the police force he was the only member of the Church on a force of 1,000 men, and did they have a good time with him. They made life hard and difficult for him. I said, "Do they still do it?" He said, "No. Now they respect me. They look up to me." So it will be with you, my dear young friends.

(*Discourses of President Gordon B. Hinckley*, 1995–99 [Salt Lake City: The Church of Jesus Christ of Latter-day Saints, 2004], 1:553)

Mosiah 13:16, 18–19 • REMEMBER THE SABBATH DAY

(Refer in this text to Jarom 1:5.)

When I was leaving to go to law school in Chicago . . . . [my mother] told me for the first time that in his graduate studies my father never studied on Sunday. He felt that he could do more in six days with the help of the Lord than he could do in seven days without it. He believed that by refraining from studying on the Sabbath—even in the difficult challenges of medical school far from home—he would receive the blessings of the Lord. It was a new time in my life, and that simple new challenge caused me to do the same. Study was my work, and the Lord had commanded us to labor for six days and rest on the seventh. I followed my mother's simple teaching about that commandment, and I was richly blessed for it.

(Dallin H. Oaks, "Be Wise," BYU–Idaho Devotional, 7 Nov. 2006, 4)

Mosiah 13:20 • HONOR THY FATHER & MOTHER

(Refer in this text to 1 Nephi 17:55.)

Mosiah 13:21 • THOU SHALT NOT KILL

I have discovered that on those occasions when I hastily digest the hurtful words of others without making the effort to look for the best in the person who delivered them, I am sometimes left with the false conclusion that I am a child of God while the person who has injured me is not. The logical extension of this improper thinking is that I feel no obligation to practice Christian injunctions, which would prevent me from judging or even hating this person who has wrongfully injured me. When I allow myself to travel this mental path, it becomes impossible for me to exercise any kind of charitable compassion toward others, and often times my only emotional response is to judge or verbally attack the person who has threatened me. Thus, I become more connected to the problem than to the solution; I have justified my own misbehavior by thinking, "He did it to me first."

It is difficult to see clearly when our first reaction in a conflict is to place blame. Placing blame or attacking verbally takes no skill because these are the reactions of the "natural man" (Mosiah 3:19). The ultimate result of this kind of thinking, when spread throughout the world, is that the commandment "thou shalt not kill" is true, except for bad guys because they are not children of God like us. It is hard for some people to see that the physical violence in our world today is inseparably connected to the passive violence we have toward others in our attitudes as well as in our conversations.

(K. Douglas Bassett, *The Barber's Song* [Springville, Utah: Cedar Fort, 2005], 166–167)

Mosiah 13:22 • THOU SHALT NOT COMMIT ADULTERY

(Refer in this text to Alma 39:4–6.)

Though ours is a time of conflict, quietly caring

for "the life of the soul" is still what matters most. . . . Outward commotions cannot excuse any failure of inward resolve. . . . If hostilities break our covenants! For example, adultery cannot be rationalized merely because there is a war on and some wives and husbands are separated. There is no footnote to the seventh commandment reading "Thou shalt not commit adultery except in times of war" (see Exodus 20:14). . . .

Let us, therefore, be like the young man with Elisha on the mount. Though he was at first intimidated by the surrounding enemy chariots, his eyes were mercifully opened and he saw "horses and chariots of fire," verifying that "they that be with us are more than they that be with them" (2 Kings 6:16, 17). Brothers and sisters, the spiritual arithmetic has not changed!

(Neal A. Maxwell, in Conference Report, Apr. 2003 [Salt Lake City: The Church of Jesus Christ of Latter-day Saints, 2003], 71–72)

———————

Once a man received as his inheritance two keys. The first key, he was told, would open a vault which he must protect at all cost. The second key was to a safe within the vault which contained a priceless treasure. He was to open this safe and freely use the precious things which were stored therein. He was warned that many would seek to rob him of his inheritance. He was promised that if he used the treasure worthily it would be replenished and never be diminished, not in all eternity. He would be tested. If he used it to benefit others, his own blessings and joy would increase.

The man went alone to the vault. His first key opened the door. He tried to obtain the treasure with the other key, but he could not, for there were two locks on the safe. His key alone would not open it. No matter how he tried, he could not open it. He was puzzled. He had been given the keys. He knew the treasure was rightfully his. He had obeyed instructions, but he could not open the safe.

In due time, a woman came into the vault. She too held a key. It was noticeably different from the key he held. Her key fit the other lock. It humbled him to learn that he could not obtain his rightful inheritance without her.

They made a covenant that together they would open the treasure and, as instructed, he would watch over the vault and protect it; she would watch over the treasure. She was not concerned that, as guardian of the vault, he held two keys, for his full purpose was to see that she was safe as she watched over that which was most precious to them both. Together they opened the safe and partook of their inheritance. They rejoiced, for, as promised, it replenished itself.

With great joy they found that they could pass the treasure on to their children; each could receive a full

measure, undiminished to the last generation.

Perhaps some few of their posterity would not find a companion who possessed the complementary key, or one worthy and willing to keep the covenants relating to the treasure. Nevertheless, if they kept the commandments, they would not be denied even the smallest blessing.

Because some tempted them to misuse their treasure, they were careful to teach their children about keys and covenants.

There came, in due time, among their posterity some few who were deceived or jealous or selfish because one was given two keys and another only one. The selfish ones reasoned, "Why cannot the treasure be mine alone to use as I desire?"

Some tried to reshape the key they had been given to resemble the other key. Perhaps, they thought, it would then fit both locks. And so it was that the safe was closed to them. Their reshaped keys were useless, and their inheritance was lost.

On the other hand those who received the treasure with gratitude and obeyed the laws concerning it knew joy without bounds through time and all eternity.

(*Memorable Stories and Parables by Boyd K. Packer* [Salt Lake City: Bookcraft, 1997], 95–97)

———————

I was appalled to read not long ago that, in one community, a proposal was made that young women be paid a dollar a day for not becoming pregnant. How pathetic! Where is our sense of values? . . .

Both experience and divine wisdom dictate that moral virtue and cleanliness pave the way that leads to strength of character, peace of mind and heart, and happiness in life.

According to a 1997 nationwide survey, divorce is 32 percent more likely among those who engaged in premarital sex than it is among the general population. And almost three times as many separated or divorced Americans have committed adultery, compared to the general population. Further, 82 percent of adults who rate their marriage as "very strong" (9 or 10 on a 10–point scale) did not engage in premarital sex. This should not surprise us. Immorality is a breach of integrity of the highest order. On the other hand, those who have demonstrated sexual purity are also likely to have cultivated other moral virtues that contribute to the success of any relationship, particularly marriage. . . .

Personal virtue is worth more than any salary, any bonus, any position or degree of prominence.

(Gordon B. Hinckley, *Standing For Something* [New York: Times Books, 2000], xx, 31, 34, 44)

Mosiah 13:23 • THOU SHALT NOT BEAR FALSE WITNESS

Are we not false witnesses if we are untrue to gospel principle we profess but do not practice?

Most damage to the collective reputation of the Church is done by those members who want to straddle the line, with one foot in the kingdom and the other foot in spiritual Babylon. Those who so compromise their principles want to play for both teams at once—the Lord's and Satan's—as if to say, "I want to wait and see which side is winning before I declare myself."

There are some members who are not concerned about their outward appearances and actions, rationalizing that they know what they really are on the inside. These individuals inevitably are judged "guilty by association." To be judged fairly, we must avoid the very appearance of evil. We would do well to remember the words quoted by President McKay: "Whate'er thou art, act well thy part" (see *Cherished Experiences from the Writings of President David O. McKay*, comp. by Claire Middlemiss [Salt Lake City: Deseret Book, 1955], 174–75).

(J. Richard Clarke, in Conference Report, Apr. 1985 [Salt Lake City: The Church of Jesus Christ of Latter-day Saints, 1985], 95)

Mosiah 13:24 • THOU SHALT NOT COVET

It is very probable that most of our crimes are born of covetousness. Many forms of evil grow out of our desire to get something for nothing. Most of the stealing, lying, cheating, deceiving and even killing takes place because we long inordinately for something that doesn't belong to us. . . .

In spite of the fact that "covetousness" is so deeply involved in our present-day problems, yet this destructive little word has practically disappeared from our present-day vocabulary and conscious thinking. . . .

The popularity of the slot machine bears testimony of our insane hope to get something for nothing. . . . Sometimes we say that our economic system has broken down. It is not the system that has broken down, rather our human character has disintegrated under our desire to get something for nothing. . . .

We have over-emphasized the American standard of living and under-emphasized the American standard of character and the sound religious principle on which morality is based. . . .

It seems that we are becoming more and more reluctant to accept the old-fashioned virtues of thrift and individual responsibility under which both character and wealth are most effectively created. . . . Even the great Church welfare program has had great difficulty in teaching people the importance of their own labor as a basis for their daily bread. . . .

Things always follow *talents*. We need only develop the *talents,* and the *things* will follow. But when we covet the *things* first, we destroy the *talents*, which in turn make the *things* possible. . . . It is always better to serve than to covet. The abundant life comes not from the things that we get, but from the things that we give. And giving helps us to avoid the awful sin, and giant evil of covetousness.

(Sterling W. Sill, *The Law of the Harvest* [Salt Lake City: Bookcraft, 1963], 360–365)

Mosiah 13:29–31 • THE LAW OF MOSES

In a sense the Law of Moses was given as a type of 'spiritual busywork' a system and pattern that would keep the people constantly involved; with everything pointing toward the coming Savior and Redeemer.

(Robert Millet, CES Symposium, Aug. 1986, 99)

Mosiah 13:33–34 • FORM OF MAN

(Refer in this text to 1 Nephi 19:10.)

Note that Abinadi did not say He [Christ] would be a man, but rather, He would have the *form* of a man. King Limhi picked up on this nuance, explaining that Abinadi taught "that Christ was the God, the Father of all things," and He would "take upon him the image of a man" (Mosiah 7:27). Again, the scriptures clearly distinguish between what the Savior was and what we are. Jesus may have shared our *image*, but He still retained His position as God.

It was because He was God and not man that Jesus could minister as He did. King Benjamin was told by an angel that the Savior would "suffer temptations, and pain of body, hunger, thirst, and fatigue, *even more than man can suffer*, except it be unto death" (Mosiah 3:7; emphasis added). The reason we could not endure the Savior's suffering, hunger, thirst, or fatigue is that we do not possess the divine power He did.

(Richard D. Draper, *Ensign*, Jan. 2000 [Salt Lake City: The Church of Jesus Christ of Latter-day Saints, 2000], 8)

Mosiah 14 • ISAIAH'S TESTIMONY OF THE COMING MESSIAH

(Isaiah 53.)

Now Bible commentators will tell you that this [Isaiah 53] has nothing to do with the life of Jesus Christ. To them this story is one concerning suffering Israel. I want to tell you that it is a story, a synopsis of the life of our Redeemer, revealed to Isaiah 700 years before the Lord was born.

(Joseph Fielding Smith, *Doctrines of Salvation* [Salt Lake City: Bookcraft, 1954], 1:23)

ABINADI'S COMMENTARY ON ISAIAH IS FOUND IN MOSIAH 15

(This grid shows the verses in chapter 15 that give commentary to the verses shown in chapter 14.)

Isaiah 53	Abinadi's Commentary
Mosiah 14:2	Mosiah 15:2–4
Mosiah 14:3	Mosiah 15:5
Mosiah 14:4–6	Mosiah 15:9
Mosiah 14:7	Mosiah 15:6
Mosiah 14:8	Mosiah 15:10, 12–13
Mosiah 14:10	Mosiah 15:11–12, 23

It should be noted that the entire chapter of Isaiah 53 in Mosiah 14 is a poem in four stanzas of three verses each (vv. 1–3, 4–6, 7–9, 10–12), constructed with well-known Hebrew parallelism. . . . Jews read Isaiah 53 as a prophecy directed to the Suffering Servant as the house of Israel. While it is clear the whole of chapter 53 is about the mortal ministry of the Messiah, . . . Abinadi's interpretation of Isaiah 53 precedes the coming of Christ by almost 150 years and yet remains the most clear and full interpretation of this prophetic chapter anywhere in the scripture.

(David Rolph Seely, *The Book of Mormon: The Foundation of Our Faith*, The 28th Annual Sidney B. Sperry Symposium [Salt Lake City: Deseret Book, 1999], 204–205)

———————

Abinadi was, of course, a prefiguration, a type and shadow of the Savior, a fact that makes his moving tribute to Christ even more powerful and poignant (if that is possible) than when Isaiah wrote it.

(Jeffrey R. Holland, *Christ and the New Covenant* [Salt Lake City: Deseret Book, 1997], 89)

Mosiah 14:1 • WHO HATH BELIEVED . . . TO WHOM IS REVEALED

(Isaiah 53:1.)

The opening lines of this chapter pose two questions: Who will believe what will be recounted here? And To whom is the "arm of the Lord" revealed? The sense of the first question can be taken in several different ways. Most obviously it appears to be a rhetorical question—expecting a negative answer—that no one has or will believe this incredible report of God coming to earth as a mortal. On the other hand, it may be an invitation to all who hear the report to consider it and to accept and believe it.

(David Rolph Seely, *The Book of Mormon: The Foundation of Our Faith*, The 28th Annual Sidney B. Sperry Symposium [Salt Lake City: Deseret Book, 1999], 206)

When John's disciples questioned whether he was or was not the One to come, he asked them simply to follow him around. And then he said: Tell John what things ye have seen and heard (Luke 7:23). On another occasion, he said: I told you [that is, gave you the report] and ye believed not: the works that I do in my Father's name, they bear witness of me [that is, reveal the Father]. But ye believe not (John 10:25–26; see also 10:5–7; Matt. 12:24). Why do ye not understand my speech? Even because ye cannot hear my word (John 8:43). When they refused to see God revealed by his words and works, Jesus called them blind and deaf. Thus John could say: Though he had done so many miracles before them, yet they believed not on him: That the saying of Esaias [Isaiah] the prophet might be fulfilled, which he spake, Lord, who hath believed our report? and to whom hath the arm of the Lord been revealed?" (John 12:37–38).

(Keith H. Meservy, *A Witness of Jesus Christ*, The 1989 Sperry Symposium on the Old Testament, ed. Richard D. Draper [Salt Lake City: Deseret Book, 1990], 157)

———————

That is, To whom has God revealed his priesthood, his gospel, those things wherein is found the power of God unto salvation?

(Joseph Fielding McConkie and Robert L. Millet, *Doctrinal Commentary on the Book of Mormon* [Salt Lake City: Bookcraft, 1987–1992], 2:221)

———————

Now, as Isaiah expressed it, "Who hath believed our report? And to whom is the arm of the Lord revealed?" (Isa. 53:1).

If you believe the words of Joseph Smith, you would have believed what Jesus and the ancients said.

If you reject Joseph Smith and his message, you would have rejected Peter and Paul and their message. . . . We invite all . . . to ponder. . . . Do I have the moral courage to learn whether Joseph Smith was called of God? . . . Am I willing to pay the price of investigation and gain a personal revelation that tells me what I must do to gain peace in this world and be an inheritor of eternal life in the world to come?

(Bruce R. McConkie, *Ensign*, Nov. 1981 [Salt Lake City: The Church of Jesus Christ of Latter-day Saints, 1981], 48)

———————

"Who hath believed our report, and to whom is the arm of the Lord revealed?" (Mosiah 14:1). Surely he was delivering a report. This query might be a common cry from every prophet who ever revealed to his people the coming of the Messiah. In this instance it is both Isaiah's and Abinadi's cries that may echo Christ's own lament when he used Isaiah's words to describe the people's rejection of him even though he had done so many miracles in their sight (see John 12:37–38).

(Ann Madsen, "What Meaneth the Words That Are Written?," *Journal of Book of Mormon Studies* [Salt Lake City: Deseret Book, 1989], 10, no. 1:9)

———————

Leaders receive revelation for their own stewardships. Individuals can receive revelation to guide their own lives. But when one person purports to receive revelation for another person outside his or her own stewardship—such as a Church member who claims to have revelation to guide the entire Church or a person who claims to have a revelation to guide another person over whom he or she has no presiding authority according to the order of the Church—you can be sure that such revelations are not from the Lord. . . .

Satan is a great deceiver, and he is the source of some of these spurious revelations. Others are simply imagined. If a revelation is outside the limits of stewardship, you know it is not from the Lord, and you are not bound by it. I have heard of cases in which a young man tells a young woman that she should marry him because he has received a revelation that she is to be his eternal companion. If this is a true revelation, it will be confirmed directly to the woman if she seeks to know. In the meantime, she is under no obligation to heed it. She should seek her own guidance and make up her own mind. The man can receive revelation to guide his own actions, but he cannot properly receive revelation to direct hers. She is outside his stewardship.

(Dallin H. Oaks, *With Full Purpose of Heart* [Salt Lake City: Deseret Book, 2002], 161)

Mosiah 14:2 • TENDER, DRY GROUND, NO BEAUTY THAT WE SHOULD DESIRE HIM
(Isaiah 53:2.)

Under the watchful eye of his Heavenly Father, he was "tender" in at least two ways—he was young, pure, innocent, and particularly vulnerable to the pain of sin all around him, and he was caring, thoughtful, sensitive, and kind—in short, tender.

(Jeffrey R. Holland, *Christ and the New Covenant* [Salt Lake City: Deseret Book, 1997], 90)

———————

In a garden setting, plants do not normally take root and grow up in dry ground. The tender plant is symbolic of Christ; the dry ground is apostate Judaism. . . . If the religion of the day did not nourish Jesus, what

was his source of spiritual growth and sustenance? His Father in Heaven was the source. Jesus would grow up before his Heavenly Father as a tender plant and would be nourished and strengthened by the true source of strength, not the dried-up religion of the times.

(S. Brent Farley, in *A Symposium on the Old Testament* [Salt Lake City: The Church of Jesus Christ of Latter-day Saints, 1983], 65)

———————

Isaiah uses two plant metaphors to portray the young mortal Jesus: "tender plant" and "root." Jesus was like a tender plant, untouched by corruption and sin. . . .

Jesus came forth not in fertile land, but in "dry ground," both temporally and spiritually. . . . The dry ground represents the spiritual barrenness of apostate Judaism.

(Donald W. Parry, *Visualizing Isaiah* [Provo, Utah: The Foundation for Ancient Research and Mormon Studies, 2001], 89)

———————

We have no reason to believe that Christ was unattractive physically, but this verse may suggest that he was plain—as in "plain and precious." In any case we know that his power was an inner, spiritual gift, and that as the son of a mortal mother, he did not stand out in any distinctive physical way, leading his surprised and offended contemporaries of the day to say of him and his messianic announcement, "Is not this Joseph's son?" He certainly did not come to them in a way that filled the people's traditional hopes and views of a Messiah who would be striking in visage or powerful in politics.

(Jeffrey R. Holland, *Christ and the New Covenant* [Salt Lake City: Deseret Book, 1997], 90–91)

———————

In appearance he was like men; and so it is expressed here by the prophet that he had no form or comeliness, that is, he was not so distinctive, so different from others that people would recognize him as the Son of God. He appeared as a mortal man.

(Joseph Fielding Smith, *Doctrines of Salvation: Sermons and Writings of Joseph Fielding Smith*, ed. by Bruce R. McConkie [Salt Lake City: Bookcraft, 1954–1956], 1:23)

———————

"He shall grow up . . . as a tender plant, and as a root out of a dry ground"—"not like a stately tree, but like a lowly plant, struggling in arid soil. So the human life of the Messiah was one of obscurity and humility" (Dummelow, 446). Or: "Messiah grew silently and insensibly, as a sucker from an ancient stock, seemingly dead (viz., the house of David, then in a decayed state)"

(Jamieson, 490). Or: Perhaps better still, he grew up as a choice and favored plant whose strength and achievement did not come because of the arid social culture in which he dwelt; it was not poured into him by the erudition of Rabbinical teachers; but it came from the divine Source whence he sprang, for as the Inspired Version has it, "He spake not as other men, neither could he be taught; for he needed not that any man should teach him" (JST, Matt. 3:25).

There is no mystique, no dynamic appearance, no halo around his head, thunders do not roll and lightnings do not flash at his appearance. He is the Son of the Highest, but he walks and appears as the offspring of the lowest. He is a man among men, appearing, speaking, dressing seeming in all outward respects as they are.

(Bruce R. McConkie, *The Promised Messiah* [Salt Lake City: Deseret Book, 1978], 477–78)

This verse describes the early childhood or upbringing of Jesus. Scholars agree that this does not describe his physical appearance, but rather teaches that people would misjudge him because they were expecting their Messiah to come in a more glorious or supernatural way. His growing up would be watched over by the Father, just as a gardener cares for a tender plant. Luke records that "the child grew, and waxed strong in spirit, filled with wisdom: and the grace of God was upon him" (Luke 2:40). Jesus' declaration to his mother when he was only twelve years of age is ample evidence that he had been nurtured and prepared by his Father in Heaven during his years in Nazareth (see Luke 2:41–49).

(Monte S. Nyman, *Great Are the Words of Isaiah* [Salt Lake City: Bookcraft, 1980], 207)

"Is not this the carpenter's son?" they asked. "Is not his Mother called Mary? And his brethren, James, and Joses, and Simon, and Judas? And his sisters, are they not all with us? When then hath this man all these things?" (Matt. 13:55–56).

Even within the immediate family of Jesus there was unbelief. Mary knew his identity, for the angel had declared it unto her. And Joseph, her husband, had been similarly informed. But Mary evidently did not broadcast her knowledge; she "kept all these things, and pondered them in her heart" (Luke 2:19).

Her other sons, born to her by Joseph, did not believe, at least not at first. They had grown up with Jesus. He was their older brother. They had become so accustomed to him as they all grew up together that they saw nothing unusual about him, certainly nothing divine. Jesus was so much like other men that not even his own blood brothers recognized his true status.

This was revealed in the scripture telling of their visit to Jerusalem for the Passover. The brothers planned to attend and wondered if Jesus would go also. It is not indicated whether they invited him to accompany them to Jerusalem. They knew of his reported miracles, but seemed to doubt them. They knew he had been persecuted and hence had shunned the crowds in Jerusalem.

They said to him, "Depart hence, and go into Judea that thy disciples also may see the works that thou doest. For there is no man that doeth any thing in secret, and he himself seeketh to be known openly."

Then they daringly added, "If thou do these things, shew thyself to the world." Note that "if." How much did they really doubt him? It seems that they even taunted him, "For neither did his brethren believe in him" (John 7:1–5).

(Mark E. Petersen, *Isaiah for Today* [Salt Lake City: Deseret Book, 1981], 45–46)

Jesus of Nazareth, though the literal son of God and thus possessor of the very powers of immortality, was to undergo the throes of mortality, including the tender and helpless years of infancy and childhood characteristic of all children. He would grow as a root in the arid and parched ground of apostate Judaism. This root-stock or "stem of Jesse" would develop in a sterile and barren religious soil, in the midst of great learning but gross spiritual darkness. . . .

The Son of God was not to be known or recognized by any outward beauty; rather, those with an eye of faith would know by the witness of the Spirit who it was that ministered among them.

(Robert L. Millet, in *A Symposium on the Book of Mormon* [Salt Lake City: The Church of Jesus Christ of Latter-day Saints, 1986], 99)

Mosiah 14:3 • A MAN OF SORROWS . . . ACQUAINTED WITH GRIEF
(Isaiah 53:3; Refer in this text to Alma 7:11–12.)

We will all have some adversity in our lives. . . . Some of it may even strain our faith in a loving God who has the power to administer relief in our behalf.

To those anxieties I think the Father of us all would say, "Why are ye so fearful? How is it that ye have no faith?" . . .

Jesus was not spared grief and pain and anguish and buffeting. No tongue can speak the unutterable burden he carried, nor have we the wisdom to understand the prophet Isaiah's description of him as "a man of sorrows" (Isa. 53:3). His ship was tossed most of his life, and at least to mortal eyes, it crashed fatally on the rocky coast of Calvary. . . .

Peace was on the lips and in the heart of the Savior

no matter how fiercely the tempest was raging. May it so be with us . . . We should not expect to get through life individually or collectively without some opposition.

(Howard W. Hunter, *Ensign*, Nov. 1984 [Salt Lake City: The Church of Jesus Christ of Latter-day Saints, 1984], 43)

President Brigham Young spoke of what evoked the "why" from Jesus, saying that during the axis of agony which was Gethsemane and Calvary, the Father at some point withdrew both His presence and His Spirit from Jesus (see *Journal of Discourses*, 3:205–6). Thereby Jesus' personal triumph was complete and His empathy perfected. Having "descended below all things," He comprehends, perfectly and personally, the full range of human suffering! (see D&C 88:6; 122:8). A spiritual sung in yesteryear has an especially moving and insightful line: "Nobody knows the troubles I've seen; nobody knows but Jesus" (see also Alma 7:11–12). Truly, Jesus was exquisitely "acquainted with grief," as no one else (Isa. 53:3).

(Neal A. Maxwell, *Ensign*, Nov. 1997 [Salt Lake City: The Church of Jesus Christ of Latter-day Saints, 1997], 23)

There are those who feel that if we follow the Savior, our lives will be free from worry, pain, and fear. This is not so! The Savior Himself was described as a man of sorrows. Those early disciples who followed the Christ experienced great persecution and trials. The Prophet Joseph Smith was no exception. Nor were the other early Saints of this last dispensation. And it is no different today. . . .

I have had the opportunity to speak with a woman who heard the call of the Savior when she was 18. Her father, who was a high official in another church, became angry with her and forbade her from being baptized. He let her know that if she became a member of The Church of Jesus Christ of Latter-day Saints, she would be ostracized from the family.

Even though the sacrifice was great, this young woman heeded the call of the Savior and entered the waters of baptism.

Her father could not accept her decision, however, and tried to force her into abandoning her new faith. He and his wife reviled her for her decision to become a member of the Church and demanded that she recant and forsake her new religion.

Even through the rage, the bitterness, and the indignity, her faith remained strong. She endured the verbal and emotional abuse, knowing she had heard the call of the Savior and she would follow Him, whatever the consequence.

Eventually this young woman managed to find a safe haven, a place of refuge with a kind member family far away from the threats and unkindness of her father.

She met a faithful young man, and the two of them were married in the temple, receiving the choice blessings that accompany a temple marriage.

Today she stands among the multitude of those who have sacrificed so much to follow the call of the Savior.

Yes, I do not suggest that the road will be easy. But I will give you my witness that those who, in faith, leave their nets and follow the Savior will experience happiness beyond their ability to comprehend.

(Joseph B. Wirthlin, *Ensign*, May 2002 [Salt Lake City: The Church of Jesus Christ of Latter-day Saints, 2002], 17)

I know some of you do truly feel at sea, in the most frightening sense of that term. . . . I testify of God's love and the Savior's power to calm the storm . . . in that biblical story that He was out there on the water. . . . Only one who has fought against those ominous waves is justified in telling us—as well as the sea—to "be still" (Mark 4:39). Only one who has taken the full brunt of such adversity could ever be justified in telling us in such times to "be of good cheer" (John 16:33). Such counsel is not a jaunty pep talk about the power of positive thinking, though positive thinking is much needed in the world. No, Christ knows better than all others that the trials of life can be very deep, and we are not shallow people if we struggle with them. . . . Surely His ears heard every cry of distress, every sound of want and despair. To a degree far more than we will ever understand, He was "a man of sorrows, and acquainted with grief" (Isa. 53:3).

(Jeffrey R. Holland, *Ensign*, Nov. 1999 [Salt Lake City: The Church of Jesus Christ of Latter-day Saints, 1999], 14)

On some days we will have cause to remember the unkind treatment. . . . We can remember that Christ was also troubled on every side, but not distressed; perplexed, but not in despair; persecuted, but not forsaken; cast down, but not destroyed (see 2 Cor. 4:8–9).

When those difficult times come to us, we can remember that Jesus . . . suffered pains and afflictions and temptations of every kind that he might be filled with mercy and know how to succor His people in their infirmities (see D&C 88:6; Alma 7:11–12). . . .

However dim our days may seem they have been darker for the Savior of the world.

In fact, in a resurrected, otherwise perfected body, our Lord of this sacrament table has chosen to retain for the benefit of his disciples the wounds in his hands and his feet and his side—. . . signs, if you will, that pain in this world is *not* evidence that God doesn't love you. It is the *wounded* Christ who is the captain of our soul—he who yet bears the scars of sacrifice, the lesions of love and humility and forgiveness. . . .

All this we could remember when we are invited by a kneeling young priest to remember Christ always.

(Jeffrey R. Holland, *Ensign*, Nov. 1995 [Salt Lake City: The Church of Jesus Christ of Latter-day Saints, 1995], 69)

With these words, Isaiah draws every human being into his account. We all are part of the eternal congregation who must choose to accept or reject this Savior. "He was despised, and *we* esteemed him not" (Mosiah 14:3; emphasis added). This rhetorical device is often used in Isaiah's writing and in many Jewish texts. One can hear in the Passover seder this same self-inclusive notion: "Were we not strangers in the land of Egypt . . . ?" Through this language we are participants, joined with those who were there. We are with them.

(Ann Madsen, "What Meaneth the Words That Are Written?," *Journal of Book of Mormon Studies* [Salt Lake City: Deseret Book, 1989], 10, no.1: 9–10)

Mosiah 14:4; 15:9 • BORNE OUR GRIEF AND CARRIED OUR SORROW
(Isaiah 53:4; Refer in this text to Alma 7:11–12.)

When his body was taken from the cross and hastily placed in a borrowed tomb, he, the sinless Son of God, had already taken upon him not only the sins and temptations of every human soul who will repent, but all of our sickness and grief and pain of every kind. He suffered these afflictions as we suffer them, according to the flesh. He suffered them all. He did this to perfect his mercy and his ability to lift us above every earthly trial.

(Howard W. Hunter, *Ensign*, May 1988 [Salt Lake City: The Church of Jesus Christ of Latter-day Saints, 1988], 16–17)

Interestingly, the word *forgive* does not appear in this chapter of Isaiah, though the Hebrew root *nasa*, from which the word *forgive* is usually translated, does appear twice, as "borne" in verse 4, and "bare" in verse 12. . . . Christ "bore" or carried our sins so that we do not have to carry their burden (John 1:29; see 1 Pet. 1:18–20). Or, as we say, "He has forgiven us," meaning he "gave" the price "before."

(Victor L. Ludlow, *Isaiah: Prophet, Seer, and Poet* [Salt Lake City: Deseret Book, 1982], 452; italics added)

Certainly as he bore the sins and sadness, the heart-break and hurt of every man, woman, and child from Adam to the end of the world, it is an understatement to say he was "a man of sorrows, and acquainted with grief." . . . Many thought that if there is suffering, there surely must be guilt. Indeed, there was plenty of guilt here—a whole world of it—but it fell upon the only utterly sinless and totally innocent man who had ever lived.

(Jeffrey R. Holland, *Christ and the New Covenant* [Salt Lake City: Deseret Book, 1997], 91)

When the unimaginable burden began to weigh upon Christ, it confirmed His long-held and intellectually clear understanding as to what He must now do. . . . In Gethsemane, the suffering Jesus began to be "sore amazed" (Mark 14:33), or, in the Greek, "awe-struck" and "astonished."

Imagine, Jehovah, the Creator of this and other worlds, "astonished"! Jesus knew cognitively what He must do, but not experientially. He had never personally known the exquisite and exacting process of an atonement before. Thus, when the agony came in its fulness, it was so much, much worse than even He with his unique intellect had ever imagined! No wonder an angel appeared to strengthen him! (see Luke 22:43).

The cumulative weight of all mortal sins—past, present, and future—pressed upon that perfect, sinless, and sensitive Soul! All our infirmities and sicknesses were somehow, too, a part of the awful arithmetic of the Atonement (see Alma 7:11–12, Isa. 53:3–5, Matt. 8:17). . . .

His suffering—as it were, *enormity* multiplied by *infinity*—evoked His later soul-cry on the cross, and it was a cry of forsakeness (see Matt. 27:46).

(Neal A. Maxwell, *Ensign*, May 1985 [Salt Lake City: The Church of Jesus Christ of Latter-day Saints, 1985], 72–73)

Mosiah 14:4 • SMITTEN OF GOD
(Isaiah 53:4; Refer in this text to Mosiah 3:7.)

Was He "smitten of God"? Not in the sense that His Father was meting out some kind of punishment. Yet the great Elohim knew the agony to which His Only Begotten would be subjected as He fulfilled His foreordained assignment. Of necessity, the Father of us all had to deny or to turn a deaf ear to the agonizing plea, "O my Father, if it be possible, let this cup pass from me."

(Hoyt W. Brewster, Jr., *Isaiah Plain and Simple* [Salt Lake City: Deseret Book, 1995], 251)

Mosiah 14:4 • STRICKEN

(Isaiah 53:4; Refer in this text to Mosiah 14:8.)

This particular verb is used sixty times in Leviticus 13 and 14, always with the same meaning—that of suffering the emotional pain of having leprosy. The Servant will be viewed with the same disdain as the Jews viewed a leper.

(Donald W. Parry, Jay A. Parry, and Tina M. Peterson, *Understanding Isaiah* [Salt Lake City: Deseret Book, 1998], 474)

Mosiah 14:5 • WOUNDED FOR OUR TRANSGRESSIONS

(Isaiah 53:5.)

Verse 5 speaks concerning Christ's atoning sacrifice. The expression "he was wounded for our transgressions" may better be translated from the Hebrew as "he was pierced for our transgressions." Jesus Christ was pierced for the transgressions of all mankind while on the cross. The Psalmist prophesied: "They pierced my hands and my feet" (Psalm 22:16). In April 1829, Joseph Smith received this revelation from the Lord: "Behold the wounds which pierced my side, and also the prints of the nails in my hands and feet" (D&C 6:37).

(Donald W. Parry, *Visualizing Isaiah* [Provo, Utah: The Foundation for Ancient Research and Mormon Studies, 2001], 90)

—————

On the night Jesus was betrayed, He took three of the Twelve and went into the place called Gethsemane. There He suffered the pains of all men. He suffered as only God could suffer, bearing our griefs, carrying our sorrows, being wounded for our transgressions, voluntarily submitting Himself to the iniquity of us all, just as Isaiah prophesied. . . .

It was in Gethsemane that Jesus took on Himself the sins of the world, in Gethsemane that His pain was equivalent to the cumulative burden of all men, in Gethsemane that He descended below all things so that all could repent and come to Him. The mortal mind fails to fathom, the tongue cannot express, the pen of man cannot describe the breadth, the depth, the height of the suffering of our Lord—nor His infinite love for us.

(Ezra Taft Benson, *The Teachings of Ezra Taft Benson* [Salt Lake City: Bookcraft, 1988], 14)

—————

Years ago there was a little one-room schoolhouse in the mountains of Virginia where the boys were so rough that no teacher had been able to handle them. A young, inexperienced teacher applied, and the old director scanned him and asked, "Young fellow, do you know that you are asking for an awful beating? Every teacher that we have had here for years has had to take one."

"I will risk it," he replied.

The first day of school came, and the teacher appeared for duty. One big fellow named Tom whispered, "I won't need any help with this one. I can lick him myself."

The teacher said, "Good morning, boys, we have come to conduct school." They yelled and made fun at the top of their voices. "Now, I want a good school, but I confess that I do not know how unless you help me. Suppose we have a few rules. You tell me, and I will write them on the blackboard."

One fellow yelled, "No stealing!" Another yelled, "On time." Finally, ten rules appeared on the blackboard.

"Now," said the teacher, "a law is no good unless there is a penalty attached. What shall we do with one who breaks the rules?"

"Beat him across the back ten times without his coat on," came the response from the class.

"That is pretty severe, boys. Are you sure that you are ready to stand by it?" Another yelled, "I second the motion," and the teacher said, "All right, we will live by them! Class, come to order!"

In a day or so, "Big Tom" found that his lunch had been stolen. The thief was located—a little hungry fellow, about ten years old. "We have found the thief and he must be punished according to your rule—ten stripes across the back. Jim, come up here!" the teacher said.

The little fellow, trembling, came up slowly with a big coat fastened up to his neck and pleaded, "Teacher, you can lick me as hard as you like, but please, don't take my coat off!"

"Take your coat off," the teacher said. "You helped make the rules!"

"Oh, teacher, don't make me!" He began to unbutton, and what did the teacher see? The boy had no shirt on, and removal of the coat revealed a bony little crippled body.

"How can I whip this child?" he thought. "But I must. I must do something if I am to keep this school." Everything was quiet as death.

"How come you aren't wearing a shirt, Jim?"

He replied, "My father died and my mother is very poor. I have only one shirt and she is washing it today, and I wore my brother's big coat to keep me warm."

The teacher, with rod in hand, hesitated. Just then "Big Tom" jumped to his feet and said, "Teacher, if you don't object, I will take Jim's licking for him."

"Very well, there is a certain law that one can become a substitute for another. Are you all agreed?"

Off came Tom's coat, and after five stroked the rod broke! The teacher bowed his head in his hands and thought, "How can I finish this awful task?" Then he heard the class sobbing, and what did he see? Little Jim had reached up and caught Tom with both arms around his neck.

"Tom, I'm sorry that I stole your lunch, but I was awful hungry. Tom, I will love you till I die for taking my licking for me! Yes, I will love you forever."

(Adapted from a story by Rev. A.C. Dixon, in Stan and Sharon Miller and Sherm and Peggy Fugal, *Especially for Mormons* [Provo, Utah: Kellirae Arts, 1971–87], 4:37–38; as quoted in Gordon B. Hinckley, *The Wondrous and True Story of Christmas* [Salt Lake City: Deseret Book, 2003], 5–7)

Mosiah 14:5 • BRUISED FOR OUR INIQUITIES
(Isaiah 53:5.)

The phrase "he was bruised for our iniquities" is more correctly rendered "he was crushed (Hebrew *daka'*) for our iniquities." Jesus Christ was crushed in the Garden of Gethsemane. The word Gethsemane (Hebrew *Gath Shemen*) itself signifies "oil press." Just as olives are crushed at an olive press to render pure olive oil, so the Anointed One was crushed to sanctify mankind. He suffered so mightily in the Garden of Gethsemane that he bled from every pore (Luke 22:44; Mosiah 3:7; D&C 19:18).

(Donald W. Parry, *Visualizing Isaiah* [Provo, Utah: The Foundation for Ancient Research and Mormon Studies, 2001], 91)

Mosiah 14:6 • SHEEP GONE ASTRAY
(Isaiah 53:6.)

It is very important that sheep should not be allowed to stray away from the flock, because when by themselves they are utterly helpless. In such a condition, they become bewildered, for they have no sense at all of locality. And if they do stray away, they must be brought back. The Psalmist prayed the prayer: "I have gone astray like a lost sheep; seek thy servant" (Ps. 119:176). The prophet Isaiah compared man's waywardness to that of sheep: "All we like sheep have gone astray" (Isa. 53:6). David sang of his divine Shepherd: "He restoreth my soul" (Ps. 23:3).

(Fred H. Wight, *Manners and Customs of Bible Lands* [Chicago: Moody Press, 1953], 158)

Mosiah 14:7 • OPPRESSED AND AFFLICTED
(Isaiah 53:7.)

[Isaiah says, "He was oppressed."] We may understand from these words that He was trampled down by abuse of power and authority vested in the Jewish Hierarch. Seventy-one of its elders and wise men formed a council known as the *Sanhedrin* which, under their Roman conquerors, had complete jurisdiction over the religious, civil, and criminal affairs of the people. They sought to crush Him, and scatter His followers.

He was afflicted. This same *Sanhedrin* which oppressed Him, not only permitted Him to be abused (their duty was to protect Him), but also, its members joined in the cries against Him, and suffered Him to be wounded. They heaped sorrows (pains) upon Him that amounted to physical calumny. . . .

Dr. Adam Clarke in his *Commentary on the Old Testament . . .*, gives one example of the many customs to which Jesus had an appeal, but of it He had not benefit. Dr. Clarke says:

"A learned friend has communicated to me the following passages from the Mishna, and the Gemara of Babylon, as leading to a satisfactory explication of this difficult place. It is said in the former, that before anyone was punished for a capital crime, proclamation was made before the prisoner by the public crier, in these words: 'Whosoever knows any thing of this man's innocence, let him come and declare it.' . . . On which passage the Gemara of Babylon adds, '. . . before the death of Jesus this proclamation was made for forty days; but no defence could be found.' On which words Lardner observes: 'It is truly surprising to see such falsities, contrary to well-known facts.' . . . The report is certainly false; but this false report is founded on the supposition that there was such a custom, and so far confirms the account given from the Mishna. The Mishna was composed in the middle of the second century according to Prideaux; Lardner ascribes it to the year of Christ 180."

(George Reynolds and Janne M. Sjodahl, *Commentary on the Book of Mormon*, ed. Philip C. Reynolds [Salt Lake City: Deseret Book, 1955–1961], 2:161–62)

Mosiah 14:7 • OPENED NOT HIS MOUTH
(Isaiah 53:7.)

Herod began to question the Prisoner; but Jesus remained silent. The chief priests and scribes vehemently voiced their accusations; but not a word was uttered by the Lord. Herod is the only character in history to whom Jesus is known to have applied a personal epithet of contempt. "Go ye and tell that fox" He once said to certain Pharisees. . . . As far as we know, Herod is further distinguished as the only being who saw Christ face to face and spoke to Him, yet never heard His voice. . . . Christ had words—of comfort or instruction, of warning or rebuke, of protest or denunciation—yet for Herod the fox He had but disdainful and kingly silence.

(James E. Talmage, *Jesus the Christ: A Study of the Messiah and His Mission According to Holy Scriptures Both Ancient and Modern* [Salt Lake City: The Church of Jesus Christ of Latter-day Saints, 1981], 636)

Here the image of wayward sheep in verse 6 (the human family) is shifted in verse 7 to that of an innocent sheep (Christ), who goes to the slaughter without utterance. When confronted by the high priest Caiaphas, Jesus "held his peace." Later Herod questioned with him in many words; but he answered him nothing. Finally with Pilate, the one man who could have spared his life, Jesus "gave him no answer." He was the Lamb of God prepared from before the foundation of the world for this ultimate and infinite sacrifice. In his sacrifice he was giving millennia of meaning to the untold number of lambs that had been offered on an untold number of altars in anticipation and similitude of this final blood offering of God's Firstborn."

(Jeffrey R. Holland, *Christ and the New Covenant* [Salt Lake City: Deseret Book, 1997], 92–93)

The vivid image of Christ's suffering in silence is symbolized by a sheep, which makes no sound as it is being sheared. Even though all our iniquities have been laid on him, "yet he opened not his mouth." We, the straying sheep for whom he paid the debt, can hardly understand such restraint. We cry out at the slightest hurt. He conserved his power for Gethsemane and the cross.

(Ann Madsen, "What Meaneth the Words That Are Written?," *Journal of Book of Mormon Studies* [Salt Lake City: Deseret Book, 1989], 10, no. 1:10)

Mosiah 14:7 • LAMB, SHEEP
(Isaiah 53:7.)

Isaiah uses two similes to describe Jesus Christ's atoning sacrifice: "as a lamb" and "as a sheep." Not only is Christ the Good Shepherd (John 10:14), but he is also the sacrificial lamb, who went without protest or resistance to his death. This contrasts with mankind, the sheep that willfully went astray (Isa. 53:6). The sacrifice of an unblemished lamb under the law of Moses prefigured the atoning sacrifice of Christ (Gen. 22:7–8; Ex. 12:3). The Atonement fulfills the symbolism of the lamb.

(Donald W. Parry, *Visualizing Isaiah* [Provo, Utah: The Foundation for Ancient Research and Mormon Studies, 2001], 93)

As "girls camp" concluded, my wife and I made the trip into the mountains to transport a van load of twelve-year-olds back to civilization. The fifteen miles of dusty, dirt road were uneventful, other than having to tune out the simultaneous talking, singing, and laughing of six effervescent young women.

However, entering the paved highway was another matter. The entrance onto the pavement is on a potentially dangerous turn, and this particular highway has the highest fatality rate of any highway in the state. I needed to turn left, thus having to cross the road. To my right was a sharp downhill turn preventing seeing very far for oncoming traffic. Cars and eighteen wheelers can suddenly appear and often are going too fast to safely adjust to merging vehicles. Thus I waited for a safe moment to cross the highway and rapidly accelerate to get out of the way of possible approaching traffic.

As I continued to scan left, then right, then back again, I noticed that directly across the road, though still on the pavement, was the carcass of a lamb that had apparently been struck by a vehicle. This brought a sigh of sadness into my heart, but due to the task at hand, I could do no more than just briefly glance at the damaged little body.

A break in the unusually busy traffic developed, I made one last look at the curve to the right, and quickly crossed the highway, turned left, and stomped on the accelerator to come up to highway speed as quickly as possible. Now that I was finally on the highway, heading downhill, I glanced in my rearview mirror. No threatening traffic emerged around the turn, but to my amazement, my gaze focused on the carcass of that lamb. Though I was rapidly accelerating away from that little body on the pavement, I had the distinct impression that that lamb raised its head and looked at me driving away. In fact it seemed that in that fraction of a hurried second, that lamb actually made eye contact with me. The sickening feeling in my stomach deepened as it seemed that those big brown eyes were saying, "You can't leave me like this!"

I dismissed this unlikely communication and again returned my attention to getting my van load of noisy girls safely around the next sharp turn in the road. However, as I continued to drive, I replayed in my mind what I thought had happened. What if that lamb really was still alive? After about a mile, I knew I had to turn around and go check out my impression. I asked my wife to be patient with me as I had to return to the rest area along the road and make certain that the little lamb was actually dead. My wife was understanding, and the girls were never aware of the lamb or even of the fact that we had turned around and were now going back to the intersection.

I intentionally stopped behind a parked eighteen wheeler in the rest area so that the girls could not see what I was doing when I left the van. They seemed content to continue their animated talking and laughing. My wife and I then once again waited for a break in the traffic and dashed across the highway to check on the lamb.

As we approached the animal, the first thing I noticed was that his little body was well onto the pavement and therefore likely to be hit again, perhaps had already been hit several times. The poor little animal's head was towards the far side of the road. As I bent over to look at his battered little face, those same big brown eyes opened again. He was still alive, but now couldn't even seem to raise his head.

The first order of business was to remove him and us from off the busy highway. I reached down to grab his thick wool coat and quickly lift him from off the road. However, as I lifted, the pelt peeled back exposing a torn and battered torso that was damaged even more than I had feared. The flesh was drying out and the maggots had already begun their sickening task. This poor little fellow must have already been in this condition for a painfully long time.

The caretaker of the rest area dashed across the highway and joined us. He kindly thanked us for stopping. He also said that several travelers had previously stopped, but all concurred that nothing could be done. Again he thanked us, but asked us to get off this dangerous highway. Sadly, he repeated that nothing could be done to help the critically injured lamb.

Although I had to agree that the injuries were terminal, there were a few things that could be done. Once more I bent down to lift him, this time putting my hands and arms under his body. I moved him as far off the road as the steep embankment would allow. No sound ever came from this little fellow but those gentle eyes somehow seemed to convey acceptance of the inevitable and gratitude for a little kindness and dignity. Thoughts of the Lamb of God, quietly suffering for all of us, struck me deeply.

There was one thing more I felt the lamb was asking me to do. I escorted my wife back to the van, asked her to remain with the girls, who were unaware that I had removed a pistol from its licensed concealment and returned to the suffering little lamb. Though years of military and hunting experience have placed weapons in my hand before, never before did it seem so merciful, though tearfully difficult, to pull the trigger.

In silence I returned to the van of unsuspecting girls and commenced once more the journey home. For about ten miles I sobbed uncontrollably as I thought about the willing Lamb of God, His seemingly unending suffering. . . . That He had to suffer for my sins. . . . Truly I saw the Savior in the Lamb.

(Author anonymous; as quoted in *Latter-day Commentary on the New Testament,* ed. by J. Pinegar, K. Douglas Bassett, and Ted L. Earl [American Fork, Utah: Covenant Communications, 2002], 242–244)

―――――――――

The Levitical Code often allowed the Hebrews a choice of a sheep or of a goat for the offering. "If his offering be of the flocks, namely, of the sheep, or of the goats, for a burnt sacrifice" (Lev. 1:10). On the Day of Atonement, it was required that a goat be sacrificed by the high priest, and that another goat should be "the scapegoat." "And the goat shall bear upon him all their iniquities unto a land not inhabited, and he shall let go the goat in the wilderness" (Lev. 16:22). Moses had ordered that the scapegoat should be taken out into the wilderness and turned loose. But in order to prevent its return to Jerusalem, it became customary to lead the creature to the height of a mountain, where it was pushed over and would be certainly killed. This was the symbol of the forgiveness of sin through the sacrifice of Christ. Although John the Baptist spoke of Jesus as the Lamb of God, he may have had in mind also the picture of the scapegoat when he said: (John 1:29, Centenary, Montgomery).

(Fred H. Wight, *Manners and Customs of Bible Lands* [Chicago: Moody Press, 1953], 168)

Mosiah 14:8 • STRICKEN
(Isaiah 53:8; Refer in this text to Mosiah 14:4, under STRICKEN.)

Ancient translators add to these words and render them, "He was smitten to death" (The Septuagint reads *lemaveth,* which, in the Greek into which the Old Testament was translated, means "to death.")

(George Reynolds and Janne M. Sjodahl, *Commentary on the Book of Mormon,* ed. Philip C. Reynolds [Salt Lake City: Deseret Book, 1955–1961], 2:162)

Mosiah 14:8–9 • PRISON, JUDGMENT, GENERATION, GRAVE, NO EVIL
(Isaiah 53:8–9.)

I think that the first clause means that our Lord was taken away (from life) by oppression and by a miscarriage of justice. The second clause, "and who shall declare his generation," is often taken to mean "and among his contemporaries who was concerned?" I think that "generation" here means "posterity," but in a very special sense. It has reference to the "seed" or "believers" of Jesus in the sense explained by the prophet Abinadi in Mosiah 15:10–13, or by the Savior to the brother of Jared when he said, "In me shall all mankind have light, and that eternally, even they who shall believe on my name; and they shall become my sons and my daughters [i.e., *my seed* or *my generation*] (Ether 3:14).

(Sidney B. Sperry, *Book of Mormon Compendium* [Salt Lake City: Bookcraft, 1968], 304)

———————

And who shall declare his generation? This has been interpreted, "And his manner of life who would declare?" Although we quote concerning the meaning stated of the question that is asked, we prefer to believe that it refers to the growth of the numbers of Christ's followers. "Of the increase of his government and peace there shall be no end" (Isa. 9:7). "And he shall reign over the house of Jacob for ever; and of his kingdom there shall be no end" (Luke 1:33).

(George Reynolds and Janne M. Sjodahl, *Commentary on the Book of Mormon*, ed. Philip C. Reynolds [Salt Lake City: Deseret Book, 1955–1961], 2:162)

Christ was taken prisoner by soldiers who entered the garden of Gethsemane expressly to seize him, and he spent the rest of his remaining hours in bondage and judgment at the hands of Pilate. He died with the wicked, crucified between two thieves, and found a burial place at the hand of the wealthy Joseph of Arimathea. Christ was the embodiment of truth, with no deceit of any kind ever having passed his lips. Nor would he do evil (even in word) in his time of greatest injustice, praying in the last hours of his life that his Father would forgive those involved, "for they know not what they do."

(Jeffrey R. Holland, *Christ and the New Covenant* [Salt Lake City: Deseret Book, 1997], 93)

———————

We gain an even stronger appreciation for the remarkable detail of the prophecy of Isaiah quoted by Abinadi. Jesus was indeed put to death "with the wicked," literally crucified between two thieves (see Luke 23:32). At the same time, he was buried "with the rich," in the sense that he was placed in a tomb owned by a wealthy man, Joseph of Arimathea (see John 19:38–42).

(Robert L. Millet, in *Symposium on the Book of Mormon* [Salt Lake City: The Church of Jesus Christ of Latter-day Saints, 1986], 100)

———————

Jewish tradition is heavy with the idea that a son

must somehow speak for his father after his death. There is a formal ceremony at the grave one year after the father's death in which the son speaks a formulaic prayer in his father's behalf, thus "declaring his generation" and the continuance of "his seed."

(Ann Madsen, "What Meaneth the Words That Are Written?" *Journal of Book of Mormon Studies* [Salt Lake City: Deseret Book, 1989], 10, no. 1:11)

Mosiah 14:10; 15:10 • PLEASED THE LORD TO BRUISE HIM . . . SEE HIS SEED, PROLONG HIS DAYS AND THE PLEASURE OF THE LORD
(Isaiah 53:10.)

Certainly it did not "please" the Father to bruise his Son, as we currently understand and use that word. Modern translations of Isaiah render these opening lines "it was the will of the Lord" rather than "it pleased the Lord." That gives a clearer meaning of what was meant by the word *pleased* when Joseph Smith translated this passage early in the nineteenth century. Furthermore, acknowledging Christ's submission to the will of the Father in Mosiah 14 is consistent with and sets the stage for the very teaching Abinadi was about to give to King Noah and his people in Mosiah 15. Indeed, Abinadi would give a succinct definition of those who are Christ's seed. They are those whose sins he has borne and for whom he has died. His soul truly was "an offering for sin," bringing the joy of a glorious heavenly reunion with "his seed," a reunion nowhere more movingly described than in President Joseph F. Smith's vision of the righteous dead. All of this is, indeed, a pleasure to the Lord.

(Jeffrey R. Holland, *Christ and the New Covenant* [Salt Lake City: Deseret Book, 1997], 93–94)

———————

If this prophecy was meant to be fulfilled during his mortal sojourn on earth, we would list it as having failed. He did not prolong his days; a voluntary death overtook him in the prime of life. . . . It is only in the resurrection that the pleasure of the Lord is perfected, for it is only when "spirit and element" are "inseparably connected" that either God or man can "receive a fulness of joy" (D&C 93:33). Thus, having made his soul an offering for sin; having seen his seed—all the righteous dead from the days of Adam to that moment—as they assembled to greet and worship him in the paradise of their Lord; and having thereafter risen in glorious immortality to live and reign forever, our Messiah truly fulfilled the prophetic utterance, for then his days were prolonged forever and the pleasure in his hand was infinite.

(Bruce R. McConkie, *The Promised Messiah* [Salt

Lake City: Deseret Book, 1978], 362)

———————

"It pleased the Lord to bruise him" is a declaration that Christ's sacrifice was a freewill offering, on the part of both the Father and the Son. In John 3:16–17, Jesus declared that the Father had sent his Son to be sacrificed because of his love for the world. In Doctrine and Covenants 34:3, Jesus declared that he voluntarily gave his life because of his own love for the world."

(Monte S. Nyman, *Great Are the Words of Isaiah* [Salt Lake City: Bookcraft, 1980], 210)

———————

This is a verse which requires careful consideration. God our Eternal Father loved his Only Begotten and, like any parent, surely anguished with the pain of his child. And yet, as infinitely painful as it must have been for Elohim, the hours of agony were necessary—they were a part of that plan of the Father of which Jehovah had been the chief advocate and proponent in premortality. Indeed it was needful that the "Lamb slain from the foundation of the world" be slain, in order that life and immortality might be brought to light. And thus "it pleased the Lord [the Father] to bruise him," in the sense that Jesus carried out to the fullest the will of the Father, in spite of the pain associated with the implementation of the terms and conditions of that will. "Oh," Elder Melvin J. Ballard said, "in that moment when He might have saved His Son, I thank Him and praise Him that He did not fail us, for He had not only the love of His Son in mind, but He also had love for us. I rejoice that He did not interfere, and that His love for us made it possible for Him to endure to look upon the sufferings of His Son and give Him finally to us, our Saviour and our Redeemer. Without Him, without His sacrifice, we would have remained, and would never have come glorified into His presence. And so this is what it cost, in part, for our Father in heaven to give the gift of His Son unto men" (Melvin J. Ballard—*Crusader for Righteousness* [Salt Lake City: Bookcraft, 1966], 137).

(Robert L. Millet, in *Symposium on the Book of Mormon* [Salt Lake City: The Church of Jesus Christ of Latter-day Saints, 1986], 100)

———————

Isaiah's prophecy and Abinadi's interpretation speak only of those who have been and not of those who shall yet believe. . . . Let us note the time and circumstances under which he will see them. Abinadi's rendition of Isaiah's inspired utterance says: "When his soul has been made an offering for sin he shall see his seed." In other words, he shall see his seed after he has worked out the infinite and eternal atonement . . .

(Luke 23:40–43). . . .

(1 Pet. 3:18–20; 4:6). In his glorious vision of the redemption of the dead, President Joseph F. Smith saw what transpired when the Messiah visited the departed dead. "The eyes of my understanding were opened, and the Spirit of the Lord rested upon me," he said, "and I saw the hosts of the dead, both small and great. And there were gathered together in one place an innumerable company of the spirits of the just, who had been faithful in the testimony of Jesus while they lived in mortality. . . . All these had departed the mortal life, firm in the hope of a glorious resurrection, through the grace of God the Father and his Only Begotten Son, Jesus Christ" (JFS-V 11–14). . . .

If this prophecy [Isa. 53:10] was meant to be fulfilled during his mortal sojourn on earth, we would list it as having failed. He did not prolong his days; a voluntary death overtook him in the prime of life. . . . It is only in the resurrection that the pleasure of the Lord is perfected. . . . Thus, having made his soul an offering for sin; having seen his seed—all the righteous dead from the days of Adam to that moment . . . our Messiah truly fulfilled the prophetic utterance, for then his days were prolonged forever and the pleasure in his hand was infinite.

(Bruce R. McConkie, *The Promised Messiah* [Salt Lake City: Deseret Book, 1978], 360–62)

Mosiah 14:11–12 • TRAVAIL OF HIS SOUL
(Isaiah 53:11–12.)

Christ certainly did know and feel the "travail of his soul," an anguish commencing in the garden of Gethsemane, where he "began to be sorrowful and very heavy . . . even unto death." He prayed so earnestly through the depths of that agony that his sweat became "as it were great drops of blood falling down to the ground." Later he would describe the experience of that suffering: "[It] caused myself, even God, the greatest of all, to tremble because of pain, and to bleed at every pore, and to suffer both body and spirit-and would that I might not drink the bitter cup, and shrink."

But he was faithful to the end, "satisfied" in its most literal, legal sense, having made reparation and restitution sufficient to appease the demands of justice. Because he "poured out his soul unto death" bearing the "sin of many," he received the inheritance of the great, sitting on the right hand of God, where all that the Father has was given him. True to his nature and true to his covenant, Christ will share that divine inheritance with all others who will be strong in keeping the commandments, thus making them "heirs of the kingdom of God" in precisely the way Abinadi declared this doctrine to King Noah.

For such merciful protection and glorious promises we must never again "hide our faces from him and esteem him not."

(Jeffrey R. Holland, *Christ and the New Covenant* [Salt Lake City: Deseret Book, 1997], 94)

————

His soul was made an offering for the sins of many whom he would one day see and own. The many would be those who had chosen to seek and know him and give away their sins to become like him. The day would come when he, as heir, would divide all he had been given with those who had willingly taken upon them his name.

(Ann Madsen, "What Meaneth the Words That Are Written?" *Journal of Book of Mormon Studies* [Salt Lake City: Deseret Book, 1989], 10, no. 1:10)

Mosiah 14:12 • POURED OUT HIS SOUL UNTO DEATH
(Isaiah 53:12.)

Redeeming Jesus also "poured out his soul unto death" (Mosiah 14:12; see also Isa. 53:12; D&C 38:4). As we on occasion "pour" out our souls in personal pleadings, we are thus emptied, making room for more joy!

(Neal A. Maxwell, *Ensign*, May 2001 [Salt Lake City: The Church of Jesus Christ of Latter-day Saints, 2001], 60)

Mosiah 15:1–4; 17:8 • CHRIST AS THE FATHER
(Refer in this text to 1 Nephi 19:10.)

In this powerful passage we have a wondrous summary of divine truth. Christ is God and he comes to redeem his people. He is the Son because he is born into mortality. He is the Father because he inherits from his Father all the might of omnipotence, and what he says and what he does become and are the words and works of him whose name he bears.

(Bruce R. McConkie, *The Promised Messiah* [Salt Lake City: Deseret Book, 1978], 372)

————

Christ is also our Father because his Father has given him of his fulness; that is, he has received a fulness of the glory of the Father. This is taught in Doctrine and Covenants 93:1–5, 16–17, and also by Abinadi in the 15th chapter of Mosiah. Abinadi's statement that he is "the Father, because he was conceived by the power of God," harmonizes with the Lord's own words in section 93 that he is the Father because he has received of the fulness of the Father. Christ says he is the Son because, "I was in the world and made flesh my tabernacle, and dwelt among the sons of men." Abinadi expresses this truth by saying he is "the Son because of the flesh."

The Father has honored Christ by placing his name upon him, so that he can minister in and through that name as though he were the Father; and thus, so far as power and authority are concerned, his words and acts become and are those of the Father. . . .

Our Lord is also called the Father in the sense that he is the Father or Creator of the heavens and the earth and all things.

(Joseph Fielding Smith, *Doctrines of Salvation*, comp. by Bruce R. McConkie [Salt Lake City: Bookcraft, 1954], 1:29–30)

————

We go to great lengths to use language that shows there is both a Father and a Son, that they are separate Persons. . . . Such an approach is perhaps essential in reasoning with the Gentiles of sectarianism. . . .

If we are to envision our Lord's true status and glory, we must come back to the pronouncement. . . . That Christ is God. And if it were not so, he could not save us. Let all men, both in heaven and on earth, hear the proclamation and rejoice in its eternal verity: "The Lord is God, and beside him there is no Savior" (D&C 76:1).

(Bruce R. McConkie, *The Promised Messiah* [Salt Lake City: Deseret Book, 1978], 98)

————

God himself—Jehovah, the God of ancient Israel—will come to earth, take a physical body, and bring to pass redemption for all men.

Because Jehovah, Jesus Christ, will have a physical body and dwell in the flesh—like every other mortal son and daughter of God—he will be known as the Son of God. On the other hand, because he will be conceived by the power of God, and will thus have within him the powers of the Spirit, he will be known as the Father . . . (see D&C 93:4, 12–14).

(*Symposium on the Book of Mormon* [Salt Lake City: The Church of Jesus Christ of Latter-day Saints, 1986], 101)

————

What is a father? One who begets or gives life. What did our Savior do? He begot us, or gave us life from death. . . .

The Son of God has a perfect right to call us his children, spiritually begotten. . . .

Now if these critics would read carefully the Book of Mormon they would find that when the Savior came and visited the Nephites he told them that he had been sent by his Father. He taught them to pray to his Father, but that did not lessen in the least our duty and responsibility of looking upon the Son of God as a Father to us because he spiritually begot us.

(Joseph Fielding Smith, *Answers to Gospel Questions* [Salt Lake City: Deseret Book, 1972], 4:177, 179–180)

Mosiah 15:5 • THE FLESH BECOMING SUBJECT TO THE SPIRIT

We have to fight continually, . . . to make the spirit master of the tabernacle, or the flesh subject to the law of the spirit. If this warfare is not diligently prosecuted, then the law of sin prevails. . . . When through the Gospel, the Spirit in man has so subdued the flesh . . . the Spirit of God unites with his spirit, they become congenial companions, and the mind and will of the Creator is thus transmitted to the creature. . . .

Our bodies are all important to us, though they may be old and withered, emaciated with toil, pain, and sickness, . . . for death is sown in our mortal bodies. The food and drink we partake of are contaminated with the seeds of death, yet we partake of them to extend our lives until our allotted work is finished. . . . Yet, if we live our holy religion and let the Spirit reign, . . . as the body approaches dissolution the spirit takes a firmer hold on that enduring substance behind the vail, drawing from the depths of that eternal Fountain of Light sparkling gems of intelligence which surround the frail and sinking tabernacle with a halo of immortal wisdom. . . .

Need we in spirit bow down to this poor, miserable, decaying body? We will not.

(Brigham Young, *Journal of Discourses* [London: Latter-day Saints' Book Depot, 1862], 9:287–288)

Mosiah 15:7 • SWALLOWED UP IN THE WILL OF THE FATHER

Do not ever doubt the goodness of God, even if you do not know "why." The overarching question asked by the bereaved and the burdened is simply this: Why? Why did our daughter die, when we prayed so hard that she would live and when she received priesthood blessings? Why are we struggling with this misfortune, when others relate miraculous healing experiences for their loved ones? . . . As the Son's will was "swallowed up in the will of the Father" (Mosiah 15:7), so must ours be. . . .

Humility and submissiveness are an expression of complete willingness to let the "why" questions go unanswered for now, or perhaps even to ask, "Why not?" It is in enduring well to the end that we achieve this life's purposes (see 2 Nephi 31:15–16; Alma 32:15; D&C 121:8). I believe that mortality's supreme test is to face the "why" and then let it go, trusting humbly in the Lord's promise that "all things must come to pass in their time" (D&C 64:32).

(Lance B. Wickman, in Conference Report, Oct.

2002 [Salt Lake City: The Church of Jesus Christ of Latter-day Saints, 2002], 32)

Mosiah 15:10 • HE SHALL SEE HIS SEED
(Refer in this text to Alma 7:11–12.)

There were many years in which I believed that the atoning process involved an infinite mass of sin being heaped upon the Savior. As I have become more familiar with the scriptures, my view of the Atonement has expanded. The Atonement involved more than an infinite mass of sin; it entailed an infinite stream of individuals with their specific needs. Alma records that Jesus took upon himself the pains, afflictions, temptations, and sicknesses of his people. In addition, he experienced their weaknesses so that he would know how to help them (see Alma 7:11–12). Isaiah prophesied that the Lord would bear "our griefs, and [carry] our sorrows"; that he would be "wounded for our transgressions" and "bruised for our iniquities" (Isaiah 53:45). Paul explained to the Hebrews that Jesus tasted "death for every man" and woman (Hebrews 2:9). No wonder 'his sweat was as it were great drops of blood" coming from "every pore" (Luke 22:44, D&C 19:18). Isaiah and Abinadi stated that when "his soul has been made an offering for sin he shall see his seed" (see Isaiah 53:10, Mosiah 15:10). And who are his seed? Those who follow the prophets (Mosiah 15:11–17). . . .

The Atonement was not only infinite in its expanse but intimate in the lives of God's children. The Redeemer of the world is acquainted with each person's infirmities. He knows your problems. He understands your joys as well as your sorrows. He knows the nature of the temptations that beset you and how they interface with your weaknesses. Above all he knows you and knows how and when to help you. Generally his help is given through the Holy Ghost. The Holy Spirit speaks quietly by generating thoughts and feelings within.

(Merrill J. Bateman, "One by One," *BYU Speeches of the Year*, 9 Sept. 1997 [Provo, Utah: BYU Press, 1997], 4)

Mosiah 15:21–26 • THE FIRST RESURRECTION

The righteous dead who lived from the day of Adam to the time when Christ broke the bands of death "were with Christ in his resurrection" (D&C 133:54–55). . . . All who were with Christ in his resurrection, and all who have so far been resurrected, have come forth with celestial bodies and will have an inheritance in the celestial kingdom (D&C 88:96–102). To those who lived before the resurrection of Christ, the day of his coming forth from the dead was known as the first resurrection. Abinadi and Alma, for instance, so considered it (Mosiah 15:21–25; Alma 40). To those who have lived since that day, the first resurrection is yet future and will take place at the time of the Second Coming (D&C 88:96–102).

(Bruce R. McConkie, *Mormon Doctrine* [Salt Lake City: Bookcraft, 1966], 639–640)

Mosiah 15:24 • DIED IN THEIR IGNORANCE

(Refer in this text to Moroni 8:22; 2 Nephi 9:25–27.)

If a person never had the opportunity to know anything about the plan of salvation, then surely he should not be held accountable for his deeds in the flesh on an equality with the man who knew the truth and then refused to obey it. Thousands of these people who lived in this ignorance were devout and faithful to the doctrines which they had been taught. They cannot be held accountable for their actions which were done in faith and obedience to that which they devoutly believed and had been taught.

(Joseph Fielding Smith, *Answers to Gospel Questions* [Salt Lake City: [Salt Lake City: Deseret Book, 1972], 4:77)

Mosiah 15:25 • LITTLE CHILDREN HAVE ETERNAL LIFE

(Refer in this text to Moroni 8.)

I have meditated upon the subject, and asked the question, why it is that infants, innocent children, are taken away from us. . . . The Lord takes many away even in infancy, that they may escape the envy of man, and the sorrows and evils of this present world; they were too pure, too lovely, to live on earth; therefore, if rightly considered, instead of mourning we have reason to rejoice as they are delivered from evil, and we shall soon have them again.

(*Teachings of the Prophet Joseph Smith*, comp. by Joseph Fielding Smith [Salt Lake City: Deseret Book, 1976], 196–197)

Little children who die before the age of accountability are saved in the celestial kingdom. . . . Serious thinking would tell us that if these children are saved, they are not subject to a later trial by the temptation and buffeting of Satan. . . . Revelations given in our day also show that little children who are deprived of the experiences in mortal life are, by eternal decree, redeemed from the temptation of Satan (D&C 29:46–48; Mosiah 15:24–25; Moroni 8:10–24).

(Joseph Fielding Smith, *Answers to Gospel Questions* [Salt Lake City: Deseret Book, 1957], 1:56–57)

Mosiah 15:29–31 • WATCHMEN LIFT UP THEIR VOICE . . . EYE TO EYE

3 Nephi 16:18–20 (Isaiah 52:8–10; Refer in this text to 3 Nephi 20:32–35.) 3 Nephi 20:32–35

I received, by a heavenly vision, a commandment in June following, to take my journey to the western boundaries of the State of Missouri, and there designate the very spot which was to be the central place for the commencement of the gathering together of those who embrace the fullness of the everlasting Gospel. Accordingly I undertook the journey, with certain ones of my brethren, and after a long and tedious journey, suffering many privations and hardships, arrived in Jackson County, Missouri, and after viewing the country, seeking diligently at the hand of God, He manifested Himself unto us, and designated, to me and others, the very spot upon which he designed to commence the work of the gathering, and the upbuilding of an "holy city," which should be called Zion—Zion, because it is a place of righteousness, and all who build thereon are to worship the true and living God, and all believe in one doctrine, even the doctrine of our Lord and Savior Jesus Christ. "Thy watchmen shall lift up the voice; with the voice together shall they sing: for they shall see eye to eye, when the Lord shall bring again Zion."

(*Teachings of the Prophet Joseph Smith*, comp. by Joseph Fielding Smith [Salt Lake City: Deseret Book, 1976], 79–80)

The Savior quoted all three verses twice to the Nephites and said they would be fulfilled through both the Nephites and the Jews. This again shows the dual nature of Isaiah's prophecies. The Savior first quoted this passage following his declaration that the land of America was to be given to Lehi's descendants after the Gentiles reject the fulness of the gospel and are "trodden under foot" by the house of Israel; he said this would fulfill the words of the prophet Isaiah (see 3 Ne. 16:10–20). He later quoted the passage while instructing the Nephites concerning the restoration of the Jews. He changed the wording from "thy watchmen" to "their watchmen," as he was referring to Jerusalem's watchmen in this case rather than those of Zion (see 3 Ne. 20:29–35). Abinadi also recognized the universal application of this passage in teaching that "the salvation of the Lord shall be declared to every nation, kindred, tongue, and people" and quoting these three verses as evidence (see Mosiah 15:28–31). Joseph Smith designated Jackson County, Missouri, as the Zion spoken of in verse 8 (see TPJS, 79–80). The "watchmen" are those who preach the gospel, as indicated in verse 7. The song to be sung in Zion will be a new song, sung when all will know Christ (i.e., during the Millennium). The words of the song, which will include parts of verse 8, are recorded in Doctrine and Covenants 84:99–102.

The Lord will "make bare his holy arm in the eyes of all the nations" at his second coming (see D&C 133:2–3). Doctrine and Covenants 133:4 admonishes the members of the Church to sanctify themselves in preparation for that day.

(Monte S. Nyman, *Great Are the Words of Isaiah* [Salt Lake City: Bookcraft, 1980], 199–200)

Eye to eye. This metaphor represents being united in purpose and understanding (Mosiah 16:1; Alma 36:26; D&C 84:98). Unity is one of the key characteristics of Zion, as Moses recorded: "The Lord called his people Zion, because they were of one heart and one mind" (Moses 7:18). . . .

Lord hath made bare his holy arm. In ancient times, men prepared for battle by throwing their cloak away from the shoulder of their fighting arm (Ps. 74:11). At the second coming of Christ, God will make bare his arm when he shows forth his power for all to see (D&C 133:2–3). . . .

Ends of the earth shall see the salvation. Every part of the earth will see and know the power of the Lord; all will see how he delivers those who turn to him. Joseph Smith promised the suffering Saints: "The days of tribulation are fast approaching, and the time to test the fidelity of the Saints has come. . . . but in these times of sore trial, let the Saints be patient and see the salvation of God. Those who cannot endure persecution, and stand in the day of affliction, cannot stand in the day when the Son of God shall burst the veil, and appear in all the glory of His Father, with all the holy angels" (*History of the Church*, 1:468).

(Donald W. Parry, Jay A. Parry, and Tina M. Peterson, *Understanding Isaiah* [Salt Lake City: Deseret Book, 1998], 465–66)

These prophetic words, from Isaiah 52:8–10, will be fulfilled after the Lord Jesus appears in glory, cleanses the earth, gathers his people from the four quarters of the earth, and establishes Zion, a society of the pure in heart. Then all shall see the salvation of God, meaning the victory of our Lord over the forces of evil and corruption. And then the earth shall rest (see Moses 7:60–64).

(Joseph Fielding McConkie, Robert L. Millet, and Brent L. Top, *Doctrinal Commentary on the Book of Mormon* [Salt Lake City: Bookcraft, 1987–1992], 112)

In the full and true sense, Israel shall triumph over her foes only when the Millennium is ushered in, only when her Messiah comes to deliver them from the aliens, only when the wicked are destroyed and the Lord reigns gloriously among his saints.

It is in this setting—a millennial setting; a day of millennial glory; the day when peace prevails because the wicked have been destroyed—it is in this setting that Jesus says: "Then"—in the day of which we speak— "the words of the prophet Isaiah shall be fulfilled." These are the words: "Thy watchmen shall lift up the voice; with the voice together shall they sing, for they shall see eye to eye when the Lord shall bring again Zion." We are establishing Zion now, but our Zion is only the foundation for that which is to be. We are laying a foundation; the promises relative to the glorious Zion of God which shall yet stand upon the earth shall be fulfilled after the Lord comes. "Break forth into joy, sing together, ye waste places of Jerusalem," Isaiah continues, "for the Lord hath comforted his people, he hath redeemed Jerusalem." The true and full redemption of Jerusalem must await the day of the Lord's return. "The Lord hath made bare his holy arm in the eye of all the nations; and all the ends of the earth shall see the salvation of God" (3 Ne. 16:4–20).

(Bruce R. McConkie, *The Millennial Messiah* [Salt Lake City: Deseret Book, 1982], 242)

Mosiah 16:8–9 • STING OF DEATH SWALLOWED UP IN CHRIST

I don't fear death. In fact, a scripture describes a Saint's death as "precious in the sight of the Lord" (Psalm 116:15). It will be precious to me, too, as I am reunited with our parents and our precious daughter, Emily, who died some five years ago. Her passing left her young and righteous husband with five children. I will eagerly meet my ancestors and preceding prophets and apostles. And one day Sister Nelson and I will dwell together in the presence of our family and the Lord forevermore. We will have been faithful to covenants made in the temple, and to the oath and covenant of the priesthood, which have assured us, in the words of the Lord, that "all that my Father hath shall be given unto [you]" (D&C 84:38).

(Russell M. Nelson, "Identity, Priority, and Blessings," *BYU Speeches of the Year*, 10 Sept. 2000 [Provo, Utah: BYU Press, 2000], 5)

It is hard, of course, to part with our friends. . . . It is natural for us to give expression to our feelings in tears in laying away the bodies of our beloved friends, and there is a degree to which we may go which is proper and right; but there are extremes which are often indulged in, which is neither proper nor right for Latter-day Saints to copy after. . . .

I have never felt to mourn . . . any Saint of the living God to the grave . . . who has been true and faithful to His covenants. . . . Such men and women have filled their mission here upon earth with honor, with labor, with love, until they have been called home. They have died in the faith, and they will receive a crown of glory. . . .

Where is the man who comprehends these principles that can mourn for that brother or sister?

(*Teachings of Presidents of the Church—Wilford Woodruff* [Salt Lake City: The Church of Jesus Christ of Latter-day Saints, 2004], 83)

An early Saint of the 19th century, Warren M. Johnson . . . was assigned by church leaders to operate Lee's Ferry, an important crossing over the Colorado River in the desert of northern Arizona. Brother Johnson endured great challenges yet remained faithful his entire life. Listen to Brother Johnson explain his family tragedy in a letter to President Wilford Woodruff:

"In May 1891 a family . . . came [to Lee's Ferry] from Richfield, Utah, where they . . . spent the winter visiting friends. At Panguitch they buried a child, . . . without [cleaning] the wagon or themselves. . . . They came to our house, and remained overnight, mingling with my little children. . . .

"We knew nothing of the nature of the disease [diphtheria], but had faith in God, as we were here on a very hard mission, and had tried as hard as we knew how to obey the [commandments] . . . that our children would be spared. But alas, in four and a half days [the oldest boy died] in my arms. Two more were taken down with the disease and we fasted and prayed as much as we thought it wisdom as we had many duties to perform here. We fasted [for] twenty-four hours and once I fasted [for] forty hours, but to no avail, for both my little girls died also. About a week after their death my fifteen-year-old daughter Melinda was [also] stricken down and we did all we could for her but she [soon] followed the others. . . . Three of my dear girls and one boy [have] been taken from us, and the end is not yet. My oldest girl nineteen years old is now prostrate [from] the disease, and we are fasting and praying in her behalf today. . . . I would ask for your faith and prayers in our behalf however. What have we done that the Lord has left us, and what can we do to gain his favor again[?}"

A short time later, Brother Johnson wrote a local leader and friend, expressing his faith to press on:

"It is the hardest trial of my life, but I set out for salvation and am determined that . . . through the help of Heavenly Father that I [would] hold fast to the iron rod no matter what troubles [came] upon me. I have not slackened in the performance of my duties, and hope and trust that I shall have the faith and prayers of my brethren, that I can live so as to receive the blessings."

(Joseph B. Wirthlin, in Conference Report, Oct. 2004 [Salt Lake City: The Church of Jesus Christ of Latter-day Saints, 2004], 109)

Mosiah 17 • ABINADI'S DEATH
(Refer in this text to Alma 24:20–24.)

Abinadi may have felt like a failure because he only had one convert.

(Joseph B. Wirthlin, in Conference Report, Apr. 1989 [Salt Lake City: The Church of Jesus Christ of Latter-day Saints, 1989], 11)

It is not easy to die, even to die for one's testimony, but the taste of death is so much sweeter to those whose lives bear fervent witness of Him whose servants they are. Occasionally in the overall scheme of things the Lord asks certain of his representatives to shed their own blood in a martyr's death, that their testament might be in full force (see D&C 135:5; Heb. 9:16–17).

(Robert Millet, CES Symposium, Aug. 1986, 103)

Consider yourself in that same circumstance [as Abinadi]. Would there not have been a flood of emotion pour over your body? Would there not have been, if only for a moment, a touch of panic, a desire to flee, a hope that the heavens would open and rescue would come? . . . Would you not then have seized upon the words "unless thou wilt recall all the words which thou has spoken evil concerning me and my people" [Mosiah 17:8] as the hoped-for route of escape? Would not most of us have sought to find some manner of taking advantage of that opportunity to avoid the sentence of death? Under circumstances such as that, it would not seem too difficult to clothe in respectability the desire to live by simply considering all of the good which you could continue to do if your life were prolonged, and contemplating how you might "recall all the words" in such an equivocal way as to still leave intact the teachings which you had sought to impart. . . .

While his martyrdom, described as having been "death by fire," would undoubtedly have been a physically painful experience, it is my thought that Abinadi's moment of supreme triumph occurred in those moments when he formed the phrase: "I will not recall the words which I have spoken" (Mosiah 17:9). . . .

One almost has to wonder how someone like Abinadi would feel if he were to hear some of the excuses we use for failing to do what the Lord has asked. Can you see yourself trying to explain to him why it is that you haven't been able to share the gospel with others? Why you are less than totally obedient? Or how, having taken the covenants of marriage, you can justify treating your husband or wife in less than a loving and nurturing way?

(Cree-L Kofford, *Heroes from the Book of Mormon* [Salt Lake City: Bookcraft, 1995], 71–72)

———————

The power of the priesthood is limitless but God has wisely placed upon each of us certain limitations. I may develop priesthood power as I perfect my life, yet I am grateful that even through the priesthood I cannot heal all the sick. I might heal people who should die. I might relieve people of suffering who should suffer. I fear I would frustrate the purposes of God.

Had I limitless power, and yet limited vision and understanding, I might have saved Abinadi from the flames of fire when he was burned at the stake, and in doing so I might have irreparably damaged him. He died a martyr and went to a martyr's reward—exaltation.

(Spencer W. Kimball, *Faith Precedes the Miracle* [Salt Lake City: Deseret Book, 1973], 99)

Mosiah 17:2–3 • ALMA (THE NAME)

The appearance of the two men named *Alma* in the Book of Mormon has occasioned much comment from critics. They observe that *Alma* is a woman's name and Latin rather than Hebrew. (Many recognize the phrase *alma mater*, which means "beneficent mother" and refers to the school from which someone has graduated.) They are correct, of course. If Joseph Smith knew the name *Alma* at all in the early 19th century, he would have known it as a woman's name in Latin. Recent documentary finds demonstrate, however, that *Alma* also occurs as a Semitic masculine personal name in the ancient Near East—just as it does in the Book of Mormon.

(Daniel C. Peterson, *Ensign*, Jan. 2000 [Salt Lake City: The Church of Jesus Christ of Latter-day Saints, 2000], 21)

Mosiah 17:4 • WRITE THE WORDS OF ABINADI

It is possible that some of the passages Mormon gives us were not taken from any written record but were revealed directly to him. For example, we know we receive the major portion of Abinadi's preaching from Alma's account of it (Mosiah 17:4). But who recorded Abinadi's final testimony after Alma had fled from Noah's assassins? Perhaps some bystander preserved it (or even some court recorder taking minutes of the execution), but perhaps, too, it was revealed directly to Mormon or another historian.

(Jeffrey R. Holland, *The Book of Mormon: It Begins with a Family* [Salt Lake City: Deseret Book, 1983] 225)

Mosiah 17:11–13 • PEER PRESSURE
(Refer in this text to Alma 39:4; 1 Nephi 8:25.)

I am so grateful that prophets do not crave popularity.

(Spencer W. Kimball, in Conference Report, Apr. 1978 [Salt Lake City: The Church of Jesus Christ of Latter-day Saints, 1978], 116–117)

———————

My husband said he still remembers going to his first examination at the University of Utah. . . . As the professor passed out the examination and left the room, he said some classmates started to pull out little cheat papers from pockets and from under their books. He said, "My heart began to pound as I realized how difficult it is to compete with cheaters." . . . About then a tall, thin student stood up in the back of the room and said, "I sold my farm and put my wife and three little children in an upstairs apartment to go to medical school, and I'll turn in the first one of you who cheats and YOU BETTER BELIEVE IT!" They believed it. My husband said he looked like Abraham Lincoln. There were many sheepish expressions and those cheat papers started to disappear as fast as they had appeared. . . . That man cared more about character than popularity. When I heard the name of J. Ballard Washburn to be sustained as a member of the Quorum of Seventy, I remembered that he was that medical student.

(Janette C. Hales, BYU Devotional, 16 Mar. 1993)

———————

[To the young women], Choose your friends with caution. In a survey made in selected wards and stakes of the Church, we learned a most significant fact: those persons whose friends married in the temple usually married in the temple, while those persons whose friends did not marry in the temple usually did not marry in the temple. The influence of one's friends appeared to be a highly dominant factor—even more so than parental urging, classroom instruction, or proximity to a temple.

(Thomas S. Monson, *Ensign*, May 1997 [Salt Lake City: The Church of Jesus Christ of Latter-day Saints, 1997], 94–95)

———————

Individuals who do wrong want you to join them because they feel more comfortable in what they are doing when others do it also. They may also want to take advantage of you. It is natural to want to be accepted by peers, to be part of a group—some even join gangs because of that desire to belong, but they lose their freedom, and some lose their lives. . . . You don't need to compromise your standards to be accepted by good friends. . . . No one intends to make serious mistakes. They come when you compromise your standards to be more accepted by others.

(Richard G. Scott, *Ensign*, Nov. 1994 [Salt Lake City: The Church of Jesus Christ of Latter-day Saints, 1994], 37)

———————

The year my schoolmates and I enrolled in junior high, the building could not accommodate all of the students, and it was determined that our seventh-grade class would be sent back to our old grade school.

We were insulted. We were furious. We'd spent six years in that grade-school building, and we were ready to move on. We were above going to school one more year with the younger grades. We felt we deserved something better. . . . We decided that we wouldn't tolerate this kind of treatment and that we should show our displeasure by going on strike.

The next day, we did not show up for school. But we had no place to go. . . . So we just wandered about and wasted the day.

The next morning, the principal, Mr. Stearns, whose demeanor matched the sound of his name, was at the front door of the grade school to greet us as we entered. He said some fairly straightforward things and then told us that we could not come back to school until we brought a note from our parents. . . . There was only one thing to do: go home and get the note.

I will never forget walking sheepishly into the house. Mother was, of course, surprised to see me and asked what was wrong. I told her what I had done and explained that I needed a note. She wrote this brief note, the most stinging rebuke she ever gave me:

Dear Mr. Stearns,

Please excuse Gordon's absence yesterday. His action was simply an impulse to follow the crowd. . . .

I resolved then and there that I would never do anything in which I was simply following the crowd. I determined that I would make my own decisions on the basis of their merits and my standards, and would not be pushed in one direction or another by those around me.

(Gordon B. Hinckley, *Standing for Something* [New York: Times Books, 2000], 13–14)

Mosiah 18:4, 16 • A PLACE CALLED MORMON

The word Mormon is used chronologically for the first time in Mosiah 18:4. Although the word appears earlier than this in the Book of Mormon it has always referred to the name of the great prophet, historian, and military leader who lived several hundred years after the time of Christ. The place called "Mormon" referred to in Mosiah 18:4 received its name "from the king." No further information is given concerning this king.

(Daniel H. Ludlow, *A Companion to Your Study of the Book of Mormon* [Salt Lake City: Deseret Book, 1976], 187–188)

Mosiah 18:8 • MOURN WITH THOSE WHO MOURN . . . BEAR ONE ANOTHER'S BURDENS

Every kind word spoken gives you greater ability to speak another. Every act of assistance rendered by you, through the knowledge that you possess, to aid one of your fellows, gives you greater ability to aid the next one. Good acts grow upon a person. I have sometimes thought that many men, judging from their utter lack of kindness and of a disposition to aid others, imagined that if they were to say or do a kind thing, it would destroy their capacity to perform a kind act or say a kind word in the future. If you have a granary full of grain, and you give away a sack or two, there remain that many less in your granary, but if you perform a kind act or add words of encouragement to one in distress, who is struggling along in the battle of life, the greater is your capacity to do this in the future. Don't go through life with your lips sealed against words of kindness and encouragement, nor your hearts sealed against performing labors for another. Make a motto in life: always try and assist someone else to carry his burden.

(*Teachings of President of the Church—Heber J. Grant* [Salt Lake City: The Church of Jesus Christ of Latter-day Saints, 2002], 143)

———————

Someone has said that people would rather be understood than be loved. In truth, the surest way to increase our love for someone is to listen with patience and respect. I believe that our baptismal covenant demands this. How can we "mourn with those that mourn" and "bear one another's burdens" (Mosiah 18:8–9) if we don't listen to know what those burdens are? . . . But we must be careful not to listen as Laman and Lemuel listened to each other. They encouraged mutual murmuring. When fellow ward members complain, blame others, and repeat negative tales, it takes self-discipline to stop ourselves from adding more fuel to their fire of disgruntlement. Mutual murmuring is a smoldering fire that can burst into flame and destroy a ward.

(Virginia H. Pearce, *Ensign*, Nov. 1993 [Salt Lake City: The Church of Jesus Christ of Latter-day Saints, 1993], 80)

Mosiah 18:9 • STAND AS A WITNESS

I often . . . ask what it means . . . to "stand as witnesses of God at all time and in all things, and in all places" I believe it means that we show by our behavior what we believe. Surley we are standing as witnesses of God when we sustain his living prophets, especially when we know what it means to sustain. We will abide by the direction and counsel of the prophets. We indeed become witnesses when we make this solemn covenant."

(Janette Hales Beckham, *Ensign*, May 1996 [Salt Lake City: The Church of Jesus Christ of Latter-day Saints, 1996], 84)

———————

When we covenant in the waters of baptism to "stand as witnesses of God at all times and in all things, and in all places," . . . It may not always be easy, convenient, or politically correct to stand for truth and right, but it is always the right thing to do. Always. . . . Today's young people, just as those "of the rising generation" (3 Ne. 1:30) in Book of Mormon times, are the most susceptible to the influence of gangs. . . . There is an entire subculture that celebrates contemporary gangs and their criminal conduct with music, clothing styles, language, attitudes, and behaviors. Many of you have watched as trendy friends have embraced the style as something that was 'fashionable' and 'cool,' only to be dragged into the subculture because of their identification with gangs. We've all heard the tragic stories of unsuspecting wannabes who have been victimized by gangs simply because they were wearing the wrong color in the wrong neighborhood. . . . Many of you young men of the Aaronic Priesthood may find yourself on the front line of a battle against those who intend to do things that are morally wrong. I do not believe that you can stand for truth and right while wearing anything that is unbecoming one who holds the priesthood of God. To me, it is impossible to maintain the Spirit of the Lord while listening to music or watching movies or videos that celebrate evil thoughts and use vulgar language.

(M. Russell Ballard, *Ensign*, Nov. 1997 [Salt Lake City: The Church of Jesus Christ of Latter-day Saints, 1997], 37–39)

———————

It will not be enough for anyone who desires a sense of fulfillment and purpose to be an able lawyer, a practitioner of medicine, a skilled architect, a proficient engineer, or whatever. We need another dimension in our lives, a compelling need and drive within each of us to feel that somehow, somewhere we have made a difference—that our lives have mattered.

It is not enough just to be good. We must be good for something. We must contribute good to the world. The world must be a better place for our presence. And the good that is in us must be spread to others. . . .

We can become involved and speak with a strong voice for that which is right and good.

(Gordon B. Hinckley, *Standing for Something* [New York: Times Books, 2000], 58)

———————

An experience . . . [President Hinckley] had in Korea at a servicemen's retreat:

"I have been in many inspirational meetings in my life . . . but I think I have never been in a more inspirational meeting than one I attended in Korea. . . . The bread of the sacrament was administered that morning. . . .

"Then the water was administered to us by a sergeant who in his testimony afterwards said, 'I grew up on the banks of the Susquehanna River and I almost inherited a hatred for the Mormons. I discovered when I was in the barracks in Korea that the man who was in the bunk next to mine was reading the Book of Mormon and I went over and started ribbing him. . . . I was mean and I was nasty. One night he got up out of his bed when I was saying something . . . and I have never seen a man stand so tall in all my life. And he held out the book and he said, "Have you ever read it?" I said, "No, of course not." And he said, "Here it is! Now you read it and you keep your mouth shut until you are through reading it and then we will talk about it." I didn't know what else to do—and I took it. And I began to read it, and as I read it, the Spirit of the Lord bore witness to me that it was true. And now I know why I was sent to Korea."

(Gordon B. Hinckley, *Go Forward with Faith* [Salt Lake City: Deseret Book, 1996], 286)

———————

Many years ago, Brigham Young told of an early missionary in the Church who was asked to share his testimony with a large group of people. According to President Young, this particular elder "never had been able to say that he knew Joseph [Smith] was a Prophet." He would have preferred to just say a prayer and leave, but the circumstances made that impossible. So he started to speak, and "as soon as he got 'Joseph' out, 'is a Prophet,' was . . . next; and from that, his tongue was loosened, and he continued talking until near sundown."

President Young used this experience to teach that "the Lord pours out His Spirit upon a man, when he testifies that [which] the Lord gives him to testify of" (*Millennial Star*, supplement, 1853, 30).

(M. Russell Ballard, in Conference Report, Oct. 2004 [Salt Lake City: The Church of Jesus Christ of Latter-day Saints, 2004], 44)

Mosiah 18:12 • HOLINESS OF HEART

Holiness is also a standard of righteousness. In some remarks by President Brigham Young in the Salt Lake Tabernacle, February 16, 1862, he used the expression

"Holiness to the Lord." He then further explained what "Holiness to the Lord" meant to him. I quote: "Thirty years' experience has taught me that every moment of my life must be holiness to the Lord, resulting from equity, justice, mercy and uprightness in all my actions, which is the only course by which I can preserve the Spirit of the Almighty to myself" (Deseret News, Apr. 2, 1862, 313).

(James E. Faust, *Ensign*, May 2005 [Salt Lake City: The Church of Jesus Christ of Latter-day Saints, 2005], 62, 68)

Mosiah 18:12–18 • WHERE DID ALMA GET HIS AUTHORITY? WAS ALMA BAPTIZING HIMSELF AT THIS TIME?

Alma was baptized and held the priesthood before the coming of Abinadi, but he became involved with other priests under the reign of the wicked King Noah, and when he baptized Helam, he felt he needed a cleansing himself so he buried himself in the water as a token of full repentance.

(Joseph Fielding Smith, *Doctrines of Salvation* [Salt Lake City: Bookcraft, 1955], 2:336–337)

We may conclude that Alma held the priesthood before he, with others, became disturbed with King Noah. . . . If he had authority to baptize that is evidence that he had been baptized. Therefore, when Alma baptized himself with Helam that was not a case of Alma baptizing himself, but merely as a token to the Lord of his humility and full repentance. . . . If I remember correctly, there is no reference to the baptism of Alma the elder or Helaman nor of Nephi and his brother Jacob, but we know they were baptized as were all the faithful members in the Church.

(Joseph Fielding Smith, *Answers to Gospel Questions* [Salt Lake City: Deseret Book, 1960], 3:203–204)

Mosiah 21:7, 11–12, 14–16 • LAMANITES NOT THE REAL ENEMY TO THE NEPHITES
(Refer in this text to Alma 53:8–9.)

In his book, *Caesar and Christ*, Will Durant, in summarizing the causes of the destruction of the Roman Empire, stated: "A great civilization is not conquered from without until it has destroyed itself within. The essential causes of Rome's decline lay in her people, her morals, her class struggle, her failing trade, her bureaucratic despotism, her stifling taxes, her consuming wars. . . .

(Ezra Taft Benson, *An Enemy Hath Done This*, comp. by Jerreld L. Newquist [Salt Lake City: Parliament Publishers, 1969], ix)

Mosiah 22:14 • MORE RECORDS

The early history contained in the Book of Mormon is obtained from three sets of plates: the brass plates of Laban, the small plates of Nephi, and the large plates of Nephi. However, when Limhi's people join with the people of King Mosiah in the land of Zarahemla they bring with them two additional sets of plates: (1) their own records, which are known as the record of Zeniff, and (2) the 'records which had been found by the people of Limhi,' which are later identified as the records of Ether (see Ether 1:1–2). When Alma and his people come into the land of Zarahemla, they also evidently bring their own records with them (see Mosiah 25:6).

(Daniel H. Ludlow, *Companion to Your Study of the Book of Mormon* [Salt Lake City: Deseret Book, 1976], 188)

Mosiah 23:4 • CAUGHT IN A SNARE

If you imagine that your prior sins, character flaws, and poor decisions prevent you from receiving all of God's blessings, consider the experience of Alma the Elder. Referring to his younger years as an immoral priest for the wicked King Noah, Alma admitted, "I myself was caught in a snare, and did many things which were abominable in the sight of the Lord, which caused me sore repentance" (Mosiah 23:9). Yet Alma's repentance was so complete and Christ's Atonement so infinite that Alma became a prophet and was promised eternal life (see Mosiah 26:20). As you do your best to be obedient and repentant, you too can receive a place in the celestial kingdom through the Atonement and grace of Jesus Christ (see Titus 3:7; 1 Peter 5:10; 2 Nephi 2:6–8; 10:24–25; 25:23; Enos 1:27; Moroni 7:41; D&C 138:14).

(Anthony D. Perkins, *Ensign*, Nov. 2006 [Salt Lake City: The Church of Jesus Christ of Latter-day Saints, 2006], 78)

Mosiah 23:21 • HE TRIETH THEIR PATIENCE AND FAITH
(Refer in this text to Alma 34:40–41.)

When a worthy priesthood bearers is led to pronounce specific blessings, we can be greatly comforted. Yet there is no guarantee of outcome without effort on our part. . . . We must do our part for the blessing to be realized. We must strive to be worthy and to exercise the requisite faith to do what we are able. . . . It is through the combination of our doing what is within our power to accomplish and the power of the Lord that the blessing is realized. . . .

A relative asked Elder Spencer W. Kimball for a blessing to combat a crippling disease. For some time Elder Kimball prepared himself spiritually; then, fasting, he was prompted to bless her to be healed. Some weeks later she returned, angry and complaining that she was "fed up" with waiting for the Lord to give the promised relief.

He responded: "Now I understand why you have not been blessed. You must be patient, do your part, and express gratitude for the smallest improvement noted."

She repented, followed scrupulously his counsel, and eventually was made well.

(Richard G. Scott, in Conference Report, Oct. 1991 [Salt Lake City: The Church of Jesus Christ of Latter-day Saints, 1991], 116–117)

Patience is not indifference. Actually, it is caring very much, but being willing, nevertheless, to submit both to the Lord and to what the scriptures call the "process of time."

Patience is tied very closely to faith in our Heavenly Father. Actually, when we are unduly impatient, we are suggesting that we know what is best—better than does God. Or, at least, we are asserting that our timetable is better than his. . . .

We read in Mosiah about how the Lord simultaneously tries the patience of his people even as he tries their faith (see Mosiah 23:21). One is not only to endure—but to endure well and gracefully those things which the Lord "seeth fit to inflict upon [us]" (Mosiah 3:19), just as did a group of ancient American Saints who were bearing unusual burdens but who submitted "cheerfully and with patience to all the will of the Lord" (Mosiah 24:15). . . .

Sometimes that which we are doing is correct enough but simply needs to be persisted in—patiently—not for a minute or a moment but sometimes for years. . . .

Patience is a willingness, in a sense, to watch the unfolding purposes of God with a sense of wonder and awe—rather than pacing up and down within the cell of our circumstance.

Too much anxious opening of the oven door and the cake falls instead of rising! So it is with us. If we are always selfishly taking our temperature to see if we are happy, we won't be. . . .

Whereas faith and patience are companions, so are selfishness and impatience. . . .

Patience is, therefore, clearly not fatalistic, shoulder-shrugging resignation; it is accepting a divine rhythm to life; it is obedience prolonged. Patience stoutly resists pulling up the daisies to see how the roots are doing!

(Neal A. Maxwell, *Ensign*, Oct. 1980 [Salt Lake City: The Church of Jesus Christ of Latter-day Saints, 1980], 28–30)

Recently I attended the funeral of a lifelong friend. His son told a beautiful story of parental patience. When the son was in his youth, his dad owned a motorcycle dealership. One day they received a shipment of shiny new motorcycles, and they lined them all up in the store. The boy did what every boy would like to do, and he climbed up on the closest one. He even started it up. Then, when he figured he had pushed his luck far enough, he jumped off. To his dismay, his dismount knocked the first bike down. Then, like a string of dominoes, they all went down, one after another. His dad heard the commotion and looked out from behind the partition where he was working. Slowly, smiling, he said, "Well, son, we had better fix one up and sell it, so we can pay for the rest of them."

I think my friend's response personifies parental patience.

Patience may well be thought of as a gateway virtue, contributing to the growth and strength of its fellow virtues of forgiveness, tolerance, and faith.

(Robert C. Oaks, *Ensign*, Nov. 2006 [Salt Lake City: The Church of Jesus Christ of Latter-day Saints, 2006], 16)

Mosiah 24:12 • POUR OUT THEIR HEARTS

Heavenly Father not only expects but also encourages us to plead with Him over our challenges. Our pleading is not a sign of weakness, but can reflect thoughtful submissiveness. Indeed, Jesus, who knew clearly what He faced in Gethsemane and on Calvary, nevertheless pleaded with the Lord for the cup to be removed from Him. Therefore it is what we do, during and after the pleading, that matters, especially as to our submissiveness to the Lord. But pleadings are appropriate.

(Neal A. Maxwell, *One More Strain of Praise* [Salt Lake City: Bookcraft, 1999], 8)

Mosiah 24:12 • HE DID KNOW THE THOUGHTS OF THEIR HEARTS

Satan and his followers, who have been cast out of God's presence and are dead to His spirit, are excluded from . . . the thoughts and the intents of our hearts. So, in his wisdom and mercy, God has provided a channel of communication between him and his children on earth that Satan, our common enemy, cannot invade. This is the channel of secret prayer. The significance of this to the Latter-day Saint is profound, for by this means we are able to communicate with our Heavenly Father in secrecy, confident that the adversary cannot intrude.

(Francis M. Gibbons, *Ensign*, Nov. 1991 [Salt Lake City: The Church of Jesus Christ of Latter-day Saints, 1991], 78–79)

Mosiah 24:14–15 • BURDENS EASED, THEY DID SUBMIT CHEERFULLY & WITH PATIENCE
(Refer in this text to Alma 14:11; Alma 34:40–41.)

Elder Clinton Cutler said . . . "The Lord's peace

comes not without pain, but in the midst of pain."

(Rex D. Pinegar, *Ensign*, May 1993 [Salt Lake City: The Church of Jesus Christ of Latter-day Saints, 1993], 66)

Of course the greatest trial I have is that I cannot hear, but I have so many blessings I cannot complain, but if we only will live so that we may receive the instructions of God, there is nothing we are called to pass through but will be for our good.

(Rachel Ivins Grant; as quoted in Russell M. Nelson, *Ensign*, May 1991 [Salt Lake City: The Church of Jesus Christ of Latter-day Saints, 1991], 22–25)

I do not desire trials. I do not desire affliction. . . . I used to think, if I were the Lord, I would not suffer people to be tried as they are. But I have changed my mind on that subject. Now I think I would, if I were the Lord, because it purges out the meanness and corruption that stick around the Saints, like flies around molasses. . . . I have seen men tempted so sorely that finally they would say, "I'll be damned if I'll stand it any longer." Well, you will be damned if you do not. . . . We have learned many things through suffering. We call it suffering. I call it a school of experience.

(John Taylor, *The Gospel Kingdom*, ed. by G. Homer Durham [Salt Lake City: Bookcraft, 1987], 332–334)

I rejoice in afflictions, for they are necessary to humble and prove us, that we may comprehend ourselves, become acquainted with our weaknesses and infirmities; and I rejoice when I triumph over them, because God answers my prayers, therefore I feel to rejoice all the day long.

(Brigham Young, *Journal of Discourses* [London: Latter-day Saints' Book Depot, 1855], 1:17)

[Mary Fielding Smith gave details of her trials at Far West in a letter to her non-member brother in England] I do not feel in the least discouraged. . . . We have been enabled to rejoice, in the midst of our privations and persecutions, that we were counted worthy to suffer these things, so that we may, with the ancient saints who suffered in like manner, inherit the same glorious reward. If it had not been for this hope, I should have sunk before this; but, blessed be the God and rock of my salvation, here I am, and am perfectly satisfied and happy, having not the smallest desire to go one step backward.

(Mary Fielding Smith [wife of Hyrum Smith]; as quoted in Don Cecil Corbett, *Mary Fielding Smith, Daughter of Britain* [Salt Lake City: Deseret Book, 1974], 100)

Concerning his personal suffering, Joseph was promised, "Thy heart shall be enlarged." An enlarged Joseph wrote from Liberty Jail, "It seems to me that my heart will always be more tender after this than ever it was before. . . . I think I never could have felt as I now do if I had not suffered."

(Neal A Maxwell, *Ensign*, May 1992, 39; quoting from *The Personal Writings of Joseph Smith*, Dean C. Jessee, 387)

[From Liberty Jail, in a time of anguish and deep suffering for the gospel's sake, the Prophet Joseph Smith wrote the following message to the Saints] Dear brethren, do not think that our hearts faint, as though some strange thing had happened unto us, for we have seen and been assured of all these things beforehand, and have an assurance of a better hope than that of our persecutors. Therefore God hath made broad our shoulders for the burden. We glory in our tribulation, because we know that God is with us, that He is our friend, and that He will save our souls.

(*Teachings of the Prophet Joseph Smith*, comp. by Joseph Fielding Smith [Salt Lake City: Deseret Book, 1976], 123)

Remember that this work is not yours and mine alone. It is the Lord's work, and when we are on the Lord's errand, we are entitled to the Lord's help. Remember that the Lord will shape the back to bear the burden placed upon it.

(Thomas S. Monson, *Ensign*, May 1992 [Salt Lake City: The Church of Jesus Christ of Latter-day Saints, 1992], 48)

Gratitude is a divine principle: "Thou shalt thank the Lord thy God in all things" (D&C 59:7). This scripture means that we express thankfulness for what happens, not only for the good things in life but also for the opposition and challenges of life that add to our experience and faith. We put our lives in His hands, realizing that all that transpires will be for our experience. When in prayer we say, "Thy will be done," we are really expressing faith and gratitude and acknowledging that we will accept whatever happens in our lives.

(Robert D. Hales, *Ensign*, May 1992 [Salt Lake City: The Church of Jesus Christ of Latter-day Saints, 1992], 65)

We should seek to be happy and cheerful and not allow Satan to overcome us with discouragement, despair, or depression. As President Benson said, "Of all people, we as Latter-day Saints should be the most optimistic and the least pessimistic" (*Ensign*, Oct. 1986, 2). . . . We need not feel depressed or discouraged about conditions in the world, for the Lord will help us find the good that will lead us to happiness. . . . Surely we live in troubled times, but we can seek and obtain the good despite Satan's temptations and snares. He cannot tempt us beyond our power to resist (see 1 Cor. 10:13).

(Joseph B. Wirthlin, *Ensign*, May 1990 [Salt Lake City: The Church of Jesus Christ of Latter-day Saints, 1990], 87–88)

Pay attention to what the Lord requires of you and let the balance go. He will take care of that if you will acknowledge His hand in all things. . . . Rejoice evermore, pray without ceasing, and in everything give thanks, even if you have nothing but buttermilk and potatoes.

(Brigham Young, *Journal of Discourses* [London: Latter-day Saints' Book Depot, 1856], 3:159)

If we are serious about our discipleship, Jesus will eventually request each of us to do those very things which are most difficult for us to do. . . .

Sometimes the best people have the worst experiences, because they are the most ready to learn.

(Neal A. Maxwell, *Church News*, 10 Aug. 2002 [Salt Lake City: The Church of Jesus Christ of Latter-day Saints)

There was a young college student who felt that his burden was much more than he could bear. In desperation, he decided the best alternative to his dilemma was to end his own life. He closed all the doors and windows of his garage with the intent of sitting in his car with the engine running. He had concluded that the result of such deliberate action would separate him from his troubles. After starting the vehicle, he settled into the front seat, waiting to expire.

For some reason, he looked down to his right between himself and the passenger seat. As he did so, his eyes fell upon a Book of Mormon that had been left there by one of his parents. He picked up this book that had been a stranger to him for so long. While it had always been around him, he had never been hungry enough to "sup" from its pages. He held it in his hands, letting it fall open without any textual destination in mind.

His eyes happened to fall upon one verse, which read, "And I will also ease the burdens which are put upon your shoulders, that even you cannot feel them upon your backs" (Mosiah 24:14). His desire to end his life was replaced with a hunger to find out if this promise was true. He recognized that this verse presented a divine alternative to his problems.

Quickly, he pressed the button on the garage door opener and backed the car out of the driveway. After clearing out his lungs, he followed an impression to drive to the office of a good man who had been his teacher. As he walked into the building, his youthful strides took him through the doorway of his teacher's office unannounced. Laying the book on the teacher's desk, he exposed the scripture that had caught his own eyes just minutes before. Pointing to Mosiah 24:14 he said, "Will Jesus do that for me?"

Hesitating long enough to read the verse, the teacher looked up from his desk, and proclaimed, "He certainly will."

To which the young man responded, "Can you tell me how?"

Thus began a change of heart and lifestyle that connected this young man to Christ. The months and years that have followed in his life bear witness to the change that is brought about for those who avail themselves to the gospel of Jesus Christ through the power of the Book of Mormon.

(Jack R. Christianson and K. Douglas Bassett, *Life Lessons from the Book of Mormon* [Salt Lake City: Deseret Book, 2003], 254–255)

Mosiah 24:14–15 • SUBMIT TO THE WILL OF THE LORD

The submission of one's will is really the only uniquely personal thing we have to place on God's altar. The many other things we "give," brothers and sisters, are actually the things He has already given or loaned to us. However, when you and I finally submit ourselves, by letting our individual wills be swallowed up in God's will, then we are really giving something to Him! It is the only possession which is truly ours to give!

(Neal A. Maxwell, in Conference Report, Oct. 1995 [Salt Lake City: The Church of Jesus Christ of Latter-day Saints, 1995], 30)

"Thy will be done," written in the heart, are the window to revelation.

(Henry B. Eyring, in Conference Report, Oct. 2002 [Salt Lake City: The Church of Jesus Christ of Latter-day Saints, 2002], 81)

I was thoroughly convinced in my own mind and

in my own heart, when my first wife left me by death, that it was the will of the Lord that she should be called away. . . .

About one hour before my wife died, I called my children into her room and told them that their mother was dying and for them to bid her good-bye. One of the little girls, about twelve years of age, said to me: "Papa, I do not want my mamma to die. I have been with you in the hospital in San Francisco for six months; time and time again when mamma was in distress you [have] administered to her and she has been relieved of her pain and quietly gone to sleep. I want you to lay hands upon my mamma and heal her."

I told my little girl that we all had to die sometime, and that I felt assured in my heart that her mother's time had arrived. She and the rest of the children left the room.

I then knelt down by the bed of my wife (who by this time had lost consciousness). . . . I told the Lord that I lacked the strength to have my wife die and to have it affect the faith of my little children in the ordinances of the gospel of Jesus Christ; and I supplicated the Lord with all the strength that I possessed, that He would give to that little girl of mine a knowledge that it was His mind and His will that her mamma should die.

Within an hour my wife passed away, and I called the children back into the room. My little boy about five and a half or six years of age was weeping bitterly, and the little girl twelve years of age took him in her arms and said: "Do not weep, do not cry, Heber; since we went out of this room the voice of the Lord from heaven has said to me, 'In the death of your mamma the will of the Lord shall be done.' "

Tell me, my friend, that I do not know that God hears and answers prayers! Tell me that I do not know that in the hour of adversity the Latter-day Saints are comforted and blessed and consoled as no other people are!

(*Teachings of Presidents of the Church—Heber J. Grant* [Salt Lake City: The Church of Jesus Christ of Latter-day Saints, 2002], 47–48)

_____

But we must understand that great challenges make great men. We don't seek tribulation, but if we respond in faith, the Lord strengthens us. The but if nots can become remarkable blessings. . . .

Our scriptures and our history are replete with accounts of God's great men and women who believed that He would deliver them, but if not, they demonstrated that they would trust and be true.

He has the power, but it's our test. . . .

Our God will deliver us from ridicule and persecution, but if not. . . . Our God will deliver us from sickness and disease, but if not. . . . He will deliver us from loneliness, depression, or fear, but if not. . . . Our God will deliver us from threats, accusations, and insecurity, but if not. . . . He will deliver us from death or impairment of loved ones, but if not, . . . we will trust in the Lord.

Our God will see that we receive justice and fairness, but if not. . . . He will make sure that we are loved and recognized, but if not. . . . We will receive a perfect companion and righteous and obedient children, but if not, . . . we will have faith in the Lord Jesus Christ knowing that if we do all we can do, we will in His time and in His way, be delivered and receive all that He has (D&C 84:35–38).

(Dennis E. Simmons, *Ensign*, May 2004 [Salt Lake City: The Church of Jesus Christ of Latter-day Saints, 2004], 73–75)

_____

(Luke 22:42). It appears that he did not seek to die on the cross, but he did want to do the will of the Father.

I learned this lesson from my father at a very early age. My dad was smarter than I was when I was seven years old. Of course, I was smarter than he was when I was seventeen, but that changed later, too. He said to me one time, "You are not big enough to milk the cows."

Now, I knew I was. I was seven years old, and I knew I could milk the cows. So I proved to him that I could.

My dad said, "You know, I believe you can milk. You've got the job." For the next ten years I milked eight to twelve cows night and morning. You may rest assured I got to the place where I did not want to milk, and once I said to Dad, "Dad, I don't want to milk." He said, "That's all right. You don't have to want to—as long as you do it." This seems to be what the Lord says to us at times when the going gets rough and we feel—"I really don't want to go to the temple," or "It is inconvenient to pay tithing," or "I don't want to go home teaching."

(Hartman Rector, Jr., in Conference Report, Oct. 1985 [Salt Lake City: The Church of Jesus Christ of Latter-day Saints, 1985], 96)

_____

We learn, then, that through repentance the earlier sorrow and darkness are transformed into joy and light. . . .

With that wonderful transformation comes another intriguing, even more revealing, change. . . .

Not only does our spiritual record change and our physical life become clean, but also our very desires are purified and made whole. Our will quite literally changes to receive His will.

(Jeffrey R. Holland, *The Book of Mormon: It Begins with a Family* [Salt Lake City: Deseret Book, 1983], 98–99)

———————

A person with the "my will" attitude in working with the Lord during life's challenges may view each of life's adversities, trials, or tragedies as a painful obstacle, an insurmountable wall, with God's role in the process being to remove this negative intrusion from the path. In the "my will" approach to prayer, Heavenly Father is viewed as a kind of spiritual Santa Claus. Just as St. Nick is called upon only in one particular season each year, so the "my will" attitude approaches God only in the season of affliction. Once the trial has passed, the person carries on with life, approaching God only when the brick wall of adversity looms again in the path.

Many children understand that each yuletide season, the key to receiving Santa's richest blessings is to be able to sit on his lap and say, "I've been good." Santa gives his gifts based on whether a child has been naughty or nice. The "my will" approach to opposition assumes that the person's role is to keep the commandments, and that God's gift for those who have been obedient (or "nice" in Santa terminology) is simply to make "it" (meaning adversity) go away.

When taken to the extreme, this spiritually warped view assumes that a spiritual Santa's greatest gifts come in the packages called health, wealth, worldly success, business security, and the total acceptance and appreciation of others. If this were true, then people such as Jesus Christ and Joseph Smith received few blessings from their Father in Heaven. . . .

The positive side of this two-sided coin could be termed the "thy will" approach in working with our Heavenly Father regarding life's opposition. This consecrated attitude is similar to the "my will" attitude only in that adversity, trials, or tragedies may also be seen as walls looming in the path ahead. The difference for the "thy will" person is that, with the Lord's help, the wall is not identified as being insurmountable. The view of the "thy will" person is proactive or solution oriented as opposed to the reactive nature of the "my will" mentality. But the basic difference is in a person's willingness to scale or even endure the obstacle with the help of the Lord. Any event of opposition or tragedy is dealt with by approaching Heavenly Father for strength and understanding, always seeking to recognize his will in the process. This view accepts that God's role is that of the trusted Father in Heaven, who will allow us to be tested in our best interest, with the promise that we will not be tested more than we are able to bear (see 1 Corinthians 10:13).

The "thy will" view of life's challenges and even tragedies assumes that growth often comes in the midst of the struggle, and that inner peace in mortality is obtained through commitment and consecration. However, this perspective does not rob us of initiative or agency.

The fundamental difference in this attitude, as compared to the "my will" perspective, is the willingness on the part of the person to place total trust in our Heavenly Father and his timing. The "thy will" view sees life as being more than just life here in mortality, and while the Lord may see fit to make an obstacle in life's path just go away, that is the Lord's option rather than the constant expectation on the part of the individual.

Incorporated in this concept is the doctrine of enduring to the end, which assumes the notion of being "willing to submit to all things which the Lord seeth fit to inflict upon him, even as a child doth submit to his father" (Mosiah 3:19).

(Jack R. Christianson and K. Douglas Bassett, *Life Lessons from the Book of Mormon* [Salt Lake City: Deseret Book, 2003], 151–153)

———————

We pit our will against God's. When we direct our pride toward God, it is in the spirit of my will and not thine be done. . . . The proud wish God would agree with them. They aren't interested in changing their opinions to agree with God's.

(Ezra Taft Benson, *Ensign*, May 1989 [Salt Lake City: The Church of Jesus Christ of Latter-day Saints, 1989], 4)

———————

If our spirits are inclined to be stiff and refractory, and we desire continually the gratification of our own will to the extent that this feeling prevails in us, the Spirit of the Lord is held at a distance from us; or, in other words, the Father withholds his Spirit from us in proportion as we desire the gratification of our own will"

(Erastus Snow, *Journal of Discourses* [London: Latter-day Saints' Book Depot, 1860], 7:352)

———————

We must learn to pray with meaning, "Not my will, but Thy will be done." When you are able to do this, his whisperings to you will be loud and clear. The Prophet Joseph Smith, after five months of extreme suffering in the dungeon of Liberty Jail, experienced it and he said, "When the heart is *sufficiently contrite*, then the voice of inspiration steals along and whispers, My son peace be unto thy soul" (*History of the Church*, 3:293; italics added).

(Graham W. Doxey, in Conference Report, Oct. 1991 [Salt Lake City: The Church of Jesus Christ of Latter-day Saints, 1991], 34)

Sadness, disappointment, severe challenges are events in life, not life itself. . . . A pebble held close to the eye appears to be a gigantic obstacle. Cast on the ground, it is seen in perspective. Likewise, problems or trials in our lives need to be viewed in the perspective of scriptural doctrine. . . . Some people are like rocks thrown into a sea of problems. They are drowned by them. Be a cork. When submerged in a problem, fight to be free to bob up to serve again with happiness. . . . Progress is accelerated when you willingly allow Him to lead you through every growth experience you encounter. . . . When you trust in the Lord, when you are willing to let your heart and your mind be centered in His will, when you ask to be led by the Spirit to do His will, you are assured of the greatest happiness along the way. . . . If you question everything you are asked to do, or dig in your heels at every unpleasant challenge, you make it harder for the Lord to bless you.

(Richard G. Scott, *Ensign*, May 1996 [Salt Lake City: The Church of Jesus Christ of Latter-day Saints, 1996], 24–25)

Only by aligning our wills with God's is full happiness to be found. Anything less results in a lesser portion. So many of us are kept from eventual consecration because we mistakenly think that, somehow, by letting our will be swallowed up in the will of God, we lose our individuality. It is not a question of one's losing identity but of finding his true identity! As one's will is increasingly submissive to the will of God, he can receive inspiration and revelation so much needed to help meet the trials of life. . . . Consecration, likewise, is not shoulder-shrugging acceptance, but, instead, shoulder-squaring to better bear the yoke. God seeks to have us become more consecrated by giving up everything. Then, when we come home to Him, He will generously give us "all that He hath" (see D&C 84:38). . . . The submission of one's will is really the only uniquely personal thing we have to place on God's altar. The many other things we "give," . . . are actually the things He has already given or loaned to us. However, when you and I finally submit ourselves, by letting our individual wills be swallowed up in God's will, then we are really giving something to Him! It is the only possession which is truly ours to give!

(Neal A. Maxwell, *Ensign*, Nov. 1995 [Salt Lake City: The Church of Jesus Christ of Latter-day Saints, 1995], 23–24)

Recently I met with a family who had lost a precious son through an unfortunate automobile accident. They wondered when the comforting spirit of the Holy Ghost would envelop them to sustain them. My counsel was that when they were prepared to say to the Lord, "Thy will be done," then would come the sweet peace which the Savior promised. This willing submission to the Father is what the Savior exemplified in the Garden of Gethsemane.

(James E. Faust, *Ensign*, Nov. 1996 [Salt Lake City: The Church of Jesus Christ of Latter-day Saints, 1996], 96)

Whatever happens in the life of a person, if his attitude is right, the Lord will work that experience for that person's good.

(Dennis B. Neuenschwander, Faculty Inservice, Orem Institute of Religion, Dec. 14, 1996)

It takes great faith and courage to pray to our Heavenly Father, "Not as I will, but as thou wilt." The faith to believe in the Lord and endure brings great strength. Some may say if we have enough faith, we can sometimes change the circumstances that are causing our trials and tribulations. Is our faith to change circumstances, or is it to endure them? Faithful prayers may be offered to change or moderate events in our life, but we must always remember that when concluding each prayer, there is an understanding: 'Thy will be done' (Matt. 26:42). Faith in the Lord includes trust in the Lord. The faith to endure well is faith based upon accepting the Lord's will and the lessons learned in the events that transpire.

(Robert D. Hales, *Ensign*, May 1998 [Salt Lake City: The Church of Jesus Christ of Latter-day Saints, 1998], 77)

Our capacity to love and our capacity to endure well are inextricably bound together! Real faith in God, therefore, includes not only faith in Him, but in His timing—one of the things most difficult for us to have faith in.

(Neal A. Maxwell, BYU Devotional, 12 Dec. 1984)

Healing blessings come in many ways, each suited to our individual needs, as known to Him who loves us best. Sometimes a "healing" cures our illness or lifts our burden. But sometimes we are "healed" by being given strength or understanding or patience to bear the burdens placed upon us. . . . (Mosiah 24:14). In that case the people did not have their burdens removed, but the Lord strengthened them so that "they could bear up their burdens with ease, and they did submit cheerfully and with patience to all the will of the Lord" (v. 15).

This same promise and effect applies to you mothers who are widowed or divorced, to you singles who are lonely, to you caregivers who are burdened, to you persons who are addicted, and to all of us whatever our burden.

(Dallin H. Oaks, *Ensign*, Nov. 2006 [Salt Lake City: The Church of Jesus Christ of Latter-day Saints, 2006], 7–8)

Mosiah 25:12 • CONDUCT OF THEIR FATHER
(Refer in this text to 2 Nephi 4:6.)

One of the greatest things a man can do for his children is to love his wife and let them know he loves her. A father has the responsibility to lead his family by desiring to have children, loving them, and by letting virtue garnish his thoughts unceasingly (see D&C 121:45). This is one of the great needs today.

(Ezra Taft Benson, *God, Family, Country* [Salt Lake City: Deseret Book, 1974], 185)

Husbands and wives who love each other will find that love and loyalty are reciprocated. This love will provide a nurturing atmosphere for the emotional growth of children. Family life should be a time of happiness and joy that children can look back on with fond memories and associations.

(Ezra Taft Benson, in Conference Report, Oct. 1982 [Salt Lake City: The Church of Jesus Christ of Latter-day Saints, 1982], 59)

We are actively engaged in teaching fathers to be compassionate fathers, and mothers full-time mothers in the home. Fathers are commanded to take the lead in all spiritual matters. We encourage parents to teach their children fundamental spiritual principles that will instill faith in God, faith in their family, and faith in their country. We plead with parents to spend time with their children, both in teaching them and in building positive relationships. These are the things that create and foster strong family units and a stable society.

(Ezra Taft Benson, BYU Devotional, 29 June 1986)

In the past twenty years, as homes and families have struggled to stay intact, sociological studies reveal this alarming fact: much of the crime and many of the behavioral disorders in the United States come from homes where the father has abandoned the children. In many societies the world over, child poverty, crime, drug abuse, and family decay can be traced to conditions where the father gives no male nurturing. . . . We need to honor the position of the father as the primary provider for physical and spiritual support. I state this with no reluctance because the Lord has revealed that this obligation is placed upon husbands. . . . (D&C 83:2, 4; 84:99; 29:48). No one would doubt that a mother's influence is paramount. . . . Fathers seem best equipped to prepare children to function in the environment outside the family. One authority states, "Studies show that fathers have a special role to play in building a child's self-respect. They are important, too, in ways we really don't understand, in developing internal limits and controls in children." He continues, "Research also shows that fathers are critical in establishment of gender in children. Interestingly, fatherly involvement produces stronger sexual identity and character in both boys and girls. It is well established that the masculinity of sons and the femininity of daughters are each greater when fathers are active in family life" (Karl Zinsmeister, "Do Children Need Fathers?" *Crises*, Oct. 1992). . . . I urge the husbands and fathers of this church to be the kind of a man your wife would not want to be without.

(James E. Faust, *Ensign*, May 1993 [Salt Lake City: The Church of Jesus Christ of Latter-day Saints, 1993], 35–36)

Fathers, if you wish your children to be taught in the principles of the gospel, . . . if you wish them to be obedient and united with you, love them! and prove to them that you love them by your every word or act to them. . . . However wayward they might be, . . . when you speak or talk to them, do it not in anger; do it not harshly, in a condemning spirit. Speak to them kindly. . . . Use no lash and no violence but . . . approach them with reason, with persuasion and love unfeigned. With this means, if you cannot gain your boys and girls, . . . there will be no means left in the world by which you can win them to yourselves.

(Joseph F. Smith, "The Elders' Journal," *Liahona*, 17 Oct. 1911, 260–261)

You adult brethren, may I suggest an 'I will' for us. . . . It is I will resolve that the leadership of family will be my most important and sacred responsibility; and I will not leave the teaching and governance of my family to society, to the school, or the Church. . . . Perhaps you have heard some say, "I am so busy with living and providing that I have little time to devote to my family, but I make an effort to see that my limited time is quality time." Brethren, this type of rationalization is severely flawed. Effective family leadership requires both quantity and quality time. . . . May we never be too busy to do the things that matter most; to preside in righteousness in our homes. . . .

(H. David Burton, *Ensign*, Nov. 1995 [Salt Lake City: The Church of Jesus Christ of Latter-day Saints, 1995], 44–45)

When my wife and I were first married, my parents lived in another state. . . . We decided to go visit them. . . . After sundown, with two hours of travel still to go, we decided to play a game. . . . We said to the small boy in back, "Let's play hide-and-seek." . . . We said, "Close your eyes and don't open them until we call you." A front-seat passenger would crouch down in the seat and 10 or 15 seconds later would call, "Okay." Our son would bound over the seat and say, "Aha, I found you!" We would say, . . . "Close your eyes again." A minute or more would go by. Then we would call, and again he would energetically climb over the seat to find us. Finally we said, . . . "Close your eyes and we will call you." . . . We drove along in silence. . . . We must have traveled 15 miles before we began to whisper quiet congratulations to ourselves on the success of our devious game. Then, from out of the backseat, came the sobbing voice of a heartbroken little boy. "You didn't call me, and you said you would." "You didn't do what you agreed to do." What a terrible accusation. . . . We knew that we could never play that game again.

(F. Burton Howard, *Ensign*, Nov. 1995 [Salt Lake City: The Church of Jesus Christ of Latter-day Saints, 1995], 53)

Our family had moved from California to New York. . . . We began the process of finding a new home by looking in communities closest to the city. Gradually, however, we moved farther away from the city to find a home in a neighborhood that suited our needs. We found a beautiful home some distance from New York City. . . . The final test before purchasing the home was for me to ride the commuter train into New York and check the time and see how long the commute would take. I made the trip and returned quite discouraged. The trip was one and one-half hours each way. I walked into our motel room where our family was waiting for me and presented to my children a choice.

"You can have either this house or a father," I said. Much to my surprise they responded, "We will take the house. You are never around much anyway." I was devastated. What my children were telling me was true. I needed to repent fast. My children needed a father who was home more. Eventually we reached a compromise and bought a home closer to the city, with a much shorter commute. I changed my work habits to allow me to have more time with my family.

(L. Tom Perry, in Conference Report, Oct. 2002 [Salt Lake City: The Church of Jesus Christ of Latter-day Saints, 2002], 8)

Many years ago I read a poem about a son who could not understand why his father would not accompany him to church. I wrote a spin-off to the poem, instead making application to scripture study:

> *Daddy says it's great to read the scriptures,*
> *And learn them all by heart.*
> *But when it's time for family study,*
> *We never really start.*
> *Each evening I go to my room to study on my own,*
> *While Daddy stays at the office,*
> *And elects to work alone.*
> *Sometimes I wonder, yes time and time again,*
> *Why scripture study is so good for boys,*
> *And not so good for men.*

As parents we sometimes hope that our children will rise above our failings. The evidence, as well as the counsel of our leaders, indicates that all too often this is not something we can count on.

(Jack R. Christianson and K. Douglas Bassett, *Life Lessons from the Book of Mormon* [Salt Lake City: Deseret Book, 2003], 77–78)

I once heard Elder Henry B. Eyring give a wonderful talk about teaching with the Spirit. He began his address with a story that just hit me like a sword in the heart. He mentioned a mission president who is a good friend of his. He said as they were talking he had asked the mission president how to better prepare a boy for a mission. He was expecting the mission president to mention that one should teach a boy how to work, teach him to love the scriptures, and so forth. The mission president instead told him that many missionaries come into the mission field not knowing they are accepted and loved and worthwhile, particularly by their fathers.

I thought about my son, fifteen years old, who is a good boy. He does his priesthood duty without me prodding him. He goes to church. When he goes out at night I don't worry about what he is doing. And yet I am constantly on his back. Why? Because he is not doing the little things I want him to get better at. And it occurred to me that I have never said to him, "We really love you and appreciate you."

(Selected Writings *of Gerald N. Lund* [Salt Lake City: Deseret Book, 1999], 380–381)

I have a brother who was associated with a large university. He told of a student athlete who was an outstanding hurdler. The young man was blind. Rex asked him, "Don't you ever fall?" "I have to be exact," the athlete responded. "I measure each time before I jump. One time I didn't, and I nearly killed myself." The young man then spoke of the countless hours his father had devoted over the years teaching, helping, and showing him how to hurdle, until he became one of the best.

How could this young man fail with a team like that—a father and a son.

(W. Douglas Shumway, *Ensign*, May 2004 [Salt Lake City: The Church of Jesus Christ of Latter-day Saints, 2004], 96)

President Grant was able to maintain discipline in the home without resorting to physical punishment. His daughter Lucy said: "I am afraid 'spare the rod and spoil the child' was never taken as a serious command by our father. . . . I think we were hurt worse to know that we had displeased our parents than we would have been to have felt the sting of the switch." . . .

His daughter Frances told of a time when she learned from his example:

"An incident occurred which made so profound an impression on me that I have remembered it all my life. I used some language father didn't approve of, and he told me he would have to wash such words out of my mouth. He scrubbed out my mouth thoroughly with soap and said, 'Now your mouth is clean. I don't ever want you to make it dirty with such words again.'

"Several days later at the breakfast table, father was telling a story, and in quoting someone else he used a profane expression. I was quick to pick it up.

" 'Papa,' I said, 'you washed my mouth out for saying words like that.'

" 'So I did,' he answered. 'And I shouldn't say them any more than you should. Would you like to wash out my mouth?'

"I certainly would. I got the laundry soap and did a thorough job of it.

"My father could have hedged. He could have said he wasn't really swearing, which, of course, was true; but that wasn't his way. A little child couldn't tell the difference between a quotation and the real thing, and he realized it. From that moment I knew that my father would be absolutely fair in all his dealings with me, and I never found him otherwise. After that, I never heard him even quote profane things. He loved to tell a lively story and he would say, 'John said, *with emphasis*, such and such,' but he never said the words. He was a great believer in teaching by example and never asked us to do anything he wouldn't do himself."

(*Teachings of President of the Church—Heber J. Grant* [Salt Lake City: The Church of Jesus Christ of Latter-day Saints, 2002], xvi–xviii)

Throughout Jack's life, he and his father had many serious arguments. One day when he was 17, they had a particularly violent one. Jack said to his father, "This is the straw that breaks the camel's back. I'm leaving home, and I shall never return." So saying, he went to the house and packed his bag. His mother begged him to stay; he was too angry to listen. He left her crying at the doorway.

Leaving the yard, he was about to pass through the gate when he heard his father call to him, "Jack, I know that a large share of the blame for your leaving rests with me. For this I am truly sorry. I want you to know that if you should ever wish to return home, you'll always be welcome. And I'll try to be a better father to you. I want you to know that I'll always love you."

Jack said nothing but went to the bus station and bought a ticket to a distant point. As he sat on the bus, watching the miles go by, he commenced to think about the words of his father. He began to realize how much love it had required for him to do what he had done. Dad had apologized. He had invited him back and left the words ringing in the summer air: "I love you." . . .

He knew the only way he could ever find peace with himself was to demonstrate to his father the same kind of maturity, goodness, and love that Dad had shown toward him. Jack got off the bus. He bought a return ticket and went back.

He arrived shortly after midnight, entered the house, turned on the light. There in the rocking chair sat his father, his head in his hands. As he looked up and saw Jack, he arose from the chair and they rushed into each other's arms. Jack often said, "Those last years that I was home were among the happiest of my life." . . .

Here was a father who, suppressing passion and bridling pride, rescued his son before he became one of that vast "lost battalion" resulting from fractured families and shattered homes. Love was the binding band, the healing balm. Love so often felt, so seldom expressed.

(Thomas S. Monson, in Conference Report, Oct. 2003 [Salt Lake City: The Church of Jesus Christ of Latter-day Saints, 2003], 62)

The Church has always taken a firm stand against dictatorships of any form. Any man who chooses to administer the office of his calling as a priesthood leader in the home by dictatorial methods is out of harmony with gospel teaching. He will not enjoy the spiritual rewards of reasoning together. . . .

Dictators are always quick to issue an ultimatum; and in case you have not discovered, an ultimatum to today's youth is almost guaranteed failure. It is the equivalent of waving a red flag, it is like declaring war on those you love.

(Robert L. Simpson, in Conference Report, Apr.

1982 [Salt Lake City: The Church of Jesus Christ of Latter-day Saints, 1982], 30)

Fathers, grandfathers, we have [a] . . . responsibility to guide our precious sons and grandsons. They need our help; they need our encouragement; they need our example. It has been wisely said that our youth need fewer critics and more models to follow.

(Thomas S. Monson, in Conference Report, Oct. 2004 [Salt Lake City: The Church of Jesus Christ of Latter-day Saints, 2004], 61)

In the battle of daily living, it is easy to lose focus on our ministries as fathers and priesthood holders. If we are not careful, our vocations, hobbies, recreation, and even perhaps our Church service can adversely impact our responsibility as fathers and husbands. . . .

Are we doing all we should do to give our families gospel instruction and governance, or are we leaving this responsibility to others? Leadership in the family often requires us to reorder our priorities in order to find the necessary time. Quality and quantity time are essential. . . .

Lead out in family home evening. Lead out in scripture study. Provide priesthood blessings. Lead out in personal and family prayer.

(H. David Burton, in Conference Report, Apr. 2000 [Salt Lake City: The Church of Jesus Christ of Latter-day Saints, 2000], 50–51)

In 1958, the Reader's Digest carried an article written by Judge Liebowitz, of New York City, titled "Put Father Back at the Head of the Family." In his capacity as judge, the author spent his days listening to evidence and handing down sentences. He traveled to Europe and discovered that the conditions among the youth there were often much better than in America. He investigated and thought and pondered, and out of his vast experience he came to the conclusion that the easiest, simplest way to reduce delinquency among the young was to put the father back as head of the family. . . .

I plead with fathers to resume their role as the head of their homes. Fathers have the basic and inescapable responsibility to stand as head of the family. That does not carry with it any implication of dictatorship or unrighteous dominion. It confers the mandate to provide for the needs of their families. Those needs are more than food, clothing, and shelter. Those needs include righteous direction and the teaching, by example as well as precept, of basic principles of honesty, integrity, service, respect for the rights of others, and an understanding that we are accountable, not only

to one another but also to God, for that which we do in this life. One writer observed, "It is not impossible that the true revolutionaries of the twenty-first century will be the fathers of decent and civilized children."

(Gordon B. Hinckley, *Standing for Something* [New York: Times Books, 2000] 148–150)

A father should never consciously disappoint his wife or children. In 1989 there was a terrible earthquake in Armenia that killed over 30,000 people in four minutes. A distraught father went in frantic search of his son. He reached his son's school only to find that it had been reduced to a pile of rubble. But he was driven by his promise to his son, "No matter what, I'll always be there for you!" He visualized the corner where his son's classroom would be, rushed there, and started to dig through the debris, brick by brick.

Others came on the scene—the fire chief, then the police—warning him of fires and explosions, and urging him to leave the search to the emergency crews. But he tenaciously carried on digging. Night came and went, and then, in the 38th hour of digging, he thought he heard his son's voice. "Armand!" he called out. Then he heard, "Dad!?! It's me, Dad! I told the other kids not to worry. I told 'em that if you were alive, you'd save me and when you saved me, they'd be saved. . . .

"There are 14 of us left out of 33. . . . When the building collapsed, it made a wedge, like a triangle, and it saved us."

"Come on out, boy!"

"No, Dad! Let the other kids out first, 'cause I know you'll get me! No matter what, I know you'll be there for me!"

(James E. Faust, *Ensign*, May 2001 [Salt Lake City: The Church of Jesus Christ of Latter-day Saints, 2001], 46)

Please remember the experience of a friend of mine. He had never owned a horse in his life until he married a wonderful woman who loves horses. Wanting to impress his new bride, he announced one evening that he was going to the pasture to teach a colt how to be led. He weighed more than the colt. He knew more than the colt. He assumed all he would need to do was pull on the lead rope and sooner or later the colt would follow. He was confident that the process would be short and simple.

He attached the lead rope to the halter, got in front of the colt, and pulled. The colt resisted. My friend pulled harder, and the colt planted his legs more firmly. So he really pulled, and the colt fell over. The process was repeated several times until my friend made this assessment: in just four or five minutes he had successfully taught the colt to fall over. All he had to do was get in front of the colt, pick up the rope, and over it would go.

His wife, watching this process, finally suggested that instead of getting in front of the colt and pulling, he might try wrapping the rope around the colt and simply walking alongside. To my friend's chagrin, it worked.

There seems to be something inside each of us that resists being told or pushed or pulled. But if someone puts an arm around a young man and walks alongside him, he is likely to follow along.

(M. Russell Ballard, *Ensign*, May 2005 [Salt Lake City: The Church of Jesus Christ of Latter-day Saints, 2005], 71)

———

One Saturday my father had to go to town to attend a conference, and he didn't feel like driving, so he asked me if I would drive him into town and bring him back in the evening. . . . My mom gave me a list of groceries she needed, and on the way into town, my dad told me that there were many small chores that had been pending for a long time, like getting the care serviced and the oil changed.

When I left my father at the conference venue, he said, "At 5 o'clock in the evening, I will wait for you outside this auditorium. Come here and pick me up, and we'll go home together."

I said, "Fine." I rushed off and I did all my chores as quickly as possible—I bought the groceries, I left the car in the garage with instructions to do whatever was necessary—and I went straight to the nearest movie theater. . . . I got so engrossed in a John Wayne double feature that I didn't realize the passage of time. The movie ended at 5:30, and I came out and ran to the garage and rushed to where Dad was waiting for me. It was almost 6 o'clock when I reached there, and he was anxious and pacing up and down wondering what had happened to me. The first question he asked me was, "Why are you late?"

Instead of telling him the truth, I lied to him, and I said, "The car wasn't ready; I had to wait for the car," not realizing that he had already called the garage.

When he caught me in the lie, he said, "There's something wrong in the way I brought you up that didn't give you the confidence to tell me the truth, that made you feel you had to lie to me. I've got to find out where I went wrong with you, and to do that," he said, "I'm going to walk home—18 miles. I'm not coming with you in the car." There was absolutely nothing I could do to make him change his mind.

It was after 6 o'clock in the evening when he started walking. Much of those 18 miles were through sugarcane plantations—dirt roads, no lights, it was late in the night—and I couldn't leave him and go away. For

five and a half hours I crawled along in the car behind Father, watching him go through all this pain and agony for a stupid lie. I decided there and then that I was never going to lie again. . . .

It's almost 50 years since the event, and every time I talk about it or think about it I still get goose bumps. Now, that is the power of nonviolent action. It's a lasting thing. It's a change we bring through love, not a change we bring through fear. Anything that is brought by fear doesn't last. But anything that is done by love lasts forever.

(Arun Gandhi, "Reflections of Peace," *BYU Speeches of the Year*, 23 Mar. 1999 [Provo, Utah: BYU Press, 1999], 43)

———

We have heard of men who have said to their wives, "I hold the priesthood and you've got to do what I say." Such a man should be tried for his membership. Certainly he should not be honored in his priesthood. . . .

No woman has ever been asked by the Church authorities to follow her husband into an evil pit. She is to follow him as he follows and obeys the Savior. . . . (Ephesians 5:22–24) . . .

A woman would have no fears . . . if the husband is self-sacrificing and worthy. Certainly no sane woman would hesitate to give submission to her own really righteous husband in everything. . . .

Christ loved the Church and its people so much that he voluntarily endured persecution for them, stoically withstood pain and physical abuse for them, and finally gave his precious life for them.

When the husband is ready to treat his household in that manner, not only the wife, but also all the family will respond to his leadership.

Certainly, if fathers are to be respected, they must merit respect; if they are to be loved, they must be consistent, lovable, understanding, and kind, and must honor their priesthood.

(*Teachings of Spencer W. Kimball*, ed. by Edward L. Kimball [Salt Lake City: Bookcraft, 1982], 316–317)

———

As I meet with priesthood leaders, I often ask about the priorities of their various responsibilities. Usually they mention their important Church duties to which they have been called. Too few remember their responsibilities at home. Yet priesthood offices, keys, callings, and quorums are meant to exalt families. Priesthood authority has been restored so that families can be sealed eternally.

(Russell M. Nelson, *Ensign*, May 2006 [Salt Lake City: The Church of Jesus Christ of Latter-day Saints, 2006], 37)

Mosiah 25:19 • CHURCHES IN THE LAND

(Refer in this text to 2 Nephi 5:26.)

Book of Mormon prophets gave the title priest to officers known in this dispensation as high priests. That is, they were priests of the Melchizedek Priesthood. . . .

Among the Nephites, brethren holding the Melchizedek Priesthood were selected, consecrated teachers, and given teaching and administrative powers and responsibilities. They had jurisdiction over the churches and, along with the priests, were "to preach and to teach the word of God." They had power to baptize, a privilege not enjoyed by teachers in the Aaronic Priesthood (D&C 20:58).

It should be noted that those consecrated priests and teachers among the Nephites were not receiving offices in the lesser priesthood, for there was no Aaronic Priesthood among the Nephites from the time Lehi left Jerusalem down to the ministry of Christ among them.

(Bruce R. McConkie, *Mormon Doctrine* [Salt Lake City: Bookcraft, 1966], 599, 776)

———

During the Mosaic dispensation there were no Aaronic Priesthood holders among the Nephites, for there were no Levites among them, and the Aaronic Priesthood in that day was confined to the sons of Levi. The priests and teachers among the Nephites held the Melchizedek Priesthood.

(Bruce R. McConkie, *A New Witness for the Articles of Faith* [Salt Lake City: Deseret Book, 1985], 348)

Mosiah 26:1–3 • THE RISING GENERATION DID NOT BELIEVE

The things we have done in past years are not now sufficient to protect our children in these critical times. It has long been taught in this Church that the day will come when no one will be able to stand without an individual testimony of the divinity of this work. That day is here. . . .

No longer can we expect the Church to assume the major role in teaching our children—parents have this prime responsibility.

(A. Theodore Tuttle, in Conference Report, Apr. 1984 [Salt Lake City: The Church of Jesus Christ of Latter-day Saints, 1984], 31–32)

Mosiah 26:3 • BELIEF PRECEDES UNDERSTANDING AND TESTIMONY

These words of Anselm are . . . good counsel: "Believe in order to understand," rather than "understand [in order to] believe" (*St. Anselm*, trans. Sidney Norton Deane [1903], 7).

(Neal A. Maxwell, in Conference Report, Oct. 2002 [Salt Lake City: The Church of Jesus Christ of Latter-day Saints, 2002], 17)

Mosiah 26:20 • CALLING AND ELECTION

When the Lord has thoroughly proved him, and finds that the man is determined to serve Him at all hazards, then the man will find his calling and his election made sure, then it will be his privilege to receive the other Comforter, which the Lord has promised the Saints. . . . [He then read John 14:12–27.] Now what is this other Comforter? It is no more nor less than the Lord Jesus Christ Himself; and this is the sum and substance of the whole matter; that when any man obtains this last Comforter, he will have the personage of Jesus Christ to attend him, or appear unto him from time to time. . . .

(*Teachings of the Prophet Joseph Smith*, comp. by Joseph Fielding Smith [Salt Lake City: Deseret Book, 1976], 150–151)

Mosiah 26:29, 35; 27:31, 35 • CONFESS SINS

When the apples in a barrel rot, it is not enough to throw away half of the spoiled apples from the barrel and replace them with fresh apples on top. This would result in all the apples rotting. Instead it would be necessary to empty the barrel and completely clean and scrub—perhaps disinfect—the entire inside. Then the barrel could be safely filled again with apples. Likewise in clearing up problems in our lives it is well also to go to the bottom and confess all the transgressions so that repentance begins with no half-truths, no pretense, no unclean residue.

(Spencer W. Kimball, *The Miracle of Forgiveness* [Salt Lake City, Utah Bookcraft, 1969], 180)

———

The formula for repentance requires that we confess. Our first confession is to the Lord in prayer. When our mistakes are not grievous ones and if they are personal, that may be all that is required. If our transgression includes tampering with the procreative capacities of another of either gender, then there is a necessary confession beyond prayer. The Lord has designated, from his priesthood, the bishop to be the common judge. If your transgression is serious, and your conscience will tell you whether it is or not, seek out the bishop. The bishop represents the Lord in extending forgiveness for the Church. At times he must administer bitter medicine. . . . There is the idea abroad that one can send a postcard of prayer and receive in return full forgiveness and be ready at once for a mission or for marriage in the temple. Not so, there are payments to be made. If a bishop offers comfort only and, in misguided kindness, seeks to relieve you of the painful but healing process in connection with repentance, he will not serve you well.

(Boyd K. Packer, BYU Fireside, Mar. 1992)

———————

You always need to confess your sins to the Lord. If they are serious transgressions, such as immorality, they need to be confessed to a bishop or stake president. Please understand that confession is not repentance. It is an essential step, but is not of itself adequate. . . . Essential to forgiveness is a willingness to fully disclose to the Lord and, where necessary, His priesthood judge all that you have done. Remember, "He that covereth his sins shall not prosper: but whoso confesseth and forsaketh them shall have mercy" (Prov. 28:13).

(Richard G. Scott, *Ensign*, May 1995 [Salt Lake City: The Church of Jesus Christ of Latter-day Saints, 1995], 76)

———————

Confession must be made first to the person who has been most wronged by your acts. A sincere confession is not merely admitting guilt after the proof is already in evidence. If you have offended many persons openly, your acknowledgment is to be made openly and before those whom you have offended, that you might show your shame and humility and willingness to receive a merited rebuke. If your act is secret and has resulted in injury to no one but yourself, your confession should be in secret, that your Heavenly Father who hears in secret may reward you openly. Acts that may affect your standing in the Church, or your right to privileges or advancement in the Church, are to be promptly confessed to the bishop, whom the Lord has appointed as a shepherd over every flock and whom the Lord has commissioned to be a common judge in Israel.

(Harold B. Lee, *Stand Ye In Holy Places* [Salt Lake City: Deseret Book, 1976], 221–221)

———————

Some young people assume they can romp in sinful mud until taking a shower of repentance just before being interviewed for a mission or the temple. In the very act of transgression, some plan to repent. They mock the gift of mercy that true repentance allows.

(Bruce C. Hafen, *Ensign*, May 2004 [Salt Lake City: The Church of Jesus Christ of Latter-day Saints, 2004], 98)

———————

The confession of his major sins to a proper Church authority is one of those requirements made by the Lord. These sins include adultery, fornication, other sexual transgressions, and other sins of comparable seriousness. . . .

Many offenders in their shame and pride have satisfied their consciences, temporarily at least, with a few silent prayers to the Lord and rationalized that this was sufficient confession of their sins. "But I have confessed my sin to my Heavenly Father," they will insist, "and that is all that is necessary." This is not true where a major sin is involved. Then two sets of forgiveness are required to bring peace to the transgressor—one from the proper authorities of the Lord's Church, and one from the Lord himself.

(Spencer W. Kimball, *The Miracle of Forgiveness* [Salt Lake City: Bookcraft, 1969], 179)

———————

[The] confession which precedes repentance should be to a bishop or stake presidency who has authority to forgive sins. Confessions to others, particularly confessions repeated again and again in open meetings, as is sometimes done, only demean both the confessor and the hearer.

(Theodore M. Burton, "The Meaning of Repentance," *BYU Speeches of the Year*, 26 Mar. 1985 [Provo, Utah: BYU Press, 1985], 6–7)

Mosiah 26:30–31 • FORGIVE OTHERS
(Refer in this text to 1 Nephi 7:20–21; 3 Nephi 13:14–15.)

Although there are many ecclesiastical officers in the Church whose positions entitle and require them to be judges, the authority of those positions does not necessarily qualify them to forgive or remit sins.' . . .

The bishop, and others in comparable positions, can forgive in the sense of waiving the penalties. In our loose connotation we sometimes call this forgiveness, but it is not forgiveness in the sense of "wiping out" or absolution. . . . In receiving the confession and waiving the penalties the bishop is representing the Lord. He helps to carry the burden, relieves the transgressor's strain and tension, and assures to him a continuation of Church activity.

It is the Lord, however, who forgives sin.

(Spencer W. Kimball, *The Miracle of Forgiveness* [Salt Lake City: Bookcraft, 1969], 332)

Mosiah 26:36 • BLOTTED OUT
(Refer in this text to Moroni 6:7–8.)

"The scriptures speak of Church members being 'cast out' or 'cut off,', or having their names 'blotted out.' This means excommunication."

(*Teachings of Spencer W. Kimball*, ed. by Edward L. Kimball [Salt Lake City: Bookcraft, 1982], 100)

———————

"In contrast to the punishment that is the intended result of the judgment of a criminal court, the primary purpose of church discipline is to facilitate repentance—to qualify a transgressor for the mercy of God and the salvation made possible through the atonement of Jesus Christ. . . . Church discipline is not an instrument of punishment, but a catalyst for change. . . . The major concern of the laws of God is to perfect the lives of his children."

(Dallin H. Oaks, 7 Feb. 1992, address given at the Temple Square Assembly Hall, Salt Lake City)

———————

The Lord is on your side and you must remember that numerous people are saved by excommunication. They are not lost by excommunication. They are saved through excommunication.

(*Teachings of Spencer W. Kimball*, ed. by Edward L. Kimball [Salt Lake City: Bookcraft, 1982], 98)

———————

Having one's name "blotted out" (Alma 5:57) means excommunication from the Church and elimination from the book of life (see D&C 132:19). The priesthood power to bind a person in a saving covenant is also the power to loose him from that covenant (see Matthew 16:19).

(*Book of Mormon Student Manual 121–122* [Salt Lake City: The Church of Jesus Christ of Latter-day Saints, 1989], 73)

Mosiah 27:1–2 • OPPOSITION FROM WITHIN THE NEPHITE SOCIETY
(Refer in this text to Jacob 5:77.)

Many students who enroll at LDS Church-owned universities and colleges are caught off guard when they discover opposition in what they believed would be a trouble-free environment. . . . But frequently, just when they believe they've left their opposition behind . . . these students discover that opposition has stowed away on board, for it crawls out of the closet when they have hardly unpacked their bags. There may be unstable roommates who have not yet made a genuine break from their habits of the past; there may be disappointments with what appeared to be ideal arrangements for housing or classes; or, surprisingly, there may be new forms of temptation to which the unsuspecting are especially vulnerable when they let down their normal guard. . . . But, if our Church campuses are the Garden of Eden, they unfortunately still have their share of serpents.

(Bruce C. Hafen, *The Broken Heart* [Salt Lake City: Deseret Book, 1989], 64–65)

THINK NOT, WHEN YOU GATHER TO ZION (Eliza R. Snow)

Think not when you gather to Zion
Your troubles and trials are through,
That nothing but comfort and pleasure
Are waiting in Zion for you.
Think not when you gather to Zion,
That all will be holy and pure;
That fraud and deception are banished,
And confidence wholly secure.
Think not when you gather to Zion,
The prize and the victory won.
Think not that the warfare is ended,
The work of salvation is done.
No, no; for the great prince of darkness
A tenfold exertion will make,
When he sees you go the fountain,
Where freely the truth you may take.

There was a time when we were driven by mobs, and our faith was tried in various ways. . . . There are no mobs now, we do not have our houses burnt down now, or our cattle shot down. But shall we be without trials? . . . It is necessary in the providence of God—that there should be liquor saloons, etc., so that Latter-day Saints . . . if they want to drink beer and get drunk, or go in and play billiards and gamble, or go to other places that are worse—can do so. "But," says one, "I thought in coming to Zion I was coming to a place of purity where none of these things existed." If that had been the case how would you have been tried?

(George Q. Cannon, *Journal of Discourses* [London: Latter-day Saints' Book Depot, 1882], 22:108)

Mosiah 27:11 • THE VISIT OF AN ANGEL
(Refer in this text to Alma 36:12–16.)

[An account by Wilford Woodruff.] One of the Apostles said to me years ago, "Brother Woodruff, I have prayed for a long time for the Lord to send me the administration of an angel. I have had a great desire for this, but I have never had my prayers answered." I said to him that if he were to pray a thousand years to the God of Israel for that gift, it would not be granted, unless the Lord had a motive in sending an angel to him. I told him that the Lord never did nor never will send an angel to anybody merely to gratify the desire of the individual to see an angel. If the Lord sends an angel to anyone, He sends him to perform a work that cannot be performed only by the administration of an angel. . . .

The Holy Ghost is what every Saint of God needs. It is far more important that a man should have that gift than he should have the ministration of an angel, unless it is necessary for an angel to teach him something that he has not been taught.

(Daniel H. Ludlow, *A Companion to Your Study of the Book of Mormon* [Salt Lake City: Deseret Book, 1976], 191)

Mosiah 27:14–16 • THE PRAYER OF THE RIGHTEOUS

(Refer in this text to Alma 10:22–23.)

You remember what Alma did when his son, Alma, didn't walk in the ways of the Lord and went about trying to destroy the church. He just did not give the Lord any rest about it; he took it to the Lord in mighty prayer until an angel of heaven appeared to his son. . . .

(LeGrand Richards, in Conference Report, Oct. 1947 [Salt Lake City: The Church of Jesus Christ of Latter-day Saints, 1947], 75)

[An account of Zion's Camp.] The scourge came as had been foretold, and the Camp of Zion felt its terrible effects. Moanings and lamentations filled the air. . . . Joseph and Hyrum administered assiduously to the sick, and soon they were in the grasp of the cholera. They were together when it seized them; and together they knelt down and prayed for deliverance. Three times they bowed in supplication, the third time with a vow that they would not rise until deliverance from the destroyer was vouchsafed. While they were thus upon their knees a vision of comfort came to Hyrum. He saw their mother afar off in Kirtland praying for her absent sons, and he felt that the Lord was answering her cry. Hyrum told Joseph of the comforting vision and together they arose, made whole every whit.

(George Q. Cannon, *Life of Joseph Smith* [Salt Lake City: Deseret Book, 1972], 183)

The stake president asked if I would meet with a distraught mother and father who were grieving over a son's decision to leave his mission. . . . We knelt quietly in a private place. . . . When we arose, the father said, "Brother Monson, do you really think our Heavenly Father can alter our son's announced decision to return home before completing his mission?" . . . I responded, "Where is your son serving?" He replied, "In Dusseldorf, Germany." I placed my arm around the mother and father and said to them, "Your prayers have been heard and will be answered. With more than thirty-eight stake conferences being held this day attended by General Authorities, I was assigned to your stake. Of all the Brethren, I am the only one who has the assignment to meet with the missionaries in the Germany Dusseldorf Mission this very Thursday." Their petition had been honored by the Lord. I was able to meet with their son. He responded to their pleadings. He remained and completed a highly successful mission.

(Thomas S. Monson, *Be Your Best Self* [Salt Lake City: Deseret Book, 1979], 28)

Pray for the weather. We have floods in one area and drought in another. I am satisfied that if enough prayers ascend to heaven for moisture upon the land, the Lord will answer those prayers for the sake of the righteous.

Way back in 1969 I was in South America. I flew from Argentina to Santiago, Chile. The Andes mountains were dry. There was no snow. The grass was burned. Chile was in the midst of a devastating drought. The people pleaded for help in bringing moisture.

We dedicated two new buildings on that visit. In each of those dedicatory services we pleaded with the Lord for rain upon the land. I have the testimony of many who were in those meetings that the heavens were opened and the rains fell with such abundance that the people asked the Lord to shut them off.

(Gordon B. Hinckley, in Conference Report, Apr. 2003 [Salt Lake City: The Church of Jesus Christ of Latter-day Saints, 2003], 105)

When the Prophet [Joseph Smith's] . . . enemies were threatening him with violence, he was told that quite a number of little children were then gathered together, praying for his safety. To this he commented, "Then I need have no fear: I am safe" (*Young Woman's Journal*, xvi, 550).

(Hyrum L. Andrus, *Joseph Smith, the Man and the Seer* [Salt Lake City: Deseret Book, 1970], 59)

We learn that there is majestic, undeniable power in the love and prayer of a parent. The angel who appeared to Alma and the sons of Mosiah did not come in response to any righteousness on their part, though their souls were still precious in the sight of God. He came in response to the prayers of a faithful parent. . . (Mosiah 27:14).

Parental prayer is an unfathomable source of power. Parents can never give up hoping or caring or believing. Surely they can never give up praying. At times prayer may be the only course of action remaining—but it is the most powerful of them all.

We learn that there is great power in the united faith of the priesthood. It is not only the elder Alma who prays when his son is laid helpless and insensible before him, but also the priests and, we might assume, other faithful friends and neighbors. . . (Mosiah 27:22).

Here is a majestic example of Christlike love. No

one in this group seems delighted that devastating recompense has finally come. No one here seems pleased to imagine the torment of this young spirit. Yet this is the young man who has despised their faith, harmed their lives, attempted to destroy the very church of God which they hold dearer than life itself. . . . What we all need we cannot in good conscience or integrity deny another. So they prayed for him who had despitefully used them.

(Jeffrey R. Holland, *The Book of Mormon: It Begins with a Family* [Salt Lake City: Deseret Book, 1983] 94–95)

Mosiah 27:24–27 • BORN AGAIN
(Refer in this text to Mosiah 5:2, 7.)

The Holy Ghost is a cure and a preventative. While you have the companionship of the Holy Ghost, the cleansing power of the Atonement is operating in your life.

(Henry B. Eyring, BYU Devotional, 29 Oct. 1989)

———————

The experience of each individual who is really born again is similar to this experience of Alma and the sons of Mosiah, although it may not be so dramatic. The effect upon each person's life is likewise similar.

(Marion G. Romney, in Conference Report, Oct. 1941 [Salt Lake City: The Church of Jesus Christ of Latter-day Saints, 1941], 89–91)

———————

Though they are real and powerful, they are the exception more than the rule. For every Paul, for every Enos, and for every King Lamoni [and Alma], there are hundreds and thousands of people who find the process of repentance much more subtle, much more imperceptible. Day by day they move closer to the Lord, little realizing they are building a godlike life.

(Ezra Taft Benson, *Ensign*, Oct. 1989 [Salt Lake City: The Church of Jesus Christ of Latter-day Saints, 1989], 5)

———————

The very process of being born again spiritually is not a one-time occurrence. Hence, Paul said that he died "daily" (I Cor. 15:31). Such is the process of putting off the old self as one becomes a woman or a man of God. Quick change artists are rare. I have not seen many put off the old and put on the new very rapidly.

(Neal A. Maxwell, BYU Fireside, 2 Dec. 1984)

———————

Have you ever thought, "Wouldn't it be nice to have that experience?" Well, the scriptures don't suggest that it would be nice; they say that it's necessary in order for you and me to have what it is we want, which is eternal life. . . .

The ordinances are the key to the "mighty change" spoken of in the scriptures. There may be some who feel that they've experienced a true spiritual rebirth without receiving those ordinances by proper authority, but they haven't. When I was a boy, someone who held the priesthood laid his hands on my head and told me that I had the right to the companionship of the Holy Ghost. I testify to you that had that ordinance not been performed, I wouldn't have that right today.

(Henry B. Eyring, *To Draw Closer To God* [Salt Lake City: Deseret Book, 1997], 105–107)

———————

On the evening of 10 May 1921, as they sailed toward what is now Western Samoa, Elder McKay had the following experience:

"Toward evening, the reflection of the afterglow of a beautiful sunset was most splendid! . . . Pondering still upon this beautiful scene, I lay in my [bed] at ten o'clock that night. . . . I then fell asleep, and beheld in vision something infinitely sublime. In the distance I beheld a beautiful white city. Though it was far away, yet I seemed to realize that trees with luscious fruit, shrubbery with gorgeously tinted leaves, and flowers in perfect bloom abounded everywhere. The clear sky above seemed to reflect these beautiful shades of color. I then saw a great concourse of people approaching the city. Each one wore a white flowing robe and a white headdress. Instantly my attention seemed centered upon their leader, and though I could see only the profile of his features and his body, I recognized him at once as my Savior! The tint and radiance of his countenance were glorious to behold. There was a peace about him which seemed sublime—it was divine!

"The city, I understood, was his. It was the City Eternal; and the people following him were to abide there in peace and eternal happiness.

"But who were they?

"As if the Savior read my thoughts, he answered by pointing to a semicircle that then appeared above them, and on which were written in gold the words:

"These Are They Who Have Overcome the World—Who Have Truly Been Born Again!"

(*Teachings of Presidents of the Church—David O. McKay* [Salt Lake City: The Church of Jesus Christ of Latter-day Saints, 2003], 1–2)

Mosiah 28:1–8 • SONS OF MOSIAH DESIRE TO BE MISSIONARIES

They pled with their father that they might go and do missionary work among the Lamanites. Now father Mosiah feared for his sons' safety in the land of their enemy . . . (v. 6). The first part of the Lord's answer might not have been exactly what Mosiah wanted to hear:

"Let them go up" (v. 7). But then follow three marvelous promises: the first, "For many shall believe on their words," and the second, "I will deliver thy sons out of the hands of the Lamanites," and then the third, "They shall have eternal life" (ibid.). Now, he did not promise them great wealth, but he did promise the greatest of all the gifts of God, eternal life! The four missionary sons of Mosiah did not choose the easy course. Their choice was neither convenient, nor popular: They gave up the kingship. . . . They were ridiculed even by other members of the Church. . . . (Alma 26:23) Their choice to serve a mission was not one of convenience. . . (Alma 26:29).

(Harold G. Hillam, *Ensign*, Nov. 1995 [Salt Lake City: The Church of Jesus Christ of Latter-day Saints, 1995], 41)

Mosiah 28:4 • THE VILEST OF SINNERS

If there is one lament I cannot abide, it is the poor, pitiful, withered cry, "Well, that's just the way I am." . . . I've heard it from too many people who want to sin and call it psychology. And I use the word sin to cover a vast range of habits, some seemingly innocent enough, that nevertheless bring discouragement and doubt and despair.

You can change anything you want to change, and you can do it very fast. . . . But change, growth, renewal, and repentance can come for you as instantaneously as they did for Alma and the sons of Mosiah. Even if you have serious amends to make, it is not likely that you would qualify for the term "the vilest of sinners," which is the phrase Mormon used in describing these young men. . . .

Do not misunderstand. Repentance is not easy or painless or convenient. It is a bitter cup from hell. But only Satan, who dwells there, would have you think that . . . it's too long and too hard to change.

(Jeffrey R. Holland, *However Long and Hard the Road* [Salt Lake City: Deseret Book, 1985], 6–7)

Mosiah 28:5–7 • A "MY WILL, THY WILL" COMPARISON

(Contrast with Zeniff's journey to Lehi-Nephi in Mosiah 9:3.)

Mosiah 28:6–7 • A BLESSING OF DELIVERANCE

When Elder [LeGrand] Richards left his first mission to go home, the ship's crossing proved to be rough. As they neared the American shore a terrible storm arose. Gigantic waves rolled about, and everything not attached to the deck was thrown around. A sister returning from Scandinavia said, "Brother Richards, you don't seem a bit worried."

He answered, "Well, I don't know what's going to happen to you and the rest of the passengers, but I feel just as much at ease as if I were sitting in my mother's parlor. I had a promise that if I filled an honorable mission I'd return home in safety, and I have had the assurance that my mission was acceptable to the Lord, so I am going home."

(LeGrand Richards, *Ensign*, July 1982 [Salt Lake City: The Church of Jesus Christ of Latter-day Saints, 1982], 9)

The branch of the Church at Colesville was also suffering persecution. . . . In the latter part of August, 1830, . . . such fierce threats had been uttered by the mobocrats . . . that Joseph and his brethren felt that they were risking their lives in thus journeying to Colesville. They joined together in mighty prayer, beseeching God that He would blind the eyes of their enemies, and permit them to go and come without recognition by the wicked. The Prophet informed his companions that their prayer would be answered, and the angel of the Lord would protect them and cover with a veil the vision of the murderous mob. They made no effort to disguise themselves, but traveled through Colesville to the house of Joseph Knight in broad day, meeting a score of their persecutors. A reward had been offered to anyone who would give information of Joseph's return; and among those whom they met were many who would gladly have earned the money, even at the expense of the Prophet's life. But no one said a harsh word to Joseph and his companions, and they were treated merely as ordinary strangers passing through the village. A meeting of the branch was held that night, and the Spirit of God was poured out upon the believers in rich abundance. They were all made firm by the blessing given, and filled with a determination to yield nothing of their faith.

(George Q. Cannon, *Life of Joseph Smith the Prophet* [Salt Lake City: Deseret Book, 1972], 93–94)

Mosiah 29:12–40 • NO KINGS UPON THE LAND

(Refer in this text to 2 Nephi 10:11.)

Mosiah 29:25 • NEPHITE GOVERNMENT

From a modern perspective we might think this verse tells of the establishment of a democratic or representative government very much like the one we now have in the United States. But on reflection we observe that Nephite politics were different from ours in many significant ways: the Nephites had no constitution, no bill of rights, no separate branches of government, and no parliamentary system of government. Their elected officers served for life, and apparently political parties and campaigning for election were discouraged.

Seen without modern influences, then, Nephite

democracy assumes an ancient character all its own. One the one hand, the use of popular consent among the Nephites resembles very closely the rite of royal anointing such as David experienced in ancient Israel (2 Samuel 5:1–3). This popular allegiance supplied a special bond of legitimacy between the ruler and his people. In Zarahemla, moreover, the popular voice of allegiance also included a covenant that placed a primary moral responsibility of sustaining the law upon the people themselves.

(John W. Welch, *The Book of Mormon: It Begins with a Family* [Salt Lake City: Deseret Book, 1983], 16)

Mosiah 29:26–27 • THE MAJORITY CHOOSE

(Refer in this text to Helaman 5:2; 6:31; 16:10.)

Mr. Frank Stanton, CBS president emeritus, told a Brigham Young University audience that network television standards will continue to decline because they are based on society's standards. He said, "Standards come from the audience . . . ; the audience determines the programming and program content." Further, he said, "I believe there will be more infractions with respect to immorality and violence and it will get a lot worse before it gets better because of the changing standards of our society" (*The Daily Universe*, 2 Feb 1989, 1). What a sad commentary on our society! Again we can learn a great principle from the Book of Mormon. When King Mosiah proposed that judges should rule instead of kings, he said: ". . . if the time comes that the voice of the people doth choose iniquity, then is the time that the judgments of God will come upon you (Mosiah 29:26–27)." That time of iniquity came about sixty years later and at several other times. In the book of Helaman we read that "they who chose evil were more numerous than they who chose good (Hel. 5:2)." If television viewing choices serve as a valid measure of our society, they who choose evil surely are more numerous than they who choose good.

(Joseph P. Wirthlin, *Ensign*, May 1989 [Salt Lake City: The Church of Jesus Christ of Latter-day Saints, 1989], 9)

That which is right does not become wrong merely because it may be deserted by the majority, neither does that which is wrong today become right tomorrow by the chance circumstance that it has won the approval or been adopted by overwhelmingly predominant numbers. Principles cannot be changed by, nor accommodate themselves to, the vagaries of popular sentiment.

(Albert E. Bowen, in Conference Report, Apr. 1941 [Salt Lake City: The Church of Jesus Christ of Latter-day Saints, 1941], 85)

I'll tell you how to vote. You read the 134th section of the Doctrine and Covenants and the 29th chapter of Mosiah, and then pray about it and you'll know exactly whom you should vote for at the election. That's how to vote.

(Harold B. Lee, address to Seminary and Institute Personnel, BYU, 8 July 1966)

This land, to God our Father, is a chosen land, dedicated as I have said to the principle of liberty and freedom, not license. Our fathers, under His inspiration, gave us the constitution of our country, the bill of rights which defines our privileges and places limitations beyond which we may not go. . . . there is no power that can wreck the government that God has established in this country unless it be the people themselves, and that I do not expect nor believe can occur.

(Anthony W. Ivins, in Conference Report, Oct. 1932 [Salt Lake City: The Church of Jesus Christ of Latter-day Saints, 1932], 107–108)

Voting was referred to . . . from the book of Mosiah. . . . I think that is the first record in sacred history of voting, and it occurred on this continent. We are facing an election this year. We learn from this book that man is endowed with certain rights, just as the Declaration of Independence states. We have the right to liberty, to freedom, to the pursuit of happiness. We have the right of the franchise. . . .

You know, the slaves never had the franchise. Before the Civil War they were not allowed to vote. We have voluntary slavery in this country because we have millions who will not go out to vote who have the right to do so. They are slaves of their own choosing, because if we do not participate in preserving this land choice above all other lands, then to that degree we are bringing back to this land, slavery.

(*Matthew Cowley Speaks* [Salt Lake City: Deseret Book, 1954], 111–113)

During recent years, polls and circumstances have suggested that an unprecedented majority of Americans believe that the private lives of public officials need not be considered as a factor in their eligibility for public office, and that private morality has no connection with public behavior and credibility. I am more deeply concerned about the growing moral deficit than I am about the monetary deficit.

(Gordon B. Hinckley, *Standing for Something* [New York: Times Books, 2000], xviii)

Alma

Alma 1:3–5, 16 • PRIESTCRAFT
(Refer in this text to 2 Nephi 26:29–31.)

Priesthood and priestcraft are two opposites; one is of God, the other of the devil. When ministers claim but do not possess the priesthood; when they set themselves up as lights to their congregations, but do not preach the pure and full gospel; when their interest is in gaining personal popularity and financial gain, rather than in caring for the poor and ministering to the wants and needs of their fellow men—they are engaged, in a greater or lesser degree, in the practice of priestcrafts.

(Bruce R. McConkie, *Mormon Doctrine* [Salt Lake City: Bookcraft, 1966], 593)

The anti-Christs such as Korihor and Sherem openly rebel against Christ, while the user of priestcraft claims a belief in Christ but perverts his teachings.

(Monte S. Nyman, Book of Mormon Symposium, Aug. 1982, 67)

Persons who write truth for the purpose of gain commit Priestcraft.

(Dallin H. Oaks, CES Symposium, 1985)

The scriptural word for gospel service "for the sake of riches and honor" is *priestcraft* (Alma 1:16).

(Dallin H. Oaks, *Pure in Heart* [Salt Lake City: Bookcraft, 1988], 39)

With a trained mind and a skillful manner of presentation, a teacher can become unusually popular and effective in teaching. But Satan will try to use that strength to corrupt the teacher by encouraging him or her to gather a following of disciples. A church or church education teacher or LDS university professor who gathers such a following and does this "for the sake of riches and honor" (Alma 1:16) is guilty of priestcraft. "Priestcrafts are that men preach and set themselves up for a light unto the world, that they may get gain and praise of the world; but they seek not the welfare of Zion" (2 Nephi 26:29). Teachers who are most popular (and therefore most effective) have a special susceptibility to this form of priestcraft (see Dallin H. Oaks, BYU Fireside, 7 June 1992).

Such a man or woman might serve in Church positions . . . in an effort to achieve prominence or cultivate contacts that would increase income or aid in acquiring wealth. Others might serve in order to obtain worldly honors.

(Dallin H. Oaks, in Conference Report, Oct. 1984 [Salt Lake City: The Church of Jesus Christ of Latter-day Saints, 1984], 14)

Alma 1:4 • ALL MANKIND SHOULD BE SAVED

Now, be very careful when anybody tells you about certainty in this world, because it's a very uncertain life. In fact, most of us are so worried about the fact that we don't know what's coming that we're easy prey for people who claim to be able to tell us exactly what's going to happen to us. Do you remember a man named Nehor in the Book of Mormon? He wanted to become popular and wealthy, so he preached a message that he knew people would like. He essentially said, "I'll tell you something about the future that's certain, and I'll make it very attractive." The scriptures record that he "testified unto the people that all mankind should be saved at the last day, and that they need not fear nor tremble, but that they might lift up their heads and rejoice; for the Lord had created all men, and had also redeemed all men; and, in the end, all men should have eternal life" (Alma 1:4). And many of the people believed him. If they had searched the scriptures and prayed about his message, they would have known it was a lie. But he told them a pleasant lie—don't worry, all will go well—and many believed him.

(Henry B. Eyring, *To Draw Closer to God* [Salt Lake City: Deseret Book, 1997], 82–83)

Alma 1:6; 5:53 • COSTLY APPAREL

(Contrast with Alma 1:27; 4:6; 5:53; Jacob 2:13; refer in this text to Alma 31:28; 32:2.)

[Regarding *wealth* among the Nephites during times of *pride*] Why should we labor this unpleasant point? Because the Book of Mormon labors it, for our special benefit. Wealth is a jealous master who will not be served half-heartedly and will suffer no rival—not even God: . . . Along with this, of course, everyone dresses in the height of fashion, the main point being always that the proper clothes are expensive—the expression "costly apparel" occurs 14 times in the Book of Mormon. The more important wealth is, the less important it is how one gets it.

(Hugh Nibley, *Since Cumorah* [Salt Lake City: Deseret Book, 1976], 393)

When money and possessions become the chief marks of distinction in society then the pursuit of money becomes the only action worthwhile. And if this pursuit requires the sacrifice of honesty, integrity, compassion and all other virtues, then so be it for the love of money is indeed the root of all evil. Thus the wearing of costly apparel involves the soul as much as the body.

(Mae Blanche; as quoted in *Studies in Scripture*, ed. by Kent P. Jackson [Salt Lake City: Deseret Book, 1987], 7:292)

Are not many of us materialistic? Do we not find it well-nigh impossible to raise our sights above the dollar sign? Are not many of us pragmatists—living not by principle but by what we can get away with? Are not many of us status-seekers—measuring the worth of a man by the size of his bank account, his house, his automobile? . . . surely these are among the many reasons why this is truly an era of peril. . . . Many of us imagine in the foolishness of pride, that our manifold blessings are due not to God's goodness, but to our own wisdom and virtue. . . . This is a sad commentary of a civilization which has given to mankind the greatest achievements and progress ever known. But it is an even sadder commentary on those of us who call ourselves Christians, who thus betray the ideals given to us by the Son of God himself.

(Ezra Taft Benson, in Conference Report, Oct. 1960 [Salt Lake City: The Church of Jesus Christ of Latter-day Saints, 1960], 103, 105)

Fashion is the science of appearances, and it inspires one with the desire to seem rather than to be.

(Edwin Hubbell Chapin; as quoted in Steven R. Covey, *Spiritual Roots of Human Relations* [Salt Lake City: Deseret Book, 1974], 24)

I see and admire beauty in people. I am not so concerned with the look that comes of lotions and creams, of pastes and packs as seen in slick-paper magazines and on television. I am not concerned whether the skin be fair or dark. I have seen beautiful people in all of the scores of nations through which I have walked. Little children are beautiful everywhere. And so are the aged, whose wrinkled hands and faces speak of struggle and survival. I believe in the beauty of personal virtue. There is so much of ugliness in the world in which we live. It is expressed in coarse language, in sloppy dress and manners, in immoral behavior which mocks the beauty of virtue and always leaves a scar. Each of us can and must stand above this sordid and destructive evil, this ugly stain of immorality.

(Gordon B. Hinckley, *Ensign*, Aug. 1992 [Salt Lake City: The Church of Jesus Christ of Latter-day Saints, 1992], 4)

I fear that in many cases we are rearing children who are slaves to expensive fads and fashions. Remember the scripture, "For where your treasure is, there will your heart be also." How do we determine where our treasure is? To do so, we need to evaluate the amount of time, money, and thought we devote to something. Might it not be well to evaluate how much focus we place on shopping and spending?

This does not mean that our children should not dress in some of the appropriate clothing that is in fashion because that can be very important to them. But they don't need a closet full. As members of the Church, we have a responsibility to present ourselves in a well-groomed, attractive, and modest manner. With good planning, this can be done without being driven to spend extravagantly on our clothing.

More than 10 times, the prophets in the Book of Mormon warn us about the problems of pride related to the nature of our clothing. . . .

We would do well if in all these areas of material things we and our children would follow the oft-quoted motto of our pioneer forebears to "fix it up, wear it out, make it do, or do without."

(Joe J. Christensen, *Ensign*, May 1999 [Salt Lake City: The Church of Jesus Christ of Latter-day Saints, 1999], 10–11)

I believe that nearly all of the hardships of a majority of the people would disappear if they were willing to forego the habit of wearing silk stockings, so to speak, and get back to the ordinary manner of dressing in a rather quiet, unassuming way; stay away from about nine-tenths of the picture shows that they attend; return to the ways of thrift and economy.

(*Teachings of Presidents of the Church—Heber J. Grant* [Salt Lake City: The Church of Jesus Christ of Latter-day Saints, 2002], 123)

I recall the experience of one of my students who drove to seminary in a very expensive sports car presented to her by her father on her sixteenth birthday. Along with my other students, I stood in the parking lot celebrating as well as coveting her brand new car. Later in the day she drove back to the seminary to visit with me one on one. With no other students around, she was free to share her feelings concerning this expensive gift. Surprisingly, her emotions were not based on the joy of receiving the beautiful car but of sorrow—almost mourning—regarding the distance between herself and her father. Her tears were interrupted by these words: "He gives me everything money can buy and nothing it can't."

I must admit that because of my middle-class background, I initially saw her words as those of a spoiled rich girl, until she said, "He has never told me he loves me. This car is his way of avoiding the issue. I would gladly give back all his expensive gifts just to hear him say, 'I love you.'"

Later that year her parents divorced, and from then on the geographical distance between her and her father equaled the emotional distance that had always been there. Without knowing it, she had identified his gifts as costly apparel. From this experience and so many others I have witnessed, costly apparel is used as a shield for people to hide behind so they don't have to make needed changes within themselves. When our hearts are filled with pride, we rationalize that if we surround ourselves with all the toys of success, then we will be thought of by others as being successful. This allows us not to have to deal with the real internal issues that keep us from progressing. We then begin to value personal possessions more than personal relationships. In this light, it is not hard to see the importance of ridding ourselves of costly apparel.

(Jack R. Christianson and K. Douglas Bassett, *Life Lessons from the Book of Mormon* [Salt Lake City: Deseret Book, 2003], 118–119)

We need to stand tall in following the counsel of the prophets to attire ourselves modestly. "Immodest clothing includes short shorts and skirts, tight [form-fitting] clothing, shirts that do not cover the stomach, and other revealing attire" (*For the Strength of Youth* [2001], 12). Clothing that is modest, neat, and clean uplifts. Immodest clothing degrades. If there is any question, ask yourself, "Would I feel comfortable with my appearance if I were in the Lord's presence?" (*For the Strength of Youth*, 13). Mothers, you can be our examples and conscience in this important matter. But remember, young people can detect hypocrisy as easily as they can smell the wonderful aroma of freshly baked bread.

(H. David Burton, *Ensign*, Nov. 2001 [Salt Lake City: The Church of Jesus Christ of Latter-day Saints, 2001], 66)

Marcie Matthews, a Laurel from Chicago, Illinois, shares her story: . . .

"Recently we had a Mutual activity on the importance of modesty. . . . It was the one weakness that I knew I had but had placed far behind in my head. Everyone wore short shorts, . . . and miniskirts, and I had bought mine with my own money. Then I heard the lesson on modesty. I went home wanting to go straight to my closet and throw away everything that was not modest so it wouldn't be there to tempt me. . . .

"Later that night my dad told me he was proud of me and that he would like to buy me a couple of knee-length dresses for church. The next step was to go through all my clothes and give away everything. It was hard for me to part with my favorite skirts and the shorts that I loved so much, but I did. . . .

"I have never felt better about myself. I love being able to walk into the temple and church and feel like I am a child of God and am representing Him . . . by the clothes that I wear. . . .

" . . . When we have to give up something that is a part of us, the blessings will pour in more than you can imagine" (letter in possession of Young Women office).

Marcie's great example epitomizes our Young Women theme. You know, the part that says, "We stand as witnesses of God at all times and in all things"—and in all *prom dresses*.

(Carol B. Thomas, *Ensign*, May 1999 [Salt Lake City: The Church of Jesus Christ of Latter-day Saints, 1999], 93)

President Harold B. Lee taught of the important symbolic and actual effect of how we dress and groom our bodies. If you are well groomed and modestly dressed, you invite the companionship of the Spirit of our Father in Heaven and exercise a wholesome influence upon those around you. To be unkempt in your appearance exposes you to influences that are degrading (see *The Teachings of Harold B. Lee*, ed. Clyde J. Williams [1996], 220).

Avoid immodest clothing. Dress and groom to show the Lord that you know how precious your body is.

President Hinckley has warned you not to decorate your body with pictures or symbols that will never wash off or to pierce your body with rings or jewelry after the manner of the world (see "Your Greatest Challenge, Mother," *Ensign*, Nov. 2000).

You would not paint a temple with dark pictures or symbols or graffiti or even initials. Do not do so with your body. . . . (1 Cor. 6:19–20) . . . (1 Cor. 3:16–17).

(Boyd K. Packer, "Ye Are the Temple of God," *Ensign*, Nov. 2002 [Salt Lake City: The Church of Jesus Christ of Latter-day Saints, 2002], 72)

Alma 1:14, 18 • CAPITAL PUNISHMENT

We solemnly make the following declarations, the Church's position on capital punishment: . . . That this Church views the shedding of human blood with the utmost abhorrence. That we regard the killing of human beings, except in conformity with the civil law, as a capital crime which should be punished by shedding the blood of the criminal, after a public trial before a legally constituted court of the land. . . . The revelations of God to this Church make death the penalty for capital crime, and require that offenders against life and property shall be delivered up to and tried by the laws of the land.

(Official Declaration, *Millennial Star*, 20 Jan. 1890, 33–34)

———

This divine law for shedding the blood of a murderer has never been repealed. It is a law given by the Almighty and not abrogated in the Christian faith. It stands on record for all time—that a murderer shall have his blood shed. He that commits murder must be slain. "Whoso sheddeth man's blood, by man shall his blood be shed." I know there are some benevolent and philanthropic people in these times who think that capital punishment ought to be abolished. Yet I think the Lord knows better than they. The law he ordained will have the best results to mankind in general.

(Charles W. Penrose; as quoted in Joseph Fielding Smith, *Answers to Gospel Questions* [Salt Lake City: Deseret Book, 1957], 1:189–199)

Alma 2:18, 28, 35 • THE LORD'S BATTLE STRATEGY

(Refer in this text to 1 Nephi 2:20.)

Safety can't be won by tanks and guns and airplanes and atomic bombs. There is only one place of safety and that is in the realm of the Almighty God that he gives to those who keep his commandments and listen to his voice.

(Harold B. Lee, in Conference Report, Oct. 1973 [Salt Lake City: The Church of Jesus Christ of Latter-day Saints, 1973], 169)

Alma 1:27 • NO COSTLY APPAREL, YET NEAT AND COMELY

(Refer in this text to Alma 1:6.)

Through your dress and appearance, you can show the Lord that you know how precious your body is. You can show that you are a disciple of Jesus Christ.

Prophets of God have always counseled His children to dress modestly. The way you dress is a reflection of what you are on the inside. . . . When you are well groomed and modestly dressed, you invite the companionship of the Spirit. . . .

Never lower your dress standards for any occasion. Doing so sends the message that you are using your body to get attention and approval and that modesty is important only when it is convenient. . . .

Avoid extremes in clothing, appearance, and hairstyle. Always be neat and clean and avoid being sloppy or inappropriately casual in dress, grooming, and manners.

(*For the Strength of Youth* [Salt Lake City: The Church of Jesus Christ of Latter-day Saints, 2001])

———

Mothers. . . . We will appoint you a mission to teach your children their duty, and instead of ruffles and fine dresses to adorn the body, teach them that which will adorn their minds. Let what you have to clothe them with be neat and clean and nice. Teach them cleanness and purity of body and the principle of salvation, and they will delight to come to these meetings.

(*Discourses of Brigham Young*, comp. by John A. Widtsoe [Salt Lake City: Deseret Book, 1954], 210–211)

———

It is impossible to expect children who have been taught to love to dress in the immodest style trends of the day to then change overnight to an entirely different wardrobe when they enter a Church university or a missionary training center, or when they are married in the temple, or even when they dress for the Sabbath day. Modest, proper styles must be taught almost from birth.

I know a little girl who is the last child in a large family in which the other children are all boys. I guess the shock of being a girl in this big family of boys has made her keenly aware of the fact that she is different from the other children. Her mother has wisely taught her that the boys wear trousers and that she wears dresses. Now you cannot get her to wear anything else but a modest dress. I am certain she will have no problem adjusting to Church dress standards anytime in her life because there will be no need for change. This is something she has been taught from the very beginning of her life. How easy it will be for her to accept the proper dress standards as she moves from child to youth to adult.

Now, before I receive letters from upset women telling me that I said they should not wear slacks, save your postage. I did not say that, although I don't think they are appropriate for the Sabbath day. What I am saying is that we have established a dress standard which requires a modest, wholesome style. . . . The way we dress is usually a good indicator of how we will act.

(L. Tom Perry, *Ensign*, Nov. 1988 [Salt Lake City: The Church of Jesus Christ of Latter-day Saints, 1988], 75)

The rolling forth of the restored gospel is a miracle . . . and not the least of the miracle is that a significant portion of it rolls forward on the shoulders of 19-year-olds! . . . Clean, clear, bright-eyed missionaries, . . . they themselves are the first gospel message their investigators encounter. . . .

I wish you could meet the marvelous young man who came to us from Bolivia, arriving with no matching clothing and shoes three sizes too large for him. He was a little older because he was the sole breadwinner in his home and it had taken some time to earn money for his mission. He raised chickens and sold the eggs door-to-door. Then, just as his call finally came, his widowed mother faced an emergency appendectomy. Our young friend gave every cent of the money he had earned for his mission to pay for his mother's surgery and postoperative care, then quietly rounded up what used clothing he could from friends and arrived at the MTC in Santiago on schedule. I can assure you that his clothes now match, his shoes now fit, and both he and his mother are safe and sound.

(Jeffrey R. Holland, *Ensign*, May 2004 [Salt Lake City: The Church of Jesus Christ of Latter-day Saints, 2004], 30)

Spencer [Kimball] paid little attention to his clothing, although [his wife] Camilla and [his secretary] Arthur conspired to keep him looking presentable. Spencer hated to take the time to shop, so Camilla often brought clothes home for him to try on. Arthur sometimes did the same at the office. Camilla shopped for Spencer's suits at Mr. Mac's, a downtown Salt Lake City clothier, but owner Mac Christensen refused payment. In an effort to reciprocate, Spencer sent money

to Brother Christensen's son while the young man was serving a mission in Australia.

On occasion, Spencer left home wearing pants and a coat from similar but different suits. He seldom noticed. Sometimes Spencer returned home to change, and other times he simply carried on. One trip to Arizona included an appointment with the governor. Arthur discovered on the plane that again Spencer's pants and coat did not match. Between their arrival and the appointment, Arthur managed to come up with a borrowed suit for him.

Just before a trip to Lakeland, Florida, Arthur tried to persuade Spencer to buy a new pair of shoes. Spencer protested that he liked his old, comfortable shoes and that he had no time for shopping. Arthur went to the store and obtained on approval three pairs of shoes in the President's size. Spencer chose one pair under protest but grumbled on the trip to Florida that the new shoes felt stiff and too tight. In Lakeland the resourceful Arthur enlisted a security aide with feet the right size to put on Spencer's new shoes and walk up and down the hotel corridor to break them in.

But the old shoes resurfaced. In a temple meeting, Elder Monson noticed a hole in Spencer's shoe and mentioned it to Arthur, who groaned, "Has he got that pair on again? I've taken that pair away from him and hidden them a dozen times! He's got all kind[s] of new shoes, but he loves that old pair."

In 1980, shortly after a meeting in the Rose Bowl, a letter containing a check for $40 reached Spencer's office. A man who had viewed the proceedings through binoculars had observed that Spencer's shoes showed signs of serious wear. Spencer laughed and told Arthur to put the money in the missionary fund.

Tying neckties presented a special challenge to Spencer. One Christmas day neighbor Sam Parker went to visit the Kimballs, and Spencer showed Sam his gifts. "Sam," he asked, "do you know how to tie a tie?"

"You bet. Would you like me to show you?"

"Yes, please, if you have time."

Sam selected a new tie and put it around President Kimball's neck. They stood in front of a mirror, with Sam behind and reaching over his shoulders to demonstrate how to tie a neat Windsor knot.

"How does that look?" asked Sam.

"Fine." Spencer loosened the tie and very carefully lifted it over his head, still knotted. With a smile he said, "Would you like to do another?"

Sam laughed, then proceeded to knot all the new ties and slip them off so that Spencer could simply lift one off the rack and pull it over his head. (Other times Spencer's sons performed the ritual.)

(Spencer W. Kimball; as quoted in Edward L. Kimball, *Lengthen Your Stride: The Presidency of Spencer W. Kimball* [Salt Lake City: Deseret Book, 2005], 54–55)

Some of you young men seem to delight in dressing in a slouchy manner. I know that it is a sensitive subject, but I believe it is unbecoming to young men who have been ordained to the holy priesthood of God.

(Gordon B. Hinckley, *Ensign*, Nov. 2006 [Salt Lake City: The Church of Jesus Christ of Latter-day Saints, 2006], 60)

Alma 1:30 • PROSPERITY WITHOUT SETTING HEARTS ON RICHES
(Refer in this text to Jacob 2:18–19.)

[In April 1932 . . . at a general Relief Society conference.] At that time the United States had sunk into the despair of the Great Depression, a widespread crisis of low economic activity and high unemployment. President Grant reproved the Saints for not heeding the counsel they had received from President Smith:

"If the people known as Latter-day Saints had listened to the advice given from this stand by my predecessor, under the inspiration of the Lord, calling and urging upon the Latter-day Saints not to run in debt, this great depression would have hurt the Latter-day Saints very, very little. . . . To my mind, the main reason for the depression in the United States as a whole is the bondage of debt and the spirit of speculation among the people."

Continuing with his address, President Grant emphasized the need to avoid debt. He also urged his listeners to pay tithes and offerings, even in times of financial difficulty. He referred to a time many years earlier when he went into debt to buy stock in the Salt Lake Theatre, hoping to save the building from being torn down:

"I want all the people within the sound of my voice to benefit by my experience in buying theatre stock. [For] 32 years of my life, . . . every dollar I made was lost before I made it. It is a great burden, figuratively speaking, to have a dead horse, and to have to carry the horse for 32 years before you can put it under the ground. It is a terrible condition, and all on account of debt. Since that time I have always lived within my means."

(*Teachings of Presidents of the Church—Heber J. Grant* [Salt Lake City: The Church of Jesus Christ of Latter-day Saints, 2002], 119–121)

Alma 3:6–19 • NEPHITE, LAMANITE
(Refer in this text to 2 Nephi 5:21–23; Jacob 1:13–14; Helaman 11:24.)

Here God places his mark on people as a curse, yet it is an artificial mark which they actually place upon themselves. The mark was not a racial thing but was acquired by "whosoever suffered himself to be led away by the Lamanites" (Alma 3:10); Alma moreover defines

a Nephite as anyone observing "the traditions of their fathers. . . " (Alma 3:11). Which makes the difference between Nephite and Lamanite a cultural, not a racial, one. . . . The cultural picture may not be the whole story of the dark skin of the Lamanites, but it is an important part of that story and is given great emphasis by the Book of Mormon itself.

(Hugh Nibley, *Lehi in the Desert and the World of the Jaredites* [Salt Lake City: Bookcraft, 1952], 85)

Originally, the Lamanites were the children of Laman, Lemuel, and some of the family of Ishmael; but as the centuries passed there were many defections in both nations, when the dissatisfied would join the opposing race and affiliate and intermix with them, so that the two names at last became more an indication of religion and civilization than of birth.

(George Reynolds, *A Complete Concordance of the Book of Mormon* [Salt Lake City: Deseret Book, 1973], 395)

It should be noted that the Lamanites were often absorbed by, and were called Nephites when they were righteous, and it is true also that the Nephites when they rebelled and became wicked, were often times called Lamanites, and there was undoubtedly a considerable mixture among them.

(Spencer W. Kimball, in Conference Report, Apr. 1949 [Salt Lake City: The Church of Jesus Christ of Latter-day Saints, 1949], 107)

[Lamanite] technically, if we stick to Book of Mormon usage of the term, especially in the closing centuries of that record, we find that it applies to those individuals who were not partakers of the gospel. Hence, it was the equivalent of our term, gentile.

(Dee. F. Green, "Book of Mormon Archaeology: The Myths and the Alternatives," *Dialogue* (Summer 1969), 4:78; "Gentile" to be understood in the Mormon sense; as quoted in Kirk Holland Vestal and Arthur Wallace, *The Firm Foundation of Mormonism* [Los Angeles, CA: LL Company, 1981], 101)

Alma 3:13 • THEY SET A MARK UPON THEMSELVES

I cannot understand why any young man—or young woman, . . . would wish to undergo the painful process of disfiguring the skin with various multi-colored representations of people, animals, and various symbols. . . . Fathers, caution your sons against having their bodies tattooed. . . . A tattoo is graffiti on the temple of the body.

Likewise the piercing of the body for multiple rings in the ears, in the nose, even in the tongue. Can they possibly think that is beautiful? It is a passing fancy, but its effects can be permanent. . . . The First Presidency and the Quorum of the Twelve have declared that we discourage tattoos and also the piercing of the body for other than medical purposes. We do not, however, take any position on the minimal piercing of the ears by women for one pair of earrings—one pair.

(President Gordon B. Hinckley, in Conference Report, Oct. 2000 [Salt Lake City: The Church of Jesus Christ of Latter-day Saints, 2000], 70–71; or *Ensign*, Nov. 2000, 52)

Alma 3:26–27 • RECEIVE WAGES FROM THE SPIRIT WE OBEY
(Refer in this text to Helaman 13:37; Moroni 7:29–31.)

If our eyes were open to see the spirit world around us, . . . we would not be so unguarded and careless and so indifferent whether we had the spirit and power of God with us or not but we would be continually watchful and prayerful to our Heavenly Father for His Holy Spirit and His holy angels to be around about us to strengthen us to overcome every evil influence.

(George Q. Cannon, *Gospel Truths*, ed. by Jerreld L. Newquist [Salt Lake City: Deseret Book, 1974], 1:82)

Let me read you what Parley P. Pratt said about this matter. "In all ages and dispensations God has revealed many important instructions and warnings to men by means of dreams. When the outward organs of thought and perception are released from their activity, the nerves unstrung, the whole of mortal humanity lies hushed in quiet slumbers in order to renew its strength and vigor, it is then that the spiritual organs are at liberty in a certain degree to assume their wanted functions . . . Their kindred spirits, their guardian angels, then hover about them with the fondest affection, the most anxious solicitude. Spirit communes with spirit, thought meets thought, soul blends with soul, in all the raptures of mutual pure and eternal love. In this situation the spiritual organs, . . . our spirit body has eyes to see, ears to hear, tongue to speak, and so on . . . the spiritual organs are susceptible of converse with Deity, or of communion with angels, and the spirits of just men made perfect. In this situation we frequently hold communion with our departed father, mother, brother, sister, son or daughter, or with the former husband or wife of our bosom whose affections for us, being rooted and grounded in the eternal elements, issuing from under the sanctuary of love's eternal fountain, can never be lessened or diminished by death, distance of space, or length of years." When we begin to understand that,

beyond sight, as Brigham Young said, is the spirit world right here round about us. If our spiritual eyes could be open, we could see others visiting with us, directing us. And if we will learn not to be so sophisticated that we rule out that possibility of impressions from those who are beyond sight, then we too may have a dream that may direct us as a revelation.

(Harold B. Lee, BYU Devotional, 15 Oct. 1952)

I am convinced that one of the profound themes of the Book of Mormon, one which may not yet have been developed enough in our teaching of young people, is the role and prevalence and central participation of angels in the gospel story. . . . Obviously I speak here not alone of the angel Moroni but also of those more personal ministering angels who are with us and around us, empowered to help us and who do exactly that. . . . Perhaps more of us . . . could literally, or at least figuratively, behold the angels around us if we would but awaken from our stupor and hear the words God is trying to tell us. . . . I believe we need to speak of and believe in and bear testimony to, the ministry of angels more than we sometimes do. They constitute one of God's great methods of witnessing through the veil, and no document in all this world teaches that principle so clearly and so powerfully as does the Book of Mormon.

(Jeffrey R. Holland, CES Symposium, BYU, 9 Aug. 1994, 16–17, 19)

We forget that God and angels are looking upon us; we forget that the spirits of just men made perfect and our ancient fathers . . . are gazing upon us, and that our acts are open to the inspection of all the authorized agencies of the invisible world. And, forgetting these things sometimes, we act the part of fools, and the Spirit of God is grieved; it withdraws from us, and we are then left to grope our way in the dark.

(John Taylor, *The Gospel Kingdom*, ed. by G. Homer Durham [Salt Lake City: Bookcraft, 1987], 179)

[A missionary testimony meeting while David O. McKay was serving in Scotland in 1899] During the progress of the meeting, an elder on his own initiative arose and said, "Brethren, there are angels in this room." . . . President James L. McMurrin arose and confirmed that statement by pointing to one brother sitting just in front of me saying, "Yes, brethren, there are angels in this room, and one of them is the guardian angel of that young man sitting there." And he designated one who today is a patriarch of the Church. Pointing to another elder, he said, "And one is the guardian angel of that young man there," and singled out one whom I had known from childhood. . . . He turned to me and . . . said: "Let me say to you, Brother David, . . . if you will keep the faith, you will yet sit in the leading councils of the Church."

(David O. McKay, *Cherished Experiences from the Writings of President David O. McKay,* comp. by Clare Middlemiss [Salt Lake City: Deseret Book, 1955], 13–14)

———————

The spirits of the just are . . . blessed in their departure to the world of spirits. . . . They are not far from us, and know and understand our thoughts, feelings, and motions, and are often pained therewith.

(*Teachings of the Prophet Joseph Smith,* comp. by Joseph Fielding Smith [Salt Lake City: Deseret Book, 1976], 326)

———————

Every person who desires and strives to be a Saint is closely watched by fallen spirits that came here when Lucifer fell, and by the spirits of wicked persons who have been here in tabernacles and departed from them. . . . Those spirits are never idle, they are watching every person who wishes to do right and are continually prompting them to do wrong.

(Brigham Young, *Journal of Discourses* [London: Latter-day Saints' Book Depot, 1860], 7:239)

———————

There is a vast number of fallen spirits, cast out with him here on the earth. They do not die and disappear; they have not bodies only as they enter the tabernacles of men. They . . . are not to be seen with the sight of the eye. But there are many evil spirits amongst us, and they labor to overthrow the Church and kingdom of God. There never was a prophet in any age of the world but what the devil was continually at his elbow.

(Wilford Woodruff, *Journal of Discourses* [London: Latter-day Saints' Book Depot, 1871], 13:163)

———————

If you live up to your privileges, the angels cannot be restrained from being your associates.

(*Teachings of the Prophet Joseph Smith,* comp. by Joseph Fielding Smith [Salt Lake City: Deseret Book, 1976], 226–227)

———————

Our fathers and mothers, brothers, sisters and friends who have passed away from this earth, having been faithful and worthy to enjoy these rights and privileges, may have a mission given them to visit their relatives and friends upon the earth again, bringing from the divine Presence messages of love, of warning, or reproof and instruction to those whom they had learned

to love in the flesh.

(Joseph F. Smith, *Journal of Discourses* 22:351, 29 Jan. 1882; as quoted in *Latter-day Prophets Speak,* ed. by Daniel H. Ludlow [Salt Lake City: Bookcraft, 1951], 31)

———————

One might as well undertake to throw the water out of this world into the moon with a teaspoon, as to do away with the supervision of angels upon the human mind. . . . They are the police of heaven and report whatever transpires on earth, and carry the petitions and supplications of men, women, and children to the mansions of remembrance.

(John Taylor, *The Gospel Kingdom,* ed. by G. Homer Durham [Salt Lake City: Bookcraft, 1987], 31)

———————

When my wife died, I took my three girls to visit New York, Chicago, Boston, Philadelphia, Hartford, Washington, and other cities of interest, that they might forget the sorrow of the death of their mother. While in Washington my oldest girl was taken down with diphtheria. . . . Very soon thereafter my second daughter came down with it, and they were both sick nigh unto death. . . .

I went into my room and shed some bitter tears at the thought that, in all probability, I should have to take that little girl home in a coffin. Kneeling down, I pleaded with the Lord to spare her life. . . .

The testimony of the Spirit came to me: "The power of the Priesthood is here on the earth. Send for the elders and rebuke the power of the destroyer and that girl shall live." . . .

Brother Clawson anointed her, and Brother Cannon confirmed the anointing. In that confirmation he said something that I have never heard, before or since, in my life. He said, "The adversary, the destroyer, has decreed your death and made public announcement of his decree, but by the authority of the Priesthood of God which we hold as His servants, and in the name of Jesus Christ, our Redeemer, we rebuke the decree of the destroyer and say, you shall live."

As I was leaving the boarding house where I had been with my children, after they had recovered sufficiently to travel, the husband of the woman who kept the boarding house (she was away that day) said he could not keep from telling me a joke on his wife.

"Mr. Grant," he said, ". . . She believes in spiritualistic mediums and in communication through the mediums, and when your little girls were taken down sick in the house, she went to a medium, who told her the following story:

"I see in your home two little girls; I see that the older one of the two little girls is taken sick. . . . I now see that the next little girl is taken sick. . . . I now see that both of them are sick nigh unto death. . . . I now see the second little girl die."

Then she described the journey of that body in a coffin from Washington to Salt Lake. . . . She then saw my little daughter lowered into the grave.

I knew then the meaning of the inspiration of the living God to George Q. Cannon when he said, "The adversary has decreed your death, and made public announcement of it, and we rebuke that decree." It was rebuked, and instead of the little girl being buried as the spiritualistic medium said she would be, because the devil himself had inspired her to do so; by the Priesthood of God rebuking the decree of death she is alive, healthy and strong. She is the mother of seven beautiful children, and, in the providences of God, George Q. Cannon is their great-grandfather.

(Heber J. Grant, *Gospel Standards* [Salt Lake City: An Improvement Era Publication, 1942], 362–364)

_____

One day in Salt Lake City a son kissed his mother good morning, took his dinner bucket, and went to City Creek Canyon where he worked. He was a switchman on the train that was carrying logs out of the canyon. Before noon his body was brought back lifeless. The mother was inconsolable. She could not be reconciled to that tragedy—her boy just in his early twenties so suddenly taken away. The funeral was held, and words of consolation were spoken, but she was not consoled. She couldn't understand it.

One forenoon, so she says, after her husband had gone to his office to attend to his duties as a member of the Presiding Bishopric, she lay in a relaxed state on the bed, still yearning and praying for some consolation. She said that her son appeared and said, "Mother, you needn't worry. That was merely an accident. I gave the signal to the engineer to move on, and as the train started, I jumped for the handle of the freight car, and my foot got caught in a sagebrush, and I fell under the wheel. I went to Father soon after that, but he was so busy in the office I couldn't influence him—I couldn't make any impression upon him, and I tried again. Today I come to you to give you that comfort and tell you that I am happy."

Well, you may not believe it. You may think she imagined it, but you can't make her think so, and you can't make that boy's father think it. I cite it today as an instance of the reality of the existence of intelligence and environment to which you and I are "dead," so to speak, as was this boy's father.—FS, ms., James H. Douglas, Ogden, 1943.

(*Gospel Ideals: Selections from the Discourses of David O. McKay*, sel. by G. Homer Durham [Salt Lake City: Improvement Era], 1953], 525–526)

_____

I feel quite confident that the eye of Joseph, the Prophet, and of the martyrs of this dispensation, and of Brigham [Young], and John [Taylor], and Wilford [Woodruff], and those faithful men who were associated with them in their ministry upon the earth, are carefully guarding the interests of the kingdom of God. . . . I believe they are as deeply interested in our welfare today, . . . with greater capacity, with far more interest, behind the veil, than they were in the flesh . . . they see us, they are solicitous for our welfare, they love us now more than ever.

(Joseph F. Smith, in Conference Report, Apr. 1916, 2–3; as quoted in *Latter-day Prophets Speak*, ed. by Daniel H. Ludlow [Salt Lake City: Bookcraft, 1951], 31)

_____

I called upon brother Joseph, and we walked down the bank of the river. . . . He told me that he had contests with the devil, face to face. . . . Some persons will say to me, that there are no evil sprits. I tell you they are thicker than the "Mormons" are in this country, but the Lord has said that there are more for us than there can be against us. "Who are they," says one? Righteous men who have been upon the earth.

But do you suppose that angels will pay friendly visits to those who do not live up to their privileges? . . . It is written that where the Holy Ghost takes up its abode the Father and Son will come and abide. That is the God whom I serve, one who has millions of angels at His command. Do you suppose that there are any angels here to-day? I would not wonder if there were ten times more angels here than people. We do not see them, but they are here watching us, and are anxious for our salvation.

(Heber C. Kimball, *Journal of Discourses* [London: Latter-day Saints' Book Depot, 1856], 3:229–230)

_____

An evidence that those in the Spirit World know of the work we do here in the Temples was related by President Wood of the Alberta Temple. While sealing a group of children to their parents, in the midst of the ceremony he felt an impression to ask the mother who was present, "Sister, does this list contain the names of all your children?" She said, "Yes." He began again but once more he stopped and asked if the list named all her children. She told him there were no more children. He attempted to proceed, but a third time was impelled to ask: "My Sister, have you not lost a child whose name is not on this list?" Then she said, "Yes, I do remember now. We did lose a little baby. It was born alive and then died soon after. I had forgotten to put its name down." The name was given, and then it, being the first born, was named first and all were sealed to the parents.

Then President Wood said: "Everytime I started to seal the children I heard a voice say: 'Mother, don't forget me,' and I could not go any farther." The appeal was made each time until the omission was discovered.

(Melvin J. Ballard, *Church News*, 20 Jan. 1940, 2; as quoted in *Exceptional Stories from the Lives of Our Apostles*, comp. by Leon R. Hartshorn [Salt Lake City: Deseret Book, 1973], 17)

An interesting sidelight to the Spirit of the Lord and its connection to music was reinforced over three decades ago in my mission in southern England by Elder Loren C. Dunn, who was a visiting General Authority at a zone conference. As the meeting began, he asked the mission president for the opportunity to express some of the feelings he was experiencing at the moment.

He stood in front of the missionaries and said, "Would all of the Elders called to the position of district leader please stand." One by one each was asked, "What is your favorite hymn?"

Six different district leaders chose separate hymns. There were songs of reverence and reflection such as "I Stand All Amazed" and rousing and spirited ones like "Ye Elders of Israel."

Elder Dunn then turned his attention to the rest of the missionaries seated in the chapel: "When I give the signal, I want all of you to sing the song chosen by your district leader." He continued, "And I want all of you to sing the hymns at the same time."

The instructions had barely sunk in when Elder Dunn signaled for the singing to begin. Eighty missionaries, representing six different districts, sang their hymns of praise—all at the same time. When all the verses were complete, the room was filled with an uncomfortable silence, as all the missionaries gazed toward Elder Dunn with the same thought. "Why were we asked to do such a humiliating thing?"

He looked into the faces of the confused and embarrassed missionaries and said, "What you just felt while singing these hymns is the same spirit I felt coming from you as I entered the chapel. Some of you need to rededicate yourselves so that we can all be singing the same song of service to the Lord."

Elder Dunn had done something that had completely caught the missionaries off guard. He had used the sacred hymns of Zion to illustrate that it is not enough just to sing good music, or just to be in the right place; our hearts must also be united in order to obtain the "wages" which are promised through the Spirit of the Lord.

(Jack R. Christianson and K. Douglas Bassett, *Life*

Lessons from the Book of Mormon [Salt Lake City: Deseret Book, 2003], 242–243)

We should never disappoint our Father, nor the heavenly hosts who are watching over us. We should not disappoint the millions in the spirit world, who too are watching over us with an interest and anxiety.

(*Teachings of Presidents of the Church—Wilford Woodruff* [Salt Lake City: The Church of Jesus Christ of Latter-day Saints, 2004], 44)

In the gospel of Jesus Christ we have help from both sides of the veil. When disappointment and discouragement strike—and they will—we need to remember that if our eyes could be opened, we would see horses and chariots of fire as far as the eye can see, riding at great speed to come to our protection. [2 Kings 6:14–17.] They will always be there, these armies of heaven, in defense of Abraham's seed. We have been given this promise from heaven.

(Jeffrey R. Holland, *However Long and Hard the Road* [Salt Lake City: Deseret Book, 1985], 13–14)

Alma 4:6–12 • PEOPLE OF THE CHURCH WAX PROUD
(Refer in this text to 2 Nephi 9:28–51; Jacob 2:13–17; 3 Ne. 6:10–16.)

Pride is essentially competitive in nature.... In the words of C. S. Lewis: "Pride gets no pleasure out of having something only out of having more of it than the next man.... It is the comparison that makes you proud: the pleasure of being above the rest. Once the element of competition has gone, pride has gone" (*Mere Christiantiy* [New York: Macmillan, 1852], 109–10)....

Pride is ugly. It says, "If you succeed, I am a failure."...

Pride is the great stumbling block to Zion. I repeat: Pride *is* the great stumbling block to Zion.

(Ezra Taft Benson, in Conference Report, Apr. 1989 [Salt Lake City: The Church of Jesus Christ of Latter-day Saints, 1989], 4–7)

Alma 4:9 • PRIDE OF MEMBERS EXCEED THAT OF NONMEMBERS
(Refer in this text to Mosiah 29:26–27.)

Alma 4:10–11 • EXAMPLE OF THE CHURCH

One of our best missionary tools is the sterling examples of members who live the gospel. This is what the Lord meant when He said to the Church, "Zion must increase in beauty, and in holiness.... Zion must put on her beautiful garments" (D&C 82:14).

(Ezra Taft Benson, *Ensign*, May 1985 [Salt Lake City: The Church of Jesus Christ of Latter-day Saints, 1985], 7.)

———————

How much easier it is to understand and accept if the seeker after truth can also see the principles of the gospel at work in the lives of other believers. No greater service can be given to the missionary calling of this Church than to be exemplary in positive Christian virtues in our lives.

(*Teachings of Spencer W. Kimball*, ed. by Edward L. Kimball [Salt Lake City: Bookcraft, 1982], 555)

———————

The time is coming when we will be mixed up in these now peaceful valleys to that extent that it will be difficult to tell the face of a Saint from the face of an enemy to the people of God. Then, brethren, look out for the great sieve, for there will be a great sifting time, and many will fall; for I say unto you there is a test, a TEST, A TEST coming, and who will be able to stand? . . . To meet the difficulties that are coming, it will be necessary for you to have a knowledge of the truth of this work for yourselves. The difficulties will be of such a character that the man or woman who does not possess this personal knowledge or witness will fall. If you have not got the testimony, live right and call upon the Lord and cease not till you obtain it. If you do not you will not stand. . . . The time will come when no man nor woman will be able to endure on borrowed light. Each will have to be guided by the light within himself. If you do not have it, how can you stand?

(Orson F. Whitney, *Life of Heber C. Kimball* [Salt Lake City: Stevens and Wallis Publishers, 1945], 446, 449–450)

Alma 4:15 • THE SPIRIT DID NOT FAIL HIM
(Contrast with Alma 30:60.)

Alma 4:19 • PURE TESTIMONY

Those who have prepared carefully for the fast and testimony meeting won't . . . give sermons nor exhortations nor travel reports nor try to entertain as they bear witness. Because they will have already expressed appreciation to people privately, they will have less need to do it publicly. Neither will they feel a need to use eloquent language or to go on at length. A testimony is a simple expression of what we feel . . . . Even a child can feel such things, . . . and our preparation of fasting and prayer produces in us child-like feelings. That preparation for the fast and testimony meeting is a covenant obligation for members of the Church.

(Henry B. Eyring, *Ensign*, Nov. 1996 [Salt Lake City: The Church of Jesus Christ of Latter-day Saints, 1996], 32)

———————

The fundamental principles of our religion are the testimony of the Apostles and prophets, concerning Jesus Christ, that He died, was buried, and rose again the third day, and ascended into heaven; and all other things which pertain to our religion are only appendages to it.

(*Teachings of the Prophet Joseph Smith*, comp. by Joseph Fielding Smith [Salt Lake City: Deseret Book, 1976], 12.

———————

A few years ago I conducted a church history tour and we went back east and one of the places we stopped was Niagara Falls. . . . We stayed at a hotel right on the riverbank, . . . so we were told to go check in, find out where our room was, and then meet in a large hall for dinner. As we . . . went to the dining room, the most frequent comment was, "Do you have a room with a view?" Everybody was asking everybody else, "Do you have a room with a view?" I had looked out the window. I was on the backside of the building. I had no view . . . of the falls. But the next day I was talking to the group, and I said it this way. "To have a room with a view, an office with a view, a home on the hillside with a view— that's wonderful! But if you get a testimony of the gospel, whereby you know about Jesus and you know about the Plan of Salvation, and you know about Joseph Smith and . . . [the living Prophet], you may not have a room with a view, but you will have a life with a view." And that's what you need.

(Robert J. Matthews, Devotional Address, Orem Institute of Religion, 18 Feb. 2005)

———————

We often hear some members, and especially children, bear their testimonies, listing things for which they are thankful: their love of family, the Church, their teachers, their friends. For them, the gospel is something that they are grateful for because it makes them feel happy and secure. . . .

My experience throughout the Church leads me to worry that too many of our members' testimonies linger on "I am thankful" and "I love," and too few are able to say with humble but sincere clarity, "I know." As a result, our meetings sometimes lack the testimony-rich, spiritual underpinnings that stir the soul and have meaningful, positive impact on the lives of all those who hear them.

Our testimony meetings need to be more centered on the Savior, the doctrines of the gospel, the blessings of the Restoration, and the teachings of the scriptures. We need to replace stories, travelogues, and lectures with pure testimonies. . . .

The Spirit cannot be restrained when pure testimony of Christ is borne.

(M. Russell Ballard, in Conference Report, Oct. 2004 [Salt Lake City: The Church of Jesus Christ of Latter-day Saints, 2004], 42–43)

———————

Many years ago, Brigham Young told of an early missionary in the Church who was asked to share his testimony with a large group of people. According to President Young, this particular elder "never had been able to say that he knew Joseph [Smith] was a Prophet." He would have preferred to just say a prayer and leave, but the circumstances made that impossible. So he started to speak, and "as soon as he got 'Joseph' out, 'is a Prophet,' was . . . next; and from that, his tongue was loosened, and he continued talking until near sundown."

President Young used this experience to teach that "the Lord pours out His Spirit upon a man, when he testifies that [which] the Lord gives him to testify of" (*Millennial Star*, supplement, 1853, 30).

(M. Russell Ballard, in Conference Report, Oct. 2004 [Salt Lake City: The Church of Jesus Christ of Latter-day Saints, 2004], 44)

Alma 5:7, 12–14, 26; 7:14 • CHANGE OF HEART
(Refer in this text to Mosiah 5:2, 7; 27:24–26.)

Would not the progress of the Church increase dramatically today with an increasing number of those who are spiritually reborn? Can you imagine what would happen in our homes? Can you imagine what would happen with an increasing number of copies of the Book of Mormon in the hands of an increasing number of missionaries who know how to use it and who have been born of God? . . . The Lord works from the inside out. The world works from the outside in. The world would take people out of the slums. Christ takes the slums out of people, and then they take themselves out of the slums. The world would mold men by changing their environment. Christ changes men, who then change their environment. The world would shape human behavior, but Christ can change human nature.

(Ezra Taft Benson, in Conference Report, Oct. 1985 [Salt Lake City: The Church of Jesus Christ of Latter-day Saints, 1985], 5)

Alma 5:14, 19 • THE IMAGE OF GOD ENGRAVEN UPON YOUR COUNTENANCE

We are called upon to purify our inner feelings, to change our hearts, to make our outward actions and appearance conform to what we say we believe and feel inside.

(Howard W. Hunter, *Ensign*, May 1992 [Salt Lake City: The Church of Jesus Christ of Latter-day Saints, 1992], 62)

———————

While serving my full-time mission to England, I had the privilege of meeting several General Authorities. One who made a lasting impression on me was President Gordon B. Hinckley. Oddly enough, the greatest impact he had on my life came after I returned from the British Isles to my home in Redding, California.

About a year after arriving home, I acquired a job as a waiter at a posh restaurant. The waiters were required to dress in suits with white shirts and bow ties. We were also asked to grow our hair long and wear mustaches. It does not take a lot of imagination to realize that I looked very different than I did while serving as a full-time missionary. A few months after I started the job, my father was called to be a bishop. President Hinckley was sent out from Salt Lake City to set him apart in his new calling.

My wife and I, as well as my extended family, sat in the high council room of the stake center, anxiously awaiting the arrival of Elder Hinckley. As he entered the room, the atmosphere was full of his gentle enthusiasm. Instantly, my mind was brimming with a flood of memories of England, and my heart was full. Seeing him again made me yearn for the time in England that could never be revisited.

Each person in the room felt of his special spirit as he shook their hands one by one. As he came toward me, I reached out and gave him an enthusiastic missionary handshake, which seemed to catch him off guard a little bit. My energetic greeting caused him to step back.

Smiling at me he said, "You'll have to excuse me; your greeting makes me feel like we're old friends." He inquired, "Have we met before?"

"Yes," I said. "I'm Doug Bassett; I met you in London while serving my mission."

He hesitated for a moment, perhaps to assess how teachable I was. Placing his hand on my shoulder, he drew me closer to him. Drawing his mouth near my ear, he spoke in a manner that ensured that I would hear his message. His voice came forth in a soft tone of regret: "You'll have to forgive me for not recognizing you, Elder Bassett; you no longer have the look of a missionary."

He then stepped back and studied me just long enough to make sure I understood the message he had delivered. Following a gentle squeeze on my shoulder, he moved on.

I was not upset at him; I loved and respected him too much for that. But make no mistake about it, his message had found its mark—like an arrow to my heart. He wanted me to know that while he was not judging me personally, younger men than myself would judge a mission and its ability to change the life of a missionary simply by my appearance. Just because I was not to judge others did not mean these young men would not judge me or the Church by my appearance.

(Jack R. Christianson and K. Douglas Bassett, *Life Lessons from the Book of Mormon* [Salt Lake City: Deseret Book, 2003], 115–117)

Of course returned missionaries are not expected to wear white shirts and ties all of the time. But wearing sloppy clothes and weird hairstyles to supposedly look trendy is not proper for one who holds the divine commission of the priesthood. Returned missionaries are an example to the young men of the Aaronic Priesthood, who will be the future missionaries. Often that which is *seen* by the Aaronic Priesthood is more powerful and persuasive than what is *said*.

(James E. Faust, in Conference Report, Apr. 2000 [Salt Lake City: The Church of Jesus Christ of Latter-day Saints, 2000], 55)

The pleasures of the body can become an obsession for some; so too can the attention we give to our outward appearance. Sometimes there is a selfish excess of exercising, dieting, makeovers, and spending money on the latest fashions (see Alma 1:27).

I am troubled by the practice of extreme makeovers. Happiness comes from accepting the bodies we have been given as divine gifts and enhancing our natural attributes, not from remaking our bodies after the image of the world. The Lord wants us to be made over—but in His image, not in the image of the world, by receiving His image in our countenances (see Alma 5:14, 19).

I remember well the insecurities I felt as a teenager with a bad case of acne. I tried to care for my skin properly. My parents helped me get medical attention. For years I even went without eating chocolate and all the greasy fast foods around which teens often socialize, but with no obvious healing consequences. It was difficult for me at that time to fully appreciate this body which was giving me so much grief. But my good mother taught me a higher law. Over and over she said to me, "You must do everything you can to make your appearance pleasing, but the minute you walk out the door, forget yourself and start concentrating on others." . . .

When we become other-oriented, or selfless, we develop an inner beauty of spirit that glows in our outward appearance. This is how we make ourselves in the Lord's image rather than the world's and receive His image in our countenances. . . .

The spiritual and physical truly are linked.

I remember an incident in my home growing up when my mother's sensitive spirit was affected by a physical indulgence. She had experimented with a new sweet roll recipe. They were big and rich and yummy—and very filling. Even my teenage brothers couldn't eat more than one. That night at family prayer my father called upon Mom to pray. She buried her head and didn't respond. He gently prodded her, "Is something wrong?" Finally she said, "I don't feel very spiritual tonight. I just ate three of those rich sweet rolls." I suppose that many of us have similarly offended our spirits at times by physical indulgences.

(Susan W. Tanner, *Ensign*, Nov. 2005 [Salt Lake City: The Church of Jesus Christ of Latter-day Saints, 2005], 14–15)

I do not believe that the method of accountability at the Judgment Day regarding this book will come in the form of an academic exam that will test our knowledge of the peoples, places, and events among the Nephites. However, the test may come in our willingness to expose ourselves to its pages and then to use the book to bless the lives of those around us.

Over the years I have come to understand that the real test for us personally goes beyond that of just obtaining a testimony. It does not come down to just knowing the Book of Mormon is true, but whether we are true to the Book of Mormon. In the final analysis it is not if we have digested the Book of Mormon, but if the Book of Mormon has digested us. Therein lies the test. The process becomes finalized when a person can stand before the Lord as a living witness to the power of the Book of Mormon in aiding an individual and attain "the measure of the stature of the fulness of Christ" (Ephesians 4:13).

Elder Dallin H. Oaks said: "This process requires far more than acquiring knowledge. . . . We must act and think so that we are converted by it. . . . The Final Judgment . . . is an acknowledgement of the final effect of our acts and thoughts—what we have *become*" (in Conference Report, Oct. 2000, 40–41).

(Jack R. Christianson and K. Douglas Bassett, *Life Lessons from the Book of Mormon* [Salt Lake City: Deseret Book, 2003], 267–268)

As I look at the young people I have served over the years, I get the feeling that many of them do not see themselves as dual (physical and spiritual) beings.

This brings to mind the analogy of the football coach and his staff who spend the week prior to a big game ironing their players' uniforms. I suppose the appearance of the team is important to a degree, but what about the more urgent preparations regarding the players' performance that needed to be considered for the upcoming game? Uniforms are important, but that's not really what football is all about. I feel that some of the problems with drugs, alcohol, and morality that engulf the physical lives of our youth might be avoided if they truly saw their bodies as an extension of their spirits. As parents, we may find it easy to get caught up in "ironing the uniforms" to be worn by the spirits God has placed in our care.

In this day and age it seems somewhat fashionable to speak of self-image. The world teaches that self-image is tied to the body and being productive in those things valued in a materialistic world. We . . . [need] to expand . . . [our] understanding beyond the physical realm and . . . [accept] that true self-image has much less to do with how a person views himself than it does with how he views his Heavenly Father in relation to himself. "Having the image of God engraven upon your countenances" (Alma 5:19) is the only manner in which we can truly feel good about ourselves. In this regard, self-image becomes selfish unless it becomes a God-image that reflects upon our behavior. In a sense, our bodies become the classroom where life's most important lessons are learned. But our true self here in mortality is our spiritual self, simply because our mortal bodies will separate from us at death.

(K. Douglas Bassett, *The Barber's Song* [Springville, Utah: Cedar Fort, 2005], 22–23)

There is beauty in all peoples. I speak not of the beauty or the image that comes of lotions and creams, of pastes and packs, as seen in slick-paper magazines and on television. Whether the skin be fair or dark, the eyes round or slanted, is absolutely irrelevant. I have seen beautiful people in every one of the scores of nations I have visited. Little children everywhere are beautiful. And so are the aged, whose wrinkled hands and faces speak of struggle and survival of the virtues and values they have embraced. We wear on our faces the results of what we believe and how we behave, and such behavior is most evident in the eyes and on the faces of those who have lived many years. . . .

My wife and I have walked together through much of storm as well as sunshine. Today, neither of us stands as tall as we once did. For both of us, the rivets are getting a little loose and the solder is getting a little soft. As I looked at her across the table one evening recently, I noted the wrinkles in her face and hands. But are they less beautiful than before? No; in fact, they are more so. Those wrinkles have a beauty of their own, and inherent in their presence is something that speaks reassuringly of strength and integrity, and a love that runs more deeply and quietly than ever before. I am thankful for the beauty that comes with age and perspective and

increased understanding.

(Gordon B. Hinckley, *Standing for Something* [New York: Times Books, 2000], 93–95)

Alma 5:15 • EYE OF FAITH

The "eye of faith" means the ability and capacity to keep your eyes on the power source (see Matt. 14:23–32).

(Ross Cole, address to CES Educators, Ricks College, 30 June 1995)

Alma 5:21–22, 24, 27 • GARMENTS WASHED

It is through His atoning sacrifice that our garments will be cleansed. The scriptural reference to garments encompasses our whole being. The need for cleansing comes as we become soiled through sin.

(Lynn A. Mickelsen, in Conference Report, Oct. 2003 [Salt Lake City: The Church of Jesus Christ of Latter-day Saints, 2003], 9)

Alma 5:26 • CAN YOU FEEL SO NOW

I was building a shed next to my home. . . . I asked my son to go over to the neighbors and borrow a power drill so that 'turning the screws in' would not be such a tedious job. He returned with a rechargeable power drill. . . . I found that as I tried to put in the screws the drill would take them in about half-way and then the power would give out. The battery-powered drill did not have sufficient power for the difficult task. I told my son to take the drill back and ask the neighbor for his other drill because the rechargeable one did not have enough power for the job I was doing. When he returned with the other drill, we plugged it into the outlet in our home. I found that I now had more than enough power to drive the screws all the way into the wood. Both power drills were instruments in my hands; however, only one was able to perform the task that I needed done. As [returned] missionaries and servants of the Lord we might ask ourselves, Am I like the rechargeable drill trying to get by on spirituality stored up from past experiences, or am I striving to be in tune continually so I am like a power drill that is plugged into the source of all power?

(Clyde J. Williams; as quoted in *The Book of Mormon: Alma, The Testimony of the Word*, ed. by Monte S. Nyman and Charles D. Tate [Provo, Utah: Religious Studies Center, BYU, 1992], 91)

My dear brothers and sisters who have returned from missions, if the people you helped bring into the Church were to see you today, would they recognize you? Would they see a bright countenance when they look into your eyes? Are you praying, reading the scriptures, going to the temple, and otherwise investing in your spiritual well-being? . . . I hope that worldly concerns have not kept you from investing in eternity.

(Mary Ellen Smoot, "Everything Money Cannot Buy," Satellite Broadcast, 3 Feb. 2002, Brigham Young University [Salt Lake City: The Church of Jesus Christ of Latter-day Saints, 2002], 5)

———

Come home with your heads up. Keep yourselves clean, from the crowns of your heads to the soles of your feet; be pure in heart,—otherwise you will return bowed down in spirit and with a fallen countenance, and will feel as though you never could rise again.

I wish to make this request; that the Elders who return from missions consider themselves just as much on a mission here as in England or in any other part of the world.

We frequently call the brethren to go on missions to preach the Gospel, and they will go and labor as faithfully as men can do. . . . In a few years they come home, and throwing off their coats and hats, they will say, "Religion, stand aside, I am going to work now to get something for myself and my family." This is folly in the extreme. . . . When he has been at home a week, a month, a year, or ten years, the spirit of preaching and the spirit of the gospel ought to be within him like a river flowing forth. . . . If this is not the case he does not fill his mission.

(*Discourses of Brigham Young*, comp. by John A. Widtsoe [Salt Lake City: Deseret Book, 1954], 328–329)

———

A person never learns anything until he realizes how little he knows. . . . Some quit learning about the gospel when they have completed a mission for the Church; some quit learning when they become an executive or have a prominent position in or out of the Church.

(Harold B. Lee, in Conference Report, Apr. 1971 [Salt Lake City: The Church of Jesus Christ of Latter-day Saints, 1971], 93)

———

To those of you who have already served, please remember that you were released from your missions but not from the Church. You spent two years as a representative of the Lord Jesus Christ. We expect you to always look and act like one of His disciples. Look the part. Act the part. Don't follow worldly trends and fashions. You are better than that. If you have slipped, then do what is necessary to regain your spiritual balance. The rules for happiness and success after your mission are pretty much the same as they were during your mission: pray hard, work hard, and be obedient.

(M. Russell Ballard, in Conference Report, Oct. 2002 [Salt Lake City: The Church of Jesus Christ of Latter-day Saints, 2002], 53)

———

There is no class of Elders that have occupied the public stand to whom I have listened with as much interest, none who have warmed up my heart so much as the returning missionary. They come home full of the spirit of their mission, filled with the Spirit of God and love for their fellowmen. . . . But it seems that in too many cases, in a very short time after their return home, they lose their interest and settle down, confining their labors to their own immediate affairs. . . .

There is no person who can hope to be active and strong physically unless he gets proper exercise. . . . So it is with the man who goes out to preach the Gospel and makes a successful missionary; if he does not continue to exercise himself and interest himself in the spiritual welfare of his fellow beings after he returns home, he will sooner or later lose the Spirit he had while in the missionary field.

(*Teachings of Presidents of the Church—Heber J. Grant* [Salt Lake City: The Church of Jesus Christ of Latter-day Saints, 2002], 184–185)

———

If you truly progress in the process of becoming a missionary, both before going on a mission and in the mission field, then when the day arrives for your honorable release as a full-time missionary, you will depart from your field of labor and return to your family—but you will never cease your missionary service. A priesthood holder is a missionary at all times and in all places. . . .

After coming back to your homes and families, may you returned missionaries always be missionaries.

(David A. Bednar, *Ensign*, Nov. 2005 [Salt Lake City: The Church of Jesus Christ of Latter-day Saints, 2005], 46–47)

Alma 5:27 • HUMILITY
(Refer in this text to Mosiah 2:25–26.)

You see, it's hard to feel that you are sufficiently humble. If you did, you might not be.

(Henry B. Eyring, "Come Unto Christ," address given at BYU, 29 October 1989)

———

The Prophet Joseph Smith, in our own dispensation, said this: "When the Twelve or any other witnesses stand, before the congregations of the earth, and they preach in the power and demonstration of the Spirit of God, and the people are astonished and confounded at the doctrine, and say, 'That man has preached a powerful discourse, a great sermon,' Then let that man or those men take care that they do not ascribe the glory unto themselves, but be careful that they are humble, and ascribe the praise and glory to God and the Lamb; for it is by the power of the Holy Priesthood and the Holy Ghost that they have power thus to speak. What art thou, O man, but dust? And from whom receivest thou thy power and blessings, but from God?"

Who has the right to be smug and conceited in his own powers or accomplishments or talents? God gave us our breath, our life, our talents, our brains, our capacities.

(Spencer W. Kimball, *BYU Speeches of the Year*, Jan. 1963 [Provo, Utah: BYU Press, 1963], 10–11)

———

Humility! That does not mean weakness; that does not mean lack of courage, lack of faith, lack of self-confidence; but it means the recognition of a higher power upon which we are dependent . . .

(Ezra Taft Benson, *So Shall Ye Reap* [Salt Lake City: Deseret Book, 1960], 33–34)

———

When one becomes conscious of his great humility, he has already lost it. When one begins boasting of his humility, it has already become pride—the antithesis of humility. . . . Somebody asked me this morning, "How do you keep humble?" Sometimes I am humble and sometimes I am unhumble. I think there is a formula that will never fail. First, you evaluate yourself. . . . I would be nothing without the Lord. My breath, my brains, my hearing, my sight, my locomotion, my everything depends upon the Lord. That is the first step and then we pray, and pray often, and we will not get up from our knees until we have communicated. The line may be down; we may have let it fall to pieces, but I will not get up from my knees until I have established communication—if it is twenty minutes, if it is all night like Enos. . . If it takes all day long, you stay on your knees until your unhumbleness has dissipated, until you feel the humble spirit and realize, "I could die this minute if it were not for the Lord's good grace. I am dependent upon him—totally dependent upon him," and then you read the scriptures.

(*Teachings of Spencer W. Kimball*, ed. by Edward L. Kimball [Salt Lake City: Bookcraft, 1982], 233–234)

———

Remember your indebtedness to the Lord and never become indebted to the things of the world. No person can fully and completely discharge his debt to our Savior for what He has done for us, but we can make regular payments. As we give our will to Him and do what He would have us do, we are showing appreciation for His gift of the Atonement.

(Mary Ellen Smoot, "Everything Money Cannot Buy," Satellite Broadcast, 3 Feb. 2002, Brigham Young University [Salt Lake City: The Church of Jesus Christ of Latter-day Saints, 2002], 6)

———

[David Whitmer told the following story:] At times when brother Joseph would attempt to translate . . . he found he was spiritually blind and could not translate. He told us that his mind dwelt too much on earthly things, and various causes would make him incapable of proceeding with the translation. When in this condition he would go out and pray, and when he became sufficiently humble before God, he could then proceed with the translation. Now we see how very strict the Lord is, and how he requires the heart of man to be just right in his sight before he can receive revelation. . . .

To illustrate so you can see: One morning when he was getting ready to continue the translation, something went wrong about the house and he was put out about it. Something that Emma, his wife, had done. Oliver and I went upstairs and Joseph came up soon after to continue the translation but he could not do anything. He could not translate a single syllable. He went downstairs, out into the orchard, and made supplication to the Lord; was gone about an hour—came back to the house, and asked Emma's forgiveness and then came upstairs where we were and then the translation went on all right. He could do nothing save he was humble and faithful.

(*A Comprehensive History of the Church of Jesus Christ of Latter-day Saints*, ed. by B. H. Roberts [Salt Lake City: The Church of Jesus Christ of Latter-day Saints, 1977], 1:130–131; as quoted in *The Book of Mormon: Fourth Nephi through Moroni, from Zion to Destruction*, ed. by Monte S. Nyman and Charles D. Tate [Provo, Utah: Religious Studies Center, BYU, 1995], 255–256)

———

If we were humble, nothing would change us—neither praise nor discouragement. If someone were to criticize us, we would not feel discouraged. If someone were to praise us, we also would not feel proud.

(Jose Luis Gonzalez-Balado, *Mother Teresa—In My Own Words*, [New York: Gramercy Books, 1996], 53)

———

It is of interest, however, that during the first 30 years of His life in Nazareth, Jesus apparently drew little attention to Himself even though He was living a sinless life (see Matthew 13:54–56; Mark 6:2–3). That should encourage us to do better in our own quiet and humble way without drawing attention to ourselves.

(William W. Parmley, in Conference Report, Oct. 2003 [Salt Lake City: The Church of Jesus Christ of Latter-day Saints, 2003], 99)

In the kingdom of God, greatness begins with humility and submissiveness. These companion virtues are the first critical steps to opening the doors to the blessings of God and the power of the priesthood. It matters not who we are or how lofty our credentials appear. Humility and submissiveness to the Lord, coupled with a grateful heart, are our strength and our hope. . . .

We see the prominent business executive graciously and humbly receiving and being taught by a humble, sometimes even intimidated home teacher. We see the highly educated humbly following counsel from their bishops, who sometimes have little formal education. We see former bishops and stake presidents graciously and humbly accepting callings to teach in the Primary, assist in the nursery.

(Richard C. Edgley, in Conference Report, Oct. 2003 [Salt Lake City: The Church of Jesus Christ of Latter-day Saints, 2003], 104)

Nobody likes one who is arrogant, who is conceited, who is egocentric, who is thinking only of himself. There is no place for arrogance on the part of any of us, not one. Be humble before the Lord, and be prayerful.

(*Discourses of President Gordon B. Hinckley*, 1995–99 [Salt Lake City: The Church of Jesus Christ of Latter-day Saints, 2004], 1:398)

I do not like to receive honors. Compliments always bother me because the great work of moving the gospel forward has in the past, does now, and will in the future depend upon ordinary members.

My wife and I do not expect reward for ourselves greater than will come to our own children or to our parents. We do not press nor do we really want our children to set great prominence and visibility in the world or even in the Church as their goal in life. That has so very little to do with the worth of the soul.

(Boyd K. Packer, in Conference Report, Oct. 2004 [Salt Lake City: The Church of Jesus Christ of Latter-day Saints, 2004], 92)

A story contained in the family lore of Brigham Young's descendants illustrates the submissive nature of humility. It recounts that in a public meeting the Prophet Joseph, possibly as a test, sternly rebuked Brigham Young for something he had done or something he was supposed to have done but hadn't—the detail is unclear. When Joseph finished the rebuke, everyone in the room waited for Brigham Young's response. This powerful man, later know as the Lion of the Lord, in a voice

everyone could tell was sincere, said simply and humbly, "Joseph, what do you want me to do?" (see Truman G. Madsen, "Hugh B. Brown—Youthful Veteran," *New Era*, Apr. 1976, 16).

I resonate to the English author John Ruskin's memorable statement that "the first test of a truly great man is his humility." He continued: "I do not mean, by humility, doubt of his own power. . . . [But really] great men . . . have a curious . . . feeling that . . . greatness is not *in* them, but *through* them. . . . And they see something Divine . . . in every other man . . ., and are endlessly, foolishly, incredibly merciful."

(*The Works of John Ruskin*, ed. E. T. Cook and Alexander Wedderburn, 39 vols. (1903–12), 5:331; as quoted in Merlin K. Jensen, *Ensign*, May 2001 [Salt Lake City: The Church of Jesus Christ of Latter-day Saints, 2001], 10–11)

People ask me frequently what is my favorite verse of scripture. I have many and this is one of them, "Be thou humble; and the Lord thy God shall lead thee by the hand, and give thee answer to thy prayers" (D&C 112:10). What a promise to those who walk without arrogance, to those who walk without conceit, to those who walk without egotism, to those who walk humbly. . . . What a solid and wonderful promise that is.

(*Teachings of Gordon B. Hinckley* [Salt Lake City: Deseret Book, 1997], 265)

Alma 5:28 • ARE YE STRIPPED OF PRIDE?

Adulation is poison. It is so very important that you do not let praise and adulation go to your head. Never lose sight of the fact that the Lord put you where you are according to His design, which you don't fully understand. Acknowledge the Lord for whatever good you can accomplish and give Him the credit and the glory.

(Gordon B. Hinckley, *Stand a Little Taller* [Salt Lake City: Eagle Gate, 2001], 5)

Alma 5:37 • PUFFED UP IN THE VAIN THINGS OF THE WORLD

There is nothing inherently evil about money. The Good Samaritan used the same coinage to serve his fellowman that Judas used to betray the Master. It is "the *love of money* [which] is the root of all evil" (1 Timothy 6:10; italics added). . . .

Money can make us selfish and prideful, "puffed up in the vain things of the world" (Alma 5:37). In contrast, if used for fulfilling our legal obligations and for paying our tithes and offerings, money can demonstrate integrity and develop unselfishness. The spiritually enlightened use of property can help prepare us for the higher law of a celestial glory.

(Dallin H. Oaks, in Conference Report, Oct. 1985 [Salt Lake City: The Church of Jesus Christ of Latter-day Saints, 1985], 78)

Alma 5:37–39, 57, 60 • WHO IS YOUR SHEPHERD?

[Speaking of some members of the Church] They have refused to live the gospel, when they knew it to be true; or have been blinded by tradition; or for other causes have not been willing to walk in the light. In this class we could properly place those who refuse to take upon them the name of Christ, even though they belong to the Church; and those who are not willing when called to go forth and preach to a perverse world 'Jesus Christ, and him crucified.' They may live clean lives; they may be honest, industrious, good citizens, and all that; but they are not willing to assume any portion of the labor which devolves upon members of the Church, in carrying on the great work of redemption of mankind. We have known members of the Church who have gone out in the world and have mingled with those not of our faith, and these members were ashamed to have it known that they were Latter-day Saints. Such persons certainly are not valiant in the testimony of Jesus.

(Joseph Fielding Smith, *Doctrines of Salvation*, comp. by Bruce R. McConkie [Salt Lake City: Bookcraft, 1955], 2:28–29)

Alma 5:44, 6:1 • HOLY ORDER

(Refer in this text to 2 Nephi 5:26.)

In general terms a *priest* is a minister. One so designated (if he is a true priest) must in fact hold the priesthood; yet the designation *priest*, when so used, has no reference to any particular office in the priesthood. Thus among the Nephites it was the practice to consecrate priests and teachers, give them administrative responsibility, and send them out to preach, teach, and baptize (Mosiah 23:17; 25:19; 26:7; Alma 4:7; 15:13; 23:4). These priests and teachers held the Melchizedek Priesthood.

(Bruce R. McConkie, *Mormon Doctrine* [Salt Lake City: Bookcraft, 1966], 598)

The Nephites were descendants of Joseph. Lehi discovered this when reading the brass plates. He was a descendant of Manasseh, and Ishmael, who accompanied him with his family, was of the tribe of Ephraim (Alma 10:3). Therefore there were no Levites who accompanied Lehi to the Western Hemisphere. Under these conditions the Nephites officiated by virtue of the Melchizedek Priesthood from the days of Lehi to the days of the appearance of our Savior among them. It

is true that Nephi "consecrated Jacob and Joseph" that they should be priests and teachers over the land of the Nephites, but the fact that plural terms *priests and teachers* were used indicates that this was not a reference to the definite office in the priesthood in either case, but it was a general assignment to teach, direct, and admonish the people. Otherwise the terms *priest and teacher* would have been given, in the singular. . . .

All through the Book of Mormon we find references to the Nephites officiating by virtue of the Higher Priesthood after the holy order (Alma 13:1; 43:1–2).

(Joseph Fielding Smith, *Answers to Gospel Questions* [Salt Lake City: Deseret Book, 1957], 124–125)

The Nephites did not officiate under the authority of the Aaronic Priesthood. They were not descendants of Aaron, and there were no Levites among them. There is no evidence in the Book of Mormon that they held the Aaronic Priesthood until after the ministry of the resurrected Lord among them, but the Book of Mormon tells us definitely, in many places, that the priesthood which they held and under which they officiated was the Priesthood after the *holy order,* the order of the Son of God. This higher priesthood can officiate in every ordinance of the gospel, and Jacob and Joseph, for instance, were consecrated priests and teachers after this order (2 Nephi 6:2).

(Joseph Fielding Smith, *Doctrines of Salvation*, comp. by Bruce R. McConkie [Salt Lake City: Bookcraft, 1956], 3:87)

Alma 5:45–47 • I KNOW . . . BY THE HOLY SPIRIT OF GOD

(Refer in this text to Moroni 10:3–5; Alma 17:3.)

As a youth, . . . [David O. McKay] had often prayed for a spiritual confirmation regarding his testimony. On 29 May 1899, he attended a memorable missionary meeting. He recounted: "I remember, as if it were but yesterday, the intensity of the inspiration of that occasion. Everybody felt the rich outpouring of the Spirit of the Lord. All present were truly of one heart and one mind. Never before had I experienced such an emotion. It was a manifestation for which as a doubting youth I had secretly prayed most earnestly on hillside and in meadow. It was an assurance to me that sincere prayer is answered 'sometime, somewhere.' During the progress of the meeting, an elder on his own initiative arose and said, 'Brethren, there are angels in this room.' Strange as it may seem, the announcement was not startling; indeed, it seemed wholly proper, though it had not occurred to me there were divine beings present. I only knew that I was overflowing with gratitude for the presence of the Holy Spirit."

(*Teachings of Presidents of the Church—David O. McKay* [Salt Lake City: The Church of Jesus Christ of Latter-day Saints, 2003], xviii)

———————

Alma the Younger had a personal experience with ministering angels. . . .

To be instructed by an angel would be a great blessing. However, as Alma taught us, his final and lasting conversion came only after he had "fasted and prayed many days." His complete conversion came from the Holy Ghost.

(James E. Faust, *Ensign*, May 2006 [Salt Lake City: The Church of Jesus Christ of Latter-day Saints, 2006], 51–52)

Alma 5:58 • BOOK OF LIFE
(Refer in this text to 3 Nephi 24:16.)

Alma 6:6 • GATHER TOGETHER OFT
(Refer in this text to Moroni 6:5–6.)

Alma 6:8 • AMEN

When we hear another's prayer, we audibly add our "amen," meaning, "That is my prayer too."

(Russell M. Nelson, in Conference Report, Apr. 2003 [Salt Lake City: The Church of Jesus Christ of Latter-day Saints, 2003], 5)

Alma 7:10 • CHRIST BORN AT JERUSALEM
(Refer in this text to 1 Nephi 1:4.)

It was the rule in Palestine and Syria from ancient times, . . . for a large area around a city and all the inhabitants of that area to bear the name of the city. . . . But this was quite unknown at the time the Book of Mormon was written. . . . One of the favorite points of attack on the Book of Mormon has been the statement in Alma 7:10 that the Saviour would be born "at Jerusalem which is the land of our forefathers." Here Jerusalem is not the city "in the land of our forefathers," it is the land. Christ was born in a village some six miles from the city of Jerusalem; it was not in the city, but it was in what we now know the ancients themselves designated as "the land of Jerusalem."

(Hugh Nibley, *An Approach to the Book of Mormon* [Salt Lake City: Deseret News Press, 1957], 85–86)

———————

Towns and villages which surrounded larger demographic or political centers were regarded in ancient times as belonging to those larger centers. For a major city center such as Jerusalem to be called not only a city but also a *land* was standard practice. . . . The scene of significant events in the Savior's ministry is referred to

four times as "the land of Jerusalem" (Hel. 16:19; 3 Ne. 16:1; Morm. 3:18, 19). . . .

Joseph Smith, of course, knew well that Jesus was born in Bethlehem. If he had been the author of the Book of Mormon he would have so stated the fact, since any deviation from the well-known setting would certainly draw objection and accusation. However, Joseph Smith was merely translating a geographical note from an ancient writer—a note which in itself is another evidence that the Book of Mormon derives from a Semitic background.

(D. Kelly Ogden, *Ensign,* Aug. 1984 [Salt Lake City: The Church of Jesus Christ of Latter-day Saints, 1984], 51–52)

———————

Alma 7:10 predicts that Jesus "shall be born of Mary, at Jerusalem which is the land of our forefathers." Is this a mistake? Everyone knows that Jesus was born in Bethlehem, not in Jerusalem. But it is now plain from modern evidence that Bethlehem could be, and indeed was, regarded anciently as a town in the "land of Jerusalem."

A recently released text from the Dead Sea Scrolls, for example—a text claiming origin in Jeremiah's days (and therefore in Lehi's)—says that the Jews of that period were "taken captive from the land of Jerusalem." Joseph Smith could not have learned this from the Bible, though, for no such language appears in it.

(Daniel C. Peterson, *Ensign*, Jan. 2000 [Salt Lake City: The Church of Jesus Christ of Latter-day Saints, 2000], 21–22)

———————

A careful reading of what Alma said will show that he had no intention of declaring that Jesus would be born *in* Jerusalem. Alma knew better. So did Joseph Smith and those who were associated with him in the bringing forth of the Book of Mormon. Had Alma said, "born *in* Jerusalem, the *city* of our fathers," it would have made all the difference in the world. . . .

Well, let us go back to the words of Alma. He did not say that the Lord would be born *in* Jerusalem. The preposition "at" has several meanings. The *Standard Dictionary* lists the following:

Of a point in space; on; upon; close to; by; near; within. . . . When we think merely of the local or geographical point, we use at; when we think of inclusive space, we employ in.

Alma was thinking of a geographical point, therefore he spoke properly according to the usage of language even in our own day when he said, "at Jerusalem, *the land of our forefathers.*"

(Joseph Fielding Smith, *Answers to Gospel Questions* [Salt Lake City: Deseret Book, 1957], 1:174–175)

Alma 7:11–12 • HE WILL TAKE UPON HIM THEIR INFIRMITIES

(Refer in this text to Mosiah 3:7; Mosiah 14:4.)

The Savior knows what it's like to die from cancer.

(Neal A. Maxwell, *Even As I Am* [Salt Lake City: Deseret Book, 1991], 116–117)

———

He [Christ] showed condescension when he chose to suffer, not only for our sins, but for the infirmities, sicknesses, and illnesses of mankind. But the agonies of the Atonement were infinite and first-hand! *Since not all human sorrow and pain is connected to sin, the full intensiveness of the Atonement involved bearing our pains, infirmities, and sicknesses, as well as our sins.*

(Neal A. Maxwell, *Doctrines of the Book of Mormon,* 1991 Sperry Symposium, 87)

———

Whatever the source of pain, Jesus understands and can heal the spirit as well as the body. The Savior, as a member of the Godhead, knows each of us personally. . . . In the garden and on the cross, Jesus saw each of us and not only bore our sins, but also experienced our deepest feelings so that he would know how to comfort and strengthen us.

(Merrill J. Bateman, *Ensign,* May 1995 [Salt Lake City: The Church of Jesus Christ of Latter-day Saints, 1995], 14)

———

Jesus knows and understands when we are stressed and perplexed. The complete consecration which effected the Atonement insured Jesus' perfect empathy; He felt our very pains and afflictions before we did and knows how to succor us.

(Neal A. Maxwell, *Ensign,* Nov. 1995 [Salt Lake City: The Church of Jesus Christ of Latter-day Saints, 1995], 24)

———

To succor means to "run to." I testify that in my fears and in my infirmities the Savior has surely run to me. I will never be able to thank Him enough for such personal kindness and such loving care.

(Jeffrey R. Holland, *Ensign,* Nov. 1997 [Salt Lake City: The Church of Jesus Christ of Latter-day Saints, 1997], 66)

———

For many years I thought of the Savior's experience in the garden and on the cross as places where a large mass of sin was heaped upon Him. Through the words of Alma, Abinadi, Isaiah, and other prophets, however, my view has changed. Instead of an impersonal mass of sin, there was a long line of people, as Jesus felt "our infirmities" (Hebrews 4:15), "[bore] our griefs, . . . carried our sorrows . . . [and] was bruised for our iniquities" (Isaiah 53:4–5).

The Atonement was an intimate, personal experience in which Jesus came to know how to help each of us.

The Pearl of Great Price teaches that Moses was shown all the inhabitants of the earth, which were "numberless as the sand upon the sea shore" (Moses 1:28). If Moses beheld every soul, then it seems reasonable that the Creator of the universe has the power to become intimately acquainted with each of us. He learned about your weaknesses and mine. He experienced your pains and sufferings. He experienced mine. I testify that He knows us. He understands the way in which we deal with temptations. He knows our weaknesses. But more than that, more than just knowing us, He knows how to help us if we come to Him in faith.

(Merrill J. Bateman, *Ensign,* Nov. 2005 [Salt Lake City: The Church of Jesus Christ of Latter-day Saints, 2005], 75–76)

———

I testify that the Savior's Atonement lifts from us not only the burden of our sins but also the burden of our disappointments and sorrows, our heartaches and our despair. . . .

If you are lonely, please know you can find comfort. If you are discouraged, please know you can find hope. If you are poor in spirit, please know you can be strengthened. If you feel you are broken, please know you can be mended.

(Jeffrey R. Holland, *Ensign,* May 2006 [Salt Lake City: The Church of Jesus Christ of Latter-day Saints, 2006], 70–71)

Alma 7:20 • HIS COURSE IS ONE ETERNAL ROUND

The divine delight in what seems to us to be mere repetition is one clue to the sublime character of God. Since we must, at times, accept what appears to us to be routine, repeated experiences, we too, if we try, can find fresh meaning and fresh joy in the repeated experiences. God's course is one eternal round but it is not one monotonous round. God is never bored, for one who has perfect love is never bored. There is always so much to notice, so much to do, so many ways to help, so many possibilities to pursue.

(Neal A. Maxwell, *A More Excellent Way* [Salt Lake City: Deseret Book, 1969], 84–85)

———

His *character* fits a like pattern. He was the same God before the earth was created that he now is. From everlasting to everlasting, he is merciful and gracious, slow to anger, and abundant in goodness. With him there is no variableness; he changes not; neither doth he walk in crooked paths; and his course is one eternal round. He is a God of truth; he cannot lie; his word endureth to all generations. He is no respecter of persons, and that man only is blessed who keeps his commandments. And he is love.

(Bruce R. McConkie, *The Promised Messiah* [Salt Lake City: Deseret Book, 1978], 197–198)

Alma 7:23 • FULL OF PATIENCE
(Refer in this text to Alma 34:40–41.)

Sometimes we fathers forget that once we too were boys, and boys at times can be vexing to parents.

I recall how much, as a youngster, I liked dogs. One day I took my wagon and placed a wooden orange crate in it and went looking for dogs. . . . As I would find a dog and capture it, I placed it in the crate, took it home, locked it in the coal shed, and turned the latch on the door. That day I think I brought home six dogs. . . . I had no idea what I would do with all those dogs, so I didn't reveal my deed to anyone.

Dad came home from work and, as was his custom, took the coal bucket and went to the coal shed to fill it. Can you imagine his shock and utter consternation as he opened the door and immediately faced six dogs, all attempting to escape at once? As I recall, Dad flushed a little bit, and then he calmed down and quietly told me, "Tommy, coal sheds are for coal. Other people's dogs rightfully belong to them." By observing him, I learned a lesson in patience and calmness.

It is a good thing I did, for a similar event occurred in my life with our youngest son, Clark. . . .

One day in his boyhood he came home from Provo Canyon with a water snake, which he named Herman.

Right off the bat Herman got lost. Sister Monson found him in the silverware drawer. . . . Well, Clark moved Herman to the bathtub, put a plug in the drain, put a little water in, and had a sign taped to the back of the tub which read, "Don't use this tub. It belongs to Herman." So we had to use the other bathroom while Herman occupied that sequestered place.

But then one day, to our amazement, Herman disappeared. . . . So the next day Sister Monson cleaned up the tub and prepared it for normal use. . . .

One evening I decided it was time to take a leisurely bath, so I filled the tub with a lot of warm water, and then I peacefully lay down in the tub for a few moments of relaxation. I was lying there just pondering, when the soapy water reached the level of the overflow drain and began to flow through it. Can you imagine my surprise when, with my eyes focused on that drain, Herman came swimming out, right for my face? I yelled out to my wife, "Frances! Here comes Herman!"

Well, Herman was captured again, put in a fool-proof box, and we made a little excursion to Vivian Park in Provo Canyon and there released Herman into the beautiful waters of the South Fork Creek.

(Thomas S. Monson, in Conference Report, Oct. 2002 [Salt Lake City: The Church of Jesus Christ of Latter-day Saints, 2002], 59–60)

———————

As we were busily preparing for a Christmas dinner, my teenaged sister excitedly reached into the cupboard for the silver-rimmed china. The lovely . . . set had been Grandmother's wedding present to Mom and Dad and was used only on special occasions. But as my sister removed some of the precious plates from the cupboard, she bumped her arm and the china slipped from her hands. Her desperate attempts to recover the plates were in vain, and the crash of china shattering on the floor was as heartbreaking as the look of helpless horror on her face.

Mother's meal-preparing hands stopped in midair, and the festive chatter of a bustling household ceased as we all stood frozen in awful silence. Without turning around to see the damage, Mother quietly slipped out of the room. Then . . . the rest of us tried to resume the tempo of our holiday duties.

Except my sister. She stood motionless, a big tear trickling down her cheek. As another tear fell, she mechanically found the broom and dustpan and began sweeping up the scattered chips. Then, on her knees, she slowly picked up the larger pieces and carefully placed them in the dustpan.

Within a few minutes Mother returned to the kitchen and wrapped her arms around her grieving daughter. My sister began to sob out loud. . . . Quietly [Mother] soothed, "That's all right, honey; people are more important than things."

Mother later told me that she had gone into the other room to pray and was blessed with a peaceful feeling and the inspiration of how to comfort my sister. The gift of spiritual perspective given to my mother that Christmas day became the most priceless gift our family received, as we children learned that we were more precious than fine china.

(Laura Russell Bunker, *Ensign*, Dec. 1998 [Salt Lake City: The Church of Jesus Christ of Latter-day Saints, 1998], 54–55)

———————

After that great First Vision, the Prophet Joseph received no additional communication for three years. However, he did not wonder; he did not question; he did not doubt the Lord. He waited patiently. He taught us the heavenly virtue of **patience**—by example.

(Thomas S. Monson, *Ensign*, Nov. 2005 [Salt Lake

City: The Church of Jesus Christ of Latter-day Saints, 2005], 68)

———————

One does not usually leap ahead from one capacity level to a level much farther away; we usually develop patiently by making small adjustments, gradually increasing our capacity, building a solid foundation on the most simple principles of the gospel: "Ye are not able to abide the presence of God now, neither the ministering of angels; wherefore, continue in patience until ye are perfected" (D&C 67:13).

We make spiritual progress through two means: our own agency and God's timetable. He does not always reveal his timetable. To possess some capacities, we wait on the Lord. We make a mistake if we think that by going into some kind of spiritual overdrive, we can suddenly assume great spiritual capacity or compel spiritual experience.

(Catherine Thomas; as quoted in *Studies in Scripture*, ed. by Kent P. Jackson [Salt Lake City: Deseret Book, 1988], 8:277)

Alma 8:1 • REST

We must not be too busy sawing to take time to sharpen the saw.

(Stephen R. Covey, personal communication)

Alma 8:10–15 • DISCOURAGEMENT IN THE MISSION FIELD

(Refer in this text to Alma 26:27; Helaman 10:1–4; refer to the quote by Joseph F. Smith under 1 Nephi 8:2, 36.)

In June 1830, Samuel Harrison Smith trudged down a country road in New York State on the first official missionary journey of the restored Church. He had been set apart by his brother, the Prophet Joseph. This first missionary traveled twenty-five miles that first day without disposing of a single copy of the new and strange book that he carried on his back. Seeking lodging for the night, faint and hungry, he was turned away, after briefly explaining his mission, with the words: "You liar, get out of my house. You shan't stay one minute with your books." Continuing his journey, discouraged and with heavy heart, he slept that first night under an apple tree. So began, in the most inauspicious way, the missionary work of this dispensation through the restored Church, The Church of Jesus Christ of Latter-day Saints.

(Ezra Taft Benson, *God, Family, Country* [Salt Lake City: Deseret Book, 1974], 188)

———————

One of the greatest secrets of missionary work is *work.* If a missionary works, he will get the Spirit; if he

gets the Spirit, he will touch the hearts of the people, and he will be happy. Then there will be no homesickness nor worrying about families, for all time and talents and interests are centered on the work of the ministry. Work, work, work—there is no satisfactory substitute, especially in missionary work. We must not allow ourselves to become discouraged. Missionary work brings joy, optimism, and happiness. We must not give Satan an opportunity to discourage us. Here again, work is the answer. The Lord has given us a key by which we can overcome discouragement (Matt. 11:28–30).

(Ezra Taft Benson, *Come Unto Christ* [Salt Lake City: Deseret Book, 1983], 96–97)

———————

[To missionaries] . . . you must know that Lucifer will oppose you, and be prepared for his opposition. Do not be surprised. He wants you to fail. Discouragement is one of the devil's tools. Have courage and go forward. Recognize that the gospel has been preached with some pain and sorrow from the very beginning of time. Do not expect that your experience will be otherwise.

(James E. Faust, *Ensign*, May 1996 [Salt Lake City: The Church of Jesus Christ of Latter-day Saints, 1996], 42)

———————

I received a mission when I embraced this work; it has never been taken from me yet. . . . We [John Taylor and I] have been over a great many rough roads [and] traveled hard. . . . For over thirty years we have labored to preach the gospel. . . . In my early missions . . . I have waded swamps and rivers and have walked seventy miles or more without eating. In those days we counted it a blessing to go into a place where there was a Latter-day Saint. I went once 150 miles to see one; and when I got there he had apostatized, and tried to kill me. Then, after travelling seventy-two miles without food, I sat down to eat my meal with a Missouri mobocrat, and he damning and cursing me all the time.

(Wilford Woodruff, *Journal of Discourses* [London: Latter-day Saints' Book Depot, 1869], 12:11–12)

Alma 8:10 • WRESTLING WITH GOD IN PRAYER

Except ye have the Spirit ye shall not teach. . . . Now, you have to pray for this. . . . But when you pray, do you really ask the Lord, as His servants, to speak through you, to let His power rest upon you and let the Holy Ghost bear witness to the people as you testify to them? Do you really pray that way? Have you really learned to plead with the Lord as if your very life depended upon it? It is necessary because your very life does depend on it, my brethren and sisters—your life as a missionary of the gospel of Jesus Christ.

(*Discourses of President Gordon B. Hinckley* [Salt Lake City: The Church of Jesus Christ of Latter-day Saints, 2005], 2:451–452)

Alma 8:14 • ANGUISH BECAUSE OF WICKEDNESS OF THE PEOPLE

It is interesting to note that, other than in the book of Job and a few other places, there are very few scriptural references to physical or mortal pain. The pain most frequently spoken of in the scriptures is the pain and anguish of the Lord and His prophets for the disobedient souls.

(Robert D. Hales, *Ensign*, Nov. 1998 [Salt Lake City: The Church of Jesus Christ of Latter-day Saints, 1998], 15)

Alma 8:18 • BY ANOTHER WAY

A number of years ago I was teaching . . . in a returned missionary Book of Mormon class at BYU. A student named Kristen Hall sent me . . . [a] letter. . . . The following is a portion of that letter:

"I had been in Portugal for two months, still with my first companion, and we were in the process of finding another area to proselyte. It seemed we had already worked the small city and we were absolutely stumped as to what to do. As we searched, we thought about a barrio (state funded apartments) of about fifteen buildings called Largateiro. The elders had told us never to go there because the last missionaries were driven out with rocks. We thought about working there, but were concerned because of this. It was the only place we hadn't gone. We went there and began to meet the people. They told us they knew who we were and they didn't believe in our teachings.

"The next morning as I began my personal study I prayed that the Lord would teach me through the scriptures what He would have me do. I came to Alma 8:11 and I saw where Alma had had a similar experience with the people of Ammonihah who said, "We know that thou art Alma . . . and we do not believe" (Alma 8:11). We began to pray about the area and how we should work there. As I continued to read of Alma's experience I saw something I had never seen before. After Alma had been kicked out of the city he was met by an angel who comforted him and then encouraged him to go back to Ammonihah. In verse 18 it says, 'he entered the city by another way.'

That is when it came to us; we needed to enter that barrio a different way—to proselyte it in a way that hadn't been done before. So we decided to work through the inactive members. So we began contacting them, and they began to invite their friends.

I had read Alma 8:18 many times before but had never thought of it in that way. I know that the Lord used that scripture to answer our prayer. Following this, we began to see success.

I'm confident that each person who has read the Book of Mormon with faith and diligence over the years can bear a similar testimony. . . . The Book of Mormon truly has the power to act as a Liahona in our lives."

(Jack R. Christianson and K. Douglas Bassett, *Life Lessons from the Book of Mormon* [Salt Lake City: Deseret Book, 2003], 264–266)

Alma 8:20 • NEPHITE

(*Refer in this text to Helaman 11:24; Jacob 1:13–14; 2 Nephi 5:21–23; Alma 3:6–19.*)

Alma 8:20 • GOD ANSWERS PRAYER THROUGH OTHER PEOPLE

Brother Artel Ricks tells an interesting story of an inspired Primary teacher. Artel was a little boy five or six years old. One night his family sat around the dinner table and talked about tithing. They told him "that tithing is one-tenth of all we earn and that it is paid to the Lord by those who love Him."

He loved the Lord, and so he wanted to give the Lord his tithing. He went and got his savings and took one-tenth of his small savings. He says: "I . . . went to the only room in the house with a lock on the door—the bathroom—and there knelt by the bathtub. Holding the three or four coins in my upturned hands, I asked the Lord to accept them. [I was certain He would appear and take them from me.] I pleaded with the Lord for some time, but [nothing happened. Why would He not accept my tithing?]. As I rose from my knees, I felt so unworthy that I could not tell anyone what had happened. . . .

"A few days later at Primary, the teacher said she felt impressed to talk about something that was not in the lesson. I sat amazed as she then taught us how to pay tithing [to the bishop, the Lord's servant]. But what I learned was far more important than how to pay tithing. I learned that the Lord had heard and answered my prayer, that He loved me, and that I was important to Him. . . .

So tender was the memory of that occasion that for more than thirty years I could not share it. Even today, after sixty years, I still find it difficult to tell about it without tears coming to my eyes. The pity is that a wonderful Primary teacher never knew that through her, the Lord spoke to a small boy" ("Coins for the Lord," *Ensign*, Dec. 1990, 47; "An Answer to Prayer," *Tambuli*, May 1988, 28).

(Gordon B. Hinckley, *Ensign*, May 2003 [Salt Lake City: The Church of Jesus Christ of Latter-day Saints, 2003], 117–118)

Alma 8:30–31 • ALMA AND AMULEK, MISSIONARY COMPANIONS

I hope every one of you is the kind of missionary your mother thinks you are. If you are that kind of missionary, you are all right. I hope every one of you has a great feeling of respect and love for your companion, that you work harmoniously together, because in that companionship there is strength that never can be found when you are alone. Great is the program of having missionaries work in pairs. They not only double their effectiveness, they triple their effectiveness when there are two working harmoniously together. "In the mouths of two or more witnesses shall all things be established," said the Lord (see Matthew 18:16; 2 Corinthians 13:1; D&C 6:28).

(*Discourses of President Gordon B. Hinckley*, 1995–99 [Salt Lake City: The Church of Jesus Christ of Latter-day Saints, 2004], 1:410)

———

Each of you has a companion. Why? Well, for one reason because the Savior said, "In the mouth of two or three witnesses [shall all things] be established" (Matthew 18:16). Another is for your mutual protection—so that you can protect one another. When you are together, it isn't likely that both of you will go wrong. One of you might be tempted to. The other will pull him up and straighten him out and give him strength to resist. Subtle are the ways of the world. Clever are the designs of the adversary. Be careful. You want to go home in honor.

(*Discourses of President Gordon B. Hinckley*, 1995–99 [Salt Lake City: The Church of Jesus Christ of Latter-day Saints, 2004], 1:422)

———

In the early days of the Church, missionaries worked independently; and, until relatively recent times, missionaries would go into a city, and one would go down one side of the street and one down the other side of the street. We don't do that now. We work together so that one may stand as a witness of the other should there be troubles, should there be difficulty, or should there be an opportunity to bear testimony of the truth of this work.

You will have companions all during your mission. I hope you will appreciate them. I hope you look for the good in them. You will find it if you look for it. You won't find it if you don't look for it. I will be forever grateful for my missionary companions of long ago. . . . I had 4 companions, one of them for 15 months. . . . I'll always be grateful for that young man. . . .

If you will cultivate a good companion relationship, that appreciation and respect for one another will remain with you throughout your lives. . . . What a precious thing is a good companion. He becomes your protector in times of trouble or in times of temptation.

(*Discourses of President Gordon B. Hinckley*, 1995–99 [Salt Lake City: The Church of Jesus Christ of Latter-day Saints, 2004], 1:528–530)

Alma 9:12–13, 24 • REPENT OR BE DESTROYED

(Refer in this text to Ether 14:25; Helaman 13:6.)

Alma 9:15–24 • WHERE MUCH IS GIVEN MUCH IS REQUIRED

(Refer in this text to 2 Nephi 9:25–27.)

Alma 9:16–17 • LAMANITES WON'T BE DESTROYED

At the time that the Prophet Joseph Smith translated this Book of Mormon, I suppose the impression was general, as it is today [1884] that the Indians were a perishing race, that they would soon disappear from the face of the land. . . . Joseph found . . . that we as a race and the nation to which we belong, should not have power to destroy the Indians. This was a most remarkable statement to make when we consider where Joseph was brought up, and the circumstances surrounding him.

(George Q. Cannon, *Journal of Discourses* [London: Latter-day Saints' Book Depot, 1884], 25:123)

———

When the United States became an independent nation, the number of Indians in North America was estimated at three million, and in the year 1876 at only one million three hundred thousand. In 1907 the decrease had been checked, and an increase to one million four hundred and seventy-four thousand was reported.

(Hyrum M. Smith and Janne M. Sjodahl, *The Doctrine and Covenants Containing Revelations Given to Joseph Smith, Jr., The Prophet with an Introduction and Historical and Exegetical Notes*, Rev. ed. [Salt Lake City: Deseret Book, 1955], 287; as quoted in Ross W. Warner, *The Fulfillment of Book of Mormon Prophecies* [Salt Lake City: Hawkes Publishing, 1975], 117)

———

When the Book of Mormon was published it was the prevailing opinion that the Indians were a perishing race and finally would become extinct. Book of Mormon prophecy is to the contrary. History has thus far proven this position to be right. The Indian population is increasing and the condition under which the Indian lives is improving.

(Ross W. Warner, *The Fulfillment of Book of Mormon*

Prophecies [Salt Lake City: Hawkes Publishing, 1975], 116)

Alma 9:21 • GIFT OF THE HOLY GHOST

There is a difference between the Holy Ghost and the gift of the Holy Ghost. Cornelius received the Holy Ghost before he was baptized, which was the convincing power of God unto him of the truth of the Gospel, but he could not receive the gift of the Holy Ghost until after he was baptized. Had he not taken this . . . ordinance upon him, the Holy Ghost, which convinced him of the truth of God, would have left him.

(Joseph Smith, *History of the Church of Jesus Christ of Latter-Day Saints* [Salt Lake City: Deseret Book, 1949], 4:555)

Alma 10 • CORRUPTION IN AMMONIHAH

It is in this scenario that Zeezrom appears. While the description of conditions in Ammonihah is not given in great detail, it is not difficult to fill in the pieces of the political, moral, and social mosaic from the recorded account. Corruption and dishonesty in official circles have become endemic. Grasping for material riches, the people have clamored to gain advantage one over another. Judges have become corrupt, susceptible to bribes and yielding advantage to those who can show favors. . . .

Numerous lawyers have emerged, skilled not only in the law but also in exploiting the devious legal system for the potential benefit of themselves and their clients.

It is a group of these lawyers that confront Alma and Amulek. . . .

It is significant that Zeezrom presents himself as the chief spokesman for these legalists. . . . (Alma 10:31). . . .

Not only is he acknowledged by his peers as one of the leaders in his craft, he is well known among the people generally, and apparently is one of the foremost to whom they look for legal assistance. This would indicate that he also has a comfortable relationship with the judges in the city.

(Dean L. Larsen, *Heroes from the Book of Mormon* [Salt Lake City: Bookcraft, 1995], 113)

Alma 10:3 • THE GENEALOGY OF LEHI

Earlier in the Book of Mormon it was mentioned that Lehi was a descendant of Joseph (1 Nephi 5:14). However, Joseph had two sons, Manasseh and Ephraim, and this is the first time the Book of Mormon indicates that Lehi was a descendant of Joseph's eldest son, Manasseh.

Some students of the Book of Mormon have wondered how descendants of Joseph were still living in Jerusalem in 600 BC when most members of the tribes

of Ephraim and Manasseh were taken into captivity by the Assyrians about 721 BC. A scripture in 2 Chronicles may provide a clue to this problem. This account mentions that in about 941 BC. Asa, the king of the land, gathered together at Jerusalem all of Judah and Benjamin "and the strangers with them out of Ephraim and Manasseh" (2 Chronicles 15:9). These "strangers. . . out of Ephraim and Manasseh" who were gathered to Jerusalem in approximately 941 BC may have included the forefathers of Lehi and Ishmael.

(Daniel H. Ludlow, *A Companion to Your Study of the Book of Mormon* [Salt Lake City: Deseret Book, 1976], 198–199)

It is true that Lehi and his family were descendants of Joseph through the lineage of Manasseh (Alma 10:3), and Ishmael was a descendant of Ephraim, according to the statement of the Prophet Joseph Smith. That the Nephites were descendants of Joseph is in fulfillment of the blessings given to Joseph by his father Israel. The Nephites were of the Jews, not so much by descent as by citizenship, although in the long descent from Jacob, it could be possible of some mixing of the tribes by intermarriage.

(Joseph Fielding Smith, *Answers to Gospel Questions* [Salt Lake City: Deseret Book, 1957], 1:142)

Alma 10:4–6 • RICHES BY THE HAND OF MY INDUSTRY

(Refer in this text to Jacob 2:13–17; 3 Nephi 13:19–24.)

A friend . . . proudly boasted that his climb toward wealth had come from tireless work and lessons learned in the "school of hard knocks." But his fortune had come at the expense of his spiritual development. When it was too late, he regretfully discovered that his ladder of success had been leaning against the wrong wall.

(Russell M. Nelson, *Ensign*, Nov. 1992 [Salt Lake City: The Church of Jesus Christ of Latter-day Saints, 1992], 7)

Alma 10:11; 15:16, 18 • AMULEK—BLESSED OF THE LORD, REJECTED BY FAMILY

The life of Amulek teaches us not only that obedience brings the inspiration of God, but that with that inspiration will come the power to accept the testing and the trials it will take to sanctify us. Amulek could not have foreseen the testing and the sacrifice ahead of him. . . . He says in his first sermon that the angel's promised blessing on his house and family had already been delivered. He seemed to think the blessings were delivered and assured . . . (Alma 10:11).

We don't know what Amulek thought those blessings had been, but we do know what became of his house and his family. He lost them all. We know that after he taught with such power as the companion of Alma in his own city, Ammonihah, his father and kindred repudiated him . . . (Alma 15:16).

Amulek may have lost even his wife and his children. . . .

If they had rejected the gospel of Jesus Christ they would have been killed in the prophesied destruction of Ammonihah. An invading army took the life of every soul in a single day. If Amulek's wife and children had made and kept covenants of the gospel, they would have been among the martyrs Alma and Amulek were forced to see die in the flames. . . (Alma 14:10–13).

Amulek was delivered by God from the powers of the adversary as a blessing for his obedience, but God would not compel his loved ones to obey.

(Henry B. Eyring, *Heroes from the Book of Mormon* [Salt Lake City: Bookcraft, 1995], 109–111)

Alma 10:22–23 • THE PRAYER OF THE RIGHTEOUS MINORITY

Our world is now much the same as it was in the days of the Nephite prophet who said: ". . . if it were not for the prayers of the righteous . . . ye would even now be visited with utter destruction" (Alma 10:22). Of course, there are many upright and faithful who live all the commandments and whose lives and prayers keep the world from destruction.

(Spencer W. Kimball, *Ensign*, June 1971 [Salt Lake City: The Church of Jesus Christ of Latter-day Saints, 1971], 6)

The Lord has made it plain to us that if we are not a prayerful people, if we fail to remember the king of this land, Jesus Christ, we can lose all of these blessings. . . . [Alma 10:22–23]. And so it seems to me that what we need in this fair land of ours is a shining example of prayerfulness, and the Latter-day Saints are the people who are chosen to exemplify to the world the power of prayer.

(Joseph B. Wirthlin, in Conference Report, Apr. 1949 [Salt Lake City: The Church of Jesus Christ of Latter-day Saints, 1949], 159)

Some years ago I accompanied President Hugh B. Brown on a tour of the Samoan Mission. The members and missionaries in American Samoa had advised us that a severe drought had imperiled their water supply to the point that our chapels and our school would of necessity be closed if rain did not soon fall. They asked us to unite our faith with theirs.

Signs of the drought were everywhere as we left the airport at Pago Pago and journeyed to the school at Mapasaga. The sun was shining brightly; not a cloud appeared in the azure blue sky. The members rejoiced as the meeting began. He who offered the opening prayer thanked our Heavenly Father for our safe arrival, knowing that we would somehow bring the desired rainfall. As President Brown rose to speak, the sun was soon shaded by gathering clouds. Then we heard the clap of thunder and saw the flash of lightning. The heavens opened. The rains fell. The drought ended.

Later at the airport, as we prepared for the short flight to Western Samoa, the pilot of the small plane said to the ground crew, "This is the most unusual weather pattern I have ever seen. Not a cloud is in the sky except over the Mormon school at Mapasaga. I don't understand it!"

President Brown said to me, "Here's your opportunity. Go help him understand." I did so.

(Thomas S. Monson, in Conference Report, Apr. 1984 [Salt Lake City: The Church of Jesus Christ of Latter-day Saints, 1984], 21)

Alma 11:1–19 • NEPHITE MONEY

We still get lots of letters, especially from churchmen, protesting that the mention of money in the Book of Mormon is another crude anachronism. They all point out that coinage was first invented by the Lydians in the 8th century BC. That would make coinage available to Lehi, but the Book of Mormon says nothing about coins, but only money, which is a different thing. The Egyptians and Babylonians had real money from a very early time—metal pieces of conventional shape and size whose exact value could always be determined by weighing and which often bore an official stamp or inscription. This old fashioned kind of money was favored by the Jews in Egypt even after the new modern coinage had been introduced.

(Hugh W. Nibley, *Since Cumorah* [Salt Lake City: Deseret Book, 1976], 255)

Alma 11:23–24 • THE RIGHTEOUS YIELDETH NOT TO THE LOVE OF LUCRE
(Refer in this text to 3 Nephi 13:19–24, 33; Jacob 2:18–19.)

Alma 11:38–39 • SON OF GOD, THE ETERNAL FATHER
(Refer in this text to 1 Nephi 19:10.)

Alma 11:43 • A BRIGHT RECOLLECTION OF ALL OUR GUILT
(Refer in this text to 2 Nephi 9:14, 33.)

In reality a man cannot forget anything. He may have a lapse of memory; he may not be able to recall at the moment a thing that he knows or words that he has spoken; he may not have the power of his will to call up these events and words; but let God Almighty touch the mainspring of the memory and awaken recollection, and you will find then that you have not even forgotten a single idle word you have spoken.

(Joseph F. Smith, *Man, His Origin and Destiny* [Salt Lake City: Deseret Book, 1973], 358–360)

Man himself is a self-registering machine, his eyes, his ears, his nose, the touch, the taste, and all the various senses of the body, are so many media whereby man lays up for himself a record which perhaps nobody else is acquainted with but himself; and when the time comes for that record to be unfolded all men that have eyes to see, and ears to hear will be able to read all things as God himself reads them and comprehends them, and all things, we are told, are naked and open before him with whom we have to do.

(John Taylor, *Journal of Discourses* [London: Latter-day Saints' Book Depot, 1886], 26:31)

And the memories of the wicked, after they leave this body, will be so increased that they will have a bright recollection, Alma says, of all their guilt. Here they forget a good many things wherein they have displeased God; but in that condition, even before the resurrection, they will have a bright recollection of all their guilt, which will kindle in them a flame like that of an unquenchable fire, creating in their bosoms a feeling of torment, pain and misery, because they have sinned against their own Father and their own God, and rejected his counsels.

(Orson Pratt, *Journal of Discourses* [London: Latter-day Saints' Book Depot, 1874], 16:365)

Although your spirit had a veil of forgetfulness placed over it at the time of your birth into mortality, it retained its power to remember all that happens—precisely recording each event of life. Indeed, scriptures warn "that every idle word that men shall speak, they shall give account thereof in the day of judgment" (Matthew 12:36). Prophets refer to our "bright recollection" (Alma 11:43) and "perfect remembrance" (Alma 5:18) at that day of decision.

(Russell M. Nelson, in Conference Report, Oct. 1985 [Salt Lake City: The Church of Jesus Christ of Latter-day Saints, 1985], 39)

Every deed that we have done will be brought to our recollection. Every acquaintance made will be remem-

bered. There will be no scenes or incidents in our lives that will be forgotten by us in the world to come. . . . The human mind . . . when quickened by the power of God, will make men and women recall not only that which pertains to this life, but our memories will stretch back to the life we had before we came here, with the associations we had with our Father and God and with those bright spirits that stand around His throne and with the righteous and holy ones.

(George Q. Cannon, *Gospel Truth* [Salt Lake City: Deseret Book, 1974], 60–61)

Man . . . rises . . . from the dead and goes to judgment; and then the secret thoughts of all men are revealed before Him with whom we have to do. . . . If a man has acted fraudulently against his neighbor—has committed murder, or adultery, or any thing else, and wants to cover it up, that record will stare him in the face, he tells the story himself, and bears witness against himself. . . . That record . . . is written by the man himself in the tablets of his own mind—that record that cannot lie—will in that day be unfolded before God and angels, and those who shall sit as judges.

(John Taylor, *Journal of Discourses* [London: Latter-day Saints' Book Depot, 1867], 11:78–79)

Alma 11:43–44 • RESURRECTION
(Refer in this text to Alma 40:23.)

While I was upon my knees praying, my room was filled with light. I looked up and a messenger stood by my side. I arose, and this personage told me he had come to instruct me. . . . He told me he wanted me to see with my eyes and understand with my mind what was coming to pass in the earth. . . .

He showed me the resurrection of the dead—what is termed the first and second resurrection. In the first resurrection . . . I saw legions of celestial beings, men and women who had received the gospel, all clothed in white robes. In the form they were presented to me, they had already been raised from the grave. After this, he showed me what is termed the second resurrection. Vast fields of graves were before me . . . and an immense host of human beings came forth. They were just as diversified in their dress as we are here, or as they were laid down.

(Wilford Woodruff, MS, 19 Oct. 1896, 67:612; as quoted in *Latter-day Prophets Speak*, ed. by Daniel H. Ludlow [Salt Lake City: Bookcraft, 1951], 37–38)

In the resurrection of the dead the child that was buried in its infancy will come up in the form of the child that it was when it was laid down; then it will begin to develop. From the day of the resurrection, the body will develop until it reaches the full measure of the stature of its spirit, whether it be male or female.

(Joseph F. Smith, *Improvement Era*, 12:594, June 1909; as quoted in *Latter-day Prophets Speak*, ed. by Daniel H. Ludlow [Salt Lake City: Bookcraft, 1951], 44)

The body will come forth as it is laid to rest, for there is no growth or development in the grave. As it is laid down, so will it arise, and changes to perfection will come by the law of restitution. But the spirit will continue to expand and develop, and the body after the resurrection will develop to the full stature of man.

(Joseph F. Smith, *Improvement Era*, 7:623–624, June, 1904; as quoted in *Latter-day Prophets Speak*, ed. by Daniel H. Ludlow [Salt Lake City: Bookcraft, 1951], 45)

If you see one of your children that has passed away it may appear to you in the form in which you would recognize it, the form of childhood; but if it came to you as a messenger bearing some important truth, it would perhaps come . . . in the stature of full-grown manhood . . .

The spirit of Jesus Christ was full-grown before He was born into the world; and so our children were full-grown and possessed their full stature in the spirit before they entered mortality, the same stature that they will possess after they have passed away from mortality, and as they will also appear after the resurrection, when they shall have completed their mission.

(Joseph F. Smith, *Improvement Era*, Feb. 1918, 21:570–571; as quoted in *Latter-day Prophets Speak*, ed. by Daniel H. Ludlow [Salt Lake City: Bookcraft, 1951], 45)

Many living witnesses can testify to the literal fulfillment of these scriptural assurances of the resurrection. Many, including some in my own extended family, have seen a departed loved one in vision or personal appearance and have witnessed their restoration in "proper and perfect frame" in the prime of life. Whether these were manifestations of persons already resurrected or of righteous spirits awaiting an assured resurrection, the reality and nature of the resurrection of mortals is evident. What a comfort to know that all who have been disadvantaged in life from birth defects, from mortal injuries, from disease, or from the natural deterioration of old age will be resurrected in "proper and perfect frame."

(Dallin H. Oaks, in Conference Report, Apr. 2000 [Salt Lake City: The Church of Jesus Christ of Latter-day Saints, 2000], 16–17)

Everyone's body, no matter how much appeal it may attain for the sake of vanity alone, must return to the dust from whence it came. The value of the body springs not from the physical traits we inherit from our earthly parents but in accepting the body as a gift from God, to be developed and placed into submission to our spirits, which lived before and continue to live after the death of the mortal body (Mormon 6:21; Philippians 3:21). In doing this, we better prepare ourselves to inherit the body when it becomes perfected in the resurrection. Each of us must see ourselves first as spiritual beings for the simple reason that we were spirits before we were given this mortal tabernacle, and we will continue to be spirits after our earthly body dies. Only when the resurrected body is welded to the spirit are we truly in a position to discern the body and the spirit as being a complete reflection of each other.

Elder Neal A. Maxwell alluded to this concept as he spoke of his granddaughter Anna Josephine, "who was born without a left hand. The other day a conversation was overheard between Anna Jo, almost five, and her cousin Talmage, three. Talmage said reassuringly as they played together, 'Anna Jo, when you grow up you will have five fingers.' Anna Jo said, 'No, Talmage, when I grow up I won't have five fingers, but when I get to heaven I will have a hand' " ("Content with the Things Allotted unto Us," *Ensign*, May 2000, 74).

(K. Douglas Bassett, *The Barber's Song* [Springville, Utah: Cedar Fort, 2005], 21)

Alma 12:3, 7; 10:17; 18:16, 18, 20, 32 • DISCERNMENT

[An experience of Heber C. Kimball] Being in charge of the Endowment House, while the Temple was in the process of construction, Heber C. Kimball met with a group who were planning to enter the temple for ordinance work. He felt impressed that some were not worthy to go into the temple, and he suggested first that if any present were not worthy, they might retire. No one responding, he said that there were some present who should not proceed through the temple because of unworthiness and he wished they would leave so the company could proceed. It was quiet as death and no one moved nor responded. A third time he spoke, saying that there were two people present who were in adultery, and if they did not leave he would call out their names. Two people walked out and the company continued on through the temple.

(Spencer W. Kimball, *The Miracle of Forgiveness* [Salt Lake City: Bookcraft, 1969], 112)

Often blessed with the power to know and understand beyond their experience, women draw on this strength as they visit monthly to teach in the homes or to assess needs as directed by the bishop. We use it as we nurture our children and teach them the gospel. . . . Discernment is critical for our times. President Boyd K. Packer has said, "We need women with the gift of discernment who can view the trends in the world and detect those that, however popular, are shallow" *(Ensign,* Nov. 1978, 8). That is exactly what we need.

(Elaine Jack, *Ensign,* Nov. 1996 [Salt Lake City: The Church of Jesus Christ of Latter-day Saints, 1996], 77)

While participating in an area conference in Manchester, England, in 1971, President Spencer W. Kimball, who was then acting president of the Quorum of the Twelve, confided in Dr. Nelson that he was having anginal pains. . . .

President Kimball called a special meeting with the First Presidency. Invited to the meeting in addition to the First Presidency and Sister Kimball were Dr. Ernest L. Wilkinson and myself. President Kimball began the meeting by saying, "I am a dying man. I can feel my life slipping. At the present rate of deterioration, it is my belief that I can live only about two more months. . . ."

Dr. Wilkinson reaffirmed President Kimball's statement, explaining that "because of congestive failure, . . . spontaneous recovery would be unlikely and death would ensue in the not-too-distant future."

Then President Kimball called on Dr. Nelson to speak, asking, "What can cardiac surgery offer?"

Dr. Nelson said, "I indicated that the operation, if it were to be done, would be a compound surgical procedure consisting of two components. . . .

President Lee asked, "What would the risks be with such procedures?"

Dr. Nelson replied, "We have no experience doing both operations on patients in this age group. . . . All I can say is, it would entail extremely high risk."

Then a weary President Kimball said, "I'm an old man and ready to die. It is well for a younger man to come to the Quorum and do the work I can no longer do."

Elder Nelson described the dramatic reaction of President Lee: "At that point President Harold B. Lee, speaking for the First Presidency, rose to his feet, pounded his fist to the desk, and said, 'Spencer, you have been called! You are not to die! You are to do everything that you need to do in order to care for yourself and continue to live.'"

President Kimball responded, "Then I will have the operation performed." . . .

The decision was made to perform the operation on April 12, . . .1972. . . .

Russell [M. Nelson] received a blessing from the First Presidency on the eve of the operation, under the hands of President Harold B. Lee and President N. Eldon Tanner. "They blessed me that the operation would be performed without error, that all would go well, and that I need not fear for my own inadequacies, for I had been raised up by the Lord to perform this operation."

The operation began the next morning. . . . Dr. Nelson observed, "From that very first maneuver until the last one, everything went as planned. There was not one broken stitch, not one instrument had fallen from the table, not one technical flaw had occurred in a series of thousands of intricate manipulations. I suppose my feelings at that time may have been like those of a concert pianist rendering a concerto without ever hitting a wrong note, or a baseball player who had pitched a perfect game—no hits, no runs, no errors, and no walks. For a long and difficult operation had been performed exactly in accordance with the blessing invoked by the power of the priesthood. . . .

"The feeling that came as we shocked President Kimball's heart and it resumed its beating immediately with vigor, was the manifestation of the Spirit which told me that I had just operated upon the man who would become president of the Church!

"I knew that President Kimball was a prophet. I knew that he was an Apostle, *but now it was revealed to me that he would preside over the Church!* This feeling was so strong that I could hardly contain myself as we performed the routine maneuvers to conclude the operation. Later on in the week as he convalesced, I shared these impressions with him and he and I wept." . . .

The evening after Christmas 1973, Brother Nelson heard the fateful news on television that President Lee had just died. . . .

President Kimball became the president of the Church on December 30, 1973, at age seventy-eight. . . . It would be a dozen years before he passed away at the age of ninety.

(Spencer J. Condie, *Russell M. Nelson, Father— Surgeon—Apostle* [Salt Lake City: Deseret Book, 2003], 153–158; emphasis added)

On the day I was released as a bishop, one of the ward members came to my home afterwards and said, "I know you are no longer my bishop, but could we talk just one more time? You have always spoken words I needed and given me such good counsel. The new bishop doesn't know me the way you do. Could we just talk one more time?"

Reluctantly I agreed. The member sat down in a

chair opposite mine. It seemed to be just as it had been in the hundreds of times I had interviewed members of the ward as a judge in Israel. The conversation began. There came the moment when counsel was needed. I waited for the ideas, the words, and the feelings to flow into my mind, as they always had.

Nothing came. In my heart and mind there was only silence. After a few moments I said, "I'm sorry. I appreciate your kindness and your trust. But I'm afraid I can't help you."

When you are released from your calling, you will learn what I learned then. God magnifies those He calls. . . . Give thanks while that gift is yours. You will appreciate its worth more than you can imagine when it is gone.

(Henry B. Eyring, in Conference Report, Oct. 2002 [Salt Lake City: The Church of Jesus Christ of Latter-day Saints, 2002], 82)

———————

The gift of discernment operates basically in four major ways.

First, as we "read under the surface," discernment helps us detect hidden error and evil in others.

Second, and more important, it helps us detect hidden errors and evil in ourselves. Thus the spiritual gift of discernment is not exclusively about discerning other people and situations, . . . it is also about discerning things as they really are within us.

Third, it helps us find and bring forth the good that may be concealed in others.

And fourth, it helps us find and bring forth the good that may be concealed in us.

(David A. Bednar, *Ensign*, Dec. 2006 [Salt Lake City: The Church of Jesus Christ of Latter-day Saints, 2006], 35)

Alma 12:3 • OUR THOUGHTS WILL CONDEMN US

(Refer in this text to Mosiah 4:30.)

If men's secret acts shall be revealed it is likely that their secret thoughts will also be revealed. . . .

The one who harbors evil thoughts sometimes feels safe in the conviction that these thoughts are unknown to others. . . .

Accordingly, men's deeds and thoughts must be recorded in heaven, and recording angels will not fail to make complete recordings of our thoughts and actions. . . . There will be no omissions in the heavenly records, and they will all be available at the day of judgment.

(Spencer W. Kimball, *The Miracle of Forgiveness* [Salt Lake City: Bookcraft, 1969], 108–109)

Alma 12:6, 11; 13:30 • SATAN'S CHAINS

(Refer in this text to 2 Nephi 1:13, 23.)

Alma 12:6, 32; 13:20 • SPIRITUAL DEATH, SECOND DEATH

This second death is not, then, the dissolution or annihilation of both spirit and body, but banishment from the presence of God and from partaking of the things of righteousness. . . .

It is similar to the first spiritual death, which has passed upon all men who have remained unrepentant and who have not received the gospel. Those who have suffered the first spiritual death or departure, which is a shutting out from the presence of God, have the privilege of being redeemed from this death through obedience to the principles of the gospel. Through baptism and confirmation they are *born again* and thus come *back into spiritual life.* . . .

Those who partake of the second death are those who have had the spiritual light and have rebelled against it. These *remain* in their sins in their banishment. . . . Alma in the Book of Mormon has clearly and forcefully depicted their status [see Alma 12:16–18]. . . .

Resurrection shall come unto all who have received tabernacles of flesh and this because they kept their first estate which entitled them to this mortal existence in the flesh. . . .

However, because they have failed utterly to keep their second estate, when they are raised in the resurrection with their bodies and spirits inseparably connected, they still remain, as the prophets have said, *as though there had been no redemption made for them, "Except it be the loosing of the bands of death,"* (Alma 11:41; D&C 76:42–48) that is the mortal death. Then shall the final sentence be passed upon them, and with Lucifer and those who served him in the beginning, shall they be cast out into outer darkness.

(Joseph Fielding Smith, *Doctrines of Salvation*, comp. by Bruce R. McConkie [Salt Lake City: Bookcraft, 1955], 2:222–224)

———————

Second death, What is that? After you have been redeemed from the grave, and come into the presence of God, you will have to stand there to be judged; and if you have done evil, you will be banished everlastingly from His presence, . . . this is what is called the second death.

(Orson Pratt, *Journal of Discourses* [London: Latter-day Saints' Book Depot, 1855], 1:288)

———————

At the time of the Final Judgment, after the Resurrection, the wicked will suffer a second death—not a death of the body, but a death as to righteousness—a spiritual death, meaning they will be banished from God's presence, and from his joy and happiness forever. . . .

Spiritual death does not mean the death of one's spirit, but means to be out of God's presence and to be dead as to righteousness. Every person born into the world suffers these two deaths. There are no exceptions. . . .

Every person, regardless of worthiness or unworthiness, will also be reclaimed from the spiritual death and will be brought back into the presence of God for the Final Judgment. No matter how wicked or unrepentant, every person will, after the Resurrection, be brought back into the presence of God for judgment. Thus all will be reclaimed from the two deaths that resulted from the fall of Adam. Those who are righteous will remain in his presence. Those who are still unclean and filthy at the time of judgment will be sent away from his presence a second time, and thus they die a second spiritual death. Only the sons of perdition suffer the complete second death.

(Robert J. Matthews; as quoted in *The Book of Mormon: Alma, The Testimony of the Word*, ed. by Monte S. Nyman and Charles D. Tate [Provo, Utah: Religious Studies Center, BYU, 1992], 54–55)

Alma 12:7 • ZEEZROM BEGAN TO TREMBLE

Why was this arrogant, sophisticated demagogue so susceptible to the influence of the Spirit? Other rebels in the Book of Mormon record were similarly confronted by spiritual leaders but persisted in their debauchery. Nehor, although rebuked by Alma, had no change of heart (see Alma 1), nor did Amlici (see Alma 2) or Sherem (see Jacob 7). Korihor stubbornly refused to repent (see Alma 30). What was there in the soul of Zeezrom that pressed him toward such a remarkable change? . . .

It appears that in spite of his having yielded to the influence of the environment in which he had gained notoriety, a spark of spiritual light must have endured in his soul.

(Dean L. Larsen, *Heroes from the Book of Mormon* [Salt Lake City: Bookcraft, 1995], 115–116)

Alma 12:9 • NOT IMPART ONLY . . . WHICH HE DOTH GRANT

(Refer in this text to Alma 37:28; 2 Nephi 32:7.)

It is not wise to continually talk of unusual spiritual experiences. They are to be guarded with care and shared only when the Spirit itself prompts you to use them to the blessing of others. I am ever mindful of Alma's words (Alma 12:9). I heard President Marion G. Romney once counsel mission presidents and their wives . . ., "I do not tell all I know, . . . for I found out

that if I talked too lightly of sacred things, thereafter the Lord would not trust me."

(Boyd K. Packer, *Ensign*, Jan. 1983 [Salt Lake City: The Church of Jesus Christ of Latter-day Saints, 1983], 53)

I have come to know that deeply spiritual experiences are usually given to us for our individual edification and it is best not to talk of them generally. . . . We may be prompted on occasion to tell of our spiritual experiences, but generally we should regard them as sacred. It is not out of order, however, to present some experiences from those who have lived in years past.

The fact that sacred spiritual experiences are not discussed widely—for instance, by the General Authorities—should not be taken as an indication that the Saints do not receive them. Such spiritual gifts are with the Church today as they were in years past.

Experiences which involve dreams or visions or visitations might be recorded and put away in family records to serve as a testimony and an inspiration to our descendants in the generations ahead.

(Boyd K. Packer, *The Holy Temple* [Salt Lake City: Bookcraft, 1980], 243)

Alma 12:9–11 • HARD HEARTS GIVEN A LESSER PORTION OF THE WORD

The best educated man in the world may not be able to comprehend the simple truths of the gospel because his soul is not in tune; he has not been enlightened by the Spirit of the Lord. He, therefore, fails to see and feel the significance of these principles. They cannot be seen except through the touch of the Holy Ghost. For this reason Alma explained to Zeezrom how gospel light may be known. [Alma 12:9–11.]

(Joseph Fielding Smith, *Doctrines of Salvation*, comp. by Bruce R. McConkie [Salt Lake City: Bookcraft, 1954], 1:296–297)

It is a popular notion that Jesus taught with parables to make his points clear and easy to understand, it just isn't so. . . .

Make no mistake about it, Jesus used parable to conceal the mysteries of the kingdom from the unworthy and the spiritually careless. Parables were so effective at concealing the message that Jesus often had to explain the meaning afterward even to the disciples. . . .

The deliberate withholding of spiritual information from those who do not believe is well established in scripture. There may be a merciful purpose to this, since they cannot reject what they haven't been taught. But mercy is not the only factor. There is justice also. The Lord withholds the greater spiritual truths from the proud and worldly-wise because they do not want to know, and do not value gospel truth enough to seek, ask, knock, or sacrifice anything to gain that knowledge.

(Robert J. Matthews; as quoted in *The Book of Mormon: Alma, The Testimony of the Word*, ed. by Monte S. Nyman and Charles D. Tate [Provo, Utah: Religious Studies Center, BYU, 1992], 49–50)

Alma 12:11 • LED BY HIS WILL DOWN TO DESTRUCTION

I counsel all of you . . . to avoid every kind of addiction. At this time Satan and his followers are enslaving some of our choicest young people through addiction to alcohol, all kinds of drugs, pornography, tobacco, gambling, and other compulsive disorders. Some people seem to be born with a weakness for these substances so that only a single experimentation will result in uncontrollable addiction. Some addictions are actually mind-altering and create a craving that overpowers reason and judgment. These addictions destroy the lives not only of those who do not resist them but also their parents, spouses, and children. . . .

The Lord in His wisdom has warned us that substances that are not good for us should be totally avoided. We have been warned not to take the first drink, smoke the first cigarette, or try the first drug. Curiosity and peer pressure are selfish reasons to dabble with addictive substances. We should stop and consider the full consequences, not just to ourselves and our futures, but also to our loved ones. These consequences are physical, but they also risk the loss of the Spirit and cause us to fall prey to Satan.

(James E. Faust, *Ensign*, May 2006 [Salt Lake City: The Church of Jesus Christ of Latter-day Saints, 2006], 53)

Alma 12:14 • OUR THOUGHTS WILL CONDEMN US

(Refer in this text to Mosiah 4:30.)

All evils to which so many become addicted begin in the mind and in the way one thinks. Experience teaches that when the will and imagination are in conflict, the imagination usually wins. What we imagine may defeat our reason and make us slaves to what we taste, see, hear, smell, and feel in the mind's eye. The body is indeed the servant of the mind.

(Joseph B. Wirthlin, *Ensign*, May 1982 [Salt Lake City: The Church of Jesus Christ of Latter-day Saints, 1982], 23–25)

Alma 12:22 • A LOST AND FALLEN PEOPLE

(Refer in this text to 2 Nephi 2:18–25.)

Not only had Adam and Eve fallen, but now their entire posterity would be relegated to a similar fate, to be born and raised estranged from the presence of God, a form of spiritual death. Such a universal condemnation was observed by Alma . . . .

Two of the consequences of the Fall were negatives, namely physical and spiritual death. But there was also good news. The two previous negatives of the Garden became positives. Adam and Eve were now blessed with a knowledge of good and evil, and appropriately so, for they had partaken of the tree of knowledge of good and evil. This enabled them to "[become] as Gods, knowing good from evil" (Alma 12:31). Satan had told a half-truth: "Ye shall not surely die [this was the falsehood]" but "in the day ye eat thereof, then your eyes shall be opened, and ye shall be as gods, knowing good and evil" (Genesis 3:4–5; see also Alma 42:3). The latter portion of Satan's promise was true. At least eventually, they did become like God in their understanding of good and evil; innocence was exchanged for knowledge; and the potential for joy became a reality. A negative became a glorious positive in the eternal scheme.

In addition, Adam and Eve's mortal bodies could now procreate and fulfill the divine command to multiply and replenish the earth.

(Tad R. Callister, *The Infinite Atonement* [Salt Lake City: Deseret Book, 2000], 41)

Alma 12:34, 36–37; 13:6, 12–13, 16, 29; 16:17 • ENTER INTO THE REST OF THE LORD

The ancient prophets speak of "entering into God's rest"; what does it mean? To my mind, it means entering into the knowledge and love of God, having faith in his purpose and in his plan, to such an extent that we know we are right, and that we are not hunting for something else, we are not disturbed by every wind of doctrine, or by the cunning and craftiness of men who lie in wait to deceive. . . . The man who has reached that degree of faith in God that all doubt and fear have been cast from him, he has entered into "God's rest," . . . The rest here referred to is not physical rest, for there is no such thing as physical rest in the Church of Jesus Christ. . . . We may thus enter into the rest of the Lord today, by coming to an understanding of the truths of the gospel. . . . But there are many [Saints] who, not having reached this point of determined conviction, are driven about by every wind of doctrine, thus being ill at ease, unsettled, restless. These are they who are discouraged over incidents that occur in the Church, and in the nation, and in the turmoils of men and associations. They harbor a feeling of suspicion, unrest, uncertainty. Their thoughts are disturbed, and they become excited with the least change, like one at sea who has lost his bearings. . . . Let them seek for it in the written word of God; let them pray to him in their secret chambers, where no human ear can hear . . . and they will immediately begin to grow in the knowledge of the truth. . . . Let them seek for strength from the Source of all strength, and he will provide spiritual contentment, a rest which is incomparable with the physical rest that cometh after toil. All who seek have a right to, and may enter into, the rest of God, here upon the earth, from this time forth, now, today; and when earth-life is finished, they shall also enjoy his rest in heaven.

(Joseph F. Smith, *Gospel Doctrine* [Salt Lake City: Deseret Book, 1975], 58, 126)

Phrases similar to "enter into the rest of the Lord" appear in the Old Testament, in the Book of Mormon, as well as in Hebrews chapters 3 and 4, and in D&C 84:24. As noted, "the rest of the Lord" can refer both to physical rest and to spiritual rest. In Doctrine and Covenants 84:24, *rest* is defined as the fulness of God's glory. The word can also mean *remainder*. Since God gives us only according to our readiness and diligence, what the faithful receive is "the rest of the Lord," meaning they shall receive the remainder, the rest of the knowledge and blessings God bestows upon his faithful children.

(Robert J. Matthews; as quoted in *The Book of Mormon: Alma, The Testimony of the Word*, ed. by Monte S. Nyman and Charles D. Tate [Provo, Utah: Religious Studies Center, BYU, 1992], 60)

Alma 12:36 • FIRST AND LAST PROVOCATION

The "first provocation" was in the Garden of Eden; God kept his word and brought death as a consequence. The second provocation was with the children of Israel in the wilderness. Again, God kept his word and withdrew his presence. He did not allow those who came out of Egypt to enter the promised land, but caused them to die in the wilderness without finding rest, neither rest for their bodies nor for their spirits.

Alma warns that since God was true to his word in earlier provocations, we have reason to believe that he will be equally true to his word, if we provoke him by our disobedience.

(Robert J. Matthews; as quoted in *The Book of Mormon: Alma, The Testimony of the Word*, ed. by Monte S. Nyman and Charles D. Tate [Provo, Utah: Religious Studies Center, BYU, 1992], 59)

Alma 13:3–5 • FOREORDINATION

Every . . . [person] who has a calling to minister to the inhabitants of the world was ordained to that very purpose in the Grand Council of heaven before this world was. I suppose I was ordained to this very office in that Grand Council.

(*Teachings of the Prophet Joseph Smith*, comp. by Joseph Fielding Smith [Salt Lake City: Deseret Book, 1976], 365)

Remember, in the world before we came here, faithful women were given certain assignments while faithful men were foreordained to certain priesthood tasks. While we do not now remember the particulars, this does not alter the glorious reality of what we once agreed to.

(*Teachings of Spencer W. Kimball*, ed. by Edward L. Kimball [Salt Lake City: Bookcraft, 1982], 316)

Our young people are among the most blessed and favored of our Father's children. They are the nobility of heaven, a choice and chosen generation who have a divine destiny. Their spirits have been reserved to come forth in this day when the gospel is on earth, and when the Lord needs valiant servants to carry on his great latter-day work.

(Joseph Fielding Smith, *Improvement Era*, June 1970 [Salt Lake City: The Church of Jesus Christ of Latter-day Saints, 1970], 3)

For nearly six thousand years, God has held you in reserve to make your appearance in the final days before the Second Coming of the Lord. . . . God has saved for the final inning some of His strongest and most valiant children, who will help bear off the kingdom triumphantly. That is where you come in, for you are the generation that must be prepared to meet your God. . . . Make no mistake about it—you are a marked generation. There has never been more expected of the faithful in such a short period of time than there is of us. Never before on the face of this earth have the forces of evil and the forces of good been so well organized. . . . The final outcome is certain—the forces of righteousness will finally win. But what remains to be seen is where each of us personally, now and in the future, will stand in this battle—and how tall we will stand. Will we be true to our last days and fulfill our foreordained mission?

(Ezra Taft Benson, Dedication of the Boise Institute of Religion, 20 Nov. 1983)

We are quite well aware that Joseph Smith and Jeremiah and the apostles and prophets . . . were foreordained to particular ministries. But that is only a part of the doctrine of foreordination. The whole House of Israel was foreordained, . . . millions upon millions— comparatively few compared to the total preexistent host—but millions of people were foreordained.

(Bruce R. McConkie, *BYU Speeches of the Year,* 1969 [Provo, Utah: BYU Press, 1969], 6)

The mightiest and greatest spirits were foreordained to stand as prophets and spiritual leaders, giving to the people such portion of the Lord's word as was designed for the day and age involved. Other spirits, such as those who laid the foundations of the American nation, were appointed beforehand to perform great works in political and governmental fields. In all this there is not the slightest hint of compulsion; persons foreordained to fill special missions in mortality are as abundantly endowed with free agency as are any other persons. By their foreordination the Lord merely gives them the opportunity to serve him and his purposes if they will choose to measure up to the standard he knows they are capable of attaining.

(Bruce R. McConkie, *Mormon Doctrine* [Salt Lake City: Bookcraft, 1966], 290)

We received the priesthood first in the premortal existence and then again as mortals. . . . All of us who have calls to minister in the holy priesthood were foreordained to be ministers of Christ, and to come here in our appointed days, and to labor on his errand.

(Bruce R. McConkie, in Conference Report, Apr. 1982 [Salt Lake City: The Church of Jesus Christ of Latter-day Saints, 1982], 48)

We are eternal beings. In premortal realms, we brethren were foreordained for our priesthood responsibilities. Before the foundation of the world, women were prepared that they may bear children and glorify God. [D&C 132:63.]

(Russell M. Nelson, *Ensign,* May 2004 [Salt Lake City: The Church of Jesus Christ of Latter-day Saints, 2004], 29)

God may have called and chosen men in the spirit world or in their first estate to do a certain work, but whether they will accept that calling here and magnify it by faithful service and good works while in mortality is a matter in which it is their right and privilege to exercise their free agency to choose good or evil.

(Harold B. Lee, *Decisions for Successful Living* [Salt Lake City: Deseret Book, 1973], 169)

Our privilege to bear the priesthood of God tonight has its beginnings in our premortal existence. . . .

The Lord has long intended you to be a creator or a continuer of the chain of faithful bearers in your priesthood family. It was your faith and wise exercise of free agency—in the premortal existence and here in mortality—which permitted you to receive the "holy calling" of the priesthood. . . .

We have each come to earth with a personal heritage of faithfulness and foreordination.

(Keith K. Hilbig, *Ensign,* Nov. 2001 [Salt Lake City: The Church of Jesus Christ of Latter-day Saints, 2001], 45)

Approximately 2,500 years before there were any children of Israel, God had divided Adam's sons into families to reflect the coming destiny of those same children of Israel. Jesus Christ himself came through definite lineage lines. Thus there was, and is, planning for the preservation of priesthood lineage. Alma made this clear when he said of men holding the high priesthood that they were "called and prepared *from the foundation of the world* according to the foreknowledge of God, on account of their exceeding faith and good works" (Alma 13:3; italics added) . . . .

It is a sobering and humbling thought then to realize that we have been chosen beforehand and reserved for a special purpose—to use that priesthood for the benefit of others and not for our own aggrandizement.

(Theodore M. Burton, in Conference Report, Oct. 1974 [Salt Lake City: The Church of Jesus Christ of Latter-day Saints, 1974], 75–76)

The elders of Israel bearing the holy priesthood, I believe they were ordained before they came here; and I believe the God of Israel has raised them up, and has watched over them from their youth, and has carried them through all the scenes of life both seen and unseen, and has prepared them as instruments in his hands to take this kingdom and bear it off. . . . If anything under the heavens should humble men before the Lord and before one another, it should be the fact that we have been called of God.

(Wilford Woodruff, *Journal of Discourses* [London: Latter-day Saints' Book Depot, 1881], 21:317)

Alma 13:10–12 • LOOK UPON SIN WITH ABHORRENCE

(Refer in this text to 3 Nephi 27:20.)

The Holy Ghost is a sanctifier. One of the primary assignments of this member of the Godhead is to burn dross and iniquity out of the repentant soul as though by fire. One who lives worthy of the guidance and cleansing influence of the Spirit will, in process of time, become sanctified. Sanctification is the process whereby one comes to hate the worldliness he once loved and love the holiness and righteousness he once hated. To be sanctified is not only to be free from sin but also to be free from the *effects* of sin, free from sinfulness itself, the very desire to sin. One who is sanctified comes to look upon sin with abhorrence.

(Joseph Fielding McConkie and Robert L. Millet, *Doctrinal Commentary on the Book of Mormon* [Salt Lake City: Bookcraft, 1987], 1:263)

This passage indicates an attitude which is basic to the sanctification we should all be seeking. . . . It is that the former transgressor must have reached a "point of no return" . . . where the sin becomes most distasteful to him and where the desire or urge to sin is cleared out of his life.

(Spencer W. Kimball, *The Miracle of Forgiveness* [Salt Lake City: Bookcraft, 1969], 354–355)

Alma 13:15 • TITHING
(Refer in this text to 3 Nephi 24:8–12.)

A man who has not paid his tithing is unfit to be baptized for his dead. . . . It is our duty to pay our tithing. If a man has not faith enough to attend to these little things, he has not faith enough to save himself and his friends.

(John Taylor; as quoted in Joseph Smith, *History of the Church of Jesus Christ of Latter-day Saints* [Salt Lake City: Deseret Book, 1974] 7:292–293)

Frequently we hear the expression "I can't afford to pay tithing." Persons who make such statements have not yet learned that they can't afford *not* to pay tithing. . . .

The Lord does keep his promises. He truly opens the windows of heaven and pours out his blessings upon those who are faithful and who obey his commandments but it will be done in his own way. These blessings may come in a financial or temporal way or may be realized by a spiritual outpouring, bringing strength, peace, and comfort. His blessings may come in unusual and unexpected ways so that at the time we may not even recognize them as blessings; but the promises of the Lord will be kept.

(Henry D. Taylor, *Ensign*, May 1974 [Salt Lake City: The Church of Jesus Christ of Latter-day Saints, 1974], 107–108)

A tithe is one-tenth of the wage earner's *full income.* A tithe is one-tenth of the professional man's *net income.* A tithe is one-tenth of the farmer's *net income,* and also

one-tenth of the produce used by the farmer to sustain his family which is a just and equitable requirement, as others purchase out of their income such food as is needed to provide for their families. A tithe is one-tenth of the dividends derived from investments. A tithe is one-tenth of net insurance income less premiums if tithing has been paid on the premiums.

(Joseph L. Wirthlin, in Conference Report, Apr. 1953, 98; as quoted in Henry D. Taylor, *Ensign*, May 1974 [Salt Lake City: The Church of Jesus Christ of Latter-day Saints, 1974], 107; italics added)

We do not ask anybody to pay tithing unless they are disposed to do so; but if you pretend to pay tithing, pay it like honest men.

("Brigham Young on Tithing," *Improvement Era*, May 1941, 282; as quoted in Henry D. Taylor, *Ensign*, May 1974 [Salt Lake City: The Church of Jesus Christ of Latter-day Saints, 1974], 107)

The payment of our tithing in the season thereof—when we get our income—makes it come easy. I find that those who pay tithing every month have very much less difficulty in paying it than those who postpone payment to the end of the year.

(Heber J. Grant, *Gospel Doctrine*, 9; as quoted in Henry D. Taylor, *Ensign*, May 1974 [Salt Lake City: The Church of Jesus Christ of Latter-day Saints, 1974], 108)

I recall sitting in this historical Tabernacle back on October 1948 when . . . Elder Matthew Cowley of the Council of the Twelve was speaking. . . . While serving as president of the New Zealand Mission he visited a good Maori sister who sincerely believed and observed the principle of tithing. Brother Cowley told of this experience in these words:

". . . When I visited that vicinity, to see this grand little woman, then in her eighties, and blind. She did not live in an organized branch, had no contact with the priesthood except as the missionaries visited there. We had no missionaries in those days. They were away at war.

"I went in and greeted her in the Maori fashion. . . . I reached forth my hand to shake hands with her, and I was going to rub noses with her and she said: 'Do not shake hands with me. . . .'

"I said: 'Oh, that is clean dirt on your hands. I am willing to shake hands with you. I am glad to. I want to.'

"She said: 'Not yet.' Then she got on her hands and knees and crawled over to her little house. At the corner of the house there was a spade. She lifted up that spade and crawled off in another direction, measuring the distance she went. She finally arrived at a spot and started digging down into the soil with that spade. It finally struck something hard. She took out the soil with her hands and lifted out a fruit jar. She opened that fruit jar and reached down in it, took something out and handed it to me, and it turned out to be New Zealand money. In American money it would have been equivalent to [about] one hundred dollars.

"She said: 'There is my tithing. Now I can shake hands with the priesthood of God.'

"I said: 'You do not owe that much tithing.'

"She said: 'I know it. I do not owe it now, but I am paying some in advance, for I do not know when the priesthood of God will get around this way again.' "

Then after a brief pause and with considerable emotion Brother Cowley continued: "And then I leaned over and pressed my nose and forehead against hers, and the tears from my eyes ran down her cheeks. . . ."

(In Conference Report, Oct. 1948, 159–60; as quoted in Henry D. Taylor, *Ensign*, May 1974 [Salt Lake City: The Church of Jesus Christ of Latter-day Saints, 1974], 108)

––––––––––

The principle of tithe paying is introduced as part of the Lord's plan for our own welfare and self-preservation. . . .

Tithe paying is part of the divine plan to protect us against hard times. I repeat, tithing is to protect us against hard times! . . .

Obedience to the law of tithing is a safeguard for us[.]

(Mark E. Petersen, in Conference Report, Apr. 1981 [Salt Lake City: The Church of Jesus Christ of Latter-day Saints, 1981], 83–84)

––––––––––

Many years ago John Orth worked in a foundry in Australia, and in a terrible accident, hot molten lead splashed onto his face and body. He was administered to, and some of the vision was restored to his right eye, but he was completely blind in his left. Because he couldn't see well, he lost his job. . . . He was forced to go door-to-door seeking odd jobs and handouts to pay for food and rent.

One year he did not pay any tithing and went to talk to the branch president. The branch president understood the situation but asked John to make it a matter of prayer and fasting so that he could find a way to pay his tithing. John and his wife, Alice, fasted and prayed and determined that the only thing of value they owned was her engagement ring—a beautiful ring bought in happier times. After much anguish, they took the ring to a pawnbroker, where they learned it was worth enough

to pay their tithing and some outstanding bills. That Sunday, John went to the branch president and paid his tithing. As he left the office, he happened to meet the mission president, who noticed his damaged eyes.

Brother Orth's son, now serving as a bishop in Adelaide, later wrote: "We believe that [the mission president] was an eye doctor, for he was commonly called President Dr. Rees. He spoke to Dad and was able to examine him and offer suggestions to help his eyesight. Dad followed his advice, . . . and in due course sight was restored—15 percent sight to his left eye and 95 percent sight to his right eye—and with the help of glasses he could see again." With his vision restored, John was never unemployed again; he redeemed the ring, which is now a family heirloom, and paid a full tithing for the rest of his life. The Lord knew John Orth, and He knew who could help him.

"President Dr. Rees" was my mother's father, and he probably never knew of the miracle that was wrought that day. Generations were blessed because a family decided they would pay their tithing regardless of the difficulty.

(Sydney S. Reynolds, in Conference Report, Oct. 2003 [Salt Lake City: The Church of Jesus Christ of Latter-day Saints, 2003], 79–80)

––––––––––

Compliance to the great law of tithing develops and trains men in the vital attribute of obedience, . . . and also in the vital attribute of unselfishness, man's most immediate need for solving the world's dilemmas in this day of hate, greed, and distrust. . . .

He doesn't really need our ten percent—it is all his in the first place; but we need the experience of giving. Just as the Sabbath was created for man rather than man for the Sabbath, so it is with tithing: the value of the human soul is most important.

(Robert L. Simpson, *Proven Paths* [Salt Lake City: Deseret Book, 1974], 92)

––––––––––

To pay tithes and offerings while ignoring the balance of Heavenly Father's advice concerning sound judgment in family finances will probably cause the windows of heaven to stick a little bit. The promised blessings will not likely be forthcoming as expected.

Every prophet in this dispensation has taught in clear, unmistakable terms that the Saints should stay out of debt. . . . That we should not participate in "something-for-nothing" schemes. . . . He advises us to be frugal, to save, and to earn our money the old-fashioned way, by the sweat of our face.

(Robert L. Simpson, in Conference Report, Apr. 1982 [Salt Lake City: The Church of Jesus Christ of Latter-day Saints, 1982], 31)

In October of 1998 Hurricane Mitch devastated many parts of Central America. President Gordon B. Hinckley was very concerned for the victims of this disaster, many of whom lost everything—food, clothing, and household goods. . . . This modern prophet's message in each city was similar—to sacrifice and be obedient to the law of tithing.

But how can you ask someone so destitute to sacrifice? President Hinckley knew that the food and clothing shipments they received would help them survive the crisis, but his concern and love for them went far beyond that. As important as humanitarian aid is, he knew that the most important assistance comes from God, not from man. The prophet wanted to help them unlock the windows of heaven as promised by the Lord. . . .

President Hinckley taught them that if they would pay their tithing, they would always have food on their tables, they would always have clothing on their backs, and they would always have a roof over their heads.

(Lynn G. Robbins, *Ensign*, May 2005 [Salt Lake City: The Church of Jesus Christ of Latter-day Saints, 2005], 34–35)

The harder it is for an individual to comply with the requirements of the Lord in the payment of his tithing, the greater the benefit when he finally does pay it. . . . No man living upon the earth can pay donations for the poor, can pay for building meetinghouses and temples, academics, and universities, can take of his means and send his boys and girls to proclaim this gospel, without removing selfishness from his soul, no matter how selfish he was when he started in.

(Heber J. Grant, *Gospel Standards*, comp. by G. Homer Durham [Salt Lake City: The Improvement Era Publication, 1942], 62)

Why should members worldwide, many of whom may not have enough for their daily needs, be encouraged to keep the Lord's law of tithing? As President Hinckley said in Cebu in the Philippine Islands, if members, "even living in poverty and misery, . . . will accept the gospel and live it, pay their tithes and offerings, even though those be meager, . . . they will have rice in their bowls and clothing on their backs and shelter over their heads. I do not see any other solution" ("Inspirational Thoughts," *Ensign*, Aug. 1997, 7).

Some may feel that they cannot afford to pay tithing, but the Lord has promised that He would prepare a way for us to keep all of His commandments (see 1 Nephi 3:7). . . .

We learn about tithing by paying it. Indeed, I believe it is possible to break out of poverty by having the faith to give back to the Lord part of what little we have.

(James E. Faust, in Conference Report, Oct. 1998 [Salt Lake City: The Church of Jesus Christ of Latter-day Saints, 1998], 73–74)

What does it mean to obey the law of sacrifice? Nature's law demands us to do everything with self in view. The first law of mortal life, self-preservation, would claim the most luscious fruit, the most tender meat, the softest down on which to lie. Selfishness, the law of nature, would say, "I want the best; that is mine." But God said: "Take of the firstlings of your herds and of your flocks" (Deut. 12:6).

The best shall be given to God; the next you may have. Thus should God become the center of our very being.

With this thought in view, I thank my earthly father for the lesson he gave to two boys in a hayfield at a time when tithes were paid in kind. We had driven out to the field to get the tenth load of hay, and then over to a part of the meadow where we had taken the ninth load, where there was "wire grass" and "slough grass." As we started to load the hay, Father called out, "No, boys, drive over to the higher ground." There was timothy and redtop there. But one of the boys called back, (and it was I) "No, let us take the hay as it comes!"

"No, David, that is the *tenth* load, and the best is none too good for God." . . .

I found later in life, this very principle of the law of sacrifice. You cannot develop character without obeying that law.

(David O. McKay, *Cherished Experiences from the Writings of President David O. McKay*, comp. by Clare Middlemiss [Salt Lake City: Deseret Book, 1955], 19–20)

I have seen God's promise fulfilled that He would "rebuke the devourer for [my sake]." That blessing of protection against evil has been poured out upon me and on my loved ones beyond any capacity I have to adequately acknowledge. But I believe that divine safety has come, at least in part, because of our determination, individually and as a family, to pay tithing.

(Jeffrey R. Holland, *Ensign*, Nov. 2001 [Salt Lake City: The Church of Jesus Christ of Latter-day Saints, 2001], 34)

By our decision now to be a full-tithe payer and our steady efforts to obey, we will be strengthened in our faith and, in time, our hearts will be softened. It is that change in our hearts through the Atonement of Jesus

Christ, beyond the offering of our money or goods, that makes it possible for the Lord to promise full-tithe payers protection in the last days (see D&C 64:23).

(Henry B. Eyring, *Ensign*, Nov. 2005 [Salt Lake City: The Church of Jesus Christ of Latter-day Saints, 2005], 40)

Alma 13:28 • TEMPTATION ABOVE THAT WHICH WE CAN BEAR
(Refer in this text to 2 Nephi 1:13, 23; 2 Nephi 28:19–22.)

Some transgressions are so powerful that it is unlikely that you will begin to overcome them without another's help. Seek that help. In time, with the strength that comes from continued use of agency to live truth, you will be healed through the Savior.

(Richard G. Scott, *Ensign*, Nov. 1992 [Salt Lake City: The Church of Jesus Christ of Latter-day Saints, 1992], 62)

———————

[A letter to Gordon B. Hinckley which he shared in General Conference] I am a 35-year-old male and am a convert to the Church of more than ten years. For most of my adult life I have been addicted to pornography. I am ashamed to admit this. My addiction is as real as that of an alcoholic or a drug addict. . . . I think it is ironic that those who support the business of pornography say that it is a matter of freedom of expression. I have no freedom. I have lost my free agency because I have been unable to overcome this. It is a trap for me, and I can't seem to get out of it. Please, please, please, plead with the brethren of the Church to not only avoid but eliminate the sources of pornographic material in their lives. . . . Pray for me and others in the Church who may be like me to have the courage and strength to overcome this terrible affliction.

(Gordon B. Hinckley, *Ensign*, Nov. 1992 [Salt Lake City: The Church of Jesus Christ of Latter-day Saints, 1992], 51)

———————

Often 1 Cor. 10:13 is quoted to suggest that God will somehow snatch us from any and all circumstances and not permit us to be tempted beyond our ability to withstand. Alma seems to be saying that we have a responsibility in this matter—a responsibility to earnestly strive through prayer and humility to avoid circumstances that may bring overpowering temptations.

(Larry E. Dahl; as quoted in *Studies in Scripture*, ed. by Kent P. Jackson [Salt Lake City: Deseret Book, 1987], 7:320)

———————

Sin is intensely habit-forming and sometimes moves men to the tragic point of no return . . . . As the transgressor moves deeper and deeper in his sin, and the error is entrenched more deeply and the will to change is weakened, it becomes increasingly near-hopeless, and he skids down and down until either he does not want to climb back or he has lost the power to do so.

(Spencer W. Kimball, *The Miracle of Forgiveness* [Salt Lake City: Bookcraft, 1969], 117.)

———————

All beings who have bodies have power over those who have not. The devil has no power over us, only as we permit him. The moment we revolt at anything which comes from God, the devil takes power.

(*Teachings of the Prophet Joseph Smith*, comp. by Joseph Fielding Smith [Salt Lake City: Deseret Book, 1976], 181, 187, 189)

———————

Satan is still trying to take away our free agency by persuading us to voluntarily surrender our will to his. . . . Some people are more susceptible to some addictions than other people. . . . One person has a taste for nicotine and is easily addicted to smoking. Another person cannot take an occasional drink without being propelled into alcoholism. Another person samples gambling and becomes a compulsive gambler. . . . We all seem to have susceptibilities to one disorder or another, but whatever our susceptibilities, we have the will and the power to control our thoughts and our actions. . . . A person who insists that he is not responsible for the exercise of his free agency because he was "born that way" is trying to ignore the outcome of the War in Heaven. We are responsible, and if we argue otherwise, our efforts become part of the propaganda effort of the adversary.

(Dallin H. Oaks, "Free Agency and Freedom," *BYU Speeches of the Year*, 11 October 1987 [Provo, Utah: BYU Press, 1987], 44–46)

———————

You are aware that many think that the Devil has rule and power over both body and spirit. Now, I want to tell you that he does not hold any power over man, only so far as the body overcomes the spirit that is in a man, through yielding to the spirit of evil.

In the first place the spirit is pure, and under the special control and influence of the Lord, but the body is of the earth, and is subject to the power of the Devil, and is under the mighty influence of that fallen nature that is of the earth. If the spirit yields to the body, the Devil then has power to overcome the body and spirit of that man, and he loses both.

(*Discourses of Brigham Young*, comp. by John A. Widtsoe [Salt Lake City: Deseret Book, 1954], 69–70)

———————

The only power the adversary has is power we give him when we sin or break our covenants. And we have not been left to withstand the wiles of the adversary alone, for the power of Jesus Christ is stronger than the power of the devil. Hence we have the promise that Lucifer cannot influence us when we stay on the Lord's side of the line . . . (D&C 93:49; 87:8).

Very simply, our physical and spiritual safety lies in never even getting close to the line that separates light from dark, good from evil. . . . How quickly ought we to run for our lives—our eternal lives—when confronted with even the slightest hint of evil.

(Sheri Dew, "Living on the Lord's Side of the Line," *BYU Speeches of the Year*, 21 Mar. 2000 [Provo, Utah: BYU Press, 2000], 2)

Satan . . . knows that he has no power over a righteous individual. Yet he is a master at making sin appealing to the undecided. . . .

When you really understand who you are, it is not difficult to resist Satan's temptations. Then he can't thwart the development of your true potential.

(Richard G. Scott, in Conference Report, Oct. 2003 [Salt Lake City: The Church of Jesus Christ of Latter-day Saints, 2003], 44–45)

Alma 13:28 • LEAD BY THE SPIRIT

I remember once while sitting in the State Bank I saw an aged brother passing, by the name of John Furster. He was one of the first men baptized in Scandinavia. As he passed the bank window the Spirit whispered to me "give that man twenty dollars." I went up to the teller, handed him my IOU for $20, walked down the street and overtook Mr. Furster in front of the ZCMI store. I shook hands with him and left the twenty dollars in his hand. Some years later I learned that that morning Brother Furster had been praying for sufficient means to enable him to go to Logan and do a little work in the temple there. At the time, the Salt Lake Temple was not completed. The twenty dollars was just the amount he needed, and years later he thanked me with tears running down his cheeks, for having given him this money.

One day while sitting in my office an impression came to me to go to Sister Emily Woodmansee and loan her fifty dollars. I did so, and found that she was in absolute need of the necessities of life. . . . There is nothing I desire more than to have my mind susceptible to impressions of this kind.

(*Teachings of President of the Church—Heber J. Grant* [Salt Lake City: The Church of Jesus Christ of Latter-day Saints, 2002], 142–143.)

Alma 13:28; 15:17 • WATCH AND PRAY ALWAYS
(Refer in this text to 3 Nephi 18:15, 18.)

The town that my family and I have lived in the past few years lies in a valley up against a section of one of the most beautiful peaks along the Wasatch Mountain Range. Within a few miles of my house are a number of old mining caves. When I first moved to this town, I was talking to a few of my neighbors as to the whereabouts of these wonderful places of adventure. They filled my head with stories that excited the little boy within me. Following our conversation, one of the fellows said, "Remember not to go cavin' up there in August." When I inquired as to his reasoning, he simply said, "Snakes—rattlesnakes."

His words immediately sent a chill down my spine, and I was reminded of my fear of these belly-crawling creatures. But with the passing of time, the weather began to warm up, and naturally I began to explore the territory around the nearby hills. The area just echoed adventure as my family and I used much of our free time to explore the mountains near our home. Summer continued until we found ourselves in the dry month of August. By this time I had forgotten the counsel of my neighbor. My son Blaine and I were riding motorcycles along the foothills on a hot August afternoon when my eyes caught sight of a mining cave that I had not yet shared with my son. The child within me burst forth as I exclaimed, "Let's go cavin'!" He joyfully followed my lead.

We drove our motorcycles as close to the cave as possible, parking them about a quarter mile from the cave's opening. As we hiked up the trail, we were surrounded by the sound of katydids and grasshoppers. It was a beautiful day, and we were two boys in a world of adventure. After an hour or so in the cool confines of the cave, we made our way back down to the motorcycles. My heart was full, and my eyes moved back and forth and all around in an effort to drink up all the scenery that surrounded us. When we reached a place in the trail that seemed to have the best vantage point to partake of all the natural beauty, I asked my son to stop and enjoy the sight. In my moment of wonder I proclaimed, "It doesn't get any better than this!"

My thoughts were interrupted by a sound I couldn't identify because it was so muffled by the clatter of the grasshoppers and katydids. I stepped toward a bush only a few feet away to get a better view. As I leaned over the bush, my eyes caught hold of its occupant. Staring back at me was a rattlesnake coiled and ready to strike, and there was no question as to its target.

In the newspaper a few years ago I read a movie title called *White Men Can't Jump*. In an instant I proved that movie's title false. I even proved that old white men can jump as I instantly became vertical as well as horizontal in the air, like one of those cartoon characters I had grown up seeing on TV. It was a shame the Guinness Book of World Records could not have been there to record my leap. At the very least it would have been a record for my age group.

It's amazing how quickly life can change from moment to moment. One moment I was strolling down a mountain trail with my son, soaking up the world around me, and in the next instant my heart was filled with terror. Quickly I grabbed my son's arm, and we ran down the trail to our motorcycles. As we sat there on our bikes catching our breath, those words of advice came back to me: "Remember not to go cavin' up there in August."

I had forgotten the counsel because I had been caught up in the moment. I placed myself as well as my son in a position to alter our tomorrows because of my preoccupation with the moment. We were fortunate not to have paid for my lack of obedience to the counsel of those who had been down that trail before us.

We can learn from the experiences of others, or we can make life's mistakes on our own. If I had just waited for another season, our adventure would not have been so perilous. I thought of Alma's words to the Nephites: "Watch and pray continually, that ye may not be tempted above that which ye can bear" (Alma 13:28). I had let down my guard by not watching continually, and I was fortunate to have had no more than just a story to tell.

(Jack R. Christianson and K. Douglas Bassett, *Life Lessons from the Book of Mormon* [Salt Lake City: Deseret Book, 2003], 104–106)

Alma 14:11 • WHY DOES GOD ALLOW TRAGEDY?

(Refer in this text to Mosiah 24:14–15; Alma 17:11.)

The right question to ask is not why good people have trials, but how shall good people respond when they are tried? . . . God does not deny us the experience we came here to have. He does not insulate us from tribulation or guarantee immunity from trouble. Much of the pain we suffer and inevitably impose upon others is self-induced through our own bad judgment, through poor choices. . . . But much that happens to us in this life we cannot control; we only respond. Knowing what God has promised can provide the courage and faith we need. We are assured in the scriptures that we may know of a surety that the Lord does visit his people in their afflictions. . . . Thus the promise is that in times of sorrow and affliction, if we endure and remain faithful and put our trust in him and are courageous, the Lord will visit us in our afflictions, strengthen us to carry our burdens and support us in our trials. He'll be with us to the end of our days, lift us at the last day to greater

opportunities for service, and exalt us at last with him and reunited loved ones, and he will consecrate our afflictions to our gain.

(Marion D. Hanks, *Ensign*, Nov 1992 [Salt Lake City: The Church of Jesus Christ of Latter-day Saints, 1992], 64)

———————

Now, we find many people critical when a righteous person is killed, a young father or mother is taken from a family, or when violent deaths occur. Some become bitter when oft-repeated prayers seem unanswered. Some lose faith and turn sour when solemn administrations by holy men seem to be ignored and no restoration seems to come from repeated prayer circles. But if all the sick were healed, if all the righteous were protected and the wicked destroyed, the whole program of the Father would be annulled and the basic principle of the Gospel, free agency, would be ended. If pain and sorrow and total punishment immediately followed the doing of evil, no soul would do a misdeed. If joy and peace and rewards were instantaneously given the doer of good, there could be no evil—all would do good and not because of the rightness of doing good. . . . Should all prayers be immediately answered according to our selfish desires and our limited understanding, then there would be little or no suffering, sorrow, disappointment or even death, and if these were not there would also be an absence of joy, success, resurrection, eternal life and Godhood. . . . Being human we would expel from our lives, sorrow, distress, physical pain and mental anguish and assure ourselves of continual ease and comfort, but if we closed the doors upon such, we might be evicting our greatest friends and benefactors. Suffering can make saints of people as they learn patience, long suffering and self-mastery. The sufferings of our Savior were part of his education.

(Spencer W. Kimball, *Faith Precedes the Miracle* [Salt Lake City: Deseret Book, 1973], 92–106)

———————

Yes, each of us will walk the path of disappointment, perhaps due to an opportunity lost, a power misused, or a loved one not taught. The path of temptation, too, will be the path of each. . . . Likewise shall we walk the path of pain. We cannot go to heaven in a feather bed. The Savior of the world entered after great pain and suffering. We, as servants, can expect no more than the Master. Before Easter there must be a cross.

(Thomas S. Monson, *Ensign*, Sept 1992 [Salt Lake City: The Church of Jesus Christ of Latter-day Saints, 1992], 4)

———————

We have reviewed from scriptures and from living

prophets four major reasons for suffering: (1) experience, (2) our good, (3) our own sins, and (4) accidents. It is important for our spiritual growth that [we] recognize the validity of these reasons.

(Keith W. Perkins, Sperry Symposium on the D&C and Church History, 1992, 287)

———————

I can understand why someone who lacks an eternal perspective might see the horrifying news footage of starving children and man's inhumanity to man and shake a fist at the heavens and cry, "If there is a God, how could he allow such things to happen" . . . God has put his plan in motion. It proceeds through natural laws that are, in fact, God's laws. Since they are his, he is bound by them, as are we. . . . The Lord can control the elements. For the most part, however, he does not cause but he allows nature to run its course. In this imperfect world, bad things sometimes happen. . . . [However], much adversity is man-made. . . . Much adversity has its origin in the principle of agency. . . . Often overlooked is the fact that choices have consequences. . . . At times we will be affected adversely by the way other people choose to exercise their agency. Our Heavenly Father feels so strongly about protecting our agency that he allows his children to exercise it, either for good or for evil. . . . But if we know and understand Heavenly Father's plan, we realize that dealing with adversity is one of the chief ways we are tested.

(M. Russell Ballard, *Ensign*, May 1995 [Salt Lake City: The Church of Jesus Christ of Latter-day Saints, 1995], 23)

———————

Trials, disappointments, sadness, and heartache come to us from two basically different sources. Those who transgress the laws of God will always have those challenges. The other reason for adversity is to accomplish the Lord's own purposes in our life that we may receive the refinement that comes from testing. . . . If you are suffering the disheartening effects of transgression, please recognize that the only path to permanent relief from sadness is sincere repentance with a broken heart and a contrite spirit. . . . When those trials are not consequences of your disobedience, they are evidence that the Lord feels you are prepared to grow more (see Prov. 3:11–12). . . . When you face adversity, you can be led to ask many questions. Some serve a useful purpose; others do not. To ask, Why does this have to happen to me? Why do I have to suffer this, now? What have I done to cause this? will lead you into blind alleys. . . . Rather ask, What am I to do? What am I to learn from this experience? What am I to change? Whom am I to help? How can I remember my many blessings in times of trial? Willing sacrifice of deeply held personal desires

in favor of the will of God is very hard to do. Yet, when you pray with real conviction, "Please let me know Thy will" and "May Thy will be done," you are in the strongest position to receive the maximum help from your loving Father.

(Richard G. Scott, *Ensign*, Nov. 1995 [Salt Lake City: The Church of Jesus Christ of Latter-day Saints, 1995], 16)

———————

Since we assembled in general conference last April, . . . I experienced my third heart attack. . . . While I was lying in my hospital bed and for several weeks at home, my physical activity was severely restricted by intense pain which disabled my weakened body, but I learned the joy of freeing my mind to ponder the meaning of life and the eternities. . . . I discovered that if I dwelt only upon my pain, it inhibited the healing process. I found that pondering was a very important element in the healing process for both soul and body. Pain brings you to a humility that allows you to ponder. It is an experience I am grateful to have endured. . . . I have come to understand how useless it is to dwell on the whys, what ifs, and if onlys for which there likely will be given no answers in mortality. To receive the Lord's comfort, we must exercise faith. The questions Why me? Why our family? Why now? are usually unanswerable questions. These questions detract from our spirituality and can destroy our faith. We need to spend our time and energy building our faith by turning to the Lord and asking for strength to overcome the pains and trials of this world and to endure to the end for greater understanding. . . . We must surrender ourselves to the Lord. In doing so, we give up whatever is causing our pain and turn everything over to Him. "Cast thy burden upon the Lord, and he shall sustain thee" (Psalms 55:22). . . . Healing comes in the Lord's time and the Lord's way; be patient. Our Savior waits for us to come to Him through our scripture study, pondering, and prayer to our Heavenly Father.

(Robert D. Hales, *Ensign*, Nov. 1998 [Salt Lake City: The Church of Jesus Christ of Latter-day Saints, 1998], 14–17)

———————

Since this life is such a brief experience, there must be regular exit routes. Some easy. Some hard. Some sudden. Others lingering. Therefore, we cannot presume, even by faith, to block all these exits, all the time, and for all people. . . .

Since certain recollections are withheld, we do not now see the end from the beginning. But God does. Meanwhile, we are in what might be called "the murky middle." Therein, however, we can still truly know that God loves us, individually and perfectly, even though we cannot always explain the meaning of all things happening to us or around us (see 1 Nephi 11:17).

(Neal A. Maxwell, in Conference Report, Apr. 1984 [Salt Lake City: The Church of Jesus Christ of Latter-day Saints, 1984], 29)

———————

Why death? Why sickness? Why tragedies? Why must I have suffering, and disappointment? Why must I have to face the "deep waters" of life? . . .

We know little of the will of the Lord, yet we judge the Lord often with our small wisdom. I speak to those who now walk the deep water of life or the rivers of sorrow. . . .

Elder Spencer W. Kimball said: "Being human, we would expel from our lives physical pain and mental anguish and assure ourselves of continual ease and comfort, but if we were to close the doors upon sorrow and distress, we might be excluding our greatest friends and benefactors. Suffering can make saints of people as they learn patience, long-suffering, and self-mastery" (*Faith Precedes the Miracle* [Salt Lake City: Deseret Book, 1972], 98).

I repeat: "Suffering can make saints of people as they learn patience, long-suffering, and self-mastery," as long as we live righteously.

Let's all learn from my friend Mick. One day he was swimming at a party. . . . He dove into the water and hit a shallow spot very hard. A broken neck was his diagnosis, and his whole body was immediately paralyzed. . . .

At the time of this tragic accident he had just one year left in law school at BYU. He was married and had two children. This tragic accident changed his whole life. . . . It was inconceivable, the emotional and physical pain that he must go through as a quadriplegic.

Even though he was in this condition in the University of Utah Medical Center, he was determined to graduate from law school. It was an almost impossible task, but good friends, true Samaritans, brought him notes and taped lectures from Provo. . . . He turned pages by a mouthstick, and if his book flipped shut, he waited for a long time until someone came to help him.

Finally, he graduated from law school, passed the Utah bar exam, and became a licensed attorney. While he was studying, exercising, and maintaining doctor's contact to gain strength, his wife took his two sons and divorced him. . . . But he never complained and even blessed the leaving loved ones. . . . It was his own Garden of Gethsemane, and he took his own cup and drank it as his blessing. . . .

My friend Mick met a most beautiful lady, Cheryl. They married and now the greatest joy has come to their lives. His wife is expecting a baby. It is a miracle. The Lord said, "I will be with thee, thy troubles to bless." Last Friday, they were sealed in the temple for time and for all eternity.

(Yoshihiko Kikuchi, in Conference Report, Apr. 1984 [Salt Lake City: The Church of Jesus Christ of Latter-day Saints, 1984], 99–100)

Alma 15:8 • IF THOU BELIEVEST, THOU CANST BE HEALED

As to the healing of the sick, He has clearly said, "And again, it shall come to pass that he that hath faith in me to be healed, *and is not appointed unto death*, shall be healed" (D&C 42:48; italics added). All too often we overlook the qualifying phrase "and is not appointed unto death" ("or," we might add, "unto sickness or handicap"). Please do not despair when fervent prayers have been offered and priesthood blessings performed and your loved one makes no improvement or even passes from mortality. . . . That your child did not recover in spite of all that was done in his behalf can and should be the basis for peace and reassurance to all who love him! *The Lord, who inspires the blessings and who hears every earnest prayer, called him home nonetheless.* All the experiences of prayer, fasting, and faith may well have been more for *our* benefit than for his.

(Lance B. Wickman, in Conference Report, Oct. 2002 [Salt Lake City: The Church of Jesus Christ of Latter-day Saints, 2002], 32)

———————

I have on my wall a painting that was given to me by a woman here in Hong Kong. On the back it says, "To Elder Gordon B. Hinckley, with gratitude for the restoration of my eyesight," and then her name is signed. I did not restore her eyesight; the Lord did. But she says that that administration saved her eyesight, and the doctors could not believe what happened to her. She was going blind, and they told her she would be blind in a matter of a few months. It was faith in the power of the priesthood and, most important of all, the goodness of the Lord which made possible that miracle.

President Jay Quealy, whom some of you may know, was seriously injured while he was presiding here. One morning he went over to see the missionaries on the island. He . . . rode on a scooter, which they were permitted to do in those days. He was on a road where there was some pea gravel and skidded right into a police van. . . . He was thrown right up over the hood and into the windshield. He broke both legs, an arm, and some ribs. I came over here to look after the mission for a time. He says . . . that when I administered to him I said that he would walk again on his natural legs and be unimpaired in his work. The doctors said he had gangrene in his legs and they would have to take them off. He said, "No, I won't let you take them off. I was given a promise by a servant of the Lord that I would walk again with my natural legs." The nurses, wonderful Chinese nurses, massaged his legs, and the gangrene miraculously cleared, and until the time of his death he walked on his natural legs. I have seen miracles here by the power of this priesthood, . . . and by the power of faith.

(*Discourses of President Gordon B. Hinckley*, 1995–99 [Salt Lake City: The Church of Jesus Christ of Latter-day Saints, 2004], 1:407–408)

We can . . . access His healing power through prayer. I'll never forget an experience that Sister Nelson and I had about three decades ago with President Spencer W. Kimball and his beloved Camilla. We were in Hamilton, New Zealand, for a large conference with the Saints. . . .

A Saturday evening cultural program had been prepared for this conference by local youth of the Church. Unfortunately, President and Sister Kimball both became very ill, each with a high fever. After receiving priesthood blessings, they rested at the nearby home of the president of the New Zealand Temple. President Kimball asked his counselor, President N. Eldon Tanner, to preside at the cultural event and to excuse President and Sister Kimball.

Sister Nelson went with President and Sister Tanner and other leaders to the event, while President Kimball's secretary, Brother D. Arthur Haycock, and I watched over our feverish friends.

While President Kimball was sleeping, I was quietly reading in his room. Suddenly President Kimball was awakened, He asked, "Brother Nelson, what time was this evening's program to begin?"

"At seven o'clock, President Kimball."

"What time is it now?"

"It's almost seven," I replied.

President Kimball quickly said, "Tell Sister Kimball we are going!"

I checked President Kimball's temperature. It was normal! I took Sister Kimball's temperature. It was also normal!

They quickly dressed and got into an automobile. We were driven to the stadium of the Church College of New Zealand. As the car entered the arena, there was a very loud shout that erupted spontaneously. It was most unusual! After we took our seats, I asked Sister Nelson about that sudden sound. She said that when President Tanner began the meeting, he dutifully excused President and Sister Kimball because of illness. Then one of the young New Zealanders was called upon to pray.

With great faith, he gave what Sister Nelson described as a rather lengthy but powerful prayer. He

so prayed: "We are 3,000 New Zealand youth. We are assembled here, having prepared for six months to sing and dance for Thy prophet. Wilt Thou heal him and deliver him here!" After the "amen" was pronounced, the car carrying President and Sister Kimball entered the stadium. They were identified immediately, and instantly everyone shouted for joy!"

I had witnessed the healing power of the Lord! . . .

I recognize that, on occasion, some of our most fervent prayers may seem to go unanswered. We wonder, "Why?" I know that feeling! I know the fears and tears of such moments. But I also know that our prayers are never ignored. Our faith is never unappreciated. I know that an all-wise Heavenly Father's perspective is much broader than is ours. While we know of our mortal problems and pain, He knows of our immortal progress and potential. If we pray to know His will and submit ourselves to it with patience and courage, heavenly healing can take place in His own way and time.

(Russell M. Nelson, *Ensign*, Nov. 2005 [Salt Lake City: The Church of Jesus Christ of Latter-day Saints, 2005], 85–86)

Alma 15:16, 18; 10:4 • REJECTED BY FAMILY

The Gospel of Salvation is perfectly calculated to cause division.

(Brigham Young, *Journal of Discourses* [London: Latter-day Saints' Book Depot, 1855], 1:235)

Nine days after Heber [J. Grant] was born, his father died of a combination of typhoid and pneumonia.

For much of his childhood, Heber and his widowed mother struggled to survive financially. They endured "blustery nights with no fire in the hearth, months with no shoes, never more than a single homemade outfit of homespun at a time, and except for an adequate supply of bread, a meager fare which allowed only several pounds of butter and sugar for an entire year."

Rachel was determined to support herself and her young son. She worked as a seamstress and took in boarders. Her brothers offered to give her a life of ease if she would leave the Church, but she remained true to her faith. This devotion and sacrifice made a lasting impression on Heber, who later recalled:

"My mother's brothers who were well-to-do financially offered to settle an annuity upon her for life if she would renounce her religion. One of her brothers said to her: 'Rachel, you have disgraced the name of Ivins. We never want to see you again if you stay with those awful Mormons,'—this was when she was leaving for Utah—'but,' he continued, 'come back in a year, come back in five years, come back in ten or twenty years, and no matter when you come back, the latchstring will be out, and affluence and ease will be your portion.'

"Later, when poverty became her lot, if she actually had not known that Joseph Smith was a prophet of God and that the gospel was true, all she needed to do was to return east and let her brothers take care of her. But rather than return to her wealthy relatives in the east where she would have been amply provided for, with no struggle for herself or her child, she preferred to make her way among those to whom she was more strongly attached than her kindred who were not believers in her faith."

(*Teachings of President of the Church—Heber J. Grant,* 2002 [Salt Lake City: The Church of Jesus Christ of Latter-day Saints, 2002], xi–xii)

––––––––––

I wish to tell you one story coming out of London. . . . One night, one cold, rainy winter night, there came a knock on the door. I went to the door and let a young man in. I knew him. He was soaking wet. I invited him to come over to the fire. . . . He put his soggy hat down and sat down by the fire, and I said, "What's the matter? You're in trouble. What is the problem?" . . .

He said, "I'm licked. I don't know where to turn. I don't know what to do. When I joined the Church, my father told me to leave home and never come back as long as I was a Mormon. Then the athletic club of which I was a member, when they learned I was a Mormon, told me I was no longer welcome. And not long after that my boss fired me." And he said, "Last night the girl I love told me that she would never marry me because of my religion."

I said, "If this has cost you so much, why don't you leave? Why don't you go back to your father's home? Why don't you go back to your athletic club? Why don't you ask your boss for your old job? Why don't you marry that girl?"

He put his head down in his hands and sobbed and sobbed and sobbed. Finally he stood up, picked up his soggy old hat, looked me in the eye, and said, "I couldn't do that. I couldn't do it. I know it's true, and whatever it costs I'll know it's true."

He walked to the door. I walked behind him. He opened the door and stepped out into the rain. I watched him as he walked out under the gas lights and faded into the darkness. And I said to myself, "There is the strength of this Church. Not in buildings, not in the BYU campus, not in Temple Square, but in the hearts of the people, in the conviction that says it's true. It's true, come what may. It's true."

(*Discourses of President Gordon B. Hinckley,* 1995–99 [Salt Lake City: The Church of Jesus Christ of Latter-day Saints, 2004], 1:365–366)

––––––––––

We have with us today the Area President, Elder Kwok Yuen Tai. He joined the Church in about 1959 or '60. His wife was the daughter of a Christian minister in Taiwan. She came here, and she joined the Church, which was a great offense to her family. Her father got after her. She told me today that he took from the wall a picture of her family and tore her face off that picture and said, "That is what will happen to you if you join this Church." He felt so strongly this way. She married Brother Tai, and they went on to Sydney, Australia, where he studied chemistry, and then to London, where he lived and worked. Then they came back here and then went to the States. They have a wonderful family. They are marvelous people. The night before last, her father was in the meeting in Taipei and said to his daughter and son-in-law things of a very complimentary and warm nature concerning this Church and our work.

Things happen. They do not happen very fast. . . . But if we will be patient and keep at it, the Lord will bring about the harvest.

(*Discourses of President Gordon B. Hinckley,* 1995–99 [Salt Lake City: The Church of Jesus Christ of Latter-day Saints, 2004], 1:403)

Alma 16:5–8 • PRO-KINGDOM VS. ANTI-ENEMY

(Refer in this text to Mosiah 11:19.)

Alma 17–18 • AMMON'S ROLE IN THE CONVERSION OF LAMONI

Ammon had prepared by fasting, praying, and studying the scriptures and gaining the spiritual endowment that we all need to teach. But I am struck by the way he taught. Remember, King Lamoni invited him to receive things, to have things done for him, but instead he chose to serve the people he intended to teach: . . . (Alma 17:25).

Underline that and remember it all your life if you want to know something about preparation. Ammon prepared himself, but he did more. He prepared his student to be taught the doctrines of salvation. How did he do it?

"And it came to pass that he was set among other servants to watch the flocks of Lamoni, according to the custom of the Lamanite" (v. 25).

Now, remember that he not only protected the servants and the animals at the waters of Sebus, but he drove off the enemy. When the other servants brought the evidence of what Ammon had done, King Lamoni said, "Where is he?" They said, "Oh, he is in the stables. He is doing every little thing to serve you" (see Alma 18:8–9).

Isn't that odd? He was called to teach the doctrines of salvation, but he was in the stables. Don't you think he should have been praying and fasting and polishing his teaching plan? No, he was in the stables.

King Lamoni had been brought up with a belief that there was a God but that whatever the king did was right. He had been specifically taught false doctrine that might have made him impervious to feelings of guilt. Do you remember that when he heard where Ammon was, a feeling of guilt, of fear that he had done wrong in the killing of the servants, came over him (see Alma 18:5)? Remember the effect in Alma chapter 18:

"And they answered the king, and said: Whether he be the Great Spirit or a man, we know not; but this much we do know, that he cannot be slain by the enemies of the king; neither can they scatter the king's flocks when he is with us, because of his expertness and great strength; therefore, we know that he is a friend to the king. And now, O king, we do not believe that a man has such great power, for we know he cannot be slain.

"And now, when the king heard these words, he said unto them: Now I know that it is the Great Spirit; and he has come down at this time to preserve your lives, that I might not slay you as I did your brethren" (Alma 18:3–4).

I have always focused before on how mixed up Lamoni was in his doctrine, without seeing the miracle. The miracle was that a spiritual need was created in a man, that he might be taught the gospel of Jesus Christ. His heart was broken. He felt guilt. And it came from the temporal things that Ammon had done.

I bear you my testimony that you can prepare the hearts of your students. Serve them; find little things to do for them. Pay the price of service, and God will honor it. I will make you that promise. Do not worry if your students are not lovable at times. Just do something for them, and they will seem a little more lovable to you. It will be a gift from God.

I bear my testimony that the Holy Ghost will prepare your students, as He prepared King Lamoni for Ammon. Never, never underestimate the spiritual value of doing temporal things well for those whom you serve. . . .

I hope you will prepare the hearts of your students. Be their servants, and you will love them. And they will feel your love. And more important, they will feel God's love. The Book of Mormon will help you in that.

(Henry B. Eyring, *Ensign*, Feb. 2004 [Salt Lake City: The Church of Jesus Christ of Latter-day Saints, 2004], 13–14)

Alma 17:2 • THEY HAD SEARCHED THE SCRIPTURES DILIGENTLY

(Refer in this text to 1 Nephi 19:23; 1 Nephi 8:19, 24, 30; 2 Nephi 4:15–16.)

May I suggest . . . a formula [in missionary work] that will ensure your success: Search the scriptures with diligence! . . . Your confidence will be directly related to your knowledge of God's word. Oh, I am sure you have heard of some missionaries who were lazy, less than effective, and anxious for their missions to conclude. A careful examination of such instances will reveal that the actual culprit is not laziness, nor disinterest, but is the foe known as fear. Our Father chastised such: ". . . with some I am not well pleased, for they will not open their mouths, but they hide the talent which I have given unto them, because of the fear of man" (D&C 60:2). Had not this same loving Heavenly Father provided a prescription to overcome this malady. . . . In a revelation given through Joseph Smith the Prophet, January 2, 1831, the Lord declared: ". . . if ye are prepared ye shall not fear" (D&C 38:30). This is the key. Will you use it? Let me provide but one reference that has immediate application to our lives. In the Book of Mormon, the seventeenth chapter of Alma, we read the account of Alma's joy as he once more saw the sons of Mosiah and noted their steadfastness in the cause of truth. . . . [Alma 17:2–3.]

(Thomas S. Monson, in Conference Report, Oct. 1969 [Salt Lake City: The Church of Jesus Christ of Latter-day Saints, 1969], 93–94)

———

To understand requires more than casual reading or perusal—there must be concentrated study. . . . Not only should we study each day, but there should be a regular time set aside when we can concentrate without interference. . . . The important thing is to allow nothing else to ever interfere with our study. . . . There are some who read to a schedule of a number of pages or a set number of chapters each day or week. . . . It is better to have a set amount of time to give scriptural study each day than to have a set amount of chapters to read. Sometimes we find that the study of a single verse will occupy the whole time.

(Howard W. Hunter, *Ensign*, Nov. 1979 [Salt Lake City: The Church of Jesus Christ of Latter-day Saints, 1979], 64–65)

———

I find that when I get casual in my relationships with divinity and when it seems that no divine ear is listening and no divine voice is speaking, that I am far, far away. If I immerse myself in the scriptures the distance narrows and the spirituality returns. I find myself loving more intensely those whom I must love with all my heart and mind and strength, and loving them more, I find it easier to abide their counsel.

(*Teachings of Spencer W. Kimball*, ed. by Edward L. Kimball [Salt Lake City: Bookcraft, 1982], 135)

———

It is not enough to read the scriptures. Random reading results in reduced retention.... Our spirits should never be deprived of the much-needed spiritual nourishment which comes from scripture study. Without this spiritual food our spirits become starved and weakened to temptation. President Kimball taught the principle that "no father, no son, no mother, no daughter should get so busy that he or she does not have time to study the scriptures and the words of modern prophets" (*Ensign*, May 1976, 47).

(L. Lionel Kendrick, *Ensign*, May 1993 [Salt Lake City: The Church of Jesus Christ of Latter-day Saints, 1993], 14)

When individual members and families immerse themselves in the scriptures regularly and consistently, ... other areas of activity will automatically come. Testimonies will increase. Commitment will be strengthened. Families will be fortified. Personal revelation will flow.

(Ezra Taft Benson, *Ensign*, May 1986 [Salt Lake City: The Church of Jesus Christ of Latter-day Saints, 1986], 81)

We should make daily study of the scriptures a lifetime pursuit.... The most important [thing] you can do ... is to immerse yourselves in the scriptures. Search them diligently.... Learn the doctrine. Master the principles.... You must ... see that ... searching the scriptures is not a burden laid upon [us] by the Lord, but a marvelous blessing and opportunity.

(Ezra Taft Benson, *Ensign*, Nov. 1986 [Salt Lake City: The Church of Jesus Christ of Latter-day Saints, 1986], 47)

True doctrine, understood, changes attitudes and behavior. The study of the doctrines of the gospel will improve behavior quicker than a study of behavior will improve behavior. Preoccupation with unworthy behavior can lead to unworthy behavior. That is why we stress so forcefully the study of the doctrines of the gospel.

(Boyd K. Packer, *Ensign*, Nov. 1986 [Salt Lake City: The Church of Jesus Christ of Latter-day Saints, 1986], 17)

Some may think that the language of the scriptures is too difficult for children, but ... we need to remember that the Lord has given children faculties for learning language even greater than those of adults.... It is good for children to hear their favorite passages of scripture, and their other favorite stories, too, over and over.... We should not bring up our children to respond to the exciting, the thrilling.... They are

a titillation of the nerves. To be moved is one thing; to be excited or titillated, a very different thing. If we bring up our children always to be wanting something new, ... they will have to have a stronger [and stronger] stimulus each time until they finally [burst]. But if we inure our children to stability, to repetition, to normal life ..., then they will live decent lives.

(Arthur Henry King; as quoted in Janette Hales Beckham, *Ensign*, Nov. 1997 [Salt Lake City: The Church of Jesus Christ of Latter-day Saints, 1997], 76)

Also, do not forget to read your scriptures. For the past two years my husband and I have discovered one of the best spiritual investment programs we have ever undertaken. We determined to read two chapters of the scriptures together every day. It is not a matter of how busy we are; it is simply placing a high priority on reading the word of the Lord on a daily basis. And what a difference doing this together has made! Greater harmony, peace, and insight have come into our marriage.

We are all given twenty-four hours a day. Each of us can choose what we will do with them. Decide now to read your scriptures every day. I think we all can budget ten to fifteen minutes a day to find out what the Lord wants us to know. By committing to read just two chapters a day, you can read the book of Mormon, The Doctrine and Covenants, the Pearl of Great Price, and the New Testament in one year. It works! If you are reading as a couple, it is a great bonding experience. If you are reading alone, it is a great time to commune with the Holy Ghost.

(Mary Ellen Smoot, "Everything Money Cannot Buy," Satellite Broadcast, 3 Feb. 2002, Brigham Young University [Salt Lake City: The Church of Jesus Christ of Latter-day Saints, 2002], 5)

At present, the Book of Mormon is studied in our Sunday School and seminary classes every fourth year. This four-year pattern, however, must *not* be followed by Church members in their personal and family study. We need to read daily from the pages of the book that will get a man "nearer to God by abiding by its precepts, than by any other book" (*History of the Church*, 4:461).

And when we are called upon to study or teach other scriptures, we need ... additional insights which the Book of Mormon may provide on the subject (see 1 Nephi 13:40, 2 Nephi 3:12).

(Ezra Taft Benson, in Conference Report, Oct. 1988 [Salt Lake City: The Church of Jesus Christ of Latter-day Saints, 1988], 3)

Our opportunity to study the scriptures as a family

has been strengthened by the consolidated meeting schedule. A good part of the Sabbath can very appropriately be used for both personal and family scripture study. . . .

When we as parents have a genuine *desire* to teach the gospel to our children, the Lord will give us entrance into their hearts. Then may we know that as we enter there we stand on holy ground.

(A. Theodore Tuttle, in Conference Report, Apr. 1984 [Salt Lake City: The Church of Jesus Christ of Latter-day Saints, 1984], 32–33)

Alma 17:2–5, 9, 11–12 • MISSIONARY WORK
(Refer in this text to Alma 29:1–2.)

[To the young men of the Church] You have missions to perform. Each of you should plan for missionary service. You may have some doubts. You may have some fears. Face your doubts and your fears with faith. Prepare yourselves to go. You have not only the opportunity; you have the responsibility. . . . Is it too much to ask that you give two years totally immersed in His service? . . . You know what is right. You know what is wrong. You know when and how to make the choice. You know that there is a power in heaven on which you can call in your time of extremity and need. . . . Stand up and walk as becomes the sons of God.

[Speaking of the sister missionaries] They perform a remarkable work. They can get in homes where the elders cannot. . . . Now having made that confession, I wish to say that the First Presidency and the Council of the Twelve are united in saying to our young sisters that they are not under obligation to go on missions. . . . Some of them will very much wish to go. If the idea persists, the bishop will know what to do. . . . missionary work is essentially a priesthood responsibility. As such, our young men must carry the major burden. This is their responsibility and their obligation. We do not ask the young women to consider a mission as an essential part of their life's program. Over a period of many years, we have held the age level higher for them in an effort to keep the number going relatively small. Again to the sisters I say that you will be as highly respected, you will be considered as being as much in the line of duty, your efforts will be as acceptable to the Lord and to the Church whether you go on a mission or do not go on a mission. . . . I certainly do not wish to say or imply that their services are not wanted. I simply say that a mission is not necessary as a part of their lives.

(Gordon B. Hinckley, *Ensign*, Nov. 1997 [Salt Lake City: The Church of Jesus Christ of Latter-day Saints, 1997], 52)

—————

The question is frequently asked, Should every young man fill a mission? The answer to this inquiry has been given by the Lord. It is yes. Every young man should fill a mission. While every young man should serve a mission, we realize that every young man is not physically, emotionally, nor morally prepared. As a consequence, some may be deprived of missionary opportunities. But all should prepare to go—to be worthy to serve the Lord. . . . Some young men, because of transgression, say they are not interested in serving a mission. The real reason, of course, is feelings of unworthiness. If such young men would go to their bishop, confide to him their problem, and sincerely repent, they may yet fill honorable missions.

(*Teachings of Ezra Taft Benson* [Salt Lake City: Bookcraft, 1988], 182–183)

—————

And I say to you . . . Elders, Awaken up! God has placed the priesthood upon you, and he expects you to magnify it. . . . We want some manhood, and some priesthood and power of God to be manifested in Israel. . . . And I pray God, the Eternal Father, to waken up these Elders, that the spirit of their mission may rest upon them, and that they may comprehend their true position before God.

(Brigham Young, *Journal of Discourses* [London: Latter-day Saints' Book Depot, 1880], 20:23)

—————

The Lord wants every young man to serve a full-time mission. Presently only a third of the eligible young men in the Church are serving missions. This is not pleasing to the Lord. We can do better. We must do better. Not only should a mission be regarded as a priesthood duty, but every young man should look forward to this experience with great joy and anticipation. A young man can do nothing more important. School can wait. Scholarships can be deferred. Occupational goals can be postponed. Yes, even temple marriage should wait until after a young man has served an honorable full-time mission for the Lord. . . . Remember, young women, you may also have the opportunity to serve a full-time mission. I am grateful my own eternal companion served a mission in Hawaii before we were married in the Salt Lake Temple, and I am pleased that I have had three grand-daughters serve full-time missions. Some of our finest missionaries are young sisters.

(*Teachings of Ezra Taft Benson* [Salt Lake City: Bookcraft, 1988], 190, 194)

—————

Now you young unmarried sisters from twenty-one to sixty-nine with good health, there is no obligation to serve, but you are certainly welcome and wanted if the Spirit encourages you to volunteer. . . . Now you young men, unmarried, nineteen to twenty-six (eighteen outside the United States), . . . a mission has been emphasized as a priesthood responsibility of such priority that again today we stress, *your mission comes before marriage, education, professional opportunities, scholarships, sports, cars, or girls.* . . . In twenty-four months you will have twenty-four years' worth of spiritual adventures. You will see people change; soften; become more humble, more obedient; have their prayers answered; and come to a knowledge that our message is true.

(Robert E. Wells, in Conference Report, Oct. 1985 [Salt Lake City: The Church of Jesus Christ of Latter-day Saints, 1985], 36)

————————

A mother and father were in my office accompanied by a 265-pound BYU sophomore All-WAC tackle. They had asked for an appointment to help resolve a confusing family situation. After we greeted the mother and the father and their son, Lance Reynolds, we had a few words of friendly conversation. I knew why they had come. The trying decision was does Lance go on a mission or does he stay and play football? I looked at the mother and said, "What do you think your son should do?" She said, "I think he can render a special service and example to the Church if he maintains his standards and continues to play football and hopefully help in bringing football fame to BYU and the Church. I think his football playing can be his mission." I looked at the father, and I said, "What do you think Lance should do?" He was smart enough not to disagree in that setting with his wife, so he merely said, "I'm not quite certain." I looked at Lance and I said, "Lance, what do you want to do?" He said, "I want to go on a mission." I responded with, "Why don't you?" He said, "I will." Our interview was over. Lance went on his mission, was an outstanding missionary, came back and reaped all-conference honors, and is now on BYU's football coaching staff. He is a special friend of mine today.

(Marvin J. Ashton, BYU Devotional, 24 Aug. 1992)

————————

An acquaintance of mine grew up not far from here. . . . Many universities offered him scholarships to play basketball. After his first year playing at a university, he told his coach that he would like to be excused for two years to go on a mission. The coach said, "If you leave, you can be sure of one thing: you will never again wear one of our basketball uniforms!" Many thought that his "mission" ought to be playing basketball. Even some family members, including his parents, tried to convince him not to serve a mission. But he was totally committed. . . . He was called, and he served an honorable mission. When he returned, . . . his coach decided to repent. . . . In his senior year, his team not only won the conference championship but went on to the finals in national competition. . . . Modern prophets have taught that every young man who is physically and mentally able should prepare himself to serve an honorable mission. The Lord did not say, "Go on a mission if it fits your schedule, or if you happen to feel like it, or if it doesn't interfere with your scholarship, your romance, or your educational plans." Preaching the gospel is a commandment and not merely a suggestion. . . . Even though for some of you there may be very tempting reasons for you not to serve a full-time mission, the Lord and his prophets are counting on you.

(Joe J. Christensen, *Ensign*, Nov. 1996 [Salt Lake City: The Church of Jesus Christ of Latter-day Saints, 1996], 40–41)

————————

One young man, when called on a mission, replied that he didn't have much talent for that kind of thing. What he was good at was keeping his powerful new automobile in top condition. He enjoyed the sense of power and acceleration, and when he was driving, the continual motion gave him the illusion that he was really getting somewhere. All along, his father had been content with saying, "He likes to do things with his hands. That's good enough for him." Good enough for a son of God? This young man didn't realize that the power of his automobile is infinitesimally small in comparison with the . . . priesthood power that he could have been developing in the service of the Lord. He settled for a pitiful god, a composite of steel and rubber and shiny chrome.

An older couple retired from the world of work and purchased a pickup truck and camper and, separating themselves from all obligations, set out to see the world and simply enjoy what little they had accumulated the rest of their days. They had not time . . . for missionary service. . . . Their experience and leadership were sorely needed . . . but, unable to "endure to the end," they were not available.

(Spencer W. Kimball, *Ensign*, June 1976 [Salt Lake City: The Church of Jesus Christ of Latter-day Saints, 1976], 5)

————————

I have a vision of thousands of missionaries going into the mission field with hundreds of passages memorized from the Book of Mormon so that they might feed the needs of a spiritually famished world. I have a vision of the whole Church getting nearer to God by abiding by the precepts of the Book of Mormon. Indeed, I have a vision of flooding the earth with the Book of Mormon.

(Ezra Taft Benson, *Ensign*, Nov. 1988 [Salt Lake City: The Church of Jesus Christ of Latter-day Saints, 1988], 4–6)

I throw out a challenge to every young man within this vast congregation tonight. Prepare yourself now to be worthy to serve the Lord as a full-time missionary. . . . Prepare to consecrate two years of your lives to this sacred service. That will in effect constitute a tithe on the first twenty years of your lives. . . . I promise you that the time you spend in the mission field, if those years are spent in dedicated service, will yield a greater return on investment than any other two years of your lives. . . . You will develop powers of persuasion which will bless your entire life. Your timidity, your fears, your shyness will gradually disappear as you go forth with boldness and conviction. You will learn to work with others. . . . The cankering evil of selfishness will be supplanted by a sense of service to others. You will draw nearer to the Lord than you likely will in any other set of circumstances. You will come to know that without His help you are indeed weak and simple, but that with His help you can accomplish miracles. You will establish habits of industry. You will develop a talent for the establishment of goals of effort. You will learn to work with singleness of purpose. . . . If you serve a mission faithfully and well, you will be a better husband, you will be a better father, you will be a better student, a better worker in your chosen vocation.

(Gordon B. Hinckley, *Ensign*, Nov. 1995 [Salt Lake City: The Church of Jesus Christ of Latter-day Saints, 1995], 51–52)

Prepare now to go on a mission. It will not be a burden. It will not be a waste of time. It will be a great opportunity and a great challenge. It will do something for you that nothing else will do for you. It will sharpen your skills. It will train you in leadership. It will bring testimony and conviction into your heart. You will bless the lives of others as you bless your own. It will bring you nearer to God and to His Divine Son as you bear witness and testimony of Him. Your knowledge of the gospel will strengthen and deepen. Your love for your fellowman will increase. Your fears will fade as you stand boldly in testimony of the truth.

(Gordon B. Hinckley, *Ensign*, May 1997 [Salt Lake City: The Church of Jesus Christ of Latter-day Saints, 1997], 50)

Now, my dear young friends, I hope all of you are pointed in the direction of missionary service. I cannot promise you fun. I cannot promise you ease and comfort. I cannot promise you freedom from discouragement, from fear, from downright misery at times. But I can promise you that you will grow as you have never grown in a similar period during your entire lives. I

can promise you a happiness that will be unique and wonderful and lasting. I can promise you that you will reevaluate your lives, that you will establish new priorities, that you will live closer to the Lord, that prayer will become a real and wonderful experience, that you will walk with faith in the outcome of the good things you do.

(Gordon B. Hinckley, *Ensign*, Nov. 1998 [Salt Lake City: The Church of Jesus Christ of Latter-day Saints, 1998], 52)

We must raise the bar on the worthiness and qualifications of those who go into the world as ambassadors of the Lord Jesus Christ. . . .

How can you possibly think that you can become involved in immoral practices and then go into the mission field as a representative of the Lord Jesus Christ? . . .

Stay away from the erotic stuff of the Internet. It can only pull you down. It can lead to your destruction.

(Gordon B. Hinckley, in Conference Report, Oct. 2002 [Salt Lake City: The Church of Jesus Christ of Latter-day Saints, 2002], 63, 65)

Prepare well for a mission all your life, not just six months or a year before you go. . . .

There is a difference in missionaries. Some are better prepared to serve the Lord the first month in the mission field than some who are returning home after twenty-four months.

We want young men entering the mission field who can enter the mission field "on the run," who have the faith born of personal righteousness and clean living that they can have a great and productive mission. . . .

Give me a young man who has kept himself morally clean and has faithfully attended his Church meetings. Give me a young man who has magnified his priesthood and has earned the Duty to God Award and is an Eagle Scout. Give me a young man who is a seminary graduate and has a burning testimony of the Book of Mormon. Give me such a young man, and I will give you a young man who can perform miracles for the Lord in the mission field and throughout his life.

(Ezra Taft Benson, *Ensign*, May 1986 [Salt Lake City: The Church of Jesus Christ of Latter-day Saints, 1986], 45)

A story written by Karen Nolen, which appeared in the *New Era* in 1974, tells of a Benjamin Landart who, in 1888, was 15 years old and an accomplished violinist. Living on a farm in northern Utah with his mother and seven brothers and sisters was sometimes a challenge to

Benjamin, as he had less time than he would have liked to play his violin. Occasionally his mother would lock up the violin until he had his farm chores done, so great was the temptation for Benjamin to play it.

In late 1892 Benjamin was asked to travel to Salt Lake to audition for a place with the territorial orchestra. For him, this was a dream come true. After several weeks of practicing and prayers, he went to Salt Lake in March of 1893 for the much anticipated audition. When he heard Benjamin play, the conductor, a Mr. Dean, told Benjamin he was the most accomplished violinist he had heard west of Denver. He was told to report to Denver for rehearsals in the fall and learned that he would be earning enough to keep himself, with some left over to send home.

A week after Benjamin received the good news, however, his bishop called him into his office and asked if he couldn't put off playing with the orchestra for a couple of years. He told Benjamin that before he started earning money there was something he owed the Lord. He then asked Benjamin to accept a mission call.

Benjamin felt that giving up his chance to play in the territorial orchestra would be almost more than he could bear, but he also knew what his decision should be. He promised the bishop that if there were any way to raise the money for him to serve, he would accept the call.

When Benjamin told his mother about the call, she was overjoyed. She told him that his father had always wanted to serve a mission but had been killed before that opportunity had come to him. However, when they discussed the financing of the mission, her face clouded over. Benjamin told her he would not allow her to sell any more of their land. She studied his face for a moment and then said, "Ben, there is a way we can raise the money. This family [has] one thing that is of great enough value to send you on your mission. You will have to sell your violin."

Ten days later, on March 23, 1893, Benjamin wrote in his journal: "I awoke this morning and took my violin from its case. All day long I played the music I love. In the evening when the light grew dim and I could see to play no longer, I placed the instrument in its case. It will be enough. Tomorrow I leave [for my mission]."

Forty-five years later, on June 23, 1938, Benjamin wrote in his journal: "The greatest decision I ever made in my life was to give up something I dearly loved to the God I loved even more. He has never forgotten me for it."

Learn from the past.

(Thomas S. Monson, in Conference Report, Apr. 2003 [Salt Lake City: The Church of Jesus Christ of Latter-day Saints, 2003], 19)

———

Some young men have had the notion that they can break the commandments, confess to their bishops one year before they plan to go on a mission, and then be worthy to serve. The repentance process is far more than planned confession followed by a waiting period. We often hear this question of one who has transgressed: "How long will I have to wait before I can go on my mission?" Keep in mind that repentance is not simply a waiting game. . . .

We now understand from the First Presidency's statement on missionary work that there are transgressions that will disqualify young men and women from missionary service (see "Statement on Missionary Work" attached to First Presidency letter, 11 Dec. 2002).

(Daryl H. Garn, in Conference Report, Apr. 2003 [Salt Lake City: The Church of Jesus Christ of Latter-day Saints, 2003], 50–51)

———

Why is Floriano Oliveira, a member of the high council in a stake in Brazil, so successful as a missionary? Because he *obeyed* the Lord's counsel to open his mouth and share the gospel. One day as he was driving through the congested traffic of Sao Paulo he took his eyes off the road for but a second and crashed into the car in front of him. He jumped out of the vehicle, hurried up to the car he had hit, opened the door and said, "I am so sorry I hit you. It was all my fault. I accept the full blame and will pay the total costs. I had no intention to do this, so please forgive me. Yet if I hadn't hit you, you wouldn't have received this message I have for you, the message that you have waited for all your life." He then explained the restoration of the gospel to this man, who was a medical doctor, and the man joined the Church two weeks later. Why has Brother Oliveira had so much success in baptizing more than two hundred people? Obedience—*obedience to the request of the Lord.*

(Teddy E. Brewerton, in Conference Report, Apr. 1981 [Salt Lake City: The Church of Jesus Christ of Latter-day Saints, 1981], 93)

———

I was in South America on one occasion with some missionaries who were going home. They were out shopping to buy things to take home—souvenirs—and I thought of the souvenirs that we ought to take home with us from our missions. There are 10 of these:

1. A testimony of the living reality of God. . . .
2. A greatly enlarged understanding of the gospel. . . .
3. A love for the people among whom you labor. If you don't love the people here, it isn't because there is something wrong with them. It is because there is something wrong with you. I hope and pray that for as long as you live you will never lose your love

for the people among whom you served as a missionary. . . .

4. A greater love and appreciation for your parents. Somehow, selfish, arrogant, conceited young men, when they get into the mission field, begin no longer to take their parents for granted but have come into their hearts a greater love for them. I hope you are not ashamed to write and tell your mother that you love her. And I hope you are not embarrassed even to tell your father that you love him. He might faint when he reads it, but he will appreciate it.

5. An understanding of the meaning of hard work. . . . You are learning how to work here, to get up every morning, to get out and work in the face of discouragement. The harder you work, the more you love the work. . . . This will bless your lives all of your days—this habit of work which you cultivate as a missionary in the field.

6. An enlarged understanding of the meaning and true worth and value of personal virtue. . . . Said the Lord through the Prophet Joseph Smith, "Let virtue garnish thy thoughts unceasingly" (D&C 121:45). And then He says the Holy Ghost shall distill upon you as the dews from heaven. That is a commandment with a promise. You ought to develop while you are on a mission. . . .

7. Increased poise, the ability to meet people, to converse with them, to talk with them. . . . You take on cleanliness and orderliness and neatness. I hope you won't go home and revert to the grubby ways of your lives that some of you knew before you came, but that you will take back with you that refinement which comes of service to the Lord in the mission field.

8. The courage to act. . . . When I finished my mission, I wasn't afraid to go talk to anybody.

9. The faith to do. The faith to try.

10. And finally, the humility to pray. . . .

Those are 10 gifts which I'd like to suggest to each of you to take home with you from the mission field.

(*Discourses of President Gordon B. Hinckley*, 1995–99 [Salt Lake City: The Church of Jesus Christ of Latter-day Saints, 2004], 1:429–432)

———

I would like to commend the missionaries who are here. . . . They all look very sober. Now, smile a little, you missionaries! That looks better. You are preaching the gospel of good news. The things you have to teach are good. They are designed to make people happy and live a better life. You ought to put a smile on your face and go forth to do the work which the Lord has outlined for you, and He will bless you. And the missionary's experiences which you have will become a great part of your lives, a great period in your lives to which you will look back all of your days with appreciation and gratitude. You are only on missions for a short time; make the most of it. I know that those who have just arrived think that it is a very long time. It will look like a long time for the first three months, and then suddenly it will get very short and look very brief, so enjoy it, and live it up, and be happy in the great opportunity that is yours.

(*Discourses of President Gordon B. Hinckley*, 1995–99 [Salt Lake City: The Church of Jesus Christ of Latter-day Saints, 2004], 1:511–512)

———

There is something about a mission that is different from all the other experiences of our lives. . . . You grow so fast, for one thing. . . .

[1.] Your fears leave you. You're not afraid to go up and knock on a door. That is a terrible thing the first time you try it, but your fears leave you. You are able to stand in a street meeting, if that is the practice of the mission to which you go. There comes into your heart a new assurance and a new boldness to do that which you ought to do. . . .

[2.] Don't get discouraged. That is easy to say, but you don't get discouraged in the mission field. You don't get offended. Brother Sterling Sill, who was an insurance man, once said, "I've been spit on. I've been sworn at. I've been kicked out the front door and right onto the ground. But I've never been insulted." That's the kind of attitude that we use when we are in the mission field. We may be spit on. We may be sworn at. We may be kicked off the front porch. But we'll never be insulted. . . .

[3.] I want to urge you missionaries to guard your health. Be careful of what you eat and what you do. Live in a sanitary, hygienic way. . . .

Now, missionaries are careless. My, you are careless. You are just terribly careless. Your mothers have taken care of you all your lives now, and you are going out to care for yourselves, and you don't know how to do it. Be careful. Guard your health. Eat good food—not rich food but good food. Observe good hygiene, good sanitation. Stay away from sickness. Keep your apartments tidy. Clean them up. Make your beds. . . . Make the bed, every day, and live orderly lives. . . . Live lives that will preserve your health as much as it is possible. . . . Guard your health, and be very careful and clean in your ways of doing things. . . .

[4.] Keep the rules. Every mission has some rules. . . . Observe them. There is safety in observing those rules. Be careful. Be wise. . . .

[5.] Keep your tempers. People will swear at you a little. Don't swear back. Return good for evil. Don't be like that missionary who was walking down the street and a man was sprinkling his lawn. As the missionary came along, the man turned the hose on him and said, "I understand you believe in baptism." The missionaries turned around and grabbed him and said, "Yes, and we also believe in the laying on of hands." Don't get involved in that kind of thing. . . .

[6.] I want to plead with you to keep your thoughts clean. . . . Get out of the gutter, and stand tall and clean, and keep yourselves aloof from those things. They will only destroy you. They are just like a terrible poison. They will tear you down and utterly ruin your lives. Stay above them. If you are busy with your missionary work, you won't be troubled with those things. If you are not busy, you're likely to be troubled with those things. Keep your thoughts clean, and speak clean words. . . .

[7.] Write regularly to your parents. . . . Your letters need not be long, but they ought to be informative. Tell them of what is going on, of what you are doing, of your work as a missionary, of your companion, of the ward or branch in which you are laboring, and of the great happiness that you find in the work. They will appreciate it. They are praying for you. They are sacrificing for you. They are doing everything they know how to do to back you up at home, and they are deserving of a letter at least once a week. . . .

[8.] Be happy. . . . You can't bring anybody into the Church while you are scowling. Have a smile on your face. You look better with a smile on your face. It doesn't cost you a thing. Be happy about it. Let that happiness shine through you as a radiance from your countenance. . . .

[9.] Listen to the promptings of the Spirit. Be humble. You may be led to someone by the hand of the Lord because of your spirit, your attitude, your feeling, your humility. . . .

I remember when Brother Lee set me apart as a stake president. He said, "Listen for the whisperings of the Spirit in the stillness of the night." Now, I believe in that. I have seen that in my experience, and I think I can testify that the Lord has spoken quietly. I didn't hear any words, but in the middle of the night ideas have come into my head which, I think, have been prophetic in their nature. . . .

[10.] You are not going to the mission to fall in love. You're not going on a mission to find a wife or a husband. You are going on a mission to serve the Lord—no other consideration in your lives. . . .

We know that if you are prayerful, if you are obedient, if you do what is expected of you, if you get up and go to work, if you are not lazy, the Lord will bless you and bring to you some measure of harvest for which you will be grateful all the days of your lives.

(*Discourses of President Gordon B. Hinckley*, 1995–99 [Salt Lake City: The Church of Jesus Christ of Latter-day Saints, 2004], 1:531, 534–539, 541)

Dr. William Ghormley served as president of the stake in Corpus Christi, Texas. He bought his gasoline at a particular station. Each time he filled his tank he would leave a piece of Church literature with the station owner. It might have been a tract or a Church magazine or the *Church News*, but he never went there without leaving something. The man who ran the station was converted by the power of the Spirit as he read that literature. When last I checked, he was serving as a bishop.

The process of bringing new people into the Church is not the responsibility alone of the missionaries. They succeed best when members become the source from which new investigators are found.

I would like to suggest that every bishop in the Church give as a motto to his people, "Let's all work to grow the ward." I am not sure the grammar is correct, but the idea is right.

(*Discourses of President Gordon B. Hinckley*, 1995–99 [Salt Lake City: The Church of Jesus Christ of Latter-day Saints, 2004], 1:559)

———

There are certain standards by which [bishops and stake presidents] should be guided in calling our missionaries. First, call no [missionary] for the purpose of saving him or her. The young man is getting wayward and you think a mission would do him good. It would. But that is not why you are sending him out. Choose [missionaries] who are worthy to represent the Church, see that they are sufficiently mature, and, above all, that they have character. . . .

In choosing a missionary it is well to keep in mind questions as follows:

Is he worthy to represent the Church?

Has he sufficient will power to resist temptation?

Has he kept himself clean while he has been home and by that standard proved himself capable of resisting possible temptation in the field?

Has he taken active part in Church organizations at home?

Does he at least glimpse what the Church has to offer the world? . . .

Every elder . . . must . . . have a conviction in his heart that he is preaching the truth. . . .

Every elder should be a Christian gentleman always. A gentleman—who is he? "Whoever is open"—nothing to hide, no downcast look because of the consciousness of guilt; "whoever is loyal"—loyal to the truth, to virtue, to the Word of Wisdom—". . . honorable himself and in his judgment of others, faithful to his word as to law, and faithful alike to God and to man—such a man is a true gentleman." . . .

There is no double standard of chastity, that every young man, as well as every young woman, is to keep himself free from sexual impurity. . . .

These young men . . . must possess at least one outstanding quality, and that is: trustworthiness. He was right who said, "To be trusted is a greater compliment than to be loved." And whom do these missionaries represent? First, they represent their parents, carrying the responsibility of keeping their good name unsullied. Second, they represent the Church, specifically the ward in which they live. And third, they represent the Lord Jesus Christ, whose authorized servants they are.

(*Teachings of Presidents of the Church—David O. McKay* [Salt Lake City: The Church of Jesus Christ of Latter-day Saints, 2003], 54–56)

[A missionary] couple tells of blessings that come from missionary service. They wrote: "Good people replaced our parenting functions better than we. . . . If a family problem has not yielded to prayer and fasting, a mission might be considered."

No senior missionary finds it convenient to leave. Neither did Joseph or Brigham or John or Wilford. They had children and grandchildren too. They loved their families not one whit less, but they also loved the Lord and wanted to serve Him. Someday we may meet these stalwarts who helped to establish this dispensation. Then will we rejoice that we did not seek the shadows when a call to missionary service came from the prophet, even in the autumn years of our lives.

(Russell M. Nelson, in Conference Report, Oct. 2004 [Salt Lake City: The Church of Jesus Christ of Latter-day Saints, 2004], 82–83)

I will speak on the urgent need for more mature couples to serve in the mission field. . . .

If we are willing to leave our loved ones for service in the mission field, we will bless them with a heritage that will teach and inspire them for generations to come. . . .

As we serve in the mission field, our children and grandchildren will be blessed in ways that would not have been possible had we stayed at home. Talk to couples who have served missions and they will tell you of blessings poured out: inactive children activated, family members baptized, and testimonies strengthened because of their service.

One missionary couple left a farm at home for their son to manage. During the somewhat dry year that followed, their farm had two hay cuttings while the neighbor's had only one. The neighbor asked their son why he had two cuttings compared to their one. The young man replied, "You need to send your folks on a mission."

(Robert D. Hales, *Ensign*, May 2001 [Salt Lake City: The Church of Jesus Christ of Latter-day Saints, 2001], 25)

Alma 17:3 • FASTING AND PRAYER

According to Alma, they gave themselves to much fasting and prayer. You see there are certain blessings that can only be fulfilled as we conform to a particular law. . . . Too many Latter-day Saint parents today are depriving themselves and their children of one of the sweetest spiritual experiences that the Father has made available to them.

(Robert L. Simpson, in Conference Report, Oct. 1967 [Salt Lake City: The Church of Jesus Christ of Latter-day Saints, 1967], 17–18)

Failing to fast is a sin. In the 58th chapter of Isaiah, rich promises are made by the Lord to those who fast and assist the needy. Freedom from frustrations, freedom from thralldom, and the blessing of peace are promised. Inspiration and spiritual guidance will come with righteousness and closeness to our Heavenly Father. To omit to do this righteous act of fasting would deprive us of these blessings.

(Spencer W. Kimball, *The Miracle of Forgiveness* [Salt Lake City: Bookcraft, 1969], 98)

All the principles associated with fasting seem to point to the fact that it produces (1) physical benefits; (2) intellectual activity; and (3) spiritual strength. . . .

The greatest of all benefits—the spiritual strength derived by the subjection of physical appetite to the will of the individual. "He who reigns within himself, and rules passions, desires, and fears, is more than a king." . . .

It was with the thought in mind of gaining spiritual strength that James, the psychologist, made this suggestion: "To do each day something which you do not like to do." If there were no other virtue in fasting but gaining strength of character, that alone would be sufficient justification for its universal acceptance.

(*Gospel Ideals: Selections from the Discourses of David O. McKay*, sel. by G. Homer Durham [Salt Lake City: Improvement Era, 1953], 209–210)

A few years ago, I was afforded the privilege to serve as a mission president. . . . We had one young missionary who was very ill. After weeks of hospitalization, as the doctor prepared to undertake extremely serious and complicated surgery, he asked that we send for the missionary's mother and father. He advised there was a possibility the patient would not survive the surgery.

The parents came. Late one evening, the father and I entered a hospital room in Toronto, Canada, placed our hands upon the head of the young missionary, and gave him a blessing. What happened following that blessing was a testimony to me.

The missionary was in a six-bed ward in the hospital. The other beds were occupied by five men with a variety of illnesses. The morning of his surgery, the missionary's bed was empty. The nurse came into the room with the breakfast these men normally ate. She took a tray over to the patient in bed number one and said, "Fried eggs this morning, and I have an extra portion for you!"

The occupant of bed number one had suffered an accident with his lawn mower. Other than an injured toe, he was well physically. He said to the nurse, "I'll not be eating this morning."

"All right, we shall give your breakfast to your partner in bed number two."

As she approached that patient, he said, "I think I'll not eat this morning."

Each of the five men declined breakfast. The young lady exclaimed, "Other mornings you eat us out of house and home, and today not one of you wants to eat! What is the reason?"

Then the man who occupied bed number six answered: "You see, bed number three is empty. Our friend is in the operating room under the surgeon's hands. He needs all the help he can get. He is a missionary for his church, and while we have been patients in this ward, he has talked to us about the principles of his church—principles of prayer, of faith, of fasting wherein we call upon the Lord for blessings." He continued, "We don't know much about the Mormon church, but we have learned a great deal about our friend; and we are fasting for him today."

The operation was a success. When I attempted to pay the doctor, he countered, "Why, it would be dishonest for me to accept a fee. I have never before performed surgery when my hands seemed to be guided by a Power which was other than my own. No," he said, "I wouldn't take a fee for the surgery which Someone on high literally helped me to perform."

(Thomas S. Monson, in Conference Report, Apr. 1984 [Salt Lake City: The Church of Jesus Christ of Latter-day Saints, 1984], 22–23)

———————

Self-mastery comes when you are old enough to observe the law of the fast. . . . Through your spirit, you develop personal power over your body's drives of hunger and thirst. Fasting gives you confidence to know that your spirit can master appetite.

Some time ago . . . Mother and I visited a Third World country where sanitary conditions were much poorer than ours. We joined with a delegation of other doctors from all over the world. The president of our group, an experienced traveler, warned of risks. In order to avoid water that might be contaminated, we were even counseled to brush our teeth with an alcoholic beverage. We chose not to follow that counsel, but simply

did what we had learned to do once a month. We fasted that first day, thinking we could introduce simple food and fluids gradually thereafter. Later, we were the only ones in our group without disabling illness.

Fasting fortifies discipline over appetite and helps to protect against later uncontrolled cravings and gnawing habits.

(Russell M. Nelson, in Conference Report, Oct. 1985 [Salt Lake City: The Church of Jesus Christ of Latter-day Saints, 1985], 39)

———————

If all we do is abstain from food and drink for 24 hours and pay our fast offering, we have missed a wonderful opportunity for spiritual growth. On the other hand, if we have a special purpose in our fasting, the fast will have much more meaning. . . .

Fasting can help us overcome personal flaws and sins. It can help us overcome our weaknesses—help them become strengths. Fasting can help us become more humble, less prideful, less selfish, and more concerned about the needs of others. It can help us see more clearly our own mistakes and weaknesses and help us be less prone to criticize others. Or our fast may have a focus on a family challenge. A family fast might help increase love and appreciation among family members and reduce the amount of contention in the family, or we might fast as a couple to strengthen our marriage bonds. A purpose of our fast as priesthood holders might be to seek the Lord's guidance in our callings, as President Hinckley has demonstrated, or we might fast with our home teaching companion to know how to help one of our families. . . . Fasting without prayer is just going hungry for 24 hours. But fasting combined with prayer brings increased spiritual power.

(Carl B. Pratt, in Conference Report, Oct. 2004 [Salt Lake City: The Church of Jesus Christ of Latter-day Saints, 2004], 50–51)

Alma 17:3 • SPIRIT OF PROPHECY . . . SPIRIT OF REVELATION

Chiefly the gift of prophecy is to know by revelation from the Holy Ghost of the divine Sonship of our Lord. . . . [It is] the greatest of all the gifts of the Spirit. Prophecy is revelation; it is testimony; it is Spirit speaking to spirit.

(Bruce R. McConkie, *Doctrinal New Testament Commentary* [Salt Lake City: Bookcraft, 1970], 2:384–86)

Alma 17:9 • THEY JOURNEYED MANY DAYS

We must be willing to journey. The sons of Mosiah were willing to step outside their surroundings and do that which was uncomfortable. Had Ammon not been willing to journey into a foreign land, inhabited by a wild and a hardened and a ferocious people, he never would have found and helped Lamoni and his father, and many Lamanites may have never learned about Jesus Christ. God has asked us to journey, go on missions, accept callings, invite someone to church, or help someone in need.

(Don R. Clarke, *Ensign*, Nov. 2006 [Salt Lake City: The Church of Jesus Christ of Latter-day Saints, 2006], 98)

Alma 17:10–11 • BE PATIENT IN AFFLICTION
(Refer in this text to Mosiah 24:14–15; Alma 34:40–41.)

It is easy enough to be pleasant,
When life flows by like a song,
But the man worth while is the one who will smile,
When everything goes dead wrong.
For the test of the heart is trouble,
And it always comes with the years,
And the smile that is worth the praises of earth
Is the smile that shines through tears.

—Ella Wheeler Wilcox

Suffering can make Saints of people as they learn patience, long suffering and self-mastery. The sufferings of our Savior were part of his education.

(Spencer W. Kimball, *BYU Speeches of the Year, 1955* [Provo, Utah: BYU Press, 1955], 9)

Alma 17:17 • ALONE

The word *alone* makes me think of you going into your classroom. You go alone. They went alone, among a ferocious people, with the intent to teach the gospel of Jesus Christ. (There will be days when your students may seem nearly as ferocious.)

(Henry B. Eyring, *Ensign*, Feb. 2004 [Salt Lake City: The Church of Jesus Christ of Latter-day Saints, 2004], 13)

Alma 17:18, 26; 18:17 • LEADER, SERVANT
(Refer in this text to Mosiah 2:16–17.)

(In a letter to Brother Edward Hunter, under date of January 5, 1842, the Prophet shows his humility and the love of his heart in these words): The store has been filled to overflowing and I have stood behind the counter all day, distributing goods as steadily as any clerk you ever saw, to oblige those who were compelled to go without their Christmas and New Year's dinners for the want of a little sugar, molasses, raisins, etc.; and to please myself also, for I love to wait upon the Saints and to be a servant to all, hoping that I may be exalted in the due time of the Lord.

(George Q. Cannon, *Life of Joseph Smith the Prophet* [Salt Lake City: Deseret Book, 1972], 386)

———

D. Brent Collette told a stirring story:

"Ronny was not just shy; he was downright backward. As a 17–year-old high school senior, Ronny had never really had a close friend or done anything that included other people. He was famous for his shyness. He never said anything to anybody, not even a teacher. One look at him told you a great deal of the story—inferiority complex. He slumped over as if to hide his face and seemed to be always looking at his feet. He always sat in the back of the class and would never participate. . . .

"It was because of Ronny's shyness that I was so astonished when he started coming to my Sunday School class. . . .

"His attendance in my class was the result of the personal efforts of a class member, Brandon Craig, who had recently befriended Ronny. Boy, if there had ever been a mismatch, this was it. Brandon was 'Mr. Social.' A good head taller than Ronny, he was undisputedly the number one star of our high school athletics program. Brandon was involved in everything and successful at everything. . . .

"Well, Brandon took to little Ronny like glue. Class was obviously painful for Ronny, but Brandon protected him like the king's guard. . . . I was so shocked when Brian, the class president, stood before our Sunday School class one Sunday afternoon and boldly announced that Ronny would offer the opening prayer.

"There was a moment of hesitation; then Ronny slowly came to his feet. Still looking at his shoes, he walked to the front of the room. He folded his arms (his head was already bowed). The class was frozen solid. . . .

"Then almost at a whisper I heard, 'Our Father in Heaven, thank you for our Sunday School class.' Then silence—long, loud silence! I could feel poor Ronny suffering. Then came a few sniffles and muffled sob. . . .

"I hurt for him; we all did. I opened an eye and looked up to make my way to Ronny. But Brandon beat me to it. With an eye still open I watched six-foot-four Brandon put his arm around his friend, bend down and put his chin on Ronny's shoulder, then whisper the words of a short, sweet prayer. Ronny struggled for composure, then repeated the prayer.

"But when the prayer was over, Ronny kept his head bowed and added: 'Thank you for Brandon, amen.' He then turned and looked up at his big buddy and said clear enough for all to hear, 'I love you, Brandon.'

"Brandon, who still had his arm around him, responded, 'I love you too, Ronny. And that was fun.'

"And it was, for all of us."

(*New Era*, May 1983, 18; as quoted in Robert L. Backman, in Conference Report, Oct. 1985 [Salt Lake City: The Church of Jesus Christ of Latter-day Saints, 1985], 16–17)

———

Young people are being hit on all sides by open and subtle attacks on their faith, their ideals, their morality, their self-confidence, even their identity. The typical teenager is pictured as being of the "ME" generation: self-centered, turned inward, unfeeling toward others, seeking immediate self-gratification. . . .

As a boy I sought happiness as the world measures it. I wanted acceptance, position, fame (particularly as an athlete), and wealth. I had none of these. I was very unhappy. I thought happiness was as elusive as a shadow.

It was not until I was called on a mission that I discovered the real key to happiness. To my surprise, despite the discouragement, the disappointments, and the plain hard work associated with my missionary labors, I was happy. It was then I learned that happiness is really a by-product of service. As I forgot my own desires, my own weaknesses and frailties in my missionary service, I began to understand King Benjamin's profound counsel to his people . . . (Mosiah 2:17).

That is why a missionary can return from the toughest experiences of his life and report, "These have been the happiest two years of my life!"

A life can never be happy that is focused inward. So if you are miserable now, forget your troubles. March right out your door, and find someone who needs you.

You want happiness? Find ways to serve. Your happiness will be commensurate with the service you render.

(Robert L. Backman, in Conference Report, Oct. 1985 [Salt Lake City: The Church of Jesus Christ of Latter-day Saints, 1985], 14–15)

———

I am grateful for the Book of Mormon which explains how we can repay Jesus Christ for his great mercy to us. His sacrifice atoned even for our personal sins and makes his mercy available to you and to me. King Benjamin may have explained how repayment is possible: "Behold, I tell you these things that he may learn wisdom: that ye may learn that when ye are in the service of your fellow beings ye are only in the service of your God" (Mosiah 2:17). . . .

What this scripture then means, is that you can repay Jesus for his mercy to you by being kind, thoughtful, considerate, and helpful to those around you. By such service to others, you can gradually pay back your indebtedness to your Savior. . . .

Instead of being filled with vain regrets over past deeds which are already done and which events you are powerless to change, you will now be so busy doing good deeds to others that you will not have a desire to sin or disobey, nor to recall past sin or disobedience. . . .

It stands to reason that the more serious the sin, the longer it takes to complete that repayment. If you work at repayment daily over the years, even very great sins you may have committed can eventually be repaid and you can then stand blameless before your Savior.

(Theodore M. Burton, "The Meaning of Repentance," *BYU Speeches of the Year*, 26 Mar. 1985 [Provo, Utah: BYU Press, 1985], 5–6)

———

The more we obey God, the more we desire to help others. The more we help others, the more we love God, and on and on. Conversely, the more we disobey God and the more selfish we are, the less love we feel.

Trying to find lasting love without obeying God is like trying to quench thirst by drinking from an empty cup—you can go through the motions, but the thirst remains. Similarly, trying to find love without helping and sacrificing for others is like trying to live without eating—it is against the laws of nature and cannot succeed.

(John H. Groberg, in Conference Report, Oct. 2004 [Salt Lake City: The Church of Jesus Christ of Latter-day Saints, 2004], 8)

Alma 17:27–28 • GOD'S ARMY OF ONE
(Refer in this text to Helaman 10:1–4, 16.)

What are we to fear when the Lord is with us? Can we not take the Lord at his word and exercise a particle of faith in him? Our assignment is affirmative . . . to carry the Gospel to our enemies, that they might no longer be our enemies.

(Spencer W. Kimball, *Ensign*, June 1976 [Salt Lake City: The Church of Jesus Christ of Latter-day Saints, 1976], 6)

———

[A vision the Prophet Joseph Smith had:] Also, I saw Elder Brigham Young standing in a strange land, in the far south and west, in a desert place, upon a rock in the midst of about a dozen men . . . who appeared hostile. He was preaching to them in their own tongue, and the angel of God standing above his head, with a drawn sword in his hand, protecting him, but he did not see it.

(Joseph Smith, *History of the Church of Jesus Christ of Latter-day Saints* [Salt Lake City: Deseret Book, 1976], 2:381)

———

What did Ammon say? "Be of good cheer" (Alma

17:31). Now, we may read this as a story about some shepherds trying to round up some missing sheep, but the message is much more powerful and significant than that. Ammon was a missionary with noble intentions to bring the king and his kingdom back to the fold of righteousness, to the well of living water. The challenge looked daunting to those who could see only, in everyday terms, sheep strung out on hillsides and not enough manpower to round them up. They were discouraged and fearful that the king would discover their loss. Ammon not only led the force to recapture the sheep, he drove away the evil men who caused the problems; and his heroic efforts persuaded the king to follow him and to follow the Savior. Ammon teaches us that no matter our circumstances, we can be an example to others, we can lift them, we can inspire them to seek righteousness, and we can bear testimony to all of the power of Jesus Christ.

(Robert D. Hales, *Ensign*, May 1997 [Salt Lake City: The Church of Jesus Christ of Latter-day Saints, 1997], 82)

––––––––––

In 1830 John Taylor's parents and other family members emigrated to Toronto, Canada, leaving him behind in England to sell the family farm and settle other family business. When finished, he left England on a ship bound for New York City. During the voyage, the ship encountered a severe storm that had already damaged several ships in the area. The captain and officers of the ship expected that they would sink, but the voice of the Spirit testified to John Taylor, "You must yet go to America and preach the gospel." President Taylor recalled: "So confident was I of my destiny, that I went on deck at midnight, and amidst the raging elements felt as calm as though I was sitting in a parlor at home. I believed I should reach America and perform my work." He arrived safely in New York, and after a few months rejoined his parents in Toronto.

(*Teachings of Presidents of the Church—John Taylor* [Salt Lake City: The Church of Jesus Christ of Latter-day Saints, 2001], xiii)

Alma 17:39 • MERCENARY CUSTOM

The servant of King Lamoni took the bloody stumps of the attackers' arms cut off by Ammon to the king "for a testimony of the things which they had done" (Alma 17:39). This practice finds direct analogues in the archaeology of Egypt and Syria....

The practice of cutting off the arms, hands, feet, or other body parts of vanquished enemies served several functions: to obtain an accurate count of the dead, to afford a basis for paying mercenary soldiers, or to identify the casualties.

(John W. Welsh, *Warfare in the Book of Mormon*,

ed. by Stephen D. Ricks and William J. Hamblin [Salt Lake City: Deseret Book, 1990], 20, 23)

Alma 18:14 • SILENCE

The first requirement for prayer is silence. People of prayer are people of silence.

(Jose Luis Gonzalez-Balado, *Mother Teresa—In My Own Words*, [New York: Gramercy Books, 1996], 8)

––––––––––

Holiness speaks when there is silence, encouraging that which is good or reproving that which is wrong.

(James E. Faust, *Ensign*, May 2005 [Salt Lake City: The Church of Jesus Christ of Latter-day Saints, 2005], 62)

Alma 18:16, 18, 20, 32 • DISCERNMENT
(Refer in this text to Alma 12:3, 7.)

On one occasion, while a Church security staff member was driving President Kimball home, Spencer leaned back to rest. After a bit, he suddenly sat bolt upright, took off his glasses, and looked intently at the driver. "Is this your first family?" he asked.

Taken aback, the driver answered, "No, sir, I was married before. I tried all I could, but it did not work out."

President Kimball said, "I'm sorry if I have said something to cause you pain." He lay back again briefly, then sat up again, looked intently, and asked, "How is your son?"

The driver, who had only daughters by his second marriage, explained that he had not been allowed to see the son by his first marriage since the child was an infant, nearly twenty years earlier. They arrived at the Kimball home, and Spencer, embracing him, said, "You have good things to look forward to."

Puzzled, the driver asked Arthur Haycock [President Kimball's secretary] why the President would be reading his personnel file. Arthur assured him that the President had not seen the file.

"How then," the driver asked, "did he know about my family situation?"

Arthur smiled, "That's why he's President of the Church."

About a week later the driver heard a knock at his door. A young man of about twenty introduced himself as his son. Now an adult, he had chosen to find his father and establish a relationship.

(Spencer W. Kimball; as quoted in Edward L. Kimball, *Lengthen Your Stride: The Presidency of Spencer W. Kimball* [Salt Lake City: Deseret Book, 2005], 48–49)

Alma 18:24–28 • MILK VS. MEAT

(Refer in this text to Alma 22:7–10.)

Alma 18:32 • HE KNOWS ALL THE THOUGHTS AND INTENTS OF OUR HEARTS

(Refer in this text to Mosiah 4:30.)

In the midst of . . . the universe's incredible vastness is incredible personalness. For example, "[God] looketh down upon all the children of men; and he knows all the thoughts and intents of the heart" (Alma 18:32; see also Isaiah 66:18).

Since we are thus fully accountable to Him, on Judgment Day we cannot invoke the Fifth Amendment!

(Neal A. Maxwell, in *Conference Report,* Oct. 2003 [Salt Lake City: The Church of Jesus Christ of Latter-day Saints, 2003], 107)

Alma 18:42; 19:6, 13–17; 22:18; 27:17–19 • SPIRITUAL EXHAUSTION

It appears that a trance is a state in which the body and its functions become quiescent in order that the full powers of the Spirit may be centered on the revelations of heaven. Freed from the fetters of a mortal body, a man's spirit can be ushered into the divine presence; it can hear what otherwise could not be heard and see what otherwise could not be seen—even the visions of eternity and even the Almighty himself. . . . It is of interest that the false prophet Shemaiah wrote to the priest Zephaniah, charging him to keep the temple a house of order by putting the mad prophets in prison and in stocks. His reference to mad prophets is understood to have been directed to those prophets who claimed authority through some ecstasy or trance. His purpose in so doing was to have the prophet Jeremiah imprisoned, it being well-known that Jeremiah made claim to such experiences (see Jeremiah 29:26–27). The story of Ammon and Lamoni affirms religious trances as a legitimate revelatory device. Lamoni, as already noted, came forth from his trance testifying that he had seen the Redeemer and then prophesied relative to the Savior's birth and the necessity of all mankind believing on his name. The testimony of his servants was that while they were in this state of physical insensibility, angels instructed them in the principles of salvation and their obligation to live righteously. Indeed, they experienced a change of heart and no longer had a desire to do evil. Such is the state in which the power of God overcomes the "natural frame" and one is "carried away in God."

(R. Millet and J. F. McConkie, *Doctrinal Commentary on the Book of Mormon* [Salt Lake City: Bookcraft, 1991], 3:140–141)

King Lamoni's experience of being filled with the Spirit of the Lord was something he had never felt before. It so overcame his natural body that he fell to the ground in a state of unconsciousness. It is interesting to note that similar experiences were had by Alma, Zeezrom, and King Lamoni's father. The following chart reviews these experiences.

Individual	What Initiated Conversion	The Results
Alma (Mosiah 27)	He was visited by an angel of God.	He became weak and could not speak nor move for three days. (Alma 36)
Zeezrom (Alma 11; 12)	Alma and Amulek preached the gospel to him with great power.	He became weak and was confined to bed with a burning fever. (Alma 15)
King Lamoni (Alma 17–19)	Ammon taught him the gospel.	He was overcome by the Spirit and fell to the earth as if he were dead.
King Lamoni's father (Alma 22)	Aaron taught him the gospel.	He was struck as if he was dead.

The similarity of these experiences seems to suggest that the Spirit of the Lord may have a very dramatic effect on those who have been especially wicked. Alma 19:6 explains this principle.

(*Book of Mormon Student Manual: Religion 121 and 122* [Salt Lake City: The Church of Jesus Christ of Latter-day Saints, 1979], 247–248)

Alma 19:6 • THE VEIL

Without the veil, we would lose that precious insulation, thus interfering with our mortal probation and maturation. Without the veil, our brief mortal walk in a darkening world would lose its meaning—for one would scarcely carry the flashlight of faith at noonday and in the presence of the Light of the World!

Without the veil, we could not experience the gospel of work and the sweat of our brow. If we had the security of having already entered into God's rest. . . .

And how could we learn about obedience if we were shielded from the consequences of our disobedience? And how could we learn patience under pressure if we did not experience pressure and waiting? . . .

The veil keeps the first, second, and third estates separate. . . . The veil avoids having things "compound in one" (2 Ne. 2:11)—to our everlasting detriment. We are cocooned, as it were, in order that we might truly choose. Once, long ago, we chose to come to this very setting where we could choose. It was in irrevocable choice! And the veil is the guarantor that our ancient choice is honored. . . .

Thus the veil stands—not to forever shut us out—but as a reminder of God's tutoring and patient love for us.

(Neal A. Maxwell, *Ensign*, Oct. 1980 [Salt Lake City: The Church of Jesus Christ of Latter-day Saints, 1980], 31)

Alma 19:6 • LIGHT

I recently recalled a historic meeting in Jerusalem about 17 years ago. It was regarding the lease for the land on which the Brigham Young University's Jerusalem Center for Near Eastern Studies was later built. Before this lease could be signed, President Ezra Taft Benson and Elder Jeffrey R. Holland, then president of Brigham Young University, agreed with the Israeli government on behalf of the Church and the university not to proselyte in Israel. You might wonder why we agreed not to proselyte. We were required to do so in order to get the building permit to build that magnificent building which stands in the historic city of Jerusalem. To our knowledge the Church and BYU have scrupulously and honorably kept that nonproselyting commitment. After the lease had been signed, one of our friends insightfully remarked, "Oh, we know that you are not going to proselyte, but what are you going to do about the light that is in their eyes?" He was referring to our students who were studying in Israel.

What was that light in their eyes which was so obvious to our friend? The Lord Himself given the answer: "And the light which shineth, which giveth you light, is through him who enlighteneth *your eyes*, which is the same light that quickeneth your understandings" (D&C 88:11; emphasis added). . . .

This light shows in our countenances as well as in our eyes.

(James E. Faust, *Ensign*, Nov. 2005 [Salt Lake City: The Church of Jesus Christ of Latter-day Saints, 2005], 20)

Ammon seems to be describing the Light of Christ that was working on the king, preparing him to receive the constant companionship of the Holy Ghost.

(Daniel K. Judd, *A Book of Mormon Treasury—Gospel Insights From General Authorities and Religious Educators* [Salt Lake City: Deseret Book, 2003], 446)

Alma 19:16–17, 31 • CONVERTED UNTO THE LORD

Once as President Kimball entered a missionary meeting in West Berlin he overheard one missionary comment to another, "Today I converted two people to the Church and they're going to be baptized this next week."

Spencer put his hand on the startled missionary's shoulder and said,

"Young man, I couldn't help overhearing you say you had converted two members to the Church today. I want you to know that you've never converted anybody in your life. And what's more, you never will. Conversion is an act of the Spirit and you're only an instrument in the hands of the Lord to bring this person into acceptance of the gospel."

Then Spencer hugged him, kissed him on the cheek, and expressed appreciation for his good efforts.

(Spencer W. Kimball; as quoted in Edward L. Kimball, *Lengthen Your Stride: The Presidency of Spencer W. Kimball* [Salt Lake City: Deseret Book, 2005], 105–106)

Alma 19:22–23 • DIVINE PROTECTION
(Refer in this text to 1 Nephi 22:16–17, 19; Helaman 5:20–52.)

Alma 20:10, 13 • THE BIRTHRIGHT
(Refer in this text to Mosiah 10:15.)

Alma 20:29 • PATIENT IN THEIR SUFFERING
(Refer in this text to Mosiah 24:14–15; Alma 14:11; Alma 31:31, 33, 38: Alma 34:40–41.)

Alma 21:3 • APOSTATE ATTITUDES, HARD HEARTS
(Refer in this text to Mosiah 13:4; Alma 24:30.)

Alma 22:9–10 • IS GOD THE GREAT SPIRIT?

According to Lamanite traditions, God is the Great Spirit. It is obvious that by this designation the Lamanites had in mind a personal being, for King Lamoni mistakenly supposed that Ammon was the Great Spirit (Alma 18:2–28; 19:25–27). Both Ammon and Aaron, using the same principle of salesmanship applied by Paul on Mars Hill (Acts 17:22–31), taught that the Great Spirit was the God who created the heavens and the earth (Alma 18:8–29; 22:8–11). This same Lamanite concept that God is the Great Spirit has existed among the American Indians in modern times.

(Bruce R. McConkie, *Mormon Doctrine* [Salt Lake City: Bookcraft, 1966], 340)

Alma 22:15–16 • BORN OF GOD

(Refer in this text to Alma 5:7, 12; Mosiah 5:2, 7; Mosiah 27:24–26.)

Alma 22:15 • CAST OFF AT THE LAST DAY

People quit trying to live the gospel because they believe they've gone too far. Perhaps they believe the Satanic lie that there is no forgiveness, that the Atonement applies to everyone else, not to them.

If we study the book every day, we'll learn that we're not cast off forever, that there is hope for us. We'll begin to understand what the scriptures mean when we get to Alma 22:15, where King Lamoni's father asks Aaron, "What shall I do that I may be born of God, having this wicked spirit rooted out of my breast, and receive his Spirit, that I may be filled with joy, that I may not be cast off at the last day?" We'll learn to rely upon the merits of Jesus Christ. We'll learn that the major purpose of the book is to show that Jesus is the Christ, and that as long as there's a Savior, everything will work out. . . .

Do you see why Satan doesn't want my sweet mother to read the Book of Mormon? If she reads and studies the Book of Mormon every day, she will know that her other son, who isn't the religion teacher, is not cast off forever. But if she quits studying, she may give up on her other son, whom we all pray will come back to the fold and be washed and cleansed through the holy blood of Christ.

(Jack R. Christianson and K. Douglas Bassett, *Life Lessons from the Book of Mormon* [Salt Lake City: Deseret Book, 2003], 20–22)

Alma 22:18 • I WILL GIVE AWAY ALL MY SINS TO KNOW THEE

We may not always succeed as quickly as we would want, but as we make repentance a constant part of our lives, miracles occur. This is what happens as we see that we really can overcome our sins: Our "confidence [waxes] strong in the presence of God" (D&C 121:45). We kneel in humility before our Father. We tell him openly of our progress, and also of our fears and doubts. As we draw near to him, he draws near to us. He gives us peace and encouragement. He heals our souls. As we continue inch by inch to repent, we determine that nothing will hold us back: we will do our part. We come to feel like that great Lamanite king who cried, "Oh God, . . . wilt thou make thyself known unto me, and I will give away all my sins to know thee" (Alma 22:18). With this commitment to who we can become, the spiritual doors swing open. There is a new freedom to feel and to know, a freedom to become.

(Neil L. Anderson, *Ensign*, Apr. 1995 [Salt Lake City: The Church of Jesus Christ of Latter-day Saints, 1995], 52)

We cannot know the meaning of all things *right now*. But we can know, *right now*, that God knows us and loves us individually!

But, brothers and sisters, what keeps us from knowing and loving Him more? Our reluctance to give away all our sins, thinking instead that a down payment will do.

(Neal A. Maxwell, in Conference Report, Oct. 2002 [Salt Lake City: The Church of Jesus Christ of Latter-day Saints, 2002], 17)

Alma 22:30–31 • DESOLATION

The land of Desolation was the place where the people of Jared first landed (Alma 22:30; Ether 6:12; 7:6). It was in this region that Limhi's people discovered the Jaredite ruins, describing the land as being "covered with bones of men" and "ruins of buildings" (Mosiah 8:8; ef. Ether 11:6; ca. 121 BC).

The city Desolation was built on the borders of the land Desolation, "by the narrow pass which led into the land southward" (Morm. 3:5–7). Desolation repeatedly changed hands during battles between Lamanites and Nephites near the end of the Nephite civilization (Morm. 3:7; 4:2–3, 8, 13, 19; ca. AD 361–375).

(*Book of Mormon Reference Companion*, ed. by Dennis L. Largey [Salt Lake City: Deseret Book, 2003], 231–232)

Alma 23:5–13 • CONVERSION OF THE LAMANITES

In the twenty-third and twenty-fourth chapters of Alma we have a dramatic account of the power of the gospel changing almost a whole nation from a bloodthirsty, indolent, warlike people into industrious, peace-loving people. Of these people the record says that thousands were brought to a knowledge of the Lord, and that as many as were brought to a knowledge of the truth never did fall away. . . . That is the great message I want to leave here. It is the softening of the hearts that this gospel does to the people who receive it. . . . Now this remarkable transformation wrought in the hearts of these thousands of people was done in a very short period of time under the influence and power of the gospel of Jesus Christ. It would do the same thing today for all the peoples of the earth if they would but receive it. . . .

(Marion G. Romney, in Conference Report, Oct. 1948 [Salt Lake City: The Church of Jesus Christ of Latter-day Saints, 1948], 75)

Alma 23:17 • ANTI-NEPHI-LEHIES

Dr. Hugh Nibley has found a Semitic and common

Indo-European root corresponding to anti that means in the face of or facing, as of one facing a mirror, and by extension either one who opposes or one who imitates.

(Daniel H. Ludlow, *A Companion to Your Study of the Book of Mormon* [Salt Lake City: Deseret Book, 1976], 209–210)

Alma 24 • WAR, THE LORD'S RULES
(Refer in this text Alma 43–63.)

Alma 24:9–13; 27:23 • WERE THE ANTI-NEPHI-LEHIES GUILTY OF MURDER?
(Refer in this text to Alma 39:5–6.)

We do know that there are murders committed by Gentiles for which they at least can repent, be baptized, and receive a remission of their sins.

(Bruce R. McConkie, *A New Witness for the Articles of Faith* [Salt Lake City: Deseret Book, 1985], 231)

Even among willful murderers there are grades and categories. There are . . . [those] who kill for sadistic pleasure. There are those who kill in drunkenness, in rage, in anger, in jealousy. There are those who kill for gain, for power, for fear. There are those who kill for lust. They certainly will suffer different degrees of punishment hereafter.

(Spencer W. Kimball, *The Miracle of Forgiveness* [Salt Lake City: Bookcraft, 1969], 130–131)

Alma 24:10 • TAKEN AWAY THE GUILT FROM OUR HEARTS

Eliminate guilt. I hope it goes without saying that guilt is not a proper motivational technique. . . .

As mortals, we simply cannot do everything at once. Therefore we must do all things "in wisdom and order" (Mosiah 4:27). Often that will mean temporarily postponing attention to one priority in order to take care of another. Sometimes family demands will require your full attention. Other times professional responsibilities will come first. And there will be times when Church callings will come first. . . .

We need to remember that Christ came to remove guilt by forgiving those who repent. . . .

As the power of the Atonement begins to work in our lives, we come to understand that the Savior has already born the burden of our guilt. O that we may be wise enough to understand, to repent as necessary, and to let go of our guilt. . . .

There will always be more we can do. There is always another family matter that needs attention, another lesson to prepare, another interview to conduct, another meeting to attend. We just need to be wise in

[protecting] our health and in following the counsel that President Hinckley has given often to just do the best that we can.

(M. Russell Ballard, *Ensign*, Nov. 2006 [Salt Lake City: The Church of Jesus Christ of Latter-day Saints, 2006], 19)

Alma 24:16 • WE SHALL GO TO OUR GOD

Some years ago a fire erupted in the middle of the night and completely destroyed a family's home. A neighbor came by to console a seven-year-old. . . . "Johnny, it's sure too bad your home burned down." Johnny thought a moment and then said, "Oh, that's where you're mistaken, Mr. Brown. That was not our home; that was just our house. We still have our home, we just don't have any place to put it right now."

What a great principle taught by a child about home. What does that word bring to your mind—*home*? To some, an edifice. To others, a place to sleep, a place to eat, a place where worldly goods are stored.

Yet to others more spiritually inclined, it might mean where family is, where my heart is, a sacred place, a peaceful place, an escape from a wicked world.

The still small voice whispers yet a deeper meaning. Home is heaven. We are strangers here on earth. My real home is not here, but there. My challenge is to learn how to bring about a home here on earth similar to the celestial one I left.

(Gene R. Cook, in Conference Report, Apr. 1984 [Salt Lake City: The Church of Jesus Christ of Latter-day Saints, 1984], 41)

Alma 24:17–25; 27:3 • WILLINGNESS TO DIE
(Refer in this text to Alma 25:7.)

The law of forgiveness and retribution . . . applies to individuals and to families, as well as to the Church at large. We are under commandment to forgive our enemies and suffer their abuses and smiting the first time and second time, also the third time. [D&C 98:32–38.] This is to be done in patience, and in humility and prayer, hoping that the enemy might repent. . . . For all these abuses we will be rewarded if we endure them in patience. . . . This may to the most ordinary human being be a hard law to follow; but nevertheless it is the word of the Lord. One of the best illustrations of this spirit of enduring wrong rather than retaliating is found in the story of the people of Ammon in the Book of Mormon. Because they refused to take up arms to defend themselves, but would rather lay down their lives than shed blood even in their own defense, they brought many of their enemies to repentance and to the kingdom of God. [Alma 24:17–25; 27:3.] This is the doctrine of Jesus Christ as taught in the Sermon on the Mount. [Matt. 5:21–22, 43–44.] If all peoples would accept this doctrine there could be no war, and all difficulties could be adjusted in righteousness. This doctrine was taught, so the Lord declared, to his people anciently. There are many things in the Old Testament in relation to the wars and battles of the Israelites in the meager record which has come down to us, which are made to appear to us that these people were cruel and vengeful, but the Lord says they went out to battle when they were guided by prophets and the spirit of revelation when the Lord commanded them.

(Joseph Fielding Smith, *Church History and Modern Revelation* [Salt Lake City: The Council of the Twelve Apostles, 1953], 1:434–35; as quoted in Daniel H. Ludlow, *A Companion to Your Study of the Book of Mormon* [Salt Lake City: Deseret Book, 1976], 256)

In 1979, . . . I was serving as president in the Mexico City North Mission. . . . A (community) meeting was called . . . at which Church members were given the following options : denounce the Church, leave the village, or be killed (not an idle threat). The members, particularly the women, said they knew the Church to be true and would not denounce it. They also indicated they had worked just as hard as the rest of the community to secure their homesteads, and they would not leave. Boldly stepping forward, they told their taunters if they were going to kill them, to get on with it. The moment grew tense as machetes were raised, then finally lowered while the Latter-day Saints stood up for that which the Spirit had testified to them to be true. These Saints eventually learned, as most of us do, that it is harder to live the gospel day by day than to die for it in an instant, but their early commitment came because the Spirit had touched their hearts and changed their lives.

(John B. Dickson, *Ensign*, Feb. 1995 [Salt Lake City: The Church of Jesus Christ of Latter-day Saints, 1995], 7)

A young man in Tonga by the name of Finau had heard the missionaries and believed their message and wanted to get baptized. He had a concern, however, as his father was adamantly opposed to his "becoming a Mormon." Finau was unmarried and still lived at home, even though he was old enough to be on his own. Since he was past "legal age" he did not need his father's permission to get baptized, but he loved his father and wanted to show respect for him.

Unfortunately, every time he talked to his father about getting baptized his father beat him. Even though Finau could have left home, he stayed and tried to explain to his father how he felt about the Church and how sure he was of his testimony. After several months

it became evident that his father would not give his permission, so Finau felt he had no alternative but to get baptized without his father's blessing. . . .

The missionaries . . . checked and found that he was indeed of legal age, that he had diligently though vainly tried to get his father's blessing, so they could see no reason why they should not baptize him. Thus, after sincere prayer together, they arranged for a time and place to baptize Finau. . . .

They were all dressed in white and together waded out into the ocean to get to a spot deep enough to perform the sacred ordinance of baptism.

Even though others were not told of the time or place, in some way the word had gotten to Finau's father several hours before, and in anger or desperation or both, he told his oldest son to "teach Finau a lesson." Encouraged by his father and drunken with anger, Finau's older brother got a large stick and headed for the beach.

He arrived at the beach just as the baptism was finished and Finau and the two elders were wading back to shore. In an anger-emboldened rage he uttered a blood-curdling scream and headed straight toward the threesome, who were now in fairly shallow water.

The two elders heard the scream, looked up, saw the stick and the charging brother, and quickly ran away. They yelled at Finau to follow them, but he quietly shook his head and simply stood there, his eyes full of peace. He raised his head and looked straight at his brother. The elders reached land and took cover in some nearby bushes just before the brother reached Finau. When the brother saw that Finau would not run but waited calmly for him with a look of perfect serenity, he hesitated for a moment—but only a moment. Then with a curse of anger he took the last couple of splashing steps, lifted his large stick, and sent it crashing across Finau's back. Finau still did not move. Again and again the stick smashed into Finau's back, tearing his shirt and exposing huge red welts oozing with blood and pain. At last an extra heavy blow crumpled Finau to his knees, then another and another left him sprawled face down in the water.

An exultant cry rent the air, and a man drunken from anger staggered to shore and disappeared uncertainly down the trail. He had "taught his brother a lesson" and left a seemingly lifeless form floating partially submerged in the gently rolling ocean.

The two elders who witnessed all this came from their hiding places and, somewhat embarrassed and very concerned, ran quickly to where Finau lay in the ocean, barely moving. They were grateful to see he was still breathing. They lifted him from the water and were sickened by what they saw. Getting beaten severely enough to raise welts and blood and tear fabric is painful enough, but to have that raw flesh submerged in salty ocean water and sand was more pain than they could comprehend. They shuddered, and wondered if Finau also had some broken bones or other unseen injuries.

Finau could hardly move, so they each took an arm and lifted him up and dragged him stumblingly to shore. As they got well onto land, Finau spoke for the first time and asked where they were going.

"To the hospital, of course," they replied. "We must get those wounds treated and see if there are any broken bones. You may have some serious back or rib problems."

"No," said Finau. "Not yet. I have only been baptized. I have not received the gift of the Holy Ghost nor been confirmed a member of The Church of Jesus Christ of Latter-day Saints—God's kingdom on earth. See that log over there? Take me to it, sit me down, confer upon me the gift of the Holy Ghost, and confirm me a member of the Church. I want to be part of God's kingdom now."

"We'll do that tomorrow. You need to get some medical treatment now."

"No," Finau replied firmly. "Do it now. Who knows, you may be right, there may be serious physical problems. I may not even make it to the hospital or I may not be alive tomorrow. Of course, I am in pain, but mostly I just feel numb. I am, however, in full control of my feelings and I want to become a member of God's kingdom now—please."

The two elders looked around, sensing possible danger. They saw no one else, however, so they looked at each other, then at Finau, who was patiently waiting. They saw such a fire of faith and determination coming from his eyes that they sat him down on the log, laid their hands on his head, and by the power and authority of the priesthood of God gave him the gift of the Holy Ghost, confirmed him a member of The Church of Jesus Christ of Latter-day Saints, and under the inspiration of God gave him a special blessing that no permanent physical damage from the beating would afflict his body.

As they took their hands from his head there was calmness in their eyes—no more furtive glances at the surrounding bushes, only tears of gratitude for the faith of a committed Tongan Saint in these latter days. Finally they got him to the hospital, where he was checked, given some care, and released. . . .

Finau stayed with the elders that night, but the next day he wanted to return to his home. They went with him and found his father, who, still filled with bitterness and anger, commanded him to leave home and never return. Finau's brother was nowhere to be found. The missionaries made arrangements for Finau to live with a member family. . . .

Finau was eventually reconciled with his father and his family, many of whom (including both his father

and his brother) later joined the Church. . . .

His father eventually apologized to him and sought his forgiveness, telling him that his mind had been darkened at the time. Finau willingly, even anxiously, forgave him. Finau's back carried those physical scars throughout his life; his soul, however, remained unscarred by anger or desire for revenge.

(John H. Groberg, *Heroes from the Book of Mormon* [Salt Lake City: Bookcraft, 1995], 51–54)

Alma 24:21–26 • A SILVER LINING

I have seen, at close range, the manner in which the Lord has turned disasters—war, occupation, and revolution—into blessings.

(*Teachings of Ezra Taft Benson* [Salt Lake City: Bookcraft, 1988], 168)

The wars that are now taking place will have a tendency, in some measure, to open the way for the Elders of the Church of Jesus Christ to go and establish the Church and kingdom of God among those nations.

(*Masterful Discourses of Orson Pratt* [Salt Lake City: N. B. Lundwall], 141)

[Referring to the Vietnam War] Notwithstanding the evil and the tragedy, I see a silver thread shining through the dark and bloody tapestry of conflict. I see the finger of the Lord plucking some good from the evil designs of the adversary. I see coming out of this conflict, as I have witnessed in other conflicts in Asia, an enlargement of the Lord's program.

(Gordon B. Hinckley, in Conference Report, Apr. 1968 [Salt Lake City: The Church of Jesus Christ of Latter-day Saints, 1968], 21)

Alma 24:30 • THEIR STATE BECOMES WORSE THAN THOUGH THEY HAD NEVER KNOWN

When the Prophet [Joseph Smith] had ended telling how he had been treated, Brother Behunnin remarked: "If I should leave this Church I would not do as those men have done: I would go to some remote place where Mormonism had never been heard of, settle down, and no one would ever learn that I knew anything about it."

The great Seer immediately replied: "Brother Behunnin, you don't know what you would do. No doubt these men once thought as you do. Before you joined this Church you stood on neutral ground. When the gospel was preached good and evil were set before you. You could choose either or neither. There were two opposite masters inviting you to serve them. When you joined this

Church you enlisted to serve God. When you did that you left the neutral ground, and you never can get back on to it. Should you forsake the Master you enlisted to serve it will be by the instigation of the evil one, and you will follow his dictation and be his servant."

He emphasized the fact that a man or woman who had not taken sides either with Christ or belial could maintain a neutral position, but when they enlisted under either the one or the other they left the neutral ground forever.

(Daniel Tyler, cited in "Recollections of the Prophet Joseph Smith," *Juvenile Instructor*, Aug. 1892, 492; as quoted in *Book of Mormon Student Manual: Religion 121 and 122*, 1981 edition [Salt Lake City: The Church of Jesus Christ of Latter-day Saints, 1979], 258)

Alma 25:2 • PEOPLE OF AMMONIHAH DESTROYED

(Refer in this text to Alma 16:2–3.)

Alma 25:7 • THEY SHOULD BE PUT TO DEATH

(Refer in this text to Alma 24:17–25.)

During the Mexican Revolution, Rafael Monroy was the president of the small San Marcos Mexico Branch, and Vicente Morales was his first counselor. On July 17, 1915, they were apprehended by the Zapatistas. They were told they would be spared if they would give up their weapons and renounce their strange religion. Brother Monroy told his captors that he did not have any weapons and simply drew from his pocket his Bible and Book of Mormon. He said, "Gentlemen, these are the only arms I ever carry; they are the arms of truth against error."

When no arms were found, the brethren were cruelly tortured to make them divulge where arms were hidden. But there were no arms. They were then taken under guard to the outskirts of the little town, where their captors stood them up by a large ash tree in front of a firing squad. The officer in charge offered them freedom if they would forsake their religion and join the Zapatistas, but Brother Monroy replied, "My religion is dearer to me than my life, and I cannot forsake it."

They were then told that they were to be shot and asked if they had any request to make. Brother Rafael requested that he be permitted to pray before he was executed. There, in the presence of his executioners, he knelt down and, in a voice that all could hear, prayed that God would bless and protect his loved ones and care for the little struggling branch that would be left without a leader. As he finished his prayer, he used the words of the Savior when He hung upon the cross and prayed for his executioners: "Father, forgive them; for

they know not what they do." With that the firing squad shot both Brother Monroy and Brother Morales.

(James E. Faust, *Ensign*, Nov. 2006 [Salt Lake City: The Church of Jesus Christ of Latter-day Saints, 2006], 21–22)

Alma 25:15–16 • LAW OF MOSES

(Refer in this text to Mosiah 13:29–31.)

Alma 26 • AMMON GLORIES IN THE LORD

I was reading again the twenty-sixth chapter of Alma and the story of Ammon's mission. I read out loud, as I sometimes do, trying to put myself in the position of the characters in the book, imagining that I was saying or hearing the words, that I was there . . . with a clarity which cannot be described and which would be difficult to comprehend by one who has not experienced it, the Spirit spoke to my soul, saying, *Did you notice? Everything that happened to Ammon happened to you. . . .*

It was a thought that had never occurred to me before. I quickly reread the story. Yes, there were times when my heart had been depressed and I had thought about going home. I too had gone to a foreign land to teach the gospel to the Lamanites. I had gone forth among them, had suffered hardships, had slept on the floor, endured the cold, gone without eating. I too had traveled from house to house, knocking on doors for months at a time without being invited in, relying on the mercies of God.

There had been other times when we had entered houses and talked to people. We had taught them on their streets and on their hills. We had even preached in other churches. I remembered the time I had been spit upon. I remembered the time when I, as a young district leader assigned by the mission president to open up a new town, had entered, with three other elders, the main square of a city that had never had missionaries before. We went into the park, sang a hymn, and a crowd gathered.

Then the lot fell upon me, as district leader, to preach. I stood upon a stone bench and spoke to the people. I told the story of the restoration of the gospel, of the boy Joseph going into the grove and the appearance of the Father and the Son to him. I remembered well a group of teenage boys, in the evening shadows, throwing rocks at us. I remembered the concern about being hit or injured by those who did not want to hear the message.

I remembered spending time in jail while my legal right to be a missionary in a certain country was decided by the police authorities. . . . I still remember the feeling I had when the door was closed and I was far away from home, alone, with only the mercies of the Lord to rely on for deliverance. I remembered enduring these things with the hope that "we might be the means of saving some soul" (Alma 26:30).

And then on that day as I read, the Spirit testified to me again, and the words remain with me even today: *No one but a missionary could have written this story. Joseph Smith could never have known what it was like to be a missionary to the Lamanites, for no one he knew had ever done such a thing before.*

(F. Burton Howard, *Heroes from the Book of Mormon* [Salt Lake City: Bookcraft, 1995], 124–125)

Alma 26:10–12, 16, 35–36 • BOASTING
(Refer in this text to Mosiah 11:19; Alma 39:2; Mormon 3:9.)

I would rather hear an Elder speak only five words accompanied by the power of God, and they would do more good than to hear long sermons without the Spirit.

(*Discourses of Brigham Young*, comp. by John A. Widtsoe [Salt Lake City: Deseret Book, 1954], 330)

Alma 26:23, 25 • THE WORD OR THE SWORD
(Refer in this text to Alma 31:5.)

Alma 26:27 • DEPRESSED AND ABOUT TO TURN BACK
(Refer in this text to Alma 8:10–15; Helaman 10:1, 4, 16; refer to the Joseph F. Smith quote under 1 Nephi 8:2, 36.)

There are times when you simply have to righteously hang on and outlast the devil until his depressive spirit leaves you. As the Lord told the Prophet Joseph Smith: "Thine adversity and thine afflictions, shall be but a small moment; And then, if thou endure it well, God shall exalt thee on high" (D&C 121:7–8).

To press on in noble endeavors, even while surrounded by a cloud of depression, will eventually bring you out on top into the sunshine.

(Ezra Taft Benson, *Ensign*, Nov. 1974 [Salt Lake City: The Church of Jesus Christ of Latter-day Saints, 1974], 67)

———

[An experience of Gordon B. Hinckley on his mission to England] Elder Hinckley found some of that discouragement common to missionaries facing new circumstances in a new land. He was not well physically, and as he went to his first street meeting . . . he recalls: "I was terrified. I stepped up on that little stand and looked at that crowd of people that had gathered. . . .

They looked rather menacing and mean, but I somehow stumbled through whatever I had to say." Down in spirit and facing no success in missionary endeavors, Gordon wrote a letter to his father, saying: "I am wasting my time and your money. I don't see any point in my staying here." In due course a gentle but terse reply came from his father. That letter read: "Dear Gordon. I have your letter [of such and such a date]. I have only one suggestion. Forget yourself and go to work, With love, Your Father." President Hinckley says of that moment, "I pondered his response and then the next morning in our scripture class we read that great statement of the Lord: 'For whosoever will save his life shall lose it; but whosoever shall lose his life for my sake and the gospel's, the same shall save it' (Mark 8:35). That simple statement, that promise, touched me. I got on my knees and made a covenant with the Lord that I would try to forget myself and go to work."

(Jeffrey R. Holland, *Ensign*, June 1995 [Salt Lake City: The Church of Jesus Christ of Latter-day Saints, 1995], 8)

———

As you nurture the seedlings of faith in others, you will find yourself saying, "Is it already the end of the day?" rather than "Will this day ever end?" Pioneer women did not have time to wallow in discouragement. They were too busy working their way toward Zion.

(Mary Ellen Smoot, *Ensign*, Nov. 1997 [Salt Lake City: The Church of Jesus Christ of Latter-day Saints, 1997], 13)

———

Discouragement and fear are tools of the devil.

(G. Homer Durham, *N. Eldon Tanner: His Life and Service* [Salt Lake City: Deseret Book, 1982], 315)

———

Some despondency is physically caused. Glandular maladies can poison the system and issue in melancholy moods beyond the power of anyone's satisfactory control. To the victims of such depressive states the best-intentioned counsel . . . may easily do more harm than good. To the black moods they suffer because of bodily dysfunctioning, further dejection is added when they, in their powerlessness, are held accountable.

In such cases the wise physician is an indispensable resource. The vast majority of us, however, who fall victim to occasional or settled moodiness and gloom have no such justification. . . .

Much of the depression we struggle with downstream could have been prevented upstream if we had been wise. Great convictions to live by, great resources to live from, great purposes to live for, the love of nature, the companionship of books, the nurture of friendship, the fine uses of play, the satisfactions of an unashamed conscience—such factors enter into a life that keeps its savor, and furnish an immunity to despondency which makes cure needless.

(Harry Emerson Fosdick, *On Being a Real Person* [New York: Harper & Brothers, 1943], 208–209)

In times of hurt and discouragement, it may be consoling . . . for all of us to recall that no one can do anything permanently to us that will last for eternity. Only we ourselves can affect our eternal progression.

(Marvin J. Ashton, in Conference Report, Apr. 1984 [Salt Lake City: The Church of Jesus Christ of Latter-day Saints, 1984], 12)

Without any doubt, Joseph Smith was a prophet with a great spirit of accomplishment and tenacity. On one occasion he said to his cousin, George A. Smith: "Never be discouraged. If I were sunk in the lowest pit of Nova Scotia, with the Rocky Mountains piled on me, I would hang on, exercise faith, and keep up good courage, and I would come out on top."

(John Henry Evans, *Joseph Smith, an American Prophet* [New York: Macmillan., 1946], 9; as quoted in Angel Abrea, in Conference Report, Apr. 1984 [Salt Lake City: The Church of Jesus Christ of Latter-day Saints, 1984], 97)

I hope that all of us, when the day of release comes from laboring in the . . . Mission, can say, "I have fought a good fight, I have finished my course, I have kept the faith." If you do, you'll go on to fruitful lives. I have no question about that. Your future lies in the present, in the habits of work that you establish here, in your spirit of dedication, in your ambition to achieve something. As you do in the mission field, so you are likely to do all the rest of your lives. . . .

I know it isn't easy. It's discouraging at times, sure. Aren't you glad it isn't just all fun all the time? Those valleys of discouragement make more beautiful the peaks of achievement. . . .

I am not too worried about how many baptisms you have, whether it is 1 or 100. My only concern is that you give your very best effort to the work. And whether it be 1 or 100, it is wonderful. . . . I know you get tired. I know you get discouraged sometimes. . . .

You are making a sacrifice, but it is not a sacrifice, because you will get more than you give up. You will gain more than you give, and it will prove to be an investment with tremendous returns. It will prove to be a blessing instead of a sacrifice. No one who ever served in this work as a missionary who gave his or her best efforts need worry about making a sacrifice, because

there will come blessings into the life of that individual for as long as he or she lives. I have not the slightest doubt about that.

(*Discourses of President Gordon B. Hinckley*, 1995–99 [Salt Lake City: The Church of Jesus Christ of Latter-day Saints, 2004], 1:364, 372, 375, 377)

I have seen President David O. McKay discouraged. I have seen President Joseph Fielding Smith and President Harold B. Lee and President Spencer W. Kimball discouraged. All of us can become discouraged. . . .

It is important to know, when you feel down, that many others do also and that their circumstances are generally much worse than yours. And it's important to know that when one of us is down, it becomes the obligation of his friends to give him a lift.

(*Teachings of Gordon B. Hinckley* [Salt Lake City: Deseret Book, 1997], 156)

If you are unhappy, if you are feeling weary, troubled, or disillusioned, may I ask you to try something? Instead of dwelling on your troubles, focus instead on creating something remarkable, something of eternal significance. Nurture a testimony; strengthen a relationship; write a family history; go to the temple; serve.

Read the family proclamation and the Relief Society declaration; make a commitment to live those principles and celebrate. . . .

"This is not a time for dragging feet or stooped shoulders," President Gordon B. Hinckley has counseled. "Stop seeking out the storms and enjoy more fully the sunlight."

(Mary Ellen Smoot, in Conference Report, Apr. 2000 [Salt Lake City: The Church of Jesus Christ of Latter-day Saints, 2000], 80)

It is God's work, it is not yours—and you have the right to claim from God greater power than you have in order to do his work. Always remember that!

I am not given much to worry. . . . I say to myself, " . . . if I am doing the best I know how, I am not going to worry." I am going to let Him do the worrying when I am doing the best that I know how for him. . . . Do not feel that you cannot reach out, outside and beyond yourselves for power which you do not possess in order to be successful in your work. We have to have that outside power.

(*Matthew Cowley Speaks* [Salt Lake City: Deseret Book, 1954], 354–355)

All . . . [of us] experience rejection at times. Each one of us, young or old, must deal with circumstances profitably when we are treated by others in a way that could allow us to feel insecure about ourselves. Where, then, does the strength come from to deal with rejection? It comes from within. We must be spiritually rooted. In this way we can roll with the punches of life and move forward without bitterness, anger, or self-pity.

(K. Douglas Bassett, *The Barber's Song* [Springville, Utah: Cedar Fort, 2005], 31)

Despair, Doom, and Discouragement are not acceptable views of life for a Latter-day Saint. . . .

I want you to know that there have always been some difficulties in mortal life, and there always will be. But knowing what we know, and living as we are supposed to live, there really is no place, no excuse, for pessimism and despair. . . .

So I hope you won't believe all the world's difficulties have been wedged into your decade, or that things have never been worse than they are for you personally, or that they will never get better. I reassure you that things have been worse and they *will* always get better. . . .

Here are some actual comments that have been passed on to me in recent months:

This comes from a fine returned missionary: "Why should I date and get serious with a girl? I am not sure I even want to marry and bring a family into this kind of a world. I am not very sure about my own future. . . ."

Here's another from a high school student: "I hope I die before all these terrible things happen that people are talking about. I don't want to be on the earth when there is so much trouble."

This from a recent college graduate: "I am doing the best I can, but I wonder if there is much reason to even plan for the future, let alone retirement. The world probably won't last that long, anyway."

Well, my, my, my. Isn't that a fine view of things? Sounds like we all ought to go eat a big plate of worms.

Contrary to what some might say, you have every reason in this world to be happy and to be optimistic and to be confident.

(Howard W. Hunter, *Ensign*, Oct. 1993 [Salt Lake City: The Church of Jesus Christ of Latter-day Saints, 1993], 70)

There have been numerous studies that have shown that as western culture in particular has moved into other parts of the world and been adopted by other countries, their levels of depression have risen, which would suggest . . . that there is something culturally about western civilization that tends to promote dis-couragement and despair and depression. . . . So what is it about western civilization, not just America, but western civilization in general that promotes depres-sion? There is no question that we are a very consumer driven kind of a civilization. We like things. And we live in enough luxury that we can have things. We want our fast food to come to us faster. We want bigger screened TVs. I mean if you have a 19-inch and then you walk through . . . [the mall] you see that they come this big, we're not satisfied with our 19-inch anymore. We want more room on our Ipod. We want everything bigger and faster and we want it NOW. And unfortunately we grow up with that. . . . You only have to turn the TV on or walk through . . . [the mall] to realize all you don't have. I don't like going to . . . [the mall] because I didn't realize all the things I wanted until I got there. Life's good and then I see there is an even better, bigger thing that I could have if I'd just buy it. . . . To learn to be content is a great advantage and great gain in life. And to not always be living wanting more or bigger or faster or better, but to learn to be content and to count your blessings is a great blessing in journeying through life.

(Grant C. Anderson, Orem Institute Devotional, 24 Feb. 2006)

Alma 27 • PEOPLE OF AMMON

From the Nephite sphere, too, we find that there were clear-cut tribal distinctions. For example, though the Anti-Nephi-Lehies (people of Ammon) were con-verted to the Nephite religion and came to live with the Nephites, yet they were not left to intermingle with the rest of the people. Rather, they were given a special terri-tory named Jershon (see Alma 27). That they remained separate from the main Nephite body is indicated by the statement that they continued to be called by the name of their mentor, Ammon, "ever after" (Alma 27:26–27).

Though the sons of the Ammonites, who fought under Helaman in the great war, called themselves by the more general term of Nephites (see Alma 53:16), they nevertheless appear to have been segregated from the main Nephite army. Helaman noted that his two thousand Ammonite warriors "were descendants of Laman, who was the eldest son of our father Lehi" (Alma 56:3). This implies that none of them was descended from Lemuel or the sons of Ishmael, who also formed the Lamanite league. It is true that Helaman notes that his two thousand were joined "to the army of Antipus" (Alma 56:10), but they were kept as a separate subunit. Later, six thousand replacement troops were sent from the land of Zarahemla "besides sixty of the sons of the Ammonites who had come to join their brethren, my little band of two thousand" (Alma 57:6). Clearly the Ammonites were united to Helaman's army and did not mingle with the other Nephites. This is further demonstrated by the fact that he then wrote of "my little band of two thousand and sixty" (Alma 37:19–20).

(John A. Tvedines, *Warfare in the Book of Mormon*, ed. by Stephen D. Ricks and William J. Hamblin [Salt Lake City: Deseret Book, 1990], 303)

Alma 27:9 • SLAVERY

He who would be no slave must consent to have no slave. Those who deny freedom to others deserve it not for themselves.

(Abraham Lincoln; as quoted in Paul Selby, *Lincoln's Life Stories and Speeches* [Chicago: Thompson and Thomas, 1902], 258)

Alma 27:22, 26 • JERSHON

Jershon, for instance, designates a place that was given to the people of Anti-Nephi-Lehi as a "land . . . for an inheritance" (Alma 27:22). In Hebrew, *Jershon* means "a place of inheritance." Joseph Smith simply would not have known this in the late 1820s.

(Daniel C. Peterson, *Ensign*, Jan. 2000 [Salt Lake City: The Church of Jesus Christ of Latter-day Saints, 2000], 22)

Alma 27:27 • PERFECTLY HONEST

(Refer in this text to 4 Nephi 1:2.)

Perhaps if we analyze some of the reasons people lie, we can avoid or overcome this vicious snare.

Sometimes we deceive and lie to avoid personal embarrassment. I recently heard of a young woman who had been released from her employment because of dishonesty. When she applied for another job, she told the prospective employer that her former boss had a family member he wanted to put in her place. She probably told her friends and family members the same story to avoid mortification.

Financial setbacks may be explained to others with untruths. Or have you ever heard someone say, "I was just too busy to get the job done," when, in truth, he had forgotten? Others use dishonesty to delay, to gain advantage, to impress, to flatter, or to destroy.

Consciously or unconsciously some people lie to destroy others. Jealousy or feelings of inferiority may cause us to degrade another's habits or character. Have you watched an overly ambitious person turn on false flattery for his own gain?

Lies are often excuses for lack of courage. Sometimes lies are nothing more than excuses for poor performance. Usually one lie or deception has to be covered by another. Lies cannot stand alone. Each one must continually be supported by more and more of its own kind.

(Marvin J. Ashton, in Conference Report, Apr. 1982 [Salt Lake City: The Church of Jesus Christ of Latter-day Saints, 1982], 11)

In our day, those found in dishonesty aren't put to death, but something within them dies. Conscience chokes, character withers, self-respect vanishes, integrity dies. How cheaply some men and women sell their good names! . . .

It is surely neither coincidence nor happenstance that five of the Ten Commandments deal essentially with honesty in its broadest sense. "Thou shalt not kill" (Exodus 20:13). . . . "Thou shalt not steal" (Exodus 20:15). . . . "Thou shalt not commit adultery" (Exodus 20:14). . . . "Thou shalt not bear false witness against thy neighbour" (Exodus 20:16). . . . "Thou shalt not covet thy neighbour's house, thou shalt not covet thy neighbour's wife, nor his manservant, nor his maidservant, nor his ox, nor his ass, nor any thing that is thy neighbour's" (Exodus 20:17). . . .

Why is honesty so vital? Because where honesty and integrity are present, other virtues follow. And conversely, where there are serious breaches of integrity, they are almost always accompanied by other moral lapses.

(Gordon B. Hinckley, *Standing for Something* [New York: Times Books, 2000], 13, 20–21, 23, 25)

In 1955, after my freshman year of college, I spent the summer working at the newly opened Jackson Lake Lodge, located in Moran, Wyoming. My mode of transportation was a 14-year-old 1941 Hudson automobile that should have received its burial 10 years earlier. Among the car's other identifying traits, the floorboards had rusted so badly that, if not for a piece of plywood, I could have literally dragged my feet on the highway. The positive is that unlike most 14-year-old cars in this time period, it used no oil—lots of water in the radiator, but no oil. I could never figure out where the water went and why the oil continually got thinner and thinner and clearer and clearer.

In preparation for the 185-mile (298-km) drive home at the end of the summer, I took the car to the only mechanic in Moran. After a quick analysis, the mechanic explained that the engine block was cracked and was leaking water into the oil. That explained the water and oil mystery. I wondered if I could get the water to leak into the gas tank; I would get better gasoline mileage.

Now the confession: after the miracle of arriving home, my father came out and happily greeted me. After a hug and a few pleasantries, he looked into the backseat of the car and saw three Jackson Lake Lodge towels—the kind you cannot buy. With a disappointed look he merely said, "I expected more of you." I hadn't thought that what I had done was all that wrong. To me these towels were but a symbol of a full summer's work at a luxury hotel, a rite of passage. Nevertheless, by taking them I felt I had lost the trust and confidence of my father, and I was devastated.

The following weekend I adjusted the plywood floorboard in my car, filled the radiator with water, and began the 370-mile (595-km) round trip back to Jackson Lake Lodge to return three towels. My father never asked why I was returning to the lodge, and I never explained. It just didn't need to be said. This was an expensive and painful lesson on honesty that has stayed with me throughout my life. . . .

Some 30 years ago, while working in the corporate world, some business associates and I were passing through O'Hare Airport in Chicago, Illinois. One of these men had just sold his company for tens of millions of dollars—in other words, he was not poor.

As we were passing a newspaper vending machine, this individual put a quarter in the machine, opened the door to the stack of papers inside the machine, and began dispersing unpaid-for newspapers to each of us. When he handed me a newspaper, I put a quarter in the machine and, trying not to offend but to make a point, jokingly said, "Jim, for 25 cents I can maintain my integrity. A dollar, questionable, but 25 cents—no, not for 25 cents." You see, I remembered well the experience of three towels and a broken-down 1941 Hudson. A few minutes later we passed the same newspaper vending machine. I noticed that Jim had broken away from our group and was stuffing quarters in the vending machine. . . .

My prayer is that as Latter-day Saints, we will be known as among the most honest people in the world. And it might be said of us as it was of the people of Anti-Nephi-Lehi that we are "perfectly honest and upright in all things; and . . . firm in the faith of Christ, even unto the end" (Alma 27:27).

(Richard C. Edgley, *Ensign*, Nov. 2006 [Salt Lake City: The Church of Jesus Christ of Latter-day Saints, 2006], 72–74)

Alma 27:28; 28:4–5, 11–12; 30:2 • MOURNING DEATH
(Refer in this text to Mosiah 16:8–9.)

To those who mourn we speak comfort. Know that your Savior is well acquainted with grief. He who notes the sparrow's fall is aware of you and desires to comfort and bless you. Turn to Him and lay your burden at His feet.

(Ezra Taft Benson, "First Presidency Christmas Message," *Church News*, 15 Dec. 1985, 3)

The only way to take sorrow out of death is to take love out of life. . . . As seedlings of God, we barely blossom on earth; we fully flower in heaven. . . . Think of the alternative [to death]. If all sixty-nine billion people who have ever lived on earth were still here, imagine the traffic jam! . . . Scriptures teach that death is essential to happiness: [Alma 42:8; 2 Ne. 9:6]. Our limited perspective would be enlarged if we could witness the reunion on the other side of the veil, when doors of death open to those returning home. . . . We need not look upon death as an enemy. . . . I know by experiences too sacred to relate that those who have gone before are not strangers to leaders of this Church. To us and to you, our loved ones may be just as close as the next room—separated only by the doors of death.

(Russell M. Nelson, *Ensign*, May 1992 [Salt Lake City: The Church of Jesus Christ of Latter-day Saints, 1992], 72–74)

More painful to me are the thoughts of annihilation than death. If I have no expectation of seeing my father, mother, brothers, sisters and friends again, my heart would burst in a moment, and I should go down to my grave. The expectation of seeing my friends in the morning of the resurrection cheers my soul and makes me bear up against the evils of life. It is like they're taking a long journey, and on their return we meet them with increased joy.

(*Teachings of the Prophet Joseph Smith*, comp. by Joseph Fielding Smith [Salt Lake City: Deseret Book, 1976], 296)

I once attended a funeral service with Elder M. Russell Ballard. A statement he made there has remained with me to this day. He said, "Life isn't over for a Latter-day Saint until he or she is safely dead, with their testimony still burning brightly." "Safely dead"—what a challenging concept. Brothers and sisters, we will not be safe until we have given our hearts to the Lord—until we have learned to do what we have promised.

(F. Burton Howard, *Ensign*, May 1996 [Salt Lake City: The Church of Jesus Christ of Latter-day Saints, 1996], 28)

I have thought about the lessons taught by death—particularly the death of a loved one. The first lesson is that life is short whether one dies at seventeen or at eighty. . . . Second, death reminds us that there is a spirit in man. . . . Another lesson taught by death concerns the importance of eternal families. Just as there are parents to greet a newborn on earth, the scriptures teach that caring family members greet the spirits in paradise and assist them in the adjustments to a new life (see Gen. 25:8; 35:29; 49:33). . . . A fourth lesson, and perhaps the most important, concerns the purpose of life. . . . Death, even if accidental, must be part of the plan. . . . Death teaches that we do not experience a fulness of joy in mortality and that everlasting joy can be achieved only with the assistance of the Master (see D&C 93:33–34).

(Merrill J. Bateman, *Ensign*, May 1995 [Salt Lake City: The Church of Jesus Christ of Latter-day Saints, 1995], 13)

―――――――

Mourning for the righteous dead springs from the ignorance and weakness that are planted within the mortal tabernacle. . . . No matter what pain we suffer, no matter what we pass through, we cling to our mother earth, and dislike to have any of her children leave us. We . . . do not like to part with each other; but could we have knowledge and see into eternity, if we were perfectly free from the weakness, blindness, and lethargy with which we are clothed in the flesh, we should have no disposition to weep or mourn. . . . It is a matter of rejoicing more than the day of his birth.

(*Discourses of Brigham Young*, comp. by John A. Widtsoe [Salt Lake City: Deseret Book, 1954], 370–371)

―――――――

Grief is the natural by-product of love. One cannot selflessly love another person and not grieve at his suffering or eventual death. The only way to avoid the grief would be to not experience the love; and it is love that gives life its richness and meaning. Hence, what a grieving parent can expect to receive from the Lord in response to earnest supplication may not necessarily be an elimination of grief so much as a sweet reassurance that, whatever his or her circumstances, one's child is in the tender care of a loving Heavenly Father.

(Lance B. Wickman, in Conference Report, Oct. 2002 [Salt Lake City: The Church of Jesus Christ of Latter-day Saints, 2002], 31–32)

Alma 29:1–2 • MISSIONARY WORK
(Refer in this text to Alma 17:2–5.)

We must be willing to release the death grip which we have on things, which have become as a security blanket in our lives. Count the many hundreds of needed missionary couples who would be serving in the field if that firm grip on the familiarities of home and of children and grandchildren could be loosened. The Lord is prepared to perform the miracle that will follow, which miracle is that both they and you will survive, even grow, with an eighteen-month separation.

(Graham W. Doxey, in Conference Report, Oct. 1991 [Salt Lake City: The Church of Jesus Christ of Latter-day Saints, 1991], 34)

―――――――

In addition to the need for more young men and women to serve, there is an urgent need for couples. Each time we visit a mission, the universal request is for more couples. The need is great for mature couples who are financially able, possessing strong testimonies, and with reasonably good health. Their entry into the mission field adds strength and maturity to our missionary effort. . . . Is this not the special time of decision for all of you . . . special mature older couples? Have you ever sat down and contemplated what kind of entries you will prepare for your life's history? Will yours be one comprised of slides and videos of worldly acquisitions of boats and motor homes, of travel and entertainment for personal gratification and amusement? Or will your history express the joy you have experienced in preaching and teaching the message of our Lord and Savior to all who would hear your voice?

(Angel Abrea, *Ensign*, May 1992 [Salt Lake City: The Church of Jesus Christ of Latter-day Saints, 1992], 24–25)

―――――――

The cause to which I speak is of missionary work as couples. . . . There is a need, not to leave homes forever, but for a time—then return and reap the rich harvest of the faithful labor. Your children and grandchildren will be blessed. . . . President Harold B. Lee taught the principle that only as we make ourselves totally available are we worthy disciples of Christ and obtain another promise that reaches beyond us. We worry and ache and pain over family members who have erred. The thirty-first section of the Doctrine and Covenants provides a great key in verse five: "Therefore, thrust in your sickle with all your soul, and your sins are forgiven you, and you shall be laden with sheaves upon your back, for the laborer is worthy of his hire. Wherefore, your family shall live." . . . The promise is sure, "Wherefore, your family shall live." Blessings will come to our wayward or wandering children, even those who are married and have children of their own. . . . As we come to the latter years of life, we come to a mature spiritual understanding. What better way have we to prepare to meet our God than to serve a mission when the autumn and winter of life is upon us?

(Vaughn J. Featherstone, *Ensign*, May 1992 [Salt Lake City: The Church of Jesus Christ of Latter-day Saints, 1992], 42–44)

―――――――

There is an urgent need in the Church today for missionary couples, not to go first-contacting or teaching the discussions, unless you want to do so, but for meaningful missionary service in all of the activities of the Church throughout the world. There is far greater flexibility in the service opportunities of couples than for single elders or sisters. In consultation with your bishop, you can indicate your own preferences for missionary service. We must train a growing number of fathers and mothers and priesthood and auxiliary leaders throughout the world who want very much to serve the Lord but simply do not know how to do it. You can help them as a leadership missionary couple. You can serve in temples, family history, educational and medical activities, welfare service projects, public affairs, and visitors' centers. . . . Your children and grandchildren will be positively influenced for good as witnessed by many couples who have honorably served, some on their third, fourth, or fifth mission. Don't wait to be asked. I invite each of you to come forth to participate some way in the glorious and varied opportunities for missionary service. . . .

(Richard G. Scott, *Ensign*, Nov. 1997 [Salt Lake City: The Church of Jesus Christ of Latter-day Saints, 1997], 36–37)

———

There is no other labor in all the world that brings to a human heart, judging from my own personal experience, more joy, peace and serenity than proclaiming the gospel of the Lord Jesus Christ. I remember that while I was laboring in Japan [after two years] . . . I received a cable: "Come home on the first vessel." When I arrived home President Smith told me that they had decided to send me to Europe [for at least one year] to succeed Brother Lyman. When I went into his office and bade him goodbye, and said, "I will see you in a year," he said, "We have decided to make it a year and a half." I said, "Multiply it by two and say nothing about it, and it will please me," and that is exactly what he did. I was there a little over three years, and never have I had sweeter joy, more genuine satisfaction in my life than during those three years, when I had no thought except the spreading of the gospel of the Lord Jesus Christ.

(Heber J. Grant, in Conference Report, Oct. 1926 [Salt Lake City: The Church of Jesus Christ of Latter-day Saints, 1926], 4)

———

I recall my own mission call to Argentina. After sharing the excitement of my call with my parents, I sought out my mentor, who was not a member of the Church, a former U.S. senator, to share the news of my call with him. He was not impressed, let me know in no uncertain terms that if I insisted on serving a mission, upon my return all the good jobs would be taken and I would never amount to anything. I was disappointed,

but realized that he saw my future only as the world perceives. Years later I realized that my mission had prioritized my life toward family, service, and gospel principles. As an added bonus, I was far ahead of most of my former classmates in worldly achievements. . . . The call to missionary service rarely comes when it is convenient or easy to serve.

(Gardner H. Russell, *Ensign*, Nov. 1991 [Salt Lake City: The Church of Jesus Christ of Latter-day Saints, 1991], 82)

———

I am grateful to bishops who helped me as a young man prepare to receive the Melchizedek Priesthood. One patient, loving bishop helped me understand that missionary service was far more important than perfecting my golf game, which had been the chief ambition of my teen years.

(H. David Burton, *Ensign*, May 1993 [Salt Lake City: The Church of Jesus Christ of Latter-day Saints, 1993], 47)

———

Truly effective missionaries have many talents, varied and beautiful, but one quality they all seem to have is the ability to stick with their commitments—that is, the power to do what they agree to do. They tell themselves to get up in the morning, on time, and do it. They don't depend on companions, district leaders, or anyone else. They commit to the mission president that they will follow the gospel study program every morning and not run out of steam in a few days. They understand that the Lord has called them to teach and testify, baptize and build the kingdom in His name, and they are happily at their work.

(L. Aldin Porter, *Ensign*, May 1992 [Salt Lake City: The Church of Jesus Christ of Latter-day Saints, 1992], 45)

———

I like to refer to missionary efforts as sharing the gospel. The word *sharing* affirms that we have something extraordinarily valuable and desire to give it to others for their benefit and blessing.

The most effective missionaries, member and full-time, always act out of love. I learned this lesson as a young man. I was assigned to visit a less-active member, a successful professional many years older than I. Looking back on my actions, I realize that I had very little loving concern for the man I visited. I acted out of duty, with a desire to report 100 percent on my home teaching. One evening, close to the end of a month, I phoned to ask if my companion and I could come right over and visit him. His chastening reply taught me an unforgettable lesson.

"No, I don't believe I want you to come over this evening," he said. "I'm tired. I've already dressed for bed. I am reading, and I am just not willing to be interrupted so that you can report 100 percent on your home teaching this month." That reply still stings me because I knew he had sensed my selfish motivation.

I hope no person we approach with an invitation to hear the message of the restored gospel feels that we are acting out of any reason other than a genuine love for them and an unselfish desire to share something we know to be precious.

(Dallin H. Oaks, *Ensign*, Nov. 2001 [Salt Lake City: The Church of Jesus Christ of Latter-day Saints, 2001], 8)

———————

The single most important thing you can do to prepare for a call to serve is to *become* a missionary long before you *go* on a mission. Please notice . . . I emphasized *becoming* rather than *going*. . . .

The issue is not going on a mission; rather, the issue is becoming a missionary and serving throughout our entire life with all of our heart, might, mind, and strength. It is possible for a young man to *go* on a mission and not *become* a missionary, and this is not what the Lord requires or what the Church needs.

My earnest hope for each of you young men is that you will not simply go on a mission—but that you will become missionaries long before you submit your mission papers, long before you receive a call to serve, long before you are set apart by your stake president, and long before you enter the MTC. . . .

You will not suddenly or magically be transformed into a prepared and obedient missionary on the day you walk through the front door of the Missionary Training Center. What you have become in the days and months and years prior to your missionary service is what you will be in the MTC. . . .

A key element of raising the bar includes working to become a missionary before going on a mission.

(David A. Bednar, *Ensign*, Nov. 2005 [Salt Lake City: The Church of Jesus Christ of Latter-day Saints, 2005], 45–47)

———————

I think the first time I ever attended a meeting in this building was at the funeral of my cousin, Carter Sessions, who died in the Northwestern States Mission. . . . When we go into the mission field we offer our lives, and sometimes the offer is accepted. In that instance the offer was accepted. . . .

On one of my visits to New Zealand I went to a conference. . . . The mission president called on a new missionary to get up and speak, and that boy was scared. I knew just how he felt because I had had the same experi-

ence years before. He stood up there, and he tried to say something, but he couldn't get it out. Now, some people would have said, "Why on earth did they ever send a man like that out into the mission field?" But do you know what the old native said to me sitting next to me? He whispered in my ear, "Won't he be giving us the devil in six months from now?" Why, he could see that boy. He was thrilled with that lad up there trying to express himself because he could see the end from the beginning. He could see the architect's plan, and he could see the contractor's work, the great designer's influence in building that young man to be a servant of God.

(*Matthew Cowley Speaks* [Salt Lake City: Deseret Book, 1954], 360–361)

———————

A young man recently shared with me how much he had learned from his perseverance as a missionary. I draw from his experience some of the things you can learn that would bring opportunities and blessings to you:

1. How to organize and use time wisely
2. The importance of hard work—that you reap what you sow
3. Leadership skills
4. People skills
5. The value of gospel study
6. Respect for authority
7. The importance of prayer
8. Humility and dependence on the Lord

(James E. Faust, *Ensign*, May 2005 [Salt Lake City: The Church of Jesus Christ of Latter-day Saints, 2005], 51)

———————

With reference to young women, the President said: "There has been some misunderstanding of earlier counsel regarding single sisters serving as missionaries. We need some young women. They perform a remarkable work. They can get in homes where the elders cannot. But it should be kept in mind that young sisters are not under obligation to go on missions. They should not feel that they have a duty comparable to that of young men, but some will wish to go" ("To the Bishops of the Church," Worldwide Leadership Training Meeting, June 19, 2004, 27).

(M. Russell Ballard, "One More," *Ensign*, May 2005 [Salt Lake City: The Church of Jesus Christ of Latter-day Saints, 2005], 70)

———————

All that I now hold dear in life began to mature in the mission field. Had I not been encouraged to be a missionary, I would not have the eternal companion or precious family I dearly love. I am confident that I would not have had the exceptional professional opportunities that stretched my every capacity. I am certain that I would not have received the sacred callings with opportunities to serve for which I will be eternally grateful. My life has been richly blessed beyond measure because I served a mission.

Now can you understand why I am so anxious to motivate every one of you young men to be a worthy missionary? . . .

I urge you not to pray to know whether you should go; rather, ask the Lord to guide you in whatever may be necessary to become a worthy, empowered full-time missionary. You will never regret serving a mission, but you most probably will regret not serving if that is your choice.

(Richard G. Scott, *Ensign*, May 2006 [Salt Lake City: The Church of Jesus Christ of Latter-day Saints, 2006], 89–90)

Alma 29:1–9 • BECOMING SPIRITUALLY CONTENT

In just a few words, a major insight came to the conscientious and the converted through Alma: "For I ought to be content with the things which the Lord hath allotted unto me" (Alma 29:3). However, just prior, Alma urgently desired to be the "trump of God" so that he might "shake the earth" (Alma 29:1). But not because of ego; in fact, Alma wanted to declare repentance and the plan of redemption to all mankind so that there might be no more human sorrow (see Alma 29:2). Yet Alma's contentment rested on the reality that God finally allots to us according to our wills (see Alma 29:4). What could be more fair?

Thus becoming content with his calling, Alma then meekly hoped to be an instrument to help save some soul (see Alma 29:9). A significant spiritual journey is thus reflected in but nine soliloquy-like verses.

The same contentment awaits us if our own desires can be worked through and aligned.

(Neal A. Maxwell, in Conference Report, Apr. 2000 [Salt Lake City: The Church of Jesus Christ of Latter-day Saints, 2000], 89–90)

A willingness to sacrifice all we possess in the work of the Lord is surely a strength. In fact, it is a covenant we make in sacred places. But even this strength can bring us down if we fail to confine our sacrifices to those things the Lord and his leaders have asked of us at this time. We should say with Alma, "Why should I desire more than to perform the work to which I have been called?" (Alma 29:6). Persons who consider it insufficient to pay their tithes and offerings and to work in the positions to which they have been called can easily be led astray by cultist groups and other bizarre outlets for their willingness to sacrifice.

(Dallin H. Oaks, *With Full Purpose of Heart* [Salt Lake City: Deseret Book, 2002], 169)

The Lord knows our circumstances and the intents of our hearts, and surely the talents and gifts He has given us. He is able to gauge perfectly how we have performed within what is allotted to us, including by lifting up some of the many surrounding hands that hang down. Thus, yearning for expanded opportunities while failing to use those at hand is bad form spiritually. . . .

I have a special grand-daughter, Anna Josephine, who was born without a left hand. The other day a conversation was overheard between Anna Jo, almost five, and her cousin Talmage, three. Talmage said reassuringly as they played together, "Anna Jo, when you grow up you will have five fingers." Anna Jo said, "No, Talmage, when I grow up I won't have five fingers, but when I get to heaven I will have a hand."

(Neal A. Maxwell, in Conference Report, Apr. 2000 [Salt Lake City: The Church of Jesus Christ of Latter-day Saints, 2000], 92–93)

When I arrived in Holland on my first mission I was very disappointed at being assigned to serve as secretary of the Mission. I had looked forward for years to the time I would be a missionary, and I had a strong desire to preach the gospel. Whenever the other missionaries went out I chafed at the restraint of having to stay in and do secretarial work. I wanted to be out actively bearing witness to the truth. It bothered me so much that the Lord blessed me with a dream which made me feel satisfied to do the work I had been assigned.

I dreamed that I was keeping books for my father in his implement and lumber business. I kept pleading with my father to let me leave because I wanted to go outside and work as a regular laborer. Finally, Father gave his consent and I took the train for Salt Lake. Upon my arrival I was met by a friend who took me and introduced me to the foreman of a section gang. . . . We had gone but a short distance when one of the men asked me what I had been doing. When I told him I had been keeping books, he asked me how much I had been doing. When I told him, he replied, "You are foolish. If I could keep books, I wouldn't be out here. Anyone can do this, but not everyone can keep books."

With that I awakened. . . . This satisfied me so that I was content to keep the books, realizing I was doing what I was needed to do. Later, when I was given the responsibility of presiding over that Mission, I understood all the office procedures which was a great help to me in my work.

(LeGrand Richards, *Just to Illustrate* [Salt Lake City: Bookcraft, 1961], 89–90)

Alma 29:3, 6–8 • OUR ALLOTMENT

We had our own free agency in our pre-mortal existence, and whatever we are today is likely the result of that which we willed to be heretofore. We unquestionably knew before we elected to come to this earth the conditions under which we would here exist. . . . I have a conviction deep down in my heart that we are exactly what we should be, each one of us, except as we may have altered that pattern by deviating from the laws of God here in mortality.

(Henry D. Moyle, in Conference Report, Oct. 1952 [Salt Lake City: The Church of Jesus Christ of Latter-day Saints, 1952], 71–72)

Alma 29:4 • GRANTED UNTO MEN ACCORDING TO THEIR DESIRE

Desire denotes a real longing or craving. Hence righteous desires are much more than passive preferences or fleeting feelings. Of course our genes, circumstances, and environments matter very much, and they shape us significantly. Yet there remains an inner zone in which we are sovereign, unless we abdicate. In this zone lies the essence of our individuality and our personal accountability. . . . Mostly, brothers and sisters, we become the victims of our own wrong desires. . . . Like it or not, therefore, reality requires that we acknowledge our responsibility for our desires. . . . Righteous desires need to be relentless, therefore, because, said President Brigham Young, "the men and women, who desire to obtain seats in the celestial kingdom will find that they must battle every day" (*Journal of Discourses* 11:14). Therefore, true Christian soldiers are more than weekend warriors. . . . Some of our present desires, therefore, need to be diminished and then finally dissolved.

(Neal A. Maxwell, *Ensign*, Nov. 1996 [Salt Lake City: The Church of Jesus Christ of Latter-day Saints, 1996], 21–22)

———

It was our privilege . . . to be living across the street from Elder F. Enzio Busche, now an emeritus Seventy, and his wife. One day Elder Busche taught our high priests quorum, and he cited a scripture in the book of Alma where Alma longs to have the voice of an angel. Then Alma immediately repents of those feelings and in verse four makes a remarkable statement. He suggests that we have to be careful what we desire, for the Lord grants unto us the desires of our heart. And then came what was to me almost a stunning statement: "Whether they be unto salvation or unto destruction." God will grant unto us, according to our will, the things which we desire (see Alma 29:1–5).

I went home that day—and it's not that I felt any of my desires were wrong—but in that moment I realized that those desires were *mine*. That day I began to

try to let the Lord know that what I'd like to do is fulfill *His* desires. Even then, I thought I really meant it, but I came to know that that's an easy thing to say and a difficult thing to do. As Elder Maxwell said yesterday, only when we truly yield our hearts to God can He begin to accelerate the purification and the sanctification and the perfecting process (see Hel. 3:35).

(Gerald N. Lund, *Ensign*, May 2002 [Salt Lake City: The Church of Jesus Christ of Latter-day Saints, 2002], 85)

Alma 29:8 • ALL NATIONS TAUGHT OF THEIR OWN NATION

Since about 92% of all missionaries in the field are Americans, we must call to the attention of all members in other lands that we need far more local missionaries. Through Alma the Lord said [Alma 29:8]. This scripture indicates, brethren, that every nation is to furnish its own missionaries and we expect that to follow. . . . It is all nations of their nation and tongue. We need far more, thousands—more Brazilians to preach in Brazil in Portuguese; thousands more Mexicans to preach in Spanish—Chileans, Peruvians, Bolivians, Colombians, Argentines, Venezuelans—Spanish to proselyte in Spanish—hundreds more of local men to preach in Scandinavian, German, French, Filipino, Indian and all nationalities in all tongues and nations. . . . Since the local men can better represent their own people without problems of language, visas, and other rights and services, we need soon hundreds of more young men of every race and nation.

(Spencer W. Kimball, Regional Representatives Seminar, Sept. 1977, 17)

———

We believe that Joseph Smith was called by God as the prophet to inaugurate this present era, known as "the dispensation of the fulness of times" (see Eph. 1:10; D&C 112:30; 121:31; 124:41; 128:18, 20; 138:48). . . . This modern dispensation of which I speak fulfills the biblical promise of a "restitution of all things (Acts 3:21; see also Rev. 14:6–7). It also fulfills another scriptural promise that "the Lord doth grant unto all nations, of their own nation and tongue, to teach his word" (Alma 29:8).

(Russell M. Nelson, *Ensign*, Nov. 1993 [Salt Lake City: The Church of Jesus Christ of Latter-day Saints, 1993], 104)

Alma 29:10–12 • REMEMBER
(Refer in this text to Helaman 5:5–14.)

The Book of Mormon uses terms related to *remembering* and *forgetting* well over two hundred times. . . .

The first thing to note is that "ways of remembrance" does not mean simply inner reflections, or merely awareness of or curiosity about the past, or even detailed information to be recalled. True, in a number of places the idea of remembrance in the Book of Mormon seems to carry the meaning of recalling information about the past (see, for example, Ether 4:16; Alma 33:3). More commonly, however, remembrance refers to action.

The call to remember is often a passionate plea to see God's hand in delivering his people from bondage and captivity.

(Louis Midgley, *Rediscovering the Book of Mormon*, ed. by John L. Sorenson and Melvin J. Thorne [Salt Lake City: Deseret Book, 1991], 168–169)

Alma 30:6 • ANTICHRIST

Good family life ceases when people refuse to have children as God commanded them to do, but make of marriage a sensual convenience.

The destruction of good family life is a sheer violation of the laws of God, and is one of the worst forms of anti-Christ. Behavior which eliminates good family life is nothing short of suicidal.

(Mark E. Petersen, *Family Power!* [Salt Lake City: Bookcraft, 1981], 3)

———

The Book of Mormon exposes the enemies of Christ. . . . It fortifies the humble followers of Christ against the evil designs, strategies, and doctrines of the devil in our day. The type of apostates in the Book of Mormon is similar to the type we have today. *God, with his infinite foreknowledge, so molded the Book of Mormon that we might see the error and know how to combat false educational, political, religious, and philosophical concepts of our time.*

(Ezra Taft Benson, *A Witness and a Warning* [Salt Lake City: Deseret Book, 1988], 3)

———

An antichrist is an opponent of Christ. He is one who offers salvation to men on some other terms than those laid down by Christ.

(Bruce R. McConkie, *Mormon Doctrine* [Salt Lake City: Bookcraft, 1966], 39)

———

I bless you with increased discernment to judge between Christ and anti-Christ. I bless you with increased power to do good and to resist evil. I bless you with increased understanding of the Book of Mormon. I promise you that from this moment forward, if we will daily sup from its pages and abide by its precepts, God will pour out upon each child of Zion and the Church a blessing hitherto unknown.

(Ezra Taft Benson, *Ensign*, May 1986 [Salt Lake City: The Church of Jesus Christ of Latter-day Saints, 1986], 78)

———

We're facing the same situation today in the world with anti-Christs as we did with Satan in the preexistence.

(G. Homer Durham, *N. Eldon Tanner: His Life and Service* [Salt Lake City: Deseret Book, 1982], 316)

———

Here we find an interesting definition of an anti-Christ: one who defies and denies the prophecies concerning the coming of Christ. This definition would, of course, pertain primarily to those who lived before the meridian of time. In our day we would speak of an anti-Christ as one who denies the divine birth of Jesus; who downplays the significance of his teachings; who claims that Jesus' sufferings, death, and resurrection have no significance for mankind. Many in this dispensation have been seduced into the damnable heresy that Jesus was merely a good man, a brilliant speaker, and a loving and tender example of mercy and forgiveness—these things alone.

(Joseph Fielding Smith and Robert L. Millet, *Doctrinal Commentary on the Book of Mormon* [Salt Lake City: Bookcraft, 1991], 3:201)

———

Thus Korihor's life teaches us that having the truths of the gospel and being a covenant servant of Christ are in nowise guarantees of salvation. We are also reminded that the most powerful opposition to the work of the Savior on this earth comes from those who know the truth and then deliberately turn from it and seek to destroy others. . . .

In every generation Korihor takes his toll of those who will not get themselves founded on the Rock.

(Chauncey C. Riddle, *The Book of Mormon: It Begins with a Family* [Salt Lake City: Deseret Book, 1983] 134, 142)

ALMA 30:10 • CAPITAL PUNISHMENT
(Refer in this text to Alma 1:14.)

Alma 30:12–28 • THE NINE DOCTRINES OF KORIHOR, AN ANTI-CHRIST
(1) Alma 30:12; (2) Alma 30:13–14; (3) Alma 30:15 [see also Jacob 7:7]; (4) Alma 30:16–17; (5) Alma 30:17; (6) Alma 30:17; (7) Alma 30:18; (8) Alma 30:24 [see also Moses 5:33]; (9) Alma 30:28

One of Satan's frequently used deceptions is the notion that the commandments of God are meant to restrict freedom and limit happiness. Young people especially sometimes feel that the standards of the Lord are like fences and chains, blocking them from those activities that seem most enjoyable in life. But exactly the opposite is true. The gospel plan is the plan by which men are brought to a fulness of joy. The gospel principles are the steps and guidelines which will help us find true happiness and joy.

(*Teachings of Ezra Taft Benson* [Salt Lake City: Bookcraft, 1988], 357)

———————

Societies structured by situational ethics—the belief that all truths are relative—create a moral environment defined by undistinguished shades of gray.

(Richard B. Wirthlin, *Ensign*, Nov. 1997 [Salt Lake City: The Church of Jesus Christ of Latter-day Saints, 1997], 9)

———————

Korihor was arguing, as men and women have falsely argued from the beginning of time, that to take counsel from the servants of God is to surrender God-given rights of independence. But the argument is false because it misrepresents reality. When we reject the counsel which comes from God, we do not choose to be independent of outside influence. We choose another influence. We reject the protection of a perfectly loving, all-powerful, all-knowing Father in Heaven, whose whole purpose, as that of His Beloved Son, is to give us eternal life, to give us all that He has, and to bring us home again in families to the arms of His love. In rejecting His counsel, we choose the influence of another power, whose purpose is to make us miserable and whose motive is hatred. We have moral agency as a gift of God. Rather than the right to choose to be free of influence, it is the inalienable right to submit ourselves to whichever of those powers we choose.

(Henry B. Eyring, *Ensign*, May 1997 [Salt Lake City: The Church of Jesus Christ of Latter-day Saints, 1997], 25)

———————

It is a real travesty today when we hear the voices of the atheist, the godless, and the anti-Christ who would deny us the right of public expression of our worship of the Master. First they moved against the long-established institution of prayer in our public schools. They would remove any vestige of Christianity or worship of the Savior of mankind in our public gatherings; they would remove the "In God We Trust" insignia from our nation's emblems and seals and from our national coins. The latest move of these anti-Christs would prohibit our own children from singing the beautiful and inspiring Christmas carols, relating to the Savior's birth or divinity, or "the heavenly angels singing" from our public schools.

(*Teachings of Spencer W. Kimball*, ed. by Edward L. Kimball [Salt Lake City: Bookcraft, 1982], 411–412)

———————

Isn't it interesting that these groups consider it "freedom of expression" to profane the Lord's name and use obscenities, but oppose prayer in public places. These groups combat public faith and prayer yet uphold the right of anyone to have an abortion.

(Joseph B. Wirthlin, *Ensign*, Mar. 1993 [Salt Lake City: The Church of Jesus Christ of Latter-day Saints, 1993], 72)

———————

Some of the world's most highly talented individuals believe, self-servingly, that mortals "[fare] in this life," prosper, and conquer according to their "genius" and strength (Alma 30:17). A few freewheelers even believe that whatsoever people do is "no crime," hurrying on to pleasure because they believe "when a man was dead, that was the end thereof" (Alma 30:17–18). Such selfish views are clearly not a climate in which the second commandment flourishes. . . . Pride is then mistaken for genuine individuality.

(Neal A. Maxwell, *Whom the Lord Loveth* [Salt Lake City: Deseret Book, 2003], 55–56)

———————

For a good while, there has been going on in this nation a process that I have termed the secularization of America. The single most substantial factor in the degeneration of the values and morals of our society is that we as a nation are forsaking the Almighty, and I fear that He will begin to forsake us. We are shutting the door against the God whose sons and daughters we are.

I have heard Margaret Thatcher, former Prime Minister of Great Britain, say on more than one occasion, "You use the name of Deity in the Declaration of Independence and in the Constitution of the United States, and yet you cannot use it in the schoolroom." Her words are a rebuke and an indictment of America. . . .

Several years ago, the state of New Jersey passed a law banishing the mention of God from state courtroom oaths. Following this action by the New Jersey legislature, a county judge decided to ban Bibles for such oaths "because you-know-Who is mentioned inside." And in recent years, the Boy Scouts of America have been attacked because of the language in the Scout Oath: "On my honor, I will do my best to do my duty to God and my country."

Contrast such attitudes with that of George Washington, expressed more than two hundred years ago in his First Inaugural Address:

"It would be peculiarly improper to omit, in

this first official act, my fervent supplications to that Almighty Being, who rules over the universe, who presides in the councils of nations, and whose providential aids can supply every human defect, that His benediction may consecrate to the liberties and happiness of the people of the United States a government instituted by themselves for these essential purposes."

People who carry in their hearts a strong conviction concerning the living reality of the Almighty and their accountability to Him for what they do with their lives are far less likely to become enmeshed in problems that inevitably weaken society. The loss of this conviction, the almost total secularizing of our public attitudes, has been largely responsible for the terrible social illnesses now running rampant among us. . . .

Divine law has become a meaningless phrase. What was once so commonly spoken of as sin is now referred to as nothing more than poor judgment. Blatant dishonesty is openly referred to and excused as "misleading others." Virtue is too often neglected, if not scorned or ridiculed as old-fashioned, confining, unenlightened. What was once considered transgression has now been labeled merely *misbehavior*, which we have come to not only tolerate but, in too many cases, rationalize, accept, and even embrace.

(Gordon B. Hinckley, *Standing for Something* [New York: Times Books, 2000], xviii–xix)

Secularism is expanding in much of the world today. Secularism is defined as "indifference to or rejection or exclusion of religion and religious considerations" (*Merriam-Webster's Collegiate Dictionary*, 11th ed. [2003], "secularism," 1123). Secularism does not accept many things as absolutes. Its principal objectives are pleasure and self-interest. Often those who embrace secularism have a different look about them. As Isaiah observed, "The show of their countenance doth witness against them."

(James E. Faust, *Ensign*, Nov. 2005 [Salt Lake City: The Church of Jesus Christ of Latter-day Saints, 2005], 20)

Alma 30:15 • YE CANNOT KNOW THINGS YE DO NOT SEE

We begin with Korihor's argument for naturalistic empiricism (the belief that it is possible to *know* all truth through the senses—by experience and observation). . . .

Now, it is plain that empiricism has value. It is good for us to observe our surroundings carefully and to appreciate our sensations. . . . Sense experience is indeed a valuable part of this life; the error comes in supposing that it is the *only* way of knowing what we know. . . .

None of the more important questions we ask can be solved or answered by depending solely on sensation. Is there a God? Is man immortal? Is it good to be honest? What should I do next in my life? . . . Every man answers these questions and makes the great decisions of his life on the basis of his belief in and acceptance of someone or something he cannot see. . . .

The answer to Korihor is plain and simple: Our initial acceptance of Christ is not empirical, for we do not see him. But we have received into our lives a Holy Spirit that teaches us to understand the scriptures about Christ and to believe that he lives. . . .

Korihor might by his argument be able to confuse someone who had never had revelation, but his contention is only a pathetic childishness to those who enjoy the companionship of the Holy Ghost.

(Chauncey C. Riddle, *The Book of Mormon: It Begins with a Family* [Salt Lake City: Deseret Book, 1983], 135–136)

Alma 30:17 • WHATSOEVER A MAN DID WAS NO CRIME

Relativism involves the denial of the existence of absolute truths and, therefore, of an absolute truthgiver, God. Relativism has sometimes been a small, satanic sea breeze, but now the winds of relativism have reached gale proportions. Over a period of several decades relativism has eroded ethics, public and personal, has worn down the will of many, has contributed to a slackening sense of duty, civic and personal. The old mountains of individual morality have been worn down. This erosion has left mankind in a sand-dune society, in a desert of disbelief where there are no landmarks, and no north, no east, no west, and no south! There is only the dust of despair.

(Joseph Fletcher and John Warwick Montgomery, *Situation Ethics: True or False?* [Minneapolis: Dimension Books, 1972], 55; as quoted in *Selected Writings of Gerald N. Lund* [Salt Lake City: Deseret Book, 1999], 127)

[Joseph Fletcher, a former dean of St. Paul's Cathedral in Cincinnati and a professor of social ethics at the Episcopal Theology School in Cambridge, Massachusetts.] Dr. Fletcher argues that love is the highest good and that what determines whether something is right or wrong is simply whether or not it is the "loving thing" to do. Here are some excerpts from his book *Situation Ethics: True or False?*

"Whether we ought to follow a moral principle or not *would always depend upon the situation*. . . . In some situations unmarried love could be infinitely more moral than married unlove. Lying could be more Christian that telling the truth. . . . Stealing could be better than respecting private property. . . . *No action is good or right of itself.* It depends on whether it hurts or helps. . . . We are . . . obliged in conscience sometimes to tell white lies, as we often call them, then in conscience we might be obliged sometimes to engage in white thefts and white fornications and white killings and white breakings of promises and the like."

(*Selected Writings of Gerald N. Lund* [Salt Lake City: Deseret Book, 1999], 126)

———————

There are some who would have us believe there is no right or wrong—that everything is relative. We must never allow ourselves to think proper conduct and decision making are found in a convenient path somewhere between right and wrong.

(Marvin J. Ashton, in Conference Report, Apr. 1982 [Salt Lake City: The Church of Jesus Christ of Latter-day Saints, 1982], 11–12)

———————

A third argument used by Korihor is that of relativism: ". . . and whatsoever a man did was no crime" (Alma 30:17). . . .

There are, of course, many versions of relativism. . . . One version encourages enjoyment of the Church social organization without getting uptight about theology or religious commandments. Another kind of relativism says that the commandments are great but open to broad private interpretation. A third acknowledges that there are commandments, but allows indulgence in sin since "nobody's perfect." A fourth version says that the commandments were okay when they were given, but they have become superfluous in our enlightened age. A fifth kind of relativism, that used by Korihor, says that the commandments were bad from the first; they are inhibitions on the soul of man that actually prevent him from ever achieving happiness. A sixth type, also used by Korihor, says that since one act is indifferent from another, it doesn't matter what we do.

The great power of all relativistic approaches is that they allow the individual to judge his own actions. This is why almost any of the approaches strikes a responsive, sympathetic chord in all other relativists. . . .

In stark contrast to the virtually infinite number of personal choices available in the broad way of relativism is the way of the Savior. That strait and narrow way is to do as he did. . . .

Now, it is little wonder that Korihor found much success in commending relativism to the members of the Church in his time. For while the Church is true, the members of the Church here on earth have not yet overcome the world, although most are still trying. For many, the effort is hard, the price too great. Whether they leave the Church or not, they abandon the narrow way and settle for some variety of relativism.

(Chauncey C. Riddle, *The Book of Mormon: It Begins with a Family* [Salt Lake City: Deseret Book, 1983] 137–139)

Alma 30:17 • EVERY MAN CONQUERED ACCORDING TO HIS STRENGTH

In concert with the other humanists of the world, he insists that achievement and success come by human means, such as physical strength, skill, and reason. . . .

Such persons define success in terms of wealth, social status, political power, and the glutting of the senses. . . .

Conversely, those who have accepted the gospel see that real success in this world is overcoming selfishness and turning one's strength to righteousness, to blessing others. . . .

Part of Satan's entourage includes those who know the gospel is true but who insist they really don't need much help except for a pointer or two and a little assistance in being resurrected.

(Chauncey C. Riddle, *The Book of Mormon: It Begins with a Family* [Salt Lake City: Deseret Book, 1983] 136–137)

Alma 30:17 • EVERY MAN PROSPERED ACCORDING TO HIS GENIUS

I wish to say a few words on intellectualism—that quality which some say we deny in our work. A so-called scholar recently expressed the view that the Church is an enemy of intellectualism. . . . If he meant by intellectualism that branch of philosophy which teaches "the doctrine that knowledge is wholly or chiefly derived from pure reason" and "that reason is the final principle of reality," then, yes, we are opposed to so narrow an interpretation as applicable to religion (see *The Random House Dictionary of the English Language*, 2nd ed. [1987], "intellectualism," 990).

Such an interpretation excludes the power of the Holy Spirit in speaking to and through man. Of course we believe in the cultivation of the mind. . . . But the intellect is not the only source of knowledge. There is a promise, given under the inspiration of the Almighty, set forth in these beautiful words: "God shall give unto you knowledge by his Holy Spirit, yea, by the unspeakable gift of the Holy Ghost" (D&C 121:26).

The humanists who criticize us, the so-called intellectuals who demean us, speak only from ignorance of this manifestation. They have not heard the voice of the Spirit. They have not heard it because they have not sought after it and prepared themselves to be worthy of it. Then, supposing that knowledge comes only of reasoning and of the workings of the mind, they deny that which comes by the power of the Holy Ghost.

The things of God are understood by the Spirit of

God. That Spirit is real. To those who have experienced its workings, the knowledge so gained is as real as that received through the operation of the five senses. . . .

Do not be trapped by the sophistry of the world, which for the most part is negative and which seldom, if ever, bears good fruit. Do not be ensnared by those clever ones whose self-appointed mission it is to demean that which is sacred.

(*Discourses of President Gordon B. Hinckley* [Salt Lake City: The Church of Jesus Christ of Latter-day Saints, 2005], 2:387–388)

Alma 30:18 • LIFT UP THEIR HEADS IN WICKEDNESS

This is not just wickedness, it is wickedness in which people take pride. They lift up their heads in it. And why shouldn't they? Korihor has provided the ultimate rationalization—there is no God; there is no ultimate right and wrong; man is the supreme being. All the guilt and shame people feel (psychological hang-ups) are simply the result of the foolish teachings of their parents or the designs of evil religious leaders.

(*Selected Writings of Gerald N. Lund* [Salt Lake City: Deseret Book, 1999], 123)

Alma 30:28 • NO GOD

Satan, with an illusion, leads a man to puff himself up with pride to say, "I am my own man. I know the Lord lives, but he expects me to handle this particular matter on my own and not bother him with any details." Not being familiar with the scriptures, the man may not know that Satan teaches the world there is no God. But to the Saints he simply says, "There is a God, but he is only *generally* involved in your life. He would not *specifically* help you today." Or he teaches the world not to pray, but to the Saints he simply says, "Don't pray now. You don't feel like praying right now" (see 2 Ne. 32:8–9). The net effect is the same.

(Gene R. Cook, in Conference Report, Apr. 1982 [Salt Lake City: The Church of Jesus Christ of Latter-day Saints, 1982], 36)

Alma 30:42, 47 • POSSESSED WITH A LYING SPIRIT

Not long ago a troubled friend of mine who has long suffered and continues to suffer the pains of a victim entrapped in his own snare of lies said, "I have been living lies for so long and have told so many over the years that, frankly, I don't really know when I am telling the truth." When I first heard this, I was moved with compassion; but a second thought had me wondering if this too wasn't just another lie. Lying has filled this friend's life full of trouble. . . .

He who lies is the servant of the lie. He who tells the lie must live with the results. . . . No man will ever be totally free who is living a lie. . . . A wrong isn't right just because many people do it. A wrong deed isn't right just because it hasn't become visible.

(Marvin J. Ashton, in Conference Report, Apr. 1982 [Salt Lake City: The Church of Jesus Christ of Latter-day Saints, 1982], 13–14)

Alma 30:43 • SHOW ME A SIGN

Sign seeking may be an attempt to gain faith and knowledge without humility, obedience and paying the price.

In a world filled with skepticism and doubt, the expression "seeing is believing" promotes the attitude, "You show me, and I will believe." We want all of the proof and all of the evidence first. It seems hard to take things on faith. When will we learn that in spiritual things it works the other way about—that believing is seeing? Spiritual belief precedes spiritual knowledge. When we believe in things that are not seen but are nevertheless true, then we have faith.

(Boyd K. Packer, "What Is Faith?" in *Faith* [Salt Lake City: Deseret Book, 1983], 43)

————

Show me Latter-day Saints who have to feed upon miracles, signs and visions in order to keep them steadfast in the Church, and I will show you members of the Church who are not in good standing before God, and who are walking in slippery paths. It is not by marvelous manifestations unto us that we shall be established in truth, but it is by humility and faithful obedience to the commandments and laws of God. When I as a boy first started out in the ministry, I would frequently go out and ask the Lord to show me some marvelous thing, in order that I might receive a testimony. But the Lord withheld marvels from me, and showed me the truth, line upon line, precept upon precept, here a little and there a little, until he made me to know the truth from the crown of my head to the soles of my feet, and until doubt and fear had been absolutely purged from me. He did not have to send an angel from the heavens to do this, nor did he have to speak with the trump of an archangel. *By the whisperings of the still small voice of the Spirit of the living God, he gave to me the testimony I possess. And by this principle and power he will give to all the children of men a knowledge of the truth. . . . And no amount of marvelous manifestations will ever accomplish this.*

(Joseph F. Smith, *Gospel Doctrine* [Salt Lake City: Deseret Book, 1975], 7)

————

Some great examples of this can be found in Church history. Ezra Booth, in company with others (including Mrs. John Johnson), visited Joseph Smith at his home in Kirtland in 1831. While there Ezra Booth witnessed a miracle. Mrs. Johnson, who had had a lame arm for a number of years, was healed by the Prophet Joseph. Booth was so awe-struck by this that he joined the Church. It was not long, however, until his faith waned and he finally apostatized and wrote a series of letters against the Church (see *History of the Church,* 1:215–217). Another example is that of Simonds Ryder, who joined the Church after what he felt was a supernatural experience. A short time later, he left after his name was misspelled in an inspired mission call. "He thought if the Spirit through which he had been called to preach could err in the matter of spelling his name, it might have erred in calling him to the ministry as well" *(History of the Church,* 1:261). Having lost whatever faith he had, and encouraged by Booth's letters, Simonds Ryder led a mob against the Prophet Joseph at Father Johnson's home where Joseph and Sidney Rigdon were tarred and feathered. This incident also caused the death of one of Joseph and Emma's adopted children (see *History of the Church,* 1:261–265). Whenever we base our belief on miracles, we must constantly be fed by miracles or our belief grows weak. . . . Perhaps some members of the Church today are troubled with a less dramatic form of sign seeking. In section 121 of the Doctrine and Covenants the Lord refers to members aspiring to the honors of men. One of the reasons we aspire to position is that we somehow feel that being called to a high position is a "sign" that the Lord approves of our efforts and that if we are not called, we have failed to measure up.

(Michael K. Parson, Book of Mormon Symposium, Aug. 1982, 73–75)

A Campbellite preacher . . . came to Joseph Smith, I think his name was Hayden. He came in and made himself known to Joseph, and said that he had come a considerable distance to be convinced of the truth. "Why," said he, "Mr. Smith, I want to know the truth, and when I am convinced, I will spend all my talents and time in defending and spreading the doctrines of your religion, and I will give you to understand that to convince me is equivalent to convincing all my society, amounting to several hundreds." Well, Joseph commenced laying before him the coming forth of the work, and the first principles of the Gospel, when Mr. Hayden exclaimed, "O this is not the evidence I want, the evidence that I wish to have is a notable miracle; I want to see some powerful manifestation of the power of God, I want to see a notable miracle performed; and if you perform such a one, then I will believe with all my heart and soul, and will exert all my power and all my extensive influence to convince others; and if you will not

perform a miracle of this kind, then I am your worst and bitterest enemy." "Well," said Joseph, "what will you have done? Will you be struck blind, or dumb? Will you be paralyzed, or will you have one hand withered? Take your choice, choose which you please, and in the name of the Lord Jesus Christ it shall be done." "That is not the kind of miracle I want," said the preacher. "Then, sir," replied Joseph, "I can perform none; I am not going to bring any trouble upon any body else, sir, to convince you."

(George A. Smith, *Journal of Discourses* [London: Latter-day Saints' Book Depot, 1855], 2:326)

Men who have professedly seen the most, known and understood the most, in this Church, and who have testified in the presence of large congregations, in the name of Israel's God, that they have seen Jesus, etc., have been the very men who have left this Kingdom, before others who had to live by faith.

You will recollect that I have often told you that miracles would not save a person, and I say that they never should.

(*Discourses of Brigham Young,* comp. by John A. Widtsoe [Salt Lake City: Deseret Book, 1954], 342–343)

It is common in our secular world to say that "seeing is believing." . . . The way of the Lord is best defined by a different maxim: "Believing is seeing." Faith in the Lord is the premise, not the conclusion. We *know* He lives; *therefore,* we trust Him to bless us according to His divine will and wisdom. This childlike confidence in the Lord is known in scripture simply as the "sacrifice . . . of a broken heart and a contrite spirit" (D&C 59:8).

(Lance B. Wickman, in Conference Report, Oct. 2002 [Salt Lake City: The Church of Jesus Christ of Latter-day Saints, 2002], 33.)

I sat on a plane next to a professed atheist who ridiculed my belief in God. I bore my testimony to him. . . .

He said: "You don't *know.* Nobody *knows* that. You can't *know* it." When I would not yield, the atheist posed perhaps the ultimate challenge to testimony. "All right," he said in a sneering, condescending way. "You say you know." Then, "Tell me *how* you know."

I could not do it. I was helpless to communicate. . . .

"You see," he said, "you don't really know. If you did, you would be able to tell me *how you know.*". . .

A thought, a revelation, came into my mind, and I

said to the atheist: "Let me ask you a question. Do you know what salt tastes like?"

"Of course I do," was his reply.

"When did you taste salt last?"

"I just had dinner on the plane."

"You just think you know what salt tastes like," I said.

He insisted, "I know what salt tastes like as well as I know anything."

"If I gave you a cup of salt and a cup of sugar, could you tell the salt from the sugar if I let you taste them both?"

"Now you are getting juvenile," he said. "Of course I could tell the difference. I know what salt tastes like. I know it as well as I know any thing."

"Then," I said, "assuming that I have never tasted salt, explain to me just what it tastes like."

After some thought, he ventured, "Well—I—uh, it is not sweet, and it is not sour."

"You've told me what it isn't, not what it is."

After several attempts, of course he could not do it. He could not convey, in words alone, so ordinary an experience as tasting salt.

I bore testimony to him once again and said: "I know there is a God. You ridiculed that testimony and said that if I *did* know, I would be able to tell you exactly *how* I know. My friend, spiritually speaking, I have tasted salt. I am no more able to convey to you in words alone how this knowledge has come than you are able to tell me what salt tastes like. But I say to you again, there is a God! He lives! And just because you don't know, don't try to tell me that I don't know, for I do!"

(*Memorable Stories and Parables by Boyd K. Packer* [Salt Lake City: Bookcraft, 1997], 57–59)

———

Here is the distinction between testimony-seeking and sign-seeking: the sign-seeker wants to keep his disobedient life and still have spiritual power.... The testimony-seeker wants to submit to God, repent, and live by the light that the Lord gives through the Holy Ghost.

(Catherine Thomas; as quoted in *Studies in Scripture*, ed. by Kent P. Jackson [Salt Lake City: Deseret Book, 1988], 8:275)

———

A Relief Society president or a bishop, you may some-day have to remove a diabolical doubter, just as Ammon had Korihor carried to the edge of town. Korihor could not be allowed to spread the cancer of his doubt, or the responsibility would have been Ammon's.... Korihor got what he thought he needed, a physical sign—he was struck dumb. But you remember what Alma taught us and taught him: the terrible evidence of even that

rebuke did not change Korihor's heart.

(Henry B. Eyring, *To Draw Closer to God* [Salt Lake City: Deseret Book, 1997], 145)

Alma 30:44 • ALL THINGS DENOTE GOD

All of beauty in the Earth bears the fingerprint of the Master Creator.

(Gordon B. Hinckley, *Ensign*, May 1978 [Salt Lake City: The Church of Jesus Christ of Latter-day Saints, 1978], 59)

———

Just a bit nearer to the sun, and Planet Earth's seas would soon be boiling; just a little farther out, and the whole would world become a frozen wilderness.... "If our orbit happened to be the wrong shape . . . then we should alternately freeze like Mars and fry like Venus once a year. Fortunately for us, our planet's orbit is very nearly a circle. The 21 percent of oxygen is another critical figure. Animals would have difficulty breathing if the oxygen content fell very far below that value. But an oxygen level much higher than this would also be disastrous, since the extra oxygen would act as a fire-raising material. Forests and grasslands would flare up every time lightning struck during a dry spell, and life on earth would become extremely hazardous."

(British scientist Alan Hayward; as quoted in Neal A. Maxwell, *First Nephi, The Doctrinal Foundation*, ed. by Monte S. Nyman and Charles D. Tate [Provo, Utah: Religious Studies Center, BYU, 1988], 7)

———

God has made certain decrees which are fixed and immovable; for instance, God set the sun, the moon, and the stars in the heavens, and gave them their laws, conditions and bounds, which they cannot pass, except by His commandments; they all move in perfect harmony in their sphere and order, and are as lights, wonders and signs unto us. The sea also has its bounds which it cannot pass. God has set many signs on the earth, as well as in the heavens; for instance, the oak of the forest, the fruit of the tree, the herb of the field, all bear a sign that seed hath been planted there; for it is a decree of the Lord that every tree, plant, and herb bearing seed should bring forth of its kind, and cannot come forth after any other law or principle.

(*Teachings of the Prophet Joseph Smith* [Salt Lake City: Deseret Book, 1976], 197–198)

———

Have you ever contemplated the wonder of yourself, the eyes with which you see, the ears with which you hear, the voice with which you speak? No camera ever built can compare with the human eye. No method of communication ever devised can compare with the voice and the ear. No pump ever built will run as long or as efficiently as the human heart. What a remarkable thing each of us is.

Look at your finger. The most skillful attempt to reproduce it mechanically has brought only a crude approximation. The next time you use your finger, look at it, and sense the wonder of it. . . .

I believe the human body to be the creation of Divinity. George Gallup once observed, "I could prove God statistically. Take the human body alone—the chance that all the functions of the individual would just happen is a statistical monstrosity."

(Gordon B. Hinckley, *Ensign,* Aug. 1992 [Salt Lake City: The Church of Jesus Christ of Latter-day Saints, 1992], 2)

Alma 30:52–53 • WHAT WAS KORIHOR'S MOTIVE?

The most powerful opposition to the work of the Savior on this earth comes from those who know the truth and then deliberately turn from it and seek to destroy others.

(Chauncey C. Riddle, *Ensign*, Sept. 1977 [Salt Lake City: The Church of Jesus Christ of Latter-day Saints, 1977], 18)

———

Remember that the very worst enemies that we've had are those that are within the Church. It was Judas that betrayed the Master. . . . Today it's the same. The greatest and worst enemies we have in the Church today are those within our ranks.

(Harold B. Lee, CES address, BYU, 8 July 1966)

———

Korihor is described in the heading as an Antichrist, but I'm not sure that he started out that way. Have you ever thought that possibly Korihor started out as a college student with lots of questions? Although his questioning may have begun honestly, he made two really bad mistakes. First, he denied his faith. He denied the Light of Christ that had been given to him. Second, he started to preach false doctrine to others. Alma, his leader, bore his testimony to Korihor and then Korihor made another mistake. Rather than listening to his leader and listening and relying on the Spirit, he defended his position . . . and became more argumentative. He demanded that he be given a sign. . . . He perhaps didn't intend for the sign to have such an affect on him personally, but often the consequences of our mistakes do affect us personally. Verses 52 and 53 of chapter 30 I believe are most important when Korihor acknowledges, "I always knew that there was a God, but Satan hath deceived me." Isn't that interesting? "I

always knew." He had the Light of Christ in him, but Satan deceived him.

(Janette C. Hales, BYU Devotional, 16 Mar. 1993)

Alma 30:54–56 • WHY DIDN'T ALMA HEAL KORIHOR?

Alma refuses to plead with the Lord for the curse to be taken away because he knows, by the spirit of prophecy and revelation, that should Korihor be released from his affliction he will continue in the work of rebellion against the plan and purposes of God.

(Joseph Fielding Smith and Robert L. Millet, *Doctrinal Commentary on the Book of Mormon* [Salt Lake City: Bookcraft, 1991], 3:213)

———

In real repentance, there is the actual *forsaking* of sinning. "Repent, and turn yourselves from all your transgressions; so iniquity shall not be your ruin" (Ezek. 18:30). A suffering Korihor confessed, "I always knew that there was a God," but his turning was still incomplete (Alma 30:52); hence, "Alma said unto him: If this curse should be taken from thee thou wouldst again lead away the hearts of this people" (Alma 30:55).

Thus, when "a man repenteth of his sins—behold, he will confess them and forsake them" (D&C 58:43).

(Neal A. Maxwell, *Ensign,* Nov. 1991 [Salt Lake City: The Church of Jesus Christ of Latter-day Saints, 1991] 31)

Alma 30:59 • KORIHOR'S DEATH

The Zoramites were a group of apostates who had left the Nephite religion and started their own church. In chapter 31, we are given an account of their teachings in some detail. Note the following phrases from that chapter which describe the doctrines of the Zoramites. Mormon tells us they had "fallen into great errors" (v. 9); they rejected the traditions of their Nephite brethren as being "handed down to them by the childishness of their fathers" (v. 16); they did not want to be "led away after the foolish traditions of our brethren, which doth bind them down to a belief in Christ" (v. 17); and they refused "to believe in things to come, which they knew nothing about" (v. 22).

Familiar echoes? Indeed they are. The Zoramites are a reflection of some of Korihor's primary teachings. In other words, the Zoramites represent the end result of Korihor's philosophy. . . . What an irony that Korihor should come to his end by the hands of the very people who practiced what he preached.

(*Selected Writings of Gerald N. Lund* [Salt Lake City: Deseret Book, 1999], 130–131)

Alma 30:60 • THE DEVIL WON'T SUPPORT HIS CHILDREN

Satan does not support those who follow him. He can't! It's the Lord who sustains; the Spirit sustains; righteousness sustains. That sustenance is not Satan's to give.

(Janette C. Hales, BYU Devotional, 16 Mar. 1993)

———————

At the last day the adversary "will not support" those who followed him anyway (Alma 30:60). He cannot. Jesus will triumph majestically, and the adversary's clever constructs, "pleasing [to] the carnal mind," will also collapse, and "the fall thereof [will be] exceedingly great" (Alma 30:53; 1 Nephi 11:36).

(Neal A. Maxwell, in Conference Report, Oct. 2003 [Salt Lake City: The Church of Jesus Christ of Latter-day Saints, 2003], 107)

Alma 31:5 • MORE POWERFUL THAN THE SWORD

The gospel is the only answer to the problems of the world. We may cry peace. We may hold peace conferences. And I have nothing but commendation for those who work for peace. But it is my conviction that peace must come from within. It cannot be imposed by state mandate. It can come only by following the teachings and the example of the Prince of Peace.

(Ezra Taft Benson, *Title of Liberty* [Salt Lake City: Deseret Book, 1964], 213–214)

———————

There are no armaments, no governmental schemes, no international organizations, and no mechanisms for the control of weapons which can preserve an unrighteous people. . . . Alma has given us compelling evidence of his conviction that repentance is more effectual than arms in maintaining peace. You will recall that he was the elected chief judge of the Nephite nation. As such he was the governor of the people of Nephi and commander-in-chief of their armies. Seeing many of them dissenting and conniving with the enemy, he, notwithstanding his power to strengthen and command his armies, placed the affairs of state in other hands that he himself might cry repentance unto the dissenters.

(Marion G. Romney, in Conference Report, Apr. 1950 [Salt Lake City: The Church of Jesus Christ of Latter-day Saints, 1950], 87–88)

———————

True doctrine, understood, changes attitudes and behavior. The study of the doctrines of the gospel will improve behavior quicker than a study of behavior will improve behavior.

(Boyd K. Packer, in Conference Report, Oct. 1986 [Salt Lake City: The Church of Jesus Christ of Latter-day Saints, 1986], 20)

———————

Decaying cities are simply a delayed reflection of decaying individuals. . . . The commandments of God give emphasis to improvement of the individual as the only real way to bring about the real improvement in society.

(Ezra Taft Benson, *A Plea for America* [Salt Lake City: Deseret Book, 1975], 18)

———————

The Lord works from the inside out. The world works from the outside in. The world would take people out of the slums. Christ takes the slums out of the people, and then they take themselves out of the slums. The world would mold men by changing their environment. Christ changes men, who then change their environment. The world would shape human behavior, but Christ can change human nature.

(Ezra Taft Benson, *Ensign*, Nov. 1985 [Salt Lake City: The Church of Jesus Christ of Latter-day Saints, 1985], 6)

———————

While in exile at St. Helena, Napoleon asked another man in his suite, "Can you tell me who Jesus Christ was?" Then Napoleon went on to say: "I will tell you." Napoleon compared himself and other heroes of antiquity with Christ and then showed how far Jesus surpassed them all. "I think I understand somewhat of human nature," said Napoleon, "and I tell you all these were men, and I am a man, but not one is like Him. Jesus Christ was more than man. Alexander, Caesar, Charlemagne, and myself, founded great empires; but upon what did the creation of our genius depend? Upon force. Jesus alone founded His empire upon love and to this very day millions would die for Him."

(Mary Ellen Smoot, "Everything Money Cannot Buy," Satellite Broadcast, 3 Feb. 2002, Brigham Young University [Salt Lake City: The Church of Jesus Christ of Latter-day Saints, 2002], 4)

———————

Do not expect the world's solutions to the world's problems to be very effective. Such solutions often resemble what C.S. Lewis wrote about those who go dashing back and forth with fire extinguishers in times of flood (see *The Screwtape Letters* [1959], 117–18). Only the gospel is constantly relevant, and the substitute things won't work.

(Neal A. Maxwell, *Ensign*, May 2004 [Salt Lake City: The Church of Jesus Christ of Latter-day Saints, 2004], 45)

Alma 31:21 • RAMEUMPTOM

Doing home teaching, earning a scout merit badge, or doing other assigned acts of service can become little more than offerings on the Rameumptom, if our hearts are not earnest and our daily nature not Christian.

(Elaine Shaw Sorensen; as quoted in *The Book of Mormon: Alma, The Testimony of the Word*, ed. by Monte S. Nyman and Charles D. Tate [Provo, Utah: Religious Studies Center, BYU, 1992], 131)

"Rameumptom." Although this name may look strange in English, it has appropriate Semitic roots recognizable to students of Semitic languages. The preface "ram" is frequently used to indicate a high place. For example, later in the Book of Mormon we read of the hill Ramah. Also, in modern Israel are the town of Ramallah (located in the tops of the Judean hills just north of Jerusalem) and Rameem (which literally means "the heights" and is located on the top of the hills near the Lebanese border).

(Daniel H. Ludlow, *A Companion to Your Study of the Book of Mormon* [Salt Lake City: Deseret Book, 1976], 213)

Alma 31:28; 32:2 • COSTLY APPAREL

(Contrast this with Matthew 22:9–14; Alma 5:14, 19; refer in this text to Alma 1:6.)

Our society may well be as guilty as the wealthy Zoramites of using fashion as "the science of appearances, inspiring us with the desire to seem rather than to be" (Edwin Hubbell Chapin). In our day the costly apparel syndrome may be identified as one aspect of the modern-day term "conspicuous consumption." The word *conspicuous* alludes to the visual side of vanity— the need to be seen, to be recognized. *Consumption* refers to that which we take in or that which we consume. Conspicuous consumption may be defined as that which we take to ourselves in order to be recognized and approved by others. By its very definition, the person trapped in conspicuous consumption, especially as it applies to "costly apparel," must be focused on the opinions of others, because what is "in" today may be "out" tomorrow. Vanity then becomes its own punishment, because there is never time to be satisfied—the eyes and opinions of others can turn so quickly to embrace someone else. For us, the disease that afflicted the Zoramites encompasses more than clothing. It can include cars, houses, boats, diplomas, and anything else that has a foundation where the need for the approval of man carries more weight than the need to be accepted by God.

(K. Douglas Bassett, *Doctrines of the Book of Mormon*, 1991 Sperry Symposium [Salt Lake City: Deseret Book, 1992], 18–19)

My six-year-old son Boyd, who was in the final months of a battle with cystic fibrosis, became very close to one of my students whom I will call Tom. When I would bring Boyd to seminary, he and Tom were inseparable. I'm sure Tom's major motivation for coming to class was connected with his desire to be with my son. The school where I taught was one of the wealthiest in the area, and wearing the "right" clothing was very important to the majority of the students. However, Tom's parents did not have a great deal of money, which was reflected in the clothes he wore to school. Perhaps this is one of the reasons he connected so well with my son. Tom's unfashionable apparel, as well as his social isolation in school, gave him an instant identification with this little boy whose body was not so fashionable either.

My son's condition continually grew worse, and near the end of the school year he passed away. His funeral was held at the church where I taught seminary, next to the high school. Like so many of my students, Tom came directly from his classes to attend the funeral. As he entered the chapel, he was stopped by one of the employees of the mortuary, who inquired, "Do you think you're dressed appropriately to show the necessary respect to this little boy and his family?"

Tom was devastated. He immediately left the building like a Zoramite cast out of the synagogue because of the *coarseness of his apparel*. To my knowledge he never attended seminary or church again. In his mind, this was the last straw for his already wavering testimony. As hard as I tried, I could not get him to come back. Is it possible that some of us in the Church could unwittingly be sending the same message that was given to Tom as well as to the unfashionable among the Zoramites?

President Gordon B. Hinckley has given us counsel against the improper use of body piercing and tattoos (see *Ensign*, Nov. 2000, 99). His counsel was directed to members of the Church, who are to refrain from such practices as a token of respect for our bodies, which the Savior identified as temples (see John 2:19–21). It is important to note that President Hinckley's words were meant for us personally; they were not given as a license to judge anyone else who chooses to participate in body piercing or tattoos. Someone with a nose ring or a tattoo might not feel welcome at church if we take President Hinckley's counsel incorrectly by casting judgmental glances or verbal innuendo about his or her appearance. If so, then it is we, the members of the Church, who take on the role of the prideful Zoramites in the Book of Mormon.

The challenge to us as members of the Church is to not judge others by their appearance while at the same time recognizing that the world will judge the Church by the appearance of its members. That is why students of church-owned schools as well as missionaries are required to dress and groom in a conservative fashion.

(Jack R. Christianson and K. Douglas Bassett, *Life Lessons from the Book of Mormon* [Salt Lake City: Deseret Book, 2003], 114–115)

Alma 31:31, 33, 38; 32:6; 33:23 •
AFFLICTION, SWALLOWED UP IN THE JOY OF CHRIST

(Refer in this text to Mosiah 24:14–15; Alma 14:11; 34:40–41.)

God never bestows upon His people, or upon an individual, superior blessings without a severe trial to prove them, to prove that individual, or that people, to see whether they will keep their covenants with Him, and keep in remembrance what He has shown them. . . . So when individuals are blessed with visions, revelations, and great manifestations, look out, then the devil is nigh you, and you will be tempted in proportion to the vision, revelation, or manifestation you have received.

(Brigham Young, *Journal of Discourses* [London: Latter-day Saints' Book Depot, 1856], 3:205–206)

––––––––––

It has been wisely observed that a blessing is anything that brings us nearer to God. Thus our afflictions often become our greatest blessings. It is in our extremities that most often we meet God, not in our comfort. Thus any time conditions come to pass—even what at the time might be construed as tragic or unfortunate conditions—that lead us toward the truth or contribute to our eventual well-being, we have indeed been blessed.

(Robert Millet and Joseph McConkie, *Doctrinal Commentary on the Book of Mormon* [Salt Lake City: Bookcraft, 1991], 3:224)

––––––––––

Why is non-endurance a denial of the Lord? Because giving up is a denial of the Lord's loving capacity to see us through "all these things"! Giving up suggests that God is less than He really is. . . . So much of life's curriculum consists of efforts by the Lord to get and keep our attention. Ironically, the stimuli He uses are often that which is seen by us as something to endure. Sometimes what we are being asked to endure is His 'help'—help to draw us away from the cares of the world; help to draw us away from self-centeredness; attention-getting help when the still, small voice has been ignored by us; help in the shaping of our souls; and help to keep the promises we made so long ago to Him and to ourselves. . . . Whether the afflictions are

self-induced, as most of them are, or whether they are of the divine-tutorial type, it matters not. Either way, the Lord can help us so that our afflictions, said Alma, can be "swallowed up in the joy of Christ" (Alma 31:38). Thus, afflictions are endured and are overcome by joy. The sour notes are lost amid a symphony of salvational sounds. Our afflictions, brothers and sisters, may not be extinguished. Instead, they can be dwarfed and swallowed up in the joy of Christ. This is how we overcome most of the time—not the elimination of affliction, but the placing of these in that larger context.

(Neal A. Maxwell, BYU Fireside, 2 Dec. 1984)

Alma 32 • FAITH

Belief in a sense is passive, an agreement or acceptance only; faith is active and positive embracing such reliance and confidence as will lead to works.

(James E. Talmage, *Articles of Faith* [London: The Church of Jesus Christ of Latter-day Saints, 1962], 96–97)

––––––––––

Faith, then, is the first great governing principle which has power, dominion, and authority over all things; by it they exist, by it they are upheld, by it they are changed, or by it they remain, agreeable to the will of God. Without it there is no power, and without power there could be no creation nor existence.

(Joseph Smith, *Lectures on Faith* [Salt Lake City: Deseret Book, 1985], 1:24)

––––––––––

So the combination of faith in Christ plus *faith unto repentance* is vitally important. That concept is one of the greatest insights we have into the importance of simple, clear faith—faith sufficient to repent. Apparently faith great enough to move mountains is not required; faith enough to speak in tongues or to heal the sick is not needed; all that we need is just enough faith to recognize that we have sinned and to repent of our sins, to feel remorse for them, and to desire to sin no more but to please Christ the Lord.

(Robert E. Wells, *Doctrines of the Book of Mormon*, 1991 Sperry Symposium [Salt Lake City: Deseret Book, 1992], 6–7)

––––––––––

Of all our needs, I think the greatest is an increase in faith.

(Gordon B. Hinckley, *Ensign*, Nov. 1987 [Salt Lake City: The Church of Jesus Christ of Latter-day Saints, 1987], 54)

––––––––––

Could faith be the answer? We all know that

more faith won't make our problems disappear. But I believe as our faith increases, we become more able to not only survive the hard times but become better because of them. . . . faith means that I really believe that: (1) Heavenly Father and Jesus Christ live, and they are in charge of this world. (2) They know me. (3) They love me. (4) They have a plan for my future. (5) I will obey the commandments, work hard, and trust in their plan. Sooner or later, everything will be okay.

(Virginia H. Pearce, *Ensign*, May 1994 [Salt Lake City: The Church of Jesus Christ of Latter-day Saints, 1994], 92)

[A lesson learned as a missionary on a sailboat in Tonga] Once I asked the Lord to bless us with a good tail wind so we could get to Foa quickly. As we got under way, one of the older men said, "Elder Groberg, you need to modify your prayers a little." "How's that?" I replied. "You asked the Lord for a tail wind to take us rapidly to Foa. If you pray for a tail wind to Foa, what about the people who are trying to come from Foa to Pangai? They are good people, and you are praying against them. Just pray for a good wind, not a tail wind." . . . We may pray for a particular type of weather, or to preserve someone's life, when that answer to our prayer may hurt someone else. That's why we must always pray in faith, because we can't have true, God-given faith in something that is not according to His will. If it's according to His will, all parties will benefit. I learned to pray for a good wind and the ability to get there safely, not necessarily a tail wind.

(John H. Groberg, *In the Eye of the Storm* [Salt Lake City: Bookcraft, 1993], 175)

Are you one who has tried to exercise faith and has felt no benefit? If so, you likely have not understood and followed the principles upon which faith is founded. . . .

Some of those principles are:

• Trust in God and in His willingness to provide help when needed no matter how challenging the circumstance.

• Obey His commandments and live to demonstrate that He can trust you.

• Be sensitive to the quiet prompting of the Spirit.

• Act courageously on that prompting.

• Be patient and understanding when God lets you struggle to grow and when answers come a piece at a time over an extended period. . . .

Even if you exercise your strongest faith, God will not always reward you immediately according to your desires. Rather, God will respond with what in His eternal plan is best for you. . . . Indeed, were you to know

His entire plan, you would never ask for that which is contrary to it even though your feelings tempt you to do so. Sincere faith gives us understanding and strength to accept the will of our Heavenly Father when it differs from our own.

(Richard G. Scott, in Conference Report, Apr. 2003 [Salt Lake City: The Church of Jesus Christ of Latter-day Saints, 2003], 78–79)

Faith exists when absolute confidence in that which we cannot see combines with action that is in absolute conformity to the will of our Heavenly Father. Without all three—first, absolute confidence; second, action; and third, absolute conformity—without these three, all we have is a counterfeit, a weak and watered-down faith.

(Joseph B Wirthlin, in Conference Report, Oct. 2002 [Salt Lake City: The Church of Jesus Christ of Latter-day Saints, 2002], 89)

Faith, the spiritual ability to be persuaded of promises that are seen "afar off" but that may not be attained in this life, is a sure measure of those who truly believe.

(Anne C. Pingree, in Conference Report, Oct. 2003 [Salt Lake City: The Church of Jesus Christ of Latter-day Saints, 2003], 13)

At Haun's Mill, a heroic pioneer woman, Amanda Smith, learned by faith how to do something beyond her abilities and the scientific knowledge of her time. On that terrible day in 1838, as the firing ceased and the mobsters left, she returned to the mill and saw her eldest son, Willard, carrying his seven-year-old brother, Alma. She cried, "Oh! My Alma is dead!"

"No, Mother," he said, "I think Alma is not dead. But Father and brother Sardius are [dead]!" But there was no time for tears now. Alma's entire hipbone was shot away. Amanda later recalled:

"Flesh, hip bone, joint and all had been ploughed out. . . . We laid little Alma on a bed in our tent and I examined the wound. It was a ghastly sight. I knew not what to do. . . . Yet was I there, all that long, dreadful night, with my dead and my wounded, and none but God as our physician and help. 'Oh my Heavenly Father,' I cried, 'what shall I do? Thou seest my poor wounded boy and knowest my inexperience. Oh, Heavenly Father, direct me what to do!' And then I was directed as by a voice speaking to me.

" . . . I was directed to take . . . ashes and make a lye and put a cloth saturated with it right into the wound. . . . Again and again I saturated the cloth and put it into the hole . . ., and each time mashed flesh and splinters of bone came away with the cloth; and the wound became as white as chicken's flesh.

"Having done as directed I again prayed to the Lord and was again instructed as distinctly as though a physician had been standing by speaking to me. Near by was a slippery-elm tree. From this I was told to make a . . . poultice and fill the wound with it. . . . The poultice was made, and the wound, which took fully a quarter of a yard of linen to cover, . . . was properly dressed. . . .

"I removed the wounded boy to a house . . . and dressed his hip; the Lord directing me as before. I was reminded that in my husband's trunk there was a bottle of balsam. This I poured into the wound, greatly soothing Alma's pain.

" 'Alma my child,' I said, 'you believe that the Lord made your hip?'

" 'Yes, mother.'

" 'Well, the Lord can make something there in the place of your hip, don't you believe he can, Alma?'

" 'Do you think that the Lord can, Mother?' inquired the child, in his simplicity.

" 'Yes, my son,' I replied, 'he has showed it all to me in a vision.'

"Then I laid him comfortably on his face, and said: 'Now you lay like that, and don't move, and the Lord will make you another hip.'

"So Alma laid on his face for five weeks, until he was entirely recovered—a flexible gristle having grown in place of the missing joint and socket, which remains to this day a marvel to physicians. . . .

"It is now nearly forty years ago, but Alma has never been the least crippled during his life, and he has traveled quite a long period of the time as a missionary of the gospel and [is] a living miracle of the power of God." ["Amanda Smith," in Andrew Jenson, comp., *Historical Record*, 9 vols. (1882–90), 5:84–86; paragraphing and punctuation altered.]

The treatment was unusual for that day and time, and unheard of now, but when we reach an extremity, like Sister Smith, we have to exercise our simple faith and listen to the Spirit as she did. Exercising our faith will make it stronger. As Alma taught: [Alma 32:27–29]. . . .

Righteousness is a companion to faith. Strong faith is earned by keeping the commandments.

(James E. Faust, in Conference Report, Apr. 2000 [Salt Lake City: The Church of Jesus Christ of Latter-day Saints, 2000], 22–23)

Alma 32:16, 25 • HUMBLE THEMSELVES

[From a letter to a disbeliever.] May I repeat, the time will come when there will be a surrender of every person who has ever lived on this earth, who is now living, or who ever will live on this earth; and it will be an unforced surrender, an unconditional surrender. . . . It is not *if* you will . . . [come] to the great truth; it is

when, for I know that you cannot indefinitely resist the power and pressure of truth.

(Spencer W. Kimball, *Ensign*, Sept. 1978 [Salt Lake City: The Church of Jesus Christ of Latter-day Saints, 1978], 8)

Alma 32:17 • DESIRE TO BELIEVE

The Book of Mormon encourages us: "If [you] will awake and arouse your faculties, even to an experiment upon my words, and exercise a particle of faith, . . . even if [you] can no more than desire to believe" (Alma 32:27).

Some may say, "I cannot believe; I am not a religious person." Just consider, God promises us divine help even if we have only a desire to believe, but it has to be a true and not a pretended desire.

(Dieter F. Uchtdorf, *Ensign*, Nov. 2006 [Salt Lake City: The Church of Jesus Christ of Latter-day Saints, 2006], 38)

Alma 32:19 • HE THAT KNOWETH THE WILL OF GOD AND DOETH IT NOT

When individuals are blessed with visions, revelations, and great manifestations, look out, then the devil is nigh you, and you will be tempted in proportion to the vision, revelation, or manifestation you have received. Hence thousands, when they are off their guard, give way to the severe temptations which come upon them, and behold they are gone.

(Brigham Young, *Journal of Discourses* [London: Latter-day Saints' Book Depot, 1856], 3:206)

Alma 32:21 • HOPE FOR THINGS NOT SEEN

Casual belief is a passive kind of belief that never stirs the soul to do anything more than think with the mind. It is the belief Jesus referred to when he said to those who professed faith or belief but did not want to do any works. . . (JST James 2:18–19).

Causal belief is a belief that leads to action. The scriptures equate it with faith. It is the substance of hope, the mental assurance of things hoped for but not seen (JST Heb. 11:1). Faith and causal belief are a gift of God given to men and women who live the laws which entitle them to this endowment of power, for it is a power (D&C 130:20–21). There is an uncommon dimension of faith in a few men and women that, when exercised in a true belief of Jesus Christ, causes the elements to react both physically and spiritually. This uncommon faith has a catalytic power to direct all matter and make earthly energy sources submissive. In the gospel sense this causal belief or faith generates salvation and eternal life.

(Kenneth W. Anderson, *The Book of Mormon: From Zion to Destruction* [Provo, Utah: Brigham Young University, 1995], 31–32)

Alma 32:21, 32 • REAL FAITH MUST BE BASED ON TRUTH

(Refer in this text to 3 Nephi 18:20.)

By way of illustration I borrow the following from the works of Orson Pratt: "When Europeans first began their explorations in the New World, the Indians whom they met were much amazed at the power and explosive properties of gunpowder and asked many questions respecting the manner in which it was produced. The Europeans, taking advantage of the ignorance of the . . . [Indians], and seeing an opportunity to increase their wealth by the deception, told the Indians that it was the seed of a plant which grew in the lands they had come from, and doubtless it would thrive in their land also. The Indians, of course, believed this statement, and purchased the supposed seed, giving in exchange for it large quantities of gold. In implicit faith they carefully planted the supposed seed, and anxiously watched for its sprouting and the appearance of the plant; but it never came. They had faith in the statements made to them by the Europeans, but as these statements were false, and therefore the evidence on which the Indians based their belief untrue, their faith was vain." Thus must it ever be. Only correct evidence, only truthful testimony can produce fruitful, profitable, true faith. *No matter how sincere one's belief may be in an error, that will not transform the error into truth. The sincere faith of the Indians in what the Europeans had said about the gunpowder seed did not make that substance produce a plant yielding gunpowder.* And so faith in false doctrines, founded upon false testimony, cannot savor of salvation.

(B. H. Roberts, *The Gospel and Man's Relationship to Deity* [Salt Lake City: Deseret Book, 1950], 46–47)

––––––––

Faith exists when absolute confidence in that which we cannot see combines with action that is in absolute conformity to the will of our Heavenly Father. . . . Only when our faith is aligned with the will of our Heavenly Father will we be empowered to receive the blessings we seek.

("Shall He Find Faith on the Earth?" *Ensign*, Nov. 2002, 83–84; as quoted in Joseph B. Wirthlin, *Ensign*, Feb. 2004 [Salt Lake City: The Church of Jesus Christ of Latter-day Saints, 2004], 65)

––––––––

It is impossible to exercise saving faith in that which is untrue.

(Robert L. Millet, *The Book of Mormon: Fourth Nephi through Moroni, from Zion to Destruction* [Salt Lake City: Bookcraft, 1995], 9)

Alma 32:27 • A DESIRE TO BELIEVE

During a zone conference, a missionary asked the instructor why his investigators did not receive answers to their prayers. They were reading the Book of Mormon and praying about it. The investigators were looking for the fulfillment of Moroni's promise that those who read the book and pray with real intent, with faith in Christ, will receive an answer. [See Moroni 10:3–5.] The instructor questioned the missionary regarding the prayers of the investigators. "Were they praying with real intent?" The missionary answered, "Yes, but they know they will not receive an answer!"

Alma states that unbelief causes the person to "resist the Spirit of the Lord" so that the seed is cast out before it has a chance to grow (Alma 32:28). A desire to believe is a prerequisite for an answer. Confirmations by the Holy Spirit are not given to unbelievers. They would not recognize the whisperings of the Holy Ghost. Further, praying with "real intent" implies praying with a desire to believe as well as a desire to know.

(Merrill J. Bateman, *Heroes from the Book of Mormon* [Salt Lake City: Bookcraft, 1995], 26)

Alma 32:28 • PLANT THE SEED IN YOUR HEART

(Refer to Virginia H. Pearce quote at the conclusion of Alma 32.)

To soundly plant good seeds in your heart requires prolonged, intense, unremitting pondering. It is a deep, ongoing, regenerating process which refines the soul.

(Joseph B. Wirthlin, *Ensign*, May 1982 [Salt Lake City: The Church of Jesus Christ of Latter-day Saints, 1982], 23–25)

––––––––

Just as soil needs preparation for a seed, so does a human heart for the word of God to take root. Before he told the people to plant the seed, Alma told them that their hearts were prepared. They had been persecuted and cast out of their churches. Alma with his love and the circumstances of their lives, which led them to be humble, had prepared them. They were then ready to hear the word of God. If they chose to plant it in their hearts, the growth in their souls would surely follow, and that would increase their faith. . . . First of all . . . to plant the seed, they have to try it by keeping commandments. . . . That feeling of surrender is not likely to come unless they experience some feeling of being loved and lowly of heart.

(Henry B. Eyring, *Ensign*, Nov. 1995 [Salt Lake City: The Church of Jesus Christ of Latter-day Saints, 1995], 38)

––––––––

Often in the Church, we refer to Alma 32 as being a great chapter on faith. This is not incorrect; but the seed Alma refers to is not faith, it is *the word of God* (see Alma 32:28).

(*Selected Writings of Gerald N. Lund* [Salt Lake City: Deseret Book, 1999], 119)

Alma 32:34–35 • SWELLETH SOULS AND ENLIGHTEN UNDERSTANDING

A few weeks ago our four-year-old grandson, Michael, reported to his parents, "When I pray, my heart feels like a roasted marshmallow." . . . The prophet Alma described these feelings . . . [in Alma 32:34–35]. Learning to discern the teachings of the Spirit is an important part of helping faith become a reality. My daughter Karen shared her experience. She said, "When I was just a little girl, I started reading the Book of Mormon for the first time. After many days of reading, I came one night to 1 Nephi 3:7: . . . I felt strongly impressed. . . . but the deep impression was really more of a feeling. I had seen my parents mark verses in their scriptures with red pencils. So I got up and searched through the house until I found a red pencil, and with a great sense of solemnity and importance, I marked that verse in my own Book of Mormon." Karen continued, "Over the years as I read the scriptures, that experience was repeated time and time again. . . In time I came to recognize that feeling as the Holy Ghost."

(Janette Hales Beckham, *Ensign*, Nov. 1997 [Salt Lake City: The Church of Jesus Christ of Latter-day Saints, 1997], 75)

Alma 32:39–43 • SEED, TREE OF LIFE

Alma's seed is the same as Lehi's rod of iron. . . . Alma teaches one how to find the strait and narrow path and hold on to the rod. It begins with a desire to believe [see Alma 32:27]. . . .

In Alma's experiment, a person plants a seed in his heart, and by nourishing it continually, it grows into a tree of life within. What does this mean? . . . If one has the tree (Christ) and its fruit (the Atonement and its blessings) within oneself, one's countenance will reflect Christ's image [see Alma 5:14]. Through the experiment of trying the word, one is blessed by the Holy Spirit and receives the gifts of faith, love, virtue, brotherly kindness, and so on, and one experiences the mighty change of heart—one is born of God. The person becomes a new creature in Christ, as Christ is within him. . . .

Lehi's tree is symbolic of the Savior. One obtains the fruits of the Atonement by holding to the rod of iron until one reaches the tree and partakes of the fruit. Alma teaches the same truths. By experimenting on the word (planting and nurturing the seed), a person's desire to believe is rewarded by a witness of the Spirit.

He receives truth line upon line and precept upon precept. By diligent and patient continuance, the seed matures into a tree within a person's heart and soul. By the power of the Holy Spirit, the additional light with the person causes him to reflect the Savior's characteristics in his countenance and being. He puts off the natural man and becomes a partaker of the divine nature. He receives a new heart and experiences a new birth.

(Merrill J. Bateman, *Heroes from the Book of Mormon* [Salt Lake City: Bookcraft, 1995], 27, 29–30)

Alma used a seed to stand for the word. He taught the discouraged Zoramites that if they would "give place, that a seed may be planted in [their] heart[s]" (Alma 32:28), and then notice if good feelings went with it, they would begin to understand and life would be different for them. Could that be a way of saying: "Decide, just for yourself, that you will make a place for scripture reading. And then, as you begin to do that notice what feelings go with it?" Alma then taught that "as the tree beginneth to grow" (Alma 32:37), it would need to be nourished with great care. Could that be a way of saying: "Nourish the desire to read. Do some things that will keep you reading and help you to understand in new ways. Let others keep you excited and help you learn more from the scriptures so that the word will continue to grow?" Alma taught that if this nourishing continued for a long time, there would be wonderful fruit. Please turn to Alma, chapter 32, verse 42: . . . "ye shall pluck the fruit, . . . and ye shall feast upon this fruit . . . that ye hunger not, neither shall ye thirst." Could that be a way of saying: "When you continue reading, and doing the things that you read about, eventually life will change in a way that is difficult to even imagine. Your daily discouragements will be replaced with a knowledge of how much God loves you. You will feast and be filled."

(Virginia H. Pearce, *Ensign*, May 1995 [Salt Lake City: The Church of Jesus Christ of Latter-day Saints, 1995], 89)

Alma 33 • ZENOS

When Alma went to preach in the sticks to some Zoramite outcasts who had been barred from the holy places because of their poverty he took as his text the short autobiographical hymn of the prophet Zenos, in which that Old World hero told how he too had been banished from the religious community and wandered in the desert as a despised outcast but still could call upon God wherever he was until God finally vindicated him and punished his enemies (Alma 33:3–11). . . .

Twelve times the Book of Mormon names the prophet Zenos, next to Isaiah the most conspicuous Old World prophetic figure in the book. . . . How, one wonders, could an important prophet like Zenos, if he ever existed, have simply dropped out of sight without leaving a trace of himself in the Bible or anywhere else? That, as we have seen is just the question that is being asked today about certain prophets now rediscovered in the Dead Sea Scrolls.

(Hugh W. Nibley, *Since Cumorah* [Salt Lake City: Deseret Book, 1976], 136, 322)

Alma 34:10–12 • INFINITE ATONEMENT
(Refer in this text to 2 Nephi 9:7–9.)

Alma 34:10–15 • GREAT AND LAST SACRIFICE

Elder M. Russell Ballard has taught that "the word *sacrifice* means literally 'to make sacred,' or 'to render sacred' " ("The Law of Sacrifice," *Ensign*, Oct. 1998, 8). The words *sacred* and *sacrifice* come from the same root. One may not have the sacred without first sacrificing something for it. There can be no sacredness without personal sacrifice. Sacrifice sanctifies the sacred.

(Dennis B. Neuenschwander, in Conference Report, Apr. 2003 [Salt Lake City: The Church of Jesus Christ of Latter-day Saints, 2003], 74)

Alma 34:14–16 • MERCY CAN SATISFY JUSTICE

All too often, the justice of God seems to be relegated to the back burner, while the mercy of God seems to get the lion's share of attention. I presume this is true because we are all hoping for mercy and trying to avoid justice if at all possible. But it is a fact that God is just, and mercy cannot rob justice. Justice will have her due! It is also a fact that mercy, while it cannot rob justice, can satisfy the demands of justice in one instance and one instance only. . . .

Only in the instance where we exercise faith in Jesus Christ unto repentance.

(Hartman Rector, Jr., in Conference Report, Oct. 1985 [Salt Lake City: The Church of Jesus Christ of Latter-day Saints, 1985], 98)

Alma 34:15 • FAITH UNTO REPENTANCE

A man we were teaching on the island of Maui had come to believe the gospel was true, but he couldn't find the strength to repent. He would make promises to change his ways, to get rid of habits very harmful to himself and his family, but he would break his promises and then suffer terribly from guilt. He felt ashamed, not good enough for Christ, and too weak to become good.

We tried all kinds of ways to help him be strong. . . . Nothing worked, and his family, who had joined the

Church, and we missionaries were all near despair. Then I remembered Joseph Smith's claim that the Book of Mormon was "the most correct book" in the world and that its principles provided the best way to get near to God (*Teachings of the Prophet Joseph Smith*, sel. by Joseph Fielding Smith [Salt Lake City: Deseret Book, 1938], 194). . . .

Then we read the main passages about Christ from the Book of Mormon with our friend, and he felt the spirit of complete love from his Savior. I remember when we came to the sermon of Amulek, in Alma 34, where he teaches that the suffering of Christ brings about the bowels of mercy, enough to break through the bands of justice and give us the means to have enough faith to repent. This was exactly what our friend needed—and as he read the Book of Mormon passages he finally understood and *felt* it and thus was able to accept Christ's love and repent. . . . The turning point was when he felt love from Christ, conveyed by the promises and spirit of the Book of Mormon. He said, "If Christ can have this kind of love for me, who am I to refuse to accept it—and not accept myself." With this new strength, he became a new person, almost overnight.

(Eugene England, *Converted to Christ through the Book of Mormon* [Salt Lake City: Deseret Book, 1989], 1–2)

Alma 34:18–27 • CRY UNTO HIM IN YOUR HOUSES
(Refer in this text to Alma 37:37; 3 Nephi 18:15–23.)

May I ask this important question: How many families in The Church of Jesus Christ of Latter-day Saints have regular nightly and morning family prayer? Those who neglect to do so are displeasing the Lord and are entitled to the same rebuke which the Lord gave some of the leading elders of the Church in the early days. No parent should depend solely on the organizations of the Church for the training of the children. They should be taught to pray regularly, secretly as well as in the family circle. The counsel that Alma and Amulek gave to the straying Zoramites is just as essential to the Latter-day Saints today as it was two thousand years ago.

(Joseph Fielding Smith, *Answers to Gospel Questions* [Salt Lake City: Deseret Book, 1972], 5:48)

No man can retain the Spirit of the Lord, unless he prays. No man can have the inspiration of the Holy Spirit, unless in his heart is found this spirit of prayer. . . . And if a man will pray as he is commanded to do in this passage of scripture which I have read [Alma 34:18–27], then he more than likely will be found in all things righteously keeping the commandments of the Lord. He will not be found scheming to take advantage of his neighbor in some trade of bargain, but in all things dealing justly, because he has prayed in the morning and has in his heart the spirit of prayer throughout the day, that the Lord will bless him in the increase of his goods, of his fields, of his flocks, or whatever it may be he is engaged in.

(Joseph Fielding Smith, in Conference Report, Oct. 1919 [Salt Lake City: The Church of Jesus Christ of Latter-day Saints, 1919], 142–143)

It is not such a difficult thing to learn how to pray. It is not the words we use particularly that constitute prayer. Prayer does not consist of words, altogether. True, faithful, earnest prayer consists more in the feeling that rises from the heart and from the inward desire of our spirits to supplicate the Lord in humility and in faith, that we may receive His blessings. It matters not how simple the words may be, if our desires are genuine and we come before the Lord with a broken heart and a contrite spirit to ask Him for that which we need.

(Joseph F. Smith, in Conference Report, Oct. 1899 [Salt Lake City: The Church of Jesus Christ of Latter-day Saints, 1899], 69)

Prayer should be direct and simple as if spoken to our earthly father. Routine forms of prayer should be avoided. The words spoken are less important than the humble faith in which they are uttered. "Prayer is the soul's sincere desire, uttered or unexpressed." It is the spirit of prayer that gives life to our desires. The direct simplicity of the Lords prayer should be kept in mind.

(John A. Widtsoe, *Evidences and Reconciliations* [Salt Lake City: Bookcraft, 1987], 316)

In the summer of my thirteenth year, . . . I eagerly joined some neighborhood friends to light fireworks. . . . Not all of our fireworks worked as they should have. . . . We set the duds aside until we had tried to light all of the fireworks. We had so many defective ones remaining, we wondered what to do. We couldn't just throw them away. What if we emptied the powder from all of them into the cardboard box? We could toss in a match and have one gigantic blast! . . . The match was tossed; we quickly ran away and waited. Nothing happened. . . . We tried a second time, using a makeshift fuse of rolled-up newspaper. . . . Again, to our good, nothing happened. . . . Foolishly, we gave it one more try. . . . Then it happened! The "gigantic blast" we thought we wanted exploded with fury into our faces. The force of the explosion knocked us off our feet, and flames from the ignited powder burned us severely. . . . Our friend's mother gathered us into her home. "First we will pray,"

she said, "and then we will call the doctor." That was the first of many prayers I remember being offered for us. Soon after, I felt my face, hands, and arms being wrapped in bandages. I heard the voices of my father and my doctor administering a priesthood blessing to me. I heard my mother's voice many times, pleading with Heavenly Father to please let her son see again. . . . I had felt with a surety that I would be healed. From the moment that first prayer was offered in my friend's home, I felt a comforting peace. . . . Each day when the doctor changed my bandages, my mother would ask, "Can he see?" For many days the answer was the same: "No, not yet." Finally, when all the bandages were permanently removed, my eyesight began to return. . . . The peace and comfort I had earlier felt gave me assurance that all would be well. However, when my vision cleared enough for me to see my hands and face, I was shocked, unprepared for what I saw. . . . Seeing my scarred and disfigured skin brought great fear and doubt into my mind. I can remember thinking, nothing can help this skin to be healed—not even the Lord. Gratefully, as my prayers and the prayers of others continued, I felt the gifts of faith and of peace restored, and then, in time, my eyesight and my skin were healed. . . . May we always seek to obtain the Lord's miraculous gift of peace through prayer.

(Rex E. Pinegar, *Ensign*, May 1993 [Salt Lake City: The Church of Jesus Christ of Latter-day Saints, 1993], 65–68)

Alma 34:28–29 • THE ROYAL LAW
(Refer in this text to Mosiah 2:16–17.)

We must have this law in mind in all that we do in our welfare work. We must love our neighbor as ourselves. The Savior put this law second only to the love of God. . . .

(Marion G. Romney, in Conference Report, Apr. 1978 [Salt Lake City: The Church of Jesus Christ of Latter-day Saints, 1978], 142)

One cannot ask God to help a neighbor in distress without feeling motivated to do something oneself toward helping that neighbor.

(Gordon B. Hinckley, *Ensign*, Feb. 1991 [Salt Lake City: The Church of Jesus Christ of Latter-day Saints, 1991], 2–5)

To worthy causes and needy people, we can give time if we don't have money, and we can give love when our time runs out. . . . Sister Drusilla Hendricks and her invalid husband, James, who had been shot by enemies of the Church in the Battle of Crooked River, arrived with their children at a hastily shaped dugout in Quincy,

Illinois, to live out the spring of that harrowing year. Within two weeks the Hendrickses were on the verge of starvation, having only one spoonful of sugar and a saucerful of cornmeal remaining in their possession. In the great tradition of LDS women, Drusilla made mush out of it for James and the children, thus stretching its contents as far as she could make it go. When that small offering was consumed by her famished family, she washed everything, cleaned their little dugout as thoroughly as she could, and quietly waited to die. Not long thereafter the sound of a wagon brought Drusilla to her feet. It was their neighbor Reuben Allred. He said he had a feeling they were out of food, so on his way into town he'd had a sack of grain ground into meal for them. Shortly thereafter Alexander Williams arrived with two bushels of meal on his shoulder. He told Drusilla that he'd been extremely busy but the Spirit had whispered to him that "Brother Hendricks' family is suffering, so I dropped everything and came [running]." . . . May [we] hear the whispering of the Holy Spirit when any neighbor anywhere "is suffering," and . . . "drop everything and come running."

(Jeffrey R. Holland, *Ensign,* May 1996 [Salt Lake City: The Church of Jesus Christ of Latter-day Saints, 1996], 30–31)

———

How well I remember my father, the bishop of our ward, filling my small red wagon with food and clothing and then directing me—as a deacon in the Church—to pull the wagon behind me and visit the homes of the needy in our ward.

Often, when fast-offering funds were depleted, my father would take money from his own pocket to supply the needy in his flock with food that would keep them from going hungry. Those were the days of the Great Depression, and many families were suffering.

I remember visiting one family in particular: a sickly mother, an unemployed and discouraged father, and five children with pallid faces, all disheartened and hungry. I remember the gratitude that beamed in their faces when I walked up to their door with my wagon nearly spilling over with needed supplies. I remember how the children smiled. I remember how the mother wept. And I remember how the father stood, head bowed, unable to speak.

These impressions and many others forged within me a love for the poor, a love for my father who served as a shepherd to his flock, and a love for the faithful and generous members of the Church who sacrificed so much to help relieve the suffering of others.

Brothers and sisters, in a sense, you too can bring to a needy family a wagon brimming with hope. How? By paying a generous fast offering.

(Joseph B. Wirthlin, *Ensign,* May 2001 [Salt Lake City: The Church of Jesus Christ of Latter-day Saints, 2001], 74)

———

I love that man better who swears a stream as long as my arm yet deals justice to his neighbors and mercifully deals his substance to the poor, than the long, smooth-faced hypocrite.

(Joseph Smith, *History of the Church of Jesus Christ of Latter-day Saints* [Salt Lake City: Deseret Book, 1980], 5:401)

Alma 34:32–33 • CAN YOU REPENT AFTER DEATH?
(Contrast with D&C 138:58; Moses 7:38–39.)

We know not fully on what terms repentance will be obtainable in the hereafter; but to suppose that the soul who has willfully rejected the opportunity of repentance in this life will find it easy to repent there is contrary to reason. To procrastinate the day of repentance is to deliberately place ourselves in the power of the adversary.

(James E. Talmage, *Articles of Faith* [London: The Church of Jesus Christ of Latter-day Saints, 1962], 115)

———

Now I have read to you the scripture (Alma 34:30–35). I believe it is the word of God "with the bark on it," where the prophet of the Lord declared unto apostates and those who have heard the gospel that if they did not repent and come into the Church now, in this day of repentance, but continued to procrastinate their repentance unto the end, that the night would come when no work could be done for them, and their souls would be lost. I think that is pretty good scripture. I do not know how the Lord could do otherwise in justice.

(Joseph Fielding Smith, *Doctrines of Salvation,* comp. by Bruce R. McConkie [Salt Lake City: Bookcraft, 1955], 2:189)

———

You can progress much more rapidly here on earth with your mortal body in this environment of good and evil than you will as a spirit in the spirit world.

(Richard G. Scott, *Ensign,* May 1997 [Salt Lake City: The Church of Jesus Christ of Latter-day Saints, 1997], 54)

———

If the repentance of the wayward children does not happen in this life, is it still possible for the cords of the sealing to be strong enough for them yet to work out their repentance? In the Doctrine and Covenants we are told:

"The dead who repent will be redeemed, through obedience to the ordinances of the house of God,

"And after they have paid the penalty of their transgressions, and are washed clean, shall receive a reward according to their works, for they are heirs of salvation" (D&C 138:58–59).

We remember that the prodigal son wasted his inheritance, and when it was all gone he came back into the family, but his inheritance was spent (Luke 15:11–32). Mercy will not rob justice, and the sealing power of faithful parents will claim wayward children only on the condition of their repentance and Christ's Atonement. Repentant wayward children will enjoy salvation and all the blessings that go with it, but exaltation is much more. It must be fully earned. The question as to who will be exalted must be left to the Lord in His mercy.

There are very few whose rebellion and evil deeds are so great that they have "sinned away the power to repent" (Alonzo A. Hinckley, in Conference Report, Oct. 1919, 161). That judgment must also be left up to the Lord. . . .

Perhaps in this life we are not given to fully understand how enduring the sealing cords of righteous parents are to their children.

(James E. Faust, in Conference Report, Apr. 2003 [Salt Lake City: The Church of Jesus Christ of Latter-day Saints, 2003], 68)

Alma 34:33 • DON'T PROCRASTINATE REPENTANCE
(Refer in this text to 1 Nephi 18:20; Helaman 13:38; 2:13.)

We should take warning and not wait for the death-bed to repent, as we see the infant taken away by death, so may the youth and middle-aged, as well as the infant be suddenly called into eternity. Let this, then, prove as a warning to all not to procrastinate repentance, or wait till a death-bed, for it is the will of God that man should repent and serve Him in health, and in the strength and power of his mind, in order to secure his blessing, and not wait until he is called to die.

(*Teachings of the Prophet Joseph Smith*, comp. by Joseph Fielding Smith [Salt Lake City: Deseret Book, 1976], 197)

We are concerned that some young people who are anticipating serving a mission or being married in the temple have a very lax attitude toward sin. "I'll just have a few free ones," they say, "and then I'll repent quickly, and go on my mission (or get married in the temple), and everything will be alright.". . . Such persons want the present convenience or enjoyment of sin and the future effects of righteousness, in that order. They want to experience the sin, but avoid its effects. . . . There is something very peculiar about the state of mind or heart of the person who deliberately commits sin in the

expectation that he or she will speedily and comfortably repent and continue as a servant of God, preaching repentance and asking others to come unto Christ. . . . Am I suggesting that the benefits of the atonement are not available for the person who heedlessly sins? Of course not. But, I am suggesting that there is a relationship between sin and suffering, that is not understood by people who knowingly sin in the expectation that all the burden of suffering will be borne by another, that the sin is all theirs, but the suffering is all His. That is not the way. Repentance, which is an assured passage to an eternal destination, is nevertheless not a free ride.

(Dallin H. Oaks, BYU Fireside, 5 Aug. 1990)

Yes, one can repent of . . . transgression. The miracle of forgiveness is real, and true repentance is accepted of the Lord. But, it is not pleasing to the Lord to sow one's wild oats, to engage in . . . transgression of any nature and then expect that *planned* confession and quick repentance will satisfy the Lord.

(*Teachings of Ezra Taft Benson* [Salt Lake City: Bookcraft, 1988], 70)

It is my judgment that some of our youth *do not believe* that repentance for serious transgression "is difficult and painful and may take a long time." Where has this grave misunderstanding come from? To you young people, if any of us who are older have given you the impression that it isn't too serious to disobey the commandments of God, forgive us. . . . Priesthood leaders, let us be careful that we do not permit young missionaries to go into the mission field with unresolved transgression. It is literally like going into battle without helmet, sword, or shield. Let us remember that it takes time to develop the power to resist the fires of temptation. It takes time to receive the sweet comfort that always comes to the heart of the truly penitent. Allow them sufficient time.

(L. Aldin Porter, *Ensign*, May 1992 [Salt Lake City: The Church of Jesus Christ of Latter-day Saints, 1992], 46)

As the time of repentance is procrastinated, the ability to repent grows weaker; neglect of opportunity in holy things develops inability.

(James E. Talmage, *Articles of Faith* [London: The Church of Jesus Christ of Latter-day Saints, 1962], 114)

The thought of intentionally committing serious sin now and repenting later is perilously wrong. Never do that. Many start that journey of intentional transgression and never make it back. Premeditated sin has greater penalties and is harder to overcome. If there is sin, repent now—while you can.

(Richard G. Scott, *Ensign*, Nov. 1994 [Salt Lake City: The Church of Jesus Christ of Latter-day Saints, 1994], 38)

I believe, to use an insurance phrase, we must pay the deductible. We must experience sorrow enough, suffering enough, guilt enough so we are conscious and appreciative of the heavier burden borne by the Savior. My soul pains when His atonement is treated lightly, when the blessing of repentance is reduced to simply "taking care of it with the bishop," when there is brief confession without humility or godly sorrow. This attitude of entitlement rather than privilege was recently expressed by a young Church member who wrote: "I have done bad things that I knew were bad because I've been taught that ever since I can remember. . . . I know repentance is a great gift. Without it I would be lost. I am not ready to repent of my sins; but I know that when I am ready, I can." Such indulgence in premeditated sin shows pitiful misunderstanding of repentance.

(J. Richard Clarke, *Ensign*, May 1993 [Salt Lake City: The Church of Jesus Christ of Latter-day Saints, 1993], 10)

One of the most serious human defects in all ages is procrastination, an unwillingness to accept personal responsibilities *now*. . . .

There are even many members of the Church who are lax and careless and who continually procrastinate. . . .

One Church member of my acquaintance said, as she drank her coffee: "The Lord knows my heart is right and that I have good intentions, and that I will someday get the strength to quit." But will one receive eternal life on the basis of his good intentions? . . . Samuel Johnson remarked that "[the road to] hell is paved with good intentions." The Lord will not translate one's good hopes and desires and intentions into works. Each of us must do that for himself.

(Spencer W. Kimball, *The Miracle of Forgiveness* [Salt Lake City: Bookcraft, 1969], 7–8)

Alma 34:34–35 • ATTITUDES AFTER WE DIE

Suppose, then, that a man is evil in his heart—wholly given up to wickedness, and in that condition dies, his spirit will enter into the spirit world intent upon evil. On the other hand, if we are striving with all the powers and faculties God has given us to improve

upon our talents, to prepare ourselves to dwell in eternal life. . . . With what disposition will our spirits enter their next state? They will be still striving to do the things of God, only in a much greater degree—learning, increasing, growing in grace and in the knowledge of the truth.

If we are faithful to our religion, when we go into the spirit world, the fallen spirits—Lucifer and the third part of the heavenly hosts that came with him, and the spirits of wicked men who have dwelt upon this earth, the whole of them combined will have no influence over our spirits. Is not that an advantage? Yes. All the rest of the children of men are more or less subject to them, and they are subject to them as they were while here in the flesh.

(*Discourses of Brigham Young*, comp. by John A. Widtsoe [Salt Lake City: Deseret Book, 1954], 379)

The wicked spirits that leave here and go into the spirit world, are they wicked there? Yes.

(*Teachings of Presidents of the Church—Brigham Young* [Salt Lake City: The Church of Jesus Christ of Latter-day Saints, 1997], 279)

A righteous man or woman cannot take a backward step spiritually after death; in short, the righteous have completed their days of probation in mortality. Amulek informs us that our disposition here will be our disposition hereafter (see Alma 34:32–25). Such is the case with regard to little children [who die before the age of accountability]. They were pure in this existence, will be pure in the world of spirits, and will come forth in the resurrection of the pure in heart at the appropriate time.

(Robert L. Millet, *The Book of Mormon: Fourth Nephi through Moroni, from Zion to Destruction* [Salt Lake City: Bookcraft, 1995], 13)

The active, intelligent, . . . organization that inhabited the body does not descend with it into the grave . . . but it goes to the spirit world. . . .

Suppose, then, that a man is evil in his heart—wholly given up to wickedness, and in that condition dies, his spirit will enter the spirit world intent upon evil. On the other hand, if we are striving with all the powers and faculties God has given us to improve upon our talents, to prepare ourselves to dwell in eternal life, and the grave receives our bodies . . . we . . . will be still striving to do the things of God, only in a much greater degree—learning, increasing, growing in grace and in the knowledge of the truth.

(Brigham Young, *Journal of Discourses* [London: Latter-day Saints' Book Depot, 1860], 7:333)

———

No one can repent on the cross, nor in prison, nor in custody. One must have the opportunity of committing wrong in order to be really repentant. The man in handcuffs, the prisoner in the penitentiary, the man as he drowns, or as he dies—such a man certainly cannot repent totally. He can wish to do it, he may intend to change his life, he may determine that he will, but that is only the beginning.

That is why we should not wait for the life beyond but should abandon evil habits and weaknesses while in the flesh on the earth. Elder Melvin J. Ballard pinpointed this problem:

. . . This life is the time in which men are to repent. Do not let any of us imagine that we can go down to the grave not having overcome the corruptions of the flesh and then lose in the grave all our sins and evil tendencies. They will be with us. They will be with the spirit when separated from the body (Ballard, "Three Degrees of Glory").

Clearly it is difficult to repent in the spirit world of sins involving physical habits and actions. There one has spirit and mind but not the physical power to overcome a physical habit. He can desire to change his life, but how can he overcome the lusts of the flesh unless he has flesh to control and transform? How can he overcome the tobacco or the drink habit in the spirit world where there is no liquor nor tobacco and no flesh to crave it? Similarly with other sins involving lack of control over the body.

(Spencer W. Kimball, *The Miracle of Forgiveness* [Salt Lake City: Bookcraft, 1969], 167–168)

Alma 34:40–41 • BE PATIENT IN AFFLICTION
(Refer in this text to Mosiah 24:14–15.)

Religious faith gives confidence that human tragedy is not a meaningless sport of physical forces. Life is not what Voltaire called it, "A bad joke," it is really a school of discipline whose author and teacher is God.

(Hugh B. Brown, in Conference Report, Oct. 1969 [Salt Lake City: The Church of Jesus Christ of Latter-day Saints, 1969], 105–107)

———

The great challenge in this earthly life is not to determine how to escape the afflictions and problems, but rather to carefully prepare ourselves to meet them. I say prepare ourselves because it demands persistent effort to develop patience as a personal attribute. In practicing patience, one comes to understand it and to acquire it. . . . We must have patience in order to withstand pain and grief without complaint or discouragement, which detract from the Spirit. . . . We are not talking here about a passive patience which waits only for the passing of time to heal or resolve things which happen to us, but rather a patience that is active, which makes things happen. . . (Rom. 2:7; 1 Peter 2:20). Patience in affliction and adversity means to persist firmly and never forsake that which we know to be true, standing firm with the hope that in the Lord's due time we will gain an understanding of that which we do not understand now and which causes us suffering. . . . The faithful Latter-day Saint—instead of despairing because a goal on his or her agenda was not realized, because his or her timetable does not bring a solution to the problems, or because comfort does not come to calm the troubles of today—waits patiently for fulfillment of promises, according to the Lord's timetable.

(Angel Abrea, in Conference Report, Apr. 1992 [Salt Lake City: The Church of Jesus Christ of Latter-day Saints, 1992], 34–37)

———

Mormon surely knew that no pain we suffer, no trial that we experience is wasted. It ministers to our education, to the development of such qualities as patience, faith, fortitude and humility. All that we suffer and all that we endure, especially when we endure it patiently, builds up our characters, purifies our hearts, expands our souls, and makes us more tender and charitable, more worthy to be called the children of God.

(Howard W. Hunter, *Ensign*, Nov. 1987 [Salt Lake City: The Church of Jesus Christ of Latter-day Saints, 1987], 60)

———

Sometimes we pray for the strength to endure yet resist the very things that would give us that strength. Too often we seek the easy way, forgetting that strength comes from overcoming things that require us to put forth more effort than we normally would be inclined to do.

(John H. Groberg, *Ensign*, Nov. 1993 [Salt Lake City: The Church of Jesus Christ of Latter-day Saints, 1993], 26)

———

It is easy enough to be pleasant,
When life flows by like a song,
But the man worth while is one who will smile,
When everything goes dead wrong.
For the test of the heart is trouble,
And it always comes with the years,
And the smile that is worth the praises of earth
Is the smile that shines through tears.

(Ella Wheeler Wilcox; as quoted in Thomas S. Monson, *Ensign*, Nov. 1993 [Salt Lake City: The Church of Jesus Christ of Latter-day Saints, 1993], 71)

I am grateful for the things which I have suffered in the flesh, which have been blessings in my life that have taught me patience, long-suffering, faith, and a sensitivity to those who are less fortunate. . . . I have learned in my life that trials are blessings in disguise if we accept them with humility, faith, and fortitude. All that we suffer and endure with patience will build within us a more charitable and tender person, having acquired the education we came on earth to receive.

(Lloyd P. George, *Ensign*, May 1994 [Salt Lake City: The Church of Jesus Christ of Latter-day Saints, 1994], 28)

No pain that we suffer, no trial that we experience is wasted. It ministers to our education, to the development of such qualities as patience, faith, fortitude and humility. All that we suffer and all that we endure, especially when we endure it patiently, builds up our characters, purifies our hearts, expands our souls, and makes us more tender and charitable, more worthy to be called the children of God, . . . and it is through sorrow and suffering, toil and tribulation, that we gain the education that we come here to acquire.

(Orson F. Whitney, *Improvement Era*, Mar. 1966 [Salt Lake City: The Church of Jesus Christ of Latter-day Saints, 1966], 211)

[A portion of a letter from Mary Fielding Smith from Commerce Illinois, to her brother in England. June 1839.]

I do not feel in the least discouraged. . . . We have been enabled to rejoice, in the midst of our privations and persecutions, that we were counted worthy to suffer these things, so that we may, with the ancient saints who suffered in like manner, inherit the same glorious reward. If it had not been for this hope, I should have sunk before this; but, blessed be the God and rock of my salvation, here I am, and am perfectly satisfied and happy, having not the smallest desire to go one step backward.

(Don Cecil Corbett, *Mary Fielding Smith: Daughter of Britain* [Salt Lake City: Deseret Book, 1974], 100)

No other dispensation has had the gospel without any challenge, without any opposition or resistance, without persecution from the world, and to expect that

we shall be without such conditions is to expect that which will never be. We do not hold membership in the Church and its blessings without paying a price for it.

(*Memorable Stories and Parables by Boyd K. Packer* [Salt Lake City: Bookcraft, 1997], 76)

Alma 35:15 • OFFENDED BY THE WORD
(Refer in this text to 1 Nephi 8:20.)

We may get angry with parents, or a teacher, or the Bishop, and dwarf ourselves into nameless anonymity as we shrivel and shrink under the venom and poison of bitterness, little realizing the suffering of the hater, the latter cheats himself. . . . To terminate activity in the Church just to spite leaders or to give vent to wounded feelings is to cheat ourselves.

(*Teachings of Spencer W. Kimball*, ed. by Edward L. Kimball [Salt Lake City: Bookcraft, 1982], 242–243)

Alma 36

I rejoice in the wonderful spirit of the Book of Mormon. I believe that it is one of the greatest missionaries in the hands of the elder that it is possible for him to have. I believe that no man can open that book and read it with a prayerful heart, and ask God, in the name of Jesus Christ, for a testimony regarding its divinity, but what the Lord will manifest unto him by His Spirit the truth of the book itself. . . . There is a mark of divinity on this book; and I maintain that no man can read, for instance, the thirty-sixth chapter, the commandments of Alma to his son, Helaman, without receiving an impression of this kind.

(Heber J. Grant, *Gospel Standards*, comp. by G. Homer Durham [Salt Lake City: An Improvement Era Publication, 1942], 29–30)

I had a wayward brother who took no interest whatever in the Church until he was between thirty-five and forty years of age. I received a letter from him, telling me that on account of the failure of our . . . mines in Oregon, where he had invested large sums of money—all that we had and all that we could borrow—that he had been tempted . . . to kill himself.

He went out into the woods intending to kill himself; but he got to thinking what a cowardly, dastardly act it would be for him to leave his wife and children destitute. So, instead of killing himself, he knelt down and prayed: "O God, if there is a God."

He got up weeping for joy, and he wrote me that he had become convinced of two things: that there is a God, and that there is a devil, one leading to life and the other to death. . . .

I went out and bought him a Book of Mormon,

went into my office, shut the door, and told the Lord I wanted to open the book to the chapter that would do a wayward and careless brother . . . the most good; and this is the chapter to which I opened [the thirty-sixth chapter of Alma]. . . .

I love that chapter. . . . Because, when that wayward brother of mine read it, he wrote: "Heber, I do not know the gospel is true, but I pledge the Lord, if he ever gives me, as He gave Alma of old, a knowledge of the divinity of the gospel, that I will labor as Alma of old labored, to bring souls to a knowledge of the truth." And, thank the Lord, he obtained the knowledge, and thank the Lord also, he has kept his pledge.

I know no man among all my acquaintances who . . . has become more devoted.

(George Q. Cannon, *Gospel Truth, Two Volumes in One*, ed. by Jerreld L. Newquist [Salt Lake City: Deseret Book, 1974], 29–30, 323–324)

Alma 36:1, 30; 37:13; 38:1 • NEPHI'S FREEDOM THESIS

(Refer in this text to 1 Nephi 1:20; Alma 48:15; 2 Nephi 1:7, 20, 30–32; Ether 2:7–9, 12, 15.)

Alma 36:3 • SUPPORTED IN THEIR TRIALS

(Refer in this text to Alma 36:27.)

My sister Lois, legally blind from birth, not only coped but served well as a public schoolteacher for 33 years. She had that same reflex possessed by those pioneer souls who quietly picked up their handcarts and headed west, a reflex we all need. So if various trials are allotted to you, partake of life's bitter cups, but without becoming bitter.

(Neal A. Maxwell, *Ensign*, May 2004 [Salt Lake City: The Church of Jesus Christ of Latter-day Saints, 2004], 44)

Alma 36:11 • AGENCY AND ALMA

Generally our Heavenly Father will not interfere with the agency of another person unless he has a greater purpose for that individual. Two examples come to mind: Saul, who became the Apostle Paul, and Alma the Younger. Both these men were deterred from their unrighteous objective of persecuting the trying to destroy the Church of God. Both became great missionaries for the Church. But even as the Lord intervened, they were given choices. Alma, for example, was told: "If thou wilt be destroyed of thyself, seek no more to destroy the church of God" (Alma 36:11).

(Marvin J. Ashton, "Know He Is There," *BYU Speeches of the Year,* 10 Nov. 1992 [Provo, Utah: BYU Press, 1992], 5)

Alma 36:12–16 • OPENING THE DOOR TO REPENTANCE

(Refer in this text to Alma 38:8.)

When we come to recognize our sin sincerely and without reservations, we are ready to follow such processes as will rid us of sin's effects. . . . Young Alma was so deep in his sin that it was most difficult for him to humble himself toward repentance, but when his experience broke down his resistance, softened his rebellion and overcame his stubbornness, he began to see himself in his true light and appraise his situation as it really was. His heart was softened. His repentance was being born.

(Spencer W. Kimball, *The Miracle of Forgiveness* [Salt Lake City: Bookcraft, 1969], 157–159)

———

Repentance is a very painful process. . . . No one should think that the gift of forgiveness is fully realized without significant effort on the part of the forgiven. No one should be foolish enough to sin willingly or wantonly, thinking forgiveness is easily available.

Repentance of necessity involves suffering and sorrow. Anyone who thinks otherwise has not read the life of the young Alma, nor tried to personally repent. In the process of repentance we are granted just a taste of the suffering we would endure if we failed to turn away from evil. That pain, though only momentary for the repentant, is the most bitter of cups. No man or woman should be foolish enough to think it can be sipped, even briefly, without consequence.

(Jeffrey R. Holland, *The Book of Mormon: It Begins with a Family* [Salt Lake City: Deseret Book, 1983] 95–96)

Alma 36:16–17 • RACKED, TORMENTED, HARROWED

The prophets teach how painful guilt can be. . . .

The prophet Alma, describing his feelings of guilt, said, "I was *racked* with eternal *torment*, for my soul was *harrowed up* to the greatest degree and *racked* with all my sins."

The prophets chose very graphic words.

Racked means "tortured." Anciently a rack was a framework on which the victim was laid with each ankle and wrist tied to a spindle which could then be turned to cause unbearable pain.

A harrow is a frame with spikes through it. When pulled across the ground, it rips and tears into the soil. The scriptures frequently speak of souls and minds being "harrowed up" with guilt.

Torment means "to twist," a means of torture so painful that even the innocent would confess.

(Boyd K. Packer, *Ensign,* May 2001 [Salt Lake

City: The Church of Jesus Christ of Latter-day Saints, 2001], 22–23)

Alma 36:17–19 • HARROWED UP BY THE MEMORY OF SIN

(Refer in this text to Alma 42:29.)

When we sincerely repent and exercise faith in the Lord and in the Atonement, we are forgiven. While the memory of our past sins may come to our minds from time to time, if we will also remember the reality of the Atonement, we will remember our *pains* no more. We will no longer be "harrowed up" by the memory of our sins.

Then we, too, can feel as Alma did: "And oh, what joy, and what marvelous light I did behold; yea, my soul was filled with joy as exceeding as was my pain!" (Alma 36:20).

(Craig A. Cardon, *Ensign,* June 1992 [Salt Lake City: The Church of Jesus Christ of Latter-day Saints, 1992], 31)

Alma 36:17–21 • I REMEMBERED ALSO TO HAVE HEARD MY FATHER

The teachings and testimonies of parents and other good people have an inevitable, inexorable effect. Those lessons are not lost on even the most wayward soul. Somewhere, somehow, they get recorded in the soul and may be called upon in a great moment of need.

It was in such a moment that the young Alma "remembered also to have heard my father prophesy" (Alma 36:17). That prophecy may have been uttered in a day when Alma was taunting his father, or jeering at those who believed, or willfully denying the reality of revelation. It may have come at a time when his father assumed Alma did not care or hear or understand. Or it may have come so early in life that his father might have thought he had forgotten. . . . Now it was being called forth for the very protection it had intended to give. . . . There will always be a great power—even latent, delayed, residual power—in the words of God we utter.

(Jeffrey R. Holland, *The Book of Mormon: It Begins with a Family* [Salt Lake City: Deseret Book, 1983] 97–98)

———————

Some of you have invested months and years trying to offer people you love the gospel of Jesus Christ—to people who have not yet accepted it. Take heart. Alma the Younger, when he came to the point of extremity, remembered the words of his father and it saved his eternal life. God may yet bless you with that greatest of all returns for the investment of your time, that the words of truth you spoke will be remembered in that moment of spiritual yearning by the person you loved enough to offer the most precious thing you ever received.

(Henry B. Eyring, *Because He First Loved Us* [Salt Lake City: Deseret Book, 2002], 35–36)

———————

Obviously, it was the Savior who removed the stain of sin, but consider the role of Enos' father, Jacob, in this process. Jacob could not give his son a "sacred grove" experience, but it *was his responsibility to show him the pathway there.* It would have been very difficult for Jacob to show his son the path had he not been there himself.

This is not unlike Alma the Younger, who for three long days was "racked with torment, . . . [and] harrowed up by the memory of [his] many sins" (Alma 36:17). During this time of suffering, Alma's mind turned to the words of his father: "I remembered also to have heard my father prophesy . . . concerning . . . Jesus Christ" (Alma 36:17). Upon crying out to the Savior, he stated, "I could remember my pains no more; yea, I was harrowed up by the memory of my sins no more" (Alma 36:19). Again, notice the role of the father in the process of spiritual growth. The Savior removed Alma's pain and stain of sin, but *the words of the elder Alma lead his son to the fruits of Gethsemane.* The quality of spiritual example and instruction by parents illuminated the strait and narrow path for many of those who have become our heroes in the Book of Mormon (see Helaman 5:5–6).

(Jack R. Christianson and K. Douglas Bassett, *Life Lessons from the Book of Mormon* [Salt Lake City: Deseret Book, 2003], 79–80)

Alma 36:22 • MY SOUL DID LONG TO BE THERE

Out came Alma's great soul cry: "O Jesus, thou Son of God, have mercy on me"! (Alma 36:18).

Purpose replaced pain. Joy swallowed up despair as Alma apparently viewed God upon His throne, and he longed to join God! (see Alma 36:22).

Such longing for a heavenly home is real, especially in view of how this life is designed. After all, brothers and sisters, when we rejoice in beautiful scenery, great art, and great music, it is but the flexing of instincts acquired in another place and another time.

(Neal A. Maxwell, in Conference Report, Apr. 1984 [Salt Lake City: The Church of Jesus Christ of Latter-day Saints, 1984], 28)

Alma 36:27 • SUPPORTED UNDER TRIALS

If we do our best to keep the commandments of God, come what may, we will be all right. Of course, that does not necessarily mean that we will be spared personal suffering and heartache. Righteousness has never precluded adversity. But faith in the Lord Jesus

Christ—real faith, whole-souled and unshakable—is a power to be reckoned with in the universe. . . . It can be a source of inner strength, through which we find peace, comfort, and the courage to cope.

(M. Russell Ballard, *Ensign*, Nov. 1992 [Salt Lake City: The Church of Jesus Christ of Latter-day Saints, 1992], 32)

———————

Many are sorely tried and tempted before their baptism, thinking such temptations will cease once they have been baptized. From my observation, this is not the case. The temptations often increase, although they may change in character. The greater the growth, the more subtle the temptation. Yet we are told that we are never tempted beyond our capacity to endure and overcome, so no one can say he was forced or seduced by a temptation.

(Stephen R. Covey, *Spiritual Roots of Human Relations* [Salt Lake City: Deseret Book, 1974], 19)

———————

God never bestows upon his people, or upon an individual, superior blessings without a severe trial to prove them, to prove that individual, or that people, to see whether they will keep their covenants with him, and keep in remembrance what he has shown them. Then the greater the vision, the greater the display of the power of the enemy.

So when individuals are blessed with visions, revelations, and great manifestations, look out, then the Devil is nigh you, and you will be tempted in proportion to the visions, revelation, or manifestation you have received.

(*Discourses of Brigham Young*, comp. by John A. Widtsoe [Salt Lake City: Deseret Book, 1954], 338)

———————

In March 1835, while serving his first mission, Wilford Woodruff had to travel through rivers and swamps in the southeastern United States. To traverse the swamps, he and his companion cut down a tree and made it into a canoe. They rowed safely for about 150 miles before abandoning the canoe and walking. President Woodruff later recalled that they took a road that "lay through swamps, and was covered with mud and water most of the way, for one hundred and seventy miles. We walked forty miles in a day through mud and water knee-deep. On the 24th of March, after traveling some ten miles through mud, I was taken lame with a sharp pain in my knee. I sat down on a log."

At this point in the journey, his companion, who had become weary of the work and had decided to return home, left him there, sitting on log in an alligator swamp. Undaunted, Wilford Woodruff turned to the Lord. He said, "I knelt down in the mud and prayed, and the Lord healed me, and I went on my way rejoicing."

(*Teachings of Presidents of the Church—Wilford Woodruff* [Salt Lake City: The Church of Jesus Christ of Latter-day Saints, 2004], 109)

———————

When I was a young man, I served as counselor to a wise district president in the Church. He tried to teach me. One of the things I remember wondering about was this advice he gave: "When you meet someone, treat them as if they were in serious trouble, and you will be right more than half the time."

I thought then that he was pessimistic. Now, more than 40 years later, I can see how well he understood the world and life. As time passes, the world grows more challenging, and our physical capacities slowly diminish with age. It is clear that we will need more than human strength. The Psalmist was right: "But the salvation of the righteous is of the Lord: he is their strength in the time of trouble" (Psalms 37:39).

(Henry B. Eyring, *Ensign*, May 2004 [Salt Lake City: The Church of Jesus Christ of Latter-day Saints, 2004], 16)

———————

In November 1835, when Wilford Woodruff was serving a mission in the southern part of the United States, he and his traveling companions received the Lord's guidance in a time of trial. He wrote: "While traveling in the night, . . . a tremendous storm of wind and rain overtook us. We came to a creek which had swollen to such an extent by the rain, that we could not cross without swimming our horses. . . . We undertook to head the stream, to ford it; but in the attempt, in the midst of the darkness and the raging of the wind and rain, we were lost in the thick woods, amidst the rain, wind, creeks and fallen treetops. We crossed streams nearly twenty times. . . . But the Lord was merciful unto us in the midst of our troubles, for while we were groping in the dark, running the risk of killing both ourselves and [our] animals, by riding off precipitous bluffs, a bright light suddenly shone round about us, and revealed our perilous situation, as we were upon the edge of a deep gulf. The light continued with us until we found a house, and learned the right road."

(*Teachings of Presidents of the Church—Wilford Woodruff* [Salt Lake City: The Church of Jesus Christ of Latter-day Saints, 2004], 217–218)

Alma 36:27 • GOD HAS DELIVERED ME

During the month of January, 1856, the weather was very cold, the temperature ranging 20 to 30 degrees below zero at times. On one occasion I found myself in the canyon alone, as it was so cold not one else cared to risk going out in the canyon that day. I was at that time hauling house logs. . . . After getting my logs cut and dragged down to the loading place I commenced loading them on my bob sled. . . . The loading place being very slippery, . . . after getting the first one loaded on the sled I turned around to load another one. The one I had on the sled slipped off like it was shot out of a gun and struck me in the hollow of the legs and threw me forward on my face across the four logs lying on the ground, or ice.

In falling, . . . I found myself with my body lying face downwards across the four logs and the fifth log lying across my legs, and I was pinned to the ground with a heavy red pine log 10 inches through at the large end and 22 feet long lying across my legs. And there I was with no visible means to extricate myself and there was no aid at hand, as no one but myself was in the canyon that day. I made up my mind that I must freeze and die all alone in the mountains of Utah. Many serious thoughts passed through my mind, as you may imagine. In falling on the logs my breast and stomach were hurt and it was difficult for me to breathe. I did not conceive what to do under the trying ordeal, but concluded to ask the Lord to help me, which I did in earnest prayer. After calling upon the Lord for some time I began to make an effort to extricate myself but all in vain, as I could not move the log that was lying on me. I, however, continued my efforts until I was exhausted and lost all recollection of my situation.

And the first I remembered afterward I was one mile down the canyon sitting on my load of logs and the oxen going gently along. . . . I spoke to my oxen and stopped them and looked around in wonder and astonishment. Then I remembered being under the log at the loading place some time previous. But how long I was there I could not determine, but supposed about two hours, as I was two hours later getting home than usual. . . . I made an effort to get off the load and put on my overcoat but found I could not do it, as I was so sore in my legs and breast that it was with great difficulty that I could move at all. . . .

My oxen being gentle and tractable and the road smooth and all down hill, I arrived home without difficulty. On arriving there I found my wife was anxiously waiting for me and quite uneasy about me, as I was so much later than usual. She . . . helped me into the house, placed me by the fireside and made me as comfortable as possible and took care of my team. I was confined to the house for some days before I could get around again.

Who it was that extricated me from under the log, loaded my sled, hitched my oxen to it, and placed me on it, I cannot say, as I do not know, or even then at the time, remember seeing any one, and I know for a surety no one was in the canyon that day but myself. Hence I

give the Lord . . . credit for saving my life in extricating me from so perilous a situation.

(Merrill, *Utah Pioneer and Apostle Marriner Wood Merrill and His Family*, 44–46; as quoted in Marriner W. Merrill, *Exceptional Stories from the Lives of Our Apostles*, comp. by Leon R. Hartshorn [Salt Lake City: Deseret Book, 1973], 160–162)

Alma 37:6–7 • SMALL AND SIMPLE THINGS

I should like to emphasize the importance of watching the little things in our lives. Have you ever noticed a large gate in a farm fence? As you open it or close it there appears to be very little movement at the hinge. But there is great movement at the perimeter.

Speaking to the Prophet Joseph Smith in 1831, the Lord said: "Out of small things proceedeth that which is great" (D&C 64:33). It is so with good or evil, my brothers and sister. Small, kind acts can grow into mammoth good institutions. The Boy Scout movement is an example of this as is known by anyone acquainted with the history of this great institution.

(Gordon B. Hinckley, in Conference Report, Apr. 1984 [Salt Lake City: The Church of Jesus Christ of Latter-day Saints, 1984], 109)

———————

The course of our lives is seldom determined by great, life-altering decisions. Our direction is often set by the small, day-to-day choices that chart the track on which we run. This is the substance of our lives—making choices.

(Gordon B. Hinckley, *Stand a Little Taller* [Salt Lake City: Eagle Gate, 2001], 13)

———————

At times we have the tendency to think that the more serious the problem, the bigger and more complex the solution should be. That idea can lead us, for example, to seek help from people or institutions outside the home when in reality the most effective solution will come by applying the glorious principles of the gospel in our homes in the small actions and duties of everyday life. The scriptures remind us "that by small and simple things are great things brought to pass" (Alma 37:6). . . .

Any hurts caused by the friction of living together will heal. Offenses will be forgiven. Pride and selfishness will be replaced by humility, compassion, and love.

(Francisco J. Vinas, *Ensign*, May 2004 [Salt Lake City: The Church of Jesus Christ of Latter-day Saints, 2004], 38)

———————

As women we are pretty hard on ourselves! Believe me when I say each of us is much better than we think. We need to recognize and celebrate what we're doing right. Much of what we do seems small and insignificant—just a part of daily living. . . .

Let me give you an example. Recently I asked Elder William W. Parmley about his memories of his mother, LaVern Parmley, who served as the Primary general president for 23 years. He didn't refer to her talks at conferences or the many programs she implemented. He spoke of one of his sweetest moments when he was 17 and preparing to go away to college. He remembered sitting with his mother as she taught him how to sew on a button. With children of all ages, small and simple acts have lasting impact.

(Bonnie D. Parkin, *Ensign*, Nov. 2005 [Salt Lake City: The Church of Jesus Christ of Latter-day Saints, 2005], 107)

Alma 37:23 • GAZELEM

Gazelem is a name given to a servant of God. The word appears to have its roots in Gaz—a stone, and Aleim, a name of God as a revelator, or the interposer in the affairs of men. If this suggestion is correct, its roots admirably agree with its apparent meaning—a seer.

Liahona. This interesting word is Hebrew with an Egyptian ending. It is the name which Lehi gave to the ball or director he found outside his tent. . . .

L is a Hebrew preposition meaning "to," and sometimes used to express the possessive case. *Iah* is a Hebrew abbreviated form of "Jehovah," common in Hebrew names. *On* is the Hebrew name of the Egyptian "City of the sun." . . . *L-iah-on* means, therefore, literally, "To God is Light"; or, "of God is Light." That is to say, God gives light, as does the Sun. The final *a* reminds us that the Egyptian form of the Hebrew name *On* is *Annu*, and this seems to be the form Lehi used.

(G. Reynolds and J. Sjodahl, *Commentary on the Book of Mormon* [Salt Lake City: Deseret Book, 1977], 4:162, 178)

Strange and unusual names were placed by the Prophet in some of the early revelations so that the individuals whom the Lord was then addressing would not be known to the world. The purpose for keeping these identities secret from their enemies having long since passed, the true names are now found in the Doctrine and Covenants.

Two of the names which identified the Prophet himself were *Gazelam* and *Enoch* (D&C 78:9; 82:11; 104:26, 43, 45, 46). Presumptively these and other names used at the same time have particular meanings, which are not now known to us.

With reference to the name Gazelam, it is interesting to note that Alma in directing Helaman to preserve both the Urim and Thummim and the plates containing the Book of Ether, says that such record will be brought to light by the Lord's servant *Gazelem,* who will use "a stone" in his translation work (Alma 37:21–23). It may be that *Gazelem* is a variant spelling of *Gazelam* and that Alma's reference is to the Prophet Joseph Smith who did in fact bring forth part at least of the Ether record. Or it could be that the name Gazelem (Gazelam) is a title having to do with power to translate ancient records and that Alma's reference was to some Nephite prophet who brought the Book of Ether to light in the golden era of Nephite history.

(Bruce R. McConkie, *Mormon Doctrine* [Salt Lake City: Bookcraft, 1966], 307–308)

Alma 37:25, 28, 31 • A CURSE UPON THE LAND
(Refer in this text to Helaman 1:11–12; Ether 8:18–25.)

Alma 37:27, 29, 32 • DO NOT TEACH DARKNESS

It is not necessary that our young people should know of the wickedness carried on in anyplace. Such knowledge is not elevating and it is quite likely that more than one young man can trace the first step of his downfall to a curiosity which led him into questionable places.

(Joseph F. Smith, *Gospel Doctrine* [Salt Lake City: Deseret Book, 1975], 373–374)

As I have met with many groups of missionaries throughout the mission, I find a tendency for missionaries to tell their faults to their companions, their friends, and sometimes in public. There is no place in the mission field to publicize your weaknesses. . . . There is no reason why you should tell every companion the fact that you might have smoked a few cigarettes in your life before you came, or that you had taken the name of the Lord vain, or any other of your weaknesses. We go forward on the assumption that you are worthy to do this work. If there is something of major importance in your life that had not been adjusted before your coming into the mission field, then certainly you should make those adjustments through your president. Don't tell the saints. That does not do anyone any good. It does not mean you are being hypocritical. You had some weaknesses, you repented, and those weaknesses are no longer a part of your life.

(*Teachings of Spencer W. Kimball*, ed. by Edward L. Kimball [Salt Lake City: Bookcraft, 1982], 96)

The study of the doctrines of the gospel will improve behavior quicker than a study of behavior will improve behavior. Preoccupation with unworthy behavior can lead to unworthy behavior. That is why we stress so forcefully the study of the doctrines of the gospel.

(Boyd K. Packer, in Conference Report, Oct. 1986 [Salt Lake City: The Church of Jesus Christ of Latter-day Saints, 1986], 20)

Members of the Church [are] not to affiliate in any way with the occult or those mysterious powers it espouses. . . . these things should not be pursued as games, be topics in church meetings, or be delved into in private, personal conversations.

(First Presidency Letter, 18 Sept. 1991; as quoted in Clyde J. Williams, *Doctrines of the Book of Mormon,* The 1991 Sperry Symposium [Salt Lake City: Deseret Book, 1992], 243)

Alma 37:33 • MEEKNESS AND LOWLINESS OF HEART

(Refer in this text to 3 Nephi 12:5.)

The person who obtains meekness and lowliness of heart and who enjoys the company of the Holy Ghost will have no desire to offend or hurt others, nor will he feel affected by any offenses received from others. He will treat his spouse and children with love and respect and will have good relationships with everyone he associates with. In occupying positions of leadership in the Church, he will apply the same principles as he does in the home, showing that there is no difference between the person he is when within the walls of his own home and the person he is in his relationship with the members of the Church.

(Francisco J. Vinas, *Ensign,* May 2004 [Salt Lake City: The Church of Jesus Christ of Latter-day Saints, 2004], 39–40)

Alma 37:34 • REST TO THEIR SOULS

In the midst of a very unsettled world one can be at peace. That peace is made possible through the Savior and his gospel that we call the plan of salvation. If we are not at peace then either our perceptions or our behavior (or both) needs adjusting.

(Larry E. Dahl, BYU Religious Education Faculty Pre-School Meeting, 27 Aug. 1992)

The man or woman who enjoys the spirit of our religion has no trials; but the man or woman who tries to live according to the Gospel of the Son of God, and at the same time clings to the spirit of the world, has trials and sorrows acute and keen, and that, too, continually. This is the deciding point, the dividing line. They who love and serve God with all their hearts rejoice evermore, pray without ceasing, and in everything give thanks; but they who try to serve God and still cling to the spirit of the world, have got on two yokes—the yoke of Jesus and the yoke of the devil . . . They will have a warfare inside and outside, and the labor will be very galling, for they are directly in opposition one to the other. Cast off the yoke of the enemy, and put on the yoke of Christ, and you will say that his yoke is easy and his burden is light. This I know by experience.

(Brigham Young, *Journal of Discourses* [London: Latter-day Saints' Book Depot, 1874], 16:123)

The ancient prophets speak of "entering into God's rest"; what does it mean? To my mind, it means entering into the knowledge and love of God, having faith in his purpose and in his plan, to such an extent that we know we are right, and that we are not hunting for something else, we are not disturbed by every wind of doctrine, or by the cunning and craftiness of men who lie in wait to deceive. . . . The man who has reached that degree of faith in God that all doubt and fear have been cast from him, he has entered into "God's rest," . . . The rest here referred to is not physical rest, for there is no such thing as physical rest in the Church of Jesus Christ. Reference is made to the spiritual rest and peace which are born from a settled conviction of the truth in the minds of men. We may thus enter into the rest of the Lord today, by coming to an understanding of the truths of the gospel. . . . But there are many [members] who, not having reached this point of determined conviction, are driven about by every wind of doctrine, thus being ill at ease, unsettled, restless. These are they who are discouraged over incidents that occur in the Church, and in the nation, and in the turmoils of men and associations. They harbor a feeling of suspicion, unrest, uncertainty. Their thoughts are disturbed, and they become excited with the least change, like one at sea who has lost his bearings. . . . Let them seek for it in the written word of God; let them pray to him in their secret chambers, where no human ear can hear, and in their closets petition for light; let them obey the doctrines of Jesus, and they will immediately begin to grow in the knowledge of the truth. . . . Let them seek for strength from the Source of all strength, and he will provide spiritual contentment, a rest which is incomparable with the physical rest that cometh after toil. All who seek have a right to, and may enter into, the rest of God, here upon the earth, from this time forth, now, today; and when earth-life is finished, they shall also enjoy his rest in heaven.

(Joseph F. Smith, *Gospel Doctrine* [Salt Lake City: Deseret Book, 1975], 58, 126–127)

Alma 37:35; 38:2 • YOUTHFUL OBEDIENCE
(Refer in this text to 1 Nephi 3:7.)

I have said again and again that I believe this is the best generation [in the Church] we have ever had. . . . You live in a world of terrible temptations. Pornography, with its sleazy filth, sweeps over the earth like a horrible, engulfing tide. It is poison. Do not watch it or read it. It will destroy you if you do. It will take from you your self-respect. It will rob you of a sense of the beauties of life. It will tear you down and pull you into a slough of evil thoughts and possibly of evil actions. Stay away from it. Shun it as you would a foul disease, for it is just as deadly. Be virtuous in thought and in deed. God has planted in you, for a purpose, a divine urge which may be easily subverted to evil and destructive ends. When you are young, do not get involved in steady dating. When you reach an age where you think of marriage, then is the time to become so involved. But you boys who are in high school don't need this, and neither do the girls. We receive letters, we constantly deal with people who, under the pressures of life, marry while very young. . . . Have a wonderful time . . . but do not get too serious too soon. You [young men] have missions ahead of you. . . . Stay away from alcohol. Graduation from high school is no reason for a beer bust. Better stay away and be thought a prude than go through life regretting it ever afterwards. Stay away from drugs. You cannot afford to touch them. They will utterly destroy you. The euphoria will quickly pass, and the deadly, strangling clutches of this evil thing will embrace you in its power. You will become a slave, a debauched slave. You will lose control of your life and your actions. Do not experiment with them. Stay free of them! Walk in the sunlight, strength, and virtue of self-control and of absolute integrity. Get all the schooling you can. Education is the key that unlocks the door of opportunity.

(Gordon B. Hinckley, *Ensign*, Nov. 1997 [Salt Lake City: The Church of Jesus Christ of Latter-day Saints, 1997], 51–52)

———

Charting the course prevents one from living an unplanned, haphazard life—a tumbleweed existence.

(Spencer W. Kimball, *The Miracle of Forgiveness* [Salt Lake City: Bookcraft, 1969], 233–234)

———

The decisions we make, individually and personally, become the fabric of our lives. That fabric will be beautiful or ugly according to the threads of which it is woven. I wish to say particularly to the young men who are here that you cannot indulge in any unbecoming behavior without injury to the beauty of the fabric of your lives. Immoral acts of any kind will introduce an ugly thread. Dishonesty of any kind will create a blemish. Foul and profane language will rob the pattern of its beauty. "Choose the right when a choice is placed before you" is the call to each of us (*Hymns,* 1985, no. 239).

(Gordon B. Hinckley, *Ensign*, May 1995 [Salt Lake City: The Church of Jesus Christ of Latter-day Saints, 1995], 53)

———

How glorious and near to the angels is youth that is clean. This youth will have joy unspeakable here and eternal happiness hereafter.

("First Presidency Message," *Improvement Era*, May 1942 [Salt Lake City: The Church of Jesus Christ of Latter-day Saints, 1942], 273)

———

Give me a young man who has kept himself morally clean and has faithfully attended his Church meetings. Give me a young man who has magnified his priesthood and has earned his Duty to God Award and is an Eagle Scout. Give me a young man who is a seminary graduate and has a burning testimony of the Book of Mormon. Give me such a young man and I will give you a young man who can perform miracles for the Lord in the mission field and throughout his life.

(*Teachings of Ezra Taft Benson* [Salt Lake City: Bookcraft, 1988], 197)

———

During an autumn evening in the early 1900s, Orville Allen stopped by Andrew Kimball's home to deliver some pumpkins. As the two men unloaded the pumpkins, they overheard Andrew's son Spencer in the barn, singing as he milked the cows. Brother Allen remarked to Andrew, "Your boy must be happy." Andrew responded: "Yes, he is always happy. He is a clean and obedient boy and always minds what I ask him to do. I have dedicated him to the Lord and to His service. He will become a mighty man in the Church."

(*Teachings of Presidents of the Church—Spencer W. Kimball* [Salt Lake City: The Church of Jesus Christ of Latter-day Saints, 2006], xiv)

———

Young [people], the family unit is forever, and you should do everything in your power to strengthen that unit. In your own family, encourage family home evenings and be an active participant. Encourage family prayer. Be on your knees with your family in that sacred circle. Do your part to develop real family unity and solidarity. In such homes there is no generation gap. That is another tool of the devil. Your most important friendships should be with your own brothers and sisters and with your father and mother. Love your family. Be loyal to them. Have a genuine concern for your brothers and sisters. Help carry their load.

(Ezra Taft Benson, *Ensign*, Nov. 1986 [Salt Lake City: The Church of Jesus Christ of Latter-day Saints, 1986], 81)

———————

Never feed the foxes! What does that mean? Breaking commandments is like feeding foxes. In England where we live, my wife and I had heard that foxes were right in town. We wanted to see a fox. A neighbor told us that if we left food for the foxes we probably would see one. Our butcher gave us some bones. Each night we would place some bones out in the backyard. Soon a fox came to eat. Then a few more. Now we have at least five foxes racing through our flower garden, digging up the lawn, and leaving a shamble every night, sort of like a furry Jurassic Park. What started out as a curiosity is now a problem, and sin is much the same. An indiscretion can begin a process that can make a mess of a whole life. Remember, if you don't start feeding the foxes, they will never tear up your yard. If you avoid making the seemingly small and harmless mistakes, your life will be free of many larger problems later on.

(Hugh W. Pinnock, *Ensign*, Nov. 1993 [Salt Lake City: The Church of Jesus Christ of Latter-day Saints, 1993], 41)

———————

It is an odd thing, in a way, how each generation seems to feel that each preceding generation is somewhat old fashioned. . . . Youth is so sure the rules have changed. Age is sure they haven't. Youth feels it knows how far it can go. Age is deeply aware of the danger. Youth feels it can always apply the brakes in time to save itself. Age knows it isn't always so. . . . Why should you suppose that the basic rules have really changed in the few short years since your parents were as young as you? The road seems new to you. It isn't new to them. They've been over it . . . and it is still essentially the same. . . . Remember, too, that parents have hearts that can be hurt; that they, like you, are sensitive to ill-timed criticism and to misunderstanding of their motives.

(Richard L. Evans, *Improvement Era*, May 1956; as quoted in *Living Truths from the Book of Mormon* [Salt Lake City: The Church of Jesus Christ of Latter-day Saints, 1970], 81–82)

———————

There is a line of demarcation, well defined, between the Lord's territory and the devil's. If you will stay on the Lord's side of the line, you will be under his influence and will have no desire to do wrong: but if you cross to the devil's side of the line one inch, you are in the tempter's power, and if he is successful, you will not be able to think or even reason properly, because you will have lost the Spirit of the Lord.

(George Albert Smith; as quoted in Spencer W. Kimball, *The Miracle of Forgiveness* [Salt Lake City: Bookcraft, 1969], 232)

———————

There are many who have made a wonderful record in the battle of life even after they have done things in their youth that were not pleasing in the sight of our Heavenly Father or for their own good; but it is far better if it is possible for us to start the children out in the battle of life with nothing recorded on the pages of their years, except good deeds and faith-promoting thoughts.

(*Teachings of President of the Church—Heber J. Grant* [Salt Lake City: The Church of Jesus Christ of Latter-day Saints, 2002], 205)

———————

A dozen years ago, in one of the countries of Africa, . . . I went to that country to see if we could receive permission from the government to bring in missionaries and establish the Church. I met with a high-ranking government minister. He gave me 20 minutes to explain our position.

When I finished he said, "I do not see where anything you have told me is any different from what is currently available in our country. I see no reason to approve your request to bring missionaries into our country."

He stood up to usher me out of his office. I was panic-stricken. I had failed. In a moment our meeting would be over. What could I do? I offered a silent prayer.

Then I had an inspired thought. I said to the minister, "Sir, if you will give me five more minutes, I would like to share one other thought with you. Then I will leave." He kindly consented.

I said, "This is a little booklet of standards we give all of the youth in our Church." . . .

When I finished he said, "You mean to tell me you expect the youth of your church to live these standards?"

"Yes," I replied, "and they do."

"That is amazing," he said. "Could you send me some of these booklets so that I could distribute them to the youth of my church?"

I replied, "Yes," and I did.

Several months later we received official approval from the government of that country to come and establish the Church.

(Earl C. Tingey, *Ensign*, May 2004 [Salt Lake City: The Church of Jesus Christ of Latter-day Saints, 2004], 50)

I shall tell you boys a story about a horse I once owned and had great pleasure in training. He had a good disposition, a clean, well-rounded eye, was well-proportioned, and, all in all, a choice equine possession. Under the saddle he was as willing, responsive, and cooperative as a horse could be. He and my dog Scotty were real companions. I liked the way he would go up to something of which he was afraid. He had confidence that if he would do as I bade him, he would not be injured.

But Dandy resented restraint. He was ill-contented when tied and would nibble at the tie-rope until he was free. He would not run away—just wanted to be free. Thinking other horses felt the same, he would proceed to untie their ropes. He hated to be confined in the pasture, and if he could find a place in the fence where there was only smooth wire, he would paw the wire carefully with his feet until he could step over to freedom. More than once my neighbors were kind enough to put him back in the field. He even learned to push open the gate. Though his depredations were provoking and sometimes expensive, I admired his intelligence and ingenuity.

But his curiosity and desire to explore the neighborhood led him and me into trouble. Once on the highway he was hit by an automobile, resulting in a demolished machine, injury to the horse, and slight, though not serious, injury to the driver.

Recovering from that, and still impelled with a feeling of wanderlust, he inspected the fence throughout the entire boundary. He even found the gates wired. So for awhile we thought we had Dandy secure in the pasture.

One day, however, somebody left the gate unwired. Detecting this, Dandy unlatched it, took his companion with him, and together they visited the neighbor's field. They went to an old house used for storage. Dandy's curiosity prompted him to push open the door. Just as he had surmised, there was a sack of grain. What a find! Yes, and what a tragedy! The grain was poison bait for rodents! In a few minutes Dandy and his companion were in spasmodic pain, and shortly both were dead.

How like Dandy are many of our youth! They are not bad; they do not even intend to do wrong; but they are impulsive, full of life, full of curiosity, and they long to do something. They too are restive under restraint, but if they are kept busy, guided carefully and rightly, they prove to be responsive and capable; if left to wander unguided, they all too frequently violate principles of right, which often leads to snares of evil, disaster, and even death.

(David O. McKay, in Conference Report, Oct. 1978 [Salt Lake City: The Church of Jesus Christ of Latter-day Saints, 1978], 87)

We have never had a better generation of youth than we have in the Church today. I am satisfied of that. They are better schooled. They are better trained. They know the scriptures better. They are just wonderful young people, but unfortunately too many are falling through the cracks. They are being enticed by these evil things. They are watching video tapes. They are playing the Internet. They get involved in some of this trashy stuff—trashy entertainment, sleazy entertainment that is brought into this part of the country.

Get close to them, please. You bishoprics, . . . reach down and be close to these young people. You may have to neglect some of the old wood, which is pretty much lost anyway. But reach down to this coming generation, and love them and reach out to them and help them and give them encouragement. . . .

See that the girls receive the kind of attention that they need, because the performance of the girls, which used to be above the boys, has come down now, until, generally across the Church they are about the same—and not as good as they ought to be.

(*Discourses of President Gordon B. Hinckley* [Salt Lake City: The Church of Jesus Christ of Latter-day Saints, 2005], 2:464–465)

Alma 37:37 • COUNSEL WITH THE LORD
(Refer in this text to 3 Nephi 18:15–23; Alma 34:18–27.)

Successful people need counsel. Unsuccessful people need counsel. The hasty impulse, the know-it-all attitude, the pride that keeps us from asking—these are the dangerous approaches to any problem from the youngest in years to the oldest of age, there is no one who can be always sure he is right, no one who has learned so much of life that he doesn't need the counsel of others and a prayerful approach to all problems. "Counsel with the Lord in all thy doings," said Alma, "and he will direct thee for good. . . ." (Alma 37:37). There is safety in counsel, no safety without it. They that will not be counseled, cannot be helped.

(Richard L. Evans, in Conference Report, Apr. 1968 [Salt Lake City: The Church of Jesus Christ of Latter-day Saints, 1968], 86)

Remember to say your prayers—morning and night (Alma 37:37). . . .

When you pray, have you ever considered not only pleading for help but also reporting for duty? Ask for the Spirit to guide you. If you will pray for direction and listen for promptings, you will become familiar with those promptings and learn to act on them. The gospel will come alive in your life. You will have more of those "aha" experiences that help you see what really matters.

(Mary Ellen Smoot, "Everything Money Cannot Buy," Satellite Broadcast, 3 Feb. 2002, Brigham Young University [Salt Lake City: The Church of Jesus Christ of Latter-day Saints, 2002], 4–5)

Alma 37:46 • THE EASINESS OF THE WAY

Several years ago while my husband, Ed, and I were serving in the England London South Mission, there was an unexpected storm. All night the winds raged. . . . Many trees throughout . . . all of southern England had been uprooted. It was amazing to see the fallen trees with their gigantic root systems, still intact, jutting into the air. I came to the conclusion that because of the "easiness of the way" (Alma 37:46)—rain is plentiful in England—the trees had no need to sink their roots deep into the earth to get the nourishment they needed. Their roots were not strong enough or deep enough to withstand the hurricane-force winds. On the other hand, the giant redwood trees that grow in northern California also have a very shallow root system. But when they are surrounded by other redwood trees, the strongest, fiercest wind cannot blow them over. The roots of the giant redwood trees intertwine and strengthen each other. When a storm comes, they actually hold each other up.

(Patricia P. Pinegar, *Ensign*, Nov. 1994 [Salt Lake City: The Church of Jesus Christ of Latter-day Saints, 1994], 78)

Alma 37:47 • LOOK TO GOD AND LIVE

Please know that we are not without understanding of some of your problems. We are aware that many of you carry very heavy burdens. We plead with the Lord in your behalf. We add our prayers to your prayers that you may find solutions to your problems. We leave a blessing upon you, even an apostolic blessing. We bless you that the Lord may smile with favor upon you, that there may be happiness and peace in your homes and in your lives, that an atmosphere of love and respect and appreciation may be felt among husbands and wives, children and parents. May you "look to God and live (Alma 37:47) with happiness, with security, with peace, with faith.

(Gordon B. Hinckley, *Ensign*, May 1995 [Salt Lake City: The Church of Jesus Christ of Latter-day Saints, 1995], 88)

Alma 38:5 • TRUST IN GOD, DELIVERED OUT OF TRIALS

President Woodruff showed his faith as he, his wife, and several others traveled by boat to serve in England. "We had been traveling three days and nights in a heavy gale, and were being driven backwards," he recounted. "Finally I asked my companions to come into the cabin with me, and I told them to pray that the Lord would change the wind. I had no fears of being lost; but I did not like the idea of being driven back to New York, as I wanted to go on my journey. We all offered the same prayer, both men and women; and when we got through we stepped on to the deck and in less than a minute it was as though a man had taken a sword and cut that gale through, and you might have thrown a muslin handkerchief out and it would not have moved it."

(*Teachings of Presidents of the Church—Wilford Woodruff* [Salt Lake City: The Church of Jesus Christ of Latter-day Saints, 2004], 109–110)

Alma 38:8 • RECOGNITION OF THE SAVIOR
(Refer in this text to Alma 36:12–16.)

Of all the necessary steps to repentance, I testify that the most critically important is for you to have a conviction that forgiveness comes because of the Redeemer. It is essential to know that only on His terms can you be forgiven. Witness Alma's declaration: [Alma 38:8]. That means you trust Him and you trust His teachings. Satan would have you believe that serious transgression cannot be entirely overcome. The Savior gave His life so that the effects of all transgression can be put behind us, save the shedding of innocent blood and the denial of the Holy Ghost.

(Richard G. Scott, *Ensign*, May 1995 [Salt Lake City: The Church of Jesus Christ of Latter-day Saints, 1995], 76–77)

Alma 38:12 • BOLDNESS, NOT OVERBEARANCE

We do not argue and fight with other churches. We do not. We simply go forward preaching, in a positive way, our doctrine. We say to people, in effect, "You bring with you all the good that you have, and then you come and let us see if we can add to it." Now, that is our purpose, and that is our mission.

(*Discourses of President Gordon B. Hinckley*, 1995–99 [Salt Lake City: The Church of Jesus Christ of Latter-day Saints, 2004], 1:518)

When you go into a neighborhood to preach the Gospel, never attempt to tear down a man's house, so to speak, before you build him a better one; never, in fact, attack anyone's religion, wherever you go. Be willing to let every man enjoy his own religion. It is his right to do that. If he does not accept your testimony with regard to the Gospel of Christ, that is his affair, and not yours. Do not spend your time in pulling down other sects and parties. . . . It is never right to do that. . . . Religions of other men are as dear unto them as ours are unto us.

(*Teachings of Presidents of the Church—Wilford Woodruff* [Salt Lake City: The Church of Jesus Christ of Latter-day Saints, 2004], 96)

Alma 38:12 • BRIDLE YOUR PASSIONS
(Refer in this text to Alma 39:9.)

What is a bridle for? To kill, to diminish, or even to limit the spirit and power of the steed? Never. Once you have trained your pony you can direct him with the merest nudge. Eventually you can "give him his head" and ride free, bareback like the wind. We are given our bodies and our emotions not to destroy but to ride. The bridle warns you that to get excited without listening to the voice of the Spirit (the rider) will bring a complaint, "Hey wait for me!" When the body is susceptible to the Spirit, it can always catch up to the Spirit. But I defy anyone to get the Spirit in harmony with the runaway body.

(Truman G. Madsen, *Four Essays on Love* [Salt Lake City: Bookcraft, 1971], 36)

It is the habit of self denial which gives the advantage to men we call self-made. . . If he is successful in any way in life he has learned to resist. He has learned to say no at the right time and then to stand by it. Life is such that he cannot escape temptation but as he faces it and masters it, he learns the true way to righteousness.

(Alvin R. Dyer, *The Challenge* [Salt Lake City: Deseret Book, 1968], 159–160)

The world needs self-discipline. You can find it in fasting and prayer. Our generation is sick for lack of self-control. Fasting and prayer help to instill this virtue.

(Robert L. Simpson, in Conference Report, Oct. 1967 [Salt Lake City: The Church of Jesus Christ of Latter-day Saints, 1967], 18–19)

The notion that you can endanger your physical and mental health by letting strong passions go unsatisfied is a vicious falsehood. Self-control is one mark of a mature person; it applies to control of language, physical treatment of others, and the appetites of the body.

(Joseph B. Wirthlin, *Ensign*, Mar. 1993 [Salt Lake City: The Church of Jesus Christ of Latter-day Saints, 1993], 71)

Patience is another form of self-control. It is the ability to postpone gratification and to bridle one's passions. In his relationships with loved ones, a patient man does not engage in impetuous behavior that he will later regret. Patience is composure under stress. A patient man is understanding of others' faults. A patient man also waits on the Lord. We sometimes read or hear of people who seek a blessing from the Lord, then grow impatient when it does not come swiftly. Part of the divine nature is to trust in the Lord enough to "be still

and know that [He is] God" (D&C 101:16). A priesthood holder who is patient will be tolerant of the mistakes and failings of his loved ones. Because he loves them, he will not find fault nor criticize nor blame.

(Ezra Taft Benson, *Ensign*, Nov. 1986 [Salt Lake City: The Church of Jesus Christ of Latter-day Saints, 1986], 47)

Men are prone to gloat over their immoral conquests. What a cheap and sullied victory! . . . The only conquest that brings satisfaction is the conquest of self. It was said of old that "he that governeth himself is greater than he that taketh a city."

Are not the words of Tennyson still appropriate? "My strength is as the strength of ten, Because my heart is pure" ("Sir Galahad"). . . .

Self-discipline was never easy. I do not doubt that it is more difficult today. We live in a sex-saturated world. . . .

Nakedness has become the hallmark of much public entertainment. . . .

We need to read more history. Nations and civilizations have flowered, then died, poisoned by their own moral sickness. . . .

No nation, no civilization can long endure without strength in the homes of its people. That strength derives from the integrity of those who establish those homes. . . .

There cannot be peace where there is not trust; there cannot be freedom where there is not loyalty. The warm sunlight of love will not rise out of a swamp of immorality. . . .

To hope for peace and love and gladness out of promiscuity is to hope for that which will never come. To wish for freedom out of immorality is to wish for something that cannot be.

(Gordon B. Hinckley, *From My Generation to Yours . . . with Love!* [Salt Lake City: Deseret Book, 1973], 4–6)

To progress, to become what you want to be, and to serve the Lord the way you should—requires that you discipline yourself constantly, discipline yourself while in your youth so that it will become a habit that will sustain you in later years.

(G. Homer Durham, *N. Eldon Tanner: His Life and Service* [Salt Lake City: Deseret Book, 1982], 313)

What is the tradition of discipline in our homes? Is our child pampered, indulged, permitted in a moment of crisis to transfer his guilt to others—his parents, peers, family, the age he lives in, society? How will he handle disappointment and failure if he is not taught to face up to his mistakes honestly? . . . "Self-respect," someone said, "is the fruit of discipline; the sense of dignity grows with the ability to say NO to one's self" (Abraham J. Herschel, *The Insecurities of Freedom*).

(Marion D. Hanks, in Conference Report, Oct. 1978 [Salt Lake City: The Church of Jesus Christ of Latter-day Saints, 1978], 117)

———

Self-mastery is essential to invoke the power of the priesthood of God. This is because this great, divine agency can be exercised only in righteousness. . . . It enhances our own gifts and talents in a remarkable way. It is the power of noble manhood. . . .

Self-mastery cannot be bought by money or fame. It is the ultimate test of our character. . . .

As full-time missionaries we learn great lessons in self-mastery. We learn to get up when we should get up, to work when we should work, and to go to bed when we should go to bed. . . .

I testify with all my heart and soul that through the power of self-mastery we will inherit the blessings our heavenly Father has for his faithful sons.

(James E. Faust, in Conference Report, Apr. 2000 [Salt Lake City: The Church of Jesus Christ of Latter-day Saints, 2000], 54–55, 58)

———

An individual who is violating commandments of the Lord will find it very difficult to discern a prompting of the Spirit from the powerful emotions that can be stimulated through transgression. I am confident that is one of the reasons that some marriages fail. Two individuals who have allowed themselves to violate the laws of chastity during courtship cannot expect to clearly perceive the answer to their prayer regarding marriage. Under such circumstances, seeking to discern the guidance of the Spirit is like trying to savor the delicate flavor of raspberry while chewing on a red hot jalapeno pepper.

(Richard G. Scott, CES Fireside for Young Adults, 13 Jan. 2002)

———

Some will gain celestial bodies with all the powers of exaltation and eternal increase. . . . [Whereas terrestrial and telestial bodies] will not have the power of increase, neither the power or nature to live as husbands and wives, for this will be denied them and they cannot increase.

Some of the functions in the celestial body will not appear in the terrestrial body, neither in the telestial body, and power of procreation will be removed.

(Joseph Fielding Smith, *Doctrine of Salvation* [Salt Lake City: Bookcraft, 1955], 2:287–88)

Alma 39:2; 38:11–14 • BOASTING
(Refer in this text to Mosiah 11:19; Mormon 3:9.)

Boasting in the arm of flesh, one of the commonest of all sins among worldly people is a gross evil; it is a sin born of pride, a sin that creates a frame of mind which keeps men from turning to the Lord and accepting his saving grace. When a man engages in self exultation because of his riches, his political power, his worldly learning, his physical prowess, his business acumen, or even his works of righteousness, he is not in tune with the Spirit of the Lord.

(Bruce R. McConkie, *Mormon Doctrine* [Salt Lake City: Bookcraft, 1966], 93–94)

———

I heard Joseph Smith say that Oliver Cowdery, who was the second apostle in this Church, said to him, "If I leave this Church it will fall."

Said Joseph, "Oliver, you try it." Oliver tried it. He fell; but the kingdom of God did not. . . .

I have seen Oliver Cowdery when it seemed as though the earth trembled under his feet. I never heard a man bear a stronger testimony than he did when under the influence of the Spirit. But the moment he left the kingdom of God, that moment his power fell. . . . He was shorn of his strength, like Samson in the lap of Delilah. He lost the power and testimony which he had enjoyed, and he never recovered it again in its fulness while in the flesh, although he died [a member of] the Church.

(*Teachings of Presidents of the Church—Wilford Woodruff* [Salt Lake City: The Church of Jesus Christ of Latter-day Saints, 2004], 104–105)

Alma 39:3–4 • FORSAKE THE MINISTRY, BE WHERE YOU ARE SUPPOSED TO BE

I wish that every Latter-day Saint could say and mean it with all his heart: "I'll go where you want me to go. I'll say what you want me to say. I'll be what you want me to be" (*Hymns* [1985], 270). If we could all do that, we would be assured of the maximum of happiness here and exaltation in the celestial kingdom of God hereafter.

(*Teachings of Ezra Taft Benson* [Salt Lake City: Bookcraft, 1988], 344)

———

Never go to any place that you wouldn't take your priesthood with you. Stay out of such places. Someone said, when you find a place that is labeled "adults only; no children or youth allowed," no adults should be allowed either, if you will be safe from the pitfalls of the devil. We are members whom the Lord expects to be a light unto the world, and to set a standard for people to seek to it.

(Harold B. Lee, *Ensign*, Nov. 1971 [Salt Lake City: The Church of Jesus Christ of Latter-day Saints, 1971], 14)

You may have heard of Elder Alma Sonne, a former Assistant to the Twelve Apostles, but you may not be familiar with his life. He was a magnificent General Authority for many years and a great preacher of righteousness. Back in the early 1900s he went on a mission to the British Isles. He left behind a dear friend named Fred Dahle, whom Elder Sonne was later able to persuade to serve a mission. Fred then had the opportunity to serve in the British Isles at the same time Elder Sonne served.

Elder Sonne, as a young missionary, kept writing his friend, Fred Dahle, and pleading with him to come on a mission, but Brother Dahle expressed little interest. Eventually, however, he gave in to Elder Sonne's pleading and, as was mentioned, he was called to serve in the British Isles. He later wrote to Elder Sonne, "Thank God, you were on the map when I was supposed to be a missionary." Think of that. Elder Dahle's gratitude knew no bounds because Elder Sonne helped him be on a mission when the Lord wanted him to be there.

One of Elder Sonne's principal responsibilities on his mission was to plan travel arrangements for new converts traveling to America and the missionaries as they arrived and left the mission field. At the conclusion of his mission Elder Sonne was able to secure passage for himself, Elder Dahle, and other missionaries on a brand new ocean liner that was scheduled to make its maiden voyage from England to New York City. The year was 1912. The new ocean liner was the *Titanic*. Arrangements were made for a train to pick them up in New York, and they would travel across the United States on their way back to Cache Valley, Utah.

A few days before the great trip across the ocean and then across the United States, Elder Dahle sent a wire indicating that he could not make the scheduled departure and suggesting that the elders go on without him. However, Elder Sonne, for some inexplicable reason that would be known only later, canceled their bookings on the *Titanic* and rebooked them all on another ship, the *Mauretania*, leaving a day later. The others in the group manifested resentment because they were not sailing on the *Titanic*.

While they were en route, the purser of the *Mauretania* told Alma in confidence that the *Titanic* had struck an iceberg and sunk on the 15th of April, with the loss of 1,517 passengers and crew and only 705 survivors. The elders were stunned by the news. As Elder Sonne and Elder Dahle walked on the deck, gazing into the dark waters of the Atlantic, Alma remembered Fred's letter. He turned to Elder Dahle and said, "Thank God, Fred, you were on the map when I was supposed to be on the *Titanic*" (Galyn Hopkins, Presentation to the Alma Sonne Family Reunion and a Faculty Inservice Meeting, Orem Institute of Religion).

(Jack R. Christianson and K. Douglas Bassett, *Life Lessons from the Book of Mormon* [Salt Lake City: Deseret Book, 2003], 43–44)

Forty-four years ago I heard William J. Critchlow Jr., then president of the South Ogden Stake, speak to the brethren in the general priesthood session of conference, and retell a story concerning trust, honor, and duty. . . . Its simple lesson applies to us today. . . .

"Rupert stood by the side of the road watching an unusual number of people hurry past. At length he recognized a friend. 'Where are all of you going in such a hurry?' he asked.

"The friend paused. 'Haven't you heard?' he said.

"'I've heard nothing,' Rupert answered.

"'Well,' continued [the] friend, 'the King has lost his royal emerald. Yesterday he attended a wedding of the nobility and wore the emerald on the slender golden chain around his neck. In some way the emerald became loosened from the chain. Everyone is searching, for the King has offered a reward . . . to the one who finds it. Come, we must hurry.'

"'But I cannot go without asking Grandmother,' faltered Rupert.

"'Then I cannot wait. I want to find the emerald,' replied his friend.

"Rupert hurried back to the cabin at the edge of the woods to seek his grandmother's permission. 'If I could find it we could leave this hut with its dampness and buy a piece of land up on the hillside,' he pleaded with Grandmother.

"But his grandmother shook her head. 'What would the sheep do?' she asked. 'Already they are restless in the pen, waiting to be taken to the pasture—and please do not forget to take them to water when the sun shines high in the heavens.'

"Sorrowfully, Rupert took the sheep to the pasture, and at noon he led them to the brook in the woods. There he sat on a large stone by the stream. 'If I could only have had a chance to look for the King's emerald,' he thought. Turning his head to gaze down at the sandy bottom of the brook, suddenly he stared into the water. What was it? It could not be! He leaped into the water, and his gripping fingers held something that was green, with a slender bit of gold chain. 'The King's emerald!' he shouted. 'It must have been flung from the chain when the King [astride his horse, galloped across the bridge spanning the stream, and the current carried] it here.'

"With shining eyes Rupert ran to his grandmother's hut to tell her of his great find. 'Bless you, my boy,' she said, 'but you never would have found it if you had not been doing your duty, herding the sheep.' And Rupert knew that this was the truth" (in Conference Report, Oct. 1955, 86).

The lesson to be learned from this story is found in the familiar couplet: "Do your duty; that is best. Leave unto the Lord the rest."

(Thomas S. Monson, *Ensign*, Nov. 1999 [Salt Lake City: The Church of Jesus Christ of Latter-day Saints, 1999], 49–50)

———

I hope we will not be . . . too proud to accept the assignments we are given. I pray that we will not be like the person in the well-known poem who said:

Father, where shall I work today?
And my love flowed warm and free.
Then He pointed out a tiny spot
And said, "Tend that for me."
I answered quickly, "Oh no; not that!
Why, no one would ever see,
No matter how well my work was done;
Not that little place for me."
And the word He spoke, it was not stern;
He answered me tenderly:
"Ah, little one, search that heart of thine.
Are thou working for them or for me?
Nazareth was a little place,
And so was Galilee.

—Meade McGuire

(James E. Faust, in Conference Report, Oct. 2002 [Salt Lake City: The Church of Jesus Christ of Latter-day Saints, 2002], 56)

———

We have inspiring examples of the submissive, faithful service of Latter-day Saints. One of the best known was that of President J. Reuben Clark. After he had served over 16 years as an extra-ordinarily influential first counselor, the First Presidency was reorganized and he was called as second counselor. Offering an example of humility and willingness to serve that has influenced generations, he said to the Church:

"In the service of the Lord, it is not where you serve but how. In the Church of Jesus Christ of Latter-day Saints, one takes the place to which one is duly called, which place one neither seeks nor declines" (in Conference Report, Apr. 1951, 154). . . .

Still, there is room for improvement in the commitment of some. When I ask stake presidents for suggestions on subjects I should treat at stake conferences, I often hear about members who refuse Church callings or accept callings and fail to fulfill their responsibilities. . . . But this is not without consequence. . . .

My brothers and sisters, if you are delinquent in commitment, please consider who it is you are refusing or neglecting to serve when you decline a calling or when you accept, promise, and fail to fulfill.

(Dallin H. Oaks, in Conference Report, Oct. 2002 [Salt Lake City: The Church of Jesus Christ of Latter-day Saints, 2002], 72–74)

———

Sister Hinckley likes to tell the story of a missionary sister who stood up in one of our testimony meetings here and said, "I am from New Zealand. When I left for my mission, at my farewell the people sang, 'I'll go where you want me to go, dear Lord . . . ; I'll be what you want me to be' " (*Hymns*, no. 270). She said, "That never crossed my mind again, that song, until one day, when we had been tracting in the rain all day long and were soaking wet, we came to another resettlement flat where refugees lived. My companion said, 'We are soaking wet. Let's go home.' " She said, 'We started for home, and the words of that song came into my mind: 'I'll go where you want me to go, dear Lord; I'll say what you want me to say . . . ; I'll be what you want me to be.' " She pulled the arm of her companion's slicker and said, "We have to go back. I don't know why, but we have to go back." They went back, and there was a light up on the fifth or sixth or seventh floor. They climbed the stairs and knocked on the door. There was a family who subsequently were baptized—a father, a mother, and three children. "I'll go where you want me to go, dear Lord . . . ; I'll say what you want me to say . . . ; I'll be what you want me to be."

(*Discourses of President Gordon B. Hinckley*, 1995–99 [Salt Lake City: The Church of Jesus Christ of Latter-day Saints, 2004], 1:410–411)

———

When I was in the seventh grade, in a health class, the teacher read an article. A mother learned that the neighbor children had chicken pox. She faced the probability that her children would have it as well, perhaps one at a time. She determined to get it all over with at once.

So she sent her children to the neighbor's to play with their children to let them be exposed, and then she would be done with it. Imagine her horror when the doctor finally came and announced that it was not chicken pox the children had; it was smallpox.

The best thing to do then and what we must do now is to avoid places where there is danger of physical or spiritual contagion.

(Boyd K. Packer, *Ensign*, May 2004 [Salt Lake City: The Church of Jesus Christ of Latter-day Saints, 2004], 78)

Alma 39:4 • THE MANY IS NO EXCUSE FOR THEE

(Refer in this text to 1 Nephi 8:25; Mosiah 17:11–13.)

Oh, if our young people could learn this basic lesson to always keep good company, never to be found with those who tend to lower their standards! Let every youth select associates who will keep him on tiptoe, trying to reach the heights. Let him never choose associates who encourage him to relax in carelessness.

(*Teachings of Spencer W. Kimball*, ed. by Edward L. Kimball [Salt Lake City: Bookcraft, 1982], 287)

Genuine friends often can provide spiritual shepherding. Note that I refer to genuine friends in the category of spiritual shepherds. Notice also that I did not include peers in that group. I readily acknowledge that peers in some cases can be and are an influence for good.... Unfortunately, so many times there are situations where peer influence has a definite negative effect. We read and hear of so many surveys and interviews where youth disclose that it was the influence and pressure of peers that led them to immoral and foolish behavior. Satan knows this.... He is aware of the tremendous influence a group of peers can have on an individual. There is a compelling desire to belong—to be one of the group.... Often the easiest and simplest nudging is that "everyone is doing it" or "it's the cool thing" or "how do you know it's bad if you haven't tried it?" Don't be deceived. Don't be influenced with this kind of enticement. Keep your eyes above the crowd.

(W. Eugene Hansen, *Ensign*, May 1996 [Salt Lake City: The Church of Jesus Christ of Latter-day Saints, 1996], 38–39)

We know that we are often judged by the company we keep. We know how influential classmates, friends, and other peer groups can be. If any of our companions are prone to be unrighteous in their living, we are better off seeking new associations immediately. Our friends should be companions who inspire us, who help us rise to our best.

(Joseph B. Wirthlin, *Ensign*, Nov. 1997 [Salt Lake City: The Church of Jesus Christ of Latter-day Saints, 1997], 34)

Face reality. Sometimes we wish we could fly from our troubles. King David did. He had been a good man, but he engulfed himself in great difficulties. It seemed to be more than he could bear. One day he cried, "Oh that I had wings like a dove! For then would I fly away, and be at rest" (Ps. 55:6). His guilt-fired emotions had gained the upper hand. He wanted to get away from

everything. Some try to fly away physically, and others try to do so emotionally. That does not solve problems. The only true escape route is marked with the sign "personal responsibility."

(Hugh W. Pinnock, in Conference Report, Apr. 1982 [Salt Lake City: The Church of Jesus Christ of Latter-day Saints, 1982], 17)

Alma 39:4–6 • ADULTERY (IMMORALITY)

(Refer in this text to 1 Nephi 22:23; Moroni 9:9.)

There are at least three dangers that threaten the Church within.... They are flattery of prominent men in the world, false educational ideas, and sexual impurity. But the third subject mentioned—personal purity, is perhaps of greater importance than either of the other two. We believe in one standard of morality for men and women. If purity of life is neglected, all other dangers set in upon us like the rivers of waters when the flood gates are opened.

(Joseph F. Smith, *Gospel Doctrine* [Salt Lake City: Deseret Book, 1975], 313)

Do not be misled by Satan's lies. There is no lasting happiness in immorality. There is no joy to be found in breaking the law of chastity. Just the opposite is true. There may be momentary pleasure. For a time it may seem like everything is wonderful. But quickly the relationship will sour.... Love begins to die. Bitterness, jealousy, anger, and even hate begin to grow. All of these are the natural results of sin and transgression. On the other hand, when we obey the law of chastity and keep ourselves morally clean, we will experience the blessings of increased love and peace, greater trust and respect for our marital partners [and] deeper commitment to each other....

(Ezra Taft Benson, *BYU Speeches of the Year*, 1987–88 [Provo, Utah: BYU Press, 1987–88], 51)

A quarter of a century ago historian John Lukacs perceptively warned that sexual immorality was not merely a marginal development but, instead, was at the center of the moral crisis of our time. Some thought Lukacs was overstating it, but consider the subsequent and sobering tragedy of children having children, of unwed mothers, of children without parents, of hundreds of thousands of fatherless children, and of rampant spousal infidelity. These and related consequences threaten to abort society's future even before the future arrives! Yet carnalists are unwilling to deny themselves, even though all of society suffers from an awful avalanche of consequences!

(Neal A. Maxwell, *Ensign*, May 1995 [Salt Lake

City: The Church of Jesus Christ of Latter-day Saints, 1995], 67)

_____

Whenever you step over the line in an immoral act or in doing any other evil thing, the Church is that much weaker. . . . When you stand true and faithful, it is that much stronger. Each one of you counts. . . . If any of you has stepped over the line, please do not think all is lost. The Lord reaches out to help you, and there are many willing hands in the Church also who will help. Put evil behind you. Pray about the situation, talk with your parents if you can, and talk with your bishop. You will find that he will listen and do so with confidentiality. . . . There is hope for you. Your lives are ahead, and they can be filled with happiness, even though the past may have been marred by sin. . . . This is the time, this is the very hour, to repent of any evil in the past, to ask for forgiveness, to stand a little taller and then to go forward with confidence and faith.

(Gordon B. Hinckley, *Ensign*, May 1996 [Salt Lake City: The Church of Jesus Christ of Latter-day Saints, 1996], 94)

_____

One who prays to know if another is to be the eternal companion while violating in any degree the law of chastity has little hope of receiving confirmation without repentance.

(Richard G. Scott, in Conference Report, Oct. 1991 [Salt Lake City: The Church of Jesus Christ of Latter-day Saints, 1991], 117)

Alma 39:5 • MURDER
(Refer in this text to Alma 24:9–13.)

If a member of our Church, having received the light of the Holy Spirit, commits this capital crime [murder], he will not receive forgiveness in this world nor in the world to come. The revelations of God to the Church abound in commandments forbidding us to shed blood.

(Wilford Woodruff; as quoted in *Messages of the First Presidency of the Church of Jesus Christ of Latter-day Saints, 1833–1964*, comp. by James R. Clark [Salt Lake City: Bookcraft, 1965], 3:205)

_____

[The Telestial Kingdom] embraces those who on earth willfully reject the GOSPEL OF JESUS CHRIST, and commit serious SINS such as MURDER, ADULTERY, lying, and loving to make a lie (but yet do not commit the UNPARDONABLE SIN), and who do not repent in mortality. They will be cleansed in the postmortal SPIRIT WORLD or spirit prison before the resurrection (D&C 76:81–85, 98–106; Rev. 22:15).

Telestial inhabitants as innumerable as the stars will come forth in the last resurrection and then be "servants of the Most High; but where God and Christ dwell they cannot come" (D&C 76:112).

(*Encyclopedia of Mormonism*, ed. by Daniel H. Ludlow [New York: Macmillan Publishing, 1992], 4:1443)

_____

"Thou shalt not kill; and he that kills shall not have forgiveness in this world, nor in the world to come" (D&C 42:18). . . . At least concerning members of the Church, to whom this revelation, which is entitled "the law of the Church," was addressed. We do know that there are murders committed by Gentiles for which they at least can repent, be baptized, and receive a remission of their sins (see 3 Nephi 30:1–2).

(Bruce R. McConkie, *A New Witness for the Articles of Faith* [Salt Lake City: Deseret Book, 1985], 231)

_____

Even among willful murderers there are grades and categories. . . . There are those who kill in drunkenness, in rage, in anger, in jealousy. There are those who kill for gain, for power, for fear. There are those who kill for lust. They certainly will suffer different degrees of punishment hereafter.

(Spencer W. Kimball, *The Miracle of Forgiveness* [Salt Lake City: Bookcraft, 1969], 129–130)

Alma 39:5–6 • DENY THE HOLY GHOST

What must a man do to commit the unpardonable sin? He must receive the Holy Ghost, have the heavens opened unto him, and know God, and then sin against Him. After a man has sinned against the Holy Ghost, there is no repentance for him. He has got to say that the sun does not shine while he sees it; he has got to deny Jesus Christ when the heavens have been opened unto him, and to deny the plan of salvation with his eyes open to the truth of it; and from that time he begins to be an enemy.

(*Teachings of the Prophet Joseph Smith*, comp. by Joseph Fielding Smith [Salt Lake City: Deseret Book, 1976], 358)

_____

The eyes can be deceived, as can the other physical senses, but the testimony of the Holy Ghost is certain. The sin against the Holy Ghost requires such knowledge that it is manifestly impossible for the rank and file to commit such a sin. Comparatively few Church members will . . . deny the Holy Ghost.

(*Teachings of Spencer W. Kimball*, ed. by Edward L. Kimball [Salt Lake City: Bookcraft, 1982], 23)

A sin that is unpardonable cannot be paid for either by the atoning blood of Christ or by the personal suffering of the sinner. The only sin that falls into this category is denying the Holy Ghost. . . . Alma identified denying the Holy Ghost as the most abominable sin. According to the Lord, individuals committing this sin do five things: (1) They "know my power, and (2) have been made partakers thereof, and (3) suffered themselves through the power of the devil to be overcome and (4) to deny the truth and (5) defy my power" (D&C 76:31). The key to these requirements appears to be the power of the priesthood. An individual must bear and be a partaker of the priesthood and then defy that power. . . . A person must have made priesthood covenants with God and then have received knowledge and power beyond what the vast majority of us have received. . . . If they have lived on this earth and have received a mortal body, they shall come forth in the last resurrection with an immortal body; but that body will not be glorified. Instead they "go away into the lake of fire and brimstone, with the devil and his angels" (D&C 76:36).

(Dean Garrett; as quoted in *The Book of Mormon: Alma, The Testimony of the Word*, ed. by Monte S. Nyman and Charles D. Tate [Provo, UT: Religious Studies Center, BYU, 1992], 157–160)

We are sent to one of four places: the celestial kingdom, the terrestrial kingdom, the telestial kingdom, or outer darkness. Section 76 of the Doctrine and Covenants teaches that the only people who qualify for outer darkness are those who have a full knowledge of the truth and then turn away from it, who have received all the ordinances and then become enemies to righteousness and would kill the Savior if he were here, or consent to his death.

(Jack R. Christianson and K. Douglas Bassett, *Life Lessons from the Book of Mormon* [Salt Lake City: Deseret Book, 2003], 45–46)

[Denying the Holy Ghost] is more than denial; it is more than inactivity in the church; it is more than losing one's testimony. As the revelations attest, such a person comes to *defy* the truth, to wage war against the Lord, His servants, and His work.

(Joseph Fielding McConkie and Robert L. Millet, *The Holy Ghost* [Salt Lake City: Bookcraft, 1989], 146)

Alma 39:8 • YE CANNOT HIDE YOUR CRIMES

Do not take comfort in the fact that your transgres-sions are not known by others. That is like an ostrich with his head buried in the sand. He sees only darkness and feels comfortably hidden. In reality he is ridiculously conspicuous. Likewise our every act is seen by our Father in Heaven and His Beloved Son. They know everything about us. . . . I invite each one of you to thoughtfully review your life. . . . Is there a dark corner that needs to be cleaned out? . . . When it is quiet and you can think clearly, does your conscience tell you to repent?

(Richard G. Scott, *Ensign*, May 1995 [Salt Lake City: The Church of Jesus Christ of Latter-day Saints, 1995], 77)

Alma 39:9 • LUST OF YOUR EYES
(Refer in this text to 1 Nephi 22:23.)

The lust of your eyes. In our day, what does that mean? Movies, television programs, and video recordings that are both suggestive and lewd. Magazines and books that are obscene and pornographic. We counsel you young men, not to pollute your minds with such degrading matter, for the mind through which this filth passes is never the same afterwards. Don't see R-rated movies or vulgar videos or participate in any entertainment that is immoral, suggestive, or pornographic.

(Ezra Taft Benson, *Ensign*, May 1986 [Salt Lake City: The Church of Jesus Christ of Latter-day Saints, 1986], 45)

Turn it off, walk away from it, burn it, erase it, destroy it. I know it is hard counsel we give when we say movies that are R-rated, and many with PG-13 ratings, are produced by satanic influences. Our standards should not be dictated by the rating system. I repeat, because of what they really represent, these types of movies, music, tapes, etc. serve the purposes of the author of all darkness.

(H. Burke Peterson, *Ensign*, Nov. 1993 [Salt Lake City: The Church of Jesus Christ of Latter-day Saints, 1993], 43)

There is neither happiness nor peace to be gained from surrendering to the weakness of indulging in these things which degrade and destroy. When such material is on television, turn off the set. Stop being a boob in front of the tube. Avoid titillating videotapes as you would a foul disease. They are in the same category. Stay away from pornographic magazines and other destructive literature. There is too much of good to see, there is too much of wonderful reading to be experienced to waste time and destroy character and willpower in submitting to such destructive rot.

(Gordon B. Hinckley, *Ensign*, Nov. 1992 [Salt Lake City: The Church of Jesus Christ of Latter-day Saints, 1992], 51–52)

——————

Each person must keep himself clean and free from lusts. . . . He must shun ugly, polluted thoughts and acts as he would an enemy. Pornographic and erotic stories and pictures are worse than polluted food. Shun them. The body has power to rid itself of sickening food. The person who entertains filthy stories or pornographic pictures and literature records them in his marvelous human computer, the brain, which can't forget such filth. Once recorded, it will always remain there, subject to recall.

(Spencer W. Kimball, *Ensign*, July 1978 [Salt Lake City: The Church of Jesus Christ of Latter-day Saints, 1978], 3–7)

——————

We are surrounded by the promotional literature of illicit sexual relations, on the printed page and on the screen. For your own good, avoid it. Pornographic or erotic stories and pictures are worse than filthy or polluted food. The body has defenses to rid itself of unwholesome food. With a few fatal exceptions bad food will only make you sick but do no permanent harm. In contrast, a person who feasts upon filthy stories and pornographic or erotic pictures and literature records them in this marvelous retrieval system we call a brain. The brain won't vomit back filth. Once recorded, it will always remain subject to recall, flashing its perverted images across your mind and drawing you away from the wholesome things in life.

(Dallin H. Oaks, *New Era*, Feb. 1974 [Salt Lake City: The Church of Jesus Christ of Latter-day Saints, 1974], 18)

——————

Be clean. I cannot emphasize that enough. Be clean. It is so very very important and you at your age are in such temptation all the time. It is thrown at you on television. It is thrown at you in books and magazines and videos. You do not have to rent them. Don't do it. Just don't do it. Don't look at them. If somebody proposes that you sit around all night watching some of that sleazy stuff, you say, "It's not for me." Stay away from it.

(Gordon B. Hinckley, Denver, Colorado, Youth Meeting, 14 Apr. 1996)

——————

A bishop reported that he had observed that the spiritual level of the young priesthood bearers in his ward was declining. Through his personal interviews with them, he discovered that many of them were watch-

ing R-rated movies. When he asked them where they went to see such trash, they said, ". . . We watch them at home. We have cable television, and when our parents are gone we watch anything we want to." . . . The Lord and his living prophets are counting on you to avoid the trash that surrounds you in the media. . . . Temptations are all around us, and today with the advent of the Internet, they are increasing. There is much that is positive in the world of the media, but here is so much that is negative. If we permit ourselves to become involved with the negative, there will be much more cause for the devil to laugh and his angels to rejoice.

(Joe J. Christensen, *Ensign*, Nov. 1996 [Salt Lake City: The Church of Jesus Christ of Latter-day Saints, 1996], 40)

——————

The girl you marry can expect you to come to the marriage altar absolutely clean. She can expect you to be a young man of virtue in thought and word and deed. I plead with you boys tonight to keep yourselves free from the stains of the world. . . . You must not fool around with the Internet to find pornographic material. . . . You must not rent videos with pornography of any kind. . . . Stay away from pornography as you would avoid a serious disease. It is as destructive. It can become habitual, and those who indulge in it get so they cannot leave it alone. It is addictive. . . . It seduces and destroys its victims. . . . I plead with you young men not to get involved in its use. You simply cannot afford to. The girl you marry is worthy of a husband whose life has not been tainted by this ugly and corrosive material.

(Gordon B. Hinckley, *Ensign*, May 1998 [Salt Lake City: The Church of Jesus Christ of Latter-day Saints, 1998], 49)

——————

The great apostle of love, John, reminded us that this world will pass away "and the lust thereof" (see 1 John 2:17). This means, quite frankly, that not only can lust ruin this life, but it is also a pandering to an appetite that will have *no* existence at all in the next world!

(Neal A. Maxwell, *Notwithstanding My Weakness* [Salt Lake City: Deseret Book, 1981], 100)

——————

Recently a certain moving picture was acclaimed the best of the year. I have not seen it, nor do I anticipate doing so. But I am told that it is laden with sex, that the use of profanity runs throughout.

Pornography . . . producers grow rich on the gullibility of those who like to watch it. . . . You do not need a road map to foretell where indulgence will take you. Contrast that with the beauty, the peace, the wonderful feeling that comes of living near to the Lord and rising above. . . .

This applies to you, my dear boys who are in this meeting. You are particular targets for the adversary. If he can get you now, he knows he may win you for a lifetime. There has been implanted within you wondrous powers and instincts for a divine purpose. However, when these are perverted, they become destroyers rather than builders.

(Gordon B. Hinckley, in Conference Report, Apr. 2003 [Salt Lake City: The Church of Jesus Christ of Latter-day Saints, 2003], 63)

———————

If we do not make good choices, the media can devastate our families and pull our children away from the narrow gospel path. In the virtual reality and the perceived reality of large and small screens, family-destructive viewpoints and behavior are regularly portrayed as pleasurable, as stylish, as exciting, and as normal. Often the media's most devastating attacks on family are not direct or frontal or openly immoral. Intelligent evil is too cunning for that, knowing that most people still profess belief in family and in traditional values. Rather, the attacks are subtle and *amoral*—issues of right and wrong don't even come up. Immorality and sexual innuendo are everywhere, causing some to believe that because everyone is doing it, it must be all right. This pernicious evil is not out in the street somewhere; it is coming right into our homes, right into the heart of our families. . . .

The new morality preached from the media's pulpit is nothing more than the old immorality. It attacks religion. It undermines the family. It turns virtue into vice and vice into virtue. . . .

The long-cherished values of abstinence from intimate relationships before marriage and complete fidelity between husband and wife after marriage are denigrated and derided. . . .

We see a rapid increase in cyberporn, involving sexual addiction over the Internet. Some become so addicted to viewing Internet pornography and participating in dangerous online chat rooms that they ignore their marriage covenants and family obligations and often put their employment at risk. . . .

According to one social observer: "Television . . . has replaced the family, the school, and the church—in that order—as the principal [instrument] for socialization and transmission of values. . . . Greed, debauchery, violence, unlimited self-gratification, absence of moral restraint . . . are the daily fare glamorously dished up to our children" (*At Century's End: Great Minds Reflect on Our Times*, ed. by Nathan P. Gardels [1995], 53).

(M. Russell Ballard, in Conference Report, Oct. 2003 [Salt Lake City: The Church of Jesus Christ of Latter-day Saints, 2003], 15–17)

———————

In its simplest terms, self-mastery is doing those things we should do and not doing those things we should not do. It requires strength, willpower, and honesty. As the traffic on the communications highway becomes a parking lot, we must depend more and more on our own personal moral filters to separate the good from the bad. Marvelous as it is, in many ways, there is something hypnotic about using the Internet. I refer specifically to spending endless time in chat rooms or visiting the pornography sites.

(James E. Faust, in Conference Report, Apr. 2000 [Salt Lake City: The Church of Jesus Christ of Latter-day Saints, 2000], 56)

———————

[A letter received by Gordon B. Hinckley.]

"My husband of 35 years died recently. . . . He had visited with our good bishop as quickly as he could after his most recent surgery. Then he came to me on that same evening to tell me he had been addicted to pornography. He needed me to forgive him [before he died]. He further said that he had grown tired of living a double life. [He had served in many important] Church callings while knowing [at the same time] that he was in the grips of this 'other master.'

"I was stunned, hurt, felt betrayed and violated. I could not promise him forgiveness at that moment but pleaded for time. . . . I was able to review my married life [and see how] pornography had . . . put a stranglehold on our marriage from early on. We had only been married a couple of months when he brought home a [pornographic] magazine. I locked him out of the car because I was so hurt and angry. . . .

"For many years in our marriage . . . he was most cruel in many of his demands. I was never good enough for him. . . . I felt incredibly beaten down at that time to a point of deep depression. . . . I know now that I was being compared to the latest 'porn queen.' . . .

"We went to counseling one time and . . . my husband proceeded to rip me apart with his criticism and disdain of me. . . .

"I could not even get into the car with him after that but walked around the town . . . for hours, contemplating suicide. [I thought,] 'Why go on if this is all that my "eternal companion" feels for me?'

"I did not go on, but zipped a protective shield around myself. I existed for other reasons than my husband and found joy in my children, in projects and accomplishments that I could do totally on my own. . . .

"After his 'deathbed confession' and [after taking time] to search through my life, I [said] to him, 'Don't you know what you have done?' . . . I told him that I had brought a pure heart into our marriage, kept it pure during that marriage, and intended to keep it pure ever after. Why could he not do the same for me? All I ever wanted was to feel cherished and treated with the smallest of pleasantries . . . instead of being treated like some kind of chattel. . . .

"I am now left to grieve not only for his being gone but also for a relationship that could have been [beautiful, but was not]. . . .

"Please warn the brethren (and sisters). Pornography is not some titillating feast for the eyes that gives a momentary rush of excitement. [Rather] it has the effect of damaging hearts and souls to their very depths, strangling the life out of relationships that should be sacred, hurting to the very core those you should love the most."

And she signs the letter. . . .

Suppose a storm is raging and the winds howl and the snow swirls about you. You find yourself unable to stop it. But you can dress properly and seek shelter, and the storm will have no effect upon you.

Likewise, even though the Internet is saturated with sleazy material, you do not have to watch it. You can retreat to the shelter of the gospel and its teaching of cleanliness and virtue and purity of life. . . .

We do not have to view salacious magazines. We do not have to read books laden with smut. We do not have to watch television that is beneath wholesome standards. We do not have to rent movies that depict that which is filthy. We do not have to sit at the computer and play with pornographic material found on the Internet. . . .

It will be amen to the effectiveness of that priesthood for anyone who engages in the practice of seeking out pornographic material.

(Gordon B. Hinckley, in Conference Report, Oct. 2004 [Salt Lake City: The Church of Jesus Christ of Latter-day Saints, 2004], 63–65)

———

Select with care the information you allow to enter your mind. . . . Television, movies, and especially the Internet can provide an open window through which you can peer into the far reaches of the world. They can bring to you information that is uplifting, good, and inspiring. But if used improperly, these media technologies can fill your mind with such unwholesome thoughts that you will be unable to hear the gentle prompting of the Spirit.

(Harold G. Hillam, in Conference Report, Apr. 2000 [Salt Lake City: The Church of Jesus Christ of Latter-day Saints, 2000], 11)

———

Pornography, which is a seedbed for more blatant immorality, is no longer regarded as back-alley fare. In too many homes and lives, it is now regarded as a legitimate slice of entertainment. Pornography robs its victims of self-respect and of an appreciation of the beauties of life. It tears down those who indulge and pulls them into a slough of evil thoughts and possibly evil deeds. It seduces, destroys, and distorts the truth about love and intimacy. It is more deadly than a foul disease. Pornography is as addictive and self-destructive as illicit drugs, and it literally destroys the personal relationships of those who become its slaves.

Not one of us can afford to partake of this rubbish. We cannot risk the damage it does to the most precious of relationships—marriage—and to other interactions within the family. We cannot risk the effect it will have on our spirit and soul. Salacious videotapes, 900 telephone numbers, the filth found on the Internet, sensual magazines and movies—all are traps to be avoided like the deadliest of plagues.

(Gordon B. Hinckley, *Standing for Something* [New York: Times Books, 2000], 36–37)

———

Let me read to you from a letter I received from a victim:

"I would like to share something with you that I have not been able to share with anyone else. I am a 35-year-old male. For most of my adult life I have been addicted to pornography. I am very ashamed to admit this, . . . but for the most part, my addiction is as real as that of an alcoholic or a drug addict. . . .

"The main reason for my writing is to tell you that the Church can't do enough to counsel the members to avoid pornography. I was first introduced to this material as a child. I was molested by an older male cousin, and pornography was used to attract my interest. I am convinced that this exposure at an early age to sex and pornography is at the root of my addiction today.

"I think it is ironic that those who support the business of pornography say that it is a matter of freedom of expression. I have no freedom. I have lost my free agency because I have been unable to overcome this. It is a trap for me, and I can't seem to get out of it. *Please, please, please* plead with the brethren of the Church not only to avoid but eliminate the sources of pornographic material in their lives. Besides the obvious things like books and magazines, they need to turn off cable movie channels in their homes. I know many who have these services and claim that they are able to screen the bad things out, but this is not true. . . .

"Pornography and perversion have become so commonplace in our lives that the sources of this material are everywhere. I have found pornographic magazines by the roadside and in dumps. We need to talk to our children and explain how evil these things are and encourage them to avoid looking at them when they come across them. . . .

"Finally, President Hinckley, please pray for me and others in the Church who may be like me to have the courage and strength to overcome this terrible affliction.

"I am unable to sign my name, and I hope that you will understand."

The computer is a wonderful instrument when it is properly used. But when it is used to deal with pornography or so-called chat rooms or for any other purpose that leads to evil practices or evil thoughts, then there must be self-discipline enough to turn it off.

(Gordon B. Hinckley, *Ensign*, Nov. 2006 [Salt Lake City: The Church of Jesus Christ of Latter-day Saints, 2006], 60–61)

Alma 39:9 • CROSS YOURSELF
(Refer in this text to Moroni 10:32.)

It is not possible to have a free ride on the road to joy, and there is no real joy that does not involve self-denial and self-discipline.

(Joseph B. Wirthlin, in Conference Report, Apr. 1982 [Salt Lake City: The Church of Jesus Christ of Latter-day Saints, 1982], 33)

———————

Some say they are born with some tendency. Whether you are born with them or you acquired them or you got them through over-medication, addiction, or any other way, what should you do? Resist them! You resist them and push them away. How long? As long as you live. There are some things that are a life-long battle.

(Boyd K. Packer, CES Fireside for Young Adults, 2 Feb. 2003, 6; as quoted in Jack R. Christianson and K. Douglas Bassett, *Life Lessons from the Book of Mormon* [Salt Lake City: Deseret Book, 2003], 52)

Alma 39:10 • COUNSEL
(Refer in this text to 2 Nephi 28:30.)

Some counselors want to delve deeper than is emotionally or spiritually healthy. They sometimes want to draw out and analyze and take apart and dissect.

While a certain amount of catharsis may be healthy, overmuch of it can be degenerating. It is seldom as easy to put something back together as it is to take it apart.

By probing too deeply, or talking endlessly about some problems, we can foolishly cause the very thing we are trying to prevent.

You probably know about the parents who said, "Now, children, while we are gone, whatever you do, don't take the stool and go into the pantry and climb up to the second shelf and move the cracker box and get that sack of beans and put one up your nose, will you?"

There is a lesson there.

(Boyd K. Packer, in Conference Report, Apr. 1978 [Salt Lake City: The Church of Jesus Christ of Latter-day Saints, 1978], 138–139)

Alma 39:11 • EXAMPLE
(Refer in this text to Alma 4:10–11.)

The Lord says if we labor all our days and save but one soul, how great will be our joy with him; on the other hand how great will be our sorrow and our condemnation if through our acts we have led one soul away from this truth. . . . For the destruction of a soul is the destruction of the greatest thing that has ever been created.

(Joseph Fielding Smith, *Doctrines of Salvation*, comp. by Bruce R. McConkie [Salt Lake City: Bookcraft, 1954], 1:313–314)

———————

Never before has the Church had a better reputation than it has now. This is because of you, my brethren and sisters. The opinions of people concerning us for the most part arise out of personal and individual experiences. It is your friendliness, your concern for others, and the good examples of your lives that result in the opinions held by others concerning the Latter-day Saints.

(Gordon B. Hinckley, *Ensign*, Nov. 1997 [Salt Lake City: The Church of Jesus Christ of Latter-day Saints, 1997], 4)

———————

Just the way you smile or the way you offer to help someone can build their faith. And should you forget who you are, just the way you speak and the way you behave can destroy faith.

(Henry B. Eyring, in Conference Report, Oct. 2002 [Salt Lake City: The Church of Jesus Christ of Latter-day Saints, 2002], 81)

———————

Years ago, when we didn't have as many cars in the states as missionaries have now, or in England, some parents were permitted to furnish cars to their sons. I was then in charge of the Missionary Department, and a man came in, a contractor, road builder, and said, "I have a son in California riding a bicycle, and he's going to get killed if he isn't careful. I'd like to take a car to him." And so permission was granted for him to take a car. He came back a week later, and he said, "Can I tell you what happened?"

He said, "I drove all the way to Los Angeles and found the place where he lived. It was about five or six in the afternoon. I knocked on the door. He came to the door, and he said, 'Gee, Dad, is that the car? Thanks. Can I have the keys?' " And his father handed him the keys, and he said, "We've got to go to a baptism. Why don't you go around the corner; there's a little restaurant. Get something to eat, and then come to the such and such meetinghouse, and we'll have a baptismal service, and you can be there."

The father said, "This boy's mother died when he was a child. I married again. There was somehow a great chasm of difference that grew between us, and I said to myself as he took the keys, 'He's the same selfish boy he always was.' "

He said, "I thought I wouldn't go to the baptismal service: I'd go back home. And then I thought, 'Well, I'd better go.' So I went around and got something to eat and arrived at the service late. And they were having a testimony meeting, and those who had been baptized were giving their testimonies. And a man stood up and said, 'I am an old man, 75 years of age. I hold two university degrees. I have been a professional man. I've made good in the world. I thought I knew everything. And one day that young man and his companion knocked on my door. I invited them in because I didn't have anything else to do, and he told me things I had never heard before. Today I have literally been born again. I don't know who is responsible for his being in the mission field, but I'd like to thank whoever sent him. He has brought a new life to me.' And then he bore testimony of the gospel. And then a woman stood and bore her testimony similarly."

And the man who was telling me the story said, "They were talking about my son." He said, "I left there and threw away my cigarettes, and when I got home I threw out the coffeepot. I'm going to try to live worthy of my son." I saw that man in the Salt Lake Temple a year and a half later.

(*Discourses of President Gordon B. Hinckley*, 1995–99 [Salt Lake City: The Church of Jesus Christ of Latter-day Saints, 2004], 1:361–362)

[Gordon B Hinckley related:] I talked with a young man recently returned from the war. He too had walked the jungle patrols, his heart pounding with fear. But reluctantly he admitted that the greatest fear he had was the fear of ridicule.

The men of his company laughed at him, taunted him, plastered him with a nickname that troubled him. They told him the things they reveled in. Then on one occasion when the going was rough, he faced them and quietly said, "Look, I know you think I'm a square. I don't consider myself any better than any of the rest of you. . . . But I grew up in a different way. I grew up in a religious home and a religious town. I went to church on Sundays. We prayed together as a family. I was taught to stay away from these things. It's just that I believe differently. With me it's a matter of religion, and it's kind of a way of respecting my mother and my dad. All of you

together might force me toward a compromising situation, but that wouldn't change me, and you wouldn't feel right after you'd done it."

One by one they turned silently away. But during the next few days each came to ask his pardon, and from his example others gained the strength and the will to change their own lives. He taught the gospel to two of them and brought them into the church.

(*Church News*, 29 Apr. 1972, 14; as quoted in J. Richard Clarke, in Conference Report, Apr. 1985 [Salt Lake City: The Church of Jesus Christ of Latter-day Saints, 1985], 95)

Following the renovation of the Mesa Arizona Temple some years ago, clergy of other religions were invited to tour it on the first day of the open house period. Hundreds responded. In speaking to them, I said we would be pleased to answer any queries they might have. Among these was one from a Protestant minister.

Said he: "I've been all through this building, this temple which carries on its face the name of Jesus Christ, but nowhere have I seen any representation of the cross, the symbol of Christianity. I have noted your buildings elsewhere and likewise find an absence of the cross. Why is this when you say you believe in Jesus Christ?"

I responded: "I do not wish to give offense to any of my Christian colleagues who use the cross on the steeples of their cathedrals and at the altars of their chapels, who wear it on their vestments, and imprint it on their books and other literature. But for us, the cross is the symbol of the dying Christ, while our message is a declaration of the Living Christ."

He then asked: "If you do not use the cross, what is the symbol of your religion?"

I replied that the lives of our people must become the most meaningful expression of our faith and, in fact, therefore, the symbol of our worship.

(Gordon B. Hinckley, *Ensign*, Apr. 2005 [Salt Lake City: The Church of Jesus Christ of Latter-day Saints, 2005], 3)

LeGrand's [Richards] father's daily teachings so impressed the boy that he took responsibility to safeguard his mind by controlling what he allowed to enter it. He tells how one day "I walked away from the old Co-op corner, where we used to play our first games, and I resolved that no friend of mine would ever be able to accuse me of befouling his mind with dirty stories like I had heard there." And he has many times repeated the classic statement, "I can go back to the town where I was raised as a boy and can tell parents how to raise their children, and I don't need to worry about old women my age sitting down in the back saying, 'Yes, but you should have known him when we knew him as a boy.' "

(LeGrand Richards, *Ensign*, July 1982 [Salt Lake City: The Church of Jesus Christ of Latter-day Saints, 1982], 7; material in this article comes from Lucile C. Tate's *LeGrand Richards: Beloved Apostle*)

———————

That summer we took our Explorers down the Snake River in canoes. Each night on this trip we had a campfire, and around the fire one of the leaders gave a spiritual thought. He began: "Possibly you would be interested in something that happened to me when I was your age."

He continued: "I played on a high-school basketball team, and we made it to the state tournament. On the last night, while we were warming up before the final game, one of the popular girls in the school came down on the gymnasium floor and invited the whole team to her house after the game. . . . We played the game and won.

"In the locker room afterwards we were deciding what we would do to celebrate, when someone remembered the invitation we had received to go to the home of this girl. So we all went to her house. It turned out that her parents were gone for the weekend. She had rolled back the rug and had invited exactly twelve girls, one for each team member. We went in and sat down in a large circle. The stereo was turned up loud and we were all talking about the game.

"After a while our hostess walked over to the stereo and turned the volume down. 'Listen, fellows,' she said, 'the basketball season is over. You don't need to worry about training any more—you can let your hair down and relax tonight.' Then she pulled out a carton of cigarettes, opened a package, and started it around the circle."

All eyes were on the man telling the story as he went on. "We lived in a Latter-day Saint community. Almost everyone was LDS. Yet as the cigarettes were passed from one to another, every person was taking one. The package was getting closer to me with every second. I didn't want to smoke, but I didn't want to be embarrassed either, by being the exception. I decided to smoke along with the rest.

"By now the cigarettes had reached the fellow next to me. But he merely said 'No, thanks,' and passed them on to me. It was my friend's courage that gave me courage, and I too said 'No, thanks,' and passed the package on."

The storyteller looked intently into the faces lit by the flickering campfire. "My young friends," he said softly, "I have many times wondered what would have happened to me if I had been sitting on the other side of my friend."

(Vaughn J. Featherstone, *Do-It-Yourself Destiny*, 21–22; as quoted in *Latter-Day Commentary on the New Testament*, ed. by J. Pinegar, K. Douglas Bassett, and Ted L. Earl [American Fork, Utah: Covenant Communications, 2002], 104–105)

Alma 39:13 • CONFESS
(Refer in this text to Mosiah 26:29.)

Alma 40:6–14 • SPIRIT WORLD
(Refer in this text to 2 Nephi 9:13.)

Spirits will be familiar with spirits in the spirit world—will converse, . . . as familiarly and naturally as while here in tabernacles. . . . You will there see that those spirits we are speaking of are active; they sleep not. And you will learn that they are striving with all their might—laboring and toiling diligently as any individual would to accomplish an act in this world.

(*Teachings of Presidents of the Church—Brigham Young* [Salt Lake City: The Church of Jesus Christ of Latter-day Saints, 1997], 281)

———————

In every death there is a birth; the spirit leaves the body dead to us, and passes to the other side of the veil alive to that great and noble company that are also working for the accomplishment of the purposes of God. . . .

There is rejoicing when the spirit of a Saint of the Living God enters into the spirit world and meets with the Saints who have gone before.

(*Teachings of Presidents of the Church—Wilford Woodruff* [Salt Lake City: The Church of Jesus Christ of Latter-day Saints, 2004], 80–81)

———————

If you see one of your children that has passed away it may appear to you in the form in which you would recognize it, the form of childhood; but if it came to you as a messenger bearing some important truth, it would perhaps come as the spirit of Bishop Edward Hunter's son (who died when a little child) came to him, in the stature of full-grown manhood, and revealed himself to his father, and said: "I am your son."

Bishop Hunter did not understand it. He went to my father and said: "Hyrum, what does that mean? I buried my son when he was only a little boy, but he has come to me as a full-grown man—a noble, glorious, young man, and declared himself my son. What does it mean?"

Father (Hyrum Smith, the Patriarch) told him that the Spirit of Jesus Christ was full-grown before he was born into the world; and so our children were full-grown and possessed their full stature in the spirit, before they entered mortality, the same stature that they will possess after they have passed away from mortality, and as they will also appear after the resurrection, when they shall have completed their mission.

Joseph Smith taught the doctrine that the infant child that was laid away in death would come up in the resurrection as a child; and, pointing to the mother of a lifeless child, he said to her: "You will have the joy, the pleasure, and satisfaction of nurturing this child, after its resurrection, until it reaches the full stature of its spirit." There is restitution, there is growth, there is development, after the resurrection from death.

(Joseph F. Smith, *Gospel Doctrine* [Salt Lake City: Deseret Book, 1975], 455–456)

I lost a son six years of age, and I saw him a man in the spirit world after his death, and I saw how he had exercised his own freedom of choice and would obtain of his own will and volition a companionship, and in due time to him, and all those who are worthy of it, shall come all of the blessings and sealing privileges of the house of the Lord. Do not worry over it. They are safe; they are all right.

(Bryant S. Hinckley, *Sermons and Missionary Services of Melvin Joseph Ballard* [Salt Lake City: Deseret Book, 1949], 260)

Apparently, there are no infants or children in the spirit world. All who reside there possess the stature of adult men and women, the same appearance they possessed prior to mortal birth. If infants or children die, their spirits immediately resume their former adult stature while in the spirit world. However, when they regain their bodies during the resurrection, they naturally come forth as children to be raised to maturity by righteous and worthy parents.

(Dale C. Mouritsen, *Ensign*, Jan. 1977 [Salt Lake City: The Church of Jesus Christ of Latter-day Saints, 1977], 50)

There is no baptism in the spirit world any more than there is any marrying and giving in marriage.

Some person or persons dwelling in the flesh must attend to this part of the work for them; for it takes just as much to save a dead man who never received the gospel as a living man. And all those who have passed away without the gospel have the right to expect somebody in the flesh to perform this work for them.

(*Teachings of Presidents of the Church—Wilford Woodruff* [Salt Lake City: The Church of Jesus Christ of Latter-day Saints, 2004], 188)

Where is the spirit world? It is right here. . . . Can you see it with your natural eyes? No. Can you see spirits in this room? No. Suppose the Lord should touch your eyes that you might see, could you then see the spirits? Yes, as plainly as you now see bodies. . . .

(*Discourses of Brigham Young*, comp. by John A. Widtsoe [Salt Lake City: Deseret Book, 1954], 376–377)

[Following death] The spirits of the just are . . . blessed in their departure to the world of spirits. . . . They are not far from us, and know and understand our thoughts, feelings, and motions, and are often pained therewith.

(*Teachings of the Prophet Joseph Smith*, comp. by Joseph Fielding Smith [Salt Lake City: Deseret Book, 1976], 326)

Many spirits of the departed, who are unhappy, linger in lonely wretchedness about the earth, and in the air, and especially about their ancient homesteads, and the places rendered dear to them by the memory of the former scenes.

(Parley P. Pratt, *Key to the Science of Theology* [Salt Lake City: Deseret Book, 1978], 117)

We have more friends behind the veil than on this side, and they will hail us more joyfully than you were ever welcomed by your parents and friends in this world; and you will rejoice more when you meet them than you ever rejoiced to see a friend in this life; and then we shall go on from step to step, from rejoicing to rejoicing, and from one intelligence and power to another, our happiness becomes more and more exquisite and sensible as we proceed.

(*Discourses of Brigham Young*, comp. by John A. Widtsoe [Salt Lake City: Deseret Book, 1954], 379–380)

Brother Joseph Smith gave an explanation of [evil influences]. There are places in the Mississippi Valley where the influence or the presence of invisible spirits are very perceptibly felt. He said that numbers had been slain there in war and that there were evil influences or spirits which affect the spirits of those who have tabernacles on the earth. I myself have felt those influences in other places besides the continent of America; I have felt them on the old battle grounds on the Sandwich Islands. I have come to the conclusion that if our eyes were open to see the spirit world around us, we should feel differently on this subject than we do; we would not be so unguarded and careless and so indifferent whether we had the spirit and power of God with us or not; but we would be continually watchful and prayerful to our Heavenly Father for His Holy Spirit and His holy angels to be around about us to strengthen us to overcome every evil influence.

(George Q. Cannon, *Gospel Truths*, ed. by Jerreld L. Newquist [Salt Lake City: Deseret Book, 1974], 1:82)

Does spirit prison include paradise and outer darkness?

I know it is a startling idea to say that the Prophet and the persecutor of the Prophet all go to prison together. What is the condition of the righteous? They are in possession of the spirit of Jesus—the power of God. . . . Jesus will administer to them; angels will administer to them; and they have a privilege of seeing and understanding more than you or I have, in the flesh; but they have not got their bodies yet, consequently they are in prison. . . . What is the condition of the wicked? They are in prison. Are they happy? No.

(Brigham Young, *Journal of Discourses* [London: Latter-day Saints' Book Depot, 1856], 3:95)

How is living without a body like being in prison?

When our spirits leave these bodies, will they be happy? Not perfectly so. Why? Because the spirit is absent from the body; it cannot be perfectly happy while a part of the man is lying in the earth.

(Orson Pratt, *Journal of Discourses* [London: Latter-day Saints' Book Depot, 1855], 1:289–290)

Can spirits progress in spirit prison?

Every man that has been baptized and belongs to the kingdom has a right to be baptized for those who have gone before; and as soon as the law of the Gospel is obeyed here by their friends who act as proxy for them, the Lord has administrators there to set them free.

(*Teachings of the Prophet Joseph Smith*, comp. by Joseph Fielding Smith [Salt Lake City: Deseret Book, 1976], 367)

Many other great truths not known before have been declared to the people, and one of the greatest is that to hell there is an exit as well as an entrance. Hell is no place to which a vindictive judge sends prisoners to suffer and to be punished principally for his glory; But it is a place prepared for the teaching, the disciplining of those who failed to learn here upon the earth what they should have learned. . . . No man will be kept in hell longer than is necessary to bring him to a fitness for

something better. When he reaches that stage the prison doors will open and there will be rejoicing among the hosts who welcome him into a better state.

(James E. Talmage, in Conference Report, Apr. 1930 [Salt Lake City: The Church of Jesus Christ of Latter-day Saints, 1930], 97)

The work of the righteous is to preach the gospel to as many as will receive it, so that whosoever receives it unto repentance may leave the spirit prison and enter into paradise when the ordinances have been done vicariously for them on earth. Through the institution of baptism for the dead, the Church is able to open the gate of baptism, which allows the repentant spirits to exit the spirit prison of hell, the state of the wicked in the spirit world.

(Richard O. Cowan; as quoted in *The Book of Mormon: Alma, The Testimony of the Word*, ed. by Monte S. Nyman and Charles D. Tate [Provo, Utah: Religious Studies Center, BYU, 1992], 184)

Alma 40:8 • TIME MEASURED UNTO MAN

Abraham was told that one revolution (or day) on Kolob equals a thousand of our years (Abraham 3:4). If one were to carry the ratio down to smaller units of time we see some interesting implications.

Kolob Time	Earth Time
1 day	1,000 years
1 hour	41.67 years
1 minute	253 days
1 second	4.22 days
.25 second	1.1 days
.01 second	1 hour

Think of the implications of that. While a person on Kolob takes a two-hour nap, a person on Earth is born, lives to the age of eighty, and dies before the other awakens. One blink on the part of a Kolobian and he misses one whole day of ours.

(Gerald Lund; as quoted in *First Nephi, The Doctrinal Foundation*, ed. by Monte S. Nyman and Charles D. Tate [Provo, Utah: Religious Studies Center, BYU, 1988], 158–159)

The great Jehovah contemplated the whole of the events connected with the earth, pertaining to the plan of salvation, before it rolled into existence, . . . "the morning stars sang together" for joy; the past, the present, and the future were and are, with Him, one eternal "now."

(*Teachings of the Prophet Joseph Smith* [Salt Lake City: Deseret Book, 1976], 220)

When we pray "Thy will be done," our submission includes yielding to God's timing. He lives in a unique circumstance wherein the past, present, and future blend in an "eternal now." Those of us who need to wear mere wristwatches should be reluctant, therefore, to insist on our timetables for Him.

(Neal A. Maxwell, *Whom the Lord Loveth* [Salt Lake City: Deseret Book, 2003], 18)

Alma 40:11 • TAKEN HOME TO GOD

These words of Alma as I understand them, do not intend to convey the thought that all spirits go back into the presence of God for an assignment to a place of peace or a place of punishment and before him receive their individual sentence. "Taken home to God," simply means that their mortal existence has come to an end, and they have returned to the world of spirits, where they are assigned to a place according to their works with the just or with the unjust, there to await the resurrection. "Back to God" is a phrase which finds an equivalent in many other well-known conditions. For instance: a man spends a stated time in some foreign mission field. When he is released and returns to the United States, he may say, "It is wonderful to be back home"; yet his home may be somewhere in Utah or Idaho or some other part of the West.

(Joseph Fielding Smith, *Answers to Gospel Questions* [Salt Lake City: Deseret Book, 1958], 2:84–86)

———

It does not mean . . . that people who return into his presence are immediately placed within a few yards or rods, or within a short distance of his person. . . .

Supposing . . . that there was a principle . . . of light of a more refined nature, that could penetrate from London to this point, so that it would affect our eyes, enabling us to see persons there, then we could both see and hear them at eight or nine thousand miles distant. Would we not be in their presence? Would it be really necessary for us to travel eight or nine thousand miles to get into the same room with them, in order to get into their presence? We should consider ourselves in their presence if we could see them; and if in addition to this we could communicate with and make them hear us, we should feel all that familiarity and sociability that we should if we were within a few steps of them.

(Orson Pratt, *Journal of Discourses* [London: Latter-day Saints' Book Depot, 1874], 16:365–366)

———

As for my going into the immediate presence of God when I die, I do not expect it, but I expect to go into the world of spirits and associate with my brethren, and preach the Gospel in the spiritual world, and pre-pare myself in every necessary way to receive my body again, and then enter through the wall into the celestial world. I never shall come into the presence of my Father and God until I have received my resurrected body, neither will any other person.

(Heber C. Kimball, *Journal of Discourses* [London: Latter-day Saints' Book Depot, 1856], 3:112–113)

———

You read in the Bible that when the spirit leaves the body it goes to God who gave it. Now tell me where God is not, if you please; you cannot. . . . The Lord Almighty is here by His Spirit, by His influence, by His presence. I am not in the north end of this bowery, my body is in the south end of it, but my influence and my voice extend to all parts of it; in like manner is the Lord here.

(Brigham *Journal of Discourses* [London: Latter-day Saints' Book Depot, 1856], 3:368)

———

Alma, when he says that "the spirits of all men, as soon as they are departed from this mortal body, . . . are taken home to that God who gave them life," has the idea, doubtless, in his mind that our God is omnipresent—not in His own personality but through His minister, the Holy Spirit.

He does not intend to convey the idea that they are immediately ushered into the personal presence of God. He evidently uses that phrase in a qualified sense. Solomon . . . makes a similar statement: "Then shall the dust return to the earth as it was: and the spirit shall return unto God who gave it" (Ecclesiastes 12:7). The same idea is frequently expressed by the Latter-day Saints. In referring to a departed one it is often said that he has gone back to God, or he has gone "home to that God who gave him life." . . .

Alma says plainly that the spirits of the righteous go into a state of happiness, etc. He says the spirits of the wicked are cast into outer darkness, etc. Now, then, how can those spirits who are cast into outer darkness be in the personal presence of God? God does not dwell where they are, and they certainly do not go where He is.

(George Q. Cannon, *Gospel Truth*, comp. by Jerreld L. Newquist [Salt Lake City: Deseret Book, 1957], 58)

———

To pass from this state of existence . . . [at the time of death]. My spirit is set free, I thirst no more, I want to sleep no more, I hunger no more, I tire no more, I run, I walk, I labor, I go, I come, I do this, I do that, whatever is required of me, nothing like pain or weariness, I am full of life, full of vigor, and I enjoy the presence of my heavenly Father, by the power of his Spirit. . . . When you close your eyes upon mortality you wake up right in the presence of the Father and the Son if they are disposed to withdraw the vail, they can do as they please with regard to this; but you are in the spirit world and in a state of bliss and happiness.

(Brigham Young, *Journal of Discourses* [London: Latter-day Saints' Book Depot, 1875], 17:142)

Alma 40:12 • PARADISE, REST, PEACE

The spirits of all men, as soon as they depart from this mortal body, whether they are good or evil, we are told in the Book of Mormon, are taken home to that God who gave them life, where there is a separation, a partial judgement, and the spirits of those who are righteous are received into a state of happiness which is called paradise, a state of rest, a state of peace, where they expand in wisdom, where they have respite from all their troubles and where care and sorrow do not annoy. The wicked, on the contrary, have no part nor portion in the Spirit of the Lord, and they are cast into outer darkness, being led captive, because of their iniquity, by the evil one. And in this space between death and the resurrection of the body, the two classes of souls remain, in happiness or in misery, until the time which is appointed of God that the dead shall come forth and be reunited both spirit and body, and be brought to stand before God, and be judged according to their works.

(Joseph F. Smith, *Gospel Doctrine* [Salt Lake City: Deseret Book, 1975], 448)

———

Those things which burdened the obedient—the worldly cares and struggles, the vicissitudes of life—are shed with the physical body. Paradise is a place where the spirit is free to think and act with a renewed capacity and with the vigor and enthusiasm which characterized one in his prime. Though a person does not rest per se from the work associated with the plan of salvation, (. . . that labor goes forward with at least an equal intensity in the spirit world), at the same time he is delivered from those cares and worries associated with a fallen world and a corrupt body.

(Robert L. Millet and Joseph Fielding McConkie, *The Life Beyond* [Salt Lake City: Bookcraft, 1986], 18)

———

Wilford Woodruff . . . continued to receive instruction from Joseph Smith, even after the Prophet's death. He told of a vision he received in which he spoke with Joseph Smith: "I saw him at the door of the temple in heaven. He came to me and spoke to me. He said he could not stop to talk with me because he was in a hurry. The next man I met was Father Smith [Joseph Smith Sr.]; he could not talk with me because he was in a hurry. I met half a dozen brethren who had held high positions on earth, and none of them could stop to talk with me because they were in a hurry. I was much astonished. By and by I saw the Prophet again and I got the privilege of asking him a question.

" 'Now,' said I, 'I want to know why you are in a hurry. I have been in a hurry all my life; but I expected my hurry would be over when I got into the kingdom of heaven, if I ever did.'

"Joseph said: 'I will tell you, Brother Woodruff. Every dispensation that has had the priesthood on the earth and has gone into the celestial kingdom has had a certain amount of work to do to prepare to go to the earth with the Savior when he goes to reign on the earth. Each dispensation has had ample time to do this work. We have not. We are the last dispensation, and so much work has to be done, and we need to be in a hurry in order to accomplish it.' "

(*Teachings of Presidents of the Church—Wilford Woodruff* [Salt Lake City: The Church of Jesus Christ of Latter-day Saints, 2004], 26)

Alma 40:15 • PARTIAL JUDGMENT

Death itself is an initial *day of judgment* for all persons, both the righteous and the wicked. When the spirit leaves the body at death, it is taken home to that God who gave it life, meaning that it returns to live in the realm of spiritual existence (Eccles. 12:7). At that time the spirit undergoes a partial judgment and is assigned an inheritance in paradise or in hell to await the day of the first or second resurrection.

(Bruce R. McConkie, *Mormon Doctrine* [Salt Lake City: Bookcraft, 1966], 402)

———

When the spirit leaves the body, it returns, says the prophet, immediately to God, to be assigned to its place, either to associate with the good and the noble ones who have lived in the paradise of God, or to be confined in the "prison-house" to await the resurrection of the body from the grave. Therefore we know that Brother Clayton has gone to God, gone to receive the partial judgment of the Almighty which pertains to the period intervening between the death of the body and the resurrection of the body, or the separation of the spirit from the body and their uniting together again. This judgment is passed upon the spirit alone. But there will come a time which will be after the resurrection, when the body and spirit shall be reunited, when the final judgment will be passed on every man.

(Joseph F. Smith, *Gospel Doctrine* [Salt Lake City: Deseret Book, 1975], 449)

Alma 40:23 • RESURRECTION: A HAIR WON'T BE LOST

(Refer in this text to Alma 11:43–44.)

A man who has lost a leg in childhood will have his leg restored. . . . Deformities and the like will be corrected, if not immediately at the time of the uniting of the spirit and body, so soon thereafter [almost instantly] that it will make no difference. . . . Infants and children do not grow in the grave, but when they come forth, they will come forth with the same body and in the same size in which the body was when it was laid away. After the resurrection the body will grow until it has reached the full stature of manhood or womanhood.

(Joseph Fielding Smith, *Doctrines of Salvation*, comp. by Bruce R. McConkie [Salt Lake City: Bookcraft, 1955], 2:293–294)

———————

The question frequently arises as to whether a child that died in infancy will remain a child in the hereafter, and whether in the resurrection the spirit will take up the same body that it tabernacled in the flesh. . . . . The late President Joseph F. Smith in an editorial in the *Improvement Era*, June 1904, . . . stated, "The body will come forth as it is laid to rest, for there is no growth or development in the grave. As it is laid down, so will it arise, and changes to perfection will come by the law of restitution. But the spirit will continue to expand and develop, to the full stature of man." Parents, therefore, who have been parted from their children by death may rest assured that, if worthy through obedience to the principles of the gospel, they will not only meet their children in the spirit world, but will also recognize them and know them as they knew them in this life. Parents too, have even a greater comfort in the fact that their little ones whose lives on earth were cut short will continue to grow and develop, and receive every blessing to which their inheritance and faithfulness will entitle them.

(*Gospel Ideals: Selections from the Discourses of David O. McKay*, sel. by G. Homer Durham [Salt Lake City: Improvement Era, 1953], 75)

———————

Man is a dual being, a spirit within a mortal body. It is difficult to teach about the intangible, spiritual part. But there are ways to do it. . . . A personal computer made of metal, plastic, glass and a dozen other materials will hold an astonishing amount of information. All of the standard works can be stored there, and in addition, sets of encyclopedias, dictionaries, books on a whole library of subjects, even illustrations and mathematical formulas. With the press of a few keys one can select any part of what is stored and see it instantly on a screen. One may, by pressing a few more keys, rearrange, add to, or subtract from what is stored in the computer. Press

another key or two and you can print a copy of whatever you desire, even in full color. You then can hold in your hand tangible, absolute proof of what is inside there and how it is arranged. However, if you should take the computer completely apart, you could not find one word of it, not one illustration, not one tangible evidence that there are volumes, verses, poems, and illustrations inside the computer. You could dissolve the computer with acids or burn it and you would not find one tangible word of evidence. You could no more find words in the ashes of a computer than you can find the spirit in the ashes of a cremated human body. No one doubts that this great base of information is actually stored in the computer. It should not be too difficult to teach each youngster that there is within the human body a spirit.

(Boyd K. Packer, CES Symposium, 10 Aug. 1993)

———————

When the angel who holds the keys of the resurrection shall sound his trumpet, the peculiar fundamental particles that organized our bodies here, if we do honor to them—though they be deposited in the depths of the sea, and though one particle is in the north, another in the south, another in the east, and another in the west—will be brought together again in the twinkling of an eye, and our spirits will take possession of them.

(Brigham Young, *Journal of Discourses*, 8:28, 25 Mar. 1860; as quoted in *Latter-day Prophets Speak*, ed. by Daniel H. Ludlow [Salt Lake City: Bookcraft, 1951], 42)

———————

I know that some people . . . will say that all the parts of the body cannot be brought together, for, say they, the fish probably have eaten them up, or the whole may have been blown to the four winds of heaven, etc. It is true the body, or the organization, may be destroyed in various ways, but it is not true that the particles out of which it was created can be destroyed. They are eternal; they never were created. . . . It is in accordance with acknowledged science. You may take, for instance, a handful of fine gold, and scatter it in the street among the dust; again, gather together the materials among which you have thrown the gold, and you can separate one from the other so thoroughly, that your handful of gold can be returned to you; yes, every grain of it. You may take particles of silver, iron, copper, lead, etc., and mix them together with any other ingredients, and there are certain principles connected with them by which these different materials can be eliminated, every particle cleaving to that of its own element.

(John Taylor, *Journal of Discourses*, 18:333–334, 31 Dec. 1876; as quoted in *Latter-day Prophets Speak*, ed. by Daniel H. Ludlow [Salt Lake City: Bookcraft, 1951], 43)

I think it has been taught by some that as we lay our bodies down, they will so rise again in the resurrection with all the impediments and imperfections that they had here. . . . This is not so. Those who attain to the blessing of the first or celestial resurrection will be pure and holy, and perfect in body. Every man and woman that reaches to this unspeakable attainment will be as beautiful as the angels that surround the throne of God.

(Brigham Young, *Journal of Discourses* [London: Latter-day Saints' Book Depot, 1856], 10:24)

Will the veil of forgetfulness be lifted in the spirit world?

There are those who suppose that death brings with it a restoration of pre-earth knowledge. The scriptures do not sustain such an idea. Were this the case, those in the spirit world who had not heard the gospel could hardly be judged according to men in the flesh, as revelation ancient and modern asserts (see 1 Peter 4:6; D&C 138:10).

(Robert L. Millet and Joseph Fielding McConkie, *The Life Beyond* [Salt Lake City: Bookcraft, 1986], 62)

Alma 40:26 • SECOND DEATH

Thus, eventually, all are redeemed from spiritual death except those who have "sinned unto death" (D&C 64:7), that is, those who are destined to be sons of perdition.

(Bruce R. McConkie, *Mormon Doctrine* [Salt Lake City: Bookcraft, 1966], 758)

Alma 41:1–15; 42:27–28 • RESTORATION

When we hear the term *restoration* we typically think of the latter-day return of the Church and the revelation of the gospel in its fulness. Book of Mormon prophets, however, use this term in a rather different sense. They teach that every individual will receive a temporal as well as a spiritual restoration, good for good, evil for evil.

(Richard O. Cowan; as quoted in *The Book of Mormon: Alma, The Testimony of the Word*, ed. by Monte S. Nyman and Charles D. Tate [Provo, UT: Religious Studies Center, BYU, 1992], 198)

We know from the Book of Mormon that the resurrection is a *restoration* that brings back "carnal for carnal" and "good for that which is good" (Alma 41:13; see also verses 2–4 and Helaman 14:31). The prophet Amulek taught, "That same spirit which doth possess your bodies at the time that ye go out of this life, that

same spirit will have power to possess your body in that eternal world" (Alma 34:34). As a result, when persons leave this life and go on to the next, "they who are righteous shall be righteous still" (2 Nephi 9:16), and "whatever principle of intelligence we attain unto in this life . . . will rise with us in the resurrection" (D&C 130:18).

The principle of restoration also means that persons who are not righteous in mortal life will not rise up righteous in the resurrection (see 2 Nephi 9:16; 1 Corinthians 15:35–44; D&C 88:27–32). Moreover, unless our mortal sins have been cleansed and blotted out by repentance and forgiveness (see Alma 5:21; 2 Nephi 9:45–46; D&C 58:42), we will be resurrected with a "bright recollection" (Alma 11:43) and a "perfect knowledge of all our guilt, and our uncleanness" (2 Nephi 9:14; see also Alma 5:18). The seriousness of that reality is emphasized by the many scriptures suggesting that the resurrection is followed immediately by the Final Judgment (see 2 Nephi 9:15, 22; Mosiah 26:25; Alma 11:43–44; 42:23; Mormon 7:6; 9:13–14). Truly, "this life is the time for men to prepare to meet God" (Alma 34:32).

(Dallin H. Oaks, in Conference Report, Apr. 2000 [Salt Lake City: The Church of Jesus Christ of Latter-day Saints, 2000], 17–18)

Alma 41:7 • THEY ARE THEIR OWN JUDGES
(Refer in this text to Alma 11:43.)

The great misery of departed spirits in the world of spirits, where they go after death, is to know that they come short of the glory that others enjoy and that they might have enjoyed themselves, and they are their own accusers.

(*Teachings of the Prophet Joseph Smith*, comp. by Joseph Fielding Smith [Salt Lake City: Deseret Book, 1976], 310–311)

The reality is that there will be a whole hierarchy of judges who, under Christ, shall judge the righteous. He alone shall issue the decrees of damnation for the wicked.

(Bruce R. McConkie, *The Millennial Messiah* [Salt Lake City: Deseret Book, 1982], 520)

Alma 41:10 • WICKEDNESS NEVER WAS HAPPINESS

You can never get enough of what you don't need, because what you don't need will never satisfy you.

(Dallin H. Oaks, in Conference Report, Oct. 1991 [Salt Lake City: The Church of Jesus Christ of Latter-day Saints, 1991], 104)

You cannot do wrong and feel right. It is impossible.

(Ezra Taft Benson, *New Era*, June 1986 [Salt Lake City: The Church of Jesus Christ of Latter-day Saints, 1986], 5)

Happiness is the object and design of our existence; and will be the end thereof, if we pursue the path that leads to it; and this path is virtue, uprightness, faithfulness, holiness, and keeping all the commandments of God.

(Joseph Smith, *History of the Church of Jesus Christ of Latter-day Saints* [Salt Lake City: Deseret Book, 1980], 5:134–135)

So many of us are fearful of what our peers will say, that we will be looked upon with disdain and criticized if we stand for what is right. But I remind you that "wickedness never was happiness" (Alma 41:10). Evil never was happiness. Sin never was happiness. Happiness lies in the power and the love and the sweet simplicity of the gospel of Jesus Christ. We need not be prudish. We need not slink off in a corner, as it were. We need not be ashamed. We have the greatest thing in the world, the gospel of the risen Lord.

(Gordon B. Hinckley, *Ensign*, May 1997 [Salt Lake City: The Church of Jesus Christ of Latter-day Saints, 1997], 49)

Laws do not change. A law, like truth, "abideth and hath no end" (D&C 88:66). A theory is tentative, subject to change, and may or may not be true. A theory is a means to an end, not the end in itself. . . . Laws governing spiritual things were irrevocably decreed in heaven before the foundation of the earth (D&C 130:20). Often young people fail to accept moral and spiritual laws because the laws are not measured by methods they have been accustomed to using. Physical or natural laws are much easier to demonstrate, and can be useful in teaching about spiritual things. Let me illustrate. At 32 degrees Fahrenheit, water freezes and changes from a liquid to a solid. At 212 degrees Fahrenheit it turns into a gas. Your students know that and there isn't anything they can do about it—they can't change it. It can be described accurately or inaccurately, in complicated measurements in Fahrenheit or centigrade or anything else, and nothing that is said about it is going to change it because it operates according to law. It will freeze or evaporate according to the law. It should not be difficult to understand that there are basic spiritual laws that have always existed, that never change, that beget consequences, and we can't change them. The wonder is

that we can depend on these spiritual laws. "Wickedness never was happiness," and anybody that has tried to find out, has found out. It is a law.

(Boyd K. Packer, CES Symposium, 10 Aug. 1993)

There is nothing gained by doing wrong. Lying, stealing, blaspheming, drunkenness, backbiting, and denying the Lord Jesus Christ bring sorrow and remorse; they debase man who is organized in the image of God; but to do right, to obey the commandments of God, to be charitable and kind, brings joy and peace and the Holy Ghost, and an eventual exaltation is our Father's kingdom.

(*The Discourses of Wilford Woodruff* [Salt Lake City: Bookcraft, 1946], 23)

I once heard a man say that there are two doors to sin—the front door is pride and the back door is low self-esteem. Many times people sin not because they really want to or because they are rebellious, but because they are so discouraged, so filled with hopelessness, or so desirous of meeting their basic needs that they go after them in unwise ways.

Someone once noted that the majority of sins committed by people are an inadequate or misguided attempt to meet our basic needs. Most sins are not committed by evil people, just misguided people.

(*Selected Writings of Gerald N. Lund* [Salt Lake City: Deseret Book, 1999], 378)

Modern day advertisements and movies portray evil as the source of happiness. Alcohol, tobacco, and infidelity are all represented as bringing easy and immediate pleasure and satisfaction. Many media sponsors and producers maximize pleasure and minimize consequences. Seldom do we see portrayed the pain, sorrow, and suffering caused by sin. Satan plays upon these scenes of artificial bliss and entices many to do evil.

(Clyde J. Williams, *Doctrines of the Book of Mormon*, 1991 Sperry Symposium, ed. by Bruce A. Van Orden and Brent L. Top [Salt Lake City: Deseret Book, 1992], 248)

Some years ago, I was invited to speak to the inmates at the Utah State Penitentiary. . . .

I was invited . . . to talk to the Alcoholics Anonymous group at the prison, which I did. When I turned to the man in charge of that group and said, "I would like to hear from you. I would like to know something about you men and what your aims and your ambitions are." The man stood up and said something like this, "I thank God for the privilege of being in this institution." Then he proceeded to explain: He said, "Before I came here, I was no good to my family, to my church, to my country. I was just no good period. Now I have hopes that when I leave here, I will be worth something to somebody." I couldn't help but think, "Isn't it pitiful when a man becomes a slave to strong drink to the point that he can thank God for the privilege of being behind prison bars for the help he can get!"

(LeGrand Richards, *Just to Illustrate* [Salt Lake City: Bookcraft, 1961], 94–95)

The gravitation of sin to sorrow is as certain as that of the earth to the sun.

(*Gospel Ideals: Selections from the Discourses of David O. McKay*, sel. by G. Homer Durham [Salt Lake City: Improvement Era, 1953], 492)

Wickedness and righteousness are not legislated by majority vote. Right and wrong are not determined by polls or pundits, though many would have us believe otherwise. Evil never was happiness. Happiness lies in the power and the love and the sweet simplicity of virtue.

(Gordon B. Hinckley, *Standing for Something* [New York: Times Books, 2000], 44)

Alma 42

Alma was in an interview with a doubter, his son Corianton. As you read the early parts of the interview, you become sure that he had listened carefully to his son. Alma saw that Corianton had a question. Corianton doubted the justice of God; it seemed too severe because of his own sins. To those with unrepented sins, the truth always seems hard, so doubt is a natural defense.

(Henry B. Eyring, *To Draw Closer to God* [Salt Lake City: Deseret Book, 1997], 149)

Alma 42:2–3 • CHERUBIM AND FLAMING SWORD

"A *cherub* is an angel of some particular order or rank to whom specific duties and work are assigned" (McConkie, Bruce R. *Mormon Doctrine.* 2d ed. Salt Lake City: Bookcraft, 1966, 124). *Cherubim* is the Hebrew plural of *cherub*. The beings who guarded the tree of life were "faithful personages belonging to this world who had not, at the time, received the privilege of partaking of mortality" (Smith, Joseph Fielding. *Answers to Gospel Questions.* Compiled by Joseph Fielding Smith Jr. 5 vols. Salt Lake City: Deseret Book, 1957–66, 2:97). While the presence of a flaming sword was evidence of divine protection of the tree of life after the Fall, the scriptures

are silent regarding its nature and appearance.

The Bible states that God placed cherubim and a flaming sword "to keep the way of the tree of life," but it does not explain why this was done (Gen. 3:24). The Book of Mormon provides this explanation and teaches how this act was essential to the plan of salvation. If Adam and Eve had been permitted to eat from the tree of life after their transgression, there would have been no death, contrary to God's word. In addition, "our first parents" would have been "forever miserable, having no preparatory state," or "time to prepare to meet God" (Alma 12:22–26)—"to repent and serve God" (Alma 42:2–5—and "thus the plan of redemption would have been frustrated" (Alma 12:26).

(*Book of Mormon Reference Companion*, ed. by Dennis L. Largey [Salt Lake City: Deseret Book, 2003], 182)

Cherubim is the (Hebrew) plural of *cherub*, though it is used in the scriptures as a singular noun. "In the celestial hierarchy, cherubs are represented as spirits next in order to seraphs" (Webster's Dictionary, 1828). Regarded as chief among their duties is that of guarding the holy place, or the place where God dwells.

(Joseph Fielding McConkie and Robert L. Millet, *Doctrinal Commentary on the Book of Mormon* [Salt Lake City: Bookcraft, 1991], 3:310–311)

Alma 42:3 • AND LIVE FOREVER

The thought would be more complete were it to read "and live forever *in his sins.*" It is not endless life that the Lord sought to prevent by placing the cherubim and a flaming sword to guard the tree of life; rather, it was endless life in an unrepentant state. Thus God in his mercy granted Adam "a probatory time, a time to repent and serve God."

(Joseph Fielding McConkie and Robert L. Millet, *Doctrinal Commentary on the Book of Mormon* [Salt Lake City: Bookcraft, 1991], 3:311)

Alma 42:8, 16 • THE GREAT PLAN OF HAPPINESS

The prophet Alma called the plan the "great plan of happiness." It is known more commonly as the plan of salvation. . . . The plan teaches that all who have or will live on earth are the spirit children of heavenly parents. We lived with them before coming to this earth to receive our bodies of flesh and bone. . . . Our Father's plan provides for redemption from the Fall through the atonement of Jesus Christ. . . . All shall rise from the dead with immortal bodies as a result of the Atonement. However, the Atonement is conditional as it pertains to each person's individual sins. It touches everyone to the degree that he or she has faith in Jesus Christ, repents, and obeys the gospel. Exaltation and eternal life with God are reserved for those who keep the commandments. Mortality, then, is the time to test our ability to understand our Heavenly Father's plan and, of course, our willingness to be obedient.

(M. Russell Ballard, *Ensign*, May 1995 [Salt Lake City: The Church of Jesus Christ of Latter-day Saints, 1995], 22–23)

———

In obedience there is joy and peace unspotted, . . . and as God has designed our happiness—and the happiness of all His creatures, he never has—He never will institute an ordinance or give a commandment to His people that is not calculated in its nature to promote that happiness which He has designed, and which will not end in the greatest amount of good and glory to those who become the recipients of his laws and ordinances.

(*Teachings of the Prophet Joseph Smith*, comp. by Joseph Fielding Smith [Salt Lake City: Deseret Book, 1976], 256–257)

———

Divine justice assures that there are no loopholes through which the not-fully-worthy would slip undeservedly into the celestial kingdom, where they would not be fully happy anyway. The plan of happiness is carefully gauged, blessing all, but especially those who have "faith unto repentance."

(Neal A. Maxwell, *One More Strain of Praise* [Salt Lake City: Bookcraft, 1999], 39)

———

The plan cannot bring true happiness to anyone whose life is grossly inconsistent with its standards. . . . It has no place of honor for one too concerned with losing his place in the secular synagogue (see John 12:42–43). . . .

Believers in the plan are not automatically immune to the consuming cares of the world. . . .

Some of our present circumstances may reflect previous agreements, now forgotten, but once freely made.

The plan always points the way, but does not always smooth the way.

(Neal A. Maxwell, in Conference Report, Apr. 1984 [Salt Lake City: The Church of Jesus Christ of Latter-day Saints, 1984], 29–30)

———

In the plan of happiness, the Great Shepherd, Jesus, will neither drive nor even herd us along the straight and narrow path. Doing such would be against God's agency-drenched plan. Instead, exemplifying and beck-

oning, Jesus says, "Come, follow me" (Luke 18:22), the very words and the manner of a true Shepherd. . . .

Meanwhile, strange, is it not, how we are willing to settle for so much less? We are like an eager child at a candy store who will settle for just "one of these and one of those," when the Owner desires to give us the whole store (D&C 84:38).

(Neal A. Maxwell, *Whom the Lord Loveth* [Salt Lake City: Deseret Book, 2003], 73–74)

———

You have a choice. You can wring your hands and be consumed with concern for the future or choose to use the counsel the Lord has given to live with peace and happiness in a world awash with evil. . . .

Now the brighter side. Despite pockets of evil, the world overall is majestically beautiful, filled with many good and sincere people. God has provided a way to live in this world and not be contaminated by the degrading pressures evil agents spread throughout it. You can live a virtuous, productive, righteous life by following the plan of protection created by your Father in Heaven: His plan of happiness. It is contained in the scriptures and in the inspired declarations of His prophets. . . .

Our Father knew of our day. He prepared the scriptures and provided continuing divine guidance to sustain us. That help will assure that you can live with peace and happiness amid increasing evil.

(Richard G. Scott, *Ensign*, May 2004 [Salt Lake City: The Church of Jesus Christ of Latter-day Saints, 2004], 100–101)

———

When we understand the great plan of happiness, we are gaining an eternal perspective, and the commandments, ordinances, and covenants, and the experiences, trials, and tribulations can be seen in their true and eternal light. . . .

Satan will dim the brightness of hope and eternal perspective by the dark, compelling urgency of now. Such is the case with those mentioned in the Book of Mormon who "turned out of the way" (Helaman 6:31) and "became for themselves" (3 Nephi 1:29).

Laman and Lemuel turned out of the way and complained of their sufferings because they did not have their possessions, with which they said they "might have been happy" (1 Nephi 17:21). . . .

Still others are described by Nephi, who said that the devil will "stir them up to anger against that which is good . . . and lull them away into carnal security" (2 Nephi 28:20–21).

Those without an eternal perspective, or those who lose sight of it, make their own standards to benefit themselves and their own selfish interests. Their mortal perspective becomes their standard and for some their god.

(Jay E. Jensen, in Conference Report, Apr. 2000 [Salt Lake City: The Church of Jesus Christ of Latter-day Saints, 2000], 33)

Alma 42:13–31 • JUSTICE, MERCY AND THE ATONEMENT

Justice requires that God must be a God of order and that he must be just and impartial. Mercy agrees with justice; however, mercy introduces the possibility of vicarious payment of the laws that have been transgressed. The law of mercy paraphrased as follows: Whenever a law is broken, a payment (or atonement) must be made; however the person does not need to make payment if he will repent and if he can find someone who is both able and willing to make payment. Note the law of mercy insists the demands of justice be met fully.

(Daniel H. Ludlow, *A Companion to Your Study of the Book of Mormon* [Salt Lake City: Deseret Book, 1976], 176–177)

Justice has many meanings. One is balance. A popular symbol of justice is scales in balance. Thus, when the laws of man have been violated, justice usually requires that a punishment be imposed, a penalty that will restore the balance. . . . Punishments prescribed by the laws of man only follow the judge's action, but under the laws of God the consequences and penalties of sin are inherent in the act. . . . By itself, justice is uncompromising. The justice of God holds each of us responsible for our own transgressions and automatically imposes the penalty. . . . If we are to return to the presence of our Heavenly Father, we need the intervention of some powerful influence that transcends justice. That powerful intervention is the atonement of Jesus Christ. The good news of the gospel is that because of the atonement of Jesus Christ there is something called *mercy*. Mercy signifies an advantage greater than is deserved. . . . If justice is balance, then mercy is counterbalance. If justice is exactly what one deserves, then mercy is more benefit than one deserves. In its relationship to justice and mercy, the Atonement is the means by which justice is served and mercy is extended.

(Dallin H. Oaks, Address given to CES Religious Educators, Temple Square Assembly Hall, 7 Feb. 1992)

If a person pays for his or her own sins can they enter the celestial kingdom?

I once wondered if those who refuse to repent but who then satisfy the law of justice by paying for their own sins are then worthy to enter the celestial kingdom. The answer is no. The entrance requirements for celestial life are simply higher than merely satisfying the law of justice. For that reason, paying for our sins will not bear the same fruit as repenting of our sins. Justice is a law of balance and order and it must be satisfied, either through our payment or his. But if we decline the Savior's invitation to let him carry our sins, and then satisfy justice by ourselves, we will not yet have experienced the complete rehabilitation that can occur through a combination of divine assistance and genuine repentance. Working together, those forces have the power permanently to change our hearts and our lives, preparing us for celestial life.

(Bruce C. Hafen, *The Broken Heart* [Salt Lake City: Deseret Book, 1989], 7–8)

I believe that our Heavenly Father wants to save every one of his children. I do not think he intends to shut any of us off because of some slight transgression, some slight failure to observe some rule or regulation. . . . I believe that in his justice and mercy, he will give us the maximum reward for our acts, give us all that he can give, and in the reverse, I believe that he will impose upon us the minimum penalty which it is possible for him to impose.

(J. Reuben Clark Jr., in Conference Report, 30 Sept. 1955 [Salt Lake City: The Church of Jesus Christ of Latter-day Saints, 1955], 24)

All of us have made wrong turns along the way. I believe the kind and merciful God, whose children we are, will judge us as lightly as He can for the wrongs that we have done and give us the maximum blessing for the good that we do.

(James E. Faust, *Ensign*, Nov. 1996 [Salt Lake City: The Church of Jesus Christ of Latter-day Saints, 1996], 53)

Mercy, detached from Justice, grows unmerciful. That is the important paradox. As there are plants which flourish only in mountain soil, so it appears that Mercy will flower only when it grows in the crannies of the rock of Justice.

(C.S. Lewis, "The Humanitarian Theory of Punishment" [1949], in *God in the Dock: Essays on Theology and Ethics*, ed. Walter Hooper [Grand Rapids, Michigan: Eerdmans, 1970], 294; as quoted in Neal A. Maxwell, *One More Strain of Praise* [Salt Lake City: Bookcraft, 1999], 8)

One thing we should remember is that the Lord does not punish us for our sins. He simply withholds his blessings and we punish ourselves. The scriptures tell us again and again that the wicked are punished by the wicked.

A simple illustration can show how easily that is done. If mother would tell me not to touch a hot stove for it would burn and hurt me, she would only be stating the law. If I should forget or deliberately touch that hot stove, I would be burned. I could cry and complain of my hurts, but who would be punishing me? Would it be mother—or the hot stove? I would be punishing myself. Even after my finger healed, I would have to remember the law, for every time I would touch that hot stove I would be burned, again and again until I could learn to obey the law. It was and is the law, and justice would have to be done. This illustration, however, disregards the important element of mercy.

(Theodore M. Burton, "The Meaning of Repentance," BYU Devotional Talk, 26 Mar. 1985 [Provo, Utah: Brigham Young University, 1985], 4)

Alma 42:16 • REPENTANCE AND PUNISHMENT

Alma bluntly told his wayward son that "repentance could not come unto men except there were a punishment." The punishment may, for the most part, consist of the torment we inflict upon ourselves. It may be the loss of privilege or progress. . . . We are punished by our sins, if not for them.

(Boyd K. Packer, *Ensign*, Nov. 1995 [Salt Lake City: The Church of Jesus Christ of Latter-day Saints, 1995], 19)

Alma 42:29 • TROUBLE YOU DOWN UNTO REPENTANCE

(Refer in this text to Alma 24:10.)

Alma desired that his son experience appropriate guilt—no more than was requisite, but surely no less than is needful to bring about change.

(Robert Millet; as quoted in *Studies in Scripture*, ed. by Kent P. Jackson [Salt Lake City: Deseret Book, 1987], 8:51)

———

Alma didn't promise that Corianton would forget. He taught him how to live with his memories, productively, humbly, continually appreciative for the mercy and long-suffering and forgiveness of God. "You'll remember your sins" we can almost hear Alma saying. "You probably won't ever forget. But remember in the right way for the right reasons."

(Marion D. Hanks, *Improvement Era*, Mar. 1966 [Salt Lake City: The Church of Jesus Christ of Latter-day Saints, 1966], 246)

———

Sometimes even after confession and penalties the most difficult part of repentance is to forgive oneself. President Joseph Fielding Smith, a man whom I

love—great friend, told of a woman who had repented of immoral conduct and was struggling to find her way. She asked him what she should do now. In turn, he asked her to read to him from the Old Testament the account of Sodom and Gomorrah, of Lot and of Lot's wife who was turned to a pillar of salt (see Gen. 19:26). Then he asked her what lesson did those verses hold for her. She answered, "The Lord will destroy those who are wicked." "Not so," President Smith told this repentant woman, "The lesson for *you* is *'Don't look back!'* "

(Boyd K. Packer, BYU Fireside, 29 Mar. 1992)

———

At times the statement is made, "I never can forgive [this person or that person]." Such an attitude is destructive to an individual's well-being. It can canker the soul and ruin one's life. In other instances, an individual can forgive another but cannot forgive himself. Such a situation is even more destructive. Early in my ministry as a member of the Council of the Twelve, I took to President Hugh B. Brown the experience of a fine person who . . . could not show mercy to himself. He could forgive others but not himself. . . . President Brown suggested that I visit with that individual and counsel him along these lines: . . . "Tell that man that he should not persist in remembering that which the Lord has said He is willing to forget" (D&C 64:10). Such counsel will help to cleanse the soul and renew the spirit of any who applies it.

(Thomas S. Monson, *Ensign*, May 1995 [Salt Lake City: The Church of Jesus Christ of Latter-day Saints, 1995], 59–60)

———

Guilt should lead to repentance. Unfortunately, guilt can be like a two-edged sword—functional or dysfunctional. Satan can pervert this divine tool by tempting the sinner to become discouraged rather than motivated. . . . Guilt, as a divinely designed consequence of sin, is meant to impel individuals to come unto Christ and repent.

(Philip Allred, *The Book of Mormon: The Foundation of Our Faith*, The 28th Annual Sidney B. Sperry Symposium [Salt Lake City: Deseret Book, 1999], 26)

———

The natives out in the islands . . . know how to repent. . . . They know how to be forgiven, and they know how to forgive themselves. . . . Why, they can come in . . . and repent . . . and if you forgive them, they go out walking on air, the happiest people you ever saw; but over here I have talked to people who have been forgiven thirty-five years ago and who have been almost perfect ever since, and they are still saying, "I'll never forgive myself. I'll never forgive myself." Brothers and sisters, teach these youngsters how to forgive themselves when they are forgiven.

(*Matthew Cowley Speaks* [Salt Lake City: Deseret Book, 1954], 133–134)

Now if you are one who cannot forgive yourself for serious past transgressions—even when a judge in Israel has assured that you have properly repented—if you feel compelled to continually condemn yourself and suffer by frequently recalling the details of past errors, I plead with all of my soul that you ponder this statement of the Savior:

"He who has repented of his sins, the same is forgiven, and I, the Lord, remember them no more.

"By this ye may know if a man repenteth of his sins . . . he will confess them and forsake them" (D&C 58:42–43).

To continue to suffer when there has been proper repentance is not prompted by the Savior but the master of deceit, whose goal is to bind and enslave you. Satan will press you to continue to relive the details of past mistakes, knowing that such thoughts make forgiveness seem unattainable. In this way Satan attempts to tie strings to the mind and body so that he can manipulate you like a puppet.

I testify that when a bishop or stake president has confirmed that your repentance is sufficient, know that your obedience has allowed the Atonement of Jesus Christ to satisfy the demands of justice for the laws you have broken. Therefore, you are now free. Please believe it. To continually suffer the distressing effects of sin after adequate repentance, while not intended, is to deny the efficacy of the Savior's Atonement in your behalf.

(Richard G. Scott, in Conference Report, Oct. 2004 [Salt Lake City: The Church of Jesus Christ of Latter-day Saints, 2004], 17)

To me, none of the many approaches to teaching repentance falls more short than the well-intentioned suggestion that "although a nail may be removed from a wooden post, there will forever be a hole in that post."

We know that repentance (the removal of that nail, if you will) can be a very long and painful and difficult task. . . . But where repentance *is* possible and its requirements are faithfully pursued and completed, there is no "hole left in the post" for the bold reason that it is no longer the same post. It is a new post. We can start again, utterly clean, with a new will and a new way of life.

(Jeffrey R. Holland, *The Book of Mormon: It Begins with a Family* [Salt Lake City: Deseret Book, 1983] 96–97)

If the time comes when you have done all that you can to repent of your sin. . . . if it be something that will affect your standing in the Church and you have gone to the proper authorities, then you will want that confirming answer as to whether or not the Lord has accepted of you. In your soul-searching, if you seek for and you find that peace of conscience, by that token you may know that the Lord has accepted of your repentance. Satan would have you think otherwise and sometimes persuade you that now having made one mistake, you might go on and on with no turning back. That is one of the great falsehoods. The miracle of forgiveness is available to all of those who turn from their evil doings and return no more, because the Lord has said in a revelation to us in our day: ". . . go your ways and sin no more; but unto that soul who sinneth [meaning again] shall the former sins return, saith the Lord your God" (D&C 82:7). Have that in mind, all of you who may be troubled with a burden of sin.

(Harold B. Lee, in Conference Report, Apr. 1973 [Salt Lake City: The Church of Jesus Christ of Latter-day Saints, 1973], 177–178)

Alma 43–63 • WAR

The most famous maxim of the nineteenth century military theorist Karl von Clausewitz defined war as the continuation of politics by other means.

(Ric Burns, Ken Burns, and Geoffrey C. Ward, *The Civil War* [New York: Alfred A. Knoff, 1990], 350)

We recognize the battle-field as a reality, but it stands as a remote one. It is like a funeral next door. It attracts your attention, but it does not enlist your sympathy. But it is very different when the hearse stops at your own door and the corpse is carried over your own threshold.

(A *New York Times* reporter, 1862, *The Civil War*, Burns, Burns, and Ward [New York: Alfred A. Knoff, 1990], 161)

Latter-day Saints know this earth will never again during its Telestial existence, be free from civil disturbance and war.

(Marion G. Romney, *Improvement Era*, June 1967 [Salt Lake City: The Church of Jesus Christ of Latter-day Saints, 1967], 77)

If men of good will can bring themselves to do so, they may save the world from a holocaust, the depth and breadth of which can scarcely be imagined. We are confident that when there is enough of a desire for peace and a will to bring it about, it is not beyond the possibility of attainment.

(First Presidency Statement, *Church News*, 20 Dec. 1980, 3)

War doesn't solve a single human problem, and yet the one place where our generation excels most is in its ability to make war. . . . Our failure has been that while we have perfected weapons, we have failed to perfect the men who may be asked to use them.

(Sterling W. Sill, in Conference Report, Apr. 1966 [Salt Lake City: The Church of Jesus Christ of Latter-day Saints, 1966], 20–21)

In our society today, we find that we are very well prepared for war. However, in that preparation for war we have lost the spiritual strength necessary to prevent it.

(Dean Garrett, CES Book of Mormon Symposium, 1986, 52)

There is great wisdom and restraint in turning the other cheek and, in the process, trying to overcome evil with good. General Omar Bradley is quoted as having said: "We have grasped the mystery of the atom and rejected the Sermon on the Mount. . . . Ours is a world of nuclear giants and ethical infants. We know more about war than we know about peace, more about killing than we know about living."

(Gordon B. Hinckley, *Standing for Something* [New York: Times Books, 2000], 71)

Every gun made, every warship launched, every rocket fired signifies, in the final sense, a theft from those who hunger and are not fed, those who are cold and are not clothed. This world in arms is not spending money alone. It is spending the sweat of its laborers, the genius of its scientists, the hopes of its children.

(Dwight D. Eisenhower; as quoted in *Studies in Scripture*, ed. by Kent P. Jackson [Salt Lake City: Deseret Book, 1987], 8:78)

Victory and defeat alike leave countries devastated and the conqueror and the conquered reduced. Wickedness brings war, and war vomits destruction and suffering, hate and bloodshed upon the guilty and the innocent. This impressive book [the Book of Mormon] should convince all living souls of the futility of war and the hazards of unrighteousness.

(*Teachings of Spencer W. Kimball*, ed. by Edward L. Kimball [Salt Lake City: Bookcraft, 1982], 414)

I would like to share an incident which took place during the Vietnam War. . . . President Harold B. Lee was the President of the Church at the time. While at an area conference in another country he was interviewed by reporters from the international news services. One reporter asked President Lee, "What is your church's position on the Vietnam War?" Some recognized the question as a trap—one which could not be answered without a very real risk of being misunderstood or misinterpreted. If the prophet answered, "We are against the war," the inter-national media could state, "How strange—a religious leader who is against the position of the country he is obliged to sustain in his own church's Articles of Faith" (Article of Faith 1:12). On the other hand, if President Lee answered, "We are in favor of the war," the media could question, "How strange—a religious leader in favor of war?" Either way, the answer could result in serious problems regarding public opinion both inside and outside the Church. President Lee, with great inspiration and wisdom, answered as would a man who knows the Savior: "We, together with the whole Christian world, abhor war. But the Savior said, 'In me ye might have peace. In the world ye shall have tribulation' (John 16:33)." And then the prophet quoted that other comforting scripture from John: "Peace I leave with you, my peace I give unto you: not as the world giveth, give I unto you" (John 14:27). President Lee then explained: "The Savior was not talking about the peace that can be achieved between nations, by military force or by negotiation in the halls of parliaments. Rather, he was speaking of the peace we can each have in our own lives when we live the commandments and come unto Christ with broken hearts and contrite spirits."

(Robert Wells, *Ensign*, May 1991 [Salt Lake City: The Church of Jesus Christ of Latter-day Saints, 1991], 86)

Alma 43–63 • WHY SO MUCH WAR IN THE BOOK OF MORMON?

In Alma 1–42, Mormon emphasized priestcraft, materialism, social-economic inequality, and other social problems. This period is followed in Alma 43–63 by a period of war and civil disruptions. This dissension led to a corruption of civil government (as described in the book of Helaman) and to the eventual collapse of the government (see 3 Nephi 1–10). At this point, the Savior visited the people.

A similar pattern of social problems, priestcrafts, materialism, wars, government corruption, and disrupted life is prophesied for the last days leading to the

Savior's second coming (D&C 45:16–48; D&C 87; Mormon 8:26–41). As indicated, Mormon and his successor, Moroni, saw our day (see Mormon 8:27–31) and took from the history and prophecies of the Nephites those events that would best help the readers of their record in the day in which it would come forth.

(H. Dean Garrett; as quoted in *Studies in Scripture*, ed. by Kent P. Jackson [Salt Lake City: Deseret Book, 1988], 70)

Alma 43:23, 45–47 • BASIC STRATEGY IN WAR

When threatened, we become anti-enemy instead of pro-kingdom of God. . . . We forget that if we are righteous the Lord will either not suffer our enemies to come upon us—and this is the special promise to the inhabitants of the land of the Americas (2 Ne. 1:7)—or he will fight our battles for us.

(Spencer W. Kimball, *Ensign*, June 1976 [Salt Lake City: The Church of Jesus Christ of Latter-day Saints, 1976], 6)

We love peace, but not peace at any price. There is a peace more destructive of the manhood of living man than war is destructive of the body. Chains are worse than bayonets.

(David O. McKay, in Conference Report, Apr. 1955 [Salt Lake City: The Church of Jesus Christ of Latter-day Saints, 1955], 24)

The so-called "Battle Scroll" from Qumran throws a flood of light on peculiar military practices described in the Book of Mormon especially those of Moroni. . . . His consultation with a prophet before the battle to learn by divine revelation the enemy's disposition and what his own movements should be. This is standard practice in the Book of Mormon (Alma 43:23) and we now learn . . . especially of the Battle Scroll that it was also the regular practice in ancient Israel.

(Hugh Nibley, *Since Cumorah* [Salt Lake City: Deseret Book, 1976], 273–274)

Our best defense is the quiet offense of allegiance to the teachings which have come to us from those whom we have sustained as prophets of God.

(Gordon B. Hinckley, *Ensign*, Jan. 2005 [Salt Lake City: The Church of Jesus Christ of Latter-day Saints, 2005], 4)

Alma 43:45–47; 48:14–16 • JUSTIFIED TO GO TO WAR

When I was 18 years old, I was inducted into the military. While I had no reason to wonder about it before, I became very concerned if it was right for me to go to war . . . [World War II]. In time, I found my answer in the Book of Mormon:

"They [the Nephites] were not fighting for monarchy nor power but they were fighting for their homes and their liberties, their wives and their children, and their all, yea, for their rites of worship and their church.

"And they were doing that which they felt was the duty which they owed to their God; for the Lord had said unto them, and also unto their fathers, that: Inasmuch as ye are not guilty of the first offense, neither the second, ye shall not suffer yourselves to be slain by the hands of your enemies.

"And again, the Lord has said that: ye shall defend your families even unto bloodshed. Therefore for this cause were the Nephites contending with the Lamanites, to defend themselves, and their families, and their lands, their country, and their rights, and their religion" (Alma 43:45–47).

Knowing this, I could serve willingly and with honor.

(Boyd K. Packer, *Ensign*, May 2005 [Salt Lake City: The Church of Jesus Christ of Latter-day Saints, 2005], 7–8)

We recognize and teach that all the people of the earth are of the family of God. . . .

But as citizens we are all under the direction of our respective national leaders. . . . Those in the armed services are under obligation to their respective governments to execute the will of the sovereign. . . .

One of our Articles of Faith, which represent an expression of our doctrine, states, "We believe in being subject to kings, presidents, rulers, and magistrates, in obeying, honoring, and sustaining the law" (Articles of Faith 1:12). . . .

However, we all must also be mindful of another over-riding responsibility, which I may add, governs my personal feelings and dictates my personal loyalties in the present situation.

When war raged between the Nephites and Lamanites, the record states . . . [President Hinckley then quoted Alma 43:45–47 and Alma 46:12–13].

It is clear from these and other writings that there are times and circumstances when nations are justified, in fact have an obligation, to fight for family, for liberty, and against tyranny, threat, and oppression. . . .

We are a freedom-loving people, committed to the defense of liberty wherever it is in jeopardy. I believe that God will not hold men and women in uniform responsible as agents of their government in carrying forward that which they are legally obligated to do. It may even be that He will hold us responsible if we try to impede or hedge up the way of those who are involved in a contest with forces of evil and repression. . . .

Never let us become a party to words or works of evil concerning our brothers and sisters in various nations on one side or the other. Political differences never justify hatred or ill will.

(Gordon B. Hinckley, in Conference Report, Apr. 2003 [Salt Lake City: The Church of Jesus Christ of Latter-day Saints, 2003], 83–84)

———————

There are, however, two conditions which may justify a truly Christian man to enter—mind you, I say enter, not begin—a war: (1) An attempt to dominate and to deprive another of his free agency, and (2) Loyalty to his country. Possibly there is a third, viz., Defense of a weak nation that is being unjustly crushed by a strong, ruthless one.

(David O. McKay, in Conference Report, Apr. 1942 [Salt Lake City: The Church of Jesus Christ of Latter-day Saints, 1942], 72)

Alma 44:5 • SACRED SUPPORT WE OWE TO OUR WIVES AND CHILDREN
(Refer in this text 1 Nephi 5:2, 7.)

A wonderful sister recently said to a dear friend:

"I want to tell you about the moment I ceased resenting my husband's time and sacrifice as a bishop. . . .

"One day I poured out my frustration, and my husband agreed we should guarantee, in addition to Monday nights, one additional night a week just for us. Well, the first 'date night' came, and we were about to get into the car for an evening together when the telephone rang.

" 'This is a test,' I smiled at him. The telephone kept ringing. . . .

"My poor husband looked trapped between me and a ringing telephone. . . .

" 'I'd better at least check,' he said with sad eyes. 'It is probably nothing at all.'

" 'If you do, our date is ruined,' I cried. 'I just know it.'

"He squeezed by hand and said, 'Be right back,' and he dashed in to pick up the telephone.

"Well, when my husband didn't return to the car immediately, I knew what was happening. I got out of the car, went into the house, and went to bed. The next morning he spoke a quiet apology, I spoke an even quieter acceptance. . . .

"Several weeks later. . . . The memory was still fresh when I came upon a woman in the ward I scarcely knew. Very hesitantly, she asked for the opportunity to talk. She then told of becoming infatuated with another man, who seemed to bring excitement into her life of drudgery, she with a husband who worked full-time and carried a full load of classes at the university. . . . She had small children who were often demanding, noisy, and exhausting. . . . 'My situation was such that I felt I deserved better than what I had. My rationalization persuaded me to think I could walk away from my husband, my children, my temple covenants, and my Church and find happiness with a stranger.' . . .

"She said, 'The plan was set; the time for my escape was agreed upon. Yet, as if in a last gasp of sanity, my conscience told me to call your husband, my bishop. . . . The telephone rang and rang and rang. Such was the state of my mind that I thought, "If the bishop doesn't answer, that will be a sign I should go through with my plan." The phone kept ringing, and I was about to hang up and walk straight into destruction when suddenly I heard your husband's voice. It penetrated my soul like lightning. Suddenly I heard myself sobbing, saying, "Bishop, is that you? I am in trouble. I need help." Your husband came with help, and I am safe today because he answered that telephone. . . .

" 'I love my husband and my children with all my heart. I can't imagine the tragedy my life would be without them. . . .' Then she said, 'I don't know you well, but I wish to thank you for supporting your husband in his calling. I don't know what the cost for such service has been to you or to your children, but if on a difficult day there is a particularly personal cost, please know how eternally grateful I will be for the sacrifice people like you make to help rescue people like me.' " . . .

I testify of home and family and marriage. . . . I testify of the need to protect and preserve them while we find time and ways to serve faithfully in the Church. In what I hope are rare moments when these seem to be in conflict, when we find an hour or a day or a night of crisis when duty and spiritual prompting require our response, in those situations I pay tribute to every wife who has ever sat along while dinner got cold, every husband who has made his own dinner, . . . and every child who has ever been disappointed in a postponed camping trip or a ball game a parent unexpectedly had to miss (and that better not be very often!). . . . I thank all who, in challenging circumstances across the Church, do the best they can to build the kingdom of God on earth.

(Jeffrey R. Holland, in Conference Report, Oct. 2002 [Salt Lake City: The Church of Jesus Christ of Latter-day Saints, 2002], 38–40)

Alma 44:8, 11, 14, 15, 19–20; 46:35; 48:13; 49:13, 17, 27; 50:36, 39; 51:6 • OATH TAKING
(Refer in this text to 1 Nephi 4:32, 37.)

Alma 45:15–16 • CONDITIONAL FREEDOM OF THIS LAND
(Refer in this text to 2 Nephi 1:7.)

I know, too, that if we will keep the commandments of God—live as he has directed and does now direct, through his prophets—we will continue to have His protecting hand over us. But we must be true to the eternal verities, the great Christian virtues that God has revealed. Then, and only then, will we be safe as a nation and as individuals. God grant that the faithfulness of the Latter-day Saints will provide the balance of power to save this nation in time of crisis.

(Ezra Taft Benson, *This Nation Shall Endure* [Salt Lake City: Deseret Book, 1977], 145)

Alma 45:16 • THE LEAST DEGREE OF ALLOWANCE

The Lord can forgive our sins, yet He "cannot look upon sin with the least degree of allowance," hence the unclean and unrepentant, though resurrected, will not be exalted (D&C 1:31).

(Neal A. Maxwell, *One More Strain of Praise* [Salt Lake City: Bookcraft, 1999], 34)

Alma 45:19 • TAKEN UP BY THE SPIRIT . . . BURIED BY THE LORD

Now, there was a *reason* for the translation of Elijah. *Men are not preserved in that manner unless there is a reason for it. . . . Moses, like Elijah, was taken up without tasting death, because he had a mission to perform. . . . The Savior, Moses, and Elias [Elijah, in other words] gave the keys to Peter, James, and John, on the Mount when they were transfigured before him. . . . They had a mission to perform,* and it had to be performed *before* the crucifixion of the Son of God, and *it could not be done in the spirit.*

(Joseph Fielding Smith, *Doctrines of Salvation,* comp. by Bruce R. McConkie [Salt Lake City: Bookcraft, 1955], 2:107, 110)

There are several important prophets who were granted the privilege of remaining on the earth. John the Revelator was one of these, and in the Doctrine and Covenants, section seven, is an account of this. Elijah evidently was another, for no living soul could have received the resurrection until after our Redeemer had opened the graves. . . .

It is a very reasonable thought to believe that both Moses and Alma, like Elijah and John, were translated to accomplish some work which the Lord had in store for them at some future day.

(Joseph Fielding Smith, *Answers to Gospel Questions,* comp. and ed. by Joseph Fielding Smith Jr. [Salt Lake City: Deseret Book, 1972], 5:38)

On Sunday, July 2, 1972. . . . Shortly before ten o'clock that evening, a Church spokesman called to tell him that President Joseph Fielding Smith had passed away at nine-thirty. "This was shocking news because he has not been ill," Elder Hunter wrote. Then, after describing what he had been told about President Smith's final few hours, he concluded, "I have often wondered about the condition of persons who are translated, and tonight I have had the feeling that this was the course the President has followed from mortality to immortality without tasting of death."

(Eleanor Knowles, *Howard W. Hunter* [Salt Lake City: Deseret Book, 1994], 237)

Alma 45:23 • HEED
(Refer in this text to 1 Nephi 15:25.)

Alma 46:8 • FORGET THE LORD
(Refer in this text to Helaman 12:2–5.)

Alma 46:9 • THE POWER OF ONE
(Refer in this text to Alma 17:27–38.)

One of the talks that has had an everlasting impression on me is one given in a Saturday evening session of a stake conference years ago. The talk was given by a young mother. Here's what she said: "I have been doing the genealogy of my great-grandfather. . . .

"My great-grandfather," she said, "left church one Sunday with his family, and they never returned—no indication why."

She then said, "In my research, I have found that my great-grandfather has over 1,000 descendants."

And then she said, and this is the part I have not been able to forget, "Of those 1,000 descendants, I am the only one active in the Church today."

As she said these words, I found myself thinking, "Is it only 1,000, or could it be more?"

The answer is apparent. The spiritual influence that family might have had on their neighbors and friends did not happen. None of his sons nor any of his daughters served as missionaries, and those they would have touched with their testimonies were not baptized, and those who were not baptized did not go on missions. Yes, there are probably many thousands who are not in the Church today, and not in this very meeting, because of that great-grandfather's decision.

As I heard her talk I found myself thinking, "What a tragedy!"

(Harold G. Hillam, *Ensign,* May 2005 [Salt Lake City: The Church of Jesus Christ of Latter-day Saints, 2005], 32)

Alma 46:12–13, 21, 36; 62:4–5 • THE TITLE OF LIBERTY

We as a people have never known bondage. Liberty has always been our blessed lot. Few of us have ever seen people who have lost their freedom—their liberty. And when reminded of the danger of losing our liberty and independence our attitude has usually been: "It cannot happen here." We must never forget that nations may, and usually do, sow the seeds of their own destruction while enjoying unprecedented prosperity. . . . This is our need today—to plant the standard of liberty among our people throughout the Americas.

(Ezra Taft Benson, in Conference Report, Oct. 1962 [Salt Lake City: The Church of Jesus Christ of Latter-day Saints, 1962], 14–15)

Of course, the war in heaven over free agency is now being waged here on earth, and there are those today who are saying, "Look, don't get involved in the fight for freedom. Just live the gospel." That counsel is dangerous, self-contradictory, unsound. . . . Now part of the reason we may not have sufficient priesthood bearers to save the Constitution, let alone to shake the powers of hell, is because unlike Moroni, I fear, our souls do not joy in keeping our country free, and we are not firm in the faith of Christ, nor have we sworn with an oath to defend our rights and the liberty of our country. Moroni raised a title of liberty and wrote upon it these words: "In memory of our God, our religion, and freedom, and our peace, our wives, and our children." Why didn't he write upon it: "Just live your religion; there's no need to concern yourselves about your freedom, your peace, your wives, or your children"? The reason he didn't do this was because all these things were a part of his religion, as they are of our religion today. Should we counsel people, 'Just live your religion. There's no need to get involved in the fight for freedom"? No, we should not, because our stand for freedom is a most basic part of our religion; this stand helped get us to this earth, and our reaction to freedom in this life will have eternal consequences. Man has many duties, but he has no excuse that can compensate for his loss of liberty.

(Ezra Taft Benson, in Conference Report, Oct. 1966 [Salt Lake City: The Church of Jesus Christ of Latter-day Saints, 1966], 122)

Young women, you are like titles of liberty as you strive to protect your families from such intruders as selfishness, harshness, anger, and strife. Your banner stands for peace and love and service to your families.

(Sharon G. Larson, *Ensign*, May 1998 [Salt Lake City: The Church of Jesus Christ of Latter-day Saints, 1998], 93)

As a teacher, I have struggled to satisfactorily explain the background of Moroni's title of liberty, which was obviously not a part of Joseph Smith's America, or our own, for that matter. However, in 1990 while teaching at BYU, I had an experience that opened the door of understanding for me.

With my limited background, I was teaching Alma 46 to a Book of Mormon class. Sensing my lack of cultural understanding on the subject, an Iranian student who was not of our faith and who had never before been exposed to the Book of Mormon raised his hand and said that he understood what Captain Moroni had done and why the people reacted the way they did.

He related to the class that he had demonstrated many times during the Iranian Revolution of 1979 using this custom we were calling the title of liberty. I invited him to come forward and share with the class his understanding of the custom. He began by drawing what looked like a wagon wheel on the board, fully equipped with a hub and spokes extending from the middle, tied to a rim surrounding the spokes. He then told the class that this was an aerial view of the city of Isfahan, which is laid out with streets that resemble a wagon wheel, with all major streets intersecting in the middle of the wheel, and extending to a major street that circled the city like the rim of the wagon wheel. The hub of the wheel is known as the government gate or city square. He explained that the outskirts of the city extended about one mile in all directions from the hub or city square.

He told how he and his companions made a cloth banner, approximately fifteen feet by three feet, and attached it to poles on both ends to be held overhead as these protesters marched through the streets. The purpose of this march was to protest Pahlavi, the Iranian Shah. A group of about fifty people divided into four to seven processions and marched from the outskirts of town down the streets that connected to the city square. Carrying a banner, each procession walked the one-mile distance in approximately an hour and a half. He indicated that with the use of these banners they typically gathered a group of 100,000 to 150,000 to the city square.

He explained that the purpose of the poles was not just to hold the banner, but this custom of "raising the pole" was used to gather an army. I asked him why then was there a need for a banner. "To state the cause," he responded.

I inquired, "What was written on these banners that would bring so many people together in such a short time?"

"Liberty," was his simple reply.

He paused as all of us recognized the obvious similarity between the word he chose and its tie to the title of liberty. He continued, "We would write in the Persian language; Liberty, Independence, and Islamic Law."

I then asked, "What is the origin of the custom?"

He responded, "I don't know; it is a widely understood custom among my people." He continued, "My grandfather used the same custom to gather people to demonstrate four decades earlier." . . .

Obviously, from a strictly military standpoint it is difficult to generalize this custom to the rituals that are encompassed within our faith. However, the application becomes clearer when viewed in a spiritual perspective. Are we not gathered together as members of the Church in a spiritual army through the symbolic act of raising our right arm to the square as a united body in support of our leaders? Elder Angel Abrea said, "The raised hand becomes a symbol of the covenant we make to support [our leaders]. Each time we criticize or condemn them, we become literally covenant breakers" (*Ensign*, Nov. 1981, 24).

(Jack R. Christianson and K. Douglas Bassett, *Life Lessons from the Book of Mormon* [Salt Lake City: Deseret Book, 2003], 179–181)

This is our need today—to plant the standard of **LIBERTY** among our people throughout the Americas.

(Ezra Taft Benson, *A Nation Asleep* [Salt Lake City: Bookcraft, 1963], 22)

Alma 46:13–16 • CHRISTIAN

Harry Emerson Fosdick once wrote: "Some Christians carry their religion on their backs. It is a packet of beliefs and practices which they must bear. At times it grows heavy and they would willingly lay it down, but that would mean a break with old traditions, so they shoulder it again. But real Christians do not carry their religion, their religion carries them. It is not weight; it is wings. It lifts them up, it sees them over hard places, it makes the universe seem friendly, life purposeful, hope real, sacrifice worthwhile. It sets them free from fear, futility, discouragement, and sin—the great enslavers of men's souls. You can know a real Christian, when you see him, by his buoyancy" (*Twelve Tests of Character* [1923], 87–88).

I hope it is clearly evident when the world looks at us that we are known for our buoyancy—that we live, believe, and practice real Christian ideas and doctrine.

(L. Tom Perry, *Ensign*, Nov. 1999 [Salt Lake City: The Church of Jesus Christ of Latter-day Saints, 1999], 77)

Alma 46:39–41 • THERE WERE MANY WHO DIED

Clearly there are different individual exit routes from life. Some people go suddenly and quickly, leaving survivors in a state of shock and with almost no time to prepare. Others die only after prolonged suffering. It is best that we leave to the Lord the variations in both the timing and the exit routes. He and He alone can make those decisions, and He does so out of His individualized perfect love and mercy. . . .

In any case, uncertainty as to longevity leaves a balance to be struck by us all. We are to salute the Lord for the gift of life, for as long as it lasts, and yet, at the same time, to be spiritually submissive as it ends. . . . Especially to those valiants who reach that point where they are sick of being sick.

(Neal A. Maxwell, *One More Strain of Praise* [Salt Lake City: Bookcraft, 1999], 9, 12)

Alma 47:22 • REVERENCE

Reverence is profound respect mingled with love. It is "a complex emotion made up of mingled feelings of the soul." [One writer] says it is "the highest of human feelings." I have said elsewhere that if reverence is the highest, then irreverence is the lowest state in which a man can live in the world. . . .

Reverence is the fundamental virtue in religion. It is "one of the signs of strength; irreverence, one of the surest indication of weakness. No man will rise high," says one man, "who jeers at sacred things." . . .

Parents, *Reverence*, as charity, begins at home. . . .

Three influences in home life awaken reverence in children and contribute to its development in their souls. These are: *first,* firm but *Gentle Guidance; second, Courtesy* shown by parents to each other, and to children; and *third, Prayer* in which children participate. . . .

I look upon reverence as one of the highest qualities of the soul. An irreverent man is not a believing man. . . .

I am prompted to place reverence next to love. Jesus mentioned it first in the Lord's prayer: "Our Father which art in heaven, hallowed by thy name . . ." (Matthew 6:9). *Hallow*—to make holy—to hold in reverence.

If there were more reverence in human hearts, there would be less room for sin and sorrow.

(*Teachings of Presidents of the Church—David O. McKay* [Salt Lake City: The Church of Jesus Christ of Latter-day Saints, 2003], 30–31)

Alma 48:11–18 • MORONI

The Book of Mormon provides a classic example of one who in large part bound Satan in his life. In Alma 48:11–13 we read:

"And Moroni was a [1] strong and a mighty man; he

was a man of [2] a perfect understanding; yea, a man that [3] did not delight in bloodshed; a man whose soul did [4] joy in the liberty and the freedom of his country, and his brethren from bondage and slavery; yea, a man whose [5] heart did swell with thanksgiving to his God, for the many privileges and blessings which he bestowed upon his people; a man who did [6] labor exceedingly for the welfare and safety of his people. Yea, and he was a man who was [7] firm in the faith of Christ, and he had sworn with an [8] oath to defend his people, his rights, and his country, and his religion, even to the loss of his blood."

The qualities of Captain Moroni . . . all contributed to his ability to bind Satan in his life.

(Clyde J. Williams, *Doctrines of the Book of Mormon*, 1991 Sperry Symposium, ed. by Bruce A. Van Orden and Brent L. Top [Salt Lake City: Deseret Book, 1992], 254)

―――――――

This man was a brilliant military commander, and he rose to be supreme commander of all the Nephite forces at the age of twenty-five. For the next fourteen years he was off to the wars continuously except for two very short periods of peace during which he worked feverishly at reinforcing the Nephite defenses. When peace finally came, he was thirty-nine years old, and the story goes that at the age of forty-three he died. Sometime before this he had given the chief command of the armies of the Nephites to his son Moronihah. Now, if he had a son, he had a wife. I've often wondered where she was and how she fared during those fourteen years of almost continuous warfare, and how she felt to have him die so soon after coming home. I am sure there are many, many stories of patience and sacrifice that have never been told.

(*Glimpses into the Life and Heart of Marjorie Pay Hinckley,* ed. by Virginia H. Pearce [Salt Lake City: Deseret Book, 1999], 188)

―――――――

It is of interest to note that approximately one out of every ten pages of the Book of Mormon deals with the life and times of Captain Moroni, which we read in Alma chapters 43–63. Given the number of people and events described in the Nephite writings, have you ever wondered why so much of what we have in the Book of Mormon is dedicated to this individual and the experiences that surrounded his life?

Apparently, the prophet Mormon had many of the Nephite records available to him from which he made his abridgement. With divine guidance he selected and included those portions of the records that would be most valuable to us in our day. What are the messages from Captain Moroni and his time that have applicability to us at the present time?

First, in Captain Moroni we are provided with an authentic hero. . . .

Our young people today need heroes who go beyond the popular musicians, comedians, great athletes, the rich, and the famous. They . . . need to know of people like Captain Moroni, whose influence will live long after the applause of those who are currently popular has faded away.

(Joe J. Christensen, *Heroes from the Book of Mormon* [Salt Lake City: Bookcraft, 1995], 128, 133)

―――――――

The idea of total victory was alien to him—no revenge, no punishment, no reprisals, no reparations, even for an aggressor who had ravaged his country. He would send the beaten enemy home after the battle, accepting their word for good behavior or inviting them to settle on Nephite lands, even when he knew he was taking a risk. Even his countrymen who fought against him lost their lives only while opposing him on the field of battle: There were no firing squads, and conspirators and traitors had only to agree to support his popular army to be reinstated. . . .

. . . By all means, let us take Captain Moroni for our model and never forget what he fought for—the poor, outcast and despised; and what he fought against— pride, power, wealth and ambition.

(Hugh Nibley, *BYU Today,* Feb. 1984, 16–19, 45, 46; as quoted in Joe J. Christensen, *Heroes from the Book of Mormon* [Salt Lake City: Bookcraft, 1995], 130)

―――――――

Here [Alma 48:17–18] Mormon likens Captain Moroni to Ammon and the sons of Mosiah, as well as to Alma and his sons. . . .

Well, what do we know about Ammon? In the book of Mosiah, we learn that he was one of the "vilest of sinners" (Mosiah 28:4), but now he's being compared to Captain Moroni! Mormon continues, ". . . yea, and even the other sons of Mosiah." What do we know about them? Again, "they were the very vilest of sinners" (Mosiah 28:4). ". . . yea, and also Alma and his sons." And what do we know about Alma the younger? He was the worst of the lot! What about Corianton, the immoral missionary? He too is included with the group described by Mormon as being "all men of God" (Alma 48:18). How could that be? When the atoning blood of Christ, the blood of the Lamb, cleanses us, we are no longer, as Elder Scott says, "second-class citizen[s] in the kingdom of God" (*Ensign,* Nov. 2000, 26). We are cleansed and made whole through the holy blood of the Lamb. This is one of the greatest passages in all of holy writ about the atonement of Christ. . . .

It is easy to understand why Satan doesn't want a young man who is involved with drugs to read the Book of Mormon, because he'll realize that if Alma and the sons of Mosiah could be forgiven, then so can he. We can see why Satan doesn't want a young woman who has had a baby out of wedlock to read the Book of Mormon, because then she too will learn that she's not "cast off forever" (Mosiah 28:4); if Corianton can be forgiven and become a man of God, then she can be forgiven and become a woman of God.

(Jack R. Christianson and K. Douglas Bassett, *Life Lessons from the Book of Mormon* [Salt Lake City: Deseret Book, 2003], 21–22)

Find encouragement in the lives of Alma the Younger and the sons of Mosiah. They were tragically wicked. [Mosiah 28:4.] Yet their full repentance and service qualified them to be considered as noble as righteous Captain Moroni.

(Richard G. Scott, *Ensign*, Nov. 2000 [Salt Lake City: The Church of Jesus Christ of Latter-day Saints, 2000], 26)

Alma 48:12 • HIS HEART DID SWELL WITH THANKSGIVING
(Refer in this text to Moroni 10:3.)

"Thank you" frequently expressed will cheer your spirit, broaden your friendships, and lift your lives to a higher pathway as you journey toward perfection.

(Thomas S. Monson, *Ensign*, Nov. 1998 [Salt Lake City: The Church of Jesus Christ of Latter-day Saints, 1998], 17)

[Luke 17:11–19.] Through divine intervention, those who were lepers were spared from a cruel, lingering death and given a new lease on live. The expressed gratitude by one merited the Master's blessing, the ingratitude shown by the nine, His disappointment.

Like the leprosy of yesteryear are the plagues of today. They are to be found everywhere. Their pervasiveness knows no boundaries. We know them as selfishness, greed, indulgence, cruelty, and crime, to identify but a few. Surfeited with their poison, we tend to criticize, to complain, to blame, and slowly but surely, to abandon the positives and adopt the negatives of life.

A popular refrain from the 1940s captured the thought:

Accentuate the positive;
Eliminate the negative.
Latch on to the affirmative:
Don't mess with Mr. In-between.
Good advice then. Good advice now. . . .

If ingratitude be numbered among the serious sins,

then gratitude takes its place among the noblest of virtues.

(Thomas S. Monson, in Conference Report, Apr. 1992 [Salt Lake City: The Church of Jesus Christ of Latter-day Saints, 1992], 79–80)

We ought to express our gratitude daily in countless ways—to each other. . . .

Gratitude is a sign of maturity. It is an indication of sincere humility. It is a hallmark of civility. And most of all, it is a divine principle. I doubt there is anything in which we more offend the Almighty than in our tendency to forget His mercies and to be ungrateful for that which He has given us. . . .

Where there is gratitude, there is humility instead of pride, generosity rather than selfishness. . . .

We would do well, also, to cultivate within ourselves a spirit of thanksgiving for the blessing of life itself and for the marvelous gifts and privileges we enjoy.

(Gordon B. Hinckley, *Standing for Something* [New York: Times Books, 2000], 89–90)

Alma 48:14–16 • NEPHITES FIGHT DEFENSIVELY
(Refer in this text to 3 Nephi 3:20–21; Mormon 3:10.)

Alma 48:15, 25; 50:19–22 • NEPHI'S FREEDOM THESIS
(Refer in this text to 1 Nephi 1:20; Alma 36:1.)

I do not believe the greatest threat to our future is from bombs or guided missiles. I do not think our civilization will die that way. I think it will die when we no longer care—when the spiritual forces that make us wish to be right and noble die in the hearts of men.

(Ezra Taft Benson, Annual Boy Scouts Banquet, Commerce, Texas, 13 May 1968)

Despite the world's crises . . . the greater crisis by far is that we might forget the Lord. How much protection would our missiles and nuclear weapons prove to be if we did not take at face value the Lord's injunction: "Thou shalt love the Lord thy God with all thy heart, and with all thy soul, and with all thy strength, and with all thy mind; and thy neighbor as thyself" (Luke 10:27)?

(Ezra Taft Benson, *Crossfire: The Eight Years with Eisenhower* [Garden City, New York: Doubleday, 1962], 441)

We are a warlike people easily distracted from our assignment of preparing for the coming of the Lord.

When enemies rise up, we commit vast resources to the fabrication of gods of stone and steel—ships, planes, missiles, fortifications—and depend on them for protection and deliverance. When threatened, we become anti-enemy instead of pro-kingdom of God; we train a man in the art of war and call him a patriot, thus, in the manner of Satan's counterfeit of true patriotism, perverting the Savior's teaching: "Love your enemies, bless them that curse you, do good to them that hate you, and pray for them which despitefully use you, and persecute you; That ye may be the children of your father which is in heaven" (Matt. 5:44–45). We forget that if we are righteous the Lord will either not suffer our enemies to come upon us—and this is the special promise to the inhabitants of the land of the Americas (see 2 Ne. 1:7)—or he will fight our battles for us (Exodus 14:14; D&C 98:37, to name only two references of many).

(Spencer W. Kimball, *Ensign*, 1976 [Salt Lake City: The Church of Jesus Christ of Latter-day Saints, 1976], 6)

Alma 50:21–23 • IN THE DARKEST TIME THE OBEDIENT WERE HAPPY

As some things clearly worsen in the world, the true Saints will simply get better.

(Neal A. Maxwell, *One More Strain of Praise* [Salt Lake City: Bookcraft, 1999], 18)

God will give us priceless, personal assurances through the Holy Ghost (see John 14:26; D&C 36:2). Whether in tranquil or turbulent times, our best source of comfort is the Comforter. . . .

Brothers and sister, though living in a time of commotion, we can stand in holy places and not be moved (see D&C 45:32; 87:8). Though living in a time of violence, we can have that inner peace that passeth understanding (see Philippians 4:7).

(Neal A. Maxwell, in Conference Report, Oct. 2002 [Salt Lake City: The Church of Jesus Christ of Latter-day Saints, 2002], 15, 17)

We must constantly remember it is not our situation or problems that make us unhappy; it is our failure to properly resolve them.

Someone has said that happiness is like a butterfly. The more you chase it, the more it will elude you. But if you turn your attention to other things, it comes and sits softly on your shoulder (see Nathaniel Hawthorne; as quoted in *Reader's Digest*, Apr. 1982, 148).

(Marvin J. Ashton, in Conference Report, Apr. 1984 [Salt Lake City: The Church of Jesus Christ of Latter-day Saints, 1984], 12)

Alma 51:13–20 • ANSWERING THE CALL TO MILITARY SERVICE

Even though we sense the hellish origin of war, even though we feel confident that war will never end war, yet, under existing conditions, we find ourselves as a body committed to combat this evil thing. With other loyal citizens we serve our country as bearers of arms, rather than to stand aloof to enjoy a freedom for which others have fought and died.

(David O. McKay, *Man May Know for Himself*, ed. by Clare Middlemiss [Salt Lake City: Deseret Book, 1967], 365–368)

We have been asked today [1942] to be patriotic. This Church, as has been read by President McKay, has a record of accomplishment that is a . . . testimony to the world of the patriotism of this people. We have been sending our boys into the army, and will continue to do so. We will buy war bonds and stamps. We will pay inordinate taxes, for the carrying on of the work for the buying of planes and munitions of war. We will produce and conserve foodstuffs, that there may be sufficient of the necessities to carry on, as we have been requested by our government. But beyond all that, the Latter-day Saints have a responsibility, that may be better understood when we recall the prophecy of Joseph Smith who declared that 'the time would come when (the destiny and) the Constitution of these United States would hang as it were by a thread, and that this people, the sons of Zion, would rise up and save it from threatened destruction' (*Journal of Discourses* 7:15). I want to ask you to consider the meaning of that prophecy, in the light of the declaration of the prophets of the Book of Mormon times, who declared that this land was a choice land above all other lands, and would be free from bondage and from captivity, and from all other nations under heaven, if they will but serve the God of this land, even our Savior, Jesus Christ (Ether 2:12). This is a people whom the Lord has chosen to preach the gospel of righteousness. We talk of security in this day, and yet we fail to understand that here on this Temple Block we have standing the holy temple wherein we may find the symbols by which power might be generated that will save this nation from destruction. Therein may be found the fulness of the blessings of the Priesthood.

(Harold B. Lee, in Conference Report, Apr. 1942 [Salt Lake City: The Church of Jesus Christ of Latter-day Saints, 1942], 87)

A Latter-day Saint must give allegiance to (his) sovereign and render it loyal service when called thereto. This includes military service. The attitude of a Latter-day Saint should be fully to render loyalty to (his) country and to free institutions which the loftiest patriotism calls for. . . . The Church is and must be against war. . . . It cannot regard war as a righteous means of settling international disputes; these should and could be settled—the nations agreeing—by peaceful negotiation and adjustment. But the Church membership are citizens or subjects of sovereignties over which the Church has no control. . . . When, therefore, constitutional law, obedient to these principles, calls the manhood of the Church into the armed service of any country to which they owe allegiance, their highest civic duty requires that they meet that call.

(Heber J. Grant, J. Reuben Clark Jr., and David O. McKay, in Conference Report, Apr. 1942 [Salt Lake City: The Church of Jesus Christ of Latter-day Saints, 1942], 92–95)

_____

The Church is opposed to war because it causes the blood of brothers and sisters to be shed. It opposes war because wars destroy spirituality. . . . But notwithstanding the horrors and evils of war and the beauty of peace, there is a greater purpose in life than merely remaining peaceful. Life calls for growth of the soul. The opportunities for growth requires that man shall retain his freedom, his free agency, his right to live and work and worship according to the dictates of his own conscience. . . . The right to a world where the individual is recognized, the right to protect our loved ones, our liberties and our religion is more important than the keeping of peace.

(William E. Berrett, *Teachings of the Book of Mormon* [Salt Lake City: Deseret News Press, 1952], 177–178)

_____

Certainly a true American cannot have too much patriotism. Surely Americans who have respect for our traditions, who support our freedoms and are willing to fight to preserve them have been called patriots from the very beginning of our nation. I am proud to be called a patriot, for it correctly denotes one who loves his country. I love America's traditions and its freedoms and I believe they are well worth fighting for, against all that which threatens from within as well as from without.

(Ezra Taft Benson, *The Red Carpet* [Salt Lake City: Bookcraft, 1962], 199)

_____

The only real peace—the one most of us think about when we use the term—is a peace with freedom. A nation that is not willing, if necessary, to face the rigors of war to defend its real peace-in-freedom is doomed to lose both its freedom and its peace! These are the hard facts of life. We may not like them, but until we live in

a far better world than exists today, we must face up to them squarely and courageously.

(Ezra Taft Benson, *An Enemy Hath Done This*, comp. by Jerreld L. Newquist [Salt Lake City: Parliament Publishers, 1969], 161–162)

_____

A man does not necessarily have to volunteer. In fact, it would be hoped that young members of the Church would have the strengthening stabilizing development of missionary service, and perhaps some schooling, before they enter the service, if indeed they are required to do so at all. And sometimes they are required to serve. If so, the brethren have said: ". . . the members of the Church have always felt under obligation to come to the defense of their country when a call to arms was made . . ." (*Improvement Era*, May 1942, 346, 348–49). Though all the issues of the conflict are anything but clear, the matter of citizenship responsibility is perfectly clear.

(Boyd K. Packer, *Improvement Era*, June 1968 [Salt Lake City: The Church of Jesus Christ of Latter-day Saints, 1968], 58, 60–61)

_____

Someone asked me once how I felt about amnesty for the draft card burner and the deserter. I told him that I thought every one of them should be taken before General Moroni to be judged.

(Vaughn J. Featherstone, *Ensign*, Nov. 1975 [Salt Lake City: The Church of Jesus Christ of Latter-day Saints, 1975], 7–10)

_____

Is it murder when a soldier kills in battle?

There are many persons who are engaged in wars who are devout Christians. They are innocent instrumentalities—war instrumentalities, for the most part—of their warring sovereignties. On each side, people believe that they are fighting for a just cause, for defense of home and country and freedom. On each side they pray . . . for victory. Both sides cannot be wholly right; perhaps neither is without wrong. God will work out in his own due time and in his own sovereign way, the justice and right of the conflict. But he will not hold the innocent instrumentalities of the war—our brethren in arms—responsible for the conflict.

(Harold B. Lee, *From the Valley of Despair to the Mountain Peaks of Hope* [Salt Lake City: Deseret News Press, 1971], 3)

_____

If, harkening to that call [to serve one's country] and obeying those in command over them, they shall take the lives of those who fight against them, that will not make them murderers, nor subject them to the penalty that

God has prescribed for those who kill. . . . For it would be a cruel God that would punish His children as moral sinners for acts done by them as the innocent instrumentalities of a sovereign whom He had told them to obey and whose will they were powerless to resist. . . . In this terrible war now waging, thousands of our righteous young men in all parts of the world and in many countries are subject to a call into the military service of their own countries. . . . That in their work of destruction they will be striking at their brethren will not be held against them. That sin, as Moroni of old said, is to the condemnation of those who "sit in their places of power in a state of thoughtless stupor," those rulers in the world who in a frenzy of hate and lust for unrighteous power and dominion over their fellow men, have put into motion eternal forces they do not comprehend and cannot control. God, in His own due time, will pass sentence upon them.

(Heber J. Grant, J. Reuben Clark Jr., and David O. McKay, in Conference Report, Apr. 1942 [Salt Lake City: The Church of Jesus Christ of Latter-day Saints, 1942], 92–96)

The time was World War II. Fierce battles raged in various parts of the world.

Tragically, the Borgstroms [family in northern Utah] lost four of their five sons who were serving in the armed forces. Within a six-month period, all four sons gave their lives—each in a different part of the world.

Following the war, the bodies of the four Borgstrom brothers were brought home to Tremonton, and an appropriate service was conducted, filling the Garland Utah Tabernacle. General Mark Clark attended the service. He later spoke with tenderness these words: "I flew to Garland the morning of June 26. Met with the family, including among others the mother, father, and two remaining sons, . . . one a lad in his teens. I had never met a more stoic family group.

"As the four flag-draped coffins were lined up in front of us in the church, and as I sat by these brave parents, I was deeply impressed by their understanding, by their faith, and their pride in these magnificent sons who had made the supreme sacrifice for principles which had been instilled in them by noble parents since childhood.

"During the luncheon period, Mrs. Borgstrom turned to me and said in a low voice, 'Are you going to take my young one?' I answered in a whisper that as long as I remained in command of the army on the West Coast, if her boy were called I would do my best to have him assigned to duty at home.

"In the middle of this whispered conversation with the mother, the father suddenly leaned forward and said to Mrs. Borgstrom: 'Mother, I have overheard your conversation with the general about our youngest. We know that if and when his country needs him, he will go.'

"I could hardly contain my emotions. Here were parents with four sons lying dead from wounds received in battle and yet were ready to make the last sacrifice if their country required it."

(Thomas S. Monson, *Ensign*, Nov. 1999 [Salt Lake City: The Church of Jesus Christ of Latter-day Saints, 1999], 20)

I want to call on everyone . . . to be men and women of loyalty to the nation of which you are a part. Love of country is a great thing. It is a good thing. If we want to change the world, we begin with ourselves, and then we move out to include our fellow citizens and build goodness among the people.

(*Discourses of President Gordon B. Hinckley*, 1995–99 [Salt Lake City: The Church of Jesus Christ of Latter-day Saints, 2004], 1:511)

Alma 53:4–7 • FORTIFICATIONS

Resisting the temptations of today's electronic media is not easy. It takes focused courage and effort. In the small town where I grew up, one had to drive at least an hour to find trouble. But today on the Internet, trouble is just a few mouse clicks away. To avoid such temptations, be like Captain Moroni of old; set up "fortifications" to strengthen your places of weakness. Instead of building walls of "timbers and dirt" to protect a vulnerable city, build "fortifications" in the form of personal ground rules to protect your priceless virtue (see Alma 53:4, 7). When you're on a date, plan to be in groups and avoid being alone. I know men, young and old, who have simply determined not to turn on the TV or surf the Internet anytime when they are alone. Fathers, it is wise to keep computers and televisions in the family room or other high-traffic areas in your home—not in children's bedrooms. I also know of fathers who, while on business trips, wisely choose not to turn on the hotel television.

Remember, such "fortifications" are not a sign of weakness. On the contrary, they show strength. . . . Remember Moroni's "strongholds" (see Alma 53:4–5). were the key to his success. Creating your own "strongholds" will be the key to yours.

(David E. Sorensen, *Ensign*, May 2001 [Salt Lake City: The Church of Jesus Christ of Latter-day Saints, 2001], 41–42)

Alma 53:8, 9; 54:6, 9, 10; 55:28, 31; 56:8, 19, 46; 57:35; 58:9–11, 33, 37; 59:11–12; 17, 20–21, 60:11, 14–28; 61:13, 21 • LAMANITES NOT A THREAT WHEN NEPHITES ARE RIGHTEOUS

(Refer in this text to Mosiah 21:7.)

So it was a blessing to the Nephites after all to

have the Lamanites on their doorstep to stir them up to remembrance. . . . No matter how wicked and ferocious and depraved the Lamanites might be (and they were that!), no matter by how much they outnumbered the Nephites, . . . they were not the Nephite problem. They were merely kept there to remind the Nephites of their real problem, which was to walk uprightly before the Lord.

(Hugh Nibley, *Since Cumorah* [Salt Lake City: Deseret Book, 1976], 376)

Alma 53:16–21; 56:45–48, 55–56; 57:21, 25–27; 58:40 • THE STRIPLING WARRIORS, THE SONS OF HELAMAN

In the spiritual battles you are waging, I see you as today's sons of Helaman.

(*Teachings of Ezra Taft Benson* [Salt Lake City: Bookcraft, 1988], 520)

The 2,000 stripling warriors not only made covenants, they kept them. . . . Very simply, they did what they said they would do. They weren't always looking for ways to straddle the line between right and wrong.

After President Hinckley was interviewed by Mike Wallace for *60 Minutes*, I had occasion to talk with Mr. Wallace about their conversation. Do you know what Mike Wallace seemed most impressed with? That President Hinckley had done everything in connection with the interview that he had promised to do. When I later offered to show Mr. Wallace how I intended to quote him in President Hinckley's biography, he replied, "That's not necessary. You're a Mormon, I trust you." . . . His expression was not a reflection of me, it was a reflection of his experience with President Hinckley. In effect, he was saying, "If you are associated with *that* man, then I assume that you, too, will do what you have said you will do."

(Sheri Dew, "Living on the Lord's Side of the Line," *BYU Speeches of the Year*, 21 Mar. 2000 [Provo, Utah: BYU Press, 2000], 4)

Thankfully we have a tremendous army of latter-day sons and daughters of Helaman, stripling "Saturday's warriors," who are not ashamed of the gospel of Jesus Christ. . . .

Steve Hawes is the student body president at New Canaan High School in Connecticut. Of its twenty-three hundred students, only twenty-four are Latter-day Saints. Steve ran unopposed in a landslide election. This is impressive. But even more impressive is Steve's moral courage—his commitment to living the principles of the gospel.

The Hawes family lived for a time in Tampa, Florida.

Steve played junior high football and basketball. When his family was preparing to move to Connecticut, the coach told Steve's father how much he appreciated and admired Steve, not just because he is a fine athlete, but because of his deep religious convictions.

"He doesn't preach sermons; he just quietly lives his religion each day. I remember," said the coach, "a group of us were in the squad room, and one of the boys pulled out a copy of *Playboy* magazine. They opened to the center-fold and began to make some vulgar comments.

"I noticed Steve walk away, so I followed him and asked if anything was wrong. He said, 'I'm okay, Coach, but that just isn't my kind of thing.'"

The coach said, "Steve made us all better people. When he joined us, most of the guys were swearing. Then they stopped swearing around Steve, and after a while, they pretty well stopped swearing altogether."

(J. Richard Clarke, in Conference Report, Apr. 1985 [Salt Lake City: The Church of Jesus Christ of Latter-day Saints, 1985], 95–96)

Who can help but be inspired by the lives of the 2,000 stripling sons of Helaman who taught and demonstrated the need of courage to follow the teachings of parents, the courage to be chaste and pure? . . .

In our lives . . . we will face fear, experience ridicule, and meet opposition. . . . Courage, not compromise, brings the smile of God's approval. . . . A moral coward is one who is afraid to do what he thinks is right because others will disapprove or laugh. Remember that all men have their fears, but those who face their fears with dignity have courage as well. . . .

Someone has said that courage is not the absence of fear but the mastery of it (see Mark Twain, in Gorton Carruth and Eugene Ehrich, eds., *The Harper Book of American Quotations* (1988), 111). At times, courage is needed to rise from failure, to strive again.

(Thomas S. Monson, *Ensign*, May 2004 [Salt Lake City: The Church of Jesus Christ of Latter-day Saints, 2004], 55–56)

"What does it mean to be true to the faith? That word *true* implies *commitment, integrity, endurance,* and *courage.* It reminds us of the Book of Mormon's description of the 2,000 young warriors: [in Alma 53:20–21]. In the spirit of that description I say to our returned missionaries—men and women who have made covenants to serve the Lord and who have already served Him in the great work of proclaiming the gospel and perfecting the Saints—are you being true to the faith? Do you have the faith and continuing commitment to demonstrate the principles of the gospel in your own lives, consistently? You have served well, but do you, like the pioneers, have the courage and the consistency to be true to the faith and to endure to the end?"

(Dallin H. Oaks, *Ensign*, Nov. 1997 [Salt Lake City: The Church of Jesus Christ of Latter-day Saints, 1997], 73)

Alma 55:28, 31 • VICTORY AND REMEMBERING THE LORD
(Contrast with Mosiah 9:3.)

Alma 56:11 • DEATH, THEY ARE HAPPY
(Refer in this text to Alma 27:28.)

Alma 56:16 • DEPRESSED IN BODY AND SPIRIT
(Refer in this text to Alma 26:27.)

At some time in our lives, each of us needs to be lifted from a depression, from a sense of foreboding or inadequacy, or just from a plateau of spiritual mediocrity. Because the feeling of uplift raises our spirits and helps us resist evil and seek good, I believe that the uplift communicated by reading the scriptures and enjoying wholesome music, art, or literature is a distinct purpose of revelation.

(Dallin H. Oaks, *With Full Purpose of Heart* [Salt Lake City: Deseret Book, 2002], 152)

———————

When you go to a multi-screen theater, you select a movie that will help you to feel what you want to feel. If you want to cry and feel sad, you will select a "tearjerker." If you want to laugh, you will go to a comedy. Likewise, you can select the internal movies you view. . . . If you want to intensify anger, guilt, shame, and/or depression . . . you will choose to select movies that will reinforce your negative judgment of self (for guilt, shame, and depression) or of others (for anger). . . .

Suppose that you have just completed an abominable game of golf, and you tell yourself: "I really screwed that up! Once again, I didn't do it well enough. The harder I try, the worse I get. I keep failing, and I guess that I'm just a failure!" This internal expression . . . generates shame ("I'm a failure") and contributes to depression. . . .

Unfortunately, people who specialize in anger have impressive [internal] movie collections of examples of other people's wrongdoings and few—if any—movies of being treated well by others. People who specialize in depression, on the other hand, have massive movie collections of personal inadequacies and misdeeds and few—if any—movies of personal successes and validation by other people. It may be difficult, therefore, for such people to select positive [internal] movies, since they may not have collected them.

(Philip Roos, *The Osiris Factor* [Springville, Utah: Bonneville Books, 2002], 49)

———————

I know of nothing that Satan uses quite so cunningly or cleverly in his work on a young man or woman. I speak of doubt (especially self-doubt), of discouragement, and of despair. . . .

I wish at the outset, however, to make a distinction that F. Scott Fitzgerald once made: "Trouble has no necessary connection with discouragement—discouragement has a germ of its own, as different from trouble as arthritis is different from a stiff joint." We all have troubles, but the "germ" of discouragement, to use Fitzgerald's word, is not in the trouble; it is in us—or to be more precise, I believe it is in Satan, the prince of darkness, the father of lies. . . . It's frequently a small germ, hardly worth going to a doctor for, but it will work and it will grow and it will spread. In fact, it can become almost a habit, a way of living and thinking, and there the greatest damage is done. Then it takes an increasingly severe toll on our spirit. . . . We turn inward and look downward. . . . We become unhappy and soon make others unhappy, and before long Lucifer laughs.

(Jeffrey R. Holland, *However Long and Hard the Road* [Salt Lake City: Deseret Book, 1985], 1–2)

———————

On that Friday the Savior of mankind was humiliated and bruised, abused and reviled.

It was a Friday filled with devastating, consuming sorrow that gnawed at the souls of those who loved and honored the Son of God.

I think that of all the days since the beginning of this world's history, that Friday was the darkest.

But the doom of that day did not endure.

The despair did not linger because on Sunday, the resurrected Lord burst the bonds of death. . . .

Each of us will have our own Fridays—those days when the universe itself seems shattered and the shards of our world lie littered about us in pieces. We all will experience those broken times when it seems we can never be put together again. We will all have our Fridays.

But I testify to you in the name of the One who conquered death—Sunday will come. . . .

No matter our desperation, no matter our grief, Sunday will come. In this life or the next, Sunday will come.

(Joseph B. Wirthlin, *Ensign*, Nov. 2006 [Salt Lake City: The Church of Jesus Christ of Latter-day Saints, 2006], 29–30)

Alma 56:47–48 • RIGHTEOUS MOTHERS
All that I am, or hope to be I owe to my angel mother.

(Abraham Lincoln; as quoted in Paul Selby, *Lincoln's Life Stories and Speeches* [Chicago: Thompson and Thomas, 1902], 221)

———————

[Referring to the stripling warriors and their mothers] I think that is one of the greatest tributes that has ever been paid to motherhood—that in circumstances such as they were experiencing, when they were surrounded by enemies, they could train their children to have that faith in God that would carry them through and would bring them home without losing their lives. . . . I realize that there is a force in the Latter-day Saint homes where our wives and mothers and daughters are, and when it comes to faith in God and prayer it is equal to anything that the men may be able to muster. I fear that sometimes we neglect them. . . . [Speaking to the Priesthood] I am asking myself the question, "How many of you who are here tonight, before you came here to wait upon the Lord, put your arms around the woman who stood by your side, the mother of your children, and told her that you were grateful that she would keep the home-fires burning when you couldn't be there?" I wonder if we appreciate the daughters of God as He appreciates them. Do we treasure their virtues and their faith and their devotion and their motherhood as our Heavenly Father does?

(George Albert Smith, in Conference Report, Apr. 1943 [Salt Lake City: The Church of Jesus Christ of Latter-day Saints, 1943], 89–90)

———————

It is the mothers of young children I would like to address first. . . . These are years when you will probably do the most important work of your lives. Don't wish away your years of caring for small children. Life is what happens to you while you are making other plans. This is a time of great opportunity for you to build the Kingdom. When you teach children to love their Heavenly Father, you have done one of the greatest things you will ever do. If you can be a full-time homemaker, be grateful. If not, you must do what is best. . . . I for one have never felt a need to apologize for my role as a full-time homemaker.

(Marjorie Hinckley; as quoted in *Ensign*, May 1995 [Salt Lake City: The Church of Jesus Christ of Latter-day Saints, 1995], 74)

———————

Suggestions for mothers as they guide their precious children:

1. Take time to always be at the crossroads in the lives of your children, whether they be six or sixteen.
2. Take time to be a real friend to your children.
3. Take time to read to your children. Remember what the poet wrote:

You may have tangible wealth untold:
Caskets of jewels and coffers of gold.
Richer than I you can never be—
I had a mother who read to me.

4. Take time to pray with your children.
5. Take time to have a meaningful weekly home evening. Make this one of your great family traditions.
6. Take time to be together at mealtimes as often as possible.
7. Take time daily to read the scriptures together as a family.
8. Take time to do things together as a family.
9. Take time to teach your children.
10. Take time to truly love your children. A mother's unqualified love approaches Christlike love.

(Ezra Taft Benson, *Come Listen to a Prophet's Voice* [Salt Lake City: Deseret Book, 1990], 32–36)

———————

If I were asked to name the world's greatest need, I should say unhesitatingly *wise mothers*; and the second greatest, *exemplary fathers*. . . . The noblest calling in the world is that of mother. True motherhood is the most beautiful of all arts, the greatest of all professions. She who can paint a masterpiece or who can write a book that will influence millions deserves the plaudits and admiration of mankind; but she who rears successfully a family of . . . sons and daughters whose immortal souls will be exerting an influence throughout the ages long after painting[s] shall have faded, and books and statues shall have been destroyed, deserves the highest honor that man can give.

(David O. McKay, *Secrets of a Happy Life*, comp. by Llewelyn R. McKay [Salt Lake City: Bookcraft, 1967], 2–4)

———————

Recently I reviewed the history of many missionaries and found a powerful correlation between exceptional missionaries and mothers who chose to remain home, often at great financial and personal sacrifice. . . . President Benson has taught that a mother with children should be in the home. He also said, 'We realize . . . that some of our choice sisters are widowed and divorced and that others find themselves in unusual circumstances where, out of necessity, they are required to work for a period of time. But these instances are the exception, not the rule' (Ezra Taft Benson, *To the Mothers in Zion*, pamphlet, 1987, 5–6). You in these unusual circumstances qualify for additional inspiration and strength from the Lord. Those who leave the home for lesser reasons will not.

(Richard G. Scott, *Ensign*, May 1993 [Salt Lake City: The Church of Jesus Christ of Latter-day Saints, 1993], 33–34)

In ten years, one-half of all children born in America will be illegitimate. More and more children have no functioning fathers. Already 70% of our juvenile criminals come from fatherless homes. Less than half of the children born today will live continuously with their own mother and father throughout childhood. One-fourth of all adolescents contract a sexually trans-mitted disease before they graduate from high school. Fifty-five percent of American children under the age of six have both parents or their only parent working in the labor force.... Annually in America there are four million reports of domestic violence, rivaling the number of births in America! Violence in America now kills 'the equivalent of a classroomful' of children 'every two days.' In the face of such challenges, we need more mothers who know the truth, whose children do not doubt their mothers know it (see Alma 56:48).

(Neal A. Maxwell, *Ensign*, May 1994 [Salt Lake City: The Church of Jesus Christ of Latter-day Saints, 1994], 88–90)

A man who holds the priesthood does not have an advantage over a woman in qualifying for exaltation. The woman, by her very nature, is also co-creator with God and the primary nurturer of the children. Virtues and attributes upon which perfection and exaltation depend come naturally to a woman and are refined through marriage and motherhood.... During World War II, men were called away to fight. In the emergency, wives and mothers worldwide were drawn into the work force as never before. The most devastating effect of the war was on the family. It lingers to this generation. In the October 1942 general conference, the First Presidency delivered a message to the Saints in every land.

"... This divine service of motherhood can be ren-dered only by mothers. It may not be passed to others. Nurses cannot do it; public nurseries cannot do it; hired help cannot do it—only mother, aided as much as may be by the loving hands of father, brothers, and sisters, can give the full needed measure of watchful care.... The mother who entrusts her child to the care of others, that she may do non-motherly work, whether for gold, for fame, or for civic service, should remember that *a child left to himself bringeth his mother to shame* (Prov. 29:15). In our day the Lord has said that unless par-ents teach their children the doctrines of the Church *the sin be upon the heads of the parents* (D&C 68:25). Motherhood is near to divinity. It is the highest, holiest service to be assumed by mankind. It places her who honors its holy calling and service next to the angels."

That message and warning from the First Presidency is needed more, not less, today than when it was given. Any soul who ... must act alone in rearing children,

working to support them will not be denied in the eter-nities any blessing—provided they keep the command-ments.

(Boyd K. Packer, *Ensign*, Nov. 1993 [Salt Lake City: The Church of Jesus Christ of Latter-day Saints, 1993], 22–23)

As I visit the missions in the world, I hear the young men bear their testimonies. They say, "My mother told me this. ... my mother is prime, she's first." She really is first, and if all women could understand this, they would want to have families instead of following the present fad. . . It has been said that "When you educate a man, you educate an individual; but when you educate a woman, you educate a whole family" (Dr. Charles D. McIver). We want our women to be well educated, for children may not recover from the ignorance of their mothers. After marriage young wives should be hap-pily occupied in bearing and rearing children.... You sometimes read things quite different from that. But it is still true, and it will be true when the last trumpet is sounded. I know of no scriptures nor authorities which authorize young wives to forego families purposely. Young married couples can make their way and reach their educational heights if they are truly determined.

(Spencer W. Kimball, Charge to Religious Educa-tors, 1982, 43–47)

Government and social plans will not effectively correct [violence], . . . nor can the best efforts of schools and churches fully compensate for the absence of the tender care of a compassionate mother and wife in the home. . . . As a mother guided by the Lord, you weave a fabric of character in your children from threads of truth through careful instruction and worthy example.... No day-care center can do that. It is your sacred right and privilege. Of course, as a woman you can do excep-tionally well in the work-place, but is that the best use of your divinely appointed talents and feminine traits? As a husband, don't encourage your wife to go to work to help in your divinely appointed responsibility of pro-viding resources for the family, if you can possibly avoid it. . . . Don't be lured away from the plan of our God to the ways of the world, where motherhood is belittled, femininity is decried, and the divinely established role of wife and mother is mocked. Let the world go its way. You follow the plan of the Lord. . . ."

(Richard G. Scott, *Ensign*, Nov. 1996 [Salt Lake City: The Church of Jesus Christ of Latter-day Saints, 1996], 74–75)

Some years ago President Benson delivered a message to the women of the Church. He encouraged them to leave their employment and give their individual time to their children. I sustain the position which he took. Nevertheless, I recognize, as he recognized, that there are some women (it has become very many in fact) who have to work to provide for the needs of their families. To you I say, do the very best you can. I hope that if you are employed full-time you are doing it to ensure that basic needs are met and not simply to indulge a taste for an elaborate home, fancy cars, and other luxuries. . . . It is well-nigh impossible to be a full-time homemaker and a full-time employee. I know how some of you struggle with decisions concerning this matter. I repeat, do the very best you can. You know your circumstances, and I know that you are deeply concerned for the welfare of your children.

(Gordon B. Hinckley, *Ensign*, Nov. 1996 [Salt Lake City: The Church of Jesus Christ of Latter-day Saints, 1996], 69)

———

[To the young women] Becoming like men is not the answer. Rather, the answer lies in being who you are and living up to your divine potential by fulfilling eternal commitments. You cannot trust the many conflicting voices that clamor about what women should or should not do in today's society. Some of the loudest voices are echoes of those others who are out of harmony with themselves and out of tune with life in general rather than being unhappy with their role as women. . . . Entreating voices may tell you that what you have seen your mothers and grandmothers do is old-fashioned, unchallenging, boring, and drudgery. . . . Homemaking is whatever you make of it. Every day brings satisfaction along with some work which may be frustrating, routine, and unchallenging. But it is the same in the law office, the dispensary, the laboratory, or the store. There is, however, no more important job than homemaking. As C.S. Lewis said, "A housewife's work . . . is the one for which all others exist." . . . Women today are encouraged by some to have it all: money, travel, marriage, motherhood, and separate careers in the world. For women, the important ingredients for happiness are to forge an identity, serve the Lord, get an education, develop your talents, serve your family, and if possible to have a family of your own. However, you cannot do all these things well at the same time. . . . You cannot be a 100–percent wife, a 100–percent mother, a 100–percent Church worker, a 100–percent career person, and a 100–percent public-service person at the same time. How can all of these roles be coordinated? I suggest that you can have it sequentially. *Sequentially* is a big word meaning to do things one at a time at different times. The book of Ecclesiastes [3:1] says: "To every thing there is a season, and a time to every purpose under . . . heaven."

(James E. Faust, *Ensign*, May 1998 [Salt Lake City: The Church of Jesus Christ of Latter-day Saints, 1998], 96)

———

As young mothers . . . evaluate the cost of working outside the home, I deeply hope they will not sell themselves short. I am so proud of those who clearly see the importance of their role. Mothers who make the choice to stay home with their children, teaching by precept and example, make lasting investments in eternal accounts. Their preparation and education does so much more than draw a paycheck. It enriches the whole family and shapes the lives of their children. Such mothers become refined by their righteous choice. They love and serve and sacrifice, and they are blessed in ways that they could not otherwise be. Disability, death, or other circumstances may necessitate individual adaptation.

(Mary Ellen Smoot, "Everything Money Cannot Buy," Satellite Broadcast, 3 Feb. 2002, Brigham Young University [Salt Lake City: The Church of Jesus Christ of Latter-day Saints, 2002], 2)

———

You sisters . . . belong to the great sorority of saviorhood. You may not hold the priesthood. Men are different, men have to have something given to them to make them saviors of men, but not mothers, not women. You are born with an inherent right, an inherent authority, to be the saviors of human souls. You are the co-creators with God of his children.

(*Matthew Cowley Speaks* [Salt Lake City: Deseret Book, 1954], 109)

———

Your mother is your best friend. Never forget that. She gave you life. She cared for you, nurtured you, nursed you when you were sick, and looked after your every need. Listen to her now. Talk with her candidly and confidentially. You will find that she will keep your confidence and that her wisdom will prove to be wonderful.

(Gordon B. Hinckley, *Ensign*, May 1996 [Salt Lake City: The Church of Jesus Christ of Latter-day Saints, 1996], 93)

———

Research conducted by the Church indicates that the single biggest factor affecting a child's participation in and attendance at church is the mother's attendance. This is not to say that the father's activity and participation are unimportant, but it is principally mothers who help their children prepare talks for Primary, who make sure their youth make it to girls camp and Mutual and youth conference, who help their children get ready on Sunday morning. Mothers are the emotional glue that holds the family together.

(Sheri Dew, *No Doubt About It* [Salt Lake City: Bookcraft, 2001], 63)

_____

The mother in the family far more than the father, is the one who instills in the hearts of the children, a testimony and a love for the gospel of Jesus Christ. . . . Wherever you find a woman who is devoted to this work, almost without exception you will find that her children are devoted to it.

(Heber J. Grant, *Gospel Standards*, comp. by G. Homer Durham [Salt Lake City: Improvement Era Publication, 1941], 150)

_____

If there is any man who ought to merit the curse of Almighty God it is the man who neglects the mother of his child, the wife of his bosom, the one who has made sacrifice of her very life over and over again, for him and his children. That is, of course, assuming that the wife is a pure and faithful mother and wife. . . . There are people fond of saying that women are the weaker vessels. I don't believe it. Physically, they may be; but spiritually, morally, religiously and in faith, what man can match a woman who is really convinced?

(Joseph F. Smith; as quoted in *Priesthood and Church Government*, comp. by John A. Widtsoe under the direction of The Council of the Twelve [Salt Lake City: Deseret Book, 1954], 86)

_____

The family proclamation declares, "God's commandment for His children to multiply and replenish the earth remains in force" (*Ensign*, Nov. 1995, 102). . . . Many in the world . . . see children only as an inconvenience. It is true that parenting is physically exhausting, emotionally draining, and mentally demanding. No one will give you good grades or blue ribbons for what you do as a mother. . . .

It is worth it! All latter-day prophets have borne witness to the sacred role of motherhood. President Spencer W. Kimball said, "It is important for you Latter-day Saint women to understand that the Lord holds motherhood and mothers sacred and in the highest esteem" ("Privileges and Responsibilities of Sisters," *Ensign*, Nov. 1978, 105). The Spirit testifies to my soul that this is true. . . .

Parenting is not only challenging, but it provides life's greatest joys.

(Susan W. Tanner, in Conference Report, Apr. 2003 [Salt Lake City: The Church of Jesus Christ of Latter-day Saints, 2003], 76–77)

_____

Our wives are often inspired but sometimes in counterintuitive ways—a reality, young men, which your fathers may be brave enough to explain to you sometime.

(Neal A. Maxwell, *Ensign*, May 2004 [Salt Lake City: The Church of Jesus Christ of Latter-day Saints, 2004], 46)

_____

"I, of course, owe everything to my mother, because my father died when I was only nine days of age; and the marvelous teachings, the faith, the integrity of my mother have been an inspiration to me." Referring to his decision to marry in the temple, he said: "I was very grateful for the inspiration and determination I had to start life right. Why did it come to me? It came to me because my mother believed in the gospel, taught me the value of it, gave me a desire to get all of the benefits of starting life right and of doing things according to the teachings of the gospel." . . .

Motherhood is near to divinity. It is the highest, holiest service to be assumed by mankind. It places her who honors its holy calling and service next to the angels.

(*Teachings of President of the Church—Heber J. Grant* [Salt Lake City: The Church of Jesus Christ of Latter-day Saints, 2002], 199, 203)

_____

Some mothers seem to have the capacity and energy to make their children's clothes, bake, give piano lessons, go to Relief Society, teach Sunday School, attend parent-teacher association meetings, and so on. Other mothers look upon such women as models and feel inadequate, depressed, and think they are failures when they make comparisons.

We should not allow ourselves to be trapped into such damaging inferiority feelings. This is another tool of Satan. Many seem to put too much pressure on themselves to be a "supermom" or "superwoman."

Sisters, do not allow yourselves to be made to feel inadequate or frustrated because you cannot do everything others seem to be accomplishing. Rather, each should assess her own situation, her own energy, and her own talents, and then choose the best way. . . . Only you and your Father in Heaven know your needs, strengths, and desires. Around this knowledge your personal course must be charted and your choices made.

(Marvin J. Ashton, in Conference Report, Apr. 1984 [Salt Lake City: The Church of Jesus Christ of Latter-day Saints, 1984], 11)

_____

It was about the 22nd day of June, 1834, when the cholera appeared in Zion's Camp at Fishing River. During the next week it raged in the midst of the party. Sixty-eight of the Saints were attacked and thirteen of

them died. . . . Joseph and Hyrum administered assiduously to the sick, and soon they were in the grasp of
the cholera. They were together when it seized them;
and together they knelt down and prayed for deliverance. Three times they bowed in supplication, the third
time with a vow that they would not rise until deliverance from the destroyer was vouch-safed. While they
were thus upon their knees a vision of comfort came to
Hyrum. He saw their mother afar off in Kirtland praying for her absent sons, and he felt that the Lord was
answering her cry. Hyrum told Joseph of the comforting
vision and together they arose, made whole every whit.

(George Q. Cannon, *Life of Joseph Smith the Prophet*
[Salt Lake City: Deseret Book, 1972], 182–183)

———

Put your homes in order. If Mother is working outside of the home, see if there are ways to change that,
even a little. It may be very difficult to change at the
present time. But analyze carefully and be prayerful
(see D&C 9:8–9). . . . Expect intervention from power
from beyond the veil to help you move, . . . to what is
best for your family.

(Boyd K. Packer, *Ensign*, May 2004 [Salt Lake
City: The Church of Jesus Christ of Latter-day
Saints, 2004], 79)

———

Mothers have no more compelling responsibility,
nor any laden with greater rewards, than the nurture
given their children in an environment of security,
peace, companionship, love, and motivation to grow
and do well. . . .

My life has been influenced in a profound and
penetrating way by good, talented, faithful, devoted
women. Though my mother died when I was twenty,
her influence and even the feeling of her presence have
stayed with me to the present day. . . .

If anyone can change the dismal situation into
which we are sliding, it is the good women of this country. . . .

The nurture and upbringing of children is more
than a part-time responsibility. It is a fact of life that
some mothers must work, but far too many do so only to
get the means for a little more luxury and a few fancier
toys—all at the sacrifice of their children. Mothers who
must work have an increased load to bear. Nevertheless,
they cannot afford to neglect their children. Children
need a mother's supervision in studying, in working
inside and outside the home, in the nurturing that only
she can adequately give—the love, the blessing, the
encouragement, and the closeness of a mother. . . .

Although the contributions of women in all walks
of life are respected, I hope we will never look down on
a homemaker.

(Gordon B. Hinckley, *Standing for Something* [New
York: Times Books, 2000], 150–151)

———

One of my white students entered an elevator that
I was in already, and I removed my hat. "Dr. Proctor,"
she said, "why . . . did you take your hat off when I got
on the elevator? You're living in the Victorian age." She
laughed congenially.

"If you'll get off the elevator with me for a moment,
I'll tell you." At my stop, we both stepped off.

"I'm not a Victorian," I said, "but some things stay
in place from one generation to another, and certain
manners stand for values that I hold dear. I believe that
a society that ceases to respect women is on its way out.
Women bear and raise our children, they are bound
to them in early infancy; they need our support and
security through this process. When we forget that, the
keystone of family and home is lost. When we neglect
and abuse women, the family falls apart and children
are less well parented, and they fill up the jails and are
buried in early graves. I believe that respect for women
is the linchpin of the family and the society. Therefore,
when you entered the elevator, I wanted you to have
automatic, immediate, unqualified assurance that if the
elevator caught fire, I would help you out through the
top first. If a strange man boarded and began to slap
you around and tear your clothes off, he would have
to kill me first. If the elevator broke down and stopped
between floors, I would not leave you in here. If you
fainted and slumped to the floor, I would stop everything and get you to a hospital. Now, it would take a lot
of time to say all of that, so when I removed my hat, I
meant all of the above."

Tears sprang to her eyes. There are some values that
abide. They have no racial or ethnic label.

(Samuel DeWitt Proctor, *The Substance of Things
Hoped for: A Memoir of African-American Faith*
[Valley Forge: Judson Press, 1999], 151–152)

———

I was talking the other day to one of my friends, . . .
who was drunk for twenty-seven years, and then finally
turned his life back to God. He is now active in the
Church and has not had a drink for fifteen years. I
asked him how he was able to overcome that habit. . . .
He said to me: "Matt, if I had not had the fortification
which came to me in my childhood from a righteous
mother, I never would have been able to overcome this
terrible habit. The influence of that mother in my home
is what has given me the courage and the strength and
the fortitude to overcome this drinking habit."

What a tribute to a mother! Now, you sisters, you
are the mothers of men, and you may not live to see the
fruits of your teaching in the lives of your children. . . .

You may not see them turn their lives back to God, but the day will come, if you give them the fortification in their childhood, in those years when their souls and minds are pliable, the day will come when they will have the strength, because of you, to turn their lives and their characters back to God and be influenced by him.

(*Matthew Cowley Speaks* [Salt Lake City: Deseret Book, 1954], 108–109)

———

I share with you an account described in a mother's letter to me relating to prayer. She wrote:

"Sometimes I wonder if I make a difference in my children's lives. Especially as a single mother working two jobs to make ends meet, I sometimes come home to confusion, but I never give up hope.

"My children and I were watching a television broadcast of general conference, and you were speaking about prayer. My son made the statement, 'Mother, you've already taught us that.' I said, 'What do you mean?' And he replied, 'Well, you've taught us to pray and showed us how, but the other night I came to your room to ask something and found you on your knees praying to Heavenly Father. If He's important to you, He'll be important to me.' "

The letter concluded, "I guess you never know what kind of influence you'll be until a child observes you doing yourself what you have tried to teach him to do."

(Thomas S. Monson, in Conference Report, Oct. 2003 [Salt Lake City: The Church of Jesus Christ of Latter-day Saints, 2003], 71–72)

Alma 56:47–48 • A BLESSING OF DIVINE PROTECTION

The Lamanite converts of the sons of Mosiah . . . took on the name of Anti-Nephi-Lehies. Some 2,000 of their sons became the "stripling warriors" when they enlisted in the Nephite army. These youthful patriots were untested in battle yet they illustrated no fear at the prospect of death. The reason for this being that "they had been taught by their mothers, that if they did not doubt, God would deliver them" (Alma 56:47). Notice if they did not doubt *something* then God would deliver them. What was it that they were not to doubt? That their mothers were telling the truth? That the gospel was true? Not to doubt Helaman their military leader, and obey with exactness? (see Alma 57:21). Not to doubt the oath they had taken to defend the freedom of their fathers and the Nephites? (see Alma 53:17; 56:47). Not to doubt that God would deliver them? Yes, perhaps the answer encompasses all of these—but there is more.

Remember, that at an earlier time their parents were a part of the Anti-Nephi-Lehies, many whom were slaughtered by their brethren, the Lamanites, because they would not take up arms to defend themselves (see Alma 24:13–23). Those who lived through the slaughter eventually went to Ammon and asked him to "inquire of the Lord" as to what to do (see Alma 27:10). The Lord responded to his inquiry by giving a blessing of protection to the parents of these stripling warriors: "Blessed are this people . . . I will *preserve* them" (Alma 27:12; italics added). In this context *preserve* meant to deliver or to protect. And that was just what he did. The text records no more slaughter among these newly converted Lamanites. This became the same promise given to the stripling warriors by their mothers that "God would deliver them" (Alma 56:47). This promise was not new to the stripling warriors when they went to battle for the first time; they grew up with it because it was the promise given to their parents by the Lord. It was not hard for them to believe in "deliverance" in battle because *this promise of "preservation" had been true in their families long before they became warriors. . . .* Ammon, the missionary who had received the revelation giving the Anti-Nephi-Lehi's their blessing of "preservation" (see Alma 27:12), received the same blessing from the Lord many years earlier when he and the other sons of Mosiah inquired of their father if they could preach the gospel to the Lamanites. The Lord spoke these words to Mosiah: "I will deliver thy sons out of the hands of the Lamanites" (Mosiah 28:7). The sons of Mosiah received the same blessing given later to their converts the Anti-Nephi-Lehies, which naturally carried over to their sons, the stripling warriors. The faith of these youthful sons mirrors the faith of their parents and the missionaries who taught them.

(Jack R. Christianson and K. Douglas Bassett, *Life Lessons from the Book of Mormon* [Salt Lake City: Deseret Book, 2003], 80–81)

Alma 57:20–21 • OBEY WITH EXACTNESS
(Refer in this text to 1 Nephi 3:7.)

Who wants the family unit to end at death? Our happiness and joy is in our families. But how do we get this major blessing? Obedience—obedience to the requirements of the restored Church of Jesus Christ. In the Brazil Sao Paulo South Mission there was an Elder Malheiros who entered into the field not being able to read or write very proficiently. He was even a little fearful of giving a prayer in public. But this young man, according to his mission president, Wilford Cardon, became one of the very greatest missionaries imaginable. (He had baptized more than two hundred people and had baptized every week for fifty-two consecutive weeks.) In a very humble manner Elder Malheiros answered, 'Well, president, I never doubted you. You said one could baptize every week, so I knew

I could baptize every week. I never doubted. It was not always easy, *but I tried to obey.*'... In Alma 57 we read about the 2,060 sons of Helaman who fought valiantly in many wars.... Yet not one lost his life because they knew 'that if they did not doubt, God would deliver them.' (Alma 56:47). In Alma 57:21 we read: 'Yea, and they did *obey and observe to perform every word of command with exactness.' They were totally obedient.* Hence, they had unbelievable protection and success.

(Teddy E. Brewerton, *Ensign*, May 1981 [Salt Lake City: The Church of Jesus Christ of Latter-day Saints, 1981], 69)

––––––––––––

The stripling warriors not only kept their covenants, but they performed "every word of command with exactness" (Alma 57:21). In other words, they kept their covenants with precision. A half-hearted effort to keep the Sabbath day holy or be morally clean or tell the truth or dress modestly is really no effort at all. Joseph Smith didn't say that we *sort of* believe in being "honest, true, chaste, benevolent [and] virtuous" (Articles of Faith 1:13). On Mount Sinai the Lord didn't declare, "Thou shalt not steal—unless you're in a real bind." He didn't say, "Thou shalt *rarely* covet." He didn't say, "Thou shalt not commit adultery—very often." He said, *"Thou shalt not,"* clearly delineating lines we are not to cross....

Men and women who sell their birthright for a mess of pottage will tell you that their demise began with something small, with some seemingly insignificant breach of integrity that escalated. The little things *do* matter.

(Sheri Dew, "Living on the Lord's Side of the Line," *BYU Speeches of the Year*, 21 Mar. 2000 [Provo, Utah: BYU Press, 2000], 4)

––––––––––––

In the late 1970s, as an instructor at the Missionary Training Center, I sat at the feet of Elder Marion D. Hanks while he gave commentary on ... [the] concept of obeying with exactness by standing by our leaders. He related a true story shared with him by Elder Hugh B. Brown shortly before the passing of this great apostle, who had served in the Canadian military:

The story is of a young officer in the First World War. He was second-in-command of a cavalry unit. His commanding officer was killed, and he was then summoned and asked if he could follow orders. He responded that he could. The query was repeated twice, and he answered affirmatively and with some impatience. Of course he could follow orders.

He was then told to lead his troops to the top of a long hillcrest overlooking a deep ravine on the other side. At the crest of the hill he was to turn his troops to the left and at hard gallop proceed for ten minutes by the clock. Nothing was to interfere, no diversions were to distract him; he was to lead his troops without fail at full gallop for ten minutes. He assured the general over the field telephone that he could do this.

The order was given, the troops mounted, the mission begun. At the crest of the hill the young major turned his troops to the left, ordered full gallop, and began the maneuver. Just as he began, he noticed a peculiar sight in a ravine to their right. Some of the bushes seemed to be moving. He paused, took the field glasses, and was electrified to see the enemy in great numbers infiltrating in camouflage up the ravine.

He was a soldier; there was the enemy; the action was plain. His repeated promise to follow orders was forgotten. He stopped his troops, turned them to the right, ordered them to draw sabers, and at full gallop charged his cavalry unit down the ravine to meet the enemy. At exactly ten minutes from the time when he was supposed to begin his full gallop away from the scene, his troops were engaged in a fierce battle with an enemy force. At that moment his own artillery, far back of the lines, opened up on the spot and killed every man in the ravine, his own soldiers as well as the enemy.

Allied intelligence had informed the army of enemy infiltration. The major and his cavalry unit were to be the diversion that would keep the enemy coming. They were to be clear of the scene when the artillery delivered its payload and the strong unit of the enemy would be wiped out. As it was, not only that unit but also the young officer along with his men paid the price of his not being able to obey with exactness. (This story was recorded by Elder Hank's secretary and sent to me in January 1991.)

Elder Hanks did not use this story to illustrate that every order, in every situation, given by every leader, in every army must be obeyed with exactness in order to have the Lord's approval. But he used it to show that the need for total obedience to authority by the sons of Helaman was directly connected to the promise of deliverance given them by their mothers. Deliverance for these young warriors, as well as ourselves, is directly tied to our obedience to those called to preside over us.

(Jack R. Christianson and K. Douglas Bassett, *Life Lessons from the Book of Mormon* [Salt Lake City: Deseret Book, 2003], 174–175)

Alma 57:36 • FILLED WITH JOY

Joy and righteousness are inseparably connected—though Satan would have us believe otherwise, that joy and worldly pleasures are one and the same. But they are not. Likewise, Satan would have us believe that happiness cannot be found in obedience, which he portrays as confining rather than liberating. But that is a lie....

I have never known anyone who was happier or who felt better about themselves or who had greater peace of mind as a result of immorality. Never.

As someone who has remained unmarried two-and-a-half decades beyond a traditional marriageable age, I know something about the challenge of chastity. It is not always easy, but it is far easier than the alternative. Chastity is much easier than regret or the loss of self-respect, than the agony of breaking covenants, than struggling with shallow and failed relationships. This is not to say there are never temptations. Even at forty-six, having long ago decided how I wanted to live my life, I have to be careful all the time. There are things I simply cannot watch, cannot read, cannot listen to because they trigger thoughts and instincts that drive the Spirit away and that edge me too close to the moral line. But those supposed sacrifices are well worth it.

It is so much more comforting to live with the Spirit than without, so much more joyful to have relationships of trust and true friendship than to indulge in a physical relationship that would eventually crumble anyway.

(Sheri Dew, "Living on the Lord's Side of the Line," *BYU Speeches of the Year*, 21 Mar. 2000 [Provo, Utah: BYU Press, 2000], 6–7)

Alma 58:9–11, 34–35, 37 • WE DO NOT DESIRE TO MURMUR
(Refer in this text to 1 Nephi 18:16.)

If our lips are closed to murmuring, then our eyes will be open.

(Neal A. Maxwell, *Ensign*, Nov. 1989 [Salt Lake City: The Church of Jesus Christ of Latter-day Saints, 1989], 82–84)

Your criticism may be worse than the conduct you are trying to correct.

(James E. Faust, *Ensign*, Nov. 1987 [Salt Lake City: The Church of Jesus Christ of Latter-day Saints, 1987], 35)

The primary reason we are commanded to avoid criticism is to preserve our own spiritual well-being, not to protect the person whom we would criticize. . . . Does this counsel to avoid faultfinding and personal criticism apply only to statements that are false? Doesn't it also apply to statements that are true? The fact that something is true is not always a justification for communicating it. . . . For example, it is wrong to make statements of fact out of an evil motive, even if the statements are true. One who focuses on faults, though they be true, tears down a brother or a sister. . . . Even though something is true, we are not necessarily justified in communicating it to any and all persons at any and all times. . . . One who focuses on faults, though they be true, fosters dissensions and divisions among fellow Church members in the body of Christ.

(Dallin H. Oaks, *Ensign*, Feb. 1987 [Salt Lake City: The Church of Jesus Christ of Latter-day Saints, 1987], 68–69)

Helaman understood the principle that the Lord stands by us as we stand by those in authority over us. He continued his letter to Moroni by asking why the government had not sent the requested assistance. Then, almost as an apology for being negative, he wrote, "We do not desire to murmur" (Alma 58:35). Notice how Helaman shared an unpleasant truth in a manner that would still allow the lines of communication to remain open. His sensitivity to his leaders, as well as his subordinates, is commendable. His was not the expression of a weak-kneed foot soldier trying not to be responsible for the bad news he had born. While he was not blind to the problem, he chose to relate the details to Moroni and at the same time reinforce his own support. . . . recognizing full well that he could not expect God to stand by him if he didn't stand by his leaders. He concluded his letter by reaffirming his testimony of the source of his small army's strength: "We trust God will deliver us, notwithstanding the weakness of our armies, yea, and deliver us out of the hands of our enemies" (Alma 58:37). It is apparent that he believed that the blessings of deliverance were in direct correlation with his support of those who presided over him.

(Jack R. Christianson and K. Douglas Bassett, *Life Lessons from the Book of Mormon* [Salt Lake City: Deseret Book, 2003], 175–176)

Alma 58:11 • PEACE TO OUR SOULS
(Refer in this text to Mosiah 4:3.)

Peace of conscience relates to your inner self and is controlled by what you personally do. Peace of conscience can come only from God through a righteous, obedient life. It cannot exist otherwise.

On the other hand, peace of mind is most often affected by external forces such as concern for a wayward child, economic pressures, real of imagined offenses, deteriorating world conditions, or more to do than sufficient time to do it. . . .

Peace of mind is restored by resolving the external forces that disturb it. Not so with a troubled conscience, for it is unrelenting, ever present, a constant reminder of the need to correct your past mistakes, to resolve an offense to another, or to repent of transgression.

(Richard G. Scott, in Conference Report, Oct. 2004 [Salt Lake City: The Church of Jesus Christ of Latter-day Saints, 2004], 14–15)

Alma 58:37 • WE TRUST GOD

When the things you realistically can do to help

are done, leave the matter in the hands of the Lord and worry no more. Do not feel guilty because you cannot do more. Do not waste your energy on useless worry.

(Richard G. Scott, in Conference Report, Apr. 1988 [Salt Lake City: The Church of Jesus Christ of Latter-day Saints, 1988], 70)

Alma 60:13 • THE LORD SUFFERETH THE RIGHTEOUS TO BE SLAIN IN BATTLE
(Refer in this text to Helaman 12:1–6.)

Recently I received a letter from parents in California whose son had written home just before last Christmas and then shortly thereafter his life was taken in the war in Vietnam. This is part of what he wrote: "War is an ugly thing, a vicious thing. It makes men do things they would not normally do. It breaks up families, causes immorality, cheating, and much hatred. It is not the glorious John Wayne type thing you see in the movies. It is going a month without a shower and a change of clothing. It is fear creeping up your spine when you hear a mortar tube in the jungle. It is not being able to get close enough to the ground when coming under enemy fire; hearing your buddy cry out because of being ripped with a hot piece of shrapnel. You . . . be proud of your American citizenship, because many brave and valiant men are here preserving your freedom. God has given you the gift of a free nation, and it is the duty of each of you to help in whatever way you can to preserve it. America is the protector of our Church, which is dearer to me than life itself." And then this young man said this very significant thing: "I realize now that I have already received the greatest gift of all, and that is the opportunity to gain exaltation and eternal life. If you have this gift, nothing else really matters."

(Harold B. Lee, *From the Valley of Despair to the Mountain Peaks of Hope* [Salt Lake City: Deseret News Press, 1971], 5–6)

It is my conviction that the present devastating scourge of war in which hundreds of thousands are being slain, many of whom are no more responsible for the causes of the war than are our own boys, is making necessary an increase of missionary activity in the spirit world and that many of our boys who bear the Holy Priesthood and are worthy to do so will be called to that missionary service after they have departed this life.

(Harold B. Lee, in Conference Report, Oct. 1942 [Salt Lake City: The Church of Jesus Christ of Latter-day Saints, 1942], 72–73)

Alma 61:9, 19 • SUPPORTING EACH OTHER IN TOUGH TIMES
(Refer in this text to 1 Nephi 16:20, 23.)

The men under you will never be loyal to you if they see that you are disloyal to those who preside in authority over you.

(Harold B. Lee, BYU Speech to CES, 8 July 1966)

It is better to carry out a plan that is not so wise, if you are united on it. Speaking generally, a plan or a policy that may be inferior in some respects is more effective if men are united upon it than a better plan would be upon which they were divided. . . . When they carry that counsel out unitedly and in the same spirit, they will be blessed, and the Church will be blessed, and, as I have said, God will supplement our weakness by His strength and our want of knowledge by His infinite knowledge and His great power.

(George Q. Cannon, *Gospel Truths*, ed. by Jerreld L. Newquist [Salt Lake City: Deseret Book, 1974], 163–164)

God will not ennoble a person, man or woman, who refuses to uphold by faith, prayer, and works those whom God has called and ordained to preside over them.

(James E. Faust, *Ensign*, May 1998 [Salt Lake City: The Church of Jesus Christ of Latter-day Saints, 1998], 97)

I have worked with seven Presidents of this Church. I have recognized that all have been human. But I have never been concerned over this. They may have had some weaknesses. But this has never troubled me. I know that the God of heaven has used mortal men throughout history to accomplish His divine purposes. They were the very best available to Him, and they were wonderful.

(Gordon B. Hinckley, *Ensign*, May 1992 [Salt Lake City: The Church of Jesus Christ of Latter-day Saints, 1992], 53)

What is meant by sustaining a person? . . . For instance, if a man be a teacher, and I vote that I will sustain him in his position. . . . I will do everything I can to sustain him. . . . I would not say anything derogatory to his character. . . . And then if anybody in my presence were to whisper something about him disparaging to his reputation, I would say, Look here! are you a Saint? Yes. Did you not hold up your hand to sustain him? Yes. Then why do you not do it? . . . If any man make an attack upon his reputation—for all men's reputations are of importance to them—I would defend him in some such way. When we vote for men in the solemn way in which we do, shall we abide by our covenants? or shall we violate them? If we violate them we become covenant-breakers.

(John Taylor, *Journal of Discourses* [London: Latter-day Saints' Book Depot, 1881], 21:207–208)

Our critics at home and abroad are watching us. In an effort to find fault, they listen to every word we say, hoping to entrap us. We may stumble now and again. But the work will not be materially hindered. We will stand up where we fell and go forward. We have nothing to fear and everything to gain. God is at the helm. We [the leaders] will seek His direction. We will listen to the still, small voice of revelation. And we will go forward as He directs. His Church will not be misled. Never fear that. If there were any disposition on the part of its leaders to do so, he could remove them.

(Gordon B. Hinckley, *Ensign*, May 1997 [Salt Lake City: The Church of Jesus Christ of Latter-day Saints, 1997], 83)

In my lifetime, there have been very few occasions when I questioned the wisdom and inspiration given by key priesthood leaders. I have always tried to follow their counsel, whether I agreed with it or not. I have come to know that most of the time they were in tune with the Spirit and I was not. The safe course is to sustain our priesthood leaders and let God judge their actions. In the early days of the Church, many fell away because they would not sustain Joseph Smith as the Lord's anointed. In fact, the Prophet Joseph said of some of the leaders in Kirtland that 'there have been but two but what have lifted their heel against me—namely Brigham Young and Heber C. Kimball' (*History of the Church*, 5:412). Because of their faithful loyalty, the Lord called Brigham Young to lead the Church west, and when the First Presidency was reorganized, Heber C. Kimball was called as First Counselor to Brigham Young. I do not speak of blind obedience, but rather the obedience of faith, which supports and sustains decisions with confidence that they are inspired. I advocate being more in tune with the Spirit so we may feel a confirming witness of the truthfulness of the direction we receive from our priesthood leaders. There is great safety and peace in supporting our priesthood leaders in their decisions.

(James E. Faust, *Ensign*, May 1997 [Salt Lake City: The Church of Jesus Christ of Latter-day Saints, 1997], 42–43)

People are not necessarily called to positions of responsibility because they are the most qualified, the most talented, or the best informed. Our challenge is to sustain, that is, give our full loyalty and support, to people who are often less than perfect, even people that we might feel to be less capable than ourselves.

(Robert L. Millet, CES Symposium, BYU, Aug. 1993)

A few do's and don'ts may be helpful: • **Do** learn to take counsel. Seek direction from file leaders and receive it willingly. • **Don't** speak ill of Church leaders. • **Don't** covet a calling or position. • **Don't** second-guess who should or should not have been called. • **Don't** refuse any opportunity to serve. • **Don't** resign from a call. • **Do** inform leaders of changing circumstances in your life, knowing that leaders will weigh all factors when prayerfully considering the proper timing of your release.

(Russell M. Nelson, *Ensign*, May 1993 [Salt Lake City: The Church of Jesus Christ of Latter-day Saints, 1993], 39)

One who rationalizes that he or she has a testimony of Jesus Christ but cannot accept direction and counsel from the leadership of His church is in a fundamentally unsound position and is in jeopardy of losing exaltation.

(Ezra Taft Benson, *Ensign*, May 1982 [Salt Lake City: The Church of Jesus Christ of Latter-day Saints, 1982], 64)

I remember years ago when I was a Bishop I had President [Heber J.] Grant talk to our ward. After the meeting I drove him home. . . . Standing by me, he put his arm over my shoulder and said: "My boy, you always keep your eye on the President of the Church, and if he ever tells you to do anything, and it is wrong, and you do it, the Lord will bless you for it." Then with a twinkle in his eye, he said, "But you don't need to worry. The Lord will never let his mouthpiece lead the people astray."

(Marion G. Romney, in Conference Report, Oct. 1960 [Salt Lake City: The Church of Jesus Christ of Latter-day Saints, 1960], 78)

Rejection of or murmuring against the counsel of the Lord's servants amounts to actions against the Lord himself. How could it be otherwise? The Lord acts through his servants. . . . His servants are not perfect. . . . But if we murmur against the Lord's servants, we are working against the Lord and his cause and will soon find ourselves without the companionship of his Spirit. So what do we do when we feel that our Relief Society president or our bishop or another authority is transgressing or pursuing a policy of which we disapprove? . . . The question is not whether we have such differences, but how we manage them. . . . We should conduct ourselves in such a way that our thoughts and actions do not cause us to lose the companionship of the Spirit of the Lord. The first principle in the gospel procedure for managing differences is to keep our personal differences private. . . . We know that such differences are discussed, but not in public. . . . All of this is done quietly and loyally. . . . Why aren't these differences discussed in public? Public debate—the means of resolving differences in a democratic government—is not appropriate in our Church government. We are all subject to the authority of the called and sustained servants of the Lord. They and we are all governed by the direction of the Spirit of the Lord, and that Spirit only functions in an atmosphere of unity. That is why personal differences about Church doctrine or procedure need to be worked out privately. There is nothing inappropriate about private communications concerning such differences, provided they are carried on in a spirit of love.

(Dallin H. Oaks, *Ensign*, Feb. 1987 [Salt Lake City: The Church of Jesus Christ of Latter-day Saints, 1987], 71)

We have a stewardship for a season, then move on to other things and sustain someone else in his or her stewardship, with perhaps a different style for another season. It seems that is as it should be. In all of this shifting we should be loyal to one another and to ourselves. If we do not understand, or if we disagree with those who currently administer a program, let us do as the Lord directs and go to them privately and discuss the matter. To do otherwise seems out of harmony with gospel teachings, does not resolve the issues at hand, and does not bring peace. What I am asking for is that we help one another move individually and collectively to a higher level than we are now—that we strive for more meekness.

(Larry E. Dahl, address given to BYU Religious Educators, 27 Aug. 1992)

While in Kirtland, John Taylor encountered much criticism of the Prophet Joseph Smith. Frequently, outspoken apostates held meetings in which they would criticize the Prophet. Toward the end of one such meeting in the Kirtland Temple, Elder Taylor requested permission to speak, and he fearlessly defended the Prophet. "It was Joseph Smith, under the Almighty, who developed the first principles," he said, "and to him we must look for further instructions. If the spirit which he manifests does not bring blessings, I am very much afraid that the one manifested by those who have spoken, will not be very likely to secure them. The children of Israel, formerly, after seeing the power of God manifested in their midst, fell into rebellion and idola-

try, and there is certainly very great danger of us doing the same thing." While many of the apostates continued their same course, the faithful Saints were strengthened by Elder Taylor's loyalty and conviction.

(*Teachings of Presidents of the Church—John Taylor* [Salt Lake City: The Church of Jesus Christ of Latter-day Saints, 2001], xiv–xv)

Whenever stake presidencies and bishoprics call new leaders and teachers in stake and ward organizations, it's a time of testing for the members. . . . On occasion, you may have wondered about a person who was called whose weaknesses you knew. Perhaps someone was called . . . whom you didn't admire or perhaps didn't ever like. . . .

Doctrine and Covenants [sec. 1], verse 23, which says the Lord intended "that the fulness of my gospel might be proclaimed by the weak and the simple unto the ends of the world, and before kings and rulers."

Now, why in the world would the weak and the simple be sent to kings and rulers? You and I sometimes feel that we are wise and we know a good deal. We have increasing experience. So why should a Sunday School teacher who seems to us weak and simple and less experienced be called by inspiration to teach us?

One reason is that it requires humility on our part. It requires a humble heart to believe that you can be taught by someone who apparently knows a good deal less than you do, and perhaps seems less likely to get revelation. . . .

Clearly, my problem and your problem is to hear the word of God from and through imperfect teachers and leaders. That is your test and mine. . . . God has said that if we are going to make it home again, we must not only hear his voice privately by our own effort, but also through the voice of his servants who, when they speak by the power of the Spirit, speak as if it were his voice. [D&C 1:38.]

(Henry B. Eyring, *To Draw Closer to God* [Salt Lake City: Deseret Book, 1997], 9, 11–13)

About 1896, Moses Thatcher, an apostle of the Church, was suspended from service in the Quorum of the Twelve Apostles. Brother Thatcher, a man of unusual gifts and most charming personality, was very popular in his home town of Logan, as throughout the Church. His suspension caused widespread discussion, and many of his intimate Logan friends felt that he had been treated unjustly, and took his side against the action of the authorities of the Church. The temporary upheaval was tempestuous. Men's feelings ran high. While the excitement was at its height, two of the ward elders called at the Widtsoe home as ward teachers. The widow's two sons were home, and the whole family assembled to be instructed by the visiting teachers. Soon the visitors began to comment on the "Thatcher episode," as it was called, and explained how unjustly Brother Thatcher had been treated. The widow answered not a word, but there was a gathering storm in her stern eyes and high-held head. After some minutes of listening to the visitors find fault with the Quorum of the Apostles with respect to Brother Thatcher, she slowly rose from her chair and as slowly walked to the entrance door of the house which she threw wide open. With eyes now blazing she turned to the two brethren and said: "There is the door. I want you to leave this house instantly. I will not permit anyone in this house to revile the authorities of the Church, men laboring under divine inspiration. Nor do I wish such things spoken before my sons whom I have taught to love the leaders of the Church. And don't come back until you come in the right spirit to teach us the gospel. Here is the door. Now, go!" The visitors hurried out shamefacedly, for the widow had chastised them thoroughly. In defense of the gospel, Sister Widtsoe knew no fear.

(Anna Karine Gaarden Widtsoe; as quoted in John A. Widtsoe, *In the Gospel Net* [Salt Lake City: The Improvement Era, 1941], 97–98)

————————

A story is told of an encounter between the Prophet Joseph Smith and Brigham Young. In the presence of a rather large group of brethren, the Prophet severely chastised Brother Brigham for some failing in his duty. Everyone, I suppose somewhat stunned, waited to see what Brigham's response would be. After all, Brigham, who later became known as the Lion of the Lord, was no shrinking violet by any means. Brigham slowly rose to his feet, and in words that truly reflected his character and humility, he simply bowed his head and said, "Joseph, what do you want me to do?" The story goes that sobbing, Joseph ran from the podium, threw his arms around Brigham, and said in effect, "You passed, Brother Brigham, you passed" (see Truman G. Madsen, "Hugh B. Brown—Youthful Veteran," *New Era*, Apr. 1976, 16).

(Richard C. Edgely, in Conference Report, Oct. 2003 [Salt Lake City: The Church of Jesus Christ of Latter-day Saints, 2003], 103–104)

————————

One of the first conditions that will bring about disunity will be selfishness; another will be envy: "Brother So-and-so passed me by and said nothing to me about the matter." "The bishopric chose Sister So-and-so to be organist, and she can't play half as well as I." "I'm not going to priesthood meeting any more because the bishopric appointed a certain man to act as adviser of the priests." "The Sunday School chose So-and-so as a teacher." . . . "The presidency of the stake

has never recognized me, and I feel offended." "The General Authorities do not always see eye to eye." Oh! a hundred and one little things like that may come up—little things, insignificant in themselves when we compare them with the greater and more real things of life. And yet, I know from experience that the adversary can so magnify them that they become mountains in our lives, and we are offended, and our spirituality starves because we entertain those feelings.

There is another element—fault-finding—associated with that spirit of envy. We find fault with a neighbor. We speak ill of each other. . . .

May we go forth with greater resolution . . . not to speak against our neighbors, nor against authorities of the Church, local, stake, or general. Let us avoid evil speaking; let us avoid slander and gossip. These are poisons to the soul to those who indulge. Evil speaking injures the reviler more than the reviled.

There are destructive termites of homes, as well as of houses, and some of these are backbiting, evil-speaking, faultfinding on the part either of parents or of children. . . . In the ideal home, there is no slanderous gossip about . . . schoolteachers, about public officials, or Church officials. I am more grateful now, as years have come and gone, to my father, who with hands lifted said, "Now, no faultfinding about your teacher or anybody else."

(*Teachings of Presidents of the Church—David O. McKay* [Salt Lake City: The Church of Jesus Christ of Latter-day Saints, 2003], 42–43)

————————

Follow the leaders who are called to preside over you, for the promise is given: "If my people will hearken unto my voice, and unto the voice of my servants whom I have appointed to lead my people, behold, verily I say unto you, they shall not be moved out of their place" (D&C 124:45).

(Boyd K. Packer, *Ensign*, May 2004 [Salt Lake City: The Church of Jesus Christ of Latter-day Saints, 2004], 80)

————————

It has always been hard to recognize in fallible human beings the authorized servants of God. . . . Joseph Smith's cheerful disposition was seen by some as not fitting their expectations for a prophet of God. . . .

The warning for us is plain. If we look for human frailty in humans, we will always find it. When we focus on finding the frailties of those who hold priesthood keys, we run risks for ourselves. When we speak or write to others of such frailties, we put them at risk. . . .

To keep ourselves grounded in the Lord's Church, we can and must train our eyes to recognize the power of the Lord in the service of those He has called.

(Henry B. Eyring, in Conference Report, Oct.

2004 [Salt Lake City: The Church of Jesus Christ of Latter-day Saints, 2004], 29–30)

———————

A word to those of us who are served by those who are newly called. . . . Most of us carry . . . the attitudes we learn in the world, where we may be quick to notice inferior service. . . .

One [way] is to express or show our displeasure. I've been the beneficiary of another way, the better way. I've sensed when I was not doing very well when I was speaking or teaching or leading in a meeting. . . . I have been able to tell when I have been not doing well, and I've looked out and seen someone in the audience . . . with eyes closed. . . . And then they've opened their eyes and smiled at me, with a look of encouragement that was unmistakable. It was a look that said as clearly as if they had spoken to me: " . . . I'm praying for you." . . . You could serve that way when you see people struggling in their service.

(Henry B. Eyring, in Conference Report, Apr. 2000 [Salt Lake City: The Church of Jesus Christ of Latter-day Saints, 2000], 83–84)

———————

Criticism, fault-finding, evil speaking—these are of the spirit of the day. . . . There is heard so much the snide remark, the sarcastic jibe, the cutting down of associates—these, too often, are the essence of our conversation. . . . Criticism is the forerunner of divorce, the cultivator of rebellion, sometimes the catalyst that leads to failure. In the church, it sows the seed of inactivity and finally apostasy. . . .

I am suggesting that as we go through life we try to "accentuate the positive." I am asking that we look a little deeper for the good, that we still our voices of insult and sarcasm, that we more generously compliment virtue and effort. . . .

When I was a young man and was prone to speak critically, my wise father would say, "Cynics do not contribute. Skeptics do not create. Doubters do not achieve."

(*Discourses of President Gordon B. Hinckley* [Salt Lake City: The Church of Jesus Christ of Latter-day Saints, 2005], 2:383–384)

———————

While the commandments of God are to all the world, there are some special commandments that are applicable to the Latter-day Saints only. What are they? One of these commandments is, that we shall honor those who preside over us; in other words, we shall honor the Priesthood. . . .

When a man says: "I am a Latter-day Saint; I am a member of the Church, in good standing, because I know what the principles of the gospel are, and I know

what the principles of government are in the Church," for that man to say, "I oppose the bishop because I don't like him" or "because I haven't faith in him," is proof by that very act that he does not understand the principle of government and submission to divine authority. . . .

Therefore, I say to you, honor the Presidency of the Stake and your Bishops, and all who are placed to preside in your midst. Sustain them in their positions by your faith and your prayers, and show them that you will help them in every good word and work, and God will bless you for it.

(*Teachings of Presidents of the Church—Joseph F. Smith* [Salt Lake City: The Church of Jesus Christ of Latter-day Saints, 1998], 212, 217)

———————

Moroni was not the first underinformed leader to conclude that another leader was not doing enough (see Alma 60). Nor was Pahoran's sweet, generous response to his "beloved brother" Moroni the last such that will be needed (see Alma 61).

(Neal A. Maxwell, *Peace, Essays of Hope and Encouragement* [Salt Lake City: Deseret Book, 1998], 115)

———————

One of the greatest weaknesses in the leadership of this Church throughout its stakes of Zion, its wards and mission fields, is the weakness, you might call it in crude terms "back-biting" or criticizing. I suppose we are all more or less guilty of that, but when we acknowledge the fact that God calls us to these positions . . . then we are not fighting against men who may have their weaknesses; we are fighting against God and his will.

(*Matthew Cowley Speaks* [Salt Lake City: Deseret Book, 1954], 232)

———————

I have watched it from the time I became a member of this Church, there is no man who undertakes to run counter to the counsel of the legally authorized leader of this people that ever prospers. . . .

When men went contrary to the counsel of their leaders, . . . they always became entangled and suffered a loss by so doing.

(*Teachings of Presidents of the Church—Wilford Woodruff* [Salt Lake City: The Church of Jesus Christ of Latter-day Saints, 2004], 202)

———————

When we believe or say we have been offended, we usually mean we feel insulted, mistreated, snubbed, or disrespected. . . . However, it ultimately is impossible for another person to offend you or to offend me. Indeed, believing that another person offended us is fundamentally false. To be offended is a *choice* we make; it is not a *condition* inflicted or imposed upon us by someone or something else. . . .

To believe that someone or something can *make* us feel offended, angry, hurt, or bitter diminishes our moral agency and transforms us into objects to be acted upon. . . . However, you and I have the power to act and to choose how we will respond to an offensive or hurtful situation. . . .

In many instances, choosing to be offended is a symptom of a much deeper and more serious spiritual malady. . . .

In some way and at some time, someone in this Church will do or say something that could be considered offensive. Such an event will surely happen to each and every one of us—and it certainly will occur more than once.

Though people may not intend to injure or offend us, they nonetheless can be inconsiderate and tactless.

You and I cannot control the intentions or behavior of other people. However, we do determine how we will act. Please remember that you and I are agents endowed with moral agency, and we can choose not to be offended.

During a perilous period of war, an exchange of letters occurred between Moroni, the captain of the Nephite armies, and Pahoran, the chief judge and governor of the land. Moroni, whose army was suffering because of inadequate support from the government, wrote to Pahoran "by the way of condemnation" (Alma 60:2) and harshly accused him of thoughtlessness, slothfulness, and neglect. Pahoran might easily have resented Moroni and his message, but he chose not to take offense. Pahoran responded compassionately and described a rebellion against the government about which Moroni was not aware. And then he responded, "Behold, I say unto you, Moroni, that I do not joy in your great afflictions, yea, it grieves my soul. . . . And now, in your epistle you have censured me, but it mattereth not; I am not angry, but do rejoice in the greatness of your heart" (Alma 61:2, 9).

One of the greatest indicators of our own spiritual maturity is revealed in how we respond to the weaknesses, the inexperience, and the potentially offensive actions of others. A thing, an event, or an expression may be offensive, but you and I can choose not to be offended—and to say with Pahoran, "it mattereth not." . . .

If a person says or does something that we consider offensive, our first obligation is to refuse to take offense and then communicate privately, honestly, and directly with that individual. Such an approach invites inspiration from the Holy Ghost and permits misperceptions to be clarified and true intent to be understood.

(David A. Bednar, *Ensign*, Nov. 2006 [Salt Lake City: The Church of Jesus Christ of Latter-day Saints, 2006], 90–92.)

Alma 62:40 • THE PRAYERS OF THE RIGHTEOUS MINORITY
(Refer in this text to Alma 10:22–23.)

There are many upright and faithful who live all the commandments and whose lives and prayers keep the world from destruction.

(Spencer W. Kimball, *Ensign*, June 1971 [Salt Lake City: The Church of Jesus Christ of Latter-day Saints, 1971], 16)

Alma 62:41 • MANY HARDENED, MANY SOFTENED
(Contrast 1 Nephi 16:8 with 1 Nephi 17:21.)

The same testing in troubled times can have quite opposite effects on individuals. . . .

Surely you know some whose lives have been filled with adversity who have been mellowed and strengthened and refined by it, while others have come away from the same test bitter and blistered and unhappy.

(*Memorable Stories and Parables by Boyd K. Packer* [Salt Lake City: Bookcraft, 1997], 93–94)

It's not so much what happens to us but how we deal with what happens to us. That remind me of a passage from Alma. After a long war, "many had become hardened," while "many were softened because of their afflictions" (Alma 62:41). The same circumstances produced opposite responses. . . .

Thomas Giles, a Welsh convert who joined the Church in 1844, also suffered much in his lifetime. He was a miner, and while he was digging coal in the mine, a large piece of coal hit him on the head and inflicted a wound nine inches long. The doctor who examined him said the injured man would not live longer than 24 hours. But then the elders came and administered to him. He was promised that he would get well, and that "even if he would never see again, he would live to do much good in the Church." Brother Giles did indeed live but was blind the rest of his life. Within a month of his injury, "he was out traveling through the country attending to his ecclesiastical duties."

In 1856 Brother Giles and his family immigrated to Utah, but before he left his homeland, the Welsh Saints presented him with a harp, which he learned to play skillfully. At Council Bluffs he joined a handcart company and headed west. "Though blind he pulled a handcart from Council Bluffs to Salt Lake City." While crossing the plains his wife and two children died. "His sorrow was great and his heart almost broken, but his faith did not fail him. In the midst of his grief he said as did one of old, 'The Lord giveth, and the Lord taketh away; blessed be the name of the Lord' (Job 1:21)." When Brother Giles arrived in Salt Lake City, President

Brigham Young, who had heard his story, loaned Brother Giles a valuable harp until his own arrived from Wales. Brother Giles "traveled from settlement to settlement in Utah, . . . gladdening the hearts of the people with his sweet music" (see Andrew Jenson, *Latter-day Saint Biographical Encyclopedia*, 4 vols. (1901–36), 2:507–8).

(James E. Faust, in Conference Report, Oct. 2004 [Salt Lake City: The Church of Jesus Christ of Latter-day Saints, 2004], 19–20)

Alma 63:5–10 • NEPHITE MIGRATIONS BY SEA

In the 63rd chapter of Alma, there is a little story which tells of Hagoth who was such an exceedingly curious man that he built a boat, and he went out on the seas, and he came back. . . . We are told in The Book of Mormon the place where those ships were built was near a narrow neck of land.

When I was on my first mission as a young boy, I used to ask the oldtimers out there, "Where did you come from?" They would say (in Maori), "We came from the place where the sweet potato grows wild, where it is not planted, does not have to be cultivated."

There is only one place in all the world where the sweet potato grows wild, and that is within the environs of that narrow neck of land where Hagoth built his ships. . . .

The Maori scholars tell you that . . . (spoken in Maori) means a place where the spirits are joined. . . .

The Maori scholars say that they came from a far distant place, where the spirits are joined, or where the body returns to the spirit. But I say, knowing the story of Hagoth as I do, that they came from the joining of two waters, a narrow neck of land between two bodies of water which joins those two great continents.

(*Matthew Cowley Speaks* [Salt Lake City: Deseret Book, 1954], 114–115)

———

Now where would the west sea be? The west sea would be the Pacific Ocean, and the narrow neck of land leading into the land northward must mean the Panama Canal area. . . .

In a great gathering of Polynesians held in Salt Lake City just prior to 1915, a prophet of the Lord, President Joseph F. Smith, . . . made the statement that without a doubt this man Hagoth and his company were the progenitors of the Polynesian races, and that this migration was the beginning of the Polynesian population in the South Pacific.

Now up until very recently men of science have said no, the Polynesians have come from the Malay states, they have come from the Asian side of Africa, and they have migrated from a westerly direction to the Polynesian islands—not from the Americas. This was popular thinking until about 1940, when a very bold scholar by the name of Thor Heyerdahl made the observation that indeed these people must be from the Americas. He set out to prove this by building some balsa rafts on which he set himself adrift off the shores of South and Central America. He and his companions drifted for about one hundred days; and depending only on the prevailing tides and winds of that area, they found themselves cast upon the shores of these South Pacific islands, not far from Tahiti. . . .

The Lord was mindful of Hagoth. The Lord guided Hagoth.

(Robert L. Simpson, *Proven Paths* [Salt Lake City: Deseret Book, 1974], 53–54, 60)

———

Speaking of Hagoth and his party, President Spencer W. Kimball said: "President Joseph F. Smith, the president of the Church reported, 'You brethren and sisters from New Zealand, I want you to know that you are from the people of Hagoth.' For New Zealand Saints, that was that. A prophet of the Lord had spoken."

(New Zealand Area Conference Report, 20–22 Feb. 1976, 3; as quoted in *Book of Mormon Student Manual: Religion 121 and 122* [Salt Lake City: The Church of Jesus Christ of Latter-day Saints, 1989], 104)

INDEX

Note: Entries in the index refer to subjects as well as phrases within the Book of Mormon.

About the Author

K. Douglas Bassett earned a bachelor's degree in psychology and a master's degree in youth leadership from Brigham Young University. He earned his doctoral degree in education from the University of New Mexico. A former seminary instructor, he has taught religion classes at BYU and currently teaches at the Orem Institute of Religion. He served a full-time mission in southern England.

He has written several books, including *The Barber's Song, Life Lessons from the Book of Mormon, Commentaries on Isaiah in the Book of Mormon*, and the best-selling *Latter-day Commentary on the Book of Mormon*.

He and his wife, the former Arlene Chapman, live in Mona, Utah. They are the parents of eight children.